The Language of Sailing

The Language of

Sailing

Richard Mayne

FITZROY DEARBORN PUBLISHERS
CHICAGO • LONDON

© Richard Mayne 2000

Published in the United States of America by
Fitzroy Dearborn Publishers
919 North Michigan Avenue
Chicago, Illinois 60611

Published in the United Kingdom by
Carcanet Press Ltd
4th floor, Conavon Court
12–16 Blackfriars Street
Manchester M3 5BQ

Typeset in 10pt Plantin by XL Publishing Services, Tiverton, and
printed and bound in Great Britain by SRP Ltd, Exeter

A Cataloging-in-Publication record for this book is available from the
Library of Congress

ISBN 1-57958-278-8 Fitzroy Dearborn

General Editors' Preface

This series offers a new conception and analysis of the vocabularies used in our sports, pursuits, vocations and pastimes. While each book contains an essential lexicon of words and phrases – explored historically and in depth – each also contains generous quotation, practical reference, anecdote and conjecture. The result is more than a dictionary: specific, inclusive, thought-provoking, each volume offers the past and present through a weave of words, in all their curiosity and delight.

Those intrigued by the language particular to their area of interest will find the relevant book a coherent and challenging treatment of the topic; those interested in the English language itself will find the series yielding significant material on semantic scope and change; and general readers who wish to understand the vocabularies of human endeavour will find the series tracing the necessary but implacable relationships between words and world.

Editors, chosen because of their intimate enthusiasm for their subjects, have been encouraged to be comprehensive in their coverage: vocabularies typically range from the demotic to the esoteric, from slang to the technical and specialised. Within that range, emphasis is also placed on *how* each lexicon developed, and why its terms acquired their peculiar descriptive power. These are books to read with pleasure as well as keep on the reference shelf.

Gerald Hammond
C. B. McCully

Abbreviations

The following abbreviations are used in the text:

c.   circa
cf.   compare

ME   Middle English
OE   Old English
OF   Old French
ON   Old Norse

EETS   Early English Text Society
STS   Scottish Text Society

OED   *Oxford English Dictionary*

Introduction

A shy non-sailor was invited to address a stag dinner at his local yacht club. Looking for an alluring topic, he decided to talk about sex: but he told his wife that his subject was 'Sailing'. The day after the dinner, she met the yacht club's secretary, who enthused at her husband's brilliant talk. 'That's funny,' she said. 'He's only done it three times. The first time, he was sick; the second time, his hat blew off; and the third time he got tangled up in the sheets.'

So the language of sailing is not quite the language of sex. Diligent readers will find words here with sexual connotations; but many sailing terms, like *sheets*, are familiar words with quite different maritime meanings. A roughly alphabetical list might include: *after, block, cheese, dodger, elbow, fetch, gingerbread, hounds, in irons, jumper, knee, lizard, mouse, nettles, otter boards, palm, quiff, roach, sole, traveller, unbend, viol, wangle, yard* and *zulu* – all used in different senses ashore and afloat. Other nautical expressions are pretty unfamiliar on land: *abox, bowse, clew, dipsey, euphroe, futtock, gashions, harpings, inwales, jill about, kedge, lasket, marl, nugger, outlicker, parbuckle, quoin, rigol, skeg, thole pins, ullage, vang, woolding, yuloh, z-twist.* This book does its best to explain them. Unlike other nautical dictionaries, it also gives some idea of their origin.

Nor is the book only nautical. English is awash with the sea, often in dead metaphors. *Anchor man, by and large, chock-a-block, the devil to pay, on an even keel, fag-end, blow the gaff, half seas over, in the offing, jump ship, keel over, at loggerheads, masthead, overboard, part brass rags, pooped, rocking the boat, steering committee, taken aback, under way...* not everyone who uses these expressions may taste their salty tang.

The language of sailing is also international. Words may change their meanings as they cross frontiers: *mizen* is not at all the same as *misaine* in French. Mishearing may lead to distortion: *Mater Cara* sounds more homely as *Mother Carey*. And national maritime rivalry breeds memorable insults: a *Dutchman* masks a defective joint, an *Irish hurricane* is a flat calm, and both an *Irishman's reef* and a *Spanish reef* are knots in the sail to be shortened. But the sea unites people as well as dividing them; and similar expressions, often from common roots, sometimes as old as Sanskrit, abound among Europe's seafarers. Many date from years of maritime exploring; some bring back to Europe words from very distant shores. *Catamaran* is a more recent example, giving birth in turn to *trimaran*, which is less anomalous than it may seem – an instance of the inventiveness that gave us *pushpit* as the aftermost counterpart of *pulpit*, as well as the still only oral *gennaker*, combining *spinnaker* with *Genoa* – pronounced '*genOa*' by all but the most Italophile.

Anyone compiling a specialised etymological dictionary feels like a flea riding on an elephant. The mount is the OED, the *Oxford English Dictionary*. Its skin is surely proof against fleabites; but no rider can resist a futile peck on finding a word omitted or an etymology implausible. Equally, many nautical words were quite obviously in use long before they first appeared in writing, whether manuscript or print. That said, the OED is indispensable, and sometimes even eloquent – for instance in the near-impossible task of describing, in words without pictures, a complex knot. For its support in my linguistic travels I am duly grateful – as I am to other toilers of the sea. Among them, I must especially mention two, whom I have taken the liberty of quoting. One is the late Peter Kemp, editor of another invaluable Oxford publication, *The Oxford Companion to Ships and the Sea*; the other is the founder and first editor of that lively and practical monthly, *Practical Boat Owner*, Denny Desoutter, whose *The Boat-Owner's Practical Dictionary* is a model of good sense and good fun. May *The Language of Sailing* earn its place beside them – and the works of Patrick O'Brian – on the shelf above the chart table, alongside the sticky chocolate bars and the dog-eared pilot books.

R.M.

Aback   (of *sails*) with the wind on the *fore side*, pressing the *sail* back, slowing the *ship*, giving it *sternway,* or driving it to *leeward.*

Sails may be 'laid aback' to slow down or to help in *tacking.* In *square-rigged vessels* the *yards* may be *trimmed* for this purpose: the order 'lay all flat aback' is to stop the *ship.* In *fore-and-aft rigs* such as the familiar *Bermuda sloop* a *headsail* may be *sheeted* aback to counter the pressure on the *mainsail* and thus to *heave to.* When lying to a single *anchor*, a *square-rigged ship* may spread a *mizen topsail* aback to prevent the *ship's* surging forward and making the *cable foul* the *anchor.*

A *ship* may be taken aback by *steering* or a *wind* shift.

It is this sense of 'taken unawares' that has acquired general currency outside nautical circles. Its first known use in this sense is in 1840, in Thomas Hood's *Up the Rhine*, 21: 'The boy, in sea phrase, was taken all aback.' When the landlubber Charles Dickens used it two years later, in *American Notes*, 52, it had evidently become a dead or accepted metaphor: 'I don't think I was ever so taken aback in all my life.'

Derived from 'a-' (preposition of state) and OE 'on baec', 'backward', and transferred from the sense of 'backward' to its specific and still current nautical usage by the late seventeenth century. Thus Jumper in the *London Gazette* No. mmmcccxv, 1 (1697): 'I braced my topsails aback.'

First attested in 1754 in Eeles, Let. 2 in *Transactions of the Philological Society*, XLIX, 144.

abaft   behind, to the rear of. The opposite used to be *afore*, but is now usually *forward* or 'forrard'.

From the preposition of state 'a-' and OE 'be-aefan', 'behind', 'back'. Its disused predecessor 'baft' dates back at least as far as the fourteenth century, as in the *Early English Psalter* (c.1300), lxxviii, 66, and is found as late as 1837, in Marryat, *The Dog Fiend*, xiii.

First attested in Hakluyt, 1589, II, 187. It was originally also used in the same sense as *aft*, as in Digby, *Voyage, 1628–29* (Camden Society, 1868), 46, and as late as 1863 in Kingsley, *Water Babies*, 271. Nowadays, the word is usually relative to something else, as in 'abaft the *beam*', which in the case of *compass bearings* means more than 90 degrees from *dead ahead.*

abeam   in a line at right angles to the mid-point of the *fore* and *aft* line.

Derived, with 'a-' as preposition of state, from the *beams*, which are at right angles to that line. See Scott, *Midge 1834–35* (1863), 23: '"What is that abeam of us?" said Mr Sprawl.'

Although Mr Sprawl was no doubt speaking loosely, the navigator would have to be more precise.

aboard   on, on to, in, or into a *ship* (but see also below).

The common meaning of the word, most often heard in the cry 'All aboard', is not the only one. From the fifteenth century onwards it also meant *alongside*, as in Robert Fabyan, *Newe Cronycles* (1494), VII, 372. 'To lay a *ship* aboard' was to come *alongside*, with a view to fighting or boarding; 'to fall aboard' is to collide sideways. In *square-rigged vessels*, 'to haul the *tacks* aboard' is to *brace* the *yards* round so as to *sail close-hauled*.

From the preposition of state 'a-' and 'board' (of Teutonic origin and in OE meaning a plank, table, shield or, poetically, *ship*; cf. the French 'à bord').

First attested in 1508 in Barclay's translation of Brant, *Narrenschiff*, vi. Shakespeare used the word in *Hamlet* (I, iii, 56), *Henry VI Part 2* (IV, I, 25), and *The Tempest* (I, iii, 56).

about   on or to the opposite *tack*, across the *wind*.

When *sailing upwind*, a *ship* goes about by changing direction sufficiently to bring the *wind* to the other side. The corresponding manoeuvre when *sailing downwind* is *gybing*. Announcing the intention to go about, the order is 'ready about'; when the *helm* is to be put *down* to *leeward* to make the move, the call in a small boat or yacht is 'lee-oh', and in a larger *sailing vessel*, 'about ship'. Once the manoeuvre is completed, the *boat* is said to 'be about'. *Skippers* rapidly tired of *crew* whose response to 'ready about' is 'about ready'.

From OE 'on-butan', outside of.

First attested in a nautical sense in 1588 in the *Orders for the Spanish Fleet*.

abox, a-box   braced flat *aback* or square to the *mast* (of head-*yards* in a *square-rigged vessel*.

From the preposition of state 'a-' and the verb 'box' (in the sense of 'to turn a *ship*), and thence from the noun (OE 'box' from the Latin *buxus*, a box-tree). However, as the OED admits, this 'yields a large number of disconnected senses'.

First attested in 1801 in Ferris, *Naval Chronicle*, VI, 245: 'With an intent to brace the head yards abox.' This meant flat *aback*, so as to bring the *ship* on to the required *tack*; to *lay* them abox would have been to lay them square to the *foremast*, so as to begin to *heave-to*.

abreast, in line   forming a line of (usually equidistant) *ships* at right angles to their course.

From the preposition of state 'a-' and 'breast', whose source is OE 'breost' and the Old Teutonic '*brust*'.

First attested in 1697 in Potter, *Archaeologica Graecae*, III, xx, 150.

aburton, a-burton   (of *cask stowage*) *athwartships* rather than *fore-and-aft*.

From the preposition of state 'a-' and 'burton' (etymology unknown), a small *tackle* of two or three *blocks*.

When *casks* were the only means of carrying fresh water, as well as meat pickled in brine, their *stowage* was vital, to keep them secure, save space, and ensure easy access.

First attested in Harris, *Lexicon Technicum* (1704–10) and defined in Young, *Nautical Dictionary* (1846): 'Casks are said to be stowed a-burton, when placed athwartships in the hold.'

a-cock-bill (also *a-cock-bell*)   with the *bills* or tapering ends cocked or pointing upwards, as when a (*fisherman's* type) *anchor* is hung from the *cathead* or the *hawsehole* with the *flukes* pointing upwards, ready to drop. Also used of the *yards* when topped up at an angle to the *deck*, traditionally in mourning.

The source of the word 'cock' in this sense of sticking up is most probably (and certainly most decorously) the head and crest of the male fowl.

First attested in the *Sea Dictionary*, 1708.

admiral   commander of a *fleet* or squadron.

The origin of the word lies in a misunderstanding of the Arabic word *'amir'*, commander, used especially in the twelfth century in the Mediterranean in the form *amir-al-bahr*, commander of the sea. Christian writers took the *'al'* in this and similar expressions to be part of the original word, and gave it Latin or vernacular forms, often confusing it with words of the 'admirable' family: hence, it is said, the red and white 'admiral' butterflies. In English, the word derives directly from the old (and modern) French *amiral*. By the sixteenth century it was pronounced 'amrel', as by some it still is. Originally applied to a chieftain of any kind, it acquired its specifically naval connotation in the late fifteenth century.

The four active ranks of admiral in the Royal Navy are Admiral of the Fleet (originally entitled to fly the Royal Standard, but from the end of the seventeenth century flying the *Union Flag*, Admiral, Vice Admiral, and Rear Admiral. The first female admiral, in 1972, was Miss Alene Duerk of the US Navy Nurse Corps.

In Elizabethan times, the word was often applied to the chief *commander's ship*, he himself being called 'general', '*captain*', or '*captain* general'.

The Admiral's Cup, a biennial award established in 1957 by

the Royal Ocean Racing Club, was named after Sir Miles Wyatt, who in that year was the Club's 'admiral'. An admiral is also the largest size of *fid* or wooden *marline-spike*.

First attested in a nautical sense in Capgrave, *Chronicle* (1460), 250, who qualifies it ('The Earl of Arundel, Richard, was mad [made] amyrel of the sea'), whereas Caxton, *Chronicles* (1480), cclxiii, 290 does not, referring to the Earl of Kent's being made 'Admyrel of England.'

admiralty, the   the governing authority of the Royal Navy, as well as its building – although the old Admiralty building in the Mall in London is now occupied by the Foreign and Commonwealth Office.

Expressions derived, sometimes derisively, from the word include: 'admiralty ham' (tinned corned beef); 'admiralty *hitch*' (made by laying a *marline-spike* through a jamming *bight*); 'admiralty pattern *anchor*' (one whose *stock* can be folded down); 'admiralty *sweep*' (an extra large turning circle made so as to come *alongside*); and 'admiralty weather' (fine when on duty, foul when free).

From *admiral*.

adrift   floating unsecured, at the mercy of *wind*, *waves*, and *current*.

By extension, the word 'adrift' has two other nautical meanings: it applies to any object unfastened, mislaid, or broken, and to any *seaman* absent without leave from his work, his *watch*, or his *ship*.

From the preposition of state 'a-' (here denoting in or on) and 'drift', originally Old Frisian for a passage for driven cattle, and in ON a snow-drift.

First attested, as meaning 'a slow current', in 1562 in Heywood, *Epigrammes*, 149; in the sense of 'deviation from the true course' in 1671 in Narborough, *Journal* (1674), 174.

adze (also *adz*, *addes*, etc)   a shipbuilding tool for slicing the surface of wood.

Its OE origin as 'adesa' is unknown; but the word is attested very early, notably *c*. AD 880 in Aelfred's Bede, *Historia ecclesiastica*, IV, 3: 'He baer him aecse and adesan on hands.'

afloat   floating, at *sea*.

From the preposition of state 'a-' and 'float', the latter derived from OE 'flot', from the Teutonic roots *'fleut-'*, *'flaut-'* and *'flot-'*, and therefore cognate with *fleet*.

First attested in 993 in *The Battle of Maldon*, 4l as 'on flot' and in a 1023 Charter of King Canute as 'aflote'.

afore   *forward* of, ahead of (but only *on board ship*).

Although the word survives in the Bible and the Book of

Common Prayer, it is now chiefly confined to dialect; it has become uncommon even in nautical parlance, except in a set phrase like 'afore the mast'. It remains embedded, as it were, like a fossil in the still more or less current word 'pinafore', whose only nautical connections are through Gilbert and Sullivan.

From OE 'on foran'. Not until the fourteenth century did 'aforn' and 'afore' replace 'forn' and 'fore'.

First attested in 1523 in Berners, *Froissart* (1523–5), I, cccl, 561.

aft (an adverb; the corresponding adjective is *after*)   toward, at, or near the *stern*.

Cf. *abaft*. From OE 'aeftan', cognate with the Gothic '*aftana*' (from behind), which in turn is from '*afta*' (behind), itself formally a superlative of '*af*' (off, away).

First attested in 1628–9 in Digby, *Journal*, 3.

after   nearer the *stern*.

Nautically, it is now used mainly in combination with other words, joined or separate, with or without hyphens. The after *cabin*, in a *yacht* like the Warrior, lies *aft* of the centre *cockpit;* the after end of a *vessel* is the part *abaft* the beam; the after *jiggermast*, in a six-*masted vessel*, is the after *mast* (the rearmost); the after *mizenmast*, in such a *vessel*, is the fourth; the after part is that near the *stern*; the after *peak* is a small space *forward* of the *stern* frame, usually enclosed by a *bulkhead* on its *fore* side; the after *swim* is the curvature of the *hull* that guides the water towards the *screw* and the *rudder*.

From the same roots as *aft*, of which it may have been seen as a comparative (i.e., 'further aft').

First attested in its present nautical sense in the *Trinity College Homilies*, 199.

afterbody   that part of a *ship's hull* which lies *aft* of the *midship* section, from the upper *deck* to the *keel*.

afterguard   formerly, the team of men on the *poop* or the *quarterdeck* working the *after* gear; now sometimes applied to the owner of a *yacht* and his guests or, in racing, the *helmsman* and his advisers. (See *after* above.)

afterturn   the twist given to *rope*, when the *strands* are laid up to form it, in the opposite direction to their twist.

aground   touching or resting on the *bottom* when still in the water; otherwise, *ashore*.

When a *vessel* is put aground deliberately, she 'takes the ground'; when by mischance, she 'runs aground' or is *stranded*. When taking the ground on a drying *mooring*, she is aground when her weight begins to supported on the *bottom* and 'dried out' when all the water has retreated from her *hull*.

From the preposition of state 'a-' and *'ground'*, itself from OE 'grund' and a common Teutonic root.

First attested, as two words, *c.* 1500 in *Cocke Lorelles bote*, 6: 'Some at saynt Kateryns stroke a grounde' – where more recently many more have found themselves *becalmed.* The expression appears as one word in 1719 in Defoe, *Robinson Crusoe*, 264.

ahoy   a hail to attract attention, as in *'ship* ahoy!'

A combination of the interjection 'a' with what the OED calls the 'natural exclamation' 'hoy'.

First attested as a complete expression in 1751 in Smollett, *Peregrine Pickle*, I, ii, 12: 'Ho! the house a hoy.' The OED traces 'hoy' to 1393 in Langland, *Piers Plowman*, C, ix, 123: 'And holpen to crie his half acre with "hoy! troly! lolly!"' But this is dubious: Skeat's edition reads 'how! trolli-lolli!' and sees it as the chorus of a song, as in Ritson, *Ancient Songs*, and in the *Chester Plays*. Skeat argues that the line refers to what might be termed 'armchair ploughmen' drunkenly singing rather than dutifully ploughing. The OED by contrast links the cry 'hoy!' to hog-calling. Sailors may take their pick.

ahull, a-hull (as in lying a-hull)   lying to the *wind* with no *sail set*, usually with the *wind broadside* on or, with the *helm a-lee*, with the *wind* on the *quarter.*

The term is sometimes used, loosely, as a synonym for *hove-to*; but the latter involves at least some *canvas set*, whereas lying ahull is done under *bare poles.* What they have in common, of course, is very heavy *weather.*

The preposition of state 'a-' with 'hull'. The origin of 'hull' as a nautical word remains obscure; but commonsense suggests that it may be derived, owing to its shape, from 'hull' in these sense of 'shell, pod, or husk' – that of peas and beans being somewhat like a *boat.* This word is descended from OE 'hula', covering.

First attested in a nautical sense surprisingly late, in 1571 in Digges, *Pantometria*, I, xxi, G J a. However, W. Towrson (1558) in Hakluyt, *Divers Voyages* (1582), 130 gives the meaning of 'ahull': 'We lost our maine sails, foresails, and spreetsails, and were forced to lye a hulling.' The modern form of the expression is first attested in 1582 in Lichefield (transl.), *Lopez de Castanheda*, 73: 'All this time the shippes lay a hull.'

alee, a-lee   on or towards the *lee* or sheltered side of the *ship*, away from the *wind*, to *leeward.*

Preposition of state 'a-' with *'hle'*, ON for 'shelter'.

First attested in English in its Norse form in the ninth century, in Cynewulf, *Crist*, 605. The expression a-lee is first recorded in 1399 in Langland *Richard the Redeless*, IV, 74. In a nautical context, it is attested *c.* 1575 in Hickscorner (Dodsley, *Select Collection of Old Plays*, Hazlitt, 1874–5): 'Ale the helm.' *Helmsmen* should not be misled by this spelling.

all fours   *moored* with four *lines*, one from each *bow* and *quarter*. The practice is most common in *mud berths*.

Originally applied to animals, and originally singular, the expression is first attested in 1563 in *Certayne sermons, the second tome of homelyes*, II, xiii, ii, 184: 'a bruit beast, creeping upon all foure'. The plural first appears in the nineteenth century. The OED omits the nautical sense, first attested in 1961 in Burgess, *Dictionary*, 11.

all hands   usual abbreviation for the command 'all hands on *deck*', calling for *seamen* of all *watches* immediately to muster on *deck*.

From the familiar word, whose source is OE 'hand' and a common Teutonic root.

First attested as denoting a manual employee in 1655, in Somerset, *Inventions*, 14; its nautical use is recorded soon afterwards, in 1669, in Sturmy, *Mariners Magazine*, I, 18.

all in the wind   *head* to *wind*, with the *sails* shaking.

Of obvious derivation. First attested in 1961 in Burgess, *Dictionary*, 11.

all standing   fully *rigged*; (of persons) fully dressed; fully equipped; (of *anchoring* or *gybing*) without preparation. It applies most often when the *anchor* is dropped with too much *way* on the *vessel*, or when a *gybe* takes place without preparing the *sheets* or *runners* for the shock.

From OE 'standan' and a common Teutonic root with offshoots in several other Germanic languages. An interesting case of extended figurative meanings. Originally, the phrase referred to *spars*: Smeaton, *Narrative* (1793), #259: 'Found all standing as we had left it.' In Dana, *Two Years* (1840), xxxi, 231, it applies to clothes: 'The mate... turned in "all standing".'

First attested in the sense of 'without preparation' in 1867 in Smyth, *Sailor's Wordbook*.

aloft   above – usually high above – the *deck*. The opposite of 'aloft' is '*alow*', meaning on, near, or below the *deck*; but this is now little used except in the phrase 'alow and aloft'. When a *ship* is carrying all *sail* alow and aloft, she has all *sails set*, including her *studding-sails*, and all *reefs* shaken out.

From ON '*a lopt*' (of motion) and '*a lopti*' (of position) via the Early English 'o loft' and 'o lofte'.

First attested in a general, non-nautical sense *c.* AD 1200, meaning 'up in the air' – usage faintly echoed in the phrase 'gone aloft', i.e. dead; in its nautical sense, in 1338 in Brunne,

Langtoft's Chronicle, 169: 'The sails was hie o loft.' By the sixteenth century the expression had become 'a loft', and by the eighteenth 'aloft'.

alongside   beside (a *quay* or a *ship*).

From OE 'and-lang' and 'side', itself from a common Teutonic root. The 'a' may, however, have been thought to be a preposition of state, the 'long side' being presented to the point of observation, in the sense of 'showing its (or her) long side'.

First attested, in three words, in 1707 in the *London Gazette*, mmmmccclxxx, 2: 'The Enemy would not come up a long Side.' By the time of Coleridge, *Ancient Mariner* (1798), iii, 13, the three words had become one: 'The naked hulk alongside came.'

aloof   to *windward*, towards the *wind*.

From the prepositiom of state 'a-' and 'loof' (meaning *luff*, weather-gage, or *windward* direction), the latter from the Dutch *'loef'*.

First attested in its nautical sense (now largely obsolete) in 1532 in More, *Confutation*, viii (*Works*, 1557, 759/2). The modern figurative sense derives from an earlier, completely obsolete nautical meaning of the word, i.e. 'distant'. This figurative meaning is probably due to the notion of 'higher' (i.e. closer to the wind).

amidships   in the middle of the *ship*, either laterally or longitudinally. The command 'amidships', usually shortened to 'midships', requires the *helm* or *tiller* to bring the *rudder* in line with the *keel*.

The preposition of state 'a-' with 'mid' (from a common Teutonic root) and 'ship' (from OE 'scip' and a common Teutonic root).

First attested (very late) in 1692 in Smith, *Seaman's Grammar*, I, xvi, 76.

anchor   heavy metal hook used to fix the *vessel* temporarily to the seabed or riverbed; to anchor is to *cast* or drop it for this purpose. The *anchor bed* is not the seabed or riverbed but a fitting in which it can be stowed. An *anchor bell* can be either one rung at anchor in fog or one rung to denote the number of *shackles* out on the *cable*. An *anchor buoy* is one marking the anchor's position. The *anchor chain*, usually known as the *cable*, is that to which it is attached. *Anchor ice* is ice that encloses objects on the bottom, breaking into blocks as the temperature rises, and sometimes floating away with the anchor embedded in it. The *anchor light*, often known as the *riding light*, is an all-round white light used when at anchor between dusk and dawn, usually *hoisted* on the *forestay*, and in *ships* over 150 feet long backed up by a similar light *aft*, 15 feet lower than the other. An *anchor pocket* is a recess at the *hawse pipe* enabling the anchor's *flukes* to be *stowed* flush with the *ship*'s side. The *anchor rode* is an old term for the *cable*. An *anchor tripping line* is attached to the *crown* of the anchor and secured to the *anchor buoy*, so as to free the anchor if this is difficult. An *anchor warp* is a rope attached to the *cable*, used as a temporary cable, or in smaller boats replacing it. The *anchor watch* is a precaution against the anchor's *dragging*: those on duty take bearings, feel for vibration or slackening and tautening, and either work the cable or, if necessary, use an extra anchor. To *swallow the anchor* is to retire from *sailing*.

The 'h' in this ancient word is what the OED calls a 'pedantic corruption', imitating the erroneous Latin spelling 'anchora'. The OE 'ancor' is cognate with the Latin *'ancora'* and its Greek source, whence the word 'angle, and with the Old High German *'anchar'*, the Low German and Middle High German *'ankar'*, and less directly with ON *'akkeri'*; cf. the Swedish *'ankare*, the Danish *'anker'*, and the French *'ancre'*. First attested *c.* AD 880 in King Aelfred's translation of Boethius, *De consolatione philosophiae*, x, 30, in the form 'ancor'.

anchorage   a place suitable to anchor in.

From *anchor*; marked on charts with a drawing of a *fisherman's anchor*. It used also to denote a royal levy on *ships* seeking shelter in *port* or *roads*.

apeak   (of the *anchor*) directly below the *bows*, usually with the *cable hove* short ready to break the anchor out. Also used of *oars* held vertically.

From the French *'a pic'*. This is confirmed by the first attested use of the term, in 1596, in Vere, *Commentaries*, 30: '... my Anchor a pike'. Later spellings include 'a Peek', perhaps confusing for dog-owners.

aplustre   the curved ornamental *stern* of an ancient Greek or Roman *vessel*; the ornamental piece on top of a *stern-post*.

From the Latin plural *'aplustria'* and hence from the Greek. First attested in 1705 in Addison, *Remarks on Italy*, 344.

apron   a broad, thick, straight-grained *timber* strengthening the *stem*, fitted between it and the *keel* and receiving the *plank* ends; of a naval gun, the lead sheet over the touch-hole to keep the vent dry; the *leadsman*'s safety screen; of a *dock*, the platform rising when the gates are closed; the surface of a concrete *slipway*; or the raked *forward* face of the bridge-*deck* on a *catamaran*.

This multi-purpose extension of a homely word should begin with the letter 'n', which it lost when 'a napron' was taken to be 'an apron': the word's origin is OF *'naperon'*. The reason for this particular extension, as for its use in the theatre and in architecture, particularly military architecture, is no doubt the resemblance in shape (squareish), position (in front), and function (protective) to those of an apron in the domestic sense. First attested in 1307 in Whitaker, *History and Antiquities*, cited in Beck, *Draper's Dictionary*.

archboard   the formed *timber* immediately under the *knuckles* of the *stern*-timbers of a *counter stern*; with the *transom* it forms the *after* end. An up-sloping and overhanging *counter* may end in a small archboard, often miscalled a *transom*.

From 'arch' and 'board', the former from the Latin '*arca*', a chest, and '*arcus*', a bow; the latter from OE 'bord'.

First attested in 1867 in Smyth, *Sailor's Word-book*.

argosy   a Mediterranean trading *carrack* in the Middle Ages, and by extension any *ship* richly laden.

Although some have suggested that this is derived from Jason's *ship* the *Argo*, its true origin is almost certainly the port of Ragusa (now Dubrovnik), which in sixteenth-century English appears as 'Aragouse', 'Arragouese', and 'Aragosa'. Roberts, *A Map of Commerce* (1683), 237, substantiates this: 'Rhagusa... from hence was the original of those great ships here built, and in old times vulgarly called Argoses properly Rhaguses.' Twelve *ships* from Ragusa, generically known as argosies, were included in the 130-strong Spanish Armada of 1588.

First attested in 1577 in Dee, *Memorials*, 9. Hooker and Fleming's 1587 continuation of Holinshed's *Chronicles*, III, 313/2, mentions 'A great argosie'.

arm, to   to fill the cavity at the base of the *lead* with tallow, putty, or stiff grease so as to find out whether the seabed is sand, gravel, shingle, mud, etc.

From the French '*armer*' and the Latin '*armare*'. The OED gives no instance of this specific nautical extension of the verb.

arms   of an *anchor*, the parts between the *crown* and the *flukes*; of a *boom* or *yard*, the extremities.

An obvious figurative use of the familiar word, whose source is the Old Teutonic '*armoz*', cognate with the Latin '*armus*', shoulder.

First attested in a nautical context in 1665 in Pepys, *Diary*, 18 September; of an anchor, in 1706 in Phillips, *New World*.

Armstrong's patent   jocular expresssion for machinery requiring muscle-power.

From 'arm' and 'strong'.

First attested in 1961 in Burgess, *Dictionary*, 15, but almost certainly a nineteenth-century invention.

arse   the lower end of a *block*.

By extension from the original meaning of 'buttocks' or 'rump', and from a common Teutonic root, *'ars'*, found in Old High German, ON, etc.

The OED gives no specific nautical application of the word; but its figurative use, indicating the lower part of anything, dates back at least to *c.* AD 1400. In its original spelling, the word is no longer in ultra-polite use; mis-spelt and pronounced as 'ass', it remains current in North America.

First attested in a nautical sense in 1961 in Burgess, *Dictionary*, 15.

artemon   a small square *sail set* on a *yard* and carried below a *bowsprit*-like *spar* over the *bows* of an ancient Roman merchant *vessel*. Used as a *steering* aid, it resembled the later *spritsail*. The word was also used, mistakenly, to describe the *mainsail* of ancient *ships*.

Adopted directly from Latin, in which it also sometimes denoted a *topsail set* above the *main*. In some usages (see below) it may have been derived from the French *'artimon'*, *mizen*. The artemon *mast* was set up in the *bows* of late medieval *ships* with a *sail* to help the *helmsman* avoid coming *head to wind*. In the nineteenth and early twentieth centuries, the expression was sometimes applied to the fourth *mast* of a four or five *mast*ed *ship*: here, the source may well have been the French *'artimon'*.

First attested in the *Digesta* and the Vulgate, but unaccountably absent from the OED.

artificial eye   an *eye* made in the end of a *rope* by *unlaying* one of its *strands*, forming the *eye*, then relaying the *strand* in the opposite direction.

From 'artificial' and *eye*.

First attested in 1961 in Burgess, *Dictionary*, 15. The OED omits this nautical sense of the phrase, restricting itself to the cosmetic palliative for visual handicap. The expression has been borrowed as the title of a British film-distribution company, in whose usage it denotes a cine-camera.

ashore   on to, or on, the land. A person *'goes* ashore'; a *ship runs* ashore' when she strikes the land rather than a submerged or separate bank, in which case she 'runs *aground.*' A 'run ashore' is a brief shore leave or *liberty*.

From 'a-' (preposition of state) and 'shore', whose source is ME 'schore', but whose earlier etymology is obscure.

First attested in 1586 in Bowes (transl.), *French Academie* (1589 edition), 341.

asleep   (of a *sail*) not pulling, and so doing no work, although (in usual use) not flapping or *flogging*: a common situation when *going about*.

Figurative use of the familiar word, whose source is 'a-' plus OE 'slapan': in OE, 'on slaepe' meant 'in sleep'.

First attested in this sense in 1867 in Smyth, *Sailor's Word-book*, which however defines it as 'filled with wind just enough for swelling' – a more active situation than the word now suggests.

astay   (of the *anchor cable*) at angle putting it roughly in line with a *stay*, usually the *forestay*. Cf. *apeak*.

From 'a-' plus '*stay*', whose source is OE 'staeg' and seems to have been first used in its nautical sense.

First attested in 1867 in Smyth, *Sailor's Word-book*.

astern   behind or backwards. As an order to the engine-room, is means 'go astern'.

From 'a-' plus *stern*, whose source is probably ON '*stjorn*'.

First attested, in both the above senses, in the seventeenth century: in 1627 in Smith, *Sea Grammar* (in the sense of 'behind'), and in 1681 in *The London Gazette* (meaning 'backwards').

athwart   at right angles to the centre line or the *course* of a *ship*.

From 'a-' plus '*thwart*', the latter derived from the early ME 'thwert': see *thwart*.

First attested, in a non-nautical sense but with the same general meaning, in 1470. The nautical sense is first attested in 1593 in Hawkins, *Observations* (1622), 232: 'If this Spanish shippe should fall athwart his King's armado'.

atrip, a-trip   (of an *anchor*), broken out of the *ground*; of *topsails* in a *square-rigged ship*) fully *hoisted* and ready for *trimming* or *sheeting home*; (of *yards*) *swayed up* with their *stops* out ready for *crossing*; of a *topmast* or *topgallant mast*) with the *fid* loosened ready for it to be *struck* or lowered. As can be seen from these usages, the underlying general notion is of readiness.

From 'a-' plus '*trip*', whose source is OF '*treper*', to kick the ground or hop: see *trip*.

First attested in 1626 in Sandys (transl.), *Metamorphoses*, xi, 228.

avast   (as an order) stop, cease, or hold fast.

Rather implausibly thought by some to be derived from the Italian '*basta*', 'that's enough'; but more likely to be a corruption of the Dutch '*hou'vast*' or '*houd vast*', meaning precisely 'hold fast'.

First attested in 1681 in Otway, *The Souldier's Fortune*, iv, 1: 'Hoa up, hoa up; so, avast there, Sir.' Perhaps more common on the stage than on the sea.

aweigh, a-weigh   (of an *anchor*) broken out of the *ground* when being *weighed*. Although well known to *landlubbers*, this expression can cause confusion with 'away' and '*under way*' (sometimes mis-spelled 'weigh'); non-professional *sailors* therefore tend to avoid it.

From 'a-' plus '*weigh*', whose source is OE 'wegan', from a common Teutonic root: see *weigh*.

First attested with this spelling in 1670 in Dryden, *Tempest*, I, I.

ay, ay, Sir or **aye, aye, Sir**   the correct and obedient response to an order *on board ship*. In the Royal Navy, it is also the correct response to a hail from another *ship* when the *ship* responding has an officer *on board* below the rank of *captain*. If a *captain* is *on board* the response should be the name of his *ship*; if an *admiral*, 'flag'; if no commissioned officer is *on board* the reply is 'No, no'.

As an affirmative, 'ay' is first attested in the late sixteenth century, of origin unknown. Its use is now restricted to dialect, the Navy, and the House of Commons.

Baboon watch   harbour *watch*, or watchman left on *deck* to safeguard a *ship* in harbour.

The word 'baboon' is derived from the 13th-century French '*babuin*', associated with grimacing and with the inclusion of grotesques in manuscript illumination. As well as describing one of the divisions of *Simiadae* or monkeys, it was used figuratively as a term of abuse from the sixteenth century onwards. The nautical implication was that the person on *watch* in such easy circumstances could be a simpleton: in the days of the old *square-riggers* he was usually an apprentice.

Not in the OED; first attested in 1976 in Kemp, *Oxford Companion*, 51.

back, to   (of *wind*) to shift direction counter-clockwise in the Northern hemisphere (i.e., contrary to its normal shift), and clockwise in the Southern hemisphere (where the normal shift is counter-clockwise); (of a *sail*) to *sheet* to *windward*, or (in a *square-rigger*) to *brace* the *yards* so as to press the *canvas* against the *mast* or ensure that the *wind* presses on the *forward* side of the *sail* to take *way* off the *ship*; (of an *anchor*) to lay out another, usually a *kedge* or a *stream anchor*, to increase holding power: in the US the expression also denotes *rigging* a 'sentinel' (in the UK an *anchor* weight) on the *rode*; (in *rowing*) to back *oars* or to back water is to push instead of pulling.

From the familiar word, whose source as a noun is OE 'baec' and a common Teutonic root (Old Teutonic *'bako'*).

First attested as applied to the wind in 1860 by Admiral Robert Fitzroy in *The Mercantile Marine Magazine*, VII, 40.

back splice   a means of preventing a *rope* from unlaying other than by *whipping*; it depends on forming a *crown knot*, with the *strands* tucked back. The disadvantage is its diameter.

From *back* plus *splice*, the latter adapted from the Middle Dutch *'splissen'*, possibly linked with 'split'.

Not in OED; first attested in 1961 in Burgess, *Dictionary*, 17.

backboard   a large board, often removable, fitted *athwartships* across the *transom* of a small *boat* as a backrest for the passengers or (if under *sail*) for the *helmsman*.

From *back* plus 'board'.

First attested in this sense in 1769 in Falconer, *Dictionary*.

backstay   part of the *standing rigging* that helps support the *mast* when the *wind* is *abaft* the *beam*. In fully *rigged ships*, backstays from each *mast* are led to the *ship*'s side *abaft* the *mast*; in smaller *boats*, they may be known as *runners*, of which the *lee runner* can be slackened off. In *Bermuda-rigged* (in the US, *Marconi-rigged*) *yachts*, the backstay or backstays may be led to a *chain plate* at the *stern*, or to a *bumpkin*. In heavy *weather* an additional *preventer* may be *rigged*.

From *back* plus *stay*, whose source is OE 'staeg'.

First attested in 1626 in Smith, *Accidence*, 29.

baggywrinkle   padding to prevent chafe, made up of bunches of old *rope yarn*, *sennet*, etc., often knotted across two *strands* of *marline*. Also spelt 'bag-o'-wrinkle', 'baggy rinkle', 'bag a wrinkle', etc; not applied to the wrinkled sagging of a badly cut or stretched *sail*.

The spelling 'bag-o'-wrinkle' is the most likely etymology on offer. The word is not in the OED.

First attested in 1961 in Burgess, *Dictionary*, 18.

bail   to empty water from a *boat*, usually by hand. Sometimes erroneously spelt 'bale'. Confusion of the two words can lead to ambiguity, as in one recorded instance in which the command 'bail out' led its recipient to jump *overboard*, thinking it an order to 'bale out', as when jumping by parachute from an aircraft.

From the French *'baille'*, the word originally denoted what is now known as a *bailer* (the implement, not its user).

First attested in its nautical sense in 1613 in Purchas, *Pilgrimage,* ix, xiv, 91.

baldheaded   originally applied to a *square-rigged vessel* with *stump topgallant masts*, which carry no *sails* above the *topgallants*; now, any *boat* with no *headsails set*.

By obvious figurative extension from the familiar words: 'bald' beingderived from ME 'balled' (i.e. like a ball), and 'head' from OE 'heafod'.

Not in OED. First attested in 1961 in Burgess, *Dictionary*, 19.

baldie   a double-ended *fishing-boat*.

Etymology unknown.

Not in OED, First attested in 1961 in Burgess, *Dictionary*, 19.

balinger   small *sea*-going *vessel* without a *forecastle*, with either a *square sail* or one extended by a *sprit* on a single *mast*, used in the fifteenth and sixteenth centuries, mainly for coastal trade but sometimes transporting some forty troops.

Although she was not used for whaling, the origin of her name was OF *'baleinier'*, whaler. By 1670 the name had dropped out of use.

First attested in 1391 in *Testamenta Eboracensia*, I, 67.

ballast   additional weight carried low in a *vessel* to improve stability.

Ballast may be liquid or solid: water in the tanks of a large *vessel*, or stone, gravel, concrete (sometimes with scrap iron in it), iron or lead. A ballast *keel* of lead or cast iron is often used for racing *yachts*, leaving the inside of the *hull* uncluttered. Ballast logs may be lashed alongside a *sailing ship*; ballast tanks are fitted in submarines. 'In ballast' means carrying no *cargo*.

A truly European word, found in similar form in most languages; probably originating in Old Swedish and Old Danish as *'barlast'* in the fourteenth century.

First attested in English in 1530 in Palsgrave, *Lesclaircissement*, 196/2.

banderole   small swallowtail *flag* flown at the *masthead* as a *weather vane*. Also spelt 'badrol' and 'bannerol'.

Originally, it was carried in battle, as can be seen in many naval paintings. Today, many *yachts* use a *burgee* as a *weather vane*. The word 'banderole' is also in use, on land, to describe a small ornamental streamer, as on a lance or trumpet; a scroll; a flat band with an inscription on Renaissance buildings; or a pall laid over a coffin.

From the fifteenth-century French *'banerolle'*, which became *'banderolle'* in the sixteenth century and *'banderole'* later. It is a diminutive of the Italian *'bandiera'*, still the word for *flag*.

First attested in 1562 in Legh, *Accedens*, 189, where it appears as 'Banaroll'.

Barber hauler   nothing to do with either a *bosun's chair* or *crossing-the-line* shaving, this is an extra line attached to the *clew* of a *headsail* in racing *dinghies*, in addition to the *sheet*, so as to adjust the fullness of the *sail*.

From the name of its inventors, Manning and Merritt Barber of California.

Not in OED; first attested in 1978 in Desoutter, *Dictionary*, 22.

bareboat (also *bare hull*, *bare pole*) chartered for use without crew or consumable stores; *under bare poles* means with no *sails set*.

From the familiar word, whose OE origin is 'baer', from a common Teutonic root of which the Old Teutonic form was '*baz-oz*', plus 'boat', from OE 'bat'. The OED gives no nautical reference to any of these expressions with regard to chartering.

'Bare pole' is first attested in 1961 in Burgess, *Dictionary*, 20, 'bareboat' and 'bare hull' in 1976 in Kemp, *Oxford Companion*, 59. 'Under bare poles' is first attested in 1697 in Dampier, *Voyage* (1699), 415.

barge a *flat-bottomed vessel* of shallow *draught*; a long narrow *craft* for canal work; a ceremonial *boat* (like Cleopatra's); in the US, a double-decker *vessel* propelled by another; in the past, the second *boat* of a *warship*, with fourteen *oars*; later, the largest *boat* of a *warship* also with fourteen *oars*, but having a *mast*, *sails*, and drop *keel*. In addition to its multiple modern meanings, the word originally denoted a small *vessel* with *sails*, one size bigger than a *balinger*. As a verb, it has a specific sense in *yacht* racing: to force a passage, illegally, between a *boat* to *leeward* and the starting mark at the beginning of a race.

From the Latin '*barca*', a *boat*, via OF '*barge*'.

First attested *c.* 1300 in *Cursor Mundi* (EETS, 1874–92), 24840.

bark originally, a small *sailing ship* of any *rig*; now synonymous with the more specific *barque*.

Like *barge*, from the Latin '*barca*', a *boat*.

First attested in 1475 in Caxton (transl.), *Historie of Jason*, 104, where it figures as 'barque': the replacement of 'qu' by 'k' is first attested in 1494.

barque a three-, four- or five-*mast sailing vessel*, *square-rigged* but with *fore-and-aft sails* on the *mizen*, furthest *aft*.

Although this was the original spelling of *bark*, it was later used, according to the OED, to distinguish the *vessel* from the larger '*bark*', which began to be built in the mid nineteenth century, becoming as big as 3,000 or 5,000 tons, especially for the grain and nitrate trade to South America via Cape Horn. Some barques are still used as training *ships*, and a few small ones are believed to carry inter-island trade in the Pacific. In the US, the word is spelled 'bark'.

Like *barge* and *bark*, from the Latin '*barca*', a *boat*.
First attested in 1475 in Caxton, *Jason*, 104.

barquentine   similar to a *barque*, except that only the *fore-mast* is *square-rigged*.

Diminutive of *barque*, perhaps on the model of *brigantine*.
First attested in 1693 in *Colonial Records of Pennsylvania*, I, 379, where it is spelled 'barkenteen'.

barricado   Seventeenth-century naval term for a *tender*, powered by *oar* or *sail*, attending *warships* in harbour but not one of the *ships*' own *boats*; also, a wooden rail across the *forward* part of the *quarterdeck*.

From the Spanish '*barrica*' and French '*barrique*', a *cask*, whence the familiar word 'barricade', since casks filled with earth or stones were used (among other objects) to form street and other improvised barricades. The nautical sense of the word may derive from the fact that such *tenders* carried provisions in casks, or possibly from their being strengthened by wooden barricados.

The OED omits the 'tender' sense, first attested in 1976 in Kemp, *Oxford Companion*, 62. The 'rail' sense is first attested in 1675 in Teonge, *Diary* (1825), 52.

barrico   a small *cask* for use in *ships*' *boats*, often to carry water. In English nautical use, pronounced 'breaker', and sometimes thus spelt.

From the Spanish '*barrica*' a *cask*.
First attested in 1607 in Smith, *Works*, Introduction, p. 54.

batten   thin iron bar securing the *tarpaulin* over a *cargo hatch*; thin wooden or (more recently and, to some, regrettably) plastic strip used to stiffen a *sail* by being slipped into a pocket on its surface at the *leech. Hatches* are *battened* down when the battens are secured with wedges in the batten *cleats* on *deck*.

The word is a variant of 'baton', which in technical use was long pronounced 'batten', although in general use the pronunciation 'battoon' (to rhyme with 'spittoon') later became fashionable until a quasi-French sound was adopted for the baton of an orchestral conductor. The expression 'to batten on' in the sense of 'exploit' comes from a quite different source, ON '*batna*', to improve.

First attested in its nautical sense in 1769 in Falconer, *Dictionary* (1789).

bawley   an English shrimping or *trawling vessel* or oyster dredger once common at Rochester and Whitstable, Kent, and at Leigh-on-Sea and Harwich, Essex, in the Thames Estuary area: it was beamy, with a modest *draught*, a high *freeboard* *forward* and a raked *transom*; it could be *sloop-* or *cutter-rigged*, with a short *mast* and *topmast*, its *mainsail loose-footed* on a very long *gaff*.

Also spelled 'bauley' and 'baully', its etymology is unknown, although conceivably connected with 'bowly' (bowl-shaped), describing the *lines* of the *hull*.

First attested in 1887 in Parish and Shaw, *Dictionary*, 9.

beak   the metal point or ram on the *bow* of a war *galley*.

By extension from a bird's beak, whose source is the French *'bec'*; of interest mainly owing to its derivative *beakhead*.

First attested in 1550 in Nicolls (transl.), *Hystory*, 183.

beakhead   the space in a *sailing warship* immediately *forward* of the *forecastle*, fastened to the *stem* and supported by the main *knee*. In older *ships* it was open to the *sea* and accessible by doors from the *forecastle* or by ladders from the *forecastle deck;* it was used as the *crew's* lavatory, and in some cases decked with gratings to that the *sea* could wash it. Hence the term *heads*, still used in this sense in the navy.

From *beak* plus *head*.

First attested in 1580 in North (transl.), *Plutarch's Lives* (1676), 423.

beam   one of the transverse *timbers* or steel bars holding a *vessel* together sideways and supporting a *deck*; also, the breadth of the *ship* at its widest part. It can also refer to the wooden or metal bar that spreads the mouth of a *trawl* when used for *fishing*, and to the *stock* of an *anchor*.

By 1613 it was used to refer to a large bar of metal, whence its meaning of an *anchor's stock*. From 1627 onwards it occurs in the other two senses above, which are in much more common use.

The beam is also used as a reference point and direction. *'Abaft* the beam' refers to the arc of a semi-circle extended to the horizon from one beam and around the stern to the other. *'Before* the beam' refers to a similar semi-circle around the *bows*. 'On the beam' means at right angles to the *fore-and-aft* line of the *ship*. A 'beam *reach'* is *sailed* with the *wind* on the beam. A 'beam *sea'* rolls at right angles to the *ship's course*. A 'beam *wind'* blows at right angles to the *keel*. 'On her beam ends' means *heeling* so that the *deck* beams are nearly vertical and there is no *righting* momentum; figuratively it means destitute, the analogy probably being with a *ship* lying on her side *ashore* rather than *heeling* at *sea*. 'Beamy' means wide. An 'x-beam' *vessel* (where 'x' may denote any number) is one whose length is x times her beam measurement.

Derived from OE 'beam' and cognate with the Dutch *'boom'*

and the German '*Baum*', the word originally meant 'tree' (as in 'hornbeam') and hence various kinds of pole.

bean-cod   a small Portuguese river and estuary *fishing-boat* with a sharp and very high *inboard*-curving *bow*; it was single-*masted* with a large *lateen sail*. Ashore, a 'bean-cod' (from two very similar OE words) is a bean pod: the nautical application is imitative and no doubt originally jocular.

First attested in its nautical sense in 1769 in Falconer, *Dictionary* (1789).

bear[1]   a heavy *coir* mat laden with sand and dragged to and fro to scour the *deck*.

Unlike *bear* as a nautical verb, this noun is derived (by obvious shaggy analogy) from the animal, and hence from OE 'bera'.

Also sometimes denoting a doormat, it is first attested in 1795 in Aikin, *Manchester*, 349.

bear[2]   to lie in a certain direction; that direction (*bearing*). Most commonly used in compounds; e.g. 'bear away' (to *point* further off the *wind*), 'bear down' (approach from *windward*, always followed by 'on'), 'bear up' ('bear away' by putting the *tiller* to *windward* – the opposite of *luffing up* by putting the *helm down* which is *not* called 'bearing down').

From the familiar word meaning to carry, whose source is a common Teutonic root and OE 'ber-an', and ultimately the Sanskrit '*bhar-*'. The nautical senses arise from a further nuance in the word, implying also to thrust or push, displacing the object of the action otherwise than by carrying it, and indicating the direction in which displacement occurs. First attested in a nautical context in 1605 in Shakespeare, *The Tempest*, III, ii, 3.

bearing   the direction in which an object lies, expressed as the horizontal angle (in degrees) between that direction and north. A 'bearing *compass*', unlike the fixed *steering compass* which shows the magnetic *heading* of the *vessel*, is normally hand-held: it shows the magnetic bearing of the object observed through it.

From the verb *bear*.

First attested in this nautical sense in 1635 in Carpenter, *Geography*, I, vii, 171.

beat   to *sail close-hauled* to *windward*. Some use this word to denote zig-zagging on alternate *tacks*, which others may call *tacking*, although others again confine this word to meaning changing from one *tack* to the other. Another term for such zig-zagging is 'beating up' – equally ambiguous in a quite different, intimidating sense.

Probably from the familiar word (from OE 'beatan') meaning

to strike – as anyone who has struggled against a Force 7 head-wind will appreciate. It remains just possible, however, that the word is derived from some nautical use of the Icelandic *'baita'*, to bait. Both etymologies fit the trying nature of the action.

First attested in its nautical sense in 1720 in *The London Gazette*, 5827/1.

Beaufort scale   a table of *wind* speeds, names, and numbers devised by Rear-Admiral Sir Francis Beaufort (1774–1857, Hydrographer of the Navy, although possibly also inspired by his predecessor Alexander Dalrymple (1737–1808), the first Hydrographer.

beaupers, bewpars, or **bewpers**   a fabric or *bunting* used for *flags*.

Almost certainly a corruption of the name of the French textile town, Beaupréau, Maine-et-Loire.

First attested in 1592 in *Wills and Inventories*, II, 211.

becket   a short length of *rope* with its ends *spliced* together to make a circle (cf. *grommet*); a similar length of rope with an *eye splice* in one end and possibly a *stopper knot* at the other, to make a loop for securing *spars*, etc.; a short length of rope with an eye splice in each end to secure a *sprit* against the *mast*; a loop or small *eye* at the end of a rope; the eye at the base of a *block*. A 'becket bend' is a *sheet bend*; a 'becket block' is one fitted with a becket; a 'becket rowlock' is a small *rope strop* used on a *thole pin* to contain the *oar* when *rowing*.

The word's etymology is speculative. It may be related to 'beck', from the Celtic root 'bacc-', meaning a hook; but it has been linked more plausibly with the Dutch *'bogt'* or *'bocht'*, meaning the 'bend' of a rope, with which the word *bight* is also cognate.

First attested in 1769 in Falconer, *Dictionary*: he believed the word to be a corruption of 'bracket' – an implausible idea.

becue   to *scow* an *anchor* for use on rocky *ground* by *making fast* a *rope* to the *flukes* and leading it to the *ring*, where it is secured by a light *seizing*: the anchor can then be *tripped* by a sharp jerk, breaking the seizing and hoisting by the flukes.

Etymology unknown: omitted from the OED. Possibly connected with the notion that the flukes are the 'tail' or 'queue' of the anchor.

First attested in 1961 in Burgess, *Dictionary*, 24.

bee   a ring or hoop of metal; one of the pieces of hard wood bolted to the outer end of the *bowsprit*, through which the *fore-topmast stays* are *rove* before being brought in to the *bows*.

'Bee blocks' are similar wooden swells on either side of the

The Beaufort scale

Number	Speed (mph)	Description	Sea Wave height (m.) ave.	max.	
0	0	Calm			Sea like a mirror
1	1–3	Light	0.1	0.1	Ripples with the appearance of scales formed
2	4–6	Light breeze	0.2	0.3	Small wavelets, more pronounced. Crests glassy appearance, do not break.
3	7–10	Gentle breeze	0.6	1.0	Large wavelets. Crests begin to break. Foam of glassy appearance. Occasional white horses.
4	11–16	Moderate breeze	1.0	1.5	Small waves, becoming longer. Fairly frequent white horses.
5	17–21	Fresh breeze	2.0	2.5	Moderate waves, more pronounced long form. Many white horses. Some spray.
6	22–27	Strong breeze	3.0	4.0	Large waves, white foam crests more extensive everywhere. Spray.
7	28–33	Near gale	4.0	5.5	Sea heaps up and white foam from breaking waves begins to blow in streaks along the direction of the wind. Some spindrift.
8	34–40	Gale	5.5	7.5	Moderately high waves of greater length; edges of crests break into spindrift. Foam blown in well-marked streaks.
9	41–47	Strong gale	7.0	10.0	High waves. Dense streaks of foam. Sea begins to roll. Spray may affect visibility.
10	48–55	Storm	9.0	12.5	Very high waves with long overlapping crests. Foam in great patches blown in dense white streaks. Surface of sea takes white appearance. Rolling of sea becomes heavy. Visibility affected.
11	56–63	Violent storm	11.5	16.0	Exceptionally high waves. Small and medium-sized ships lost to view behind waves. Sea is completely covered with long white patches of foam. Edges of wave crests blown into froth. Visibility affected.
12	64–71	Hurricane	14.0	—	Air filled with foam and spray. Sea completely white with driving spray. Visibility seriously affected.

13 to 17 may be used for even worse conditions.

after end of the *boom*, with *sheaves* for leading through the *leech reef pendants* or *reefing tackle*; at one time, the term also applies to the bowsprit bees.

The word is unconnected with stinging, honey-gathering insects or with the letter B: its ultimate source is OE 'beag' or 'beah', a ring, although the OED dismisses this primary sense as obsolete.

First attested in its nautical sense in 1860 in Stuart, *Catechism*, 74.

beetle   heavy wooden mallet used to drive *reeming irons* into the *seams* of wooden *ships* in order to *caulk* them with *oakum* and pitch.

More entomology-free etymology: like *bee*, this word has nothing to do with insects (or with beetle brows). Its source is OE 'bietel', a hammer or mallet, clearly cognate with 'beat'.

First attested in *c*. AD 897 in King Aelfred (transl.), *Gregory's Pastoral Care* (EETS, 1871), xxxvi, 253.

before   ahead of, on the *forward* side of.

Most commonly used in set phrases. 'Before the *beam*' means *forward* of it; 'before the *mast*' means literally forward of it, but is used in two figurative senses, to describe *seamen* since their quarters used to be in the *forecastle*, and to refer to where dead men's effects were sold; while 'before the wind' means with the wind *aft*, or *running*. For etymology, see *afore*.

First attested in a nautical context is 1598 in Phillip, *Linschoten*, III, 23.

belay   to *make fast* a *rope* or *line* by taking turns round a *cleat* or *belaying pin*; also, as a command, 'stop' or 'cease'. A *belaying pin* is a short bar of wood, iron, or brass, several of which may be arranged side-by-side in a rack, *pin-rail*, *fife-rail*, or *spider band*. They are used for *running rigging*; larger *ropes* and *cables* are not belayed but *bitted*, i.e. brought through to the *bitts*.

The remote origin of the word, which has a very early history in the ninth century, meaning at that time 'to beset', is OE 'belecgan'; it has also been suggested that the nautical use of the term may derive from the Dutch '*beleggen*', to cover, cognate with the German '*belegen*'. The obsolete and possibly erroneous form of 'belay' was 'belage'.

First attested in a nautical sense in 1549 in the *Complaynt of Scotlande* (EETS, 1872), vi, 41.

bellum   long *canoe*-shaped *boat paddled* or poled and used in Persian Gulf *ports* and the Shatt-al-Arab and adjacent Iraqui waters.

The word does not denote a 'war canoe': its source is not the

Latin '*bellum*' but the Persian '*balam*'.

First attested in English surprisingly late, in 1901 in *World Wide Magazine*, VI, 464/1.

belly the fullness of a *sail*; to swell when filled with *wind* (referring to sailing, not digestion). A *belly band* is an extra strip of *canvas* etc., fitted to a *sail* to strengthen it for the *reef points*; a *belly stay* is an extra support for a *mast* or *spar* at its centre; a *belly tackle* is used to support *sheer legs* halfway up when lifting heavy weights.

From the familiar word, whose source is ME 'bali', a bag; only later was it applied to animals, including humans.

First attested in a nautical sense in 1697 in Potter, *Archaeologia* (1715), III, xiv, 123, referring to the *hold*; and as a noun applied to a sail, in 1840 in Dana, *Two Years*, V, 12, although the verb is attested in 1718 in Pope, *Iliad*, I, 626.

below under the *deck*, in or into a *cabin* or *hold*.

From the familiar word, which combines 'be-' and '-low' from ME 'loogh'; but the word was not common until the sixteenth century, when it began to acquire a prepositional as well as adjectival and adverbial use; previously, the more frequent word was *alow*.

First attested in roughly its present sense in 1598 in Shakespeare, *Merry Wives*, II, ii, 150; and in a nautical context in 1600 in Ritson, *Robin Hood* (1795; 1884 edition), II, xvi, 90.

belting heavy *timber rubbing-strake* fitted round large *vessels* at or near the *waterline*.

From the familiar word 'belt', whose source is OE 'belt' and the Old Teutonic '*baltjo-z*' – as well as, probably, the medieval Latin '*balteum*'.

First attested in its nautical sense as late as 1898 in the *Westminster Gazette*, 14 January, 9/3.

bend a *hitch* or *knot*, especially one easily *cast off*, but seldom used except in set phrases such as 'bends and hitches', *fisherman's bend*, etc., and mainly current as a verb meaning to tie or *make fast*, particularly securing a sail (although nowadays tying has largely been replaced by *hanks,* metal *runners,* etc.) or securing a *cable* to an *anchor*.

From OE 'bend', meaning essentially a bond, bind, or tie: a case of nautical terminology's retaining the original sense that is otherwise lost.

First attested in 1399 in Langland, *Richard the Redeless* (EETS, 1867–85; 1886), IV, 72.

beneaped having run *aground* at the top of *spring tides* and so obliged to wait through about two weeks of *neap tides* before the next tide high enough to float the *vessel* off. Near the *equinoctial* spring tides the wait may be for six months.

From OE 'nep', but otherwise of unknown origin and obscure meaning.

First attested in 1692 in Smith, *Seaman's Grammar* (enlarged), I, xvi, 80.

bergantine   small fourteenth to sixteenth-century Mediter-ranean *rowing* and *sailing vessel*. Like the British *pinnace*, bergantines were carried unassembled in the *holds* of exploring ships such as those of Columbus; they were then put together and used in estuaries and rivers, where they *drew* only up to 18 inches. They could be as long as 40 feet, with eight to sixteen rowing benches and one or two short *masts* with *lateen sails*.

The word is obviously cognate with *brigantine*, but its spelling is derived from the Spanish 'bergantin' and the Old Spanish 'vergantin'. The OED considers 'bergantine' and 'brig-antine' to denote the same (various) kinds of vessel, deriving their name from the Provençal *'bregan'*, irregular soldier, and such relatives as the Italian *'brigante'*: the implication is that these were skirmishing vessels, associated with brigands. Other authorities, however, distinguish between the two. No doubt 'exploring' sometimes involved 'infiltrating'.

First attested as 'bergantine' in 1555 in Eden, *Decades*, 108.

Bermuda, Bermudan, or **Bermudian**   a *rig* with a tall, tapering, roughly triangular *jib-headed* rather than *gaff main-sail*. Used in and around the West Indies from about 1800 onwards, introduced into Britain for small racing craft in 1911–12, and adopted by larger racing and cruising *yachts* between the two World Wars. Since the tall *mainmast* needed *staying*, it was thought by some to resemble a wireless aerial, and was nicknamed *Marconi rig*, still its normal name in the US. The adjective can be applied also to a *mast*, a *cat*, a *cutter*, a *sloop*, a *schooner*, a *ketch*, or a *yawl*.

Named after the eponymous group of islands.

First attested, as applied to the rig rather than the provenance, in 1853 in Kipping, *Mast-making*, II, 5.

berth   a place to sleep *on board*; a position in a *ship*'s company, with or without a sleeping-place; a place in harbour where a *boat* can be *moored* or secured *alongside*, or *ride* to her *anchor*. Nowadays, a berth on board is usually a *bunk* or even a *cabin*; in the past, it could be merely a place to sling a *hammock*.

Almost certainly unconnected with 'birth', the word is prob-ably a derivative from the nautical meaning of *bear*. Its original meaning was 'convenient sea-room' (whence the expression 'to give a wide berth', i.e. to avoid).

First attested in 1622 in Hawkins, *Observations* (1593), 117, where the spelling is 'byrth'.

Berthon boat   collapsible wood-and-canvas *dinghy* invented in 1849 by the Rev. Edward Lyon Berthon (1813–99). As with others of Berthon's inventions, the British Admiralty at first ignored the boat; but the reformer Samuel Plimsoll took an interest in its life-saving potential, and the Navy finally bought a developed version of it. Some are still in use; it has also been imitated, notably in France.

From the name of its inventor.

First attested in 1878 in Nares, *Narrative* (1875–6), I, i, 20.

bezan, bizan   small seventeenth-century *yacht*, usually a *ketch*.

From the Dutch '*bezaan*', *mizen sail*, cognate with the Spanish '*mesana*', the French '*misaine*' (although this means 'foremast'), and the Italian '*mezzana*', the word being transferred from the sail to the vessel itself. King Charles II gave the name *Bezan* to one of his yachts, a 35-tonner given him by the Dutch in 1661; and he had a second, named *Isabella Bezan*, built for him in 1680 by Phineas Pett. The former was that mentioned by Samuel Pepys, below: he sailed in her, and even used her as a floating office.

First attested in Pepys, *Diary*, 5 September 1662.

bibbs   timber supports bolted to the *hounds* of a *mast* in a *square-rigged ship*, to support the *trestle-trees*.

From the familiar word 'bib', itself possibly connected with the Latin '*bibere*', to drink, but also perhaps onomatopoeic for dribbling: the word is so used because the position of the bibbs resembles that of the bib on a baby.

First attested in 1779–80 in Cook, *Voyage to the Pacific* (1776–80), II, 271, where it is spelt 'bib'.

Bible   slang for the block of sandstone used for scrubbing wooden *decks*.

So called because those using it had to kneel: hence the name *holystone* for the same thing. Smaller blocks, used for awkward corners, were known as 'prayerbooks'.

First attested in this nautical sense in 1867 in Smyth, *Sailor's Word-book*, 98, which gives the 'kneeling' explanation.

bight   a loop in a *rope*; a sag in a rope or *canvas*; a large wide bay.

From OE 'byht', originally (in the tenth century) meaning 'band'.

First attested, as a coastline feature, in 1481 in *Ripon Acts* (1452–1506), 344; as a loop in rope, in 1622 in Hawkins, *Observations*, 132.

bilge   the rounded part of the *hull* where the side and bottom plates meet; (also 'bilges') the bottom part of the *boat* (between the two bilges) under the *cabin sole*; the widest part of a *cask* near the bung. As a verb, the word may mean to *stave in* or to be *stove in* at the bilge. A 'bilgeboard' is one of two *keels* situated at the bilges and raised or lowered like a *centreboard*. 'Bilge blocks' are supports placed at the bilges when in *dock*. 'Bilge free' (of a *cask*) means so *stowed* as to avoid pressure on its widest part. 'Bilge keels' are non-retractable bilgeboards, often replacing but sometimes merely supplementing the centre *keel*. A 'bilge *keelson*' is a *stringer* set across the *frames* at the bilge. 'Bilge paint' is synthetic resin paint applied to the inside of the bilges as a protection against oil, grease, and fuel in the bilge water. A 'bilge pump' is that used to clear the bilges. 'Bilge water' (seldom all water) is that which the bilge pump is intended to remove. 'Bilge ways' are the *timbers* used to support the bilge during construction.

Probably a corruption of 'bulge', itself derived from OF '*boulge*', whose modern French form '*bouge*' still means 'bilge' in all its senses except the colloquial meaning of 'nonsense', itself probably from 'bilge water'.

First attested in its nautical sense in 1513 in Douglas (transl.), *Virgill*, V, iv, 78.

bill   the pointed end of an *anchor*'s *fluke*. An offshoot of the word is 'bill-board', meaning not a large poster but a board fitted to protect the *timbers* when the *anchor* is *weighed*.

Derived by analogy from the bill of a bird.

First attested in this sense in 1769 in Falconer, *Dictionary*.

binge   to soak and rinse out a *cask*. Hence its colloquial use to mean carouse or carousal.

The origin of this word remains obscure: it may possibly be derived from Lincolnshire dialect, and has no connecion with 'binge' meaning to bow, analogous with 'bend' and 'cringe'.

First attested in its carousal sense in 1854 in Baker, *Glossary*, and in its nautical senes in 1961 in Burgess, *Dictionary*, 27.

binnacle   the wooden or other housing for the *steering compass*, its light and correctors.

Originally and at least until 1839, the word was 'bittacle', derived via the Spanish '*bitacula*' or '*bitacora*' from the Latin '*habitaculum*', habitation. The French for 'binnacle' is still '*habitacle*'.

First attested in 1762 in Falconer, *Shipwreck*, II, 458.

bird's nest   a small look-out position, usually round and sometimes a *cask,* placed at the *masthead* and smaller than the *crow's nest*, to help locate whales in Northern waters.

By obvious analogy from the familiar words.

First attested in 1867 in Smyth, *Sailor's Word-book*.

bitter end   not a tearful conclusion, but the inboard end of a *cable* when made fast to the *bitts*, i.e. with all the cable paid out. To 'bend to the bitter end' is to reverse the cable so as to shift the point of chafe. From *bitts*.

First attested in 1627 in Smith, *Seaman's Grammar*, VII, 30.

bitts   pairs of timber or iron posts to which the *cable* or *mooring warp* is made fast. To 'bitt' is to secure to the bitts. A 'bitts stopper' or 'bitts compressor' is used to hold the *outboard* end of the cable while the *inboard* end is bitted.

The derivation of the word remains obscure, but may be Teutonic, related to '*bitan*', to bite. Corresponding terms occur in many European languages: in French, '*bitte*'; in Italian, '*bitta*'; in Spanish, '*bita*'; in Swedish, '*beting*'; in Danish, '*beding*'; in Dutch, '*beting*'; in German, '*Baeting*' – which resembles OE 'baeting', anything that holds or restrains, including a rope. But in medieval Latin '*bitus*' was a whipping-post. So speculation continues.

First attested in 1593 in Nichols, *Drake*, V, 509.

Blackwall hitch   a quick and simple way of attaching a *rope* to a hook, passing a *bight* round the neck of the hook and crossing the two parts so that the part under strain jams the other. A *clove hitch* is a refinement on this principle.

Of unknown derivation, but almost certainly connected with Green and Wigram's shipbuilding yard at Blackwall, London, where the nineteenth-century Blackwall *frigates* were built for the India trade after the expiry of the East India Company's monopoly in 1833.

Not in OED. First attested in 1961 in Burgess, *Dictionary*, 28.

block   a pulley. Except in the expression 'block and tackle', the word in this sense is now almost always confined to nautical use.

From OF '*bloc*' and perhaps the Old High German '*bloh*'.

First attested in its nautical sense in 1622 in Malynes, *Consuetudo*, 143.

bloody flag   colloquial term for the big square red *flag* that British *warships* used to *hoist* at the *masthead* when going into battle. The red signal flag for the letter B is still used to indicate 'I am taking on, or discharging, explosives'; but now warships of all nations hoist their national *ensigns*, known as 'battle ensigns', at the beginning of naval action.

From OE 'blodig' and a common Teutonic root plus *flag*, of immensely complex and uncertain etymology.

Not in the OED; first attested in 1976 in Kemp, *Oxford Companion*, 89–90.

blue ensign   since 1864, that of Naval Reserve and naval auxiliary vessels. Originally, in the seventeenth century, the fleet was divided into three fairly small squadrons: the rear *admiral*'s flew a blue *ensign*, the vice-admiral's a white, and the admiral's a red. Although this division is said to have originated with Elizabeth I, the earliest surviving instructions on the wearing of coloured *flags* date from 1617. In 1864 the red ensign was allocated to the merchant navy, the white was adopted by the Royal Navy, and the blue was assigned to auxiliaries. It may nevertheless be worn by merchant vessels and by owners of *yachts* registered with certain clubs, provided they have a warrant from the Admiralty and include some insignia or design in the *fly*.

From ME 'blew' and OF '*bleu*' plus *ensign*, from Latin '*insignia*' via OF '*enseigne*'.

'Ensign' is first attested in this sense in 1707 in the *London Gazette* No.4356/1.

Blue Peter   the *signal flag* for P (a blue flag with a white rectangular centre), mainly used to indicate imminent departure. It can also be used at sea to signal 'Your lights are out or burning badly' (although this will presumably be hard to see in the dark), by *fishing vessels* to indicate 'My nets have become fast on an obstruction', or at the start of a race with or instead of the five-minute gun. The term is also used for the naval long-service and good conduct medal, whose ribbon is blue and white.

From ME 'blew' and OF '*bleu*' plus 'Peter', the old phonetic alphabet word for the letter P. In the present international phonetic alphabet, 'Peter' has been replaced by 'Papa'.

First attested in 1823 in Byron, *Don Juan*, XI, 83.

bluejacket   a British naval *rating*, as distinct from a Royal Marine.

From the Navy List's 1858 rules for uniform, including a jacket 'to be made of navy blue cloth double-breasted, with stand and fall collar... to reach the hips... one inside breast-pocket and seven black horn crown and anchor buttons'.

Previously, sailors were known as *tars*, from *tarpaulin*. The current uniform is a jumper and bell-bottom trousers, with a blue jean collar with three white stripes. New recruits scrub their collars in the hope of making them look faded and themselves old salts.

First attested in 1830 in Marryat, *King's Own*, ii.

board   the side of a *ship*, leading to the expression 'go by the board', i.e. *overboard*; a *tack* when *close-hauled*.

From OE 'bord', one of whose meaning's was already a ship's side, and the French '*bord*', as in the expression '*virer de bord*', to turn the ship's side in another direction.

First attested in English in 1533 in Bellenden (transl.), *Livy's Rome*, I, 73.

boat strictly, a small open man-made *craft* with no *decking*, usually propelled by *oars* or an *outboard* engine, sometimes with a *lugsail* on a short *mast*. However, *fishing boats* are often half- or fully decked, and propelled by *inboard* engines or full suits of *sails*; while submarines are also known as 'boats' since they were originally called 'submarine boats'. Further exceptions were the original 'torpedoboats', forerunners of destroyers and *frigates*, as well as the World War II motor torpedo-boats and motor gunboats that have given way to the current fast patrol boats. Otherwise, sea-goers normally use the word *ship*, even of mail and packet boats; *landlubbers* use the word 'boat' more extensively. *Yacht* owners self-deprecating refer to their own craft as 'boats', although they may call a friend's vessel a 'yacht'; and they will sometimes use the word 'ship' of either, in what might be called 'forgotten jocular' vein. No one hoping to be respected would ever refer to 'my yacht'. Naturally enough, the word has given rise to a multitude of related expressions. A 'boat boom' is a long *spar* swung outwards from a vessel's side, from which it keeps boats not in use. 'Boat chocks' or 'cradles' are on-deck supports for boats. The 'boat deck' is that from which *lifeboats* are manned. 'Boat drill' is lifeboat or 'abandon ship' practice. A 'boat-hook' is a pole with a hook at one end for picking up *moorings*, etc. A 'boatkeeper' is the member of a boat's crew who stays in the boat to look after her when the rest have left. 'Boatpox' is an affliction of GRP *hulls*, beginning with underwater blisters that burst and remove the gel coat. A 'boatrope' can be a *painter*, a *hoist,* or a rope with which to secure a vessel. A 'boat's bag' is a holdall for tools, etc. The 'boat's box' is a sealed container for *flares*, rockets, etc. 'Boat your *oars*' is the command to *unship* the oars and lay them *fore* and *aft* within the boat; this is not to be confused with '*ship* your oars', meaning to place them in the *crutches* ('*rowlocks*') ready for use.

The word's etymology is as complicated as its use. Its origin is OE 'bat'. This would have corresponded to an Old Teutonic '*baito*' or an ON '*beit-r*'; but the ON word for a small boat was '*bat-r*', which would have corresponded to an OE 'baet' or 'bet', giving the modern English 'beet'. The OED concludes that the ON word was a borrowing from OE. The same root appears in Romance languages such as '*bateau*' in French (from OF '*batel*'), '*batello*' in Italian, etc.

First attested in OE in 891 in the *Anglo-Saxon Chronicle*; in its modern spelling in 1591 in Shakespeare, *Henry VI*, IV, vi, 33.

boatswain   (pronounced 'bo'sun' and often so spelt) the officer or warrant officer in charge of *sails*, *rigging*, *anchors*, *cable*, etc., but not normally *boats*. A 'boatswain's call' or 'pipe' is a small, oddly-shaped whistle that can produce a variety of tones or trills and was used for giving orders (now only on ceremonial occasions): until Tudor times it was the insignia of the Lord High *Admiral*. A 'boatswain's chair' is a short board slung in *bridle* and used to *hoist* a man *aloft*. The 'boatswain's chest', 'locker' or 'store' is that reserved for *stowing blocks*, *ropes*, *canvas*, spikes, etc.

'Boat' (from OE 'bat') plus 'swain' (from OE 'swan'): in its original sense, now obsolete, 'swain' meant a young man attendant on a knight, and hence of lower degree.

First attested *c*. 1450 in *Pilgrims Sea-voyage*, 21.

bobstay   a *stay*, usually of *chain* or heavy wire *rope*, but sometimes a solid rod, from the end of the *bowsprit* to the *stem* or *cutwater*, to counteract the upward strain. The original reason for fitting a bobstay was that the *foretopmast* was *stayed* to the *bowsprit* and exerted powerful lifting force when the sails were full. *Square-rigged* training ships still carry bobstays; otherwise they are now mainly confined to *yachts* with bowsprits, and not to all of these.

An etymological half-mystery. The original meaning of *Stay* is nautical, first found in *c*. AD 1100: but lexicographers remain baffled as to which of the many meanings of 'bob' is here coupled with it.

The 'bobstay piece' is the wooden support at the *stem* to which the bobstay may be attached.

First attested in 1769 in Falconer, *Dictionary*.

bollard   a vertical piece of wood or iron fixed to the ground for securing *mooring* lines; *aboard ship*, usually in pairs.

Of unknown derivation, but possibly based on the familiar word 'bole' for the trunk of a tree.

First attested, surprisingly late, in 1844 in Key, *Gorgon*, 67.

bolt   a roll of *canvas*, 39 yards long but of no fixed width, although generally of 22–30 inches.

From OE 'bolt', an arrow (as in 'bolt from the blue'), by transference in the fourteenth and fifteenth centuries to its textile sense, possibly connected with the use of 'clothyard' to describe an arrow's length, although the Middle Low German '*bolte*', '*bolten*' also meant a piece of linen rolled up.

First attested in 1407 in Wollebergh, *Will*.

boltrope   a rope sewn round the edge of a *sail* to prevent its tearing. On square sails, it is fitted to the *after* edge; on *fore-and-aft* sails, to the *port* side. It may also be subdivided (omitting the 'bolt-') according to where on the sail it is fitted: e.g. *luffrope* (or *headrope*), *footrope*, etc. A footrope should therefore not be confused with a *toestrap*, used by *dinghy sailors* to hook their feet in when *heeling*. In dinghies and small *cruisers*, the luffrope may have the additional function of holding the *mainsail* to the *mast*, whose *after* side has a groove into which it slides.

From *bolt* plus *rope*.

First attested in 1626 in Smith, *Accidence*.

bone   the foam and spray seen at the *bows* of a fast-moving *vessel*. Usually used in such expressions as 'a bone in her teeth', which makes obvious the figurative likeness to a beast of prey carrying a white bone jutting out on either side of its jaws.

From the familiar word, whose source is OE 'ban' from a common Teutonic root and the Old Teutonic '*baino*'.

First attested in 1627 in Smith, *Seaman's Grammar*, II 10.

bonnet   an additional strip of *canvas laced* to a *sail*, usually in *square-riggers*, to catch extra *wind*; a cover for the *navel pipe*. The OED believes that bonnets were originally fitted at the top of sails, or that they may have been *topsails*. Later they were certainly fitted at the *foot*. Nowadays, those seeking to increase sail area are more likely to use a *watersail*, e.g. below the main *boom*.

From the familiar word, whose source is ME and OF 'bonet', head-dress.

First attested in its nautical sense in 1399 in Langland, *Richard the Redeless*, IV, 72.

booby-hatch   an additional small *companion-way*; the *hatch* on the *cabin* top of a small *cruiser*.

From the primary meaning of the word 'booby', a fool, which is probably derived from the Spanish '*bobo*', meaning both a fool and a species of gannet. The German '*Bube*', a fool, seems to be a separate word, since its Low German form was '*boeve, boef*' and its Middle High German form '*buobe*'. The combination 'booby-hatch' may have analogies with 'booby-hutch' or 'booby-hut'; but why a second means of ingress and egress should be regarded as reserved for those 'with learning difficulties' remains obscure, unless the *skipper*, who presumably used the main companion-way, despised (or affected to despise) the *crew*.

First attested in 1840 in Dana, *Two Years*, XXXIV, 130.

boom   a long *spar* used to extend the *foot* of a *sail*; a pole used to mark a *channel*; a barrier of connected spars, poles, logs, etc., used to restrict or retain floating timber; a spar *rigged* horizontally to *moor boats*. In *square rig*, booms are usually temporary, and rigged in light airs, like a *spinnaker boom*; in *fore-and-aft rig* the booms are usually permanent. Most *mainsails* now have booms, as do some *staysails*, to facilitate *tacking*. On a *sailboard*, the boom is of *wishbone* shape. In the plural, the word denotes a part of the *deck* where spare spars are stowed. As a verb, 'to boom off' means to *fend* off with spars. Anyone struck by the boom in an accidental or unexpected *gybe* will recall a very different sense of the word.

Associated expressions include: 'boom boats' (the larger ship's boats stowed aboard in *crutches* between the fore- and main masts, while the smaller are secured on *davits*); 'boom crotch' or 'crutch' (a support for the boom when moored or anchored, in place of a *topping lift*); 'boom defence' (placed across a harbour entrance); 'boom horse' (an iron band fitted to the boom for the *block* of the *sheets* to travel on); 'boom irons' (metal rings fitted to the *yard-arms* of *square-riggers* through which the *studdingsail* booms are traversed); 'boom strap' (a metal fitment to which the *mainsheet block* is *shackled*: since it prevents *roller reefing*, the sail has to be reefed by points); 'boom vang' (the *martingale* or *kicking strap* used to prevent the boom from rising).

From the Dutch '*boom*', tree, beam or pole, corresponding to the Old and Middle High German '*boum*', the modern German '*Baum*', OE 'beam' and the modern English 'beam'.

First attested as a barrier in 1645; as a spar in 1662 in Birch, *History*, 1756–7, I, 91; as a timber retainer in North America in 1702; and in the plural in 1762.

boomkin (also *bumkin, bumpkin*)   a short *spar* projecting from the *stern* on which to attach the *backstay* or the *mizen sheets*; formerly a short spar projecting from the *quarters* for the *main brace block* or (as a *bowsprit*) from the *stem* for the *foresail clew* line.

A diminutive of *boom*, probably related to the Dutch '*boomken*'.

First attested in a nautical sense in 1611 in Cotgrave, *Dictionarie* and in 1632 in Sherwood, *Dictionarie*. 'Bumpkin', in its sense of a rustic clown, is first attested rather earlier, in 1570 in Levins, *Manipulus*, 133. This usage, conceivably insulting to the Dutch, may be derived from the Middle Dutch '*bommekijn*', little barrel.

boot-top   the part of the *hull* which lies between the *load waterline* and the *light waterline*. 'Boot-topping' is the paint applied along the boot-top and also on the ship's *bottom*: it used to be composed of tallow, rosin and sulphur or lime, to give a smooth surface and act as anti-fouling, for which modern compounds are now used, although sometimes still referred to by the original name.

Derived by extension from the polished upper part of a top-boot. First attested in 1764–6 in Croker, *Dictionary*.

bottle-screw   (also known as a *rigging screw* or *turnbuckle*) a tensioning device for *shrouds*, etc., consisting of two eyebolts threaded at opposite ends, and on opposite threads, into a central sleeve which when turned clockwise or anticlockwise tightens or loosens the tension.

Derived by obvious analogy from 'bottle', whose source is the Old (and modern) French *'bouteille'*. The OED gives only the definition 'corkscrew'; but whether this is an intermediary remains uncertain.

First attested in its nautical sense in 1961 in Burgess, *Dictionary*, 33–4.

bottom   the *keel* of a *ship*; all the *hull* below the *waterline*; the *sea*bed; the ship herself.

From OE 'botm'.

First attested as the seabed in the late eighth century in *Beowulf*, 3016; as the lowest part of a ship in 1382 in Wyclif, *Wisdom*, v, 10; and as the whole ship in 1522 in Fiddes, *Wolsey* (1724), 64. The best remembered use of the word in this last sense is in George Canning's 'A Political Despatch' (31 January 1826):

> In matters of commerce, the fault of the Dutch
> Is giving too little and asking too much;
> With equal advantage the French are content,
> So we'll clap on Dutch bottoms a twenty per cent.

bottomry   (also spelled 'bottomarie', 'bodomery', 'bottomree', 'bottomary' and 'bottomery' – see also Pepys, below): a mortgage on a *ship* (or its contents, in which case the proper term is 'respondentia'). Unlike a mortgage on real property, bottomry is risky to the lender, who loses his security if the ship is lost at sea. Hence the story told by Samuel Pepys in his *Diary* for 30 November 1663: 'I heard the best story of a cheat entended by the Maister of a ship, who had borrowed twice his money upon Bottomaryne, and as much more insured upon his ship and goods as they were worth, and then would have cast her away upon the coast of France and there left her, refusing any pilott which was offered him; and so the Governor of the place took her and sent her over hither to find an Owner; and so the ship is come safe, and goods and all – not worth 500*l*, and he had one way or other taken 3000*l*.' Pepys attended Guildhall the next day to hear the case tried at King's Bench, where the jury found for the plaintiff.

From *bottom*, but after the Dutch '*bodmerij*'.

First attested in 1622 in Malynes, *Consuetudo*, 171.

bow   the *forward* part of the *vessel*, just *abaft* of the *stem*. In the plural, a warning order given in a boat going alongside, telling the foremost member of the crew to ship his *oar* and man his *boathook*.

A 'bow and beam bearing' is the American expression for a *four point bearing*, a method of finding distance *off* by taking two bearings of an object on shore, one when it *bears* four points or 45 degrees on the bow, the other when it is *abeam* and bears 90 degrees. 'Bow chasers' were two long guns mounted in the *bow-ports* of sailing warships. 'Bower anchors' are the two main anchors, permanently attached to their cables and kept at the bows. A 'bow fender' is self-explanatory. A 'bow lantern' is a bi-colour lantern that may be mounted forward (usually on the *pulpit*) on the centreline of a boat under 20 metres long, showing red to *port* and green to *starboard*. A 'bow-line' (to rhyme with 'cow-line' and not to be confused with the knot *bowline*, pronounced 'bo-lin') is a *mooring warp* at the bows. A 'bowman' (to rhyme with 'cow-man' and nothing to do with archery) is the foremost man of a boat's crew, pulling the 'bow oar'. The 'bow plate' is the metal fitting at the *stem* to which the *headsail* is *tacked* down and the *forestay* attached. The 'bow ports' were square holes in the bows of sailing warships through which the *port-chasers* were fired. The 'bow rail' is the US term for the *pulpit*. A 'bow rudder' is a rudder forward of the *keel*, used to improve the turning circle. The 'bow sheets' or 'headsheets' are *not* lines controlling sails, but the floorboards, benches and space in the *fore* part of the ship. 'Bows on' is said of a vessel approaching from any direction when her centreline points at the observer. A '*bowsprit*' is a *spar* projecting from the *stem*: it has a different derivation and a separate entry. The 'bow wave' is that on each bow generated as the *stem* cuts through the water: when a boat is *planing*, the bow wave shifts *aft*.

Also spelled 'bowe' and 'bough', this word corresponds in form and sense to the Low German '*bug*', the Dutch '*boeg*', the Danish '*boug*' and '*bov*', and the Swedish '*bog*', all of which mean both the shoulder of a human or beast and the bow of a ship. The word is of the same family as 'bough', which comes directly from OE, whereas 'bow' comes through the other languages.

First attested in 1626 in Smith, *Accidence*, 11.

bowline   a knot used to make a secure loop or *bight* in a rope, the large loop being secured by two small interlocking bights, making it non-slip but easy to undo.

Although the word might be thought to be derived from *bow*, it is pronounced 'bo-lin', and it appears in English several centuries earlier, referring to a rope passing from the middle of the perpendicular edge on the *weather* side of *square sails* (to which it was fastened by three or four *bridles*) to one or other of the bows. Hence the modern sense of the word: bowlines were used to secure the bridles to *cringles* in the sail.

Early spelling included both 'bolin' and 'bowling', from which Tobias Smollett drew the name of his nautical character 'Tom Bowling' in *Roderick Random* (1748) – a name adopted by Charles Dibdin (1745–1814) in a sea-song portraying his brother Captain Thomas Dibdin. Compare the similar use of the word *cringle* by Michael Scott (1789–1835) in his book *Tom Cringle's Log*, and the pseudonym *Taffrail* adopted (from his nickname) by the nautical author Captain Henry Taprell Dorling (1883–1968).

First attested *c.* 1450 in *Early English Alliterative Poems* (EETS, 1864–9), 104.

bowse (also *bouse*)   to achieve the final degree of tautness on a rope such as a *halyard*, often using a *tackle* for the purpose.

An etymological mystery. Although the word is often confused with its obsolete twin 'bouse' or 'bowse', meaning 'to booze', no true connection can be found or even surmised.

First attested in 1593 as quoted from Sir Francis Drake in Arber, *Garner* (1877–96), V, 497.

bowsprit   *spar* projecting forward from the *stem*, to which the *foremast stays* are attached. The bowsprit may be extended by a *jib-boom* if a *fore-topgallant mast* is set, and on it will be set the *flying jibs*. A 'running bowsprit' (used on smaller *cutter-rigged* vessels) can be run in or *furled* by sliding *inboard*; a 'steeving bowsprit' can be hinged up to or beyond the vertical; a 'standing bowsprit' is fixed.

From Low German, Dutch, or OE: its counterpart is found in all modern Teutonic languages – e.g. Dutch '*boegspriet*', German '*Bug-* or *Bogspriet*', Swedish '*bogsproet*', Danish '*bogspryd*'. 'Bow' in this context appears late in English, and a number of peverted versions such as 'boltsprit' made an early appearance.

First attested in 1338 in Brunne (ed.), Langtoft, *Chronicle*.

box   the space between the *backboard* and the *sternport* where the *coxswain* sits.

A nautical application, owing to its shape, of the familiar word, whose etymology is disputed by at least three competing theories. The first would derive it from the variety of wood, whose source is OE 'box' from the Latin '*buxum*'. A second proposes a direct independent descent from the Latin. A third suggests derivation from the Latin *'pyxis'*, a box, also *'puxis'* and medieval Latin *'buxis'*. Some Teutonic forms of the word may confirm this third hypothesis.

First attested in 1867 in Smyth, *Sailor's Word-book*.

box-haul   to *veer* a ship round on her *heel* when it is impracticable to *tack* or make a great *sweep*. The *helm* is put down as if to *tack*, so as to bring the *bows* up into the *wind*; the waves drive the bow down to *leeward*; the *aftermost* sails are *brailed* up to spill the wind and give the *foresails* more turning moment; then, as the *stern* goes through the wind the aftermost sails are *braced* to catch it until it is *forward* of the *beam* and the *yards* can be braced again. The manoeuvre thus includes a *gybe*. In small boats it is sometimes known as 'a wheelbarrow turn'.

From 'box' in the special nautical sense of making a 360-degree turn (familiar from 'boxing the compass' and probably derived from the notion of going round all the inner surfaces of a box in its familiar sense), plus 'haul'.

First attested in 1769 in Falconer, *Dictionary*.

box off   to *pay off* from the wind by hauling *head-sheets* to *windward* (and, in *square-rigged* ships, laying the *head-yards* flat *aback*) when the *helm* alone cannot manage it.

From 'box' in its special nautical sense of making a 360-degree turn, as in *box-haul*.

First attested in 1832 in Marryat, *Newton Forster*, xxii.

box the compass   to name all the consecutive *points* and *quarter-points* of the compass from north to south and up to north again both ways; also applied to anything that turns full circle, or to a *fluky* wind.

From 'box' in its special nautical sense, as in *box-haul*.

First attested in 1753 in Chambers, *Cyclopaedia*; first attested in a figurative, non-nautical sense in 1815 in Ireland, *Scribbleomania*, 213.

brace   rope secured near each end of a *yard* in *square-rigged* vessels so as to alter its angle to the *fore-and-aft* line; to 'brace' is to use the braces for this purpose. Yards are 'braced *aback*' to bring the wind on to the *forward* side of the sail and take *way* off the ship; they are 'braced about' to bring the ship on to the opposite *tack*; they are 'braced *abox*' to bring the *head-yards* flat aback to top the ship; they are 'braced by' in order to *heave to*; they are 'braced in' to bring the yards *athwartships* when *running*; they are 'braced sharp' or 'braced up' to make the yards as close as possible to fore-and-aft when sailing *close-hauled*.

To 'splice the mainbrace' is slang, originally naval, for serving

drink, originally rum or *grog*. Some suggest that it was a reward
for hauling on the main-braces, a heavy task; others that it was
for emergency repair that needed both watches (which seems
more likely, since both rarer and involving *splicing* rather than
simply hauling). With the replacement of sail by steam, splicing
the mainbrace became limited to special occasions; and, in the
British Navy, it lapsed in 1970 with the end of issuing rum.

The expression 'a brace of shakes'(a very short space of time)
derives from a different 'brace', the word for 'a pair' – possibly
originating in the 'brace' with which a pair of dogs were leashed
when coursing. The 'shakes' were the shaking of a sail as the
ship came into the wind.

From the French '*bras*' (*de vergue*), with the same meaning.

First attested in 1626 in Smith, *Accidence*, 28.

brails   ropes led from the *leech* on both sides of a *fore-and-
aft loose-footed* sail and secured to the *mast* at *deck* level, to
gather the sail close to the mast, spilling wind and thereby
slowing the ship. To 'brail' or 'brail up' is to use them thus.

From OF '*brail*', earlier '*braiel*', from the Latin '*bracale*', a
waist-belt.

First attested in 1450 in *Pilgrimes Sea-Voyage*, 33.

brassbounder   originally, a *midshipman*; later, an officer
apprentice in a British merchant ship.

The OED claims that this name came from brass on the
uniform; but Kemp (ed.), *Oxford Companion* (1976), 105, more
plausibly suggests that it was derived from the fact that 'in most
companies of ship-owners the apprentices wore caps with thin
gold *lace* binding round them'. 'Lace' here is used in the nautical
sense, also applied to rings of rank on sleeves, etc.

First attested in 1890–1904 in Fraser and Henley, *Slang*; the
locus classicus is the title of Sir David Bone's account of his early
years at sea in *The Brassbounder* (1910).

break   the point where a *deck* changes level, e.g. the break of
the *poop,* where the poop deck descends to the upper deck. As
a noun and verb, 'break' has many other nautical applications.
To 'break bulk' is to begin to unload *cargo*. To 'break ground'
is to begin to break out the *anchor*, heaving it out of the ground.
To 'break' or 'break out' a *flag* is to let it *fly* from having been
hoisted in a roll tied with a slipknot. A vessel is said to 'break
her back' when the *keel* droops at each end. To 'break sheer'
when at *anchor* is to be forced by wind or current to swing
across the anchor and risk *fouling* it with the *cable* – the opposite of 'keeping her sheer'. To 'break off' is to be *headed* by a
wind when sailing *close-hauled* and be forced to sail to
leeward: the wind is the said to 'break her off'. To 'break *tacks*'

is to go from one tack to the other, i.e. to *go about*.

'Breaking ground' by *weighing anchor* and shifting to a new position was sometimes done on a Saturday to avoid the ill-luck thought to attend beginning a voyage on a Sunday.

Like all other senses of the word, this descends ultimately from OE 'brecan'.

First attested in 1725 in Defoe, *New Voyage*, 264.

breaker   a wave that curls and breaks on the shore; a small cask.

In the first case from 'break' and thence from OE 'brecan'; in the latter from *barrico* (from the Spanish *'bareca'* or *'barrica'*.

First attested in in the former sense in 1684 in Mather, *Providences* (1856), 43; in the latter in 1834 in Marryat, *Peter Simple*, xxxiii.

breakwater   structure designed to break the force of the sea and provide shelter for vessels in harbour; a low *bulkhead athwartships* to break the force of any *seas* that are *shipped*; (on smaller vessels) a *coaming* for the same purpose.

From 'break' (from OE 'brecan') plus 'water' (from OE 'waeter').

First attested in 1769 in Falconer, *Dictionary*.

bream   to singe marine growth off a ship's *bottom*.

Of uncertain origin: some derive it from 'broom' (the plant), from the Dutch *'brem'*; others (more dubiously, though plausibly) from the German *brennen*', to burn.

First attested in 1626 in Smith, *Accidence*, 3.

breast backstays   a pair of *stays* led from the *head* of a *topmast* or a *topgallant mast* in a *square-rigged* ship to *chain-plates* forward of the standing *backstays*.

The word 'breast' figures in many other nautical expressions. A 'breast band' is a wide band of *sennit* used to support the *leadsman* when taking *soundings* by hand – sometimes called a 'breastrope'. A 'breastfast', also sometimes (confusingly) called a 'breastrope' or even a 'breast', is a *hawser* from any part of a vessel to a *jetty,* more or less at right angles to the ship's side. A 'breast hook' is a steel or wooden strengthener in the shape of a V secured internally across the *stem* of a ship; it may also denote a hook fitted internally on either bow of a *dipping lug cutter,* to which the *tack* of the *foresail* can be hooked when the wind is *abaft* the *beam.* To 'breast off' is to move off from *alongside* sideways. 'Breastwork' describes the rails and *stanchions* placed *athwartships,* or any ornamentation on them.

From the familiar word 'breast', whose source is OE 'breost', from the Old Teutonic *'brust'*, plus *backstay*.

First attested in 1769 in Falconer, *Dictionary* (1789), E ij.

breech   the opening in a *block* opposite the *swallow*. The rope can pass through the swallow, but not through the smaller breech.

Ultimately from the Old Teutonic '*brok*', meaning an article of clothing for the loins and thighs, i.e. breeches or britches; the word was applied in general to the posterior part of anything. The OED omits this specific nautical use of the word.

First attested in 1961 in Burgess, *Dictionary*, 37.

breeches buoy   a ring *lifebuoy* with canvas trunks attached, used mainly to transfer survivors from a wrecked vessel to the shore along a *jackstay*. Ultimately derived, like *breech*, from the Old Teutonic '*brok*', breeches, plus *buoy*.

First attested in 1880 in *Boy's Own Paper*, III, 52/1.

bridge   the raised platform from which the *captain* controls the ship.

Originally (and still) meaning a structure carrying a road, etc., over a gap, ravine, river, etc., its current nautical use arose when steamships with *paddle-wheels* replaced sailing ships, in which the captain had commanded from the *quarterdeck*. Now, the platform bridging the gap between the two paddle-wheels gave a better all-round view; and this 'bridge' was retained when the *propeller* replaced them.

In modern small sailing *cruisers*, the 'bridge-deck' is the transverse structure at the forward end of the *cockpit* forming the top of the *cabin* steps and often housing the engine.

From the Old Teutonic via OE 'brycg'.

First attested in 1843 in Bailey, *Pegasus*, 44.

bridle   a length of rope, wire or chain secured at each end to a *spar*, etc., to the *bight* of which a *purchase* can be hooked (e.g. in the case of a *spinnaker* pole to spread the load of the *downhaul*); the upper end of fixed *moorings*, terminating in the mooring *buoy*. A ship *riding* to two *anchors* is said to be 'on a bridle'. The 'mainsheet bridle' (also known as the *horse* or the *traveller*) is the transverse wire or other fitment on which the mainsheet *block* travels from side to side above the *tiller*. 'Bridle-ports' were square *ports* cut in the bows of wooden ships at main deck level for the *mooring warps*.

A nautical extension (like *martingale*) of the familiar equestrian word, from OE 'bridel', derived in turn from the earlier 'brigdel' and formed (like 'handle', 'saddle', etc.) by adding the instrumental suffic to the root word 'bregd-an', to pull or twitch.

First attested in 1626 in Smith, *Accidence*, 15.

brig   originally an abbreviation for *brigantine*, but later denoting a ship with a different *rig*, a two-masted vessel with *square sails* on both masts, and on the mainmast a lower mainsail with *gaff* and *boom*. Brigs may have been developed as men-of-war because of their extra sail power; but this may not have increased their manoeuvrability. In practice they were used mainly for short trips and coastal trading, and later as training ships, even after the days of sail. The last training brigs for boy sailors in the British Navy were phased out in the first decade of the twentieth century. Also (from US slang) a place of detention on board or ashore.

A 'hermaphrodite brig', sometimes called a 'brig-schooner', has a brig's *square-rigged* foremast but a *schooner*'s mainmast, with a *fore-and-aft* mainsail and *square topsails*.

From *brigantine*.

First attested as a ship in 1720 in the *London Gazette* No. 5848/4; as a prison, in 1852 in *The Knickerbocker*, XXXIX, 404.

brigantine   two-masted sailing vessel *square-rigged* on the foremast but *fore-and-aft rigged* on the mainmast.

Although a medieval Latin form of the word, '*brigantinus*' is found *c.* AD 1400, the English word seems to be derived from the French '*brigandin*', now '*brigantin*' and the Italian '*brigantino*'. All are associated with both 'brigade' and 'brigand', and probably denoted skirmishing vessels: cf. *bergantine*. In the Mediterranean, where they originated, they often also had *oars*.

First attested in 1525 in Berners, *Froissart* (1812), II, clxxi (clxvii), 498.

brightwork   the varnished wooden parts of a boat above decks. This is one of the few words on which the OED is in error, alleging that 'bright work' denotes 'polished metal-work on ships, etc.'

From 'bright' (from OE 'beorht') plus 'work' (from OE 'weorc').

First attested in 1841 in the *Southern Literary Messenger*, VII, 769/2.

bring   to cause to come or go in a certain direction. To 'bring by the board' is to carry *overboard*. To 'bring by the lee' is to alter course to *leeward* when *running* so that the *lee* side is suddenly to *windward*: watch out for the *boom*. To 'bring (up) to the wind' is to *luff up*. To 'bring home the anchor' is to shift the anchor to the ship instead of vice versa. To 'bring home the log' is to recover and set up a *logship* (or *logchip*) when the pin slips. To 'bring to' is to check the *way* on a ship, in *square-rigged* vessels by *bracing* the *foremast yards aback*, in *fore-and-aft* rigged ships by coming *head to wind*. To 'bring to' can also mean to check another vessel by firing a shot across her *bows*. To 'bring to an anchor' is the traditional expression for anchoring, since in the days of sail the ship would be 'brought to' beforehand so as to slow her down. To 'bring up' is to moor or anchor. To be 'brought up all standing' is to be halted, e.g. by a wind shift or by running *aground*. From a common Teutonic root and OE 'bring-an'.

First attested in a nautical sense in 1695 in Luttrell, *Historical Relation* (1678–1714), III, 437.

Bristol fashion   spick and span, neat and *seamanlike* (usually 'shipshape and Bristol fashion').

From the high reputation of the city which before the rise of Liverpool was Britain's major West Country port.

First attested in 1840 in Dana, *Two Years*, XX, 61.

broach, broach to   to become unmanageable by slewing round against the *helm*, *luffing up* uncontrollably, *heeling* dangerously, and swinging broadside on to the wind and sea, liable to be dismasted, *capsize*, or roll over. Probably from the apparently identical word 'broach', which means among other things to pierce with a spit as a preliminary to roasting; this word in turn is derived from the noun 'broach', meaning a tapering pointed instrument, and from the same ME 'broche' as the modern word 'brooch', which despite its distinctive spelling is pronounced in the same way as 'broach'.

First attested in its nautical sense in 1705 in Dampier, *New Voyage* (1697, 1699, 1703–9 (1720), II, iii, 6.

broad   (in various phrases) at a wide angle to the *stem*. Thus 'broad on the bow' is at roughly 45 degrees from right ahead, and 'broad on the quarter' is at roughly the same angle from dead *astern*. A 'broad reach' is the point of sailing at which the wind is just *abaft* the *beam*. 'Broadside on' or 'broadside to' is sideways on to. Two other nautical uses of the word carry its more common sense of 'wide'. A 'broad *pennant*' is a wide swallow-tailed *burgee* flown by a Royal Navy *commodore* (white with a red St George's cross) or by the *flag* officers of UK yacht clubs. In the latter case, the vice-commodore's has one ball or round patch in the *hoist* (the side nearest the *staff*) and the rear-commodore's two. The 'broad seam' is the variation in the overlap of neighbouring cloths in making a sail, so as to adjust its curve when *set*.

From OE 'brad' and thence a common Teutonic root.

First attested in a nautical sense in 1860 in the *Mercantile Marine Magazine*, VII, 82.

brow   *gangplank* from ship to shore; the hinged part of the *bow* or *stern* of a landing craft or *ferry* which is lowered to act as a ramp for access to the quay. Reports of ferry disasters, however, usually refer to 'bow doors'.

Not from the familiar word meaning a forehead, but from

ON '*bru*', bridge, which itself, however, may be cognate with ON '*brun*', the source of the familiar word 'brow'.

First attested in this nautical sense in 1867 in Smyth, *Sailor's Word-book*.

buccaneer   a piratical *privateer* on the Spanish coast of America; more generally, any such.

From the French '*boucan*' barbecue and its associated verb '*boucaner*', to grill on a barbecue: 'buccaneer' originally denoted one who hunts, dries, and smokes ox meat, especially one of the French hunters of San Domingo – a sense first attested in 1661. Some may well have sought other than oxen as their prey.

First attested in its nautical and piratical sense in 1690 in B.E., *New Dictionary*.

bulkhead   vertical partition below decks to stiffen the structure and/or divide the *hull*. In large ships, bulkheads may be *fore-and-aft* as well as *athwartships*; in smaller craft they are usually athwartships, as in the case of that separating the *cabin* from the *cockpit*. Watertight 'collision bulkheads' are fitted near the *bows* of larger ships to prevent flooding as the result of a collision.

From 'bulk' (meaning in different times and contexts both 'cargo' and 'belly'), probably of Scandinavian origin and cognate with ON '*bulki*', plus 'head', from OE 'heafod'.

First attested in 1496 in *Naval Accounts*, 167.

bulldog grip   U-shaped steel clamp with threaded ends and a bridge fixed down with nuts, used to hold two wires together.

Obviously derived from the vice-like grip of a bulldog's jaws, a bulldog being one originally used in bull-baiting, from 'bull' (from ME 'bole') plus 'dog' (from the mid eleventh-century English 'dogge').

First attested in 1908 in *Sears, Roebuck Catalogue*, 204/3, and in a specifically nautical sense in 1923 in *Manual of Seamanship*, II, 307.

bull rope   originally a rope used for hoisting a *topmast* or *topgallant mast* in *square-rigged* vessels, this now means a rope from the end of a *yacht*'s *bowsprit* to its *mooring buoy*, to prevent the buoy striking or rubbing the *hull* in slack water or when the boat is *wind rode*.

From 'bull' (from ME 'bole') plus 'rope' (from OE 'rap'), in this case because of the resenblance to an animal's tether.

First attested in 1882 in Nares, *Seamanship* (6th edition), 173.

bullseye   wooden (or nowadays often plastic) *block* or *fair-lead* grooved to take a *strop* (but without a *sheave*) and bored to take a rope; piece of thick glass let into a deck to admit light below; the small expanse of blue sky in the centre of a tropical storm.

From 'bull' (from ME 'bole') plus 'eye' (from OE 'eage'): three of the many figurative uses of the expression, the most familiar being that denoting the centre of a target.

First attested in its 'block' sense in 1769 in Falconer, *Dictionary*; in its 'light' sense in 1825 in Gascoigne, *Path*, 64; and in its 'storm' sense in 1753 in Chambers, *Cyclopaedia*, Supplement.

bulwark(s)   (usually plural) the solid sides of a ship above the upper deck, higher than a mere *toe-rail* and far more substantial than a *guardrail* with *dodgers*, to protect against the sea and prevent things or people falling overboard.

Of either Middle High German or Scandinavian origin, the word may be derived from Middle High German '*boln*', to throw, or from the roots of the English 'bole' and 'work', meaning a work constructed from tree-trunks. The corresponding word in Dutch is '*bolwerk*', in German '*Bollwerk*', in Danish '*bulvaerk*', in Swedish '*bolverk*'. The modern French (and English) 'boulevard' is derived from the Teutonic roots.

First attested in a nautical sense in 1804 in Duncan, *Mariner's Chronicle*, II, 274.

bumboat   small boat used by local traders to sell goods to *crews* of ships lying *offshore*.

Three hypotheses contend for this word's etymology. The first (and least attractive) is that offered by the OED: that the word is derived from 'bum' in its primary and very ancient (at the latest fourteenth-century) sense of 'buttocks', because such vessels were originally used to remove 'filth' from ships in the Thames, according to the by-laws of Trinity House in 1685; they also seem to have delivered vegetables. The second and more picturesque possibility is that the word may be derived from 'bumbay', an old Suffolk dialect term for a quagmire – which itself may be derived from 'bum' as above. The most appealing theory is that 'bumboat' may be a corruption of the Dutch '*boomboot*', a broad-beamed fishing-boat.

First attested in 1671 in a *Proclamation* by Charles II on 6 April, which may tend to confirm the first of the three hypotheses above: 'Whereas several Dirt-boats, and Bum-Boats, ... under pretence of Fetching Dirt, and Furnishing necessary Provisions on Board such Ships as are in the River, do commit divers Thefts and Robberies... '

bumpkin, bumkin (or **boomkin**)   a short fixed *spar* extending over the *stern*, usually as a point of attachment for the *backstay* if the *boom* is long, sometimes to *sheet* the *mizen* *sail* if the *mizen-mast* is stepped very far *aft*. In some cases the word is also used for a short spar replacing the *bowsprit*. Originally, the term covered a short boom projecting forward on either side of the *bows*, to extend the *clew* of the *foresail* to windward, or a similar boom on each *quarter* to carry the *main brace blocks*.

The word appears to be connected with 'bumpkin' in the sense of a clownish yokel, which may be derived from the Dutch '*boomken*' or little tree; but the actual source would seem to be 'boom' in its ordinary nautical sense (also derived from the Dutch), with the diminutive added.

First attested in its nautical sense in 1632 in Sherwood, *Dictionary*; in its rustic sense slightly earlier, in 1570 in Levins, *Manipulus Vocabulorum*, 133.

bunk   a built-in sleeping-place on board ship (not a *hammock*, *pipecot*, or settee-berth). A 'bunkboard' or 'leeboard' is a hinged or removable plank stowed under the cushion or mattress when in harbour, and used at sea to prevent a sleeper rolling out of the bunk when the vessel *heels*.

Etymology unknown, even to the OED. The word may however be related to 'bank' and 'bench' as well as 'bunker'. The Old Swedish '*bunke*' meant boarding used to shield cargo from the weather.

First attested (in a land-based sense) in 1758 by Lyon in Tomlinson, *Military Journals*, 1855, 37.

bunt   the middle part of a sail, cut full to belly out; the similar part of a fishing net. In *square-rigged* ships, the *topsails* had the most bunt, and were often so heavy that a *bunt-jigger* consisting of two single blocks was fitted to enable the bunt to be hauled up to the *yard*. 'Buntlines' were ropes attached to the *footropes* of *square* sails to haul them up so as to spill the wind or to *furl* them. 'Buntline bands' were strips of canvas *tabled* to the forward side of sails to prevent the buntlines chafing them. 'Bunters' were the men in the centre of the yards who gathered in the bunt when furling. 'Bunt-fair' meant sailing *before the wind*.

Etymology unknown. It has been likened to the Danish '*bundt*' and the Swedish '*bunt*', bundle; but although the OED dismisses these as 'merely' from the German '*Bund*', that seems a quite plausible source.

First attested in its nautical sense *c.* 1582 in the *Cotton MS*, App., xlvii.

bunting   thin, light, open-weave worsted material used for *flags*; collectively, flags.

Etymology uncertain, although it may be connected with the

verb 'bunt', to sift, and its associated noun 'bunt' in its sense of a sieve, which are respectively dialect and obsolete. The French *'etamine'* means both bunting and bolting-cloth (used for sifting).

First attested in 1742 in a Navy Board letter to L.C.A. on 24 September (MS in the Public Record Office). 78 years earlier, in 1664, Samuel Pepys, then an official of the Navy Board, had speculated in buying calico for flags; but it proved too heavy and friable: he used the surplus on dresses for his wife and servants.

buoy   a floating mark *anchored* to the seabed either for navigation or to indicate a laid *mooring*. A *bell-buoy*, obviously, is one equipped with a bell, whose melancholy tolling indicates a hazard. A *cable-buoy* is used to lift a *mooring cable* from rocks on which it may chafe. A *can-buoy* is one of four main shapes of navigational buoy, the others being conical, spherical, or consisting of a *spar*. A *lifebuoy* is a life-saving flotation device, round or horseshoe-shaped: against etymology, it is free-floating. A *mooring buoy* (for large vessels usually cylindrical) marks a mooring and is used to tie up to. A *watch buoy* is a fixed mark used to ensure that a *lightship* has not drifted from its position. *Buoy-hopping*, in such well-buoyed areas as the Solent, is a lame form of navigation, picking one's way from one buoy to another. A *buoy jumper* is a seaman placed on a buoy to *shackle* on the *bridle* or to *reeve* a *slip-rope* before unshackling. A *buoy rope* attaches a buoy to any object on the seabed (including its own mooring), but usually to the *flukes* of an anchor, both to mark it and to facilitate breaking it out. *Buoyage* is a system of buoys laid out to indicate a *fairway* for shipping. *Buoyancy*, or the ability to float, is often used to describe the buoyancy bags, compartments, material, or tanks installed in a vessel to help it float. A *buoyancy test* entails filling a boat with water, to see if it will still float with its gear and crew.

Originally from the Latin *'boia'*, a halter (because the buoy is tethered), passing into English either through OF *'boye'*, which has become the modern French *'bouee'*, or via Middle Dutch, in which *'boeie'* meant both buoy and halter. Either derivation would explain both the apparently intrusive 'u' and the fact that some sticklers still pronounce the word to rhyme (more or less) with 'hooey', although most speakers now make it a homophone of 'boy'.

First attested in 1466 in *Manners and Household Expenses* (Roxburghe Club, 1841), 325.

burgee   small triangular flag flown at the *masthead*, often carrying club insignia, and useful to indicate wind direction. Club *commodores* fly swallow-tailed versions. Until recently, a square burgee was flown when racing. Etymology unknown.

First attested in 1848 in *Blackwood's Magazine* LXIII, 87.

burgoo   porridge or gruel formerly served to seamen, and made of boiled oatmeal seasoned with butter, salt, and sugar; *loblolly*.

From the Arabic *'burgul'*, cognate with the Turkish *'bulgur'*: sometimes spelt 'burgou(t)'.

First attested in 1750 in William Ellis, *Family Companion*, 206.

burton   (also *Spanish burton*) type of *purchase* using three single *blocks* or two single blocks and a hook, in which one *whip* is used to haul on the *fall* of the other.

Etymology unknown.

First attested in 1704 in Harris, *Lexicon Technicum*.

bustle   an underwater bulge at the after end of the *hull*, to diminish *drag*.

From the late eighteenth- and early nineteenth-century fashion of women's dresses' projecting at the rear—which usage is of unknown etymology.

First attested in its nautical sense in 1978 in Desoutter, *Dictionary*, 43.

butt   the squared end of a *plank* on the side of a wooden vessel where it is secured to the timbers; the space between such squared ends, secured with a *strap* across it, and *caulked*; to place end to end; a large cask. The *butt strap* is the strip of wood or plate covering and securing two planks joined at their butts. If one or both of the planks should spring loose it is said to *start a butt*.

Of uncertain and perhaps diverse derivation, this word may be from the same root as the Danish and Low German *'but'*, the Dutch *'bot'* and the Spanish and Portuguese *'boto'*, all connected with the idea of 'thick' and 'blunt'. But it may have affinities with the French *'bout'*, end. In its sense as 'cask', first found in the fifteenth century, its origin seems to be a Romanic word underlying the French *'botte'*.

First attested in 1627 in Smith, *Seaman's Grammar*, ii, 3.

butter box   an awkwardly built boat, *beamy* and/or top-heavy.

Of confused etymology, this word was first used as a derisive term for a Dutchman, owing to his supposedly excessive consumption of butter: in this sense it is first attested in 1600 in Thomas Dekker's *The Shoemaker's Holiday*, I, 21, and appears in a sea-song to commemorate the victory over the Dutch at the St James's Day battle on 25 July 1666, during the second Anglo-Dutch War (1665–7).

In its specifically shipbuilding sense, the word is first attested in 1840 in Dana, *Two Years*, ix.

buttock   the under part of the rounded after end of the *hull*, between the *keel* and the *counter* or *transom*. In ship design, the *buttock lines* are the longitudinal *fore-and-aft* lines equidistant from the centre of the hull.

A diminutive of *butt*, first attested in the thirteenth century, the word's primary anatomical meaning is the obvious source of its figurative nautical application; in French, likewise, sailors refer to '*les fesses d'un navire*'.

First attested in its nautical sense in 1627 in Smith, *Seaman's Grammar*, ii, 4.

by   (usually referring to the wind) in close relation to (but used in a number of specific expressions). *By the board* is said of anything passed, thrown, or fallen over the side of a ship, and of a mast broken off at or near deck level. *By guess and by God* is or was a primitive form of *dead reckoning*, relying on experience, instinct, and estimation rather than compass, chart, tide tables, observation and calculation. *By the head* describes a vessel whose *bows* lie lower than her *stern* owing to bad *stowage* or *ballasting*. *By and large* normally means sailing somewhat *off the wind* (about five *points* off for *fore-and-aft rig* and seven for *square rig*); but some apply it to sailing with the wind near the *beam*. *By the lee* is a situation, when *running* before the wind, in which the wind comes round to the *lee* side of the sails, risking an involuntary *gybe*: it may be caused by a wind shift or a steering error. *By the mark* is the phrase prefixed by the *leadsman* to his announcement of a *sounding*. *By-points* are the *points* of the *compass* containing the word 'by', as in 'North by East', etc. *By the stern* is the opposite of 'by the head'. *By the wind* means on or close to the wind, e.g. *close-hauled*. *Full and by* is as close to the wind as possible with the sails filled and no shivering or lifting of their *luffs*.

From OE '*bi*' and a common Old Teutonic root. The twenty or more columns devoted by the OED to 'by' and its by-products show how complex a very short word can be.

Cabin   compartment for sleeping, eating, etc. A *cabin cruiser* is a motor boat with cabin and *berths*, whereas the word 'cruiser' alone may mean a sailing craft – except on the Norfolk Broads, where it means a motor cruiser, while a sailing craft is known there as a *yacht*. The *cabin sole* is the floor of a boat's cabin: the planks are laid on the sole bearers *athwartships*.

From the late Latin '*cappana*', a small house or hut.

First attested in 1382 in Wyclif, *Bible*, Ezekiel, xxvii, 6.

cable   originally, any thick strong hemp or wire rope, now usually applied to that attached to the anchor, which almost always includes *chain*; a measure of length, one-tenth of a *nautical mile*, i.e. 608 feet or some 200 yards (183 metres), also equivalent to 100 *fathoms*. The *cable clench* or *clinch-bolt* is the fitting at the bottom of the *cable locker* for attaching the cable to the ship. A *cable holder* (usually one on each *bow* of larger ships) is a *capstan*-like drum fitted with sprockets to receive chain cable. A *cable hook* is a long iron hook used to shift cable on deck. A *cable jack* is a long mounted lever with a hook for lifting cable over a *slip*. *Cable laid* (sometimes known as 'cablet' or 'water-laid') rope is made by laying up three or more *hawser laid* ropes against their own lay, for extra strength. The *cable locker* is where the cable is stored while not at anchor: in small boats it may be no more than a bucket. The *cable party*, in large vessels, consists of the *hands* needed *forward* to work the cable. A *cable ship* is one fitted for the laying of under-sea telegraph and telephone cable. *Cable stoppers*, usually known as *slips*, are used to hold the cable either temporarily or as a standby or *preventer* when at anchor to ease the strain on the brake of the cable holder.

From the late Latin '*capulum*' or '*caplum*', a halter for cattle, itself based on the verb '*capere*', to catch. This well enough tallies with the notion of an anchor cable. But the corresponding French word '*câble*', with its circumflex indicating an omission, may be derived, through '*cadable*', from the Latin '*catabola*', a sling, itself resembling '*catapulta*', a catapult.

Although attested in its general sense as early as 1205, the word is first attested in a nautical sense in 1325 in *Early English Alliterative Poems* (EETS, 1864–9), B 418.

caboose   a small *deckhouse* originally used for cooking; any odd corner used as a store.

Of Teutonic origin, this has its counterparts in the Dutch '*kabuis*' and '*kombuis*', both including the notion of 'house', and the German '*Kabuse*'; cf. the French '*cambuse*', which Littré believed was introduced into the French navy in the eighteenth century.

First attested in 1769 in Falconer, *Dictionary*.

cabotage   coasting trade. In aviation, the word has been revived since the 1930s to mean reserving a country's airspace to its own nationals.

Possibly derived from the Spanish '*cabo*', a cape (since coasting vessels sailed from cape to cape); but a more likely source is the name of some kind of ship. A thirteenth-century copy of an earlier manuscript in the Paris *Bibliothèque nationale* has the word '*cabo*' glossed as meaning a ship; and '*cabot*' or '*chabot*' was the French term for a small slow boat.

First attested in 1831 in Sinclair, *Correspondence*, II, 186.

caique   originally, a light boat or *skiff* propelled by one or two oars and used in Turkish water, notably in the Bosporus; later, a small Levantine sailing boat, usually with a *lateen* rig; now, the word covers a range of small sailing or motor vessels plying between East Mediterranean ports and especially islands.

From the Turkish '*kaik*', also used to describe the Sultan's ceremonial *barge*.

First attested in its original sense in 1625 in Purchas, *Pilgrimes*, ii, 1623, and in the broader sense in 1666 in the *London Gazette*, No.95/2.

caisson   a fixed enclosure reaching to the bottom which can be filled with air to make possible work on under-sea structures; a similar watertight tank (sometimes known as a *camel*) which can be flooded, submerged, then pumped out and used as a buoyant lifting force to raise wrecks, etc.; also, the gate that closes a *dock* or dry dock. *Caisson disease*, like 'the bends', is a colloquial term for compression sickness, suffered by divers who surface too quickly, when bubbles of nitrogen form in the body tissues.

From the French '*caisson*', a large chest, and usually pronounced 'kayssonn', although in the eighteenth century it may have been pronounced 'cassoon'.

First attested in an aquatic sense (it has others closer to the French original) in Chambers, *Supplement* to *Cyclopaedia* (1753).

camel   originally, a wooden case in two halves fitted to the *keel* and pumped out to give extra buoyancy, for example to pass over a *shoal*; later, equivalent to a *caisson*; also, a strong wooden stage used as a *fender* in port.

The original word 'camel', indicating the animal, is probably derived from the Semitic '*gamal*', cognate with the Arabic '*jamala*', to bear; it has therefore been suggested that the first two nautical applications of the word are based on the idea of a beast of burden, lifting the ship. Might there also be an analogy with the camel's hump, filling with water? The third nautical application remains mysterious, save in so far as the structure may at first have resembled half of a camel in its original sense.

First attested in a nautical sense in 1716 in Perry, *State of Russia*, 168.

canoe   a long, narrow, light, portable open boat, normally propelled by paddles, although some Pacific island canoes are very large, as are some more modern sailing canoes. The *kayak* type of canoe is enclosed by a cover. A *canoe body* is a round-*bilge*, shallow, *beamy hull* to which a separate *keel* is bolted.

A *canoe stern* rises from the water like a *counter*, but is curved and comes to something like a point at deck level.

The original sixteenth-century form of the word was 'canoa', found in the West Indies by Columbus, and imported thus into Spanish and English, where it continued until the eighteenth century. Already by the seveneenth century 'canow' had become current, and in that century there also appeared 'caano', 'cano', 'canno', 'canoo', 'cannoe', and 'canoe', which last also appears in French *c.* 1600, while *'cano'* is found in Dutch. The modern French *'canot'*, meaning simply a small boat, is a diminutive of OF *'cane'*, a boat, which may have Teutonic roots, as does the Low German *'kane'*, like the Dutch *'kaan'* and the German *'Kahn'*; cf. also the Latin *'canna'*, also meaning a small boat or *gondola*.

First attested in 1555 in Eden, *Decades*, 45.

cant   piece of wood laid on deck to support the *bulkheads*, etc.; timber near the *bow* or *stern* sharply angled from the *keel*; to turn a ship's *head*, usually in a confined space. In whaling, the word describes the cut made in the animal between the neck and the fins, where the *cant purchase* was secured in order to turn the body while *flensing*. The *cant line* is the groove between the *strands* of a rope, a row of casks, etc. *Cant rope* is the old name for four-stranded rope *laid up* without a core.

Apparently of multiple origins, since it occurs in Teutonic, Slavonic, Romanic and Celtic, with many non-nautical meanings, but always related to the notions of edge, border, corner, etc. It seems to be distinct from 'cant' in the sense of whining, jargon, or humbug, all of which are derivatives of the Latin *'cantus'*, a song, which is also the origin of 'chant' and associated words.

First attested as a nautical noun in 1794 in *The Elements and Practice of Rigging and Seamanship*, II, 286. As a nautical verb, it is first attested in 1784 in Nelson, *Dispatches* (Nicolas, 1844–6), VII, Add. 7.

canvas   strong coarse cloth made from flax or hemp, originally used for sails and graded from 00 to 10 (very fine); still used to denote sails, although these are now more usually made of polyester (Terylene or Dacron). *Canvas climbers* were seamen in large sailing ships who went *aloft*.

In its original ME form 'canevas' (identical with the Old Northern French and modern French), the word seems to be derived from the late Latin *'cannabaceus'* (cf. 'herbaceous'), hempen, and thence from *'cannabis'*, hemp, whose Greek form was *'kannabis'*.

Although first attested in a non-nautical sense after 1260

(Rogers, *History of Agriculture*, 1866–87, II, 5ll), the word is first attested in a nautical sense *c*. 1325 in *Richard Coer de Lion*, 2645 (Weber, *Metrical Romances*, 1810).

caper   a lightly armed seventeenth-century Dutch *privateer*; also, by extension, her captain.

From the Frisian '*kapen*', to steal, rob, or plunder; cf. the modern Dutch '*kaper*'. This may have influenced the modern and mainly US use of the word to mean a heist, racket, or other underworld exploit, although 'caper' in that sense is usually held to be derived from 'caper' in the sense of a dance, from the Italian '*capriola*'.

First attested in 1657 in Colvil, *Mock Poem* (1695 ed.), 23.

capsize   to overturn when afloat; to turn over (a coil of rope). A *dinghy* is said to have capsized when its mast hits the water; a *cabin* boat in that position, if she does not right herself, is said to be on her *beam ends*, and is only capsized if bottom up.

The origin of the word is unknown, although Skeat suggested that it might be a corruption of either the Spanish '*cabezar*', to nod or pitch (of a ship), or the Spanish '*cabuzar*', to sink by the *head*. Castilian pronunciation of 'z' as 'th' may cast some doubt on this theory; but American or Southern Spanish pronunciation may in fact be the source of the English word.

First attested, late enough to for it to have been picked up from the Spanish colonies in the New World, in 1788 in Dibdin, *Musical Tour*, xxxv, 142.

capstan   a *windlass* with its shaft, barrel or spindle vertical, turned by bars radiating like spokes, for heavy work such as raising anchors and working *cables* or hauling a ship close to a *pier*. Over the centuries, the word's spellings have included 'capstain', 'capsten', 'capstone', 'capstaing', 'capstern', 'capstorm', 'capstand', and 'capstall'. There are also remoter obsolete forms such as 'capstock' and 'cablestock'.

From either the French '*capestan*' or the earlier Provençal '*cabestan*', to which are related the still earlier form '*cabestran*', the Catalan '*cabestrant*', the Spanish '*cabestrante*', '*cabestante*', and '*cabrestante*', which last is also found in Portuguese. The Portuguese '*cabresto*' is a halter or (for nautical purposes) a system of ropes relating to the *bowsprit*. It has been suggested that British seamen learned the word from counterparts in Marseille or Barcelona during the Crusades.

First attested in English *c*. 1325 in *Early English Alliterative Poems*, B, 418 – paradoxically more than a century before its first written appearance in French.

captain   senior officer in charge of a ship, regardless of rank; in all navies, the rank next below rear-*admiral*; also the title of the senior *rating* in charge of a team performing a specific task.

Ultimately derived from the Latin '*caput*', head, via the late Latin '*capitanus*', the fourteenth-century French (and modern French) '*capitaine*' and ME 'capitain'; cf. the parallel 'chieftain'.

First attested *c.* 1380 in Wyclif, *De Ecclesia*, ix in *Selected Works*, III, 360.

caravel   originally, a fairly small two-masted, *lateen-rigged* Mediterranean trading vessel of the fourteenth to seventeenth centuries, taken up in the sixteenth century by Spanish and Portuguese explorers and developed as three-masters, *square-rigged* on the two *forward* masts and with a *lateen-rigged mizen*; they had a simple curved *stem* and a plain *transom*. The average length over all, in the larger ships, was 75–80 feet, with a few exceptions up to 100 feet, as in the case of Columbus's 1492 *Santa Maria*. The word 'caravel' or 'carvel' is also used to denote the floating mollusc *Ianthina*. In French, '*caravelle*' was adopted as the name of the twin-jet *Sud-Aviation* passenger aircraft used by Air France, chiefly in the 1960s.

Ultimately derived from the late Latin '*carabus*' and the Greek '*karabos*', a light ship, via the Spanish '*caraba*' and its probable derivative '*carabela*': cf. the Portuguese '*caravela*'. Hence the French sixteenth-century (and modern) '*caravelle*' (earlier '*caruelle*') and the Italian '*caravella*'. Some identify the English word with *carvel*, which others restrict to the late-medieval two-masted Mediterranean vessel described above.

First attested in 1527 as used by R. Thorne in Hakluyt, *Divers Voyages* (1582), B, iv, b.

cardinal   relating to the four main points of the compass (North, South, East, and West) either as in cardinal points or winds, or in the cardinal system of *buoyage*, with *buoys* to the North, South, East and West of the relevant hazard.

As in its ecclesiastical sense, the word is derived from the Latin '*cardo*', a hinge: the North and South poles were '*cardines*'. Since there are four cardinal points, the word is closely associated with that number, as in 'cardinal virtues'; but 'cardinal numbers' are of course those answering the question 'How many?' rather than 'In what order?'

First attested in its nautical sense in 1549 in *The Complaynt of Scotlande*, vi (EETS, 1872), 61.

careen   to lay a vessel on her *beams ends* in order to work on her *hull*. A place where this is done is known as a *careenage*.

The verb is probably derived from the identical but now rarely used noun, denoting the careened position; this comes from the French '*carene*', keel, corresponding to similar words in other Romance languages.

First attested as a noun in 1591 and as a verb in 1600 in Hakluyt, *Principall Navigations*, III.

cargo   the merchandise or freight carried by a ship. A *cargo jack* was the large screw jack used to cram cotton, hides, etc., into a *hold*. A *cargo net* was used in the days before container ships to slingcased or packaged cargo in and out of the hold.

From the Spanish '*cargo*', loading or burthen; or perhaps from '*carga*', freight. Both are derived from the medieval Latin '*carricum*', a load, which in Italian gives the modern '*carico*' and '*caricare*', to load, almost identical with the late Latin '*carricare*'.

First attested in 1657 in Ligon, *Barbados*, 8.

Carley float   a large oval life-raft, supplied mainly to warships and used in World War II; now largely superseded by inflatable rubber craft.

Named after its inventor, the American Horace S. Carley.

First attested in 1903 when the patent was taken out by the Carley Life Float Company of Philadelphia.

carlings (also *carlins* or *carlines*)   short squared timbers fitted *fore and aft* between the *beams* to support the deck planking, especially at *hatches*. *Carling-knees* are similar timbers lying transversely from the ship's side to the hatches.

Probably derived from the French '*carlingue*', meaning the timber into which the mast is *stepped*, although according to Littre this French word is itself derived from English.

First attested in 1611 in Cotgrave, *Dictionarie*, under the word 'Aileurs'.

carrack   a large three-masted European trading vessel of the fourteenth to seventeenth centuries, *square-rigged* on the *fore-mast* and *mainmast*, *lateen-rigged* on the *mizen*, with a very high *forecastle* and *after castle*, and usually armed to protect the cargo. Superseded in the seventeenth century by the *galleon*, designed by Sir John Hawkins, with a lower forecastle, improving her windward performance.

From the medieval Latin '*carraca*', itself of uncertain origin, via OF '*carraque*' or '*caraque*'.

First attested (in one of many alternative spellings) *c.* 1386 in Chaucer, *Canterbury Tales*, 'Prologue to the Somnours Tale', line 24.

carrick bend   a round knot used to join two *hawsers* that are to go round the *capstan*, where a *reef knot* could jam between the *whelps*; unlike the reef knot, which is flat, the carrick bend weaves one of its loops between the two sides of the other, crossing itself on the way out, in this respect rather like a *figure-of-eight knot*. The OED's definition is a model of clear concision: 'Formed by looping the two ends to be joined, and interlacing them, each going at every intersection, now over, now under, the other.'

The word's origin is almost certainly *carrack*, which was frequently spelt with an 'i' in place of the second 'a'.

First attested in 1819 in Rees, *Cyclopaedia*, under 'Bend'.

carry away   to break (of a *spar*) or to part (of a rope). Although now normally intransitive in its nautical senses, the phrase was in the past also used transitively with a meaning closer to its normal, non-nautical sense.

From the late Latin '*carricare*', to convey in a cart, via the Old North French '*carier*'.

First attested as an intransitive verbal phrase in 1703 in Burchett, *Memoirs*, v, xxii, 723; its transitive use is first attested in 1840 in Dana, *Two Years*, xv, 4l.

cartel   (pronounced 'cart'l') a ship used in time of war to exchange prisoners or otherwise communicate with the enemy; identified by flying a white flag. Also sometimes known as a *cartel-ship*. Common in the days of sailing navies, the word died out soon after the advent of steam.

Like the more familiar 'cartel' (or price-ring), derived from the French '*cartel*' and thence from the Latin '*cartellus*', both diminutives of the word for paper.

First attested in 1769 in Falconer, *Dictionary*.

carvel-built   constructed with the hull planks laid edge to edge to make a flush smooth finish.

Apparently derived from *caravel* in its fifteenth- to seventeenth-century vernacular spelling of 'carvel', although its occasional spelling 'carver', as by Captain Miller in Nelson, *Dispatches* (ed. Nicolas, 1844–6), VII, clix, 1798, may suggest some mental association with carving.

First attested, in doubly erroneous fashion, in 1678 in Phillips, *New World*, which not only spells it 'carnel' but also defines it as 'the building of ships first with their Timbers, and after bringing in their planks'.

cast   (as a noun) a single *sounding* taken with the *lead*; (as a verb) to turn the vessel when *weighing anchor*, by *backing* the *headsail*. To *cast an anchor* is an obsolescent expression for dropping it or letting it go: hence the metaphor 'to cast an anchor to windward', meaning to provide for the future. To *cast loose* is to break out of its fastenings or *lashings*; to *cast off* is to let go a rope securing the ship. In modern non-nautical usage, the word is rare except in set expressions like 'cast a clout', 'cast a glance', etc.

From ME 'cast-en', itself derived from ON '*kasta*', and possibly cognate with the Latin '*gestus*'.

First attested as a noun in 1616 in Ben Jonson, 'The Forrest', and as a nautical noun in 1662 in Fuller, *Worthies* (reprinted 1840), I, 442. First attested as a nautical noun in 1776 in Falconer, *Dictionary*, under 'Jib'.

cat   the *purchase* whereby the anchor was hoisted (before *stockless* anchors); to secure the anchor on board (strictly to the *cat head* rather than the *hawse pipe*); until the nineteenth century, a sturdy Northern European collier with a *canoe stern*, projecting *quarters*, a deep *waist* and no *figurehead*; a *cat-boat*; the *cat-o'-nine-tails*; a colloquial abbreviation for a *catamaran*.

A *cat-boat* is an American sailing-boat of nineteenth-century origin with a shallow *draught* and a broad *beam*, first used for fishing in shallow waters, then as a *sandbagger* for racing, with a *cat rig*. A *cat davit* is a *davit* used in catting the anchor. A *cat head* is a wooden or metal support projecting from the *bow* to take a large *block* used in catting the anchor. *Cat holes* are holes in the *stern* for mooring or other ropes. The *cat pennant* is the rope used to raise the anchor to the cat head. *Cat rig* consists of a large quadrilateral sail, *fore-and-aft* on *gaff* and *boom*, on a mast *stepped forward* in the *bows* (also known as *Una rig*, from the name of the 16-and-a-half foot racing boat shipped to Cowes in 1852). A *cat walk* is any long narrow gangway above a deck, especially that which in older ships joined the *midships bridge* to the *forecastle* and *poop* decks.

The word, its derivation, and the reason for its nautical application, are as much a mystery as Macavity in T.S. Eliot's *Practical Cats*. The original word, in its animal usage, is itself of unknown origin, although found in languages throughout Europe.

First attested in a nautical sense in 1626 in Smith, *Accidence*, 12.

catamaran   a *raft* of two or more logs *lashed* together, used in both the East and the West Indies; a raft used in the St Lawrence River, consisting of two boats lashed together; an inert fire-ship (or proto-torpedo) used in 1804 against the French invasion fleet at Boulogne, consisting of a 21-foot lead-lined chest packed with explosives, to be towed towards its target; a small rectangular raft used as a *fender* in dockyards; a twin-hulled sailing *yacht*. By only partly bastard etymology, the word has given birth to *trimaran*, a three-*hulled* sailing vessel (three maram). Colloquially, 'catamaran' is often abbreviated to 'cat'.

From the Tamil '*katta*', to tie, and '*maram*', wood.

First attested in 1697 in Dampier, *New Voyage*, I, vi, 143. In the 1804 sense, first attested in *The Annual Register*, 1804, 419/2.

In the modern yachting sense, first attested in 1957 in *The Times*, 13 December, 15/2.

catharpings   ropes (or, later, iron fittings) under the *tops* at the lower end of the *futtock shrouds* in *square-riggers*, used to *brace* them in tighter so as to give more room for bracing in the *yards* when sailing closer to the wind.

Conjecturally from 'harp' as a musical instrument, whose origin is OE 'hearp', from a common Teutonic root whose Old Teutonic form was *'harpon'*. The 'cat' connection is more obscure still: Captain Frederick Marryat, in *Peter Simple* (1833), vii, quotes a *midshipman* as explaining that 'these were called the cat-harpings because they were so difficult to climb, that a cat would expostulate if ordered to go out by them'.

First attested in 1626 in Smith, *Accidence*, 15.

cat-o'-nine-tails   a whip with nine knotted lashes, a legal form of punishment in the British Navy and Army until 1879.

Derived from 'cat' (the animal), with what the OED calls 'grim humour' evoking scratching the back.

First attested in 1695 in William Congreve, *Love for Love*, Act III, Scene iii.

catspaw   a twisting *hitch* in the *bight* of a rope forming two *eyes* to go on the hook of a hoisting *tackle*; also, a darkening ruffle on calm water indicating a puff of wind.

Derived from 'cat' (the animal): in the former case because of its clinging ability, in the latter because of its appearance (especially if the cat be black).

First attested in the former sense (but as a verb) in 1749, in *The Elements and Practice of Rigging and Seamanship*, I, 217; in the latter sense, in 1769 in Falconer, *Dictionary*.

caulk   to make watertight the seams between planks, by driving in *oakum*, rope junk, or cotton with a *caulking iron*, struck by a *caulking mallet*, then sealing or *paying* with hot pitch, marine glue, etc; to sleep, dressed, on deck; a sleep; a dram or drop of liquor. A *caulker* has, or had, four different meanings – a caulking iron, a person who caulks, a pillow, or a dram; but all are now virtually obsolete.

From the Latin *'calcare'*, to tread, stamp, press, and OF *'cauquer'*, to tread, press, squeeze in with force, or to tent a wound. Dr Johnson spelled the word 'calk', which is clearly closer to the Latin root.

First attested as a verb in its primary sense *c.* 1500 in the *Chester Plays* (1843 edition), I, 47. As a verb meaning to sleep, in 1836 in Howard, *Rattlin the Reefer*, lxx, and with more precision (about being fully dressed) in 1867 in Smyth, *Sailor's Word-book*, 173. As a short sleep, in 1917 in *Chambers's Journal*,

14 July, 514/2. As a dram, in 1833 in *Peter Simple*, 265, by Edward Howard's shipmate Frederick Marryat.

ceiling   inside planking in the *holds* of merchant ships, carried across the floor and up as far as the *beams* on the sides.

From the obsolete verb 'ceil', first attested in 1428, although 'ceiling' in a non-nautical sense is first attested in 1380. Both words might seem to be derived from the Latin '*celare*', to conceal, although this verb acquired the sense of simply 'to cover' only in late Latin. Other proposed derivations, from the Latin '*caelare*', to carve, or '*caelum*', heaven or heavens, seem still less plausible. The fact that *c.* 1450 the word 'ceiling' was used to mean a screen of tapestry or curtain may well support '*celare*' as its source. Only later did it come to mean, except at sea, only overhead covering.

First attested in its nautical sense in 1633 in James, *Strange and Dangerous Voyage*, 50.

centreboard   retractable *keel* fitted on the centreline of the boat. The device was first used by Chinese river *junks*. Its application to small craft was pioneered in colonial America, where the need to sail to windward in shallow East Coast waters made a retractable keel an asset. In 1774 Lord Percy introduced it to Britain, in a small vessel he had had built in Boston, Massachusetts; a larger version was built at Deptford in 1789, followed by a number of experiments with three and later five centreboards. The modern form of the device, pivoted at the *foreward* end, was introduced in 1809 by Captain Shuldham of the Royal Navy. Strictly speaking, a centreboard is made of wood and a *centreplate* of metal; but the former term is loosely applied to the latter object too.

First attested in 1867 in MacGregor, *Voyage Alone*, 93.

chain   length of interlocking metal links; in the plural, a small ledge on either side of a shift just *abaft* the mast, for spreading and setting up the lower *rigging* and/or providing a platform for the *leadsman*. *Chain cable* is that used for the anchor; the *chain locker* (also known as the *cable* locker) is where it is stowed. A *chain pipe* or *navel pipe* is the pipe through which the chain passes from the chain locker to the *foredeck*. A *chain splice* is used to secure a rope to a chain. A *chain stopper* is a short length of chain used to hold a wire under stress. A *chain swivel* is a revolving link inserted to prevent kinking.

From the Latin '*catena*', chain. But 'chains' in the second sense has a more complex history. In old sailing ships, the leadsman stood between the *shrouds*, which were originally attached to chains (in the first sense) secured to the ship's side. Later, and still today, the shrouds were secured to plates of metal which are still known as *chain-plates*, although some now call them 'shroud-plates'. Similarly, *chain-wales* (pronounced 'channels' and also sometimes known, confusingly, as 'chains') are projections to carry the chain-plates clear of the *gunwales* (pronounced 'gunnels').

First attested in a plural, nautical sense – but to denote chain-plates – in 1627 in Smith, *Sea Grammar*, v, 20, and in its normally accepted sense in 1720 in Defoe, *Captain Singleton*, xi, 193 in the 1840 edition.

chantey, chanty or **shanty**   merchant seamen's work song. Broadly, there were two kinds of chanty: the *capstan* chanty, requiring continuous effort, and the *halyard* chanty, which stressed recurring moments of collective heaving. In the navy, with plenty of *hands*, they were rarer than in merchant ships, where fewer hands made co-ordination of effort more necessary. Even there, they had disappeared by about 1875, superseded by steam power.

Said (by the OED) to be 'a corruption of the French "*chantez*", imperative of "*chanter*", to sing.' The word's ultimate origin is clearly the Latin '*cantare*', to sing.

First attested in 1857 in C. Nordhoff, 'Merchant Vessel' in *Nine Years a Sailor*, iv, 40. However, the earliest known example of a chanty dates from about 1450 in the *Complaynt of Scotlande*; while 'Haul the Bowline' is only a little more recent. The reason for the late first attestation may be that when chanties were gradually dying out as routine work songs they began to attract attention from writers.

chapel   to revert to the original course after being *taken aback* (usually in the passive voice, 'to be chapelled').

Of obscure origin, although the word itself seems to be derived from the familiar noun, as witness the variant expression 'to build oneself a chapel', said of a *helmsman* whose negligence has caused the vessel to be chapelled. Alternatively, the similar French expression '*faire* (or *prendre*) *Chapelle*' was believed by Littré to be a mis-spelling for '*chapel*' or '*chapeau*' – which suggests an analogy with doffing and replacing a hat.

First attested in 1769 in Falconer, *Dictionary*.

Charley (or Charlie) **Noble**   the H-type chimney fitted to take smoke from the *galley* or stove and discharge it above decks; later, any portable chimney.

An etymological enigma, omitted from the OED.

First attested in 1961 in Burgess, *Dictionary*, 49.

chart   map of a sea area, showing coastlines, rocks, lighthouses, etc., and the depth of water. Broadly two types of chart are produced for navigation: one on the Mercator projection, in which *rhumb line* courses appear as straight lines, the other gnomic, with *great circle bearings* appearing as straight lines. *Chart datum* on any one chart is the level below which the *tide* is unlikely to fall, and from which its heights and depths are expressed; the normal chart datum (unless otherwise specified) is the mean water level at ordinary *spring tide*. The *chart-house* or *chart-room* is the room or space near or on the *bridge* reserved for the navigator and for charts, chronometer, etc. In *yachts*, the navigator has to make do with a *chart table*, usually just inside the main cabin.

From the Latin '*carta*', '*charta*', originally a leaf of paper; cf. the French '*carte*', map.

First attested in 1696 in Phillips, *New World*, fourth edition: this uses the expression 'sea-cart', which by the next century had dropped out of use since the word 'chart' had become restricted to nautical maps.

check   to ease out a rope in short lengths, maintaining the strain; to stop a vessel (with an anchor, a mooring *warp*, or a burst *astern* on the engine). In its nautical sense, the word has in effect the opposite meaning to its sense in, for instance, riding, although while 'checking a rope' means gradually *paying it out*, the rope is nevertheless continually 'checked' (in the lay sense) as it goes. A *check wire* is one sewn into the *luff* of a sail to prevent over-stretching.

From ME 'chek' or 'chak' and OF '*eschec*': cf. also the Northern French and Provençal '*escac*', the Italian '*scacco*', and the medieval Latin '*scaccus*'. All have their origin in the Persian '*shah*', king, entering Europe via Arabic and applied in the game of chess (itself of similar origin) in the phrase '*shah mat(a)*', i.e. 'the king is dead', or 'checkmate'. So the word descended from 'king' came to mean the king's defeat, and by extension any similar restraint.

First attested in a nautical sense in 1833 in Marryat, *Peter Simple*, viii.

cheeks   pieces of timber bolted to the mast of a sailing ship below the *masthead* to support the *trestle-trees*; the sides of a *block*; the rounded portions of the *bows* of fifteenth-century *men-of-war* when they were extended by building the *forecastle* above the *beakhead*; the side-pieces of wooden gun-carriages in *warships*; any pieces of wood at the sides of a spar or part, such as *rudder cheeks* on either side of the *rudder stock*.

From OE 'cece', with many cognate forms in Old German and Dutch; the nautical use of the term is by simple analogy with the sides of the face or with the buttocks.

First attested in 1627 in Smith, *Seaman's Grammar*, iii.

cheese   to *coil* down the *tail* of a rope on deck in a tight flat spiral with the tail at the centre; the resultant coil. Although decorative, a cheesed rope tends to kink.

From OE 'cese', with many cognate forms in Old German and Dutch: the nautical use of the word is by obvious analogy with a flat round cheese such as a brie. Omitted from the OED, and first attested in 1961 in Burgess, *Dictionary*, 50.

chesstrees   two oaken spurs fitted to the *topsides* of a *square-rigger* where the curve of the *bow* begins to straighten out, with either a hole or a *sheave* through which the *bow lines* run, to be hauled tight by the crew. In older ships the chesstrees were often imaginatively carved, sometimes with a face through whose mouth the bow lines were run.

Almost certainly not from the familiar word 'chess', but from 'chase' in the old sense of a hollow or groove, from the French '*chas*', originally an enclosure but later a needle-eye (cf. the Italian '*casso*').

First attested in 1627 in Smith, *Seaman's Grammar*, v, 23.

chimes   channels in the *waterways* (at the sides of and projecting above the deck) in old sailing vessels; the rims formed by the projecting ends of the *staves* of a *cask*.

Nothing to do with musical sounds (derived from the Latin '*cymbalum*'), but from ME 'chimb(e)' and sometimes indeed spelt 'chimbs': the general sense of the ME word was 'edge', comparable with OE 'cimstanas', the bases of a pillar. Smyth, *Sailor's Word-book* (1867) treats the word as a variant of *chine*.

First attested *c*. AD 800 in the *Erfurt Glossary* (EETS, 1885), 291.

chine   the angle where the bottom planks of a boat meet the side. In a hard-chined boat the angle is pronounced; in a soft-chined boat it is less so, and may involve more than one chine.

In its nautical sense the word is thought by the OED to derive from *chime*, its spelling altered by 'phonetic attraction' toward the non-nautical word 'chine' meaning 'backbone' (from OF '*eschine*'). First attested in 1833 in Richardson, *Marine Architecture*, 5.

Chinese gybe   a *gybe*, almost always accidental, in which the *boom* goes to the *lee* side, but the upper part of the sail does not.

Prima facie, the phrase might seem to imply that 'Chinese' here meant simply odd or outlandish; but Kemp, *Oxford Companion* (1976), 166, claims: 'It is so called because of its prevalence with the Chinese junk rig with its light bamboo battens and no boom to hold the foot of the mainsail steady.' However, Desoutter, *Boat-Owner's Practical Dictionary* (1978),

53, maintains: 'The term itself is an unwarranted occidental jibe, for Chinese boats with their fully battened lug-sails are incapable of getting themselves into this specifically Bermudan predicament.' The OED cannot adjudicate since it omits the expression.

First attested in Kemp, *loc.cit.*

chinse   to press *oakum* into a seam as a temporary measure before or instead of *caulking*.

Probably a corruption of 'chinch', which in turn is a dialect form of 'chink' in the sense of a cranny, which appears in the mid sixteenth century as a virtual synonym of *chine* (in Raynalde, *Byrth of Mankynd*, tr. 1545, (1564 edition), Hh.j).

First attested in its present form in 1769 in Falconer, *Dictionary*.

chip log   a simple speed-measuring device consisting of a wooden *quadrant*, weighted on the arc to remain upright and attached to a *log* line which it pulls off a drum: the length pulled off during a given time (28 seconds for a line knotted every 47 feet 3 inches) gives the speed in *knots* or nautical miles-per-hour. Although now superseded by modern technology, the chip log can still be used if all else fails. For this purpose, attach a makeshift chip to a nylon line 100 feet long, with a knot at 15 feet from the chip. Let the log run out that far, then measure with a stop-watch the time it takes to run out a further 84 feet 5 inches. Divide 50 by the number of seconds to find the speed in knots.

From the familiar word 'chip', whose source is the corresponding verb, from OE 'cippian', to cut.

First attested in 1835 in Chambers's *Edinburgh Journal*, iv, 98/2.

chock   a wedge; to secure, usually with wedges; in the US, a *fairlead*.

Fom the Old Northern French '*chuque*' and '*chouque*', a block of wood; in English originally identical with 'chuck' and influenced by 'choke'.

First attested in a nautical context in 1769 in Falconer, *Dictionary*.

chock-a-block   the position when two *blocks* of a *tackle* are so close together that no further movement or purchase is possible; full; 'fed up'. An older and now less common equivalent expression is *two blocks*.

From *chock* as an adverb, originally meaning as close or full as possible.

First attested in 1840 in Dana, *Two Years*, xxv, 82.

choke the luff   to jam a *tackle* temporarily by pushing the hauling part of the rope between the *sheave* of the *block* and the line *rove* through it: the jam can be released by a tug on the hauling part.

From the familiar word 'choke', of ME origin (as both 'choke' and 'cheke'), and from *luff-tackle*, consisting of a double and single block.

First attested in 1794 in *The Elements and Practice of Rigging and Seamanship*, I, 164.

clamp   plank laid *fore-and-aft* to support the deck beams; *timber* fixed to a mast or *yard* to prevent bursting; hinged metal hoop to secure *spars*, etc.; a *one-cheeked block*.

All derived from the familiar word, which is of English, Low German or Dutch origin; it does not appear in OE or ME, and seems to emerge (in its general sense) only in the fourteenth century.

First attested nautically in 1626 in Smith, *Accidence*, 9.

clap on   to add something briskly and often temporarily; also, a call for help in hauling on a rope.

Although now rather archaic, the expression survives today in respect of more *canvas*, an extra *purchase* to increase hauling power, and *whipping* on the end of a rope.

From the noun and verb 'clap', originally ME 'clappe' or 'cleppe', referring oto the sound typically made by the collision of two hard, flat or concave surfaces, now mainly confined to applause and thunder. In time, the word came to be applied to action resembling such collision but without necessarily involving noise.

First attested in a nautical sense, although metaphorically, in 1598 in Shakespeare, *The Merry Wives of Windsor*, II, ii, 142.

claw off   to *beat* to *windward* away from a *lee shore* or other hazard.

A vivid metaphorical extension of the familiar word, whose origin is OE 'clawu', talon. To 'claw off' was often used in the obvious sense of 'to remove something by clawing'; but the nautical usage rather suggests 'to remove oneself by clawing', especially in view of the cognate expression *clawing the wind*.

First attested in a nautical sense in 1615 in Roe, *Embassy*, edited by W. Foster, 2 vols., 1899, I, 36 (24 August 1615).

claw ring   a metal calliper-shaped device to fit round the *boom* when roller-*reefing* the *mainsail*: it takes the *mainsheet block*. Also known as a *boom claw* or *reefing claw*.

From 'claw', whose source is OE 'clawu', talon.

First attested in 1961 in Burgess, *Dictionary*, 51.

clear   to empty, unload, escape or free; the opposite of *foul*; to sail safely past anything. *Clear ahead* or *astern* (in racing) means not overlapping. '*Clear anchor*' is the report, when *weighing* anchor, that it is free of obstruction. To *clear a ship* is to pass satisfactorily through customs. A *clear berth* is room to swing at anchor without *fouling* anything. Of a rope, *clear for running* means free to run off. *Clear hawse* describes *riding* by two anchors whose *cables* are free of each other; a *clear hawse slip* is a device used to clear a foul hawse. '*Clear lower deck*' is a command for all *hands* on deck except those in charge of running machinery. '*Clear the board*' means remove all obstructions and get off the upper deck. To *clear the land* is to avoid all *reefs, shoals*, etc. A *clear view screen* is a rapidly rotating glass disc that throws off rain, sleet, snow, etc., to give the navigator better vision. A *clear wind* is one unobstructed by other sails, etc. *Clearance*, as well as its ordinary meaning of free space, is a certificate from customs showing that their requirements have been met. A *clearing bearing* or *clearing line* is a course avoiding hazards; a *clearing mark* is an object shown on a chart which may be joined to another by a clearing line.

From ME 'cler' and thence from the Latin '*clarum*'.

First attested in a nautical context in 1602 in Shakespeare, *Hamlet*, IV, vi, 19.

cleat   wooden, plastic or metal fitting with two arms or horns, around which a rope is *belayed*; a small wedge of wood fixed to the *yards* of *square-riggers* to prevent ropes, etc., slipping off; to belay round a cleat. Over the years, cleats have taken many different shapes, the latest including *jamming cleats* or *jammers*, either of the patent 'Clamcleat' variety (with a V-shaped groove) or consisting of two serrated cams with springs to keep them together. Probably derived from OE 'cleat', a hard lump, and certainly cognate with the Dutch '*kloot*' and the German '*Klosz*' (meaning respectively a ball and a clot or clod), as well as with the Norse '*klot*', a pommel.

First attested, in the sense of a wedge, in 1377 in *Political Poems* (Rolls Series, 1859–61), I 217; in the sense of a belaying cleat, in 1769 in Falconer, *Dictionary*.

clench (virtually interchangeable with *clinch*)   to rivet by beating the end of a boat nail (or *clench bolt*) over a *roove* or *rove* (a cup-shaped washer); to hammer over the *bolt* of a *shackle* to prevent its opening; (formerly) to fasten a rope such as the anchor *cable* with a *half hitch* whose end is *stopped* back on its own part with a *seizing*. See also *clinker-built*, from a dialect form of the same word.

From ME 'clenchen', associated with 'cling'. From the fifteenth century onwards, Northern English and Scottish also have 'clink', while from the sixteenth century onwards 'clinch' appears. In non-nautical usage there is a greater distinction between 'clench' and 'clinch': one clenches one's teeth but clinches a deal. All senses share the notion of fixation or firm closure.

First attested *c*. 1250 in *The Owl and the Nightingale* (Percy Society, 1843), 1206.

clew   the *after* lower corner of a sail in *fore-and-aft rig;* in *square rig*, the two lower corners; sometimes, however, applied to all corners; the *lanyards* and *nettles* by which a naval *hammock* is slung from hooks. A *clew cringle* is one of two or more *eyes* in each of the clews of a square sail to enable various ropes to pull it in different directions are needed. A *clew garnet* is the *tackle* used on a lower square sail for hauling it up to the *yard*. A *clew line* performs the same function for upper square sails. A *clew outhaul* is the tackle that tensions the *foot* of the mainsail in fore-and-aft rig.

From OE 'cliwen' a ball formed by coiling together, as in a ball of wool. From here, via such legends as that of Ariadne's thread, it came to have the figurative sense later (and still) spelt 'clue'.

First attested *c*. AD 897 in King Aelfred, *Gregory's Pastoral Care* (EETS, 1871, xxxv, 241).

clinker-built   *hull* construction in which the lower edge of each plank overlaps the upper edge of that below it, *clenched* or riveted together with copper boat nails. The corresponding US expression is 'lapstrake'. Boats thus built now tend to be small, since their hulls have a larger surface and create more friction than if they were *carvel-built*.

The origin of the expression is *clench*; variants of it, now rare, are *clinch-built* and *clencher-built*.

First attested (in the expression a 'clincher', i.e. a clinker-built vessel) in 1678 in Phillips, *New World*. 'Clincher-built' is first attested in 1769 in *St James' Chronicle*, 10/11 August, 2/2. 'Clinker-built' as first attested in 1804 in the *Hull Advertiser*, 21 January, 2/3.

clipper   fast nineteenth-century sailing ship with fine lines, a very sharp-raked *stem*, and an overhanging *counter stern*, much used for the tea trade. Historically, the word was first applied to the Virginia and Maryland *schooners* that ran the blockade in the War of 1812 and were later used as slave ships. By 1832 an enlarged Baltimore clipper, the *Ann McKim*, was given a *square rig*. The first true clipper ship was probably the *Rainbow*, built in 1845; and for some time American ship-builders dominated the scene. British (mainly Scottish) builders followed, and the 1860s became the heyday of the tea clippers until the opening of the Suez Canal in 1869 began to undermine their *raison d'être*.

The origin of the verb 'clip' is ME 'clippen', to make a sharp sound; it gradually came to include in its meaning the idea of rapid movement. It is this, as much as any notion of 'clipping the time off competitors' voyages', that seems to explain the nautical sense of the word 'clipper'.

First attested in 1830 in Marryat, *The King's Own*, xiii.

close   to move nearer to; near. The word's associated expressions are more significant than it is by itself. They include: *close aboard*, almost touching; *close harbour*, one artificially enclosed rather than natural; *close-hauled*, sailing as close to the wind as possible (4 to 6 *points* off it in a *fore-and-aft rigged* vessel, 6 points off in a *square-rigger*; *close-jammed*, sailing too close to the wind (though not *in stays*); *close linked*, said of an unstudded small chain; *close reach*, a *reach* with the eind just *before* the *beam* (the same as a *fine reach*); *close reefed*, reefed down as far as possible; *close stowing anchor* (now largely obsolete), one with a fixed *stock* and balancing band; *close up* (of a flag), hoisted as far as possible; *close-winded*, able to sail quite close to the wind.

Whether pronounced with a voiced or an unvoiced 's', the word comes from the Latin '*clausum*', closed or shut.

First attested as a nautical verb in 1673 in the reprint of Prince Rupert's 1642 *Speech to His Majesty and the Lords of his Privie Councell*, in the *London Gazette*, 788/4.

clove hitch   a *hitch* consisting of two *half hitches*, the second reversed so that its end is brought up through its own part: this will hold so long as tension be maintained.

The word 'clove' is really two. The first refers to the pungent spice, and is derived from the Latin '*clavus*', a nail, which the bud somewhat resembles. The second is derived from OE 'clufu' and is related to 'cleave' – hence a 'clove' of garlic, which although pungent is not *Caryophyllus aromaticus*. The clove hitch belongs to the second, cloven family.

First attested in 1769 in Falconer, *Dictionary*, H h 3 b.

club   a *spar* fitted to the *foot* of a triangular sail such as a *staysail* or *jib*, commoner in the US than in the UK. To *club haul* is to turn a vessel in a narrow space by using the *lee* anchor cable as a pivot thanks to a rope led *aft* to the *quarter* – a manoeuvre famously used in 1814 by Captain Hayes to extricate his ship HMS *Magnificent* from between two reefs, but unusable by *fore-and-aft rigged* vessels. A *club topsail* (see above) is one extended by clubs, sometimes replacing a *gaff* topsail. *Clubbing* is making *sternway* in a tide to reach a *berth*. *Clubfooted* describes any vessel with a wide *forefoot*.

From ME 'clubbe', 'clobbe', a thick stick (and possibly therefore associated with the verb 'clobber', to beat up, whose origin the OED says is unknown). There is also a link with 'clump', whence the meaning of a society or association.

First attested in a nautical sense in 1886 in the US magazine *Outing*, IX, 19/1.

clump   heavy concrete, iron, or stone block to which a *mooring buoy* is attached. A *clump cat head* is a stronger version of the already strong cat head.

Probably from the Low German '*Klump*', meaning clump in its general sense; possibly with older Teutonic roots, but unknown in English before the sixteenth century.

First attested, in the phrase 'clump blocks', in 1869 in Stuart, *Catechism*, 37.

coach-roof   that part of the *cabin* top that is above *deck* level, to provide headroom below. The word 'coach' in its non-nautical sense gave rise to *coachwhipping*, plaiting strips of *canvas*, etc., in fancy patterns for decorative use on *stanchions*, etc. The strips were said to resemble coach whips.

The word 'coach', which from the sixteenth century onwards finds equivalents in almost all European languages, is derived like them from the Magyar '*kocsi*' or '*kotsi*', first found in the fifteenth century as an adjective from Kocs, a place south of Komorn, between Raab and Buda: it appears in Latin in1499 as '*cocius currus*'. As well a meaning a carriage, it was used from the mid seventeenth to the mid eighteenth century to denote the *forward* part of the cabin space under the *poop* deck, and later the *fore-cabin* under the *quarterdeck*, just forward of the great cabin. It has been suggested that the origin of this usage was the ancient '*carosse*' of the *galley*, the space under the poop deck where the *captain* or *admiral* had his bed. Samuel Pepys, *Diary*, 3 May 1660, uses the word 'coach' in something like this sense. First attested in 1883 in *Harper's Magazine*, August, 450/2.

coaming   raise framework round *hatches* and other openings in the deck, or round the *cockpit*, to keep out surface water.

Etymology unknown. Although some identify it with 'combing', such spelling is not found until the late nineteenth century, and is then very occasional and probably erroneous.

First attested in 1611 in Cotgrave, *Dictionarie*.

cobbing   an unofficial and now obsolete naval punishment, consisting of blows on the buttocks with a flat piece of wood called a *cobbing board*. In the nineteenth century the wood was replaced by a *hammock clew*, which since it had 22 *nettles* was in effect a cat-of–22-tails. The practice was abolished by the British Admiralty before the century was over.

Etymology unknown, but possibly onomatopoeic. The word 'cob' in the sense of to fight or strike dates back to about 1400, as in Sir John Denham's 1636 edition of the translation of *The Destruction of Troy*, 8285.

First attested in 1769 in Falconer, *Dictionary*.

coble (sometimes *cobble*): a short flat-bottomed *rowing* boat used in salmon fishing, etc.; a broad *carvel-built* flat-bottomed fishing boat most common on the North-East coast of England, with a *forefoot* deeper than the *keel* and a deep *rudder*, carrying a *lug-sail* on her mast and occasionally a *jib* on a temporary *bowsprit*, with usually an engine plus *thole pins* for up to three pairs of *oars*.

Of Celtic origin, either from the Old Northumbrian 'cuopl' or from the Old Welsh *'caupol'* and the Breton *'caubal'*: cf. the modern Welsh *'ceubal'*, *'ceubol'*, *skiff* or *ferry-boat*. The word has also been compared to the Latin *'caupulus'*, a short boat.

First attested *c*. AD 950 in the *Lindisfarne Gospels*, Matthew viii, 23.

cocked hat   the triangle produced by plotting three *bearings* on a *chart*: with perfect precision they should all meet at one point, but never do. The centre of the triangle should be the ship's position, unless mistakes have been made. Still in use despite the advent of Decca and GPS.

Figurative use of the term originally applied to a hat with the brim permanently turned up or cocked, especially the trangular version worn at the end of the eighteenth and the beginning of the nineteenth centuries. It was later, illogically but understandably, applied to the ceremonial triangular (but now brimless) headgear pointed before, behind and at the crown.

First attested in its navigational sense in 1961 in Burgess, *Dictionary*, 55.

cockpit   the *well* of a sailing *yacht* in which the *helmsman* sits; in old sailing ships, a space on the lower deck near the *after hatchway*, originally allotted to the senior *midshipman* and later to the surgeon; in action, it became a sick bay – and in HMS *Victory* it was where Nelson died. Later applied to aircraft and to motor racing cars.

Figurative use of the term used from at the latest the sixteenth century to denote the enclosed arena used for cock-fighting. The same reasoning by likeness caused it to be applied in the theatre to indicate the pit, and in some cases to name a theatre built on the site of a former cockpit, as well as to Whitehall office buildings similarly situated.

First attested in a nautical context in 1706 in Phillips, *New World* (6th edition).

codshead and mackerel tail   with broad, raised and rounded *bows* tapering away *aft*, and the broadest *beam* well *forward*. Rare in modern *yacht* design, where the broadest beam has moved aft, markedly so in some racing craft.

Based on the shapes of the respective fish.

First attested in 1891 in *Scribner's Magazine*, X, 5.

coffee-grinder   large and expensive *winch*, with internal gears, usually on a pedestal in the centre of the *cockpit*, actuated by crank handles and used for *port* and *starboard headsail sheets* in turn; in some cases the handles are on the pedestal and operate one winch on each side.

Jocular extension of the expression's normal meaning as a mill for grinding coffee (from the Arabic '*qahwah*' via the Turkish '*kahveh*', and from OE 'grinden').

First attested in 1978 in Desoutter, *Dictionary*, 58.

cofferdam   a *caisson*; a heavy double transverse *bulkhead* to separate *holds* or oil tanks in large merchant vessels. The space between the twin bulkheads was often used to carry oil or water *ballast*.

From the two familiar words 'coffer' (from ME 'cofre') and 'dam' (from the Teutonic and Old Frisian 'dam').

First attested, in a non-nautical context, in 1736 in Hawksmoor, *London Bridge*, 26; and in a nautical context in 1890 in the *Daily News*, 28 January, 6/1.

cog   a merchant ship (occasionally a warship) of the thirteenth to fifteenth centuries, *clinker-built*, with rounded *bow* and *stern*, and a *forecastle* and *after castle*, very broad in the *beam*; also, a type of small craft formerly used for trading on the Humber and the Ouse.

From ME 'cogge' or 'kogge', which with similar Northern European words is derived from a common Old Teutonic root. OE '*cogue*', which has the same meaning, is however thought to be derived from the Latin '*coccha*', which appears to have spawned other similar words in Italian and Spanish. The relation between the two families, if such they be, remains obscure.

First attested in the former sense above *c.* 1325 in *Richard Coer de Lion* (in Henry W. Weber, *Metrical Romances*, 1810), 4784. In the latter sense above, first attested in 1531–2 in *Actis made 23 yere Henry VIII* (*Statutes of the Realm*, Record Commission, 1810–28), c. 18.

coil   to lay up a rope in concentric rings; a length of rope thus laid up. If the rope has a right-handed *lay*, it should be coiled clockwise, and *vice versa*, to keep the lay of the rope tight.

Cognate with, and probably derived from, the French '*cueillir*', to collect, cull, or cut.

First attested in 1611 in Cotgrave, *Dictionarie*.

coir   light (floatable) rope made from coconut fibre.

From the Malayalam '*kayar*', cord, which in turn is derived from '*kayaru*', to be twisted.

First attested in 1582 in Nicholas Lichefield, translation of *Lopes de Castanheda*, 14 b.

collar   originally, the lower end of the principal *stays* in a *square-rigger*; then the rope to which it was attached; the *eye* in the upper end of a stay or in the *bight* of the *shrouds* which is threaded over the *masthead*; the neck of a ring bolt. A *collar knot* is one used when *jury-rigging* or improvising shrouds: two long ropes are centred, and their bights joined in a *granny knot* which is left open and slipped over the masthead and as far down as the *hounds*.

Figurative use of the familiar word, which is derived from ME 'coler' (gradually changing its spelling by approximation towards Latin), meaning anything worn round the neck.

First attested in its primary nautical sense in 1626 in Smith, *Accidence*, 14.

colours   the national *ensign* flown by a ship; its daily hoisting and lowering. In the British Royal Navy the colours are the *jack* flown on the *jackstaff* in the *bows* and the *White Ensign* flown at the *yardarm* when at sea or, in harbour, from an ensign staff at the *stern*. The colours of a merchant (or pleasure) vessel are the *Red Ensign*. In harbour, colours are hauled down at sunset and hoisted at 8.00 a.m. in winter; at sea they remain hoisted.

Figurative plural use of the familiar word, from ME 'colur'. The plural was sometimes referred to as if it were singular.

First attested in 1590 in Smythe, *Certain Discourses*, 2 b.

colt   a knotted rope used for goading, a punishment in the British Royal Navy until officially abolished in 1809.

Somewhat obscurely derived from 'colt' in the sense of a young animal, itself originating in OE as a term for a young ass or young camel, and only later a young horse. Some references to the colt as intended for use on youngsters may be a bridge between the two meanings of the word.

First attested in its punitive nautical sense in 1769 in Falconer, *Dictionary*.

comb cleat   double-arched bridge *cleat*, also used as a *bee block* or *fairlead*. The word 'comb' has also been used to denote the crest of a wave (splitting into tine-like wavelets), whence *comber*, a long curling wave.

From the ancient (OE) word 'comb', whose meaning has

broadened, especially when used adjectivally, to include many objects resembling a comb in the original sense, however remotely.

First attested (without the noun 'cleat') in 1627 in Smith, *Seaman's Grammar*, ii, 10; with the noun, in 1794 in *Elements of Rigging and Seamanship*, I, 4.

come   move hither – in a number of nautical phrases, viz.: *Come no nearer*, sail no closer to the wind; *come on board through the cabin window*, begin as an officer, not a seaman; *come to*, sail closer to the wind; *come to an anchor*, let the anchor go; *come up to the capstan*, walk the *cable* back to ease the strain or *veer* some of it; *come up the tackle*, let go the *fall*; *come up with*, overhaul or meet; *coming home* (of an anchor), *dragging*; *coming inboard*, about to hit the ship; *coming on* (of tides) increasing daily, e.g. between *neaps* and *springs*; *coming over* (of the *boom*), about to swing across in a *gybe*.

From a common Teutonic root that appears in OE as 'cuman', and which like many apparently simple words has a very complex history.

First attested in a nautical sense in 1633 in Thomas James, *Voyage*, 23.

commander   naval officer next below *captain*; the master of a merchant ship; a large wooden-headed mallet.

From 'command', which in turn is derived from ME 'coma(u)nde-n'. The figurative application to a mallet seems not to be derived from the naval rank or from a jocular reference either to force or to wooden-headedness, but to be a throwback to one obsolete sense of the word 'command', meaning to propel mechanically.

First attested as denoting a naval rank *c.* 1450 in Wright-Wuelcker, *Vocabularies*, 579/45; as a mallet, in 1573 in Baret, *Alvearie* (1580 edition), C., 907.

commodore   naval officer between the ranks of *captain* and *rear-admiral*; the senior officer of a *yacht club*.

Etymology uncertain. Some believe it to be a corruption of the Spanish '*comendador*', but early appearances of the word or anything like it have no Spanish connections. The first approximation to the modern word appears as 'commandore' in the reign of William III, so it may have come from the Dutch '*kommandeur*'. Not until the mid eighteenth century did its present spelling appear; before that it was sometimes spelt 'commadore'.

First attested in 1695 in the *London Gazette* No. 3124/1; in the spelling 'commodore' in 1748 in Anson, *Voyage*, I, i, 5.

companion   originally, the framing and sash lights on the *quarterdeck*, etc., whereby the *cabins* and decks below are lit; the covering over an upper deck *hatchway* leading to the *companion ladder*, *companion way*, or steps going *below*; in *yachts*, the entry from the *cockpit* into the main *cabin*.

Not derived from the familiar word 'companion' meaning comrade (etymologically 'bread-sharer', since it comes from OF *'compaignon'* and the late Latin *'companio'*, made up of *'com-'*, together, and *'pan-'*, bread). The nautical word resembles rather the Dutch *'kompanje'* and OF *'compagne'*, more fully *'chambre de la compagne'*, derived from the Italian *'camera della compagna'*. This 'chamber' was where daily victuals were stored, including of course bread – which is a link with the familiar word.

First attested in 1762 in Falconer, *Shipwreck*, II, 243.

compass   the instrument indicating North and making possible the taking of *bearings*. Its inventor is unknown, but it was already in use in the Mediterranean at least as early as the twelfth century. A magnetic compass points to *magnetic North*, a gyroscopic or gyro compass to *true North*. In former times, an azimuth compass, taking bearings on the sun, the moon, or a star, was used to discover the degree of *magnetic variation*. A *compass bearing* is the direction of any object (measured in degrees from North) as indicated by the compass (often a *hand bearing compass*). The *compass card* is the round card marked off in degrees, to which the magnetic needles are fixed. The *compass corrector box* is that inside the *binnacle* containing the corrector magnets. A *compass course* is the angle between the North-South line of the compass and the *fore-and-aft* line of the ship. *Compass error* is the degree to which the compass is deflected by both *variation* and *deviation* combined. The *compass pivot* is the needle point in the centre of the compass on which the card rotates. A *compass rose* is a graduated circle printed on a *chart* showing both true and magnetic North. *Compass timber* (from an earlier and separate meaning of the word) is shipbuilding timber already steamed and curved to fit the shape of the vessel.

The history of the word, in all its applications, is obscure. Which came first – the noun or the verb? And in the case of the mariner's compass, was the term derived from the idea of a circle (as in the notion of 'encompassing') or was it, as in German, originally applied to a sundial? The original etymology of the word clearly involves stepping or pacing together (as perhaps in a pair of compasses); but this does not solve the problems posed by the word in the singular, nautical sense.

First attested, despite its much earlier use, *c*. 1515 in *Cocke Lorelles Bote* (Percy Society, 1843), 12.

con (also *cond* or *cun*)   to direct the *helmsman*. According to Smyth, *Sailor's Word-book* (1867), sailors pronounced it 'cun'. Although now largely obsolete, the word is still familiar from its use in 1883 by Robert Louis Stevenson, *Treasure Island*, III, xiii (1886 edition, 104). The basic expression survives in *conning tower*, originally the armoured control centre of a warship and now the connecting structure between the *bridge* and the pressure *hull* of a submarine, known in larger vessels as the *sail*.

Two possible derivations have been suggested for this word. One is ME 'cunnen', to know or be skilful, associated with both 'can' and 'cunning'. However, the spelling 'con' is not attested until 1699, whereas 'condue' dates from about 1330 and 'cond' from about 1400, suggesting that (if either represents the original spelling) the word's source may be the Latin '*conducere*', to lead (which also gives the English word 'conduct'). Folk etymology being what it is, the two sources may well have been confused.

First attested in a specifically nautical sense in 1609 (as 'cund') in Biddulph, *Travels* (edited by T. Lavender, 1612), Preface, 11.

concluding line   a small *line rove* through the wooden steps of a *stern* or similar rope ladder, used to haul it up for stowage, with each step collapsing on to the one below it.

From the now obsolete sense of 'conclude', meaning to close up, from the Latin '*concludere*'.

First attested in 1961 in Burgess, *Dictionary*, 60.

contline   the spiral groove between the *strands* of a rope; (formerly) the space between two casks stowed side-by-side.

'Of uncertain derivation' claims the OED; 'it has been suggested that *cont* is a variation of *cant*'. A simpler, more plausible but coarser hypothesis is that the word owes its origin to a comparison with the female genitalia: in fact, the now obsolete word 'cunting' was used by no doubt sex-starved seamen to describe the contline.

First attested in 1848 in Biddlecombe, *Rigging*, 10.

coracle   small round, or more often round-cornered, portable boat made of wickerwork, originally covered with animal hides but later made watertight with pitch or other material, used by ancient Britons for river and coastal transport; still used, mainly by salmon fishermen, on Welsh and Scottish lakes and rivers.

From the Welsh '*corwgl*' or '*cwrwgl*', possibly a diminutive but certainly a derivative of '*corwg*' or '*cwrwg*', which by the thirteenth or fourteenth century has become '*coruc*' or '*corwc*', meaning both carcass and coracle, and equivalent to the Irish '*curach*', a boat. The same word appears in the seventh century in the Latinised form '*curaca*'.

First attested in English as late as 1547, Salesbury, *Dictionary*.

Corbie's aunt   St Elmo's fire, the fiery balls that appear at the *masthead* or *yardarms* of ships when the air is full of electricity.

A wonderful corruption of a corruption. Although 'corbie' (from OF '*corb*' – cf. the Italian 'corvo' and the modern French '*corbeau*', crow) is an old word for a raven, 'Corbie's aunt' is a North-East Scottish fishermen's version of 'corposant', meaning the same mysterious fire. 'Corposant' is derived from the Italian, Old Spanish and Portuguese '*corpo santo*', or, in the original Latin, '*corpus sancti*', saint's body, or '*corpus sanctum*', holy body.

First attested in 1561 in Richard Eden, translation of Martin Cortes, *Arte of Nauigation*, II, xx, 51 b.

Corinthian   amateur, or without a professional (paid) skipper. The OED labels the word 'US', which is true of its origin; but its use in Britain is confirmed by the existence of the Royal Corinthian Yacht Club, founded in 1872 and now at Burnham-on-Crouch, Essex.

Although 'pertaining to Corinth' is the obvious meaning of the term, the logic of its meaning 'amateur' is puzzling. 'Corinthian brass' was a costly ornamental metal; a 'Corinthian style' was regarded by Matthew Arnold as over-brilliant; and in the nineteenth century 'Corinthian' implied elegant dissipation. So the word may have had overtones of dilettantism when it was adopted in the early years of *yacht* racing to describe owners who sailed their own boats rather than using professionals.

First attested in its nautical sense (except in the title of the above-mentioned Club) in 1885 in *Harper's Magazine*, June, 83/1.

corposant   see *Corbie's aunt*.

corsair   a *privateer*, i.e. a private ship licensed to operate against the merchant vessels of an enemy; a member of its crew; also, loosely, a *pirate* or pirate ship. Corsairs operated off the Barbary Coast of North Africa as late as 1825, and although widely regarded as pirates they were usually licensed by the Turkish government in Constantinople to prey on the trade of Christian states. Through French from the Latin '*cursus*', a voyage, and medieval Latin '*cursus*', a hostile excursion. As the OED remarks, 'The reference of the name to *Corsica* was a piece of Italian popular etymology and animosity.'

First attested in 1549 in Thomas, *Italie* (1561 edition), 82.

corvette   a flush-decked warship of the seventeenth and eighteenth centuries with one tier of guns, smaller than a *frigate* but *rigged* as a *barque* or a *brig*; from 1939, a small fast patrol or escort vessel used against U-boats in the Battle of the Atlantic.

From the French word, comparable with the Portuguese '*corveta*' and the Spanish '*corbeta*', and supposedly derived from the Latin '*corbita*' – although this was a slow merchant ship, said to be named from the basket (in Latin, '*corbis*') hoisted as an *ensign* or signal by Egyptian grain ships.

First attested in 1636 in a letter in the *Sidney State Papers* (edited by A. Collins, 1746), II, 436 (L.).

counter   a projecting *stern* or its under side. To *counter brace* (in the 'contrary' sense of 'counter') is to brace the *head-yards* one way and the *after-yards* the other, in a *square-rigger* *going about* or *lying to the wind*. *Counter currents* are those that for whatever reason flow against the main stream, including those under the *lee* counter of a ship under way. *Counter rails* are decorative mouldings on a ship's counter.

Almost certainly independent of a shop's or a counting-house's counter; most likely associated with the notion of 'contrary' or 'opposite', from the French '*contre*' and the Latin '*contra*': the counter being that part of the ship which projects backwards, i.e. counter to the normal forward movement.

First attested in 1626 in Smith, *Accidence*, 11.

course   direction steered from point to point; initially, the sails set on the lower *yards* of a *square-rigger* to which *bonnets* could be attached. In practice, both senses of the word need some elaboration. The *compass course* of a ship is the angle between her path and the North-South line on the compass; her *magnetic course* is the angle between her path and *magnetic North*; her *true course* is that between her path and *true North*; while her *course made good* is her progress over the seabed, or the track to be plotted on the *chart*. In the second sense of the word, its meaning was gradually extended to cover all sails set on the lower yards, whether or not they could carry bonnets, and to *staysails* set on lower masts and the main staysails of *brigs* and *schooners*; the courses were named according to the masts – *fore course*, *main course*, and *mizen course*.

From the Latin '*cursum*', running, run, race, or course; in the second sense, via the intermediate senses of 'a series' and 'a level'.

First attested in the first sense in 1553 by Sebastian Cabot in Hakluyt, *Divers Voyages* (1582 edition), 259; in the second sense, *c.* 1515, in *Cocke Lorelles Bote* (Percy Society, 1843), 12.

cow hitch   a *bend* or *hitch* not properly tied, or otherwise unfit for its purpose. Alternatively, a way of securing a doubled rope through a ring or round a pole, by passing the *bight* through the ring, then putting the *standing parts* through the bight but not through the ring (essentially, forming two half hitches tied in opposite directions), secure only so long as equal strain is placed on each standing part. Burgess, *Dictionary* (1961), 63, defines it as 'used to join two soft eyes, interlocked by thoroughfooting'.

The first sense of the term – the only one mentioned by the OED – is a derogatory extension of the word 'cow' (itself from OE 'cu' and from common Teutonic and Indo-European roots). Such extensions began in the sixteenth century, to describe a coward, in the late seventeenth century a coarse woman, and in the nineteenth century, in Australian and New Zealand slang, any objectional person or thing. The other senses reflect both the rather unseamanlike nature of the hitch and its likely use with the animal concerned.

First attested in 1867 in Smyth, *Sailor's Word-book*.

coxswain   the *helmsman* in a charge of a ship's boat; the senior *petty officer* on board small naval craft.

The original spelling 'cockswain' clarifies the etymology. One meaning of the word 'cock', now obsolete, was a small ship's boat, cognate with *cog* and first attested in the fifteenth century in the combination 'cokbote' – which combination is its only survival today. 'Swain', from ON *'sveinn'*, meaning attendant, is the same as in 'boatswain'; and, as that word is contracted in speech to 'bosun', so 'coxswain' is pronounced 'coxun'.

First attested *c.* 1463 in *Manners and Household Expenses* (Roxburghe Club, 1841), 219.

CQR   a patent *stockless* anchor whose *fluke* resembles two ploughshares set back to back and held to the *shank* a pin on which it pivot; for use by small vessels and *yachts*. Designed in 1933 by Professor (later Sir) Geoffrey Taylor, intended for use by flying boats. Known in the US as the 'plow' anchor.

A phonetic version of the word 'secure'.

First attested in 1933 when its patent was taken out.

crab   originally a wooden *capstan* with claws; later, a capstan without a *drumhead*; a portable capstan or *winch*.

A figurative use, because of its claws, of the familiar word, which is derived from OE 'crabba' and dates back at least as far as the year 1000.

First attested in its nautical sense in 1627 in Smith, *Seaman's Grammar*, I, 2.

cradle   a framework, usually wooden, to support a vessel ashore, especially on the *launching ways*, down which it slides with the ship.

A figurative extension of the familiar word, which is derived from OE 'cradol', itself probably a diminutive from the German stem '*krat*', and therefore meaning 'little basket' (cf. 'bassinet').

First attested in a nautical context in 1627 in Smith, *Seaman's Grammar*, I, 1.

craft   small vessel; later, any kind of ship.

The common Teutonic forebears of the word, including OE 'craeft', all denoted strength or force. Only in English, from the ninth century onwards, did it come to acquire the notion of 'skill'. It then came to mean the equipment used by fishing boats, and these then acquired the name 'small craft', often used as a collective noun denoting a number of vessels. As the OED observes, 'The want in English of any general collective term for all sorts of "vessels for water carriage" naturally made craft a useful stop-gap.' It then gradually began to be applied to individual boats.

First attested as a collective noun for vessels in 1671–2 by Sir C. Lyttelton in *Hatton Correspondence* (Camden Society, 1878), 75; and as denoting fishing tackle in 1688 in Randle Holme, *Armory*, III, 163/1. The fact that this first attestation slightly predates the other is of no etymological significance.

crank   (of a ship) liable to tip sideways, either at sea or on land. 'Cranky' is sometimes used in the same sense. A milder synonym is *tender*.

Unconnected with the familiar word, but almost certainly derived from the Dutch and Frisian '*krengd*', lying on its side.

First attested (in the phrase 'cranke sided') in 1626 in Smith, *Accidence*, 13; on its own, in 1696 in Phillips, *New World*.

cranse (also *crance, crans*, or *cranze*) **iron**   a metal band with *eyes*, fitted to the *bowsprit*-end to take the *bobstay*, *shrouds*, etc.

From the Old and Middle High German '*Kranz*', via the Dutch '*krans*', a wreath or garland.

First attested in 1846 in Young, *Nautical Dictionary*.

creeper   a *grapnel* to recover items from the seabed by dragging for them.

From the familiar verb 'creep', itself from OE 'creopan'.

First attested in its nautical sense *c.* 1400 in the Northern English alliterative verse on which Sir Thomas Malory based his prose work, *Morte Arthure* (EETS, 1865, revised 1871), 3667.

crew   the ship's company; to work as a member of it or, in *dinghies*, to assist the *helmsman*.

From OF '*creue*', increase, and possibly linked with the English verb 'accrue', the word originally meant military reinforcements, shifting gradually to denote a group or company, including a team of workmen. The word is quite distinct from 'crew' as a pen for animals, which comes from an early English version of the Old Welsh '*creu*' or '*crau*'.

First attested in a nautical context in 1692 in Love, *Mariner's Jewel* (5th edition, 1724), 120.

cringle   a rope loop, usually with a metal *thimble* to prevent chafe, worked into the *boltrope* at the *head*, *tack* or *clew* of a sail; those in line with the *reef points* are *reef cringles*. Michael Scott adopted the word for his *Tom Cringle's Log*, a vivid account of early nineteenth-century life in the Caribbean, first published in 1829–33 in *Blackwood's Magazine* and republished in 1836.

From the Low German '*Kringel*', a small circle or ring; cf. the word 'crinkle' from the Dutch and Low German '*krinkel*', a curve.

First attested in 1627 in Smith, *Seaman's Grammar*, v, 22.

cross   to place across the mast (originally said of sails, later of *yards*, in a *square-rigger*). The word has many other nautical applications. A *cross bar* is a long round iron bar used for turning *cables*. A *cross beam* is a strengthening timber *athwartships*. *Cross bearings* are those taken on separate objects to determine the ship's position, usually by producing a *cocked hat* on the *chart*. A *cross head* is a *rudder* head fitted to connect the *steering* gear. The *cross jack* (pronounced 'cro'-jack') is the *mizen course* or its *yard*. *Cross lashing* is not an angry naval punishment but a method of lashing in which the consecutive turns are crossed diagonally. A *cross pawl*, in ship-building, is a horizontal timber used to hold the frames temporarily in position. A *cross sea* or *cross seas* means a sea moving against the wind, and therefore choppily. To *cross someone's bows* is to pass close ahead, and (figuratively) to thwart. To *cross the T* is a battle manoeuvre whereby a fleet in line ahead crosses at right angles to the enemy's battle line, so that all its guns can be fired on the *broadside* while the enemy can reply only with those that can fire ahead. To *cross the line* is to cross the equator, when those doing so for the first time are ceremonially initiated. *Cross trees* are timber *spreaders* fixed *athwartships* across the *trestle-trees* at the upper ends of lower masts and *topmasts*.

The word is derived, by several routes, from the Latin '*crux*'.

First attested in a nautical context in 1393 in Gower, *Confessio amantis* (R. Pauli, 1857; *English Works*, EETS, 1900), I, 81.

crowfoot   a number of small cords *rove* through a long *block* or *euphroe* and radiating to support an awning, etc.

From the shape of the foot of a crow, which word, from OE

'crawe', is cognate with a number of similar words in Germanic languages, associated with verbs meaning to crow. Together with the Latin '*corvus*', this may suggest a degree of onomatopoeia. The same notion (of a crow's foot) underlies the names of various flowers that share the same generic common name. *Crow's foot* is a term also used for the method of attaching *reef points* to a sail, by unlaying the *strands* to splay them out.

First attested in 1627 in Smith, *Seaman's Grammar*, v, 24.

crown   a *knot* formed at a rope's end as the basis for a *back splice*, interweaving the *strands*; also, the base of an anchor, where the *arms* meet the *shank*. A *crown and wall* is a *wall knot* formed on a crown knot. A *crown plait* is one formed by alternate crown and *diamond* knots.

From the Latin '*corona*', garland or wreath.

First attested in the ropework sense in 1769 in Falconer, *Dictionary*; of an anchor, in 1875 in Bedford, *Sailor's Pocketbook* (2nd edition), vi, 216.

crow's nest   platform or shelter, originally made from a *cask*, high on the *foremast*, from which the *masthead* lookout would watch for the blow of a whale or for channels through ice, etc. Although now obsolete as a nautical device, the term has since been used in New Zealand for shepherds' lookouts.

From 'crow' and 'nest', but originally applied to military observation posts.

First attested in its nautical sense in 1818 in *Blackwood's Magazine*, IV, 343.

cruise   to sail to and fro over a particular area; such a voyage, especially when undertaken by tourists. Chronologically, the verb precedes the noun.

The 'to and fro' is a clue to the word's etymology: its origin is the seventeenth-century Dutch '*kruisen*', to cross, and it has similar roots to those of 'cross' and 'crucifix', notably the Latin '*crux*', a cross.

First attested in 1651 by G. Carteret in *The Nicholas Papers*, (Camden Society, 1886–1920), I, 236.

cruiser   in the days of sail, a ship detached from a fleet to *cruise* in search of the enemy; later, a generic type of warship; in *yachting*, often a motor vessel, but also a sailing boat not designed for racing. A *cruising stern* is one with a fuller form down to and at the waterline, the projecting part being under water. *The Cruising Association* was founded in 1908 to assist cruising *yachtsmen*. A *cruising chute* is a pole-less *spinnaker*.

From *cruise*.

First firmly attested in 1695 in *London Gazette*, No 3061/1.

crupper chain   chain that secures the *heel* of a *jib boom* fitted to a *bowsprit,* to prevent its rising.

Like *martingale,* this is a nautical term adapted from saddlery, the crupper being originally the strap buckled to the saddle to prevent its slipping forward, and looped under the horse's tail. The word's origin is OF *'croupiere',* from the medieval word *'crope'* or *'crupe',* meaning rump. The same source underlies 'croupier', originally one who rides behind on the horse's rump, then one standing behind a gambler, and finally the master of ceremonies who rakes in the chips at a gaming table.

First attested (without the word 'chain') in 1860 in H. Stuart, *Catechism,* 74; with the word 'chain' in 1882 in Nares, *Seamanship* (6th edition), 13.

crutch   *stanchion* topped by two short curved arms to take the main *boom* of a *yacht,* etc., when the sails are stowed; metal pin with similar arms, fitting into a socket in the *gunwale* of a boat as pivot for an *oar* (often popularly called a *rowlock*).

Figurative extensions of the familiar word, whose origin is OE 'crycc', from a common Teutonic root, and associated also with 'crotch'.

First attested in the former sense above in 1769 in Falconer, *Dictionary*; in the latter sense above, in 1869 in Bennett, *Leaves from a Log,* 127.

cuddy   originally a *cabin* under the *poop deck* in the *after* part of a sailing ship, used by the *captain* and his passengers; later a small cabin or cookhouse on board; now more often a small space, e.g. in the *forepeak* of a half-decked vessel, too small for a cabin, too big for a locker. A *cuddy jig* is the tottering of someone who has not yet 'got his sea legs'.

Of uncertain origin. Some, implausibly, compare it to 'cubby' or 'cubby-hole'; other have suggested an oriental source. The most likely is the sixteenth-century Dutch *'kaiute'* (modern Dutch *'kajuit'*), with the same meaning.

First attested in 1660 in Pepys, *Diary,* 14 May.

Cunningham (also *Cunningham eye* or *Cunningham hole*) an *eyelet* or *cringle* near the bottom of the *luff* of a *mainsail* through which a line is *rove* to tauten it when racing.

From the name of its inventor, Briggs Cunningham of New York, skipper of the 1958 America's Cup defender *Columbia*.

First attested in 1976 in Kemp, *Oxford Companion,* 218.

currach, curragh   See *coracle*.

cut and run   to depart in haste. While some believe that this might entail cutting the anchor *cable,* the cost of an anchor suggests that it more plausibly meant cutting the mooring *painter* or, in *square-riggers*, cutting the ropeyarns that held the *furled* sails *stopped* to the *yards*. The *cut of her jib,* meaning general appearance, dates from mid eighteenth-century sailing navies, when the size and shape of a vessel's jib could identify it before its national flag could be recognised: Spanish ships had small jibs or none at all, French ships often two, with short luffs. A *cut splice* is one joining two overlapping ropes to form an oval *eye*. *Cutting one's painter* meant making a secret departure from a mooring or, colloquially, dying.

As a noun meaning 'lot' or 'portion', the word 'cut' was already in use by 1300; but although the verb meaning 'to make an incision' also appears towards the end of the thirteenth century it seems to be distinct from the noun, and has no place in OE, which used the verb 'snidan' (cf. the German '*schneiden*') or 'ceorfan' (cf. 'carve'). The source of the verb 'cut' was probably an Old Teutonic stem '*kut-*' or '*kot-*'. The source of 'run' is the OE intransitive 'rinnan'.

First attested in 1704 in the *Boston News-Letter,* 12 June, 2/2.

cutch   a preparation of Acacia catechu gum used to prolong the life of canvas sails.

From the Malayalam '*kachu*', the gum in question.

First attested in 1617 in Cocks, *Diary in Japan 1615–22* (Hakluyt Society, 1883), I, 294 (Y.).

cutlass   short sword with a flat, wide, and slightly curved blade, carried on board large warships until the second decade of the twentieth century.

From the French '*coutelas*' and cognate with the Italian '*coltellaccio*', a large (and formidable) knife.

First attested (as 'coutelace') *c.* 1594 in Thomas Kyd, translation of R. Garnier, *Cornelio,* V, 189.

cutter   originally, an auxiliary boat to a *man of war*, later used by customs and as a *pilot boat*; a *clinker-built* ship's boat equipped with *oars* and two masts carrying a *dipping lug foresail* and a *standing lug mainsail*; a sailing *yacht* with a mainsail and two foresails (in the US known as a *sloop*, the term 'cutter' being used there for boats with an older *rig* and a very long *bowsprit*), usually *Bermuda-rigged*; a US Navy patrol vessel of some 2,000 tons.

Of uncertain origin. Dr Johnson called it 'a nimble boat that cuts the water', which is a plausible conjecture. The French '*cotre*' is derived from the English word, not *vice versa*.

First attested in a nautical context in 1745 in Thomas, *A True and Impartial Journal,* 284.

cutwater   the *forward* curve of a ship's *stem*, also formerly sometimes known as the *knee* of the *head* or *beakhead*.

From 'cut' (probably from an Old Teutonic stem '*kut-*' or '*kot-*') and 'water' (from a common Teutonic root and OE 'waeter').

First attested in 1644 in Winthrop, *New England* (1825–6; 1953 edition), II, 239.

Dagger-board   a drop *keel* or non-pivoting *centre-board*.

From 'dagger', since it slides from its case like the weapon from its sheath, and moves along its centreline. 'Dagger', although related to the obsolete verg 'dag', to stab, and to the French '*dague*' and the Spanish and Italian '*daga*', a dagger, seems to predate all of these, first attested as it is *c.* 1375: it has no OF equivalent, and seems to be an original English word, possibly onomatopoeic.

First attested in 1961 in Burgess, *Dictionary*, 66.

dan or **dan buoy**   small temporary marker buoy with a flag on top, secured with a weight and lines, used to mark fishermen's nets, etc., or a man overboard.

Of obscure origin; unlikely to be related to 'dan' or 'don' as an honorific from the Latin '*dominus*', lord or master.

First attested in 1687 in the *London Gazette* No. 2298/4.

dandy   a *sloop* or *cutter* with a *jigger-mast aft*, on which is set a small *lugsail*; a vessel *rigged* like a *yawl*, but with a *jib-headed mizen* and a *loose-footed mainsail*; a *ketch* or *yawl*; the sail on the mizen in a ketch or yawl; a small *winch*, as used in fishing boats for the *trawl* (also 'dandywink').

The proliferation of meanings is largely explained by the fact that all are derived from the familiar word, itself of uncertain origin but possibly descended from the seventeenth-century 'Jack-a-dandy', a fop. Current on the Scottish borders in the late eighteenth century, 'dandy' was adopted in early nineteenth-century London, to mean a swell or exquisite, whence it was extended to denote any smart contrivance.

First attested in a nautical context in 1858 in *The Mercantile Marine Magazine*, V, 134.

davit   a curved iron or timber crane for hoisting e.g. the anchor; now more usually, and often in the plural, the devices used to suspend *lifeboats* and swing them outward for lowering. A *davit-cast* is a heavy *spar* used as a crane on board ship; a *davit-guy* is a *guy-rope* used to steady a davit; the *davit-roll* is the davit's roller or *sheave*; the *davit-rope* is that which secures the davit to the *shrouds* when out of use.

Formerly also spelt 'David' and apparently an extension of that name (as is often the case with tools): the person in question, if any, remains unknown. At one time, it may have been pronounced with a long 'a', though normally this is now short.

First attested in 1373 in a Norman-French indenture in T. Riley, *Memorials* (1868), 370.

Davy Jones   the evil spirit of the sea, sometimes shortened to 'Davy'. *Davy Jones's locker* is the seabed or maritime graveyard.

Of unknown origin.

First attested in 1751 in Smollett, *Peregrine Pickle*, XIII.

dead eye   a circular *block* with no revolving *sheaves* but three holes arranged in an inverted triangle, through which *shroud lanyards* are *rove*; similar device with one hole, often for extending a *stay*.

From 'dead', already thus spelt in OE, with a common Teutonic root, the idea being that the block had no moving parts. Because such blocks were also known as 'dead men's eyes', it may be that the three holes suggested two human eyes and an open mouth.

First attested in 1748 in Anson, *Voyage*, I, viii, 78.

dead horse   period of work on board ship already paid for in advance and having to be 'worked off'.

Why 'horse'? Possibly because to sailors a horse on board represented something out of place and burdensome.

First attested in 1832 in E.C. Wines, *Two Years*, I, 73.

deadlight   wooden or metal shutter that can be used to protect a window, *scuttle* or *port* to black out its light.

Of obvious etymology.

First attested in 1726 in George Shelvocke the Elder, *Voyage* (1757 edition), 3.

dead marine   an empty bottle, sometimes simply 'marine'.

The origin of the expression is undoubtedly the low esteem in which *marine* officers were held by regular seamen. It has been alleged that the future King William IV, when serving at sea as the Duke of Clarence, ordered a steward at dinner on board to remove the 'dead marines', the bottles that had done their duty nobly and were ready to do it again. This may be a true story; but since the Duke served in the Navy only from 1779 (aged 24) and was a *midshipman* and *lieutenant* until appointed *post-captain* in 1786, it seems surprising that a lexicographer should record the expression as early as 1785. Perhaps the future Sailor King, using an existing phrase, was showing his wit by the elegance of his tribute to the fallen.

First attested in 1785 in Francis Grose, *Classical Dictionary*, under 'Marine officer': 'An empty bottle (sea wit), marine officers being held useless by the seamen.'

dead men   *reef* and *gasket* end, etc., left flapping untidily. Although ashore the expression was used for empty bottles, as in the song 'Down Among the Dead Men', the nautical equivalent for that was *dead marines*.

No doubt from the uselessness of the ends in question, possibly by analogy with felons swinging from a gibbet.

First attested (as meaning empty bottles) in 1700; but with this specific nautical meaning not until 1825 in Glascock, *Naval Sketch-Book* (1826 edition), I, 11.

dead reckoning   estimation of present position by computing speed and direction (affected by *tide* and *leeway*) from a former known position.

It is sometimes suggested that this is a contraction of 'deduced reckoning', but the conjecture seems more ingenious than plausible, although 'deduced' in this sense, attested in 1529, predates the first attestation of 'dead reckoning'. Kemp, *Oxford Companion* (1976), 234, argues that the term arose from the ancient custom of sailors' calling unknown water 'dead seas'; but, although the Greeks and Romans gave this name to the Arctic Ocean, they also applied it to the Dead Sea, which was not unknown to them. 'Dead reckoning' may therefore, perhaps, owe its origin to another overtone of 'dead', i.e. unrelieved or absolute – but not to the further sense of 'accurate'.

First attested in 1613 in Ridley, *Short Treatise*, 147.

deadrise   the rise of the bottom of a boat from the *keel* to the full breadth of the turn of the *bilge*.

Missing from the OED, this word may be related to the seventeenth-century 'deadrising', defined in 1769, in Falconer, *Dictionary*, as 'those parts of a ship's floor or bottom, throughout her whole length, where the floor timber is terminated upon the lower futtock'.

First attested in 1961 in Burgess, *Dictionary*, 68.

dead water   the *eddy* under the *counter* of a moving vessel which passes away more slowly than that along her sides.

The etymology is self-explanatory.

First attested in this precise sense in 1627 in Smith, *Sea Grammar*, ix, 42.

deadwood   heavy wedge-shaped timber filling the angle between the *keel* and the *sternpost* or the *transom* of a wooden vessel; similar *knee* at the *stem*.

The relation between this precise meaning and others, including the literal one, is probably indirect, via various nuances of the word 'dead', rather than direct and figurative.

First attested in this nautical sense in 1728 in Chambers, *Cyclopaedia*.

deck   the horizontal platforms in ships and boats corresponding to floors in a building. Reading upwards from the bottom in a large ship, the decks are the *orlop*, the lower (now sometimes combined), the main, the shelter or promenade, the bridge deck and the boat deck. In the days of the sailing navy, the upper deck was often called the *spar* deck and the main deck the gun deck. Other names, such as hurricane deck or cabin deck, are also used; so are terms for portions of the deck or part decks. Thus the *forecastle* deck is the built-up portion near the *bows*, and the *poop* deck is that near the stern, while that part of the upper deck *abaft* the mainmast is the *quarterdeck*.

A *deck hand* is a seaman over seventeen with at least a year's service, or anyone working on upper deck duties. A *deckhead* is the underside of a deck viewed from below (which a *landlubber* might just call a 'ceiling'). A *deckhouse* is a rectangular structure on the deck, known in sailing warships as a 'round house' because one could walk round in it, and usually used for accommodation. A *deck light* is a strong glass *bull's eye* or prism set in the deck to let light in below. The *deck log* is a rough *log* book recording all information about working the ship. To *deck out* is to *dress a ship overall*.

Deck passage is a passage or trip with no accommodation provided. The *deck pipe* is the *navel pipe* through which the *cable* passes up from the *chain locker*. A *deck plate* is an angled metal plate attached to the deck, to which a fitting can be *shackled* (in the US, a disc covering the opening to a fuel or water tank). A *deck shelf* is the long *fore-and-aft* timber in a wooden *yacht*, to secure the tops of the timbers and support the beams for the deck. A *deck watch* is not a task, a working party, or a stretch of time but a timepiece, a small watch synchronised with the chronometer and used to time sights, *bearings*, etc. *Decked in,* of a *dinghy*, etc., means parted-decked, the next biggest part-deck being *quarter-decked*, the next biggest *half-decked*.

Probably of Flemish or Low German origin via the Middle Dutch '*dec*', a roof or covering: cf. the modern German '*Dach*', a roof, and '*Decke*', a blanket. In Dutch, the word '*dek*' does not appear in the nautical sense until about 1675, whereas it is attested in English 162 years earlier.

First attested in 1513 in a letter to Cardinal Wolsey from Echyngham on 5 May (Cotton MSS. Calig. D. vi. 1f 110).

deep   a *channel* between *shoals*; (in *lead* and line *soundings*) a sounding between marks on the line, identified by that still visible above the surface of the water – and therefore really meaning 'shallower than' whichever number the **leadsman** calls out. Burgess, *Dictionary* (1961), 69, holds that 'the term "by the deep" is incorrect, there being no mark on the line'. Incorrect or not, it survived until at least 1882; and it seems possible that the 'correct' cry of (say) 'deep four' may be a contraction. A **deep draft route** in a traffic separation scheme is that for vessels which **draw** a lot of water. A **deep sea line** was not a shipping company but a line used for deep soundings before the days of the **echo sounder**. **Deep-vee** refers to a boat with a sharp **deadrise** angle of more than about 5 degrees.

From OE 'deop' or 'diop', with a common Teutonic root giving, for example, the modern German '*tief*'. In early nautical usage the word was often spelt 'dip'.

First attested in 1769 in Falconer, *Dictionary* (1789 edition), M m iv: 'As there is no mark at 4, 6, 8, &c., he estimates those numbers, and calls, "By the dip four, &c."'

de Horsey rig   having a triangular *foresail* and a *loose-footed gaff mainsail*. From Admiral Sir A.F.R. de Horsey (1827–1922), who introduced the rig in the early twentieth century for use in British warships' *launches*, *pinnaces*, and *cutters*.

First attested in 1905 in *A Manual of Seamanship*, iii, 47.

departure   the last firm *fix* obtained by an outward bound vessel, from which a *course* is *laid*: the number of *nautical miles* due East or West from one point to another. When two places are on the same parallel of latitide, the 'departure' or distance between them equals the difference of longitude in minutes multiplied by the cosine of the latitude. This calculation was important in the sixteenth, seventeenth, and early eighteenth centuries, when the various courses sailed during the day were resolved into their North-South and East-West components.

From 'depart', itself derived from the Latin '*dispartire*', to divide, perhaps via OF '*departir*'.

First attested in the sense of a change of longitude in 1669 in Sturmy, *Mariners Magazine*, Book IV, 158; in the sense of point of departure, in 1699 in Hacke, *Original Voyages*, I, 42.

derrick   a pivoted *spar* used for lifting weights, *stayed* from a mast and controlled by *guys* and a *topping lift*.

From the surname of a noted hangman at Tyburn *c.* 1600: its original meaning was either a hangman, a hanging, or the gallows (which a derrick obviously resembles).

First attested in the sense of a crane rather than a lethal contraption in 1756 in *The Gentleman's Magazine*, XXVI, 429.

deviation   *compass error* due to magnetism on board, which can be partly offset by corrector magnets and/or noted on a deviation card showing the degree of error on each main *heading* of the ship.

From the Latin *'deviare'*, to deviate, via the medieval Latin *'deviatio'*.

First attested in 1821 in Fisher, *Journal*, 3.

devil   the *seam* in the *upper deck* planking next to the *waterways*; also, contradictorily and confusingly, the seam on the *garboard* or *garboard strake*, i.e. the outer plank next to the *keel*. So named because of the difficulty of caulking either seam, in the one case because so often wet and in the other because so inaccessible. The phrase 'the devil to pay (and no pitch hot)' has been thought to come from either nautical use of the word, plus *pay* in its caulking sense; but it may be merely an extension of the general, financial sense of the expression, first attested in Swift, *Journal to Stella*, 28 September 1711, and referring back to some archetypal Faustian bargain. Similarly, the expression 'between the devil and the deep blue sea' (occasionally 'the dead sea') may have arisen from there being 'only the thickness of the ship's hull planking between this seam and the sea' (Kemp, *Oxford Companion* (1976), 244); but it is actually first attested, in 1637, in a non-nautical context in Monro, *Expedition*, II, 55. A *devil's claw* is a form of *cable stopper* with two prongs that pass across a horizontal link but hold that next to it, which cannot then lie flat. *Devil's smiles* are deceptive glimpses of sunlight between dark clouds.

The word itself is derived from OE 'deofol', and ultimately, via the Latin *'diabolus'*, from the Greek *'diabolos'*, which originally meant an accuser or slanderer, from the corresponding verb meaning literally to throw across. The game 'diabolo', sometimes known as 'devil on two sticks' because it involved tossing a double-headed top on a string held taut by two wooden handles, may conceivably owe its name to the original Greek verb, although the 'devil' association has always been strong, perhaps because of the difficulty of playing it.

First attested in a nautical sense in 1865 in Smyth, *Sailor's Word-book*; and in the garboard strake sense in 1893–5 in Funk & Wagnall, *Standard Dictionary*.

dghaisa   a *gondola*-like boat used in harbours and around the coast of Malta.

A Maltese word, also spelt *'dghajsa'* and *'diassa'*, but pronounced 'dysa' or 'dyso'.

First attested in 1893 in 'Sarah Grand' (Mrs M'Fall), *The Heavenly Twins*, I, ii, I, 214.

dhow   a *lateen-rigged*, single-masted trading vessel of 150–200 tons common in the Red Sea, the Persian Gulf, and the Indian Ocean, as well as on the Nile; later, any similar-sized vessel in those waters, with however many masts, and now often with a diesel engine.

Although the word exists in modern Arabic, its language of origin remains obscure.

First attested in 1799 in Jackson, *Journal from India*, 3.

diagonal-built   built with the side planking at an angle of 45 degrees from the horizontal, a second layer of planking being laid at right angles to the first (i.e. at 45 degrees from the horizontal in the opposite direction): used for some sailing *dinghies*, some *yachts* and some small naval vessels, to strengthen the *hull*. From the Greek '*diagonios*', from angle to angle, via the Latin '*diagonalis*'.

First attested in this nautical sense in 1869 in R.W. Meade, *Naval Architecture*, 416.

diamond knot   a *stopper knot* contrived in a rope by *unlaying* the *strands* to the required point, tucking them through the *bights* of each other, then *laying up* the rest of the rope again. A *diamond of error*, rather like a *cocked hat*, is the shape formed by the intersection of two position bands in a hyperbolic system of navigation such as Decca. *Diamond shrouds* or *stays*, used in some *Bermuda-rigged* boats, are carried in pairs over short struts of *spreaders* from one point on a mast to another lower down, making a diamond pattern against the sky.

By figurative extension from the familiar word 'diamond', whose source is the Latin '*adamas*', adamant, via ME 'diamant'.

First attested in 1769 in Falconer, *Dictionary*.

diaphone   low-pitched fog signal operating on compressed air, each note ending with a sharply descending 'grunt'.

From the Greek '*dia-*', through, and '*phon-*' sound.

First attested in 1906 in the *Daily Colonist*, of Victoria, British Columbia, 20 January, 6/5.

dickey, dicky   a ship's officer, sometimes the second mate; a small seat, often one of two at the rear of a large square-sterned rowing boat; a naval seaman's collar; little.

Basically a diminutive of a diminutive, from 'Richard' via 'Dick'. How it came to have so many nautical meanings, as well as so many others, remains obscure, although it has been suggested that when the word denotes an article of clothing it may have affinities with the Dutch '*dek*', a covering (itself related to *deck*).

First attested in the sense of a seat, in 1801 in *Gabrielli's Mysterious Husband*, IV, 260; as a naval officer in 1867 in Smyth,

Sailor's Word-book; and as a small *projecting* platform for the **leadsman** in 1907 in Masefield, *A Tarpaulin Muster*, iv, 57; as a collar and little, in 1961 in Burgess, *Dictionary*, 70.

dinghy   originally a small open rowing boat with one pair of *oars*, usually *clinker-built*, used as a work-boat for bigger vessels or as a *tender* to a *yacht*; later partly *decked* and used for racing under sail; now predominantly for sport, although the word still covers tenders, including inflatables, which may carry *outboard* engines. Not always originally spelt with an 'h', which seems to have been adopted (presumably to ensure pronunciation with a hard 'g') in or around 1832, although it was still being omitted some 50 years later, apparently without deleterious effect.

From the Hindi *'dengi'* or *'dingi'*, small boat – diminutives of *'denga'*, *'donga'*, a larger coastal vessel.

First attested in this specific Indian sense in 1794 in *The Elements and Parctice of Rigging and Seamanship*, I, 242; in a more general sense, in 1818 in 'Alfred Burton' (John Mitford), *Johnny Newcome*, iii, 176.

dip   (of a *compass* needle) tendency to tilt downwards towards the nearest magnetic pole; (of the horizon) correction to be made when observing altitude with a *sextant*, to allow for atmospheric refraction of light and for one's own eye's height above sea level; to lower (e.g. the *ensign*) in salute. A *dipper* is a baling ladle. *Dipping* is plunging into the trough of a wave after riding it. *Dipping a light* is sailing away from it until it disappears below the horizon, while a *dipping light* is one that does so as the ship rides to the *swell*. *Dipping lug* is a *rig* in which a *lugsail* projects *forward* of the mast and so has to be partly lowered, with the *yard* dipped round th mast, when *going about*.

From OE 'dyppan', associated with 'deep'.

First attested in the 'compass' sense in 1727–51 in Chambers, *Cyclopaedia*; in the 'horizon' sense in 1774 in Mackenzie, *Marine Surveying* (1819 edition), I, 18; in the 'lowering' sense in 1858 in Reade, *Love me little, love me long*, II, iv, 174.

dipsey, dipsie, dipsy   a deep sea *lead*; the *sinker* on a fishing line; the float on a fishing line.

From 'deep sea'.

First attested in the 'lead' sense in 1626 in Smith, *Accidence*, 29; in the first of the two mutually conflicting 'fishing' senses, in 1860 in John R. Bartlett, *Dictionary of Americanisms* (3rd ed.); in the second of these, in 1867 in Smyth, *Sailor's Word-book*.

dirk   originally, in the late seventeenth or early eighteenth century, a naval dagger worn and used in close combat; later, the small naval sword in a *midshipman*'s full-dress uniform.

Of very uncertain origin. The original spelling 'dork' (found in 1602) might conceivably be a corruption of the Danish, Dutch, and Swedish '*dolk*' or the German '*Dolch*', a dagger. From the second half of the seventeenth century the spelling 'durk' was common, but Dr Johnson ('without authority', says the reproachful OED) adopted the spelling 'dirk'. Johnson thought the word to be of Scottish Highland provenance; but it has no counterpart in Gaelic.

First attested (as 'dork') in 1602 in a *Form of Ancient Trial by Battel*, reprinted in Nicolson and Burn, *History and Antiquities*, (1777), I, 596; in a nautical context, in 1867 in Smyth, *Sailor's Word-book*.

ditty bag or **box**   receptacle for small belongings, including darning materials, and (in the case of a ditty box) personal keepsakes, usually locked.

Of unknown origin, although Smyth, *Sailor's Word-book* (1867), conjectured that the bag, at least, derived its name 'from the *dittis* or Manchester stuff of which it was once made'. The OED comments: 'No evidence of this is given, nor is anything known of the stuff alleged.'

First attested as 'ditty bag' in 1860 in Stuart, *Catechism*, 81; as 'ditty box' in 1883 in the *Pall Mall Gazette*, 2 June.

dock   the area of water in a port or harbour enclosed by *piers* or *wharves*; in the US, the piers or wharves themselves; to enter a dock. *Dock dues* are charges made for the use of docks. *Docking herself* is said of a boat's making a bed for herself in the ooze. *Docking keels*, also known as *bilge keels*, are twin keels at about the turn of the *bilge* which help support a boat's weight in *dry dock*, launching *ways* or mud. The *dockyard cat* is the phantom thief blamed when a vessel is in harbour. *Dockyard maties* are dockyard *hands*. A *dry dock* is one from which the water can be pumped. A *floating dock* is one that can be flooded to allow a ship to enter, then pumped out to raise her high and dry.

Of uncertain origin. It first appears in fifteenth-century English and Dutch, then seems to have spread. Its original meanings included a bed in mud of sand in which a vessel could sit at low water, the hollow she left in doing so, a creek or haven in which she could either settle or ride at anchor, and a trench made for that purpose. But the modern, manufactured meaning also appears from the outset, and actually predates the other quoted instances.

First attested in 1486 in *Naval Accounts* (Navy Records Society, 1896), 23.

dodger a *canvas* or similar screen to protect from spray, etc., originally used on ships' *bridges* before the introduction of reinforced glass, and now most common around the *cockpits* of *yachts*, often bearing the boat's name.

From the verb 'dodge', whose origin is mysterious: it may possibly be derived (like 'sledge' from 'sled') from a Scottish word 'dodd', to jog.

First attested in a nautical sense in 1898 in Cutcliffe Hyne, *Captain Kettle*, x, 260.

dog to fasten securely, for instance by passing a line spirally round a rope with and in the *lay*; to halve the *strands* of a rope, when completing a *splice*, and *seize* each part to its neighbouring half. The word 'dog' also appears as a nautical noun, meaning a fastening for closing watertight doors; but this is not an exclusively nautical expression, having been used for a clamp since the fifteenth century. In a *yacht*, the *doghouse* is the raised area at the *after* end of the *cabin* top which offers standing room and may also shelter the *forward* part of the *cockpit*. The *dog shores* are timbers used to support a ship on the launching *ways*. A *dog sleep* (cf. a 'cat nap') is one snatched by someone who should be awake, e.g. on *watch*. The *Dog Star* is Sirius. The *dog vane* is a form of *tell-tale*, often of *bunting*, or of cork and feathers threaded on a thin line, and attached either to the *rigging* or to a short *staff* on the *weather gunwale*, to indicate to the *helmsman* the direction of the wind. The *dog watches* are the two half watches of two hours each, into which the 4 p.m. to 8 p.m. watch is split to provide an odd number of watches each day so that no one has to keep the same watch on consecutive days: known as 'first dog' and 'second dog' they were in use by the seventeenth century, but their etymological rationale remains obscure.

From the familiar word for a canine, via the idea of jaws gripping tightly. The word itself seems to be of English origin, since the common Teutonic term was '*hund*'. 'Dogge' appears in the mid eleventh century, and when used in other languages, as perhaps also in its early English uses, seems to refer to a particular kind or breed, and is often noted as of English provenance.

First attested in a nautical context in 1847 in Key, *H.M.S. Gorgon*, 24.

dogger originally, an early fishing trawler, later applied (in English but no longer in Dutch) only to Dutch vessels; a two-masted *bluff-bowed ketch*-like boat, *square-rigged* on the main, with a *lugsail* on the *mizen* and two *jibs* on a long *bowsprit*. Believed to have given its name to the Dogger Bank (first attested in the seventeenth century).

From Anglo-French and ME 'doggere', and not in Dutch until a century later.

First attested in 1356 in a Statute of Edward III (*Act 31 Edw.III, III, c I*).

doldrums   a belt of calm near the equator, where the *trade winds* meet and tend to neutralise each other.

From the obsolete singular noun 'doldrum', a dullard, derived from the equally obsolete 'dold', dull or stupid. This gave rise to the expression 'in the doldrums', first attested in 1811 as meaning 'in the dumps' or out of sorts. From there it was applied to a ship, meaning 'almost becalmed', first attested in 1823 in Byron's poem 'The Island' (based partly on Bligh, *Bounty*), II, xxi, 8–10. The OED believes that the transfer of the expression to a geographical place was 'a misunderstanding... the state being taken as a locality'.

First attested in the geographical sense in 1855 in Maury, *Geography of the Sea*, x, f.583.

dolphin   a large wooden *pile* or cluster of piles used as a *mooring* post, or for *warping* in or out of a *dock*; a mooring *buoy*; a plaited rope strap round the mast of a *square-rigger* to prevent the lower *yard* dropping if its other supports were shot away. A *dolphin striker* is the downward-pointing *spar* fixed to and perpendicular to the bowsprit, used for holding down the *jib-boom* (with *martingales*) against the upward pull of the *fore top-gallant stay*.

Derived (allegedly owing to 'resemblance') from the familiar word for the marine mammal, which originated in the Middle Ages as 'delfyn', from the Latin '*delphinus*'.

First attested in 1764 in Coker *et al.*, *The Complete Dictionary*.

donkey   a small boiler, often portable; a sailor's sewing machine; formerly, a seaman's chest. A *donkey engine* is a small steam engine used on board for subsidiary tasks such as feeding the main boilers. A *donkey frigate* was one of a class of small ships built for the Royal Navy in the late eighteenth and early nineteenth centuries. A *donkey-house* is the structure on deck housing, if need be, the donkey engine. A *donkey pump* is an auxiliary steam pump. *Donkey's breakfast* was a merchant seaman's colloquial name for his straw-filled mattress. From the familiar word for ass: this was first pronounced to rhyme with 'monkey' and was probably derived from 'Duncan'. For a long time it was regarded as a colloquialism. In most of its figurative or transferred meanings, it seems to carry overtones of 'auxiliary', 'subsidiary', etc.

The OED gives neither definitions nor references for any of the above senses of the word 'donkey' alone, which is first attested in 1961 in Burgess, *Dictionary*, 74. 'Donkey engine', the earliest related expression cited by the OED, is first attested in 1858 in the *Mercantile Marine Magazine*, V, 49.

dory   a small flat-bottomed coastal fishing-boat, chiefly on the Grand Banks off Newfoundland, rowed but with removable *thwarts* and sailed but with a removable triangular sail, and therefore stackable inside one another on board larger vessels; more recently, a double-ended, almost rectangular *hard-chined dinghy* with shallow draught and flared sides, usually propelled by an *outboard* motor, for use by *yachtsmen* and fishermen as a workboat.

The word's derivation is uncertain, but may well be from the familiar word for the fish (*Zeus faber*), which was originally the past participle of the French verb '*dorer*', first attested in the fifteenth century as '*dorré*'. The only snag in this theory is that the fish in question is found in European, not American waters.

First attested in the sense of a boat in 1726 in *The Travels of Captain N. Uring*, 346.

double   to sail round a cape or other point of land so that it now lies between the ship's present and previous positions; to line or cover (a ship) with an extra layer of planking. *Double-banked* used to mean having two tiers of *oars*, one above the other; now, a boat is said to have her oars double-banked if there are two people pulling each oar, but is said to 'pull double-banked' if there are two oarsmen, each pulling a pair of oars. A *double bend* is a double *sheet bend*. To *double bitt* is to take an extra turn on the *bitts*. A *double block* is one with two *sheaves* on the same pin. The *double bottom* or *bottoms* refers to the space or spaces between the outer skin on the bottom of a ship and the watertight plating over the floors. A *double bowline* is a *bowline on the bight*. *Double braided* is plaited rope (as for *sheets*) with a braided core inside a braided sheath. A *double capstan* has two capstan barrels on the same central shaft to provide one on each of two adjacent decks. *Double chine* means having two chines along each side. To embark in *double clews* (i.e. with double cords for a *hammock*) meant to get married; a *double clewed jib*, however, is a four-sided jib with two clews, introduced for the America's Cup race in 1934, and nicknamed 'Greta Garbo' before it faded from the scene. A *double-ender* is any boat pointed at both *bow* and *stern*. *Double head rig* is one with two *headsails* set *forward* of the mast. A *double knot* is any knot enlarged by being repeated. A *double luff* is a *purchase* with two *double blocks*, the *standing part* of the rope being secured to the upper one. *Double-luffed* is said of a sail whose *luff* passes round a *stay* or *spar* and is then secured to itself, e.g. with a zipper or stitching. A *double tide* is one that has either two *high waters* or two *low water* in each cycle, as occurs off Cowes. *Double topsails* were a development from the old single topsail: they were bent to two *yards*. A *double topsail schooner*, however, was one with topsails on two masts, not with two topsails on one mast. A *double whip* is a rope led through a single *block*, then down and through a *hook block* and secured to or near the upper block. *Doubling* is the turned edge of a sail to which the *boltrope* is secured, any strengthening piece or strip sewn into a sail, or the overlap of an upper and a lower mast. *Doubling the angle on the bow* is a navigational calculation performed by taking the *bearing* of an object on the *bow* while approaching, keeping a steady *course* until the second bearing of the same object is twice the first, then working out the distance covered over the ground, which will be equal to the distance of the ship from the object when the second bearing is taken (because the two distances are the equal sides of isosceles triangle whose base was the distance between the ship and the object when the first bearing was taken). *Doubling up* means duplicating all ropes securing a vessel. *Doublings* is an alternative and more common expression for 'doubling' as applied to overlapping masts.

From the Latin '*duplus*', twice as much, via ME and OF 'duble', 'doble' (cf. '*paso doble*'), later 'double'; the verb follows the adjective.

First attested in 1548 in Hall, *Chronicle*, Henry VII, 11 b.

down   (of the *helm*) in the same direction as that toward which the wind is blowing; to put the helm down, or down helm, has the effect of bringing the *head* of the boat 'up' into the wind, often in the process of *going about*.

In a small boat or *yacht*, putting the helm down often means putting it literally down, since in a blow the vessel will be *heeled*. *Down along* means proceeding coastwise down a *channel*. *Down at the head* is a more self-explanatory expression for *by the head*. *Down below* is below the upper deck. A *downhaul*, originally applied to ropes used for hauling down *jibs*, *staysails* or *studdingsails*, now has a far more general meaning, including for example the rope that holds down the *spinnaker* pole, or even the *kicking strap* or *boom vang*. *Down stream* means with the *current*. *Down wind* means with the wind.

The oldest form of the word is the noun meaning a hill, which is from OE 'dun' (cf. the modern English 'dune'), first attested in the seventh century. The adverb originated in late OE, from 'of dune', off the hill or height, later turning into 'adune', then into 'dune' or 'dun', first attested in the early twelfth century.

First attested in a nautical context in 1769 in Falconer, *Dictionary* (1789 edition), F.

dowse   lower, smother, and hold down quickly (e.g. when *striking* a sail).

Probably from the Middle Dutch '*dossen*' or the early modern Dutch '*doesen*', both meaning 'to beat': when first attested in a general sense, in 1559, the English word carries this same meaning, only later coming to mean putting out a light or a fire. It is distinct from 'dowse' in the water-divining sense, which probably originated in dialect, and which is not attested until 1691, in the combination 'deusing-rod'.

First attested in its nautical sense in 1627 in Smith, *Seaman's Grammar*, xiii, 60.

drabbler   extra canvas laced to the *bonnet* of a sail in a *square-rigger* to give it extra drawing power.

From the old word 'drabble', to paddle or bespatter, first attested in the early fifteenth century and derived from ME 'drabelen' with the same meaning.

First attested *c.* 1592 in Greene and Lodge, *Looking Glasse* (*Works*, Routledge), 134/2.

drag   (of an anchor, its *flukes*, or the ship itself) to fail to hold the *ground*; to *draw* more water *aft* than *forward*. Most commonly, a ship is said to drag her anchor, and the anchor is said to drag; but colloquially the ship may be said to be dragging. A *drag anchor* is a *drogue* when used as a sea anchor. *Drag chains* are lengths of chain *shackled* to weighted drags to act as a brake when a ship has been launched. A *drag sheet* is a sail laced to a weighted *spar* to act as a drogue. In the US, especially, 'drag' is also used to denote what used to be called 'resistance' – the retardant forces working on a *hull*, consisting of *form drag* (due to the difference in pressure on the *fore* and *aft* faces), *induced drag* (due to the pressure difference between the *lee* and the *weather* sides of the *keel*), *skin drag* (akin to friction) and *wave drag* (determined by *hull* length).

From OE 'dragan', to pull. First attested about an anchor in 1694 in *Several Late Voyages and Discoveries* (1711 edition), 11.

draught   the depth of water a vessel *draws* – i.e. that needed for her to float. *Draught marks* are those on the *stem* and *sternpost* to show the ship's draught at any given state of loading.

From the early ME 'draht' and related to the origin of *drag*.

First attested in a nautical context in Shakespeare, *Twelfth Night*, v, I, 58.

draw   (of a ship) to displace a given depth of water; (of a sail) to be full of wind and hence 'drawing' the boat. A *draw knot* (which expresion has no relation to either specific sense above, but only to the general notion of pulling) is one in which one end is doubled on its *bight* so that it can quickly be pulled undone.

Like *drag*, from OE 'dragan', to pull.

First attested in respect of displacement in 1555 in Richard Eden, *Decades* (Arber, 1885), 7; relating to a sail, in 1627 in Smith, *Seaman's Grammar*, ix, 41.

dredge   a wedge-shaped metal device with a *trawling* net attached, for scraping oysters, etc., from the seabed, etc.; a *dredger*'s bucket; to *trawl* thus; to remove silt, etc., similarly from a waterway. A dredger, although the word was primarily applied to oyster dredging, is now almost exclusively a vessel built to remove mud from the bottom, by an endless chain of buckets, by a grab, or by suction.

Of uncertain origin, but possibly Scottish: the word occurs in the combination 'dreg-boat' in the *Burgh Records of Edinburgh* (Scottish Burgh Records Society 1869–82) for 16 November 1471. The OED suggests a link with the stem of *drag*; but 'dreg' in the sense of sediment (cf. the modern 'dregs') is attested as early as the fourteenth century in the *Early English Psalter*, lxxiv, 9. This the OED suggests to be 'probably from Norse', comparing it with the Icelandic '*dreggjar*' and the Swedish '*draegg*', both plural and meaning 'lees'. Coincidence? Connection? Confusion? It remains hard to say.

First attested in its modern spelling in 1602 in Carew, *Cornwall*, 30 b.

dress   (of a mast) attach the *standing* and *running rigging*; (of rigging, etc.) coat with linseed or other oil; (of a ship) decorate with flgs at the *mastheads*, or *dress overall* (at the mastheads and in a continuous line from the *jackstaff* to the *ensign staff*. When dressed overall, naval ships obey strict regulations about the order in which the flags are placed; merchant vessels and *yachts* are subject only to a recommendation. The *dressing line* is that which carries the flags when a ship is dressed overall.

From OF '*dresser*', earlier '*drecier*' or '*drescer*', to arrange (as still today).

First attested in a nautical sense in 1769 in Falconer, *Dictionary*.

drift   the distance a vessel makes to *leeward* owing to the *tide* and/or the wind; the rate in *knots* of certain ocean currents; the distance between two *blocks* in a *tackle*, etc.; the linear displacement of the lower end of a *stay* (which determines its angle); the deviation of a shell from its aimed trajectory owing to the rifling in the barrel from which it has been fired; the accumulation of small ice and debris broken away from the edges of icefields; (as a verb) to float with the wind and/or tide. A *drift anchor* is any kind of *drogue* so used. *Drift ice* means floating masses of broken ice drifting. A *drift lead* is a hand *lead* dropped on the bottom to wa*rn of dragging one's anchor*. A *drift net* or *drift of nets* is a fine-mesh net *buoyed* on the top edge and weighted on the lower edge to catch surface shoaling fish such as herring, mackerel and pilchard. A *drift sail* is one *bent* to a *spar*, weighted and *bridled* and *streamed* overboard as a drogue. A *drifter* is either a fishing boat somewhat smaller than a *trawler*, using drift nets – or an exceptionally light *headsail* for use in light airs.

From the early ME word of the same spelling, cognate with a number of others in Old Frisian, ON, Middle Dutch, Dutch, Swedish, Danish, Middle High German and German – all from 'drifan' (or similar), to drive.

First attested in a nautical context in 1562 in Heywood, *Dialogue* (1867 edition), 149; as applied to sea debris in 1600 in Hakluyt, *Principall Navigations* (1810 edition), III, 530; and as the more technical sense of deviation, in 1671 in Narborough, *Journal* in *Account of Several Late Voyages and Discoveries* (1711 edition), I, 174.

drive   to be unable to resist the forces of wind and *tide*; to *run* before a strong wind; to sail a ship *overcanvassed*; (of the wind) to propel despite human resistance; (now rare) to fish with *drift nets*. A *driver* was an extra sail hoisted as a *studding-sail*, from about 1700 onwards, to exploit a following wind: originally a high, narrow *square sail*, it was later enlarged and *bent* to the *gaff*, and from about 1790 onwards it became known as the *spanker*.

From OE 'drifan', with Teutonic roots common to similar early words in other languages, and itself the origin of 'drift' in the early sense of driven.

First attested in a nautical context in the mid eleventh century in a Charter of Edward the Confessor (1042–66) reprinted in Kemble (ed.), *Codex Diplomaticus* (1839–48), IV, 221.

drogue   *warp*, *spar*, cone, canvas bucket, etc., *towed astern* to check a boat's *way*; sometimes used, loosely, to include a sea anchor, which however is used *forward*, with the ship facing the wind rather than *running* before it, as with a drogue.

Of uncertain origin, but a probable variation of *drag*, its spelling influenced by the obsolete Scottish and modern French 'drogue', drug (itself of obscure origin and first attested *c*. 1377).

It would be far-fetched to suggest that a drogue was thought to act as a sedative on the ship: but the expression 'a drug on the market' is a further instance of apparent inter-relation among 'drag', 'drogue' and 'drug'.

First attested (to denote a device attached to a harpoon line to slow down a whale) in 1725 in *Philosophical Transactions of the Royal Society*, XXXIII, 263; in its modern boat-slowing sense, in 1875 in Bedford, *Sailor's Pocket-book* (2nd edition), vi, 220.

drop keel   originally, a portion of the *keel* in early submarines that could be detached in emergencies to increase *buoyancy*; now, although according to some 'erroneously', a retractable keel such as a *centreboard*.

The origin of 'drop' is the noun, from OE 'dropa'; the verb comes from OE 'dropian'.

First attested in 1896 in the *Westminster Gazette*, 12 May, 2/1.

drumhead   the round top of a *capstan* into which the capstan bars are fitted.

Originally denoting the skin or membrane across the top of a drum, whence the expression 'drumhead tribunal' or 'drumhead court-martial' for one conducted summarily round a drum. The word 'drum' itself is of obscure and complex origin. It is first attested around 1540, but was not in general use until about 1575. Its predecessor was 'drombyllsclad', 'drombeslade' or 'drumslade'; and it may have been on offshoot of the 'trom-' root found in other Teutonic languages, which gave rise not only to the German '*Trommel*' but also to words like 'trumpet' – suggesting that it signified any instrument making a loud noise.

First attested in its nautical sense in 1726 in Shelvocke, *Voyage* (1757 edition), 15.

dub, dubb   to smooth a plank with an *adze*, either to prepare it for the deck or sides of the vessel under construction or to examine the state of the side planking already in place by shaving off an outer layer.

Probably but not certainly from OF '*aduber*', meaning to 'dub' in the sense of investing with a title, etc. From here the word was extended to mean to dress, array, trim or crop: the word 'dubbin' (grease for leather) is an offshoot of these senses.

First attested in a shipbuilding context in 1711 in Sutherland, *Ship Builder's Assistant*, 160.

duck up   to raise with a jerk (e.g. a sail obstructing the *helmsman*'s view).

From the verb 'duck', which is descended from OE 'ducan', only emerging in its present spelling in the mid sixteenth century, probably by assimilation to the noun 'duck' in the sense of water-fowl. While the latter admittedly 'ducks' now and then, its name seems to be derived from a different OE word 'duce'; but since that word is also related to 'ducan' the quest comes full circle and again links the bird with its characteristic movement.

First attested in its nautical sense in 1706 in Phillips, *New World* (6th edition).

Duffel or **Duffle coat**   loose hooded overcoat made of thick coarse cloth and fastened by *beckets* and wooden *toggles*.

From its place of manufacture, the town of Duffel in Brabant, between Antwerp and Mechlin.

First attested, but as a noun, in 1677 in Plot, *Oxfordshire*, 279.

dunnage   loose wood, blocks, brushwood, mats, etc., stowed under, around, and among the *cargo* to protect it from wet, chafe, etc.

Of unknown origin. In the seventeenth century it was spelt 'dinnage' or 'dynnage', making just possible a link with the Low German *'duen'*, thin – *'duenne twige'* being thin twigs or brushwood: cf. also the Dutch *'dun'*.

First attested in 1497 in *Naval Accounts* (Naval Records Society, 1896), 251.

Dutchman   a Dutch vessel; a piece of wood or metal covering a defective joint. A *Dutchman's breeches* are patches of blue sky appearing before a *gale*. A *Dutchman's log* is a piece of timber thrown overboard *forward* to estimate the ship's speed by the time she takes to overtake it. A *Dutchman's purchase* is one used in reverse, the *fall* becoming the *hoist* and *vice versa*.

Associated with the Middle Dutch *'dutsch'*. The origin of the word's second meaning is unknown; but this and similar expressions and usages may possibly reflect Anglo-Dutch maritime rivalry.

First attested in its 'neutral', non-opprobrious sense in 1657 in Ligon, *Barbados* (1673 edition), 19; in the sense of covering a flaw, in 1859 in Bartlett, *Americanisms*, 134.

E**aring**   small line used to secure the corner of a sail to a *spar*, usually a *square* sail to its *yard*, but also (in the case of a *clew* earing) to haul the *foot* of the sail towards the *after* end of the *boom*. *Reef earings* are those whereby the *reef cringles* are made fast to the appropriate spar (in the case of *square-riggers*, a yard, but nowadays more often the boom.

Almost certainly not from 'ear-ring', but from 'ear' with the completing suffix '-ing'. 'Ear' is from OE 'eare', with a common Teutonic root, and cognate with the Latin *'auris'*; here it applies by transference to the two upper corners, although in later applications any corner could have an earing.

First attested in 1626 in Smith, *Accidence*, 15.

ease   in general, to lessen the strain: (of a rope or *sheet*) to slacken slightly; (of the *helm* when *close-hauled*) to *luff up* by putting the helm *down* slightly. The command *ease to ten* (or whatever number) is given when the helm is farther over, and indicates the number of degrees to aim at: it can also mean to slow the engine down to the required figure.

Probably from OF *'aisier'*, similar to the Italian *'adagiare'* (and the musical *'adagio'*) and ultimately from the Latin *'ad-'* plus the late Latin *'asium'*. The noun in this case predates the verb.

First attested in a nautical context in 1627 in Smith, *Seaman's Grammar*, v, 20.

ebb   the receding flow of the tidal stream, from the end of *slack water* at *high tide* to the beginning of slack water at *low tide*; (of the tide) to fall, recede.

The noun is from OE 'ebba', the verb from OE 'ebbian'; their Old Teutonic root might be *'abjon-'* or *'ebjon-'*, connected with the Gothic *'ibuks'*, backwards.

First attested as both noun and verb in the tenth century: the noun in 993 in *Battle of Maldon*, ed. Grein, *Bibliothek* (1883–97 edition), 65; the verb before 1000 in Caedmon, *Genesis and Exodus*, in the same collection, 1413.

eddy   local current, often circular, usually caused by obstruction or by *fluky* winds, and in a different direction from the main flow.

Of unknown origin, but possibly linked with ON *'ida'*, which had the same meaning.

First attested in 1455 in Holland, *Howlat*, lxiv.

elbow   (in the *hawse*) double twist in the two *cables* caused when a ship swings twice the wrong way. In shipbuilding, an *elbow piece* is a *knee*. In the clubhouse after a race, *elbow-bending exercise* is that involved in raising beer or wine glasses to the lips.

By transference from the familiar word, which itself is derived from OE 'elnboya' (cf. the modern German *'Ellenbogen'*, *'Ellbogen'*, from the same Teutonic root).

First attested in its nautical sense in 1769 in Falconer, *Dictionary*.

embark   (of *cargo*, etc.) to put on board; (of people) to go on board; (of a ship) to take or receive on board.

From the Latin *'in-'* and *'barca'*, which in late Latin give the verb '*imbarcare*', the source of similar words in all the Romance languages, including the French '*embarquer*', which seems to be the immediate parent of 'embark'.

First attested in 1550 in Nicolls, *Thucidides*, 20.

ensign   the national flag *worn* by a ship; a US naval rank equivalent to a *midshipman* or *sub-lieutenant*. British ships use three ensigns, each with the national flag in the upper corner of the *hoist*. The *White Ensign* is flown by a ship of the Royal Navy (or one of its shore establishments); the *Blue Ensign* by naval auxiliary vessels; the *Red Ensign* by merchant navy (and pleasure) vessels. *Yachts* of the Royal Yacht Squadron above a certain tonnage may also fly the White Ensign, and some yacht clubs and individuals have the right to fly the Blue Ensign (in the case of a club, with its badge in the *fly*). The *ensign staff* is the pole erected right *aft* to carry a ship's ensign. As a rank, an ensign was also military, and the word was sometimes corrupted to 'ancient', as in Shakespeare's 'ancient Pistol' in *2 Henry IV*, II, iv, 120.

From the Latin '*insignia*' via OF '*enseigne*', and until the seventeenth century used as a verb in the same sense as '*enseigner*' in French, to instruct.

First attested in the sense of a ship's flag (although applied to military banners since the end of the fourteenth century) in 1707 in a Royal Proclamation of 27 July printed in the *London Gazette* No. 4356/1; as a nautical rank, in 1708 in the *London Gazette* No. 4420/7.

entrance   the shape of a vessel's *bow* at and below water level. Kemp, *Oxford Companion* (1976), 288 has *entry* in place of 'entrance', and Schult, *Dictionary* (2nd edition, 1992), 90, offers both. The OED gives only 'entrance'.

An extension of meaning from the familiar word, itself derived from the similarly spelt but otherwise pronounced word in OF.

First attested in its nautical sense in 1781 on 24 August, by Nelson in Nicolas, *Dispatches and Letters*, I, 43.

Eugenie   wollen cap worn by late nineteenth-century seamen in polar regions.

From the caps presented by ex-Empress Eugenie of France to every officer and man on board the *Alert* and *Discovery* during the Royal Navy's Arctic expedition of 1875.

First attested in 1976 in Kemp, *Oxford Companion*, 291.

euphroe   a wood or metal fitting through which a number of ropes form a *crowfoot*, e.g. for suspending an awning, or as the multi-part *sheets* of a fully *battened junk* sail.

From the Dutch '*juffrouw*', literally 'maiden' (cf. the German '*Jungfrau*' and similar words in other Teutonic languages) but actually meaning 'deadeye' – the extension being perhaps associated with the lacing of a bodice or skirt.

First attested in 1815 in Burney, enlargement of Falconer, *Dictionary*, under 'Dead-eye'.

even keel, on an   not *listing*; *drawing* as much water *fore* as *aft*.

From a now largely obsolete sense of the word 'even', meaning horizontal. The word itself, apparently unconnected with that for 'evening', comes from OE 'efen'.

First attested as a nautical phrase in 1836 in Marryat, *Mr Midshipman Easy*, xxvi.

eye   originally, the round loop in a *shroud* or *stay* where it passes over the mast at the *hounds*; any loop *spliced* or *whipped* at the end of a rope or wire; the hole at the top of an anchor's *shank* that takes the ring; in meteorology, the relatively calm centre of a revolving tropical storm, or the direction from which a wind blows. An *eye-band* is a metal band with eyes for attaching *shrouds* or *stays* to a *spar*. An *eye-bolt* is a bolt with an eye in the end. An *eyebrow* is a *rigol* or lipped ledge over a *scuttle* or window to divert water. An *eyelet* is a small hole in a sail, awning, sailbag, etc., usually reinforced with a metal *grommet*. An *eye plate* is a strong fitting, e.g. bolted to the deck as anchorage for a shroud; an *eye splice* is a loop made in the end of a rope or wire, usually around a metal *thimble* and, if not, known as a 'soft' eye. *Eyes inboard* is a call to someone distracted from work by a feature of the environment, such as a female *ashore*. The *eyes of her*, based on the eyes that some fishermen and others paint on the *bows* of their boats, refers to the foremost part of any ship. The *eyes of the rigging* are the soft eyes of the shrouds (see *eye splice* above) that fit over a *masthead* and rest on the *hounds*. A *Flemish eye* was a neat but weak method of making an eye in a shroud, by dividing the *strands*, knotting each part separately, then *parcelling* and *serving*.

By extension from the familiar word, derived from OE 'eage' and linked to many other Teutonic-based words and to the Gothic '*augo*'. Etymologists have sought, not quite successfully, a further link to the Old Aryan root '*oq-*', to see (whence the Latin '*oculus*', eye, and the modern English 'ocular', 'oculist', etc); the problem is the vowel shift between 'au' or 'ea' and 'o'.

First attested in a nautical context in 1562 in the phrase 'the wind's eye'; but in its main nautical sense in 1642 in Monson, *Naval Tracts* (in *Churchill's Collection*), III, 345/2.

Fag-end   the end of a rope, especially when *unlaid* and/or frayed because *unwhipped*.

   Perhaps surprisingly, much older than its application to cigarette-ends; indeed, 'fag' for cigarette is itself an abbreviation from 'fag-end' in the earlier and now obsolete meaning of 'fag' as anything that hangs loose. Before 'fag-end' was thus circuitously applied to smoking, it denoted the last part of a piece of cloth, often of coarser texture than the rest, and hanging loose; it was then applied to rope. The obsolete verb 'fag', meaning to droop, may conceivably be derived from *flag* in a similar sense, which is comparable to OF *'flaquir'* and hence may be derived from the Latin *'flaccus'* and *'flaccidus'*, which are the source of 'flaccid'.

   First attested in a nautical context in 1775 in Ash, *Dictionary*.

fair   (of weather) favourable; (of wind) one obviating the need to *tack* or *gybe* on a given *course*.

   From OE 'fayer', which meant 'beautiful' before coming also to denote 'fair-haired'.

   First attested as regards weather *c.* 1205 in *Layamon's Brut* (Society of Antiquaries, London, 1847), 7594; as regards wind, *c.* 1384 in Chaucer, *The Hous of Fame*, 1967.

fairlead   a metal, wooden or plastic fitment, open or closed, fixed to the boat, through which a rope can be led.

   From the very general sense of *fair* as favourable.

   First attested in 1841 in Dana, *Seaman's Manual*, 104.

fairway   navigable *channel*, e.g. for entering or leaving harbour, marked by *port* and *starboard buoys*, withies, etc. From *fair* in the general sense of favourable and the particular sense of unobstructed; although sometimes spelt 'fareway', this seems to be the result of erroneous etymology.

   First attested in a nautical (as distinct from a golfing) context in 1584 in *Binnell's Description* (1758 edition), 62; in a golfing context, in 1910 in Darwin, *Courses*, I, 18.

fake   a complete turn of a rope when *coiled* on deck or on a drum; to coil a rope thus, free to run out. Cf. *flake*.

   Of uncertain origin, but quite distinct from the slang word 'fake' meaning 'counterfeit', which may be derived from the older words 'feak' and 'feague' and thence from the German *'fegen'*, to furbish. The nautical word 'fake' may be the same as the Scottish *'faik'*, a fold; alternatively, it may be related to the Middle High German *'vach'*, which meant 'fold' as well as 'compartment'. Did the OE 'faec', a space of time, have a similar additional meaning?

   First attested as a verb (although the noun is thought to pre-date it) *c.* 1400 in *Morte Arthure* (EETS 1865, revised 1871), 742.

fall   the handling end of a *tackle*; (in the plural) the complete tackles whereby a ship's boat is hoisted in or lowered from the *davits*. As a verb, 'fall' has its place in many nautical phrases. To *fall aboard* is to come into contact with another vessel broadside on. To *fall astern* is to drop back and be overtaken. To *fall away* is to sail less close to the wind than before. To *fall down* is to *drift* downstream. To *fall in with* is to sight and contact another ship at sea. To *fall off* is to sail further off the wind. A *fall tub* is a wooden container in which the falls are coiled. *Falling home* (of the upper part of a ship's side) means sloping inwards. The *falling out* (of the *bows*) is the upward and outward curve that provides additional protection from the waves.

The noun comes from the verb, whose origin is OE 'feallan'. First attested in the singular sense in 1644 in Manwayring, *Dictionary* (pre-1625), 38; in the plural sense in 1832 in Marryat, *Newton Forster*, x.

false keel   additional keel secured outside that of a wooden ship either to improve her sailing ability or to protect the true keel when going *aground*.

The word 'false' recurs in other nautical phrases, all but the last of them as innocent as the first. The *false points* of the compass are the three-letter points (ENE, etc.). A *false stem* is a fine tapered *cutwater* added to the *stem*. A *false tack* is a deceptive manoeuvre in *yacht* racing, *luffing up* as if to *go about* but then *paying off* on the same *tack*.

From the 'substitution' sub-sense of the word, which itself is from the late OE 'fals', based on the Latin '*falsus*'. The OED points out that in modern English the pejorative overtones of 'false' are more prominent than in other languages using words of similar derivation, which generally retain the older sense of 'erroneous' without necessarily connoting deceit.

First attested in 1627 in Smith, *Seaman's Grammar*, xi, 53.

fantail   a far-projecting *stern* overhang.

Clearly enough from 'fan' and 'tail', which in turn are derived from OE 'fanne' and 'taeyel': the complete word is first attested in the eighteenth century, applied to pigeons.

First attested in its nautical sense in 1882 in *Harper's Magazine*, LXIV, 174/2.

fardage   *dunnage*, i.e. loose wood or other materials used around and among items of cargo to prevent damage.

Originally applied to the impedimenta or baggage of an army, the word is derived from the French '*fardage*', associated with OF '*fardel*', burden, (in modern French '*fardeau*'), itself the source of the obsolete English word familiar from Hamlet's 'To be or not to be' soliloquy: 'Who would fardels bear?'

First attested in its military impedimenta sense in 1578. The OED, without quotations, declares that it was used in the nautical sense 'in charter parties about 1860' but is now 'obsolete among English shippers'.

fashion pieces   timbers *athwartships* at the *transom* giving extra support to the plank ends.

From the very general sense of the word, i.e. 'making', associated with OF *'facon'* (cf. 'fashioning'), and derived from the Latin *'factio'*, whence also of course 'faction.'

First attested in 1627 in Smith, *Seaman's Grammar*, ii, 2.

fast   a *hawser* securing a vessel (as in *headfast, sternfast*, etc., which although now rare in the UK are still current in the US); secured. To *make fast* is the normal nautical expression for to *tie up*. (Cf. 'fasten'.)

The adjective, from OE 'faest', seems to predate the noun, which comes from ME 'fest'. The sense of 'rapid' apparently developed from the adverbial use of the word, via the notion of 'closely packed' merging into that of 'in quick succession'.

First attested as an adjective *c.* 888 in Aelfred, Boethius, (Sedgefield, 1899), xii; as a *mooring warp, c.* 1440 in *Promptorium parvulorum* (Camden Society, 1843–65), 158/1.

fathom   (as a measure of depth or of the length of ropes and *cables*) six feet or 1.8256 metres; (now rarely) to sound the depth of; (commonly) to get to the bottom of. On modern *charts*, fathoms have largely been replaced by metres. This has not yet ousted the expressions *fathom lines*, undersea contour lines, or *fathom mark*, the six-foot measure that would sometimes be marked off for convenience with small copper nails on a deck plank.

From OE 'faedm', meaning the outstretched arms: the corresponding verb 'faedmian' meant to embrace. In the singular, 'faedm' meant chest or bosom, in the senseof clasping a person to one's body. Hence the measure of roughly six feet: compare also the nautical method of coiling a rope by separating and closing the hands holding it at arm's length.

First attested (as the measure of both outstretched arms including the middle finger-tips) *c.* 725 in the *Corpus Glossary* (Oldest English Texts, EETS, 1885).

fay   (in shibuilding) to fit two pieces of timber snugly together. A *faying edge* is one thus fayed.

From the Old Teutonic *'fogjan'* via OE 'feyan', to fit, adapt, or join.

First attested in a non-nautical context in the tenth century; but in a nautical context in 1754, in Murray, *Shipbuilding*, 188.

feather   the foamy crest of a wave; the ripple caused by a submarine's periscope; a wind strength indicator on a weather map; (of an oar or propellor) to twist to reduce resistance. *Feathers* show the wind strength on *wind arrows* of weather maps: under the World Meteorological Organization's system, half a feather indicates 5 *knots* and a full feather 10; no feathers, winds of up to 2 knots. Some countries use a system based on half a feather for each number on the *Beaufort* scale. To *feather* a sail is to bend the mast to *windward* at *spreader* level, thereby curving the *topmast* to *leeward*, increasing *sail twist* and opening the *leech* to let the air flow out more easily: the aim is to reduce *heel* without losing speed by *easing* the main *sheet*. *Feather-edged* describes any plank with one edge thinner than the other. A *featherway* is a groove cut for the key of a pin, as for instance in a *shackle*.

Figurative application of the familiar word, which is derived from a common Teutonic root and appears in OE as 'feder', like the modern German '*Feder*'; a pre-Teutonic word '*petra*' corresponds to the Greek '*pteros*' (cf. 'pterodactyl').

First attested in a nautical context as a verb, before 1740 in Tickell, *Poetical Works* (1807); as a noun, indicating the crest of a wave, in 1838 in *The Civil Engineer and Architect's Journal*, I, 272/1; indicating the ripple left by a periscope, in 1828 in the *Papers* of the *Michigan Academy*, I (1929), 292.

feaze   (obsolete in all but nautical contexts) to unravel old rope for making into *oakum* with which to *caulk* wooden vessels.

Thought to be related to OE 'faes', fringe, possibly via ME 'vese' or 'veze' with the same meaning. Possibly also related to the (originally US) 'faze', meaning to disturb or upset (or 'frazzle'), which was sometimes spelt 'feaze' and is thought by the OED to have originated in dialect: cf. 'the ravell'd sleeve of care' in *Macbeth*.

First attested in 1568 in Smith, *De Recta Lingua*, 31 b.

fend (off)   to push a boat clear and prevent a collision. A *fender* is any appliance suspended at the side of a ship to prevent chafe against a *wharf*, *pontoon*, wall, or other vessel, but removed when *under way*. A *fenderboard* is a plank hung horizontally *outboard* of two or more fenders to bridge the gap between them. *Fendering* is padding all round the *gunwale* of a *tender* or *launch*, also known as a *rubbing strake*.

Originally having a more general meaning, the word is an abbreviation of 'defend', from the Latin '*defendere*' – which itself originally meant to ward off.

First attested in a very general sense (now obsolete save in such expressions as 'fend for oneself') in the late twelfth century. The nautical 'fender' is first attested in 1626 in Smith, *Accidence*, 16; but the OED has no instance of 'fend' or 'fend off' in a nautical context until 1861 in Hughes, *Tom Brown at Oxford* (1889 edition), 127.

ferry   to carry from one place to another (now usually by water); a place where such conveyance takes place; a vessel used for that purpose. The OED claims that 'ferry' as a verb relating to water is limited to 'now only over a stream, canal, etc.': but this seems unduly restricted unless the Channel be included in 'etc'.

The verb (which appears in the late eighth century in *Beowulf*) predates the noun. Its origin is OE 'ferian', to convey, cognate with the root of the old word 'fare', as in 'thoroughfare'.

First attested as a verb in a watery context in the late tenth century in the poem *Andreas* (edited by Grein, 1888), 293; as a similar noun, *c.* 1440 in *Promptorium parvulorum* (Camden Society, 1843–65), 156/2.

fetch   (rarely now) distance sailed on a single *tack*; distance between two points (e.g. between headlands, between the origin of a wave and its arrival, between an inlet or upriver *mooring* and the open sea; to sail a distance *upwind* without *tacking*; to reach a certain point or place. To *fetch a compass* is to go round in a circle. To *fetch the pump* is to prime it. To *fetch up* is to arrive somewhere more or less unintended – the only non-nautical sense of the word still clearly linked with its nautical use.

From OE 'fecc(e)an', to seek and bring back. In its general and familiar sense, the verb predates the noun; in its nautical sense, the opposite.

First attested as a nautical noun in or before 1555 in Richard Eden, *Decades* (Arber, 1885), 231; as a nautical verb in 1556 by W. Towrson in Hakluyt, *Principall Navigations* (1589), 98.

fid   large pointed pin of hard wood used to open the *strands* of large *hawsers* for *splicing* (a *marline-spike* is a smaller metal equivalent, notoriously misdescribed, when on pocket-knives, as a device for getting stones out of horses' hooves); iron or wooden bar used to secure a *topmast stepped* on a lower mast; plug of *oakum* for the vent of a muzzle-loading gun; quid of tobacco.

Of unknown origin. The OED conjectures that its various meanings may relate to different but identical words with different lineage; but the nautical senses all seem inter-related and could perhaps be onomatopoeic.

First attested in 1615 in E.S., *Britaines Buss*, in Arber, *English Garner* (1877–96), III, 629.

fiddle   raised or adjustable rim or frame to prevent objects sliding about or off tables, shelves, etc. A *fiddle block* is a *double block* with one *sheave* over the other. A *fiddle head* is an ornamental (violin-like) scroll on the *bows* in place of a *figurehead*. *Fiddler's Green* is the sailor's paradise.

From the familiar word by analogy with the shape either of the instrument's ribs or of its scroll. The ultimate origin of the word, via ME 'fidele' is obscure. 'The Teutonic word,' says the OED, 'bears a singular resemblance in sound' to its medieval Latin synonym '*vitula*', '*vidula*' – from which are derived the various languages' words 'viol', 'viola', and 'violin'.

First attested in its nautical sense in 1865 in *The Daily Telegraph*, 21 August, 5/2.

fiddley   iron framework and grating over *hatches* above engines and boiler rooms in small steam or diesel vessels.

Of unknown origin. There seems to be no connection with the much later 'fiddly' in the sense of needing dexterity.

First attested in 1881 in *The Standard*, 17 November 2/3.

fife-rail   originally, rails on *bulwarks* round the *poop* and *quarterdeck* of sailing *men-of-war*, often used to secure the *clew* lines of sails; later, bars of wood or metal at the foot of the mast, with *belaying pins* to secure the *halyards*.

The term is said to have originated in the custom of the fifer's sitting on these rails which the anchor was being *weighed*. ('Fifer' from 'fife', a small shrill pipe, is first attested in 1540; 'fife', from either the High German '*Pfeife*' or the French '*fifre*', is first attested in 1525.)

First attested in 1721 in Bailey, *Dictionary*.

figure-of-eight knot   a *stopper knot* useful for, e.g., the ends of *jib sheets*; made like an *overhand knot* but with the end passed the opposite way through the final loop.

From its resemblance to the figure 8.

First attested *c*. 1860 in Stuart, *Catechism*, I.

figurehead   ornamental figure on the *forward* end of a ship, originally on the *beakhead*, later on a continuation of the *stem* below the *bowsprit*. Whatever the date of the word, the object has a very long history, going back as far as Ancient Egypt. With the advent of steam and iron, figureheads gradually died out, although some shipping companies such as the Fred Olson Line have reintroduced them.

The origin of 'figure', first attested in the fourteenth century, is the similar French word, from the Latin '*figura*', associated with '*fingere*', to feign. 'Head' is from OE 'heafod', with a common Teutonic root, as in the Gothic '*haubip*' and the Old Teutonic '*haubud*' – whose consonants (but not all their vowels) suggest a link with the Latin '*caput*', head.

First attested in 1765 in the *Annual Register*, 185.

filibuster   originally, a freebooter or plunderer; then a *buccaneer* in the Spanish West Indies in the seventeenth century; later, one of the bands of North American adventurers who between 1850 and 1860 fomented unrest in Latin America; a privateer; to engage in any of these activities. Figuratively, the term is now applied to delaying tactics or tacticians in the US Congress, etc. From the Dutch '*vrijbuiter*', freebooter (the 'boot', like 'booty', denoting profit and later plunder). Whether it reached English as 'filibuster' via the French '*filibustier*' or *vice versa* remains uncertain.

First attested (though here not in a specifically nautical sense) in the late sixteenth century (pre-1587) in Garrard, *Art of Warre* (1591 edition), 236.

fill   (of the wind) to cause the sails to swell; (of a sail) to become full of wind; to *brace* the sails so that they fill.

From the ME verb 'fullen', associated with the OE noun 'fyllo', 'fyllu'.

First attested in a nautical context in 1610 in the Epilogue to Shakespeare, *The Tempest*, 12.

fisgig, fizgig   a pronged *harpoon*, for spearing fish (sometimes therefore erroneously spelt 'fishgig'): Neptune's *trident* is one example.

Probably from the Spanish '*fisga*', a harpoon; but the spelling and pronunciation have been attracted back towards the first sense of a word that was later also applied to a top and a kind of firework, but which originally meant a frivolous woman. 'Fisgig' in that opprobrious sense is first attested before 1529.

First attested in its nautical sense in 1565 by J. Sparke in Hakluyt, *Principall Voyages* (1589), III, 520.

fish   to strengthen a cracked or broken mast, *yard* or *spar* by lashing curved splints around it and over the fault; such a splint. The familiar meanings of 'fish' and the associated 'fisherman' and 'fishing' give rise to a number of other nautical expressions. To *fish an anchor* is to draw up the *flukes* of a *stocked* anchor to the *cat davit* before *stowing* it on an anchor bed. The *fish front* is the rounded timber on the *fore* side of a *made mast*. A *fish hook fastening* is a way of attaching a fishing line to the hook, with a *clove hitch* jammed by a *half hitch* below it. A *fisherman's anchor* is the oldest type, with the *stock* at right angles to the *shank* (as almost invariably used in logos, etc.). A *fisherman's bend*, used for *bending* a rope to an anchor, is made by passing two *round turns* round the ring, then passing the end within them, finishing with a *half hitch* taken on the rope. *Fisherman's boots* are those that reach up to the waist. *Fisherman's grease* is salt water used for lubrication. A *fisherman's knot,* used to *bend* two lines together, consists of an *overhand knot* in the end of each, so that each contains the other, and pulled together. To use a *fisherman's reef* is to leave the *mainsail* un*reefed* but to *spill wind* by slackening the *sheet.* A *fisherman's staysail* is a large *topsail,* as in a *schooner,* set above a *main staysail.* A *fisherman's walk* is any small space on deck. *Fishing boats* may be of any size and may seek to catch crustaceans and molluscs as well as fish. *Fishing lines* are those supplied in different sizes for different kinds of catch. A *fishing smack* is a *sloop-rigged* fishing vessel with a well in which to preserve the catch alive. *Fishes royal* were whales, dolphins, and sturgeon stranded on UK shores, which under a statute of 1324, *De praerogativae regis,* belonged to the Crown until the privilege was renounced in 1971.

The familiar word is from OE 'fisc' and the pre-Teutonic *'pisko',* cognate with the Latin *'piscis'.* In the nautical sense of a splint, the word's origin is mysterious. It might be derived from the piscatorial sense of 'fish'; but, as the OED remarks, 'the appropriateness of the name on this supposition is not obvious'. It may possibly be derived from the French *'ficher',* to fix; but there is no trace of the French word *'fiche'* being used in this sense.

First attested in the nautical sense of a splint in 1666 in the *London Gazette,* No. 59/3.

fix   to ascertain one's position by whatever means; an observed position thus obtained. From the Latin *'fixus',* the past participle of *'figere'* to fix or fasten. The noun, in this nautical sense, is commoner than the verb, which (in this sense) the OED omits.

First attested as a noun in 1902 in the *Encyclopaedia Britannica,* XXXIII, 97/2.

flag   a rectangular piece of *bunting* with various colours and designs, used to indicate nationality, etc., or to convey signals, and usually *flown* on a *staff* or *halyard.* The *flag deck* is the small space near the mast reserved for flag lockers and halyards. A *flag of distress* is the national or the *Red Ensign* flown upside down or at half mast. A *flag officer* is any of the rank of rear *admiral* or above, whose presence at sea is indicated by a flag rather than a broad *pendant* such as indicates a *commodore*: hence the expression 'He has got his flag' when promoted to rear admiral, and the response 'Flag' to the hailing of a ship with a flag officer in command. A *flagship* is one *wearing* the flag of a flag officer. A *flagstaff* is a mast or pole on shore, but never at sea. *Flags of convenience* (sometimes called *flags of necessity*) are national *ensigns* flown by vessels registered in those

countries for tax or other reasons but in all other respects of
different national origin and ownership.

Three other nouns are thus spelt: they denote the quill-feathers
of a bird's wing, the flagstone, and the plant (now the iris).
Etymologically they seem to be unconnected. The nautical word
'flag' is thought to be of English origin, although it has counterparts in all modern Germanic languages. If English, it might
be a transferred use of the word for the iris, or possibly from
either OE 'flacg', a poultice, or the twelfth-century 'flage', some
kind of baby's garment. If the word is not originally English, the
OED conjectures that 'it may plausibly be supposed to be an
onomatopoeic formation, expressing the notion of something
flapping in the wind'. Attractive as this theory may be, it
contrasts oddly with the verb 'flag', suggesting flaccidity: 'but
probably,' says the OED, 'there is a mixture with an onomatopoeic formation, expressing the same notion as *flap*, *flack*, but
implying less energetic movement. What took the wind out of
the word in its transition from noun to verb remains unclear.

First attested as a noun in the present sense in 1481–90 in
the *Howard Household Books* (Roxburghe Club, 1844), 42.

flake   a *cradle* slung over the side as a work platform; a single
ring or *coil* of rope or *cable*; to lay down (a rope)on the deck
in flat loops, rings, or coils for inspection or decoration; (of a
mainsail) to stow in equal *bights* on either side of the *boom*.
See also *fake*.

'Flake' as a cradle, although not first attested until the nineteenth century, may be derived from ON *'flake'*, originally a
hurdle or wicker shield, later various kinds of framework. As a
single ring or coil, and its attendant verb, the word may be a
confusion with *fake*, whose first appearance predates that of
'flake' in this sense by two centuries. But it is certainly cognate
with the German *'Flechte'*, with the same meaning.

First attested as a cradle in 1867 in Smyth, *Sailor's Word-
book*; as a coil, in 1626 in Smith, *Accidence*, 27 – although here
the 'f' was misprinted as a long 's'.

flare   the outward and upward curve of the *hull*, the opposite of *tumblehome*; a firework *signal*, hand-held or otherwise,
to indicate position (white), distress (red), etc.

Both senses of the word, perhaps surprisingly, are of similarly unknown origin. The verb predates the noun, and has been
compared to the modern Norwegian *'flara'*, to blaze or flaunt.
The first and now obsolete meaning of 'flare' was to spread out
for display: the sense of being fanned outwards (of a flame)
emerges in the mid eighteenth century.

The noun is first attested in its fiery sense; but in a strictly nautical context the first attested sense is of 'outward curving', in 1833 in Thomas Richardson, *Mercantile Marine Architecture*, 1 – which mis-spells it 'flair', although this word, originally meaning scent, is quite distinct from 'flare'; as a burning signal, in 1883 in Russell, *Sailors' Language*, 52.

flat   a fairly level *shoal* of mud or sand uncovered at low water; a large, broad, flat-bottomed boat or *barge*; level floor-timbers *amidships*. *Flat aback* describes sails pressed to the mast by the wind. *Flat aft* or *flat in*, of a *fore-and-aft* sail, means *sheeted* in as far as possible. A *flatboat* was an eighteenth- and early nineteenth-century landing boat supplied to warships and *flat-bottomed* for landing on beaches. *Flat-bottomed* describes a boat with no curvature or *deadrise*. The *flat end* is the *stern*. A *flat knot* is a *reef knot* or *square knot*. A *flat seam* is made by overlapping two edges of *canvas*, etc., and sewing the edge of each to the body of the other. A *flat seizing* is a method of bending two ropes together when they bear equal loads, by first drawing an *eye* in a light line tight round one rope, then taking a series of *turns* round both, passing the end of the line back between the ropes and over a series of turns, finally drawing tight and finishing with a *clove hitch*. A *flat-iron* is any vessel that is wide, low, and of shallow *draught*. A *flattie* is a small flat-bottomed *dinghy* – or any kind of flat fish. *Flatting* is matt paint, often used as an undercoat for enamel.

Clearly linked with ON *'flatr'* and with similar words in Swedish and Danish. Whether it is derived from the Old Aryan *'plat-'* or *'plath-'*, the Sanskrit *'prthu'*, broad, and the Greek *'platus'*, thought to be the source of the French *'plat'*, is less certain but seems highly likely.

First attested in the sense of 'shoal' and (as very often) in the plural, in 1550 in Coke, *Debate* (1877 edition), 155, 103.

fleet   a creek; an organised group of ships; to move something along, notably to get a better haul on a rope, etc.; to begin to shift as the *tide* rises after being *aground* at low water. All these nautical senses of the word (which exclude that of 'rapid' as in 'fleet of foot') are derived from the same OE roots – the noun 'fleot'and the verb 'fleotan', with common Teutonic origins. The sense of 'creek' or 'ditch' is most obviously preserved in Fleet Street, London, named after The Fleet, a stream of water flowing into the Thames between Fleet Street and Ludgate Hill, now a covered sewer.

First attested in the late eighth century in *Beowulf* (EETS, 1882), 3822, in the virtually obsolete sense of 'to be or to get afloat', to 'sail'; in the sense of 'creek', *c*. AD 893 in King Aelfred, translation of *Orosius* (EETS, 1883), I, 1, 27; in the sense of a group of ships, before 1000; but in the sense of moving something along not until 1769 in Falconer, *Dictionary* (1789 edition), Y b – possibly because this may have been a case of substitution from the earlier non-nautical verb 'flit'.

Flemish   pertaining to or associated with Flanders or Flemings, in various nautical expressions – none of them, unlike similar 'Dutch' allusions, pejorative. A *Flemish coil* is one laid flat in a tight spiral with the end in the centre. A *Flemish eye* is a *soft eye splice* in which the *strands* and *yarns* are *unlaid*, the yarns knotted indifferent positions around a *spar*, etc., the eye bound together, the long ends tapered, and the whole neatly *served over*. *Flemish horses* are the short *foot ropes* at the end of a *yard* used by seamen in that position when *reefing* or *furling*.

All three expressions are first attested in 1840–1 by Dana, the first and third in *Seaman's Manual* (1841), 106 and 105, the second in *Two Years* (1840), xxv, 134.

Flinders bar   one of two iron bars mounted vertically on a *binnacle* to compensate for the *deviation* caused to the compass by other iron objects or features on board.

From the name of its inventor, the British navigator and explorer Matthew Flinders (1774–1814), author of *A Voyage to Terra Australis*, published on the day of his sadly early death.

First attested in 1881 by W. Thomson in the *Journal of the Royal United Services Institute*, XXIV, 408.

flog   to beat (often with a *cat-o'-nine-tails*); (of a sail) to flap violently. To *flog a dead horse* is to do work already paid for. To *flog the glass* is to try to shorten a period on *watch* by either turning or shaking the *sand-glass*. To *flog around the fleet* was to punish by taking the culprit to be flogged aboard every ship in the harbour.

Originally regarded as slang, the word may have been schoolboy slang; in which case its origin may be the Latin '*flagellare*', to beat. If not, it may be onomatopoeic, and connected with *flag*.

First attested in1676 in Elisha Coles, *Dictionary*.

flood   the rising tide; high water; (of the tide) to rise; (of a ballast tank, etc.) to fill; (of most other things, including a boat) to overfill. The roughly six-hour period of the flood tide is divided into three two-hour parts: the *young flood*, the *main flood*, and the *last of the flood*. Again roughly, the amount and speed of the rise is 1/12 for the first hour, 2/12 for the second, 3/12 for each of the third and fourth, 2/12 for the fifth, and 1/12 for the sixth. This is known as the *rule of twelfths*, and it applies equally to the six hours of the *ebb*.

From OE 'flod' and a common Teutonic root.

First attested in 1031 in the *Anglo-Saxon Chronicle*.

flotilla   originally, a small *fleet* or a fleet of small vessels, now known in the Royal Navy as a squadron; a group of chartered *yachts cruising* more or less together or to a plan, usually with a lead boat as guide.

From the diminutive of the Spanish *'flota'*, fleet; this word entered English in the seventeenth century to denote the convoys of merchant ships bringing the treasures of America and the Indies back to Spain.

First attested in 1711 in the *London Gazette* No. 4890/1.

flotsam   goods, *cargo* or wreckage found floating in the sea; (rarely) oyster spawn. Flotsam is usually contrasted with *jetsam*, material deliberately thrown overboard rather than simply lost; in 1926 in Britain, a pair of singing entertainers (B.C. Hilliam and Malcolm McEachern) adopted the names 'Mr Flotsam and Mr Jetsam'.

Ultimately from the late Latin *'flottatio'* and *'flottare'*, via the Anglo-French *'floteson'* (cf. the modern French *'flottaison'*).

First attested (as floating goods, etc.) in 1607 in Cowell, *Interpreter*; (as oyster spawn) in 1879 in *Cassell's Technical Educator*, IV, 154/1.

flower of the winds   the *fleur-de-lys* or decorative North printed on *compass cards* and *compass roses*.

'Flower', first attested in the thirteenth century, is from ME 'flour', 'flur', which like its counterparts in Latin and in other European languages is derived from the Aryan root *'bhlo-'*. The modern 'flour' is of similar origin.

The rationale of 'flower of the winds', however, remains uncertain.

First attested in 1867 in Smyth, *Sailor's Word-book*.

flowing   (of a tide) *flooding*, rising; (of *sheets*) *eased* off when the wind is on or *abaft* the *beam*; (of *yards* in a *square-rigger*) *braced* more squarely to the mast. In the nineteenth century the expression was also used in a figurative sense, meaning promptly or with ease.

From the verb 'flow' and thence from the OE strong verb 'flowan'.

First attested in a nautical context (referring to the sail rather than the sheets) in 1748 in *Anson's Voyage*, II, ii, 130.

fluke   one of the flattish, pointed, triangular ends of the arm of an anchor, designed for digging into the ground; one of the two triangular parts of a whale's tail.

Although the word's origin is uncertain, it may be a figurative or transferred use of the oldest sense of the word, meaning a flounder, which dates from the eighth century and comes from OE 'floc', flat. It is quite separate from the colloquial word 'fluke' meaning an accident (usually happy): see *flukey*, *fluky*.

First attested, regarding an anchor, in 1561 in Eden, *Arte of Nauigation*, A iij b; regarding a whale, in 1725 in *Philosophical Transactions of the Royal Society*, XXXIII, 256.

flukey, fluky   (of winds) light and unpredictably variable.

From the noun 'fluke', often used in billiards, meaning a piece of luck or a happy accident. The origin of that word is obscure: the OED suggests that it may be from English dialect, citing Robinson, *Glossary* (English Dialect Society, 1876), where it is defined as 'a guess'. 'Fluke' is first attested, in the context of billiards, in 1857 in *Notes and Queries*, Series II, IV, 208/1.

'Flukey' or 'fluky' is first attested in 1857 in reference to cricket, but in 1880 in a nautical context in *The Daily Telegraph*, 7 September.

fly   *compass card* (now largely obsolete in this sense); the part of a *flag* farthest from the *hoist* (which is the part by the *staff* or *halyard*); the horizontal dimension of a flag; the lower corner of a flag farthest from thehoist, which may be *defaced* by an emblem; a strip of *bunting* used as a *tell-tale*. A *fly-boat* was a flat-bottomed Dutch vessel of the sixteenth to nineteenth centuries used mainly for coastal traffic. A *fly-by-night* was an additional sail used by naval sloops in the eighteenth and early nineteenth centuries when *running*, acting as a *studding-sail* or a small *spinnaker*, but sometimes as an extra *jib* set from the *topmast* head and *sheeted* to the upper *yardarms* by *tack* and *clew*. A *flying bridge* is an additional lightweight structure acting as a *steering* position above the wheelhouse to give a better view. The *Flying Dutchman* is the phantom ship of various legends, the best known of which situates it off the Cape of Good Hope; but it also denotes a 19.8-foot international racing *dinghy*. A *Flying Fifteen* is a category of 20-foot racing dinghies. A *flying gybe* is one in which the *boom* has not been *trimmed amidships* and therefore flies across dangerously. A *flying jib* is the *foremost* jib, in *square-riggers tacked* down to the *jib-boom* or to the *flying jib-boom* which extends beyond it. *Flying kites* are additional upper sails used in *light airs* or fine weather. *Flying light* refers to a vessel floating high in the water. A *flying fish sailor* is one who prefers tropical climes.

All the senses of the noun, and many others with no nautical connections, are derived from the verb, whose origin seems to have been a common Teutonic root which in OE gives rise to 'fleogan' or 'fliogan', first attested in *Beowulf*.

First attested as regards a compass card in 1610 in Folkingham, *Synopsis*, II, vi, 56; as part of a flag, in 1841 in Dana, *Seaman's Manual*, 105.

foot   the lower edge of a sail (or of some other fitting). To *foot down* is to tauten a rope by standing on it. A *foot-rope* is that part of the *bolt-rope* which goes along the foot of a sail and its often fed into a groove on the *boom. Foot-ropes* (usually plural) are those slung in *stirrups* under a *yard* or boom to be stood in by those *reefing* or *furling* a sail.

Another ancient word, from a common Teutonic root, emerging in OE as 'fot' and first attested in *Beowulf*.

First attested as regards a sail in 1597 in Dampier, *New Voyage*, I, xviii, 495.

fore   (generally) front, *before* or ahead (but see specific combinations).

fore-and-aft   lengthwise on board ship. A *fore-and-after* is one *fore-and-aft rigged*, i.e. with sails fixed at their *forward* edges and *sheeted* from their *after* edges. *Fore-and-aft rigged* is also a naval term for petty officer dress as contrasted with the *square rig* worn by seamen. *Fore-and-aft seamanship* is elementary or basic seamanship. *Forebitter* denotes seamen's recreational songs, as distinct from *chanties* or *shanties*, which were work songs – the term probably arising from the habit of singing them round the *fore bitts* on the *forecastle*. The *fore bitts* are the *foremost* wooden *bitts* for securing *cables*. The *forecastle* (pronounced and sometimes spelt 'fo'c'sle') is the space underneath the *foredeck*, but was originally a castle built over the bows of early fighting ships from which archers operated, and for centuries it was the crew's quarters, usually below the deck but sometimes in a *deckhouse*. The *fore course* is the sail *bent* to the fore lower *yard*. The *foredeck* is that part of the deck forward of the *bridge* or the *foremast*. The *forefoot* is the junction of the *stem* and the *keel*. A *fore-ganger* is a 15-*fathom* length of anchor *cable* heavier than the rest, placed between the anchor and the first *shackle* to withstand extra wear in the *hawsepipe* – also, in *whalers*, a rope connecting the line with the *shank* of a *harpoon*. A *foregirst* (also spelt 'fargood') is a short *spar lashed* to the mast and used to *boom* out the *luff* of a *lugsail*. The *fore gripe* is the piece of wood *clenched* to the *keel* that takes the *stempiece*. A *fore guy* is any rope that leads forward from a boom, etc., to keep it in position. The *fore-hoods* are the foremost inner and outer planks of a wooden ship, whose ends are *rabbeted* into the *stem*. The *fore hook* is the *breast hook*. The *fore horse* is the iron bar fitted *athwartships* on the foredeck on which the *fore sheet* travels. The *forelock* is the flat splayed end of a *shackle pin*, etc., to prevent its falling out. The *foremast* is the *forward* one of two or more masts. *Foremost* is nearest the *bows*. The *forenoon watch* is that kept from 8.00 a.m. to noon or 12.30 p.m. The *fore peak* is the small space under the foredeck. *Fore-reach* is headway into the wind during *tacking* or while *hove-to*, while to *fore-reach* is either to shoot ahead in *stays* or to lie close to the wind and creep slowly ahead. A *foresail* in a *square-rigger* is the lowest *square sail* on the foremast; in a *schooner* a *gaff* fore-and-aft sail set *abaft* the mast; and in a *cutter* or *sloop jib*-shaped. *Fore-sheets* are not *sheets* (in either the nautical or the domestic sense) but the forward part of a ship, in the bows – the opposite of *stern-sheets*, and probably derived from that expression, rather as the jocular *pushpit* is derived from *pulpit*. *Fore sheets* (without the hyphen), however, are those used on the *foresail*. The *foreshore* is any part of the *shore* between low and high water marks. The *fore spring* is that led forward from *amidships*, the opposite of the *back spring*. The *forestay* is the wire rope from the *masthead* to either the *stem* or the *bowsprit* end. *Forestay sag* is the amount of droop in the forestay. A *forestaysail* is the technically correct expression for a foresail when *hanked* to the forestay, as with many *jibs*. A *fore top* is a platform at the head of the foremast. The *foretopgallantmast* is that above the *fore-topmast*, which in turn is that immediately above the foremast. The *fore-triangle* is the area in a *yacht* between the masthead, the base of the mast at deck level, and the forward end of the forestay. A *foreturn* is the twist given to the *strands* of a rope before they are *laid up* into it.

From the Sanskrit *'pura'*, which also produced the Latin *'pro'*, *'prae'* and *'per'* as well as the Greek *'pro'*, etc., and the various Teutonic forms such as *'vor'* in German. In English, the OED considers, its use as an adjective arose from analysis of words in which it was a prefix. From the sixteenth century it was thought to be an abbreviation of 'before': hence its being spelt 'fore' rather than 'for'.

Although current in non-nautical senses since 1000 or earlier, the word is first attested in a nautical context – and combination ('fore-sprit-saile') – in 1661 in Holyday, *D.J. Juvenalis and A. Persius Flaccus*, 229.

forward   in front; towards the *bows* of a ship; in the *fore* part of a ship. Sometimes still pronounced 'forrard', notably by those priding themselves on being 'old salts'. A ship moves 'ahead', not 'forward'.

From the OE 'for(e)weard', which like the modern word was

both an adjective and an adverb.

First attested in 1601 in Shakespeare, *All's Well that Ends Well*, V, iii, 39.

fothering   emergency stopping of a leak using *oakum*, etc., inside a sail, on the principle of the modern collision mat.

Probably from the Dutch '*voederen*' (now '*voeren*') or the Low German '*fodern*', equivalent to the modern German '*fuettern*', to line.

First attested in 1789 in Duncan, *Mariner's Chronicle* (1805), IV, 36.

foul   wrong, unsatisfactory, difficult; to collide with or otherwise interfere with (mostly in specific combinations). A *foul anchor* has its *cable* caught on its *flukes*, or is itself trapped by some underwater obstruction. A *foul berth* is one in which the vessel cannot keep clear of others or of neighbouring objects. A *foul bottom* is a *hull* covered with marine growth. *Foul ground* is an *anchorage* littered with obstructions that may result in a foul anchor. A *foul hawse* occurs when a ship lying to two anchors gets their *cables* intertwined. A *foul wind* is one that endangers the ship or thwarts her progress, usually by blowing dead against her intended course. To *foul* a vessel is to bump into her. To *foul* a ship's *hawse* is to let go a *cable* across it. In the US, *foul weather gear* is heavy weather gear.

From OE 'ful', whose root meant 'rotten', 'putrid'; it was associated with the Aryan '*pu*' and the Sanskrit '*pu*', to stink, whence the Latin '*putere*' with the same meaning and the English word 'putrid'. The OED regards the exclamation of disgust 'pooh!' and the slang 'poo', excrement, as 'vocal gestures' blowing away the undesirable; but such gestures may explain the original roots. The word 'foul', during its evolution, also meant 'sluggish', as of a horse: this compares with the German '*faul*', lazy.

First attested as a nautical adjective in 1622 in Hawkins, O*bservations* (Hakluyt Society, 1847), 117; as a nautical verb in 1726 in Roberts, *Four Years' Voyages*, 401.

found   (in the expression 'well found') maintained or equipped.

The past participle of 'find', whose source is OE 'findan'. The parent verb had the sense of 'equip' or 'supply' as early as the twelfth century, as in *Trinity College Homilies*, c. 1200 (EETS, 1873), 215.

First attested in a nautical context in 1793 in Smeaton, *Narrative, 1791*, 94.

founder   to fill with water and sink, usually in deep water. For no clear reason, the word is seldom used when a vessel sinks as the result of some other mishap, such as an explosion.

From OF *'fondrer'*, to sink to the bottom (in Latin, *'fundus'*). In the late Middle Ages the verb was also transitive, meaning to send to the bottom; but from 1600 at the latest it was used in the modern intransitive sense, corresponding to OF *'s'enfondrer'*.

First attested in 1589 in Hakluyt, *Principall Navigations*, III, 398.

four-point bearing   an instance of *doubling the angle on the bow* to ascertain distance from the shore: a *bearing* is taken on an object 45 degrees off the bow, then again when it is 90 degrees off; on a straight course at a steady speed, the distance *off* then equals the distance run as read from the log. The 'points' in question are *points* of the *compass*, of which there are 32 in a 360-degree circle, each therefore representing eleven-and-a-quarter degrees, so that four points are 45 degrees.

First attested in 1948 in de Kerchove, *Dictionary*, 278/2.

fractional rig   with the *forestay* extending only part of the way up the mast.

From OF *'fraccion'*, in turn derived from the ecclesiastical Latin *'fractio'*, from *'frangere'*, to break.

First attested in 1981 in Schult, *Dictionary* (1992 edition), 105/2.

frame   one (or all) of the *ribs* of a ship, running from the *keel* to the side rail and determining the shape of the *hull*. A vessel whose frames are in place ready for planking is said to be *in frame*.

From ON *'frame'*, furtherance, or possible OE *'fram'*, forward: in the twelfth and thirteenth centuries the meaning was 'advantage'. Then, through the notion of fashioning or constructing, in the sixteenth century it came to mean an established order, plan, verbal formula or set of standards. As early as the fourteenth century, however, it also had a material meaning as a structure, especially one acting as a skeleton.

First attested in its nautical sense in 1769 in Falconer, *Dictionary*, D b.

frap   bind tightly with a rope or line (e.g. secure *halyards* to prevent noise when in port). A *frapping line* is one used to frap anything.

Probably from OF *'fraper'*: the modern French *'frapper'*, knock, has a similar secondary meaning, and 'frap' in English once had the primary meaning of 'to strike'.

First attested in its nautical sense in 1548 in Hall, *Chronicle*, 22b.

free   (of wind) *abaft* the *beam*; to shift further *abeam* from ahead; (of *sheets*) to *ease*. In the seventeenth century, the verb meant 'to *bale* out'; but this is now obsolete.

From a very ancient Teutonic root whose basic meaning was 'dear' (hence 'friend'): the OE form was 'freo', 'frio' or 'frig'. Applied to members of the household, it distinguished them from serfs of slaves, who were not free. Cf. the Latin *'liberi'* children, based on the same distinction.

First attested as an adverb, in the phrase *steering free*, similar to the present-day *sailing free* (i.e. with eased sheets) or *running free* (i.e. with the wind from *astern*), in 1812 in *The Examiner*, 12 October, 649/2; as an adjective in 1840 in Dana, *Two Years*, xxv, 81.

freeboard   the distance from the water-level to the lowest point at which water could reach the deck or the *cockpit*. Normally measured at the *waist*, but more safely at the most vulnerable level.

Originally, from the fourteenth century, a legal term referring to the right to claim a margin of land outside the fence of a park or forest, and to the margin thus claimed. Its nautical application may well be a figurative adoption: according to Smyth, *Sailor's Word-book* (1867), the previous expression for the same thing was 'plank-sheer' – 'latterly... termed the freeboard'.

'Latterly' was an exaggeration: the term is first attested in 1726 in Shelvocke, *Voyage* (1757 edition), 286.

freeing ports   openings in the *bulwarks*, often hinged, through which any water *shipped* can run away into the sea.

From the now obsolete sense of *free*, meaning to bale or empty out.

First attested in 1880 in *The Times*, 23 October, 5/4.

Frenchman   a left-handed loop or turn put in when *coiling* down a rope right-handed, so as to counteract twists (especially useful with wire rope, which is less tolerant of twists).

From the familiar noun, extending the notion of 'foreign', 'exotic', 'contrary', etc., but without any particularly pejorative overtone: the phrase 'Flemish fake' was also used at one time for the same thing.

First attested in the expression *French fake* in 1846 in Young, *Nautical Dictionary*; the form 'Frenchman' does not appear in the OED.

freshen   (of the wind) to increase in strength; (in various combinations) to adjust so as to minimise chafe. To *freshen hawse* is to *pay out* a short length of *cable* to shift the section being rubbed; to *freshen the nip* is to *veer* or *haul* slightly with the same effect.

From the familiar word 'fresh' and hence from OE 'fersc', which is derived from an Old Teutonic root that has flowered in most European languages.

First attested in relation to wind in 1697 in Dampier, *New Voyage*, I, iv, 79; as applied to rope in 1867 in Smyth, *Sailor's Word-book*. However, a figurative use is attested in 1827 in Cooper, *The Red Rover* (1881 edition), iii, 51: 'Profiting by the occasion to "freshen his nip", as he quaintly called swallowing a pint of rum and water, he continued his narrative.'

freshes   (almost always plural) floods of fresh water flowing into the sea. Rivers noted for this include the Congo, the Ganges, the Indus, the Mississippi, the Rhone and the Tyne. The Nile is particularly notable for carrying quantities of sand into the sea, turning it yellow.

From 'fresh' and its OE antecedent 'fersc'.

First attested *c.* 1682 in Collins, *Salt*, 10.

frigate   originally a light, swift vessel for *rowing*, then for *sailing*; in the days of sail a three-masted ship, fully *rigged* on each mast, with 24–38 guns on a single *gundeck*, in the class next to ships of the line, and used for jobs needing quick manoeuvrability; now a small *warship*, often used for anti-submarine or anti-aircraft duties.

Although derived directly from the French '*frégate*', the word seems to have earlier antecedents in the Italian '*fregata*' and the Spanish and Portuguese '*fragata*'. The OED, discounting the theory that its origin might have been the Late Latin '*fabricata*' (constructed), declares that its ultimate etymology is unknown. Littré, however, apparently plausibly, conjectures that it may have come from the Greek '*aphrachta*', an undecked vessel, which the very earliest rowing frigates sometimes were.

First attested in this early and now obsolete sense in 1585 in Washington, *Nicolay's Nauigations*, I, ii, 2b.

frigatoon   a two-masted Venetian vessel with a square *stern*.

From the Italian '*fregatone*', big frigate, augmentative version of '*fregata*', probably from the Spanish and Portuguese '*fragata*'. It seems highly unlikely that it should be derived from the Italian '*fregare*', to rub, or '*fregata*' in the sense of rubbing or deletion.

First attested in 1721 in Bailey, *Dictionary*.

full   (of a sail) filled with wind, and *drawing*. *Full and by* is as close to the wind as possible, with the sails filled and not lifting or shaking. *Full and change* are the times of the full and the new moon, relating to *Spring* and *Neap* tides respectively. *Full-bottomed* is said of a ship with a very wide *hold*. To secure for a *full due* is to do so quasi-permanently. *Full for stays*, as an order to the *helmsman*, is to keep the sails full of wind in order to **go about** easily. A ship **full-rigged** has three or more masts with all **square sails set** on all of them. **Full sail** is with all **canvas** set.

From OE 'full' and a common Teutonic root.

First attested in 1627 in Smith, *Sea Grammar* (1692 edition), ix, 42.

furl to gather and **stow** a sail, usually along a **spar**.

Possibly from 'furdel' or 'fardel', which in turn are from OF *'fardeler'*, with the same meaning: cf. Hamlet's 'fardels' (burdens or bundles). However, Littré regards the French *'ferler'* as derived from the English 'furl'. There may also be a connection with the early modern French *'fresler'* and with the English 'frill'.

First attested in 1556 by W. Towrson in Hakluyt, *Principall Navigations*, (1589 edition), 113.

furniture the movable equipment of a ship, excluding fuel, food, and other stores.

From the French *'fourniture'*, in the thirteenth century 'forneture'.

First attested in a strictly nautical sense in 1582 in Lichefield, *Lopez de Castanheda*, xxix, 73b.

furring extra planking on a ship's side to give more **beam**. Sometimes corrupted into 'furrens'.

From 'fur', of which the verb may be older than the noun. Originally, it meant to add a lining or covering, and came from OF *'forrer'*, of which the modern form is *'fourrer'*, to stuff. The notion of 'hair' is a later accretion, and has not affected the shipwright's sense of the word.

First attested in 1622 in Hawkins, *Observations* (Hakluyt Society, 1847), 120.

futtock one of the four or five separate pieces of timber that form a **frame** or **rib** in a wooden ship, between the **floor** and the **top timbers**. A **futtock band** was a band on the lower mast to which were secured the **futtock shrouds**, of chain or large hemp, and later metal rods, running downward and inward from the **futtock plates** secured to the sides of the **top**, so as to support it. Desoutter, in *The Boat-Owner's Practical Dictionary* (1978), 89, remarks: 'The word is not likely to be important to the modern yachtsman, but a shout of "and futtocks to you!" has great force with perfect propriety.'

Almost certainly derived from 'foot-hook', as conjectured by Manwayring, *Dictionary* (1644) and again by Falconer, *Dictionary* (1769).

First attested in 1611 in Cotgrave, *Dictionary*.

Gaff   the *spar* to which the *head* of a four-sided *fore-and-aft* sail is *bent*, on the *after* side of a mast; a spar angled to a mast, on which flags are hoisted; an iron hook on a handle, often used for lifting fish *inboard*. A *gaff cutter* is one with a gaff *mainsail* and more than one *headsail*. *Gaff-headed* describes a gaff sail, i.e. four-sided, not triangular. *Gaff jaws* are wooden or metal claws at the inboard end of the gaff which partly encircle the mast. A *gaff ketch* is one with a gaff mainsail, the *mizen* being either *jib-* or gaff-headed. *Gaff-rigged* refers to fore-and-aft rig with gaff sail or sails. A *gaff-rigged cat* has no headsail but one mast with a gaff sail *stepped* near the *bow*. A *gaff sail* is a four-sided fore-and-aft sail whose head is bent to a gaff while it *foot* is extended by a *boom*. A *gaff schooner* is one with gaff sails. A *gaff sloop* has a single headsail and a gaff mainsail. A *gaff topsail*, uniquely, is triangular and owes its name to the fact that its head is extended on a gaff which is *set* frim or hoisted on a *topmast*. A *gaff yawl* is one with a gaff mainsail, the mizen being either jib- or gaff-headed.

From the French '*gaffe*', a boat-hook.

First attested (not surprisingly, in this sense) in 1656 in Blount, *Glossographia*; in the sense of a spar, in 1769 in Falconer, *Dictionary*, R r ij b.

gale   a strong wind of 34–47 *knots*, forces 8 and 9 on the *Beaufort scale*, 8 being a gale (34–40 knots) and 9 a strong gale (41–47 knots). Force 7 is a near gale (28–33 knots).

Of unknown etymology. It may originally have been an adjective: some connect it with the Danish '*gal*' (mad, furious, bad), from ON '*galenn*' (mad, frantic, possibly bewitched). However, its first spelling in English ('gaile') suggests that it was pronounced then as now, and not as in any Scandinavian language.

First attested in 1547 in Henry Howard, Earl of Surrey, rhyming *Proem. to the 73rd Psalm*.

galleass, galleasse, or **galliass**   vessel with *oars* and sails, larger than a *galley*, used for Mediterranean freight in the sixteenth and seventeenth centuries, and for a short time for war: six were in the 1588 Spanish Armada, but were unsuitable for the Channel and the North Sea.

From OF '*galeace*' and the Italian '*galeaza*', an augmentative form of '*galea*', a galley: cf. *galleon*.

First attested in 1544 in the *State Papers of Henry VIII* (1834 edition), III, 504.

galleon   a fifteenth-century development of the *carrack*, omitting the high *forecastle* which had often forced the *bows* to *leeward*; originated by Sir John Hawkins and adopted by Spain, first as a warship, then as a trader.

Like *galleass*, 'galleon' is derived from an augmentative form of the Italian '*galea*' – '*galeone*' – probably via the medieval Latin '*galeonem*'.

First attested in 1529 in Lindesay, *Complaynt*, 406.

galley   originally (from about 3000 BC to the eighteenth century) a Mediterranean fighting ship, usually *rowed* by criminals or slaves; a large open *rowing boat* used in the eighteenth and nineteenth centuries by customs officers and *press gangs*; a *warship*'s boat for the use of the *captain*; the cookhouse or kitchen on board ship. A *galley frigate* was one built for the English Navy under Charles II, with *oars* or *sweeps* as well as sails. *Galley pepper* was the soot, ashes, etc., sometimes found in the food. A *galley slave* was one condemned to row in a galley – or, in a modern *yacht*, the cook.

From OF '*galie*' and the medieval Latin '*galea*' or late Greek '*galaia*'.

First attested (as a ship) before 1300 in the metrical romance *King Horn*, 185; (as a cookhouse) in 1750 in Blanckley, *Expositor*.

galligaskins   wide *breeches* worn by sailors until the beginning of the nineteenth century; later, a derisive term for any wide breeches.

Probably a corruption of the French '*garguesque*', which itself came from '*greguesque*', from the Italian '*gregesco*', meaning 'in the Greek style'.

The 'galli-' part of the word may be a transfer from the roughly contemporary 'gally-breeches', possibly referring to *galley*; but much of this is conjectural, if not far-fetched.

First attested in 1577 in Holinshed, *The firste Volume of the Chronicles*, II, 1859/1.

galliot   originally a small *galley* used for boarding parties in the seventeenth and eighteenth centuries; from the eighteenth century, a small Dutch *barge*-like trading vessel.

From the French '*galiote*' and the Italian '*galeotta*', a diminutive of '*galea*'.

First attested in 1357 in *Political Poems* (Rolls Series, 1859–61), I, 65, Viij and xl.

gallows   in *square-riggers*, a raised wooden frame of two uprights and a cross-piece for *stowing* spare *booms* and *spars*; in small *fore-and-aft* craft, a *boom crutch*; in *trawlers*, inverted U-shaped metal frames carrying large *sheaves* for the *trawl warps*.

An extension from the macabre but familiar word, itself from OE 'galga', cognate with the Old Frisian '*galga*' and with the modern German '*Galgen*'. There may also be a connection withthe Lithuanian '*zalga*' and the Armenian '*dzalk*', a pole. There seems to be no link with 'Golgotha'.

First attested in a nautical sense in 1769 in Falconer, *Dictionary* (1789 edition), D d iij b.

gammon iron   metal band clamping the *bowsprit* to the *stem*. *Gammon lashing* or *gammoning* was performing the same function with rope.

The familiar word 'gammon' (in its porcine sense) is derived from the Old Northern French '*gambon*', in modern French '*jambon*', ham. The nautical sense of the word, originally meaning *lashing* the bowsprit to the stem, may have been a figurative extension from the tying up of a ham; but this remains highly conjectural.

First attested in its nautical sense (as a verb) in 1711 in Sutherland, *Ship Builder's Assistant*, 62.

gangplank   a plank (usually fitted with treads) for access to a vessel.

From OE 'gang' (walk, walking) and ME 'planke', from the Old Northern French (and modern French) '*planche*'.

First attested in 1846 in *The Knickerbocker*, XXVII, 469.

gangway   passageway for access to a vessel from the *quay*, of which a *gangplank* is one type. Originally, the word denoted a narrow platform in deep-waisted ships connecting the *quarter-deck* to the *forecastle*.

From OE 'gang' (walk, walking) and OE 'wey' (road).

First attested, in its 'platform' sense, in 1688 in the *London Gazette* No. 2317/1; in its 'passageway' sense, in 1780 in Falconer, *Dictionary* (new edition).

gantline   a rope *rove* through a *block* fixed *aloft*, for hoisting *standing rigging, boatswain's chairs*, etc.

A corruption of *girtline*.

First attested in 1840 in Dana, Jr, *Two Years*, viii, 18: 'A long piece of rope... is taken up to the mast-head from which the stay leads, and rove through a block for a girt-line, or, as the sailors usually call it, a gant-line.'

gantlope   naval punishment in which the culprit ran or was propelled in a half-*cask* between two rows of men armed with knotted cords or sticks, striking him on the naked back. The punishment was abolished by the Admiralty in 1806; but its figurative use, first attested in 1649, still continues, 'gantlope' being corrupted into 'gantlet'(1661) and 'gauntlet' (1676) in the phrase 'running the gauntlet'.

'Gantlope' is itself a corruption from the Swedish '*gatlopp*', from '*gata*' (lane) and '*lopp*' (course or running). The OED believes that the expression entered English during the Thirty Years' War. The corresponding verb in German is *'gassenlaufen'* (literally 'run along an alleyway').

First attested in 1646 in the Earl of Shaftesbury, *Diary*, 11 April, in Christie, *Life* (1871), I, 34.

garboard   the plank nearest the *keel* on either side of a wooden ship. In steel vessels, the equivalent are the *garboard plates*.

Probably from the Dutch *'garen'* (for *'gaderen'*), to gather, and *'boord'*, board: cf. the French *'gabord'*.

First attested (as 'Garbell') in 1626 in Smith, *Accidence*, 8.

garnet   a *tackle* used in *square-riggers*, *rigged* from a *guy* made fast to the mainmast *head* with a *block seized* to the *mainstay* over the *hatchway*, for hoisting in stores, etc. A *clew garnet* is a small tackle for hauling up the *clew* of a *course* to a *yard*, for *furling*.

The word has no connection with a mineral, a pomegranate, or a hinge: its origin is obscure, although linked with the Dutch *'garnaat'* or *'karnaat'*, whose meaning is similar.

First attested in 1485 in *Naval Accounts* (Navy Records Sciety, 1896), 68.

gash   garbage; spare or free. A *gash-bag* is a rubbish bin on board.

The OED declares the origin of both noun and adjective 'unknown', but links the former with the English dialect 'gaishen', a skeleton or silly-looking person, or obstacle. There may, however, be a connection with the French verb *'gâcher'*, to spoil, whose original meaning was 'to dilute plaster' before it acquired the figurative sense of 'working clumsily' and hence 'spoiling', from which the noun is *'gâchis'*, a mess. Littré declares that *'gâcher'* is derived from *'gâche'*, a mason's tool or spatula, and hence from the Old High German *'waskan'*, to wash.

First attested in a nautical sense in 1925, and even then in the now disused form 'gashions', in Fraser and Gibbons, *Soldier and Sailor Words and Phrases*, 103: '*Gashions*, extra of anything.' First attested in the sense of 'garbage' in 1961 in Burgess, *Dictionary*, 101.

gasket   length of rope, plaited cord, or *canvas* tape, etc., used as a *sail tie*.

The word originated in its nautical sense rather than as applied to motors; but its etymology remains obscure. The Italian *'gaschetta'*, attested in the nineteenth century, is almost certainly derived from the English word rather than *vice versa*.

The original spelling of 'gasket' as 'caskette' has been likened to the Spanish *'cajeta'*, a box; but this is not the origin of the word 'casket' in that sense, which although looking like a diminutive of *cask* in fact predates that word and remains equally mysterious. Nor is it easy to see how the word for a box might have become that for a sail tie, except in the very tenuous sense that each encloses something. 'Garter' might seem a more appropriate word, attested in the figurative sense of anything tying like a garter as early as the sixteenth century; but the words are too dissimilar for any plausible link between them.

First attested in 1622 in Hawkins, *Observations* (Hakluyt Society, 1847), 188.

gennaker   a *spinnaker rigged* like a *genoa*.

A combination or, in Lewis Carroll's word, portmanteau of the two operative nouns.

Not yet attested in print in English, but used orally in yacht-racing circles by 1995.

genoa   large *jib* or *foresail* whose *clew* extends far *aft* to overlap the *mainsail*, than which it usually has a far larger area.

From the name of the Italian city, where it was first recognised at the 1927 Genoa International Regatta: often mispronounced with the accent on the second syllable.

First attested in 1932 in *Yachting*, August, 66/2.

ghost   to make *headway* when there is little or no apparent wind. A *ghoster* is a special light sail, very like a *genoa* or a *Yankee*, but with its luff going all the way up the *stay* rather than stopping short of the *masthead*.

From OE 'gast', a spirit, and thence from a common West Germanic root which may well have the Sanskrit antecedent '*ghoizdo-z*' – although this appears to have connoted anger rather than apparitions.

First attested in its nautical sense in 1891 in *The Field*, 26 December, 967/2.

gig   a long, light, narrow ship's boat, now very rare, with four or six *oars* and *steps* for two short masts that could carry *lug* or *lateen* sails.

Of very uncertain origin. The oldest sense of the word, in the fifteenth century but now obsolete, was as a whipping-top or whirligig, whence perhaps came its late eighteenth-century (1791) sense of a light two-wheeled one-horse carriage. The idea of lightness, speed, and perhaps instability may account for its nautical use.

First attested in its nautical sense in 1790 in John Wolcot ('Peter Pindar'), *Works* (1812), II, 338.

gimbals   device for keeping a *compass*, chronometer, cooker, etc., horizontal at sea: it consists of two concentric metal rings pivoted at right angles to each other (although cookers are often only semi-*gimballed*, to counteract only *heel*).

An altered form of 'gimmal', itself an altered form of 'gemel' (pronounced with a soft 'g'), from the same word in OF and from *'gemellus'* in Latin, both meaning 'twin': cf. the modern French *'gémeaux'* for 'Gemini' as against *'jumeaux'* for twins. 'Gimmal' (also with a soft 'g') had as its primary meaning a finger-ring divisible into two or sometimes three – hence the nautical meaning; now, both 'gimmal' and 'gemel' are obsolete. The OED offers both a hard and a soft 'g' for 'gimbals'; but the hard 'g' is now the norm.

First attested in its nautical sense in 1780 in Falconer, *Dictionary* (new edition).

gingerbread (or *gingerbread work*)   decorative scroll work and carving or moulding at the *stern, bows*, or *quarters* of large ships, especially *warships* and merchant ships, of the fifteenth to eighteenth centuries. Such work was often gilded, leading at least one authority (Kemp, *Oxford Companion* (1976), 343) to imply that this was the origin of the expression 'to take the gilt off the gingerbread'. In fact, culinary gingerbread was often gilded too: see King, *Cookery,* (1708), 346: 'The enticing gold of ginger-bread.'

The word appears to be a misreading of the source-word for 'ginger' – OF *'gingembras'* or *'gingembrat'* (modern French *'gingembre'*), the third syllable being mistaken for 'bread' and the second acquiring an intrusive final 'r'. From the fifteenth century onwards it meant more than just preserved ginger, and came to denote a cake containing treacle and ginger, making the '-bread' part of the word quite plausible. The cake was often shaped into figures and letters, etc.

First attested in its nautical sense in 1748 in Smollett, *Roderick Random*, III.

gipsy, gypsy   a small drum attached to a *winch*; the sprocket wheel on a *windlass* that takes the links of the chain *cable*. In the annals of the sea, *Gipsy Moth* was the name of five yachts owned by Sir Francis Chichester, in the fourth of which he circumnavigated the globe single-handed in 1966–7. He named them after the Gipsy Moth aircraft in which he had flown solo to Australia in 1929.

The early form of the word, 'gipcyan', is an aphetic form of 'Egyptian' (i.e. having lost its first syllable). Originally meaning Romany, it acquired a number of connotations connected with gipsies' real or supposed characteristics (e.g. open-air, itinerant (including portable), wayward, dishonest), and appeared in a number of combinations. One of these was *gipsy-winch*, which later lost its second part.

First attested, in the combination 'gipsy-winch' in 1875 in Knight, *Dictionary of Mechanics* (1874–7).

girt   *moored* with two anchors by *cables* so taut that the ship cannot swing to wind or tide; (of a cable) to rub or grate against the ship; to distort a sail with a rope, etc., running across it. When a ship is girt, the remedy is of course to slacken off the cable that 'girts' against the bow or the *forefoot. Girtline* is the alternative and perhaps more authentic term for *gantline*.

The past participle of 'gird' (as in 'gird up your loins') in the case of the adjective and probably also the verb, although the latter may possibly derive from the now rare 'girt' meaning 'girth'. The common ultimate origin of both words is OE 'gyrdan', to encircle.

First attested as an adjective in 1627 in Smith, *Sea Grammar*, vii, 30; as a verb, in 1794 in *The Elements and Practice of Rigging and Seamanship*, II, 310.

glass   in the days before nautical clocks and chronometers, an hourglass or *sandglass*; until the eighteenth century, a telescope; still, a barometer or even a barograph.

All these (save the barograph) being partly made of glass, the term is derived form the substance, whose name originated in OE as 'glaes' and is probably derived from the old Teutonic '*glo*', to shine or indeed to glow. First attested, in the sense of 'hourglass', in 1557 in *Tottel's Miscellany*, Arber edition, 1870, 138; in the sense of 'telescope' in 1613–16 in Browne, *Britannia's Pastorale*, II; in the sense of 'barometer' in or after 1688 in J. Smith, *The Baroscope*, 66.

glut   a piece of strengthened *canvas* sewn into a *square sail*, with a strong *eyelet* for the *bunt jigger*; a piece of wood used as a fulcrum; to prevent slippage.

Of confused etymology. In its other, familiar sense, it comes from OF '*glout*', a gulp, and the obsolete French '*gloutir*', to swallow – both no doubt onomatopoeic; and the nautical verb is probably related to gulping with the likelihood of clogging or even choking. The nautical noun is another matter: it may conceivably be associated with *cleat*.

First attested, as a nautical noun in its 'canvas sense', in 1841 in Dana, *Seaman's Manual*, 107; as a nautical noun in its 'fulcrum' sense in 1846 in Young, *Nautical Dictionary*; as a nautical verb in 1867 in Smyth, *Sailor's Word-book*.

go   (not in itself a nautical verb, but used in a great variety of nautical phrases). To *go aboard* is to enter a ship. To *go about* is to *tack*, putting the ship's *head* through the wind so that it blows from the other side. To *go aloft* is to climb the mast, *ratlines*, or *standing rigging* – and, figuratively, to die. To *go* *ashore* is to disembark. To *go large* is to sail with the wind near the *quarter*. To *go out with the ebb tide* is to die. *Gone by the board* means disappeared *overboard*; it is also applied to a mast that has broken off at deck level.

Like most simple-seeming words, 'go' has a very complex history. Its origin is a common Teutonic defective verb, leading to the OE infinitive 'gan'.

First attested *c.* 825 in various forms in the *Vespasian Psalter*.

gobbie, gobby   a coastguard; a *quarter-deck* man; (in the US) a *bluejacket*.

Of obscure and complex origin. In the non-nautical sense, it was a slang term for smokers who spat, attested in 1890 in Farmer and Henley, *Slang*, III, 168/1. In this sense the term is clearly derived from 'gob', which has many colloquial and other meanings, including 'mouthful' (from OF *'gobe'*), 'mouth' (from the Gaelic and Irish *'gob'*, meaning 'beak' or 'mouth'), and hence to spit. Until 1923 the coastguard service in Britain was manned by naval pensioners, who may have been thought, by younger sailors or smugglers, to merit the disparaging nickname.

First attested in 1929 in Bowen, *Sea Slang*, 58.

gondola   a light, flat-bottomed, high-prowed and high-sterned *skiff*, often ornamented, propelled by a *stern oar*, used on the canals of Venice; a small coastal rowing-boat used on the shores of Italy; a small, oar-propelled wooden *warship* used on US lakes and rivers.

The word is Italian, but beyond that its origin is unknown: it is attested in Italy as early as the eleventh century.

First attested in English in 1549 in Thomas, *Italie*, 83 b.

gooseneck   jointed metal fitting which attaches the *boom* to the mast, allowing it to swivel and pivot; a ventilating cowl bent over to keep water out.

From its resemblance to the outstretched neck of a goose in flight. 'Goose', which dates from the tenth century, is derived from OE 'gos' and a common Teutonic root; 'neck' is from the (rare) OE 'hnecca', cognate with similar words in most Teutonic languages but no others. First attested in 1688 in Sewall, *Diary* (1878–82), 29 November.

goosewing   to sail *downwind* with the *mainsail* set on one side and the *foresail boomed* out on the other, usually with a *whisker pole*. Originally, 'goosewings' were the *clews* of a *course* or *topsail* in a *square-rigger*, used when the wind was too strong for the full sail, even fully *reefed*.

From the resemblance to the spread wings of the bird. 'Goose', dating from the tenth century, comes from OE 'gos' and a common Teutonic root; 'wing' is from ME 'wenge', 'wengen', 'wenges' (first attested in the plural), cognate with a number of similar words in Scandinavian languages, and all associated with ON *'vaengir'*.

First attested in its nautical sense in 1626 in Smith *Accidence*, 29.

gores   segments of a sail cut at an angle to produce the right curve; angular pieces of wood used to complete the planking. *Goring* is that part of a sail's *skirts* where, cut on the bias, it gradually widens.

A 'gore' (as distinct from 'gore' as blood, etc.) was originally a triangular piece of land: this usage was derived from OF 'gara', itself related to OE 'gar', a spear (cf. 'to gore' in the sense of 'to stab), which seems to have denoted the spear's triangular pointed end.

First attested in a nautical sense in 1794 in *The Elements and Practice of Riggings and Seamanship*, I, 91.

gorge   the groove in the *sheave* of a *block* that takes the rope.

One of the many figurative extensions of the familiar word, which since the late Middle Ages has meant both the internal and the external throat. Its origin is OF *'gorge'*, which Littré believes to be derived from the Latin *'gurges'*, meaning a gulf, whereas the OED considers that 'the possibility of connexion with the Latin *gurges*, whirlpool, is very doubtful'. In Latin, however, the word was also used figuratively: so the OED's opinion may be doubtful too.

First attested in 1812–16 in Smith, *Panorama, 308*.

grab   a shallow one- or two-masted Indian coastal vessel common during the seventeenth to nineteenth centuries, ranging between 150 and 300 tons.

From the Arabic *'yurab'*, literally 'raven', but used figuratively for a *galley*. The smaller grabs also had *sweeps* for *rowing*.

First attested in 1680 in Morden, *Geography* (1685 ed.), 405.

grapnel   a small two- to four-pronged anchor sometimes used as such by *dinghies*, etc., either on the seabed or hooked on to a bush or branch, but in the case of larger vessels originally for grappling with the enemy, holding a ship *alongside* for boarding; also used for dragging the bottom in search of objects lost overboard.

From the Anglo-French *'grapenel'*, a diminutive of the similar *'grapon'* and cognate with OF *'grapelle'*, itself a diminutive of *'grape'*, a hook, which is the source of 'grapple' in English. It is hard to resist conjecturing a possible link with 'grip', which as a noun appears to be derived from OE 'gripe', grasp, related to the Old High German '-*grif*', and (as a verb) from the Old

Northumbrian 'grippa', corresponding to the Middle High German 'gripfen'. The verb 'grab' seems to correspond to the Middle Dutch and Middle High German *'grabben'*, which may be an onomatopoeic version of the root of 'grip'. 'Grasp', on the other hand, comes from ME 'graspen', itself perhaps from OE 'graepsan' and the Old Teutonic *'graipison'*. Despite all possible reservations, the family resemblance is striking.

First attested in 1373 in Riley, *Memorials*, (1868), 369.

grass line, grass rope   a line made of *coir* or sisal, which floats: useful in rescue or salvage, or as a *drogue*.

'Grass', from OE 'graes', originally meant any kind of herbage.

First attested in a nautical context in 1882 in Nares, *Seamanship*, 6th edition, 147.

grave   to clean a ship's bottom and coat it with a protective such as tar; to replace rotten timber with a new piece. A *graving dock* is or was a dry dock in which the ship's bottom could be treated. A *graving piece* is the fresh timber replacing that removed.

The origin of 'grave' in the first sense is unknown: it may come from the French *'grave'* (= *'grève'*), a shore, since boats were often beached for the purpose. 'Grave' in the second sense may be an extension of 'grave' in the sense of 'excavate': this is also an obsolete synonym for 'engrave'. If this be the case, the origin of the word in this second sense is OE 'grafan', to dig, to engrave.

First attested in the 'cleaning and protecting' sense in 1461 in the *Tenth Report of the Royal Commission on Historical Manuscripts*, Appendix V, 301; in the 'renewing timber' sense in 1976 in Kemp, *Oxford Companion*, 350.

gribble, gribble worm   a small marine boring crustacean, the *limnoria tenebrans*, not unlike a woodlouse.

Of unknown origin; but the word appears to be cognate with 'grub', whose source is the Old Teutonic *'grab'*: cf. 'grave'.

First attested in 1838 by E. Moore in *The Magazine of Natural History*, II, 207.

grid, gridiron   wood or metal staging, above water at low tide, on to which a vessel can be floated for inspection and treatment when the tide *ebbs*.

'Grid' is a back-formation from 'gridiron', whose origin, however, is obscure: its earliest form, 'gredire', appears in the same text as 'gredile', meaning 'griddle'. Although the change from '-ile' to '-ire' may be phonetic or the result of popular etymology, '-ire' in ME was the equivalent of 'iren', 'iron'.

First attested in its nautical sense in 1846 in Young, *Nautical Dictionary*.

gripe   to carry too much *weather helm* and so tend to turn up into the wind when *close-hauled*.

Although seductively like the familiar word for complaint or discomfort, the nautical word is derived from an obsolete term for *forefoot*, originally spelt as derived from the Dutch '*greep*'.

First attested in this nautical sense in 1627 in Smith, *Seaman's Grammar, xi*, 53.

gripes   long, broad bands of *canvas*, matting or plaited rope used to secure boats on deck. A *griping spar* is a long spar with *fenders*, *shipped* between the *davits*, to which a boat is secured, and from which, in the case of *lifeboats*, a scrambling net is hung.

From OE 'gripan', to grasp.

First attested in 1762 in Falconer, *Shipwreck*, II, 102.

grog   rum-and-water. *Grog-blossom* is *acne rosacea*, or an alcohol-induced red nose. *Groggy* means tipsy. A *grog-shop* is a public house. A *grog-tub* is a barrel or other container from which grog is served. Its issue in the Royal Navy began in 1740, when Admiral Edward Vernon (1684–1757) sought to reduce drunkenness by having the daily ration of one pint of neat rum for men, and half-a-pint for boys, diluted with a quart of water. It was issued in two halves, at noon and 6.00 p.m., until 1824, when the evening issue was abolished. In 1850, the daily ration was reduced to one gill; in 1881 it ceased to be issued to officers, and in 1918 to warrant officers. Chief and petty officers had their ration undiluted, while all other ratings received one-and-a-half gills of water to half a gill of rum until 1970, when the Navy abolished the grog ration altogether.

The word is said to be an abbreviation of 'grogram' (from the French '*gros grain*') a coarse fabric of silk, of mohair and wool, or of all three. Admiral Vernon wore a grogram boat-cloak (or, some say, grogram breeches) and was consequently known as 'Old Grog' – hence the name for his diluted rum.

First attested in 1770 in an article by T. Norworth in *The Gentleman's Magazine*, 559/2.

gromet (also spelt *gromit, grummet*, or *grummett*)   in the days of the Cinque Ports navies, a boy who tended the ships in harbour (until about 1500); in the Royal Navy, a senior ship's boy in the eighteenth century rated as a volunteer 2nd class.

From OF and Anglo-French '*gromet*' or '*groumet*', meaning variously a servant, valet, shop-boy, or wine-merchant's assistant: cf. '*gourmet*'. The word recurs in a Latin version, '*grometus*' or '*gromettus*', in Anglo-Latin documents until the sixteenth century, often meaning 'groom'.

Etymological connection with the word, however, remains

uncertain (although the original French, like the Latin, would seem to connote 'little groom').

First attested as 'gromet', although in an otherwise Latin text, in 1229 in Jeake, *Charters*, translated with annotations, 1678 (1728), 25, Note; in an English-language text, in 1570–6 in Lambarde, *Perambulation* (1596, 1826), 110.

grommet (pronounced and sometimes spelt *grummet*)   a rope ring formed by *laying up* a single *strand* three times, originally used to secure the upper edge or the *luff* of a sail to its *stay*, but also sometimes replacing the *crutch* for an *oar*, or securing it to the *thole pin*, and now often used for deck quoits; a brass *eye* or *cringle* fitted into sails, *canvas*, etc., for *lacing*.

From the fifteenth-century French '*gromette*' (now '*gourmette*'), the curb of a bridle, from the verb '*gourmer*', to curb, itself of unknown origin despite its phonological resemblance to '*courber*', with the same meaning as well as the cognate 'to curve'.

First attested in 1626 in Smith, *Accidence*, 12.

ground   to touch or 'take' the seabed or shore, to run *aground*. *Ground scope* is the length of *cable* under water between two anchors or clumps used as *moorings*. *Ground sea* is a succession of breakers rolling on to the shore in calm weather. A *ground swell* is a short steep swell caused by sandbanks, etc. *Ground tackle* is that used for anchoring and mooring.

From OE 'grund' and a common Teutonic root.

First attested in 1624 in Smith, *Generall Historie*, III, v, 59.

grow   (of the anchor *cable*'s direction from the *bow* towards the anchor) to point or stretch.

From OE 'growan'.

First attested in 1780 in Falconer, *Dictionary*.

gudgeon   metal *eyelet* on the *sternpost* into which the *pintle* of the *rudder* is fitted.

Possibly from the fourteenth-century French '*goignon*', whence the modern French '*gond*' (hinge); but more likely from the OF and ME '*gojon*', which in turn is associated with '*goujon*', meaning a gudgeon in both its senses (a small freshwater fish used as bait, and a fitting for the rudder) and in its culinary sense in French a strip of fish (as described in an English menu) – but not, in French, in the colloquial English sense of a simpleton.

First attested in 1558 by W. Towrson in Hakluyt, *Principall Navigations* (1589), 124.

gunter rig   a development of the *lugsail rig* in the direction of a *Bermuda sloop*: the *luff* of the *mainsail* is very short, while its *head*, almost in line with the luff, is *laced* to a *gaff* or *yard* which when fully hoisted is almost an extension of the mainmast. This rig is especially useful for boats that are left on open moorings (where a tall mast might be vulnerable), trailed, or taken under bridges.

'Gunter', as might be guessed, is a surname – that of the English mathematician Edmund Gunter (1581–1626). He did not, as has sometimes been surmised, invent the gunter rig; but he produced the 'Gunter's scale', familiarly known as 'the gunter'. This was a flat rule, two feet long, marked on one side with scales, of chords, sines, tangents, etc., and on the other with their logarithms. When these two were marked on two separate rules, which slid alongside each other, the device was known as a 'sliding gunter'; and the ship's rig was named because of its resemblance to the two sliding rules. The rig was indeed first known as a 'sliding gunter' itself.

First attested in 1794 in *The Elements and Practice of Rigging and Seamanship*, I, 136.

gunwale   (pronounced 'gunnel' and sometimes mis-spelt 'gunwhale'): the timber or other material fitted all round the top of the *hull* linking all the *ribs* and the top plank, and usually projecting proud of the sides. In modern sailing *dinghies*, the equivalent projection is the *rubbing strake*.

From OE 'walu', the mark of a lash – i.e. a weal, which the gunwale might be thought to resemble. 'Wale' was used in the sense of 'gunwale' as early as the fourteenth century. The prefix 'gun-' is derived from the fact that guns were rested upon it.

First attested in 1466 in *Manners and Household Expenses* (Roxburghe Club, 1841), 205.

guy   a rope or *tackle* used to control lateral movement of a *derrick* or *spar*, etc. An *afterguy* leads *aft* from the *boom*, a *foreguy forward*. A *spinnaker guy* is attached to the spinnaker boom.

From OF '*gui*', associated with the Latin '*guida*' and similar words in other Romance languages, as with the Italian '*guidare*' (whence '*guido*' and '*guida*'), all connected with guidance. 'Guy' in English itself once meant 'guide', but is now obsolete in that sense.

First attested in 1620 in John Taylor ('Water Poet'), *The Praise of Hemp-seed*, 10.

gybe   to turn a sailing boat when the wind is *aft*, so that it passes from one *quarter* to the other, 'putting the *stern* through the wind'; the action of so doing; the *tack* on which the boat is, when the wind is aft (e.g. 'on the *port gybe*'). A *gybe all standing* takes place, usually by accident, when the *boom* is allowed to swing violently from one extreme to the other, without the prior precaution of hauling in the *mainsheet* to reduce the distance of travel.

From the seventeenth-century Dutch '*gijben*' (now '*gijpen*'), to gybe; cf. the German '*gieben*', '*giepen*', and the Swedish '*gippa*', '*gipa*'. How the hard 'g' in these languages became soft in English remains a mystery.

First attested in 1693 in *Minutes of the Provincial Council of Pennsylvania* (1852), I, 376.

Hack watch   not a reporter's spell on duty, but a small accurate timepiece, checked daily against the ship's chronometer, and used when taking astronomical sights; also known as the *deck watch*.

Perhaps because this instrument was used by many people, its name is associated with the various meanings of 'hack', including 'for hire', as derived from 'hackney' – not the London borough, but originally from OF '*haquenée*', a docile mount for ladies, and hence an ambling horse of the kind ofen hired out.

First attested in 1851–9 in George B. Airy, *Astronomy*, in *Manual of Scientific Enquiry*, 3.

half beams   *beams* that do not extend across the whole breadth of the ship, but stop at *hatchways*, etc. 'Half' appears in a number of other nautical expressions. A *half-breadth plan* is a design drawing showing the deck lines of a shop from *stem* to *stern* for only half the breadth of the *hull*. *Half cardinals* are not truncated churchmen, but the four points of the *compass* intermediate between the *cardinal* points (i.e. NE, NW, SE and SW). A *half-deck* was originally the space between the foremost *bulkhead* of the *steerage* and the *forward* part of the *quarter-deck*; then a structure on the upper deck of a merchant vessel, usually in the *waist*, used as a *berth* for apprentices; now often a deck extending over only part of the vessel, as in a *half-decker*, an open boat partly decked. *Half-ebb* describes a falling tide midway between high and low water; *half-flood* the equivalent on a rising tide. A *half-hitch* is a loop formed by passing the end of a rope around its *standing part* and then bringing it up through the *bight*. A *flag* or *ensign* is lowered (not raised) to *half mast* (halfway down the mast) as a token of mourning. *Half-musket shot* was the range (about 100 yards) at which British *ships of the line* traditionally preferred to fight, usually aiming at the *hull*, whereas other navies fired from further off, aiming at the *standing rigging*. *Half seas over* (of a person) means unsteady owing to strong drink. A *half-sprit* was the original term for a *gaff*. *Half tide* is the mean level of the sea during *springs* or *neaps*. A *half-tide mooring* is one on which a boat is about half the time *afloat* and half *aground*.

'Half' is from a common Teutonic root, of which the OE offshoot was 'healf': originally, in all languages, it mean 'side', as in the two sides of a coin.

First attested in 1850 in Greenwood, *Sailor's Sea-book*, 95.

halyard   (also *halliard* or *haul-yard*, often plural): rope, wire, or *tackle* used to hoist (and sometimes lower) sails, *ensigns*, or *burgees*.

Originally 'halier' or 'hallier', from 'hale' (to haul), or from OF *'halier'* or *'hallier'*: the '-yard' was a seventeenth-century corruption. First attested as 'halier' in 1373 in Riley, *Memorials*, 1868, *Indenture*, 370. The 'd' is first attested in 1611 in Randle Cotgrave, *Dictionarie*; the 'y' in 1627 in Smith, *Sea Grammar...Enlarged*, v, 21.

hamber line, hambroline, or **hambro line**   a small (4–5mm diameter) three-*strand*ed hemp line or cord, often *tarred* and always hard *laid*, used for *lacings*, *lashings*, *seizings*, etc., and usually supplied in *hanks*; sometimes known as codline.

Apparently a corruption of 'Hamburg', but any connection between the city and the object remains obscure.

First attested in 1793 in T. MacDonell, *Diary*, in Gates, *Five Fur Traders* (1933), 75.

hambone, ham-bone   slang for a sextant.

From the (very far-fetched) supposed resemblance in shape.

First attested in 1938 in Worsley, *First Voyage*, viii, 144.

hammock   a suspended swinging bed of *canvas* or netting, secured by cords at each end; the naval version was of No.0 canvas, 6 foot by 4 foot. Hammocks were also sometimes used as rough lifebuoys or as *hammock-shrouds* for burial at sea. A *hammock-batten* was one of the strips of wood nailed to the ship's *beams*, from which the hammocks were slung. The *hammock clews* were the small cords or *nettles* at each end for suspending the hammock. The *hammock nettings* were the rope nettings in which rolled-up hammocks were stored when not in use, lashed or hung to the *hammock rails* above the *bulwarks* or (in battle) placed along the sides of the upper deck and along the *break* of the *poop* as (somewhat flimsy) protection against musket fire.

From the Spanish *'hamaca'*, of Carib origin, the original Carib word being possibly *'hamorca'*.

First attested in 1555 in Eden, *Decade*, ed. Arber, 1885, 200.

hance   a curved rise from a lower to a higher part of a rail, e.g.

between the poop and the upper deck, often elaborately carved.

From the Anglo-French '*haunce*', OF '*hauce*' or '*haulce*', later '*hausse*', rise. The same root gives the familiar 'enhance'.

First attested in its original, non-nautical sense of 'lintel' in 1534 in More, *Treatice*; in its nautical sense in 1637 in Heywood, *True Description*, 41.

hand   a member of the crew, sometimes prefixed by a location (e.g. *deck hand, galley hand*); (of a sail) to *furl* or lower. 'Hand' also occurs in many nautical expressions. A *hand bearing-compass* or *hand compass* is one hand-held for taking bearings of other vessels or objects. A *hand lead and line* consists of 10–14 pounds of lead on a line for taking hand *soundings*. A *hand line* is any used by hand, for soundings, fishing, etc. A *hand mast* is a light pole mast. *Hand-over-hand* refers to rapid hauling on a line in which one hand passes over the other in turn (and also, figuratively, to rapid progress, often in overtaking another vessel). *Hand reef and steer* were formerly a seaman's basic qualifications. *Hand taut* is as taut as possible without a *winch* or *windlass*. A *handspike* is a hand lever, usually made of wood with an iron heel.

From a common Teutonic root, in OE 'hand'; its figurative use to refer to a person (whose handiwork is employed) is first attested in 1590 in Spenser, *Faerie Queene*, I, xi, 5.

First attested in its nautical sense in 1669 in Sturmy, *The Mariners Magazine*, I, 18.

handy billy   a small *jigger purchase* or *tackle*, used for handling cargo. breaking out an anchor, etc.: it consists of a rope 2 inches or under, *rove* with one double and one single *block*, each of which has a rope *tail*, though one may have a hook.

'Handy' here is in its familiar sense of 'adroit' or 'capable': its origin is *hand*. 'Billy', derived from the pet form of 'William' is often found denoting some machine or implement, including a cosh or a policeman's truncheon; but its precise *raison d'être* here remains obscure.

First attested in a non-nautical sense in 1858 in Simmonds, *Dictionary*; in its nautical sense, in Smyth, *Sailor's Word-book*.

hank   a skein or coil of small line; a ring, clip, or hoop of metal (or plastic) for *bending* the *luff* of a *staysail* or a *jib* to the *stay*, usually in the form of a piston, *double claw* or tab.

From ON '*honk*', which meant both a coil and a clasp.

First attested in the sense of a coil in 1483 in *Catholicon Anglicum*, 173/2; as a device for securing the luff, in 1711 in Sutherland, *Ship Builder's Assistant*, 134.

hard   a slipway or stretch of shore firm enough for *launching* and *landing*; firmly, as in '*hard alee*' (sometimes used as a warning instead of '*lee-o*'), *hard aport, hard astarboard, hard aweather, hard down, hard up* – all meaning that the helm is in, or should be moved as firmly and as far as possible into, the specified position. A *hard chine hull* is one in which the *topsides* and the bottom meet at an angle (along the *chine*) rather than curving to a round bilge. A *hard eye* is an *eye splice* containing a *thimble*. *Hard tack* is ship's biscuit. To *harden in* is to haul in the *sheet* so as to flatten the sail.

'Hard' is from OE 'heard', which in turn is from a common Teutonic root and from the pre-Teutonic '*kartus*', corresponding to the Greek '*kratus*', meaning powerful.

First attested as a nautical adverb in 1549 in the *Complaynt of Scotlande* (EETS, 1872), vi, 40; as a non-nautical noun, in 1576 in Turner, *Oxford* (1880), 385; as a nautical noun in 1838 in Dickens, *Nicholas Nickleby*, xxviii.

harpings   extra planking beside the *bows* of a wooden ship to strengthen her against the sea.

The OED suggests that the word may be derived from 'harp', the musical instrument; but it seems at least conceivable that itmay be related to the earlier word 'harping', a grappling-iron (cf. *harpoon*), from the French '*harpin*', a boat-hook.

First attested in 1658 in Edward Phillips, *New World*.

harpoon   a barbed spear with a line attached, for capturing whales and other large sea animals: it is either thrown or fired from a gun.

From the French '*harpon*', a cramping iron, or possibly the French '*harpin*', a grappling-iron or boat-hook.

First attested in a non-nautical sense in 1625 in Purchas, *Pilgrimes*, I, iii, 118; in its nautical sense in 1694 in *Several Late Voyages and Discoveries* (1711), II, 8.

hatch   opening in the deck for the passage of either people or objects, *cargo*, etc. In the plural, it used to be used for 'deck' (hence the expression *under hatches*); but this usage died out in the seventeenth century. In the singular, the word is still often used to denote *hatch cover*, as first attested in 1617 in John Minsheu, *The Guide into Tongues* (1627). A *hatch beam* is a removable beam fitted *fore-and-aft* to large hatches to support *hatch covers* when they are *battened down*. A *hatchboard* is a *washboard*. The *hatch coaming* is a hatch's raised framework. *Hatch covers* are those that close the hatches, in wood, tarpaulin, canvas, steel or plastic. *Hatch money* is that paid to a watchman to prevent pilfering. A *hatch roller* is a length of pipe-shaped roller to prevent chafing on the hatch coamings. A *hatchway* is a hatch with a ladder leading *below*.

From OE 'haec', originally 'a half-door', and in Southern and

Midland OE sometimes spelt 'hatch' or 'hetch'.

First attested in its precise modern nautical sense in 1793 in Smeaton, *Narrative*, 99.

haul to pull. Obvious though this may seem, the word is used in a number of less elementary nautical expressions. A wind *hauls aft* or *forward* when it changes direction; if it *hauls ahead* it is hauling forward. To *haul aft* a *sheet* is to bring the *clew* of the sail further aft. To *haul ashore* is to retire from the sea. '*Haul away*' is the order to pull. A ship *hauls her wind* when brought closer to the wind after *running free* (the appropriate command is '*haul to the wind*' or '*haul your wind*'). To *haul off* is to pull away (e.g. from a *jetty*) or to alter course away from an object. To *haul one's wind* is to dodge something by sudden change. To *haul out* is to pull a vessel out from a dock or to pull a boat from the water. To *haul taut* is to take up a rope's slack. *Haulbowlines* is an old term for seamen – presumably referring to the lines securing the *bow* rather than to the knots.

A variant, originally sixteenth-century, spelling of ME 'hale' from OF '*haler*'.

First attested (and in the specialised nautical sense of *trimming* sails) in 1557 in W.Towrson, in Hakluyt, *Principall Navigations* (1589), 113.

hawse that part of a ship's *bow* in which the *hawse holes* for the anchor *cable* are cut; by extension, the area through which the anchor cable lies, from ship to seabed or, when two anchors are in use, the whole area between both hawse holes and both anchors; to *yaw* and tauten the cable when at anchor. A ship has *clear* or *open hawse* when the two cables do not cross, a *foul hawse* when they do. A *hawse bag* was a canvas bag full of *oakum* to plug the hawse holes: a *hawse block* or *buckler*, wooden or metal, has the same function today. A *hawse-piece* was the timber through which the hawse hole was cut. The *hawsepipe* is the tube leading through the hawse hole to prevent chafe. A *hawse plug* was anything used to plug the hawse hole.

Confusion surrounds the derivation of 'hawse' and its relationship with *hawser*. 'Hawse' was used for 'hawser' in the sixteenth and seventeenth centuries; and in the sixteenth to eighteenth centuries 'hawser' was sometimes used, erroneously it would seem, for 'hawse' in the sense of an area. Since 'hawser' seems to be derived from the Anglo-French '*hauceur*', to hoist (cf. the French '*hausser*'), the word 'hawse' might be thought to spring from the same root. But the OED considers it to be 'a phonetic spelling of sixteenth c. *halse*, *haulse*', and this in turn to be linked to ON (and modern German) *'hals'*, neck. The OED concedes, however, that this linkage is only 'apparent'.

First attested in 1497 in *Naval Accounts* (Navy Records Society, 1896), 313.

hawser   heavy rope of hemp or wire, normally 4½ inches or more in circumference, used for *towing, warping,* securing *alongside* (*breast-ropes* and *springs*) or as a *warp* for a *kedge* anchor; in smaller vessels without chain cable, the main anchor warp is sometimes called a 'hawser'. A *hawser bend,* for joining two hawsers, consists of an *overhand knot* in each, or alternatively two *double round turns* and *double half hitches,* looped together, with each end *seized* back. A *hawser eye* is a *thimble eye* in the end of a hawser, or sometimes a *becket* of smaller rope *tailed* and *served* so as to *reeve. Hawser-laid* describes a rope whose three *strands* are *laid* up against the twist, usually right-handed, i.e. anti-clockwise.

For etymology, see *hawse.*

First attested in 1338 in the manuscript *Sacrist's Roll of Durham.*

haze   to persecute with overwork.

Unconnected with the familiar 'haze' (or mist), whose origin is unknown although it seems to be a back-formation from 'hazy', itself of unknown origin too. In the present nautical sense, 'haze' is derived from OF *'haser',* known as early as 1450 in the sense of 'to irritate, annoy, etc.'

First attested in its nautical sense in 1840 in Dana, *Two Years,* viii, 18.

head   the top or *forward* part – the *stem* of a boat, the upper end of a *spar* (as in *masthead*), the top edge of a sail or (if the sail is triangular) its top corner; the seaward and of a *pier* or *jetty*; (of a wind) to edge round towards a ship's *bows.* A *head-board* (in its nautical sense) is the small wooden or other insertion at the top of a *Bermuda* mainsail. The *headfast* is rope or chain securing the head of a vessel to the *quay.* A *heading* (apart from its directional sense) is the *canvas* hemmed pocket of a *flag* that contains the rope. *Head on* means *bows on. Head reaching* is the same as *forereaching.* The *headrope* is a rope headfast, and also that part of the *boltrope* of a four-sided sail that lies along its head. The *heads* is the old (and still current) naval term for the latrines, originally consisting of little more than timbers, projecting on either side of the bows, on which the crew sat to relieve themselves. *Headsails* are all those *set before* the *foremast.* A *head sea* is one whose waves approach from the direction steered. The *headstay* is that from the top of a mast to the bow. *Headway* is movement forward through the water.

Obviously a figurative extension from the head of a human being or other animal: the word itself has a common Teutonic root and appears in OE as 'heafod'. Although the consonants in this word seem to correspond to those in the Latin '*caput*', head, the vowel difference seems not to substantiate a link.

First attested (as meaning the stem of a vessel) in 1485 in *Naval Accounts* (Navy Records Society, 1896).

heart   the central core of a rope round which the *strands* are *laid* up; a form of *deadeye* used for setting up the *stays* of a *square-rigger*, often triangular but sometimes heart-shaped.

A typically figurative use of the familiar word for the vital organ, itself derived from a common Teutonic root which appears in OE as 'heorte' and is related to the Latin '*cor*', '*cordis*'. First attested, as a form of deadeye, in 1769 in Falconer, *Universal Dictionary*; as the core of a rope, in 1841 in *Penny Cyclopaedia of the Society for the Diffusion of Useful Knowledge*, 1833–43, XX, 155/2.

First attested in this sense in 1875 in Bedford, *Sailor's Pocketbook*, x, 360.

heave   the lift of a sea or swell; to pull strongly on a rope or line; to throw. To *heave ahead* is to haul a ship forward with a *warp* or (figuratively) to get on with one's work. *Heave and set* is the rising and falling of a ship on the waves. '*Heave-ho*' is a call for extra collective effort. To *heave in* is to start pulling on a rope, to back it up on a *capstan* as it starts turning, or alternatively to take in some of the anchor *cable*. To *heave in sight* is to become visible over the horizon. *Heaving down* is the *heeling* of a ship by *tackles* between the *masthead* and the shore when *careening*. A *heaving line* is a light line, often slightly weighted at the free end, thrown across a gap (e.g. between ships or between ship and shore) as a *messenger* to which a heavier line can be attached for hauling across. To *heave short* is to take up the *slack* of a rope, etc., on a capstan or *winch*. To *heave the lead* is to take *soundings* by hand *lead* and line. To *heave to* is to bring a ship as nearly as possible to a stop – with engine if available, otherwise by *trimming* the sails, typically by *backing* the *headsail(s)*, putting the *helm a-lee* and adjusting the mainsail to bring the wind on to the *weather bow* and hold that position, drifting slowly to *leeward*, despite the stormy weather that has made the tactic necessary.

From a common Teutonic strong verb, in OE 'hebban', corresponding to the Latin '*capere*', to take, but used in the ense of 'to lift' as early as the tenth century.

First attested, in the sense of 'throw', in 1592 in Robert Greene, *Orpharion* (1599 edition), XII, 68; in the sense of 'pull' in 1626 in Smith, *Accidence*, 27; in the noun sense of 'lift of the sea' in 1834 in Scott, *Midge*, 1834–5, 18.

heel   to *list* or tilt when under sail; the *after* end of a ship's *keel* and the lower end of the *sternpost*; the lower end of a mast, *boom*, or *bowsprit*.The *heel-brace* is the iron support at the bottom of a *rudder*. A *heel-chain* is that used for holding out the *jib-boom*. A *heeler* is a light sailing boat 'with a good (or clean) pair of heels' – i.e. a good turn of speed. *Heeling error* is *compass* error caused by the tilting of the ship and any nearby ironwork, etc., while the compass, being *gimballed*, remains horizontal. *Heeling force* is that component of the total aerodynamic force that acts at right angles to the boat's course. *Heeling moment* is the product of heeling force and the distance between the centre of effort and the centre of lateral resistance – in other words, a tall-masted ship with much canvas set will (surprise, surprise) heel more than one with a deep-*reefed* mainsail and, say, a *storm jib*. A *heel-jigger* is a *jigger* or light *tackle* fastened to the heel of a spar to help running it in and out. The *heel-knee* is the *compass piece* that attaches the *keel* to the *sternpost*. A *heel-lashing* is not a cruel naval punishment but the lashing which attaches the inner part of a *studding-sail boom* to the *yard*, or secures the *jib-boom*.

The verb and the noun are two distinct words. The verb (with its associated noun – rare now save in such expressions as 'angle of heel') is a corruption of the now obsolete 'hield', 'heeld' or 'heald', to tilt, from OE 'hieldan'. The more familiar noun is from OE 'hela', meaning the human heel, and extended figuratively to many uses including the two nautical sets of applications above.

First attested, in the sense of a ship's tilting, *c.* 1575 in Hooker, *Carew* (in *Archaeologia* XXVIII), 33; in the sense of the lowest part, *c.* 1602 in Marston, *Antonio and Mellida*, Part I, i, 16.

helm   the *tiller* or *wheel* controlling the *rudder;* also, to steer a boat with either. Since the tiller moves in the opposite direction to the rudder, and the wheel the same way as the rudder, orders to a helmsman at the wheel, which used to refer to the required direction of the tiller, were for many years ambiguous and confusing. '*Port* 10', for instance, meant that the wheel had to be put over 10 degrees to *starboard*. Not until the mid–1930s did all maritime nations come to relate orders to the rudder itself (and therefore not to the tiller, if any, but to the wheel, if any), so that the order instanced above was now 'starboard 10'. *Helm amidships* denotes the tiller or wheel position that puts the rudder in the *fore-and-aft* line of the vessel. A *helm angle indicator* or *helm indicator* is an anstrument with a pointer, geared to the wheel, showing the angle of the rudder relative to the fore-and-aft line – a boon to anyone more familiar with a tiller and unsure of the centre point of a wheel's turn. *Helm orders* are those given to the *helmsman*. The *helm port* is the gap through which the rudder passes through the hull. '*Helm's alee*' is a warning cry from the helmsman when *putting the helm down* to *go about*. *Putting the helm down* is the action needed to turn the rudder to windward; *putting the helm up* is the opposite: 'down' and 'up' are almost literal terms in a *dinghy* or small *yacht heeled* by the wind. The *helmsman* is the person, male or female, at the tiller or the wheel.

From OE 'helma' (weak, masculine), a handle, and totally unconnected with 'helm' in the sense of 'helmet', whose OE origin is the strong masculine 'helm', itself descended from the pre-Teutonic '*kelmo-s*', whose root '*kel-*', as in Latin ('celare'), meant to cover or conceal.

First attested *c.* AD 725 in the *Corpus Glossary* (Oldest English Texts, EETS, 1885), 4.

hemp   fibres (up to 3 metres long) from the hemp plant (*cannabis sativa*) long used for ropes, whether white or *tarred* as a preservative, because strong and not liable to stretch; now almost entirely superseded by synthetic fibres.

From OE 'henep', 'haenep', both obviously enough cognate with the Latin '*cannabis*' and the Greek '*kannabis*': cf. *canvas*.

First attested in a cordage context *c.* 1300 in *The Lay of Havelok the Dane* (EETS, 1868), 782.

hermaphrodite or **hermaphrodite brig**   a *brig-schooner* or sailing-ship with two masts, the *foremast rigged* as a *brig* with *square sails* set on *yards*, the *mainmast* rigged as a *schooner* with a square *topsail set* above a *gaff mainsail* (whereas a *brigantine* had no square sail on the main, which carried only *fore-and-aft* sails).

A figurative extension from the name of Ermaphroditos, in Greek mythology the son of Hermes and Aphrodite, who fused with the nymph Salmacis.

First attested in its nautical sense in 1794 in *The Elements and Practice of Rigging and Seamanship*, I, 220.

Highfield lever   pivoted tensioning lever, especially for *backstays*.

From the name of J.S. Highfield, rear-*commodore* of the Royal Thames Yacht Club, who invented it *c.* 1930 for his 15-metre *Dorina*.

First attested in 1976 in Kemp, *Oxford Companion*, 389.

hitch   one of a series of *knots* or *bends* whereby a rope is made fast to another or to some object, but can be released; thus to make fast. A *clove hitch* is made with two *half hitches*, the second reversed so that the *standing part* is between the hitches and tension on the rope tightens the hitch. A *half hitch* is a single turn round a *spar*, etc., with the end of the rope led back through the *bight*. A *rolling hitch* is formed by passing the end of the rope round the spar, then a second time so that it rides over the standing part and is carried across and up through the bight.

The verb seems to have preceded the noun, and originally meant 'to jerk'; it may have come from the same source as 'itch', whose origin is OE 'yicc(e)an', with the same meaning. In the sixteenth and seventeenth centuries 'hitch' seems to have been spelt without the initial 'h'.

First attested in 1627 in Smith, *Seaman's Grammar*, vii, 30.

hog   a large brush of birch twigs between two planks, for scrubbing a ship's *bottom*; the long *fore-and-aft* timber secured over the *keel*; to arch in the middle, as when the *bow* and *stern* have sagged, or the boat has been thus designed. *Hogged* describes a ship in this condition. A *hogged sheer* is a *sheer* line highly curved *amidships*, where it is high, as opposed to *bold sheer*, which is low amidships. *Hogging* is either scrubbing with a hog, or sagging amidships. A *hogging line* is a bottom line or chain *hauled* under the keel to fit collision mats or to use a hog.

All figurative extensions of the familiar word denoting a pig (or a sheep), referring to either its bristly skin or its arched back: the origin of the parent word is unknown.

First attested in 1769 in Falconer, *Dictionary* (1789 edition).

hoist   to raise (a *flag* or a sail, but not the *yard* of a *square-rigger*, which is *swayed*); a method of lifting; the *luff* of a *fore-and-aft* sail or the depth of a *square sail* at midpoint; the edge of a flag or *ensign* that lies along the *staff*, and to which the *halyards* are *bent*; a string of signal flags. To *hoist the flag* (said of an *Admiral*) means to assume command: at the start of a race, it is hoisted at the ten-minute gun. To *hoist pennants* is to make oneself known to others.

A corruption of the now obsolete 'hois' or 'hoiss', which has counterparts in most Scandinavian and Teutonic languages, although it remains uncertain which is the primary source: it may well be English. In the fifteenth and sixteenth centuries, this word was spelt 'hysse' or 'hyce': the 'oi' sound may be broad, rustic or nautical pronunciation. An obvious parallel is the French '*hisser*', with the same meaning.

First attested in 1697 in the *London Gazette* No. 3329/4.

hold   the below-decks compartment for stowing *cargo*, etc., often divided by *bulkheads* to limit shifting or rolling, and sometimes refrigerated. The verb 'hold' in its familiar sense has a few nautical applications. To *hold on to the land* is to keep near but not necessarily in sight of land. To *hold water* when *rowing* is to check *way* by keeping the *oar* blades still and vertical in the water. *Holding* or *holding ground* is the quality of the seabed for anchoring, mud, clay or sand being 'good holding', shingle the reverse.

Although the noun might appear to have a link with the verb, the former's true ancestor is the now obsolete 'holl', first attested in this sense in 1470 and sometimes (as in 1483) spelt 'hole'. The word's origin is OE 'hol': cf. the Dutch '*hol*' in the same sense. The final 'd' seems to have accrued by association with the familiar verb 'hold', derived from OE 'haldan'.

First attested as a specific nautical noun in 1591 in Ralegh, *Report*, 22.

holiday   a gap or patch unintentionally left when painting, varnishing, or *paying* a deck *seam*.

A fanciful extension from the familiar use of the word, originally a saint's day and now more often a vacation. Its OE source, 'haliydaey', existed as one word but also appeared as two: its first vowel originally gave 'haliday', but by the sixteenth century was superseded by its modern spelling.

First attested in its nautical sense in 1785 in Grose, *Classical Dictionary*.

holystone   block of soft sandstone used for scouring wet wooden decks.

At least three theories have been advanced for this word's etymology.

The least plausible is that holystones were stolen from graveyards: in fact, many tombstones were made of more durable material, up to and including granite. A common suggestion is that scrubbing either took place on Sunday or was a preparation for Sunday rounds or inspections: in fact, deck-scrubbing (like rust-chipping) was not necessarily weekly. The third possiblity is that the name arose from the need to kneel while scouring: this may be supported by the fact that seamen called large holystones 'bibles' and smaller ones 'prayer-books'.

First attested in its nautical sense in 1823 in Crabb, *Technological Dictionary*. Smyth, *Sailor's Word-book* (1867) offers the three etymological hypotheses noted above.

hooker   originally, a Dutch fishing vessel, two-masted with various *rigs*; a one-masted fishing *smack* on the Irish and South-West coast of England; a deprecating or affectionate term for a ship that is far from new. A Dutch hooker was originally *square-rigged* on the main, and had a small *topsail* above a *fore-and-aft* sail on the *mizen*, as well as two *jibs* on a *bowsprit*. Later, she was *sloop-rigged* with a *loose-footed mainsail*.

From the Dutch '*hoeker*', itself meaning a fishing boat – i.e. one that uses a hook.

First attested in 1641 in Smith, *Royal Fishings*, 4.

hoop   one of a set of wooden rings (of ash, elm or oak) riveted with copper nails, to slide up and down the *mainmast* secured to the *luff* of the *mainsail*, usually in older *gaff-rigged* craft; the square metal band that held the *stock* of an old-fashioned anchor to the *shank*; an old form of naval punishment for men accused of fighting each other, in which their left hands were bound to a wooden hoop and their right wielded a knotted cord each, to lash each other until one gave in – the loser to be given further lashes with the *cat-o'-nine-tails*.

From late OE 'hop', associated with similar words in Low German, Frisian, and Middle Dutch.

First attested, in its mast-hoop sense, in 1851 in the *Illustrated Catalogue* of the Great Exhibition, 971; as the band of an anchor, in 1867 in Smyth, *Sailor's Word-book*. The punishment is described in Kemp, *Oxford Companion*, 395.

hopper   *barge* or *lighter* to receive and take away the spoil brought up by dredging.

Indirectly from 'hop' (itself from OE 'hoppian', to jump about), because of the hopping motion of the 'hopper' in corn and other mills, similar to that of the loading device on this type of vessel.

First attested in its nautical sense in 1759 in Brand, *Newscastle-upon-Tyne* (1789), II, 588.

hornpipe   a traditional solo sailor's dance, originally three-in-a-measure, later two. Although now usually associated with sailors, the dance once had no maritime connotations – as may be conjectured from the title of one such tune, 'The Sailor's Hornpipe'.

Named after a now obsolete musical instrument not unlike a flageolet or a recorder, butwith the bell and mouthpiece made of horn (from OE 'horn', cognate with the Latin '*cornu*').

First attested *c.* 1485 in *The Digby Mysteries* (Abbotsford Club, 1835), V, final stage directions: 'Here mynstrallys, an hornpype'.

horns   the points of the *jaws* of a *boom* (or, far more usually, a *gaff*) where they meet the mast; the outer ends of the *crosstrees*; two projecting bars on the *after* part of a *rudder* as an alternative method of controlling it; the two outward-pointing parts of a *cleat*. *Horn timbers* are the pieces of wood that join the *keel* to the *transom* and form the backbone of the *counter*.

By analogy with an animal's horns (from OE 'horn', cognate with the Latin '*cornu*').

First attested in a nautical context in 1794 in *The Elements and Practice of Rigging and Seamanship*, I, 167.

horse   the *footrope* of a *yard* in a *square-rigger*; a raised metal bar running *athwartships* to which the *sheets* are led and along which they can slide or be positioned by means of a *traveller*; a *shoal* or sandbank, usually exposed at *low water*. The *horse latitudes* are those that lie between the prevailing *westerlies* and the *trade winds*, roughly between 30 degrees and 35 degrees North and South – areas of calm with light and variable winds. A *horsing iron* is a *caulking iron* for *horsing up* (i.e. compressing and hardening) the *oakum* in the *seams* of a deck.

From OE 'hors' and a common Teutonic root. The first two nautical applications seem to be based on the idea that a horse supports and carries a human or other burden, and makes travel possible. The connotation of 'shoal' is by analogy with the shape of a horse's back – which may also contribute to the (sometimes arched) bar for the sheets. As for the horse latitudes, various conjectures have been hazarded. First, that horses and other animals on the way to the Americas died from lack of food and water owing to the slow progress. Secondly, that the expression is a translation of the Spanish '*El Golfo de las Yeguas*' (the Gulf of the Mares), allegedly so named because ships were tossed about there by variable winds. Thirdly, that is these regions, sailing from Britain, seamen had just about worked off the *dead horse* for which they had been paid in advance. None of these suggestions seems altogether compelling. Might it be that in such latitudes the ship rolled and made slow headway, rather like a plodding carthorse?

First attested in a nautical context *c.* 1205 in *Layamon's Brut* (Society of Antiquaries, London, 1847), 28978.

house   to stow or secure anything in its proper place, especially against heavy weather. As an adjectival noun, the word has a number of nautical applications. A *houseboat* is a permanently *moored* or beached boat used for living in. A *houseflag* is the private *flag* used by a person, a shipping line, or a company; *houseline* (also called *housing*) is a small three-*stranded* line *tarred* and loosely made up for *lashings*, *seizings*, etc. A *housewife* (pronounced 'hussif') is a small rolled-up receptacle for sewing gear. *Housing* (when not a synonym for 'houseline') is the part of the mast between its *heel* and the upper deck.

From OE 'husian', to put in a house – which in turn is derived from the OE and common Teutonic 'hus'.

First attested as a nautical verb in 1769 in Falconer, *Dictionary* (1789 edition).

hoy   a small coastal vessel of up to 60 tons, single-decked and usually *fore-and-aft rigged* on a single mast, used mainly for carrying passengers from port to port; in the Netherlands, usually two-masted, *lug-rigged* on both.

From the Middle Dutch '*hoei*'; cf. the modern Dutch '*heu*'.

First attested in 1495 in *The Paston Letters*, No. 937, III, 388.

hulk   originally a large ship of up to 400 tons, contemporary with the *carrack* and often thus named; colloquially, any large ship with awkward-looking lines; any such vessel immobilised as, for example, a storehouse or a prison. Until the eighteenth century, the word was still being used also for *hull*, a meaning now obsolete for some 200 years. The prison hulks will be familiar to any reader of Dickens's *Great Expectations*.

From OE 'hulc', corresponding to the late Latin '*hulcus*' and perhaps related to the Greek '*holkas*', a vessel to be towed. 'Hulc' normally referred to a flat-bottomed, round-ended transport ship.

First attested *c.* 1050 in the Supplement to *Aelfric's Glossary* (Wright and Wuelcker, *Vocabularies*, second edition, 1884), 181, 28 – an exception to the normal meaning of the word, since it refers to the *Liburna*, a fast, light vessel.

hull   the body of a ship excluding her decks and superstructure, her masts, her *rigging* and all her internal fittings – in other words, her empty shell or 'hull'.

A ship is said to *hull* when moving without rudder, sail, or engine movement. To *hull* a ship is to penetrate her hull with gunfire. *Hull down*, of ships, refers to a position so far away that none of the hull is visible above the horizon. To *strike hull* is to take in all sail and *lie a-hull* with the *helm lashed a-lee*.

It seems highly likely, although unproven, that 'hull' in the nautical sense is the same word as in the sense of 'husk' or 'pod' – which is derived from OE 'hulu', with the same meaning, itself cognate with the Old High German '*hulla*' (modern German '*Huelle*', a cloak or covering). As meaning 'husk', 'hull' is first attested *c.* AD 1000.

First attested in its nautical sense *c.* 1440 in *Promptorium parvulorum* (Camden Society, 1843–65), 243/1.

hullock   a small piece of sail spread in heavy weather to keep the ship's *head* in the desired direction to the sea (either the *mizen course*, to keep her head to the sea, or the *foresail*, to lay her head the other way.

The origin of this obsolescent word remains unknown, although the diminutive '-ock' (as in 'hillock') clearly refers to the size of the scrap of *canvas*. The first part of the word seems to have only a tenuous link with *hull* unless in its use as a verb, in which the ship moves because the wind works on her hull: might the canvas be considered to act as an extra piece of hull? It seems unlikely.

First attested in 1553 in Hakluyt, *Principall Navigations* (1589), 269.

hurricane   a tropical or sub-tropical revolving *storm* with winds of *force 12* or more on the *Beaufort scale* (64 *knots* or more),

From the Spanish '*huracan*', itself from the Old Spanish '*furacan*'; in English, the word retained its Hispanic appearance until the mid seventeenth century, when the present spelling became common (and after 1688 virtually invariable).

First attested in 1555 in Eden, *Decades* (ed. Arber, 1885).

Inboard   within the framework of the ship; closer to her centre line. Originally the phrase 'in board'. (See *board*).

First attested in 1830 in Cooper, *Water Witch*, III, vii, 216.

indraft, indraught   a *current* setting towards the land in a bay or a *sound*, or up an *estuary*. From *draught*.

First attested in 1594 in Thomas Blundevil, *Exercises* (1636 edition), vii, liv, 744.

inhaul   rope used for *hauling* in anything that has been hauled *outboard*, e.g. the *jib* from the *bowsprit* end; originally known as an 'inhauler'. Cf. *downhaul, outhaul*. From *haul*.

First attested in 1860 in *The Mercantile Marine Magazine*, VII, 114.

in irons   *head to wind* and failing to *pay off* on either *tack*.

A figurative extension of the same expression in its meaning of 'fettered'; 'iron' is from OE 'iren', 'isern', and 'isen' – cf. the German '*Eisen*' and similar words in other Teutonic languages.

First attested as a nautical phrase in 1832 in Marryat, *Newton Forster*, xxii.

in soundings   in water shallow enough for *soundings* to indicate approximate position, traditionally within the 100-*fathom* line, i.e. on the continental shelf. From the verb *sound*, which in turn is an adaptation of the French '*sonder*', and in the Middle Ages had the now obsolete meaning of 'to pierce'; its nautical sense is first attested in the late fifteenth century, although 'sounding-line' dates from 1336.

'In sounding' (singular) is first attested at an unspecified date
in the fifteenth century, in *Sailing Directions* (Hakluyt Society,
1889), 21; 'in soundings' (plural) in 1694 in Narborough,
Journal (in *Several Late Voyages*, 1711), I, 18.

in stays   *head to wind* in the process of *going about* from
one *tack* to another, but not *in irons*.

'Stay' is derived from the OE 'staey', which had the modern
nautical meaning; the OED implies that 'in stays' is derived from
this primary sense of the word, but without specifying how. In
the early sixteenth century, some fifty years before anything like
the expression is first attested, the word 'stay' was being used
in the more general sense of 'a halt'; and it seems at least plausible that this was the real origin of the phrase, rather than any
direct connection with cordage.

A variant of the phrase (of which there were many, including
'at stays', 'on stays', etc.) is first attested in 1586 in Sidney,
Arcadia (1912 edition), I, I, 11. The actual phrase 'in stays' is
first attested in 1823 in Scoresby, *Journal*, 91.

inwale   a *strake* on the inner upper edge of a wooden *hull*
(cf. *gunwale*).

From 'in' and 'wale': see *gunwale*.

First attested in 1875 in Walsh, 'Stonehenge', in *Manual of
British Rural Sports*, 1859 (1875 edition), II, VIII, ii, 1, 639.

Irish horse   especially tough or pungent salt beef. One of
many expressions casting aspersions on the Irish. *Irish
pennants* are frayed or loose ends of rope, etc. An *Irishman's
hurricane* is a flat calm with perhaps some drizzle. An
Irishman's reef is the *head* of a sail tied up or knotted.

The word 'Irish' is derived from 'Ir-', the stem of OE 'I'ras',
meaning the inhabitants of Ireland.

First attested in Smollett, *Roderick Random*, I, xxxiii, 291.

Jack   a sailor in the British Navy (also *Jack Tar*, from
tarpaulin); a *schooner-rigged* vessel used in the
Newfoundland fisheries; a small nautical *flag* flown on a staff
at the *stem* when at anchor; a general diminutive or qualifier
applied to many nautical nouns. A *Jack Adams* was an argu-
mentative fool. *Jack Dusty* or *Jack of the dust*, originally the
purser's assistant in the bread room, is the *rating* dealing with
victualling stores. *Jack-in-the-basket* is a mark in coastal
waters, usually a box or basket on top of a pole, to indicate a
shoal, etc. A *jackrope* is the *lacing* used to *bend* on the *foot*
of a *boomed mainsail*. A *jackstaff* is that on which the jack

is flown. A *jackstay* is a wire rope to carry a *traveller*, etc., or a rod or rope on a *yard*, to which a sail may be bent, but now most important as a *fore-and-aft lifeline* on either side of a boat on to which the safety harness is clipped. A *Jack Strop* or *Jack my hearty* is a young boaster. A *jackyard* is a small *boom* to carry a *topsail*.

However obscurely, all these usages seems to be derived from the by-name 'Jack', used since ME as a familiar form of 'John', although originally disyllabic, as in 'Jacce', 'Jakke' or 'Jacke'.

First attested in the sense of a sailor in 1659 in Daniel Pell, *Pelagos*, Proem B iv; as a fishing vessel, in 1891 in the *Report of the United States Commissioner of Fish and Fisheries*, Appendix VI, 529; as a flag, in 1633 in *Sailing Instructions* (Sloane MS) 2682, 1f. 51.

jackass   a heavily-built Newfoundland open boat; (mainly US) a *hawse-bag*. To *jackass* a *boom* is to switch a *spinnaker* boom from one side to the other. A *jackass-barque* is a four-masted ship *square-rigged* on the two *foremost* masts and *fore-and-aft rigged* on the two *after* masts. A *jackass rig* is any such unusual combination of *rigs*. A *jackass schooner* is a three-masted *schooner* with no main *topmast* and *square sails* set on her *foremast*. From its animal meaning (a male ass), via the connotation of dullness, stupidity, stubbornness or eccentricity.

First attested in 1867 in Smyth, *Sailor's Word-book*.

Jacob's ladder   a rope ladder with wooden steps for ascending the *rigging*, e.g. on a *topgallant* mast where there are no *ratlines*; the rope ladder hanging from the *boom* of a warship, to which ship's boats are made fast in harbour; a series of shakes and fractures, one above another, in a wooden *spar*.

An allusion to *Genesis*, xxviii, 12: 'And he [Jacob] dreamed, and behold a ladder set up on earth, and the top of it reached to heaven: and behold the angels of God ascending and descending on it.'

First attested in a nautical context in 1840 in Marryat, *Poor Jack*, xxviii.

jam cleat, jamming cleat or **jammer**   a *cleat* (of various designs) with a serrated V or spring action which will hold a rope without the need to pass it round the *horns*.

From 'jam' in its sense of squeezing tightly, which in turn seems to be associated with 'champ', to chew. 'Champ' in that sense is first attested in 1530, but has no clear connection with other or anterior languages, and may well simply be onomatopoeic. This may also be the case with 'jam' in both its familiar senses (since the preserve is the result of crushing or 'champing' fruit).

'Jam' as a verb is first attested in 1706 in Sewall, *Diary* (1674–1729, published 1878–82), 1879, II, 156, entry for 6 March.

Jamie Green   a sail set below the *jib-boom* on the *dolphin striker* (in tea *clippers*).

Although obviously enough from a personal name, this expression remains of unknown origin: presumably, a *skipper* of that name originated this unusual *rig*.

First attested in 1866 in the *Journal* of a Captain Keay, reproduced in Lubbock, *China Clippers* (1914), Appendix H, p.xxi (entry for 20 June).

jaw   the distance along a rope that includes each of its *strands* once; (in the plural) the fork of a *gaff* that engages with the mast; (of a *block*) the slot for the *sheave*; (of a shackle) the space between the *lugs*. Long-*jawed* or slack-*jawed* rope is one in which the *lay* has become loose. *Jawrope* is that across the jaws of a gaff to keep it to the mast.

A figurative extension of the familiar word, which itself probably comes from ME 'chowe', mutated into 'jowe' in the fourteenth century and 'jawe' in the fifteenth.

First attested in the 'rope' sense in 1961 in Burgess, *Dictionary*, 123; in the 'gaff' sense in 1835 in Marryat, *The Pirate*, viii.

jeers   heavy *tackle* for hoisting and lowering the lower *yards*. A *jeer capstan* was fitted between the *foremast* and the main: it was here that floggings took place.

Of unknown origin: unconnected with derision.

First attested in 1495 in *Naval Accounts* (Navy Records Society, 1896) 188: 'Jeres for the Mayne takell'.

jetsam (also *jetson*)   goods or equipment deliberately thrown *overboard*.

From *jettison*: the elision of the central vowel seems to have occurred in speech in the sixteenth century, when the two words diverged towards their present meanings.

First attested in 1591 in *Articles Concerning the Admiralty*, 21 July, 6.

jettison   to throw *overboard*, sometimes in order to lighten a ship in distress. The noun, meaning the act of throwing, precedes the noun, although the latter is now more commonly used.

From the Anglo-French *'getteson'* (OF *'getaison'*), and the Latin *'jactatio'* (throwing).

First attested in English in 1425 in the *Rolls of Parliament* 1278–1503 (1767–77), IV, 394/1.

jetty   a *mole, pier*, or *wharf*.

From OF *'getée'* or *'jetée'*, the act of throwing or the 'thrown-out' (projecting) part of a building; from the eighteenth century onwards, the word was sometimes treated and spelt as French. Its further origin is obviously the French verb *'jeter'*, to throw – which is also, indirectly, the source of the English 'jut'.

First attested in 1412–20 in Lydgate, *Chronicle of Troy* (EETS, 1906–10), II, xxi (Digby MS 230) 1f. 99/1

jewel-block   each of the two small *blocks* suspended at the ends of *yards* through which the *studdingsail halyards* are *rove*. The jewel-blocks were also used for *reeving* the rope for execution by hanging at the *yard-arm*.

Thought by the OED to be a sailors' 'fanciful appellation'; but perhaps more simply a corruption of 'dual'.

First attested in 1769 in Falconer, *Dictionary* (1776).

Jew's harp   the *shackle* attaching a chain *cable* to an anchor.

So called from its resemblance in shape to the musical instrument of that name; but this in turn, originally known as a 'Jew's trump', is of uncertain origin.

The instrument may have been made, sold, or exported to England by Jews, or thought to have been; it may have been so called because of Biblical mention of harps and trumps; it may have been named thus as an opprobrious reference to its economical nature and to the alleged parsimony of Jews.

First attested in its nautical sense in 1750 in Blanckley, *Naval Expositor*, 83.

jib   originally (and, some insist, properly) the *foremost* triangular sail in a sailing vessel, set between the *foremasthead* and the *bowsprit* end – the sail *aft* of it, set on the *forestay* between the foremasthead and the *stem*, being known as the *forestaysail* or *staysail*. Nowadays, such staysails are almost universally known as 'jibs'. Large *square-rigged* ships of the late nineteenth and early twentieth centuries carried as many as six jibs: from *forward aft* they were the *jib-of-jibs*, the *spindle jib*, the *flying jib*, the *outer jib*, the *inner jib*, and the *storm jib*. A *jib-boom* is an extension of the *bowsprit* used for setting a jib. A *jib-club* is a small *boom* used on the *foot* of a jib. A *jib downhaul* is a rope used for hauling down the jib. A *jib guy* is a stout rope to support the jib-boom. A *jib halyard* is that used for hoisting the jib. *Jib-headed* (of a sail) means triangular instead of square. A *jib-header* is a *topsail* shaped like a jib. A *jib-iron* is a round iron hoop with hook and *tackle* used to haul out the *tack* of the jib. *Jib netting* is network under a jib-boom to prevent men and sails falling into the sea. The *jib sheets* are those used to control it, now via *winches* in boats of any size. The *jib stay* is that on which the jib is set. A *jib stick* is a *whisker pole*. A *jib topsail* is one set above the jib and *hanked* to the topmost *stay*. A *jib traveller* is a jib-iron.

The word's etymology remains obscure. It may be an abbreviation of 'gibbet', since it was suspended from the *masthead*. It may equally be cognate with the Danish *'gibbe'*, meaning to pull a sail or *yard* from one side of the ship to the other (itself undoubtedly related to *gybe*). However, the comparatively rare verb 'jib', which this source may supply, is not attested until 30 years after the first attestation of 'jib' as a noun, which has no counterparts in other languages.

First attested in 1661 in the *Inventory of the Swallow Ketch* in *State Papers Domestic, Charles II*, xxxv, 10, 1.

jigger   a light *tackle* with one single and one double *block*, at best multiplying the power by four; a small sail set right *aft*. A *jigger-mast* is strictly a mast for the jigger, although it has also been used for the *mizen* of a *yawl* or for the fourth mast in a five- or six-masted *schooner*.

The word's etymology is uncertain, although as in its non-nautical senses it seems connected with smallness, neatness, and often jerky motion. This last suggests an association with the noun and verb indicating dancing; but the origin of 'jig' in this sense is equally obscure, since OF *'gigue'*, meaning a crude violin, was obsolete before 'jig' appeared, and the modern French *'gigue'*, meaning the dance, seems to have been formed from the English 'jig'.

First attested as a nautical tackle in 1726 in Roberts, *Four Years' Voyages*, 119; as a sail, in 1867 in Smyth, *Sailor's Wordbook*.

jill about   to move around idly with no set course.

The etymology of this expression is complex and rather far-fetched. 'Jill' seems to be a variant of 'gill', which as a verb is thought to be derived from the noun meaning a measure (of wine, etc.), whose origin is OF *'gille'* or *'gelle'*, itself descended from the Latin *'gillo'*, *'gellus'*, a vessel or measure. The move from the noun to the verb is alleged to have occurred in the eighteenth century, when 'gilling' meant drinking white wine before dinner: this in turn appears to have spawned the expression 'gilling [or jilling] about', first attested in 1876 in Robinson, *Glossary*: *'Jilling*, "He goes gilling about", drinking his half-pints at different places, as the toper.'

First attested in a nautical context in 1955 in *The Times*, 18 July, 9/6.

jockey pole   metal *spar* to prevent the *spinnaker guy rope* *fouling* the *stanchions* or the *shrouds*: also known as a *reaching strut*, it is attached to the mast on the same side as the *spinnaker pole*.

One of the many figurative extensions of the word 'jockey' that imply riding on something or acting as an auxiliary. 'Jockey' itself began as a diminutive or by-name of John or Jack, especially in Scotland and the North of England.

First attested in 1976 in Kemp, *Oxford Companion*, 433.

jolly   a Royal Marine. Originally, all soldiers carried *on board* a British warship were known as 'jollies', a 'tame jolly' being a militiaman and a 'royal jolly' a Marine.

Of doubly uncertain origin. The original and familiar word 'jolly' is derived from ME and OF *'jolif'*, meaning festive, which in turn may be associated with ON *'jol'* – Yule. The slang expression for a shipboard soldier may be derived from a specific sense of 'jolly', i.e. 'finely dressed', or simply from its more common meaning of 'high-spirited'.

First attested in its nautical sense in 1829 in Marryat, *The Naval Officer*, xi.

jolly-boat   *clinker-built* ship's rowing-boat with a bluff *bow* and wide *transom*, usually hoisted in *davits* at the *stern* of a ship and used for inspection, landing, etc.

Possibly from a word of fifteenth-century origin, 'jolywat', which seems to have meant much the same thing, but whose derivation is obscure; but, as written, perhaps related to a number of words in Teutonic languages denoting a small boat, such as the Danish, Low German, and Swedish *'jolle'* and the Dutch *'jol'* – although the 'j' in these languages usually turns into an English 'y', as in *yawl*, which actually corresponds to these words. That might make 'jolywat' a more plausible contender for the ancestry of 'jolly-boat': but if so it explains little, since the supposed source of 'jolywat', the Spanish and Portuguese *'galeota'*, was a very different and much bigger craft; the supposed transformation of a hard Iberian 'g' into a soft, voiced English 'j' is a further argument against the hypothesis.

First attested in 1727–41 in Ephraim Chambers, *Cyclopaedia*.

Jolly Roger   a flag supposedly flown by *pirates*, consisting or a white skull (and sometimes crossed bones beneath it) on a black ground. Another version, a black skeleton on a yellow field, was perhaps a misreading of the flag of Imperial Austria, which during the eighteenth century was used as a flag of convenience by *privateers*. It seems that black flags were sometimes flown by pirates; but there is no hard evidence that the skull-and-crossbones was.

The word 'Roger', from the personal name, OF *'Roger'*, *'Rogier'* and Old High German *'Ruodeger'*, *'Hrodger'*, had by 1700 come to be slang for a penis, and may be figuratively employed in the expression 'Jolly Roger'. What made it festive

is less easy to conjecture, unless carousing over the spoils.
First attested in 1785 in Grose, *A Classical Dictionary.*

jumbo   a large *fore staysail* in a *fore-and-aft rigged* ship;
sometimes, its *club* or *boom.*

Originally, it seems, from the second part of 'mumbo-jumbo',
a word used since the eighteenth century to denote a West
African god, idol or cult. The earliest meaning of 'jumbo' was
a big or clumsy person, animal, or things: it was especially
applied to a famous elephant in the London Zoo, sold to the
showman P.T. Barnum in 1882.

First attested in its nautical sense in 1912 in *Outing,* August,
629/2.

jumper   a rope, chain, or wire made fast as a *preventer* to
stop a *yard,* mast etc., bending, jumping, or springing up under
stress: most often leading from the outer end of the *jib-boom*
in a *square-rigger* to the *dolphin striker,* helping to *stay* the
fore topgallant mast. A *jumper stay* is one that runs *forward*
from the *masthead,* over a *jumper strut* jutting forward, and
back to the *cross-trees* (or, in a racing *yacht,* often lower) to
add stiffness to the mast and prevent its bowing forward, notably
in *fractional rig,* where the *forestay* is secured well below the
masthead. *Jumper wire* (or *jumping wire*) is serrated wire
leading from the *stemhead* of a submarine back over the
conning-tower to the *stern,* and used to cut a way through
defensive netting. A *jumping ladder* is a light rope ladder used
over the side of a ship. *Jumping ship,* now normally used to
describe desertion before sailing, also sometimes denotes the
crew's jumping together to dislodge a boat that has run *aground.*

From the verb 'jump', apparently of onomatopoeic origin and
unknown before about 1500.

First attested in a nautical context in 1856 in Kane, *Arctic
Explorations,* I, viii, 87.

junk   old worn-out rope, cut into lengths for other uses, such
as *swabs, fenders,* etc.; slang for salt beef and pork used *on
board*; oriental sailing vessel, flat-bottomed, high-*sterned,* with
square *bows* and two or three masts carrying *lugsails* often made
of matting with horizontal *battens,* each sail having its own *sheet.*

In the sense of 'old rope', the word's derivation is unknown:
it is almost certainly distinct from an obsolete word 'junk'
meaning 'rush' (the plant). The food sense is a figurative extension of the 'old rope' sense. The name of the oriental vessel is
ultimately derived from the thirteenth-century (or earlier)
Javanese '*djon*', meaning a large vessel: cf. the Malayalam
'*adjong*'. In this usage, the word entered English by way of other
European languages, notably the Portuguese '*junco*'.

First attested in its 'old rope' sense in 1485 in *Naval Accounts* (Navy Records Society, 1896), 49; in its 'food' sense, in 1762 in Smollett, *Launcelot Greaves*, xiii; as a sailing vessel, with the spelling 'Giunche', in 1555 in Eden, *Decades* (Arber 1885), 215. More orthodox spellings appeared in the seventeenth century.

jury emergency makeshift: most often used in combinations such as *jury anchor*, *jury mast*, *jury rig*, *jury rudder*, *jury tiller*, etc.

Not, apparently, a contraction of 'injury', for which there is no evidence. A plausible suggestion is that the term is a jocular extension of the term for a panel of jurors. However, the word 'jurory', meaning slander or false witness, from OF *'jurerie'*, was current as early as the fourteenth century, and may have lent weight to the expression.

First attested in its nautical sense in 1616 in Smith, *New-England*.

Kayak originally, an Eskimo or Inuit wooden canoe covered with sealskin with a hole for the canoeist; now, any canoe of similar design.

From the Eskimo or Inuit word, common to all dialects from Greenland to Alaska, and pronounced with very guttural consonants. There is no connection with the Arabic *caique*. If a woman is using the canoe it is known as a *'umiak'*.

First attested in 1662 in Davies, translation of A.Olearius, *Voyages and Travels*, 71.

keckle to cover a rope *cable* with old rope, bound in the *lay* and sometimes *served* over it, to prevent chafe in the *hawse-holes*.

Of unknown etymology: the fact that it used sometimes to be spelt 'cackle' by no means implies cacchination.

First attested in 1627 in Smith, *Seaman's Grammar*, vii, 30.

kedge small auxiliary anchor, often used to *warp* a ship from one *berth* to another or to haul her off a *shoal*; thus to warp a ship.

Although occasionally spelt 'catch' and possibly assciated with 'cadge', the word's origin remains obscure. 'Cadge' sometimes meant to tie or fasten, as well as to peddle or to beg (perhaps by buttonholing); and 'cagging-anchor' is attested before the verb 'kedge', which may be a back-formation: the noun in turn is attested later than the verb.

First attested in 1627 in Smith, *Seaman's Grammar*, vii, 29.

keel the lowest main timber of a wooden ship, or the lowest continuous line of plates of an iron or steel ship; (loosely) the *ballast keel* projecting below it in a *yacht*; a small flat-bottomed *lighter*; to turn a boat keel upwards. A *ballast keel* is the projecting keel of a yacht carrying her *ballast* for stability. *Bilgekeels* are twin keels enabling a ship to be supported upright on the *launching ways*, on the floor of a *dry dock*, etc., or (in the case of a yacht) to take the *ground*. A *fin keel* (of a yacht) is a deep, narrow and short *fore-and-aft* keel, giving quick manoeuvrability. A *fin-and-bulb* keel is similar, with ballast in a bulb at its base. *Keel blocks* are those on which a ship rests on the floor of a building slip or in a dry dck. *Keel-hauling* was a naval punishment in which the culprit was hoisted on a rope to one *yard-arm*, dropped into the sea, then dragged under the keel before being hoisted to the opposite yard-arm for further similar treatment. *Keel-raking* involved, usually, only one half of this ordeal. A *keel-rope* is the *limber-rope* threaded through the *limbers* alongside the keel for clearing the *bilges*.

From ON '*kjol-r*'.

First attested in a combination (keel-rope) in 1352 in *Exchequer Accounts* Q.R. Bundle 20 in the Public Record Office.

keelson (also **kelson** and still pronounced thus)   an inner *keel* or *stringer* bolted to the keel over the floor timbers, or (in a steel ship) the metal equivalent.

Not 'son of the keel', but associated with it via the first part of the word. The nearest conjectural ancestor, unrecorded, would probably have been ON '*kjolsvin*' or '*kjalsvin*': the equivalents in other Teutonic languages are (in Swedish) '*koelsvin*', in Dutch '*kolzwijn*', in German '*Kielschwein*', etc. Here, the second part of the word is equivalent to the English 'swine'; and although no one knows how this animal reference arose, it is not an isolated instance: cf. *cat, dog, hog, horse*, all of which have their place in the language of sailing. A conjectural ME forerunner of the modern word might be 'kelswin' – the second syllable being eventually contracted, as in *boatswain*, which became in turn 'boteson', 'boson' and 'bos'n'.

First attested *c.* 1611 in Chapman, translation of *Iliads* [*sic*], I, 426.

kennet   a 1706 error for *kevel*.

kentledge   pig-iron used as *ballast*, usually on the *keelson* plates. *Limber-kentledge* was kentledge laid in the *limbers*. *Kentledge-goods* were often heavy *cargo* items used as ballast.

Of uncertain origin: possibly from 'quintal' with '-age' addded, rather as in *stowage, dunnage*, etc.

First attested in 1607 by William Keeling (discoverer of the Cocos Islands) in Purchas, *Pilgrimes* (1625–6), III, vi, 2, 191.

ketch   a two-masted sailing vessel that has undergone many
changes of size, use, and design but is now commonly a *yacht*
with the *mizen* mast *forward* of the *rudder-head* (as distinct
from a *yawl*, where the mizen is *aft* of it) and/or with a *mizen
sail* at least half the area of the main. Note, however, that this
description also fits a number of two-masted beach boats that
are nevertheless known as yawls, such as the Norfolk yawl.

Originally a 'catch', from ME 'cache', which appears in the
later fifteenth century, and in the sixteenth century as 'catch'.
The reference may just possibly be to fishing, but is more likely
to be to swift pursuit, as in the case of *yacht*, from the Dutch
'jagt', *'jacht'*, chase. In the seventeenth century, however,
ketches were thought not fast but merely handy, as witness
Glanville, *Voyage to Cadiz*, 1625 (Camden Society, 1883), 116:
'Catches, being short and round built, bee verie apt to turne up
and downe, and usefull to goe to and fro, and to carry messages
between shipp and shipp almost with anie wind.'

First attested as spelt 'ketch' in 1655 in Cromwell, *Letters and
Speeches* (ed. Carlyle, 1845), letter of 13 June.

kevel (or **kennet**)   a large *cleat*, usually on the *gunwale* of a
sailing vessel, made of two upright pieces of wood and used for
belaying ropes. *Kevel-heads* are the ends of a vessel's top
timbers continued above the gunwale to act as a kevel. *Kennet*,
although existing in two obsolete senses in its own right, was in
this nautical sense a misreading in 1706 by John Kersey in his
(the sixth) edition of Phillips, *New World*: the mistake was copied
by at least four subsequent unalert lexicographers.

From the Old Norman French *'keville'* (modern *'cheville'*), a
peg or pin.

First attested in its nautical sense *c.* 1330 in Manning, *Story
of England* (Rolls Series, 1887), 12062.

kicking strap   a rope or wire *tackle* used as a *martingale*,
to prevent the boom of a *yacht* or racing *dinghy* from lifting,
especially when *reaching* or *running*; known in the US as a
boom vang.

Originally a strap adjusted to prevent a horse from kicking
(compare a martingale, used to keep the animal's head down);
the origin of 'kick' is a ME word 'kike' or 'kyke' about which
no more is known: it has no connection with opprobrious
modern US slang, and may be onomatopoeic.

First attested in its nautical sense in 1951 in Pennant, *Young
Sailor*, v, 70.

killick (or **killock**)   originally, a heavy stone used as an anchor,
or a small real anchor; now slang for the anchor; also, naval
slang for a leading seaman, whose badge is a *foul* anchor sewn

on his sleeve. Of unknown origin.

First attested as a form of anchor in 1630 in Winthrop, *New England* (1825 edition), I, 40; as a badge in 1915 in 'Bartimeus' (Sir Lewis Ritchie), *A Tall Ship*, iii, 62.

kingpost   a short post or mast close to the *cargo hatches*, from which a cargo *derrick* is operated.

'King' is derived from a common Teutonic word which in OE was 'cyning'; by extension, it implies importance or centrality. In building carpentry, a kingpost is the perpendicular post in the centre of a roof truss. The *kingplank* is the central main plank in a deck. The *kingspoke* is the spoke in a ship's *wheel* which is upright when the *rudder* is aligned *fore-and-aft*.

First attested in its nautical sense in 1927in Bradford, *Sea Terms*, 95/2.

kite   light-weight, light-weather lofty sail – originally, all the sails in a *square-rigger* that were set above the *topsails*, but later those set above the *topgallants,* including *studding-sails* and *jib-topsails*; nowadays, loosely, a *spinnaker*. A *kite drag* is a *drogue rigged* like a kite with cross *spars* and *canvas*, plus a weight at the tail.

From the familiar word for the toy, itself derived from the bird of prey, whose name originated in OE as 'cyta', with no similar word appearing in any related language.

First attested in its nautical sense in 1856 in Emerson, *English Traits*, ii, 33.

knee   roughly L-shaped piece of wood or metal used to strengthen two parts of a vessel that meet more or less at right angles. A *bosom knee* is fixed horizontally between the *after* side of a *beam* and the ship's side. A *carling knee* strengthens the right angle between a *carling* and a beam. A *hanging knee* fits vertically under the end of a deck beam. A *lodging knee* is like a bosom knee but fixed on the *forward* side of the beam. A *stern knee* joins the *sternpost* or the*transom* to the *keel*.

From comparison with the human joint, whose name is derived from a common Teutonic root whose OE offshoot was 'cneow' or 'cneo'; in the background there is also a Sanskrit word '*janu*', related to the French '*genou*'.

First attested in a nautical context, though referring to naturally occuring, not manmade knees in the timber, in 1352 in the *Exchequer Accounts* Q.R., Bundle 20, No.27, in the Public Record Office.

knight-heads   timbers on each side of the *bow* that support the *bowsprit*; earlier, two timber frames *abaft* the *foremast* to support the ends of the *windlasses*.

Probably derived by comparison from the obsolete sense of 'knights', which were strong posts or *bitts* on the deck with *sheaves* for the *halyards*: this sense is first attested in 1495, half a century after 'knight' is first attested as a chess piece, and suggesting that the latter may have inspired the figurative nautical use. This hypothesis finds support in Falconer, *Dictionary* (1789 edition), which remarks of the bitts that 'Their upper parts only are denominated knight-heads... being formerly embellished with a figure designed to resemble a human head.' The original and familiar word 'knight', from a common West German word, in OE 'cniht' or 'cneoht', simply meant lad or boy, as it often still does in other languages.

First attested in its original sense in 1711 in Sutherland, *Ship Builder's Assistant*, 115; in the sense of supports for the bowsprit, in 1883 in *The Century Magazine*, October, 946/2.

knock-down   a *capsize* with masts and sails in the water (but not necessarily with the boat failing to right herself). To *knock down* (apart from being the verb corresponding to the noun) is also to knock the hoops off an empty *cask* so that its *staves* may be stored in a smaller space.

'Knock' is derived from the late OE 'cnocian', probably of echoic origin. Although the original verb and noun imply physical collision, often with a sharp sound, a knock-down may be the result of wind as well as wave – no less sudden and alarming.

First attested in 1888 in *Scribner's Magazine*, May, 526/1.

knot   an intertwining of one or more ropes to fasten them together or to something else, or as a *stopper* to prevent slippage; the nautical measure of speed, one *nautical mile* per hour; formerly, one division of the *log line*. Sticklers or pedants sometimes assert that in nautical terms a knot is one in which a rope is involved only with itself, to make a stopper knot (e.g. a *figure-of-eight knot*, in which one end of a *half hitch* is passed 'the wrong way' through the loop), or such complex knots as a *manrope knot* (which makes a 'clump' on the end of, e.g., a handrail rope), a *Matthew Walker* (with a similar purpose), a *Turk's head* (a continuously plaited ring), etc. But the word 'knot' can also refer to a *splice* or to a *reef knot* (in which two ropes are symmetrically joined by interlinked loops). Equally, it is sometimes said that a knot is permanent but a *bend* or *hitch* only temporary: yet the stopper knots in *jib sheets* obviously break this alleged 'rule'. In fact, the word 'knot' is commonly used for all kinds of *bend, hitch,* or *splice*. Less confusion surrounds the knot as a measure of speed. The term originated with the *chip log*, whose knots were spaced at intervals of 47 feet 3 inches: the ship's speed was reckoned by the number of these that ran out while a 28-second hourglass emptied itself, a nautical mile being 6080 feet, and the number of knots being twice the number of metres per second. This is why sticklers object to those who, equating the 'knot' to the nautical mile, refer to 'knots per hour'. However, this solecism was committed as long ago as 1748 by George Anson in his *Voyage Round the World* and in 1833 by as popular and prolific a writer as Captain Frederick Marryat in *Peter Simple* – not to mention Captain James Cook himself, in his *Voyages* (1799 edition), V, 1828. Will such instances silence *Jack Strops*?

From OE 'cnotta', a knot or knob: cf. the verb 'knit'. First attested in ropework *c.* AD 1000 in Aelfric, *Homilies* (ed Thorpe, 1844–6), II, 28; as a measure of speed, in 1633 in James, *The Strange and Dangerous Voyage*, 24.

kye   a skinflint sailor; cocoa or hot chocolate.

The word's origin is unknown; but the OED draws attention to 'kyish', which the *English Dialect Dictionary* defines as 'dirty'.

First attested as 'miser' in 1929 in Bowen, *Sea Slang*; as 'beverage', in 1943 in Hunt and Pringle, *Service Slang*, 42.

Labour   (of a ship) to roll or pitch heavily in rough seas. From the more general meaning of the verb, implying travail; the original source for the noun is OF *'labor'* (cf. Latin) and, for the verb, OF *'laborer'* modern *'labourer'*.

First attested in this nautical sense in 1627 in Smith, *Seaman's Grammar*, ix, 40.

lace   to attach a sail to a *gaff* or *boom* by passing a cord alternately through each eyelet hole and round the *spar*. The cord used in this process is *lacing*. A *lacing eye* is a bridge-shaped metal fitting attached to the structure to provide anchorage for the lacing of an awning, etc. A *lacing hook* is half of a lacing eye. *Lacing reefing* is similar to *points reefing* except that the attachment is by a continuous cord.

The original, obsolete meaning of 'lace' was a snare, hence later a draw-string: the noun was an adaptation of OF *'laz'*, *'las'*, from the popular Latin *'lacium'*. The verb has a similar derivation, being adapted from OF *'lacier'* (popular Latin *'laciare'*).

First attested in its nautical sense in 1635 in Brereton, *Travels* (Chetham Society, 1844), 169.

ladder   stairs *on board*; ranging system for naval gunnery.

From OE 'hlaed(d)er', which in turn is from a Teutonic root *'hli'*, whose source may be the Aryan *'kli-'* (cf. the Greek *'climax'* and conceivably also 'climb'). The traditional nautical use of the term, usually with a qualifying word, dates from the days when ladders in the familiar sense, either fixed or portable, were used for upward or downward access from deck to deck. As it is, many ladders in the nautical sense, which might elsewhere be called steps or stairs, are almost as steep as ladders in the familiar sense.

First attested in 1616 in Smith, *Accidence*, 13.

lagan   goods sunk at sea with a *buoy* so that they can be recovered; *cargo* inside a sunken ship; any goods lying on the seabed.

Originally perhaps from a Scandinavian root underlying the verbs 'lay' and 'lie' – cf. ON '*logn*', a net laid in the sea – but more immediately derived from OF '*lagan*', '*laguen*', '*lagand*' and from the medieval Latin '*laganum*'. The OED considers that the alternative spelling 'ligan' arose from 'pseudo-etymology'.

First attested in 1200 in the *Carta de Dunewic* in Stubbs (ed.), *Select Charters* (1895 edition), 311.

laid   (or rope) made by twisting the fibres and/or *strands* (as contrasted with braided rope, which is plaited). A *cable-laid* rope consists of three *hawser-laid* ropes twisted together. A hawser-laid rope consists of three strands twisted together against their *lay*. A *single-laid* rope is one strand, composed of twisted fibres. *Laid aback* is said of sails deliberately thus positioned. A *laid deck* is one made of narrow planks of (usually) teak, each about two inches wide, *caulked* but left unvarnished. *Laid up* refers either to the way the strands of a rope are wound together or to a ship out of commission: compare, in non-nautical parlance, the same phrase applied to an invalid.

From the verb and noun 'lay' and thence from OE 'lecgan': cf. the modern German '*legen*'.

First attested in a nautical context in 1769 in Falconer, *Dictionary* (but see also *lay*).

lammy   a Duffel-coat, sometimes quilted.

Almost certainly from 'lambie', originally a pet name for 'lamb', which itself existed in that form in OE and is attested as early as the eighth century.

First attested in 1886 in *The Gentleman's Magazine*, October, 390.

Lanby (also **Lanby buoy**)   a *buoy* carrying a light, fog signal, and radar beacon, as replacement for a *lightship*: of 12 metres diameter with a lattice mast, the Lanby is unmanned but monitored by a shore station.

An acronym for Large Automatic Navigational BuoY.

First attested in 1976 in Kemp, *Oxford Companion*, 465.

land   the overlapping part of two planks in a *clinker-built* boat. To *land* (from the familiar meaning of the noun) is to go, take, or place *ashore*. A *land breeze* is one that blows from land to seaward in the evening when the land temperature falls. *Landfall* is land first seen on approach, usually after a long voyage, and to make a good landfall is to arrive where planned. The *landing strake* is the upper strake but one on either side of a boat.

From the familiar meaning of land, via its use to denote one of the strips into which a ploughed field was divided by water-furrows. 'Land' itself was spelt thus in OE, and is derived from a common Teutonic root: it is first attested in *Beowulf.*

First attested in its nautical, boat-building sense in 1875 in Knight, *Practical Dictionary of Mechanics* (1874–7).

landlubber   seaman's derogatory term for a non-sailor or anyone inept *on board*.

The first part of the word, from OE, needs no further explanation. The second, which by the later sixteenth century had acquired the same meaning as 'landlubber', is unconnected with 'lover', but a word already attested in the fourteenth century as meaning a lout or bumpkin. Its origin is uncertain. The OED conjectures that 'the form may possibly belong to an adoption' of OF '*lobeor*', meaning a swindler, from '*lober*', to deceive. But it seems more likely to be derived from 'lob', which although not attested as meaning a bumpkin before 1533 is found as describing the cod-like pollack in 1357, five years before 'lubber'.

Although probably of onomatopoeic origin, 'lob' is associated with several Teutonic words which, as the OED puts it, 'express the general notion of something heavy, clumsy or loosely pendent'. The compound word 'landlubber' may conceivably result from a confusion with 'landloper', originally a vagabond, from the Dutch '*landlooper*': this first appears in the sixteenth century, and around 1700 was briefly recorded as synonymous with 'landlubber' or, in its nautical sense, 'lubber'.

The latter is first attested in this nautical sense in 1579 in Gosson, *Schoole of Abuse*, 33b. 'Landlubber' is first attested before 1700 in B.E., *New Dictionary*.

lanyard   a short length of rope or cord used for any purpose *on board*, but most particularly, before the days of *rigging screws* (*bottle screws*), to tauten the *shrouds*, and to secure a sailor's knife (as in the white cord of naval uniform).

The word is a second adoption from the French '*lanière*'; the first ('lainer') made its appearance in English *c.* 1386 in Chaucer, *The Knight's Tale*.

First attested in 1626 in Smith, *Accidence*, 15.

larboard   obsolete term for *port*, which was superseded in the nineteenth century owing to confusion with *starboard*.

The word's origin is uncertain. Its ME form was 'lad(d)eborde' or 'latheborde': the extra syllable was lost in the sixteenth century. This has led to speculation that the word meant 'the loading side', since many early merchant ships are said to have had a loading or lading *port* on that side. However, the corresponding OE word was 'baecborde', which (although it did not survive into ME) has its counterparts in many European languages, including French (*'babord'*). The implication seems to have been that this side was at the back of the (presumably right-handed) *steersman* using the *steering oar*, which in early Germanic ships was on the *starboard* or steering side. (The French *'tribord'* is itself a corruption of *'estribord'*, corresponding to *starboard*.)

The change from 'larboard' to *port* was made official in the British Navy in 1844. From 'larboard' comes the equally obsolete word *larbolins*, meaning those of the crew forming the *port watch*.

First attested in its ME form in or before 1300 in *Early English Alliterative Poems* (EETS, 1864–9), C 106; in its modern form in the early sixteenth century (precise date unknown) in the Surtees Society's *Miscellanea* (1888), Sir A. Barton, 8.

large   with the wind *abaft* the *beam* but not dead *astern*, i.e. on a *broad reach*. In *square-riggers*, 'large' was the point of sailing at which the *studding-sails* would begin to *draw*.

From the familiar word, which is ultimately from the Latin *'largus'*, *'larga'* – the masculine givng rise to OF *'larc'*, *'larg'*, source of ME 'larg', 'largue'. In French, this gave way to *'large'*; the modern French adjective *'largue'*, with its nautical senses of 'slack' and (respecting the wind) 'abaft the beam', was adopted, according to the OED, from Southern dialects. The feminine of the original Latin is the source of 'large' in all its various English senses.

First attested in its nautical sense in 1591 in Hakluyt, *Principall Navigations* (1598–1600 edition), III, 491.

lascar   an East Indian native employed in a British ship.

From either the Urdu *'lashkar'*, army or camp, or a shortened form of its derivative *'lashkari'*. According to Fryer, in *East India and Persia* (1698), 107, 'The Seamen and Soldiers differ only in a vowel, the one being pronounced with an *u*, the other with an *a*; as *Luscar* is a Soldier; *Lascar*, a Sailor.' Despite this precision, 'lascar' is often found referring to soldiers, and 'lashkar' occurs between 1616 and the present day as meaning a camp or body of soldiers.

First attested in its nautical sense in 1625 in Purchas, *Pilgrimes* (1625–60), i, V, 650.

lash   to secure with a rope or cord; a stroke of the *cat-o'-nine-tails*. To *lash down* is to secure firmly; a *lashing* is any rope or cord used for this purpose; a *lash-up* is anything insecurely lashed or generally untidy.

Although in appearance identical, the verb and the noun may be derived from different roots. 'Lash' in the sense of to tie is most probably associated with OF *'lachier'*, a dialect form of *'lacier'*, to lace or knot. A 'lash' is formed almost certainly from the corresponding verb, whose origin may be onomatopoeic or, just possibly, OF *'lascher'* (modern *'lâcher'*), to let loose, as in *'lâcher un coup'*, to let fly with a blow. The likelihood of an etymological link between them, as via the use of the noun to describe the thong of a whip (and hence something that could be used for tying), seems extremely remote.

First attested as a nautical verb in 1624 in Smith, *Generall Historie*, v, 194.

lask   to bowl along on a *quartering* wind.

From the OF verb *'lascher'* (modern *'lâcher'*), to let loose or relax: cf. *lash*.

First attested in 1622 in Hawkins, *Observations* (Hakluyt Society, 1847), 40.

lasket   a small cord sewn in loops to the *bonnets* and *drablers* of a *square-rigger* for *lacing* them to the *courses* and *bonnets* respectively.

Probably an adaptation (on the lines of 'gasket') of the French *'lacet'*, whose meaning is the same.

First attested in 1704 in Harris, *Lexicon Technicum*.

lateen   a large narrow triangular sail whose *foot* is nearly horizontal and whose *leech* is nearly vertical; the long *luff* is *laced* to a very long *yard* on a very short *mast*, the yard slanting upwards so that its *peak*, *abaft* the mast, rises above it. Although this *rig* is probably of Arab origin, the modern Arab version of the sail, as seen on Nile *dhows*, is usually four-sided, with a very short luff, the head of the sail in this case being what is laced to the yard: the technical name for this sail is 'seltee-lateen'.

An Anglicisation of the French feminine *'latine'*, as in *'voile latine'*, meaning Mediterranean sail: the rig would be hazardous on wilder oceans.

First attested in 1727–41 in Chambers, *Cyclopaedia* (1741 edition).

launch   to move a vessel for land to water and float her; an eighteenth- and nineteenth-century Mediterranean gunboat; the largest ship's boat of a sailing man-of-war; a small powered *tender*. *Launching ways* are the sloping timber blocks down which a ship is launched.

The verb and the noun (with the exception of 'launch' as the occasion of a launching) come from different roots. The verb is from the Old Norman French *'lancher'*, corresponding to the Old Central French *'lancier'*, originally meaning to pierce, and then to hurl. The noun is related to the Spanish *'lancha'*, a *pinnace*, which may be of Malay origin.

The verb is first attested in or before 1400 in *Morte Arthure* (EETS, 1865, revised 1871), 3921; the noun in 1697 in William Dampier, *New Voyage*, 1729 edition, I, 2.

lay   the twist, left or right, of the *strands* of a rope; with many other words, as below, to come or go, to prepare, to follow, to take, to place, to lie, etc. To *lay* (in general), is to come or go; to *lay aboard* is to come *alongside*; to *lay a course* is to sail on the course prescribed; to *lay aft* is an order to move aft; to *lay a mark* is to sail to it without having to *tack*; to *lay* (a ship) *by the lee* is to turn off the wind, bringing it round to the *lee quarter* until the sails are *aback*. To *lay back* is to apply one's full weight, e.g. in *rowing*; *lay days* are those allowed a charter party for loading or unloading *cargo*; *lay down* is an order to come down from aloft; *lay forward* is an order to move forward. *Laying along* means steeply heeled by the wind; *laying back* means leaning right back with every stroke of an oar; *laying off* is a way of developing the shape of a boat on the mould-loft floor. *Lay off* is an order to keep clear, e.g. not to bring a boat alongside a gangway; to *lay off a course* is to plan it on the *chart*; to *lay out a kedge* is to take it out by boat to drop it in the right place; to *lay out on the yards* (in *square-riggers*) is to work there handling sails; to *lay out the cable* is to arrange it lengthwise for inspection or to remove kinks; to *lay the land* is to sail away from it until it is below the horizon; to *lay to* is to stop by sailing into the wind. To *lay up* is either to take a vessel out of service, or to twist fibres and strands into a rope; *lay-up* is a glass and resin laminate for plastic *hulls*. In several of these usages, 'lay' is (mis)treated as synonymous with 'lie'.

The noun is derived from the verb, whose origin is OE 'lecgan', to cause to lie.

First attested as a nautical noun in 1800 in *The Naval Chronicle*, XII, 195 (Captain Harvey); as a verb, in 1486 in *Naval Accounts* (Navy Records Society, 1896), 13. Other nautical applications of the verb begin to be attested from the sixteenth century onwards; but the word is so adaptable and multifarious that to pinpoint them would merely be to make spot checks on very general usage.

lazaret, lazarette, lazaretto   a quarantine building or ship;
a compartment *on board* for stowing provisions or stores.

From the French '*lazaret*' and the (old) Italian '*lazzaretto*'
(now spelt '*lazzeretto*'), both of which are from 'lazar', itself
derived from the Bibilical Lazarus (*Luke*, xvi, 20), and originally meaning any poor and diseased person, then more
specifically a leper. The 'compartment' sense is an extension of
that of segregation.

First attested as a quarantine refuge in 1605 in Jonson,
Volpone, VI, i (1607 edition, I 2 b); as a storehouse, in 1711 in
Sutherland, *Ship Builder's Assistant*, 161.

lazy block   one fitted to a *deckplate* which is upright when
in use but lies down when released: an example is that used for
genoa sheets. In a nautical context, 'lazy' does not always
impute idleness to an object or its user: sometimes it implies
merely neat assistance. Thus a *lazy guy* is not an indolent fellow,
but a small rope or *tackle* restraining undue swing on a *boom*;
lazy jacks are not *tars* who neglect their duty but ropes from
the *mast* down each side of a sail to a point on the boom, used
to help gather the sail when lowering it (especially useful on
gaff-rigged boats). A *lazy lead* is a free-swivelling *block* for
wire rope used on steering gears and held up by the tension of
the *cable*. A *lazy leadsman* is not a slacker 'swinging the lead',
but a second leadsman helping to haul in the line; a *lazy painter*
is not a lethargic artist but either a smaller auxiliary painter used
to secure a boat alongside in calm weather, or a rope or wire
hanging down from a lower boom, with a *thimble* in the end,
to which a ship's boats are secured when in harbour.

By obvious analogy with a person or animal, from 'lazy' –
itself of obscure origin: it may be derived from the Middle Low
German '*lasich*', '*losich*', but may possibly come from 'lay',
formed in the same fashion as 'tipsy', 'gutsy', etc.

'Lazy block' is first attested in 1978 in Dessoutter, *Practical
Dictionary*, 123.

lead[1]   (pronounced 'led') weight (not necessarily made of
lead) attached to a line for taking *soundings*.

The *lead line* is that to which the lead is attached; a *lead
mine* is not a quarry for metal but a *yacht* with a heavy or bulb
keel; the *leadsman* is the seaman who heaves the lead (ahead
of the ship so that when it reaches the seabed it will be directly
below him); a *leadswinger* is a shirker.

From OE 'lead' and the pre-Teutonic 'loudhom'; its primary
meaning is of course the heaviest of the base metals, about seven
pounds' weight of which was used as a plummet, cup-shaped
at the bottom to take a lump of tallow, to which sand, mud, or

shingle would adhere to indicate the nature of the seabed.

First attested in this nautical context *c.* 1440 in the *York Mysteries*, 1885 edition, ix, 199.

lead[2]   (pronounced 'leed') the direction in which a rope runs. This gives rise to a number of associated words. The *leader* is the rope secured to the bottom of a *fleet* of nets; a *leader cable* is a transmitting cable laid on the bottom of a *channel* or *fairway* to guide ships along it; a *leading block* is one used to change the angle of a rope; a *leading light* is one used to set up a *transit* to guide ships clear of a local hazard; a *leading mark* serves the same purpose by day; the *leading part* is the *fall* of a rope that has been led through a leading block and which is pulled to *overhaul* it; a *leading wind* is one that enables the *sheets* to be *eased* off.

The noun, with its many other meanings, comes from the verb, which in turn has its origin in OE 'laedan', from a common Teutonic root.

First attested in its nautical sense *c.* 1860 in Stuart, *Catechism*, 37.

lee   the side away from that from which the wind is blowing, except in the expression a *lee shore*, which is one on to which a wind is blowing. A *leeboard* is one of a pair of pivoted boards on either side of a flat-bottomed vessel, the lee-side one being lowered as a form of *drop keel* to reduce *leeway*: the same word is applied to a board or other device fitted to prevent a sleeper rolling out of a *bunk*. *Leebowing* is a tactic in yacht racing, in which the 'give-way' or non-priority boat *goes about* on the lee *bow* of a competitor, which is thereby *back-winded*. *Lee edge* is the old name for *leech* (of a sail); *lee helm* is a tendency to *bear away* when the *helm* is central, so that the *helmsman* has to hold the helm *down* to maintain a straight course. *Lee-o* is the helmsman's announcement to the crew when going about: it follows the warning *ready about*. A *lee shore* (see above) is one towards which the wind is blowing, so called because it faces the lee side of the ship. *Leeward* (pronounced 'looard') is down wind (i.e. in the direction towards which it blows); *leeway* is the angle and/or distance a ship is set down to leeward of her course by the wind and/or tide.

From OE 'hleo', meaning shelter, cognate with ON '*hle*', meaning lee in the nautical sense, as also the Dutch '*lij*'.

First attested in its nautical sense *c.* 1400 in *Destruction of Troy* (EETS, 1869–74), 2806.

leech   the *after* edge of a *fore-and-aft* sail; the outer edges of a *square* sail, known respecively as the *port* and *starboard* leeches. A *leech line*, in large sailing ships, runs from the *yardarm* to the leech of a square sail to control and gather it; in smaller boats and yachts it is a very light line threaded through the hollow hem of a sail's leech to adjust its curve and tension. A *leech rope* is that part of a *boltrope* that is sewn to a leech.

Of obscure origin, but probably associated with ON *'lik'* (which the OED calls 'a nautical term of obscure meaning') and with both the Swedish *'lik'* and the Danish *'lig'*, which mean boltrope. The Dutch *'lijk'* and the German *'Liek'* both mean leech line (see above). The idea that 'leech' might be a contraction of 'lee edge', although tempting, remains fanciful – if only because it would not fit a *square-rigger*.

First attested in 1485 in *Naval Accounts* (Navy Records Society, 1896), 38.

leg   the run or distance made on a single *tack*; the side of a racing course between two *marks*; one of the wooden supports keeping a boat upright when she takes the *ground*. A *leg-of-mutton rig* has triangular *mainsails*; a fast ship has *legs*.

From ON *'legg-r'*, meaning leg in its sense of limb. Some trace the word to the West Aryan root *'laq-'*, which appears in the Greek *'laktiksein'*, to kick, and the Latin *'lacertus'*, arm.

First attested in a nautical context in 1497 in *Naval Accounts* (Navy Records Society, 1896), 324.

let draw   command to allow a *headsail* previously held *aback* now to be allowed to *fill* on the new *tack*. To *let fly* is to release the *sheet*, spilling the wind from a sail, used in the Royal Navy as a salute to a senior officer; to *let go* is to release anything, such as a rope under tension; *let go and haul*, rather like 'let draw', is a command when *tacking* a *square-rigger*, meaning to release the *fore bowline* and what are now the *weather braces*, and haul what are now the *lee braces*. To *let her fizzle* is to leave *canvas* set as long as possible despite rising winds; to *let her run* is to let out a rope of cable quickly under load rather than *paying it out* in careful stages.

From OE *'laetan'*, itself a very old and versatile word meaning among others things to release, allow, etc.

First attested in its nautical sense in 1961 in Burgess, *Dictionary*, 133.

Levanter   a strong wind from the East or North-East blowing in the Mediterranean.

From 'Levant', the countries of the Eastern Mediterranean – itself from *'levant'*, French for 'rising', referring to the sun.

First attested in 1790 in Burke, *Reflections*, 86.

liberty   shore leave. The *liberty boat* is that taking seamen on shore leave; such men are known as *liberty men*.

A nautical application of the familiar word but rare phenomenon, from the French '*liberté*' and the Latin '*libertas*'.

First attested in this specific sense in 1758 in Blake, *Plan*, 12.

lie   (of a vessel) to make no *way*. To *lie a-hull* is to lie in a heavy sea with all sails lowered and stowed; to *lie alongside* is to lie side-by-side in a harbour *berth*; to *lie at anchor* is to be anchored; to *lie a-try* is to lie as much *head-to-wind* as possible in a heavy sea, possibly under *bare poles* (as in lying a-hull), but possibly under a *mizen topsail* or *trysail* to give slight forward motion and remain within troughs; to *lie off* is to stop at some distance fom the shore or from another vessel. To *lie on your oars* is to cease *pulling* and stay seated with the *oars* horizontal. To *lie over* is to *heel*; to *lie to* is to lie a-hull or lie a-try (see above).

From OE 'licgan' and a common Teutonic root, with the ordinary sense of recumbence.

First attested in this nautical sense *c.* 1121 in *The Anglo-Saxon Chronicle* for the year 1009 (Laud MS).

lifebelt   round or horseshoe-shaped device to keep a person afloat. A *lifeboat* is one designed for saving life at sea; a *lifebuoy* is a form of lifebelt, but may be cruciform and capable of supporting two people; a *lifejacket* is a vest or jacket giving 35 lb of *buoyancy* and designed so that the wearer floats face upwards (otherwise, the device is only a buoyancy aid). *Lifeline* is an ambiguous term, denoting sometimes the guard rails, sometimes the *jackstay*, and sometimes the line linking the wearer's harness to the jackstay or anchor point. A *liferaft* is one designed to take the survivors of a vessel that has had to be abandoned.

From the familiar word 'life', in these usages denoting the preservation of life; the original is OE 'lif', cognate with many similar Scandinavian words, from the Aryan root '*leip-*', '*loip-*', '*lip-*', meaning to continue.

'Lifebelt' is first attested in 1858 in Simmonds, *Trade Products*; but the earliest record of a similar compound, 'lifeline' (see above), is in 1700, mentioned in *Notes & Queries* (1941), 12 July, 22/2.

lift   a line or wire supporting part of the *rig*, e.g. the ends of the *yardarms*. A modern example is the *topping lift* used to support and sometimes to raise the *boom* of a sailing *yacht*.

From ON '*lypta*', connected with ON '*lopt*', meaning air or sky (cf. the modern German '*Luft*'): the notion is of raising towards the sky.

First attested in this nautical sense in 1485 in the *Naval Accounts* (Navy Records Society, 1896), 36.

light   a navigation or signal lamp; to move, haul, lift, etc., usually in set phrases.

To *light along* is to move or carry in a certain direction; a *light buoy* is an anchored navigational aid carrying a light; *light dues* are charges made for the upkeep of local lights, buoys, etc. A *lighter* (first attested in this sense in 1487) is a vessel, usually a flat-bottomed *barge*, used to move *cargo* from ship to shore or vice versa (not, as the OED implies, to lighten the ship but as the agent of lighting or shifting as above); *lighterage* is such shifting or the charge made for it. A *lighthouse* is a permanent structure carrying a light for navigational purposes, first attested in the seventh century BC. *Light Lists* is a two-volume periodical published by the Hydrographic Department of the Royal Navy, showing the position and characteristics of all navigational lights. A *lightship* is a permanently moored vessel, usually non-navigable, acting as a lighthouse. To *light to* is to slacken off more or a rope or *hawser* so as to make a further turn round a *bollard* or *cleat*. A *light vessel* is the more usual present term for a lightship. The *light waterline* is that at which a vessel floats when empty of all dead weight.

Although identical in form, as their equivalents are in the Dutch '*licht*', and almost so in the German '*Licht*' and '*leicht*', the two meanings of what looks like a single word actually come from different roots. 'Light' in the sense of illumination is derived from OE 'lecht', whose origin is the Aryan root '*leuk-*' which underlies, among other things, the Latin '*lux*'. To 'light' in the sense of shifting, usually with the addition 'along', comes from OE 'lihtan': in some obsolete usages it had the sense of making less heavy: cf. 'to alight' (thereby relieving the horse or vehicle of a burden).

First attested in the sense of nautical illumination in 1604 in Grimstone, translation of *J. de Acosta's Naturall and Morall Historie*, III, xi, 155; in the sense of shifting, in 1841 in Dana, *Seaman's Manual*, 114.

limber   one of the holes cut in the *timbers* of wooden ships on either side of the *keelson* so that the *bilge* water can drain into the pump *well*. *Limber-boards* were short removable boards just above the limbers, to be lifted for unblocking them; a *limber chain*, *rove* through the limbers, was an alternative way of clearing them; *limber hole* was an early alternative to 'limber'; *limber ropes* were the rope equivalent of limber chains.

Conjecturally a corruption of the French '*lumière*', in the sense of a hole or perforation.

First attested ('limber holes') in 1626 in Smith, *Accidence*, 8.

Limey   American nickname for a British sailor, and hence for any Briton.

An abbreviation of 'lime-juicer', first attested in 1859, and derived from the issue of lime juice as an antiscorbutic in British ships, made statutory in 1854.

First attested as a general term for Britons in 188 in Australia, but in its specifically nautical usage not until 1918 in Depew, *Gunner Depew*, 18.

line   narrow-gauge rope; also various senses, mostly connected with the familiar geometrical usage. *The Line* (as in 'crossing the Line') is the Equator. *Line abeam, abreast, ahead,* or *astern* refers to the positioning of a number of ships *under way*, often in battle formation: the *line of battle* is that formed by a fleet before engaging an enemy. A *line of bearing* is that along a *bearing*; a *line of soundings* is a series at regular intervals which may be used as a guide to the vessel's position; a *line of transit* is that drawn on a *chart* to indicate a *fairway*. A *liner*, formerly a fishing-boat using lines, is a large steam or motor vessel operating by a shipping line. The *lines* of a vessel are its designer's drawings; *lines of flotation* are the horizontal indications (for various seas and seasons) that go with the *Plimsoll mark*. A *line start*, in yacht racing, is a start across a line between two points. To *line up* is to prepare.

Both these families of meaning spring from the same ultimate source, which is associated with flax and hence with the word 'linen'. 'Line' in its now largely obsolete and dialect meaning, flax, is derived from OE 'lin', which like its other Teutonic cousins is adopted from or cognate with the Latin '*linum*'. In its sense of thin cord, the word is an amalgam of two, whose ultimate etymology is the same: OE 'line' (cord or line) and ME 'ligne' (cf. the modern French equivalent), from the popular Latin '*linja*' – originally, in classical Latin, '*linia*' and later (as in modern Italian) '*linea*'. In its first usage this meant linen thread, but it later acquired the more general sense of 'line' (as in geometry), shared by the modern Italian '*linea*' and the modern French '*ligne*'.

First attested in the sense of cord before the year 1000, in *The Dialogue of Salomon and Saturnus* (Aelfric Society, 1848; Grein, 1898), Grein 294.

lipper   a ruffling of the sea's surface, from a ripple to a small wave that comes over the *lee* rail. Two very rare verbs have the same form as the noun: one means to ripple, the other to sail with the gunwale level with the water.

Conjecturally a frequentative formation related to the verb 'lap', which comes from OE 'lapian', to lick; but possibly associated with the noun 'lip' (from OE 'lippa') since a lipper may surge over the *topsides*, which may be thought to resemble a human (or simian) lower lip.

First attested in 1513 in Douglas (tr.), *Virgill*, VII, ix, 119.

list   an inclination to one side; thus to incline (in both cases permanently, as distinct from *heel* or *heeling*, which is temporary unless it ends in a *capsize*.)

Of unknown origin: the OED conjectures that it may be a use of 'list' in the sense of longing or (in the figurative sense) inclination. If so, the source is the OE verb 'lystan', associated with 'lust' in its earlier sense of pleasurable longing.

The noun is the source of the verb, but the latter is first attested in 1626 in Smith, *Accidence*, 29, while the former is not attested until 1633. In both cases, the word is spelt 'lust', perhaps confirming the conjectural etymology above.

Liverpool pennants   originally, rope yarns used instead of buttons on a sailor's coat; now, the *beckets* and wooden *toggles* on a *Duffel coat*.

From the city of Liverpool and *pennant*. As with many such geographical allusions, the original intention was no doubt derogatory.

First attested in 1933 in Masefield, *Bird of Dawning*, 287.

lizard   a short length of rope with a *thimble* or *hard eye spliced* into one end.

From the familiar word for one of the family of reptiles, whose shape it may resemble; that word is an adaptation from OF '*lesard*', from the Latin '*lacertum*' and its feminine '*lacerta*' which is the scientific name of the species.

First attested in its nautical sense in 1794 in *The Elements and Practice of Rigging and Seamanship*, I, 16.

log   device for measuring the ship's speed and progress; abbreviation for *log book*, in which these and all other significant facts, events and actions (notably meteorological and navigational data) are recorded; to enter in the log book.

The *logchip* or *logship* is the weighted wooden quadrant that *c.* 1600 replaced the board or piece of wood (see below) previously *towed* to measure boat speed. The *log glass* is a type of hourglass running out in 28 seconds, for use with the log. The *log line* is a rope of plaited flax used to tow the rotator of a patent log (evolved during the eighteenth and early nineteenth centuries).

The nautical usage arose from the earliest kind of log, which consisted of a board or piece of wood attached to a line that was allowed to run out for a specified time, the amount of line run out then indicating the speed in *knots* (themselves made at the appropriate intervals in the line). The original word 'log', however, is more obscure. It comes from late ME 'logge', but this is not derived from ON '*lag*' (felled tree), and probably not from a later Scandinavian word of similar character: it emerged in English in the late fourteenth century.

First attested in its nautical sense in 1574 in Bourne, *Regiment* (1577 edition), xiv, 42b.

loggerhead   a wooden *bitt* in a whaling ship around which the *harpooning* line was run out.

Directly from the use of the word, for example by Shakespeare, to mean 'dunderhead'. 'Logger-' is a dialect word to describe something clumsy, such as a block of wood used (like a ball and chain) to prevent a horse straying. The familiar expression 'at loggerheads' appears to be derived not from nautical usage but from a wholly different meaning of the word, describing a ball of iron on a long handle, which was heated and plunged into *tar* or pitch to melt it. The implement may have been used as a weapon. Both the implement and its figurative application are first attested in the late seventeenth century.

First attested in its nautical sense in 1850 in Cheever, *A Whaleman's Adventures* (ed. Scoresby, 1859 edition), ix, 116.

longboat   the largest ship's boat of a sailing vessel. 'Long' appears in a number of other nautical expressions. *Long in the jaw* or *long-jawed* describes a rope that is losing its twist owing to being stretched. A *long line* is a single line with mutiple hooks for fishing. A *longship* was a Norse or Viking galley. A *long-shoreman* is a person living near the shore and making a living on it. A *long splice* is one made by *unlaying* two ropes' ends to a distance eight times their circumference, then *laying up* the *strands* in the space where the opposite strands have been unlaid, so the splice can pass through a *block, fairlead*, etc.

From OE 'lang', 'long' and from a common Teutonic root, plus 'boat'.

First attested *c.* 1515 in *Cocke Lorelles Bote* (Percy Society, 1843), 12; and familiar to many from R.L. Stevenson's *Treasure Island*.

loom   the *inboard* end of an *oar*; the blurred and enlarged appearance of an object in sea mist or fog; light dimly reflected on a low cloud.

Two words, from two different roots. That referring to an oar comes from the same source as the weaving machine, i.e. ME 'lome' (from OE 'yeloma'), an implement or utensil. The word 'loom' in its optical senses is derived either from the Latin '*lumen*', light, or from Scandinavian roots meaning to move slowly (as in 'looming up'): there may well have been some confusion between the two.

First attested as pertaining to an oar in 1697 in Dampier, *New Voyage* (1729 edition), I, 54; in its optical connection at sea, in 1836 in Marryat, *Mr Midshipman Easy*, xxvi.

loose-footed   nothing to do with ill-fitting sea-boots, but (of a sail) not *laced* to a *boom*.

From ME 'los' plus 'footed'.

First attested in 1895 in *Outing* (US), XXVI, 46/1.

lop   a short choppy sea, probably in relatively sheltered waters.

Of onomatopoeic origin, but also possibly connected with 'lap' in the sense of licking, from OE 'lapian'.

First attested in its nautical sense in 1829 in Hawker, *Diary 1802–53* (published 1893), I, 360.

low and aloft   carrying all possible *canvas*. 'Low' and 'lower' also appear in a number of other nautical expressions. *Low water* is low tide. *Lower and dip* is the order given when a *dipping lug cutter goes about*, the *foresail* being lowered to unhook the *tack* and swing the sail round *abaft* the *mast* so as to secure it on the other *tack*. *Lower away* is the order to begin lowering anything. The *lower boom* is a *spar* projecting from the ship's side in harbour, to which boats may be secured; the *lower deck* is that below the main deck, used for *messing* when it ceased to be the *gun deck*, and hence still used to denote *ratings* as distinct from officers; *lower deck attitude* is that deemed unsuitable in candidates for a naval commission; the *lower mast*, in a built-up or *made mast*, is the first section from the deck upwards.

From early ME 'lah' plus aloft: the original of *alow and aloft*, rather than the other way round.

The OED records only this last phrase, first attested in 1863 in Reade, *Hard Cash*, I, 268. 'Low and aloft' is first attested in 1976 in Kemp, *Oxford Companion*, 500.

lubber   a clumsy or unseamanlike sailor (cf. *landlubber*). The *lubber's hole* was an opening in the floor of the *tops* (at the *head* of the *mast*) enabling them to be reached without having to go over the *futtock shrouds*; a *lubber's line* is the black line inside a *compass* bowl showing the direction of the ship's *head*; *lubber's points* are a lubber's line and one opposite to it; a *lubber's trademark* is the end of a rope left *unwhipped*.

Probably from OF '*lobeor*', swindler or parasite; but in sense much more like 'lob', which although perhaps onomatopoeic is paralleled by a number of similar-sounding Teutonic words with the general sense of something (as the OED puts it) 'heavy, clumsy, or loosely pendent' – e.g. modern Dutch '*lob*', '*lubbe*', a hanging lip, Danish '*lobbes*', a clown or bumpkin, and Norwegian '*lubb*', '*lubba*', a short stout person. Cf. 'lump', whose meanings as early as 1597 included a dull, heavy person.

First attested in 1597 in Gosson, *Schoole of Abuse*, 33b.

luff   the *leading* edge of a *fore-and-aft* sail; to sail closer to windward; in yacht racing, to outmanoeuvre a competitor by doing so and thus avoiding being overtaken to windward. *Luff alee* is an order to put the *helm* hard *alee*; *luff and lie* means to come as close to the wind as possible and stay there; *luff and shake*, or *luff and touch her* means to see how close to the wind one can sail by coming as far as the point when sails start shaking, then *easing off*; *luffed in* is slang for 'roped in' for some task; a *luffing match*, in yacht racing, is an effort by a *leeward* boat to luff one or more competitors; a *luff rope* is a *bolt rope* on the luff of a sail; a *luff spar* is a metal or wooden *spar*, sometimes for roller *reefing*, to which the luff of a *headsail* is attached; a *luff tackle* is a *purchase* with one single and one double *block*, originally used to haul down the *tack* of a *fore-and-aft* sail to tauten the luff; *luff tape* is tape or webbing sewn to the luff of some headsails or to the vertical edges of a *spinnaker* to reduce stretch; to *luff up* is to put the *helm* down so as to come up to the wind; *luff upon luff* means one luff *tackle* hooked to the *fall* of another to double the increase in power; *luff wire* is that running along the luff of some headsails to reduce stretch.

From early ME 'lof', 'loof', apparently adopted from OF '*lof*', later '*louf*', meaning a device for altering a ship's course. Since the normal such device is now the *rudder*, some scholars assume that 'luff' originally meant a *steering oar*. As those who have learned to sail without a rudder will know, this is by no means certainly the case. The OED, comparing the senses of the word at various times in English and other languages, suggests rather warily that 'it may have been some kind of machine for operating on the sails.' What is certain is that 'luff' also meant by turn the weather-gauge or the part of a ship towards the wind (now obsolete) and the fullest, broadest part of a ship's *bow*.

First attested in its modern sense in 1513 in Douglas (transl.), *Virgill*, v, xiv, 7.

lug   originally, the *yard* on which a *lugsail* is set; a *lugsail*, i.e. a *fore-and-aft* sail, almost *square*, *bent* to a yard and slung to *leeward* of the *mast*. A *balance lug* is *laced* to a *boom* that projects slightly *forward* of the mast, but is not attached to it, being *bowsed* down with a *lanyard*. A *Chinese lug* has a boom with *battens* from *luff* to *leech*, all extending forward of the mast. A *dipping lug* has no boom, and the yard has to be passed round the mast when *tacking*; a *gunter lug* has a yard which is virtually an extension of the mast; a *standing lug* has a boom whose forward end pivots at the mast. A *lugger* is a sailing vessel with a lugsail *rig*.

Almost certainly a figurative extension of 'lug' in its earlier –
and, surprisingly, non-jocular – sense of 'ear'. Of obscure
etymology, the word first appears in the late fifteenth century,
meaning the ear-flap of a (deerstalker-type) cap; as meaning 'ear',
it first emerges in the beginning of the sixteenth century. In
Scotland by the nineteenth century, it had superseded the word
'ear', which had become temporarily obsolete; it serves North
of the border as a very commonly used colloquialism. In the
nautical sense, it is just possible that the word is connected with
the verb 'to lug', meaning to drag: this is probably of Scandinavian origin – cf. the Swedish '*lugga*', to pull someone's hair.

First attested in its nautical sense in the combination 'lugsail'
in 1677 in the *London Gazette* No. 1194/4.

Maelstrom   originally, the strong current that *rips*
past the Southern end of Moskenaes island in the
Lofoten group off the West coast of Norway, thought
at one time to be a whirlpool sucking ships to their doom;
mentioned in Mercator's 1595 *Atlas*. Now, any great whirlpool.

Seemingly of Dutch origin: in early modern Dutch it was spelt
as in English, and meant a whirlpool; the Dutch spelling is now
'*maalstroom*'. The first part of the word appears to mean 'grind'
or 'whirl': cf. the Paeroic '*mala*' and possibly the various words
associated with 'mill'. The word's second component, unsurprisingly, means 'stream'.

First attested *c*. 1560 in Hakluyt, *Principall Navigations*, 334
(Anthony Jenkinson), where it appears as 'Malestrand' – prob-
ably a mis-hearing and a confusion with what is now known as
Marstrand, in Southern Sweden.

main   the open sea (as in 'Spanish Main'); principal or largest;
abbreviation for *mainmast*, *mainsail*, etc.; pertaining to either
of these. The *main boom* is the *spar* extending the *foot* of a
fore-and-aft mainsail. The *main brace* is the *purchase* used
to *trim* the main *yard*; since at least the early nineteenth century
to splice the main brace has been slang for serving out *grog*,
probably since hauling on the main brace called for exceptional
effort and perhaps exceptional reward. The *main deck* is that
which extends along the ship's whole length; the *main derrick*
is the largest in the ship; the *mainmast* is the tallest in the ship;
the *mainsail* is that hoisted on the mainmast, in *square-*
riggers the lowest and largest; *mainsail haul* is the order given
in *tacking* a square-rigger, to *brace* round the *after yards* once

the sails on the *foremast* have been *backed* and the ship is almost *head to wind*; the *main sheet* is that which controls the mainsail. The *main ship channel* is the deepest channel in any given area, usually marked with lights. The *main top* is the platform at the mainmast *head*. The *main yard* is the lower yard to which the mainsail is *bent*.

From OE 'mayen', a noun originally meaning strength, as still in the phrase 'with might and main'. The OED considers it 'doubtful whether the development of the English word owes anything to the influence of OF *maine, maigne* great: – Latin *magnus.*' Given the many variations in the spelling of the English word, one may perhaps doubt the doubt.

First attested as a noun meaning the open sea in 1579–80 in North (transl.), *Plutarch's Lives*, C. Marius (1595), 468; as a nautical adjective, in 1485 in *Naval Accounts* (Navy Records Society, 1896), 37.

make   reach, attain, etc., in a number of nautical phrases. *Make and mend* is the traditional half-day without work on the ship, supposedly for clothes repair, etc. To *make bad weather* (or *heavy weather*) is to labour in heavy seas. To *make fast* is to *belay* or otherwise secure; to *make headway* is to move forward through the water. To *make her number* is to identify and report the 'number' or four-letter identification (by flag signals) of a vessel. To *make port* is to reach and enter it; to *make sail* is to *set* or increase sails; to *make sternway* is to move backwards through the water; to *make the land* is to come within sight of the coast. To *make your pennants* is to identify oneself. To *make water* is to leak; a *tide is making* when rising or flooding.

From OE verb 'macian' and a common Western Germanic root.

First attested in a specifically nautical sense in the obsolete phrase 'make the tackling', i.e. make sail; this occurs *c.* 1450 in *The Pilgrims Sea-voyage* (EETS, 1867), also in Wright and Halliwell (ed.), *Reliquiae Antiquae*, 1842–3), I, 2.

manger   a small space in the *bows* just *abaft* the *hawse-holes*, with a *coaming* on its *after* end to prevent water flowing *aft*. The *manger-board* is the name for this coaming.

So called from its resemblance to an animal's manger, which in turn is derived from the French '*mangeoire*', in the twelfth century spelt '*maingeure*'; this comes from the vulgar Latin '*manducatoria*', from '*manducare*', to eat: cf. the French '*manger*' and the Italian '*mangiare*'.

First attested in this nautical sense in 1627 in Smith, *Seaman's Grammar*, ii, 10.

Manila, Manilla   rope made from the fibres of the abaca banana plant or *musa textilis*, which does not rot in seawater and has no need to be tarred as hempen rope does (although both are now superseded by synthetics).

From the name of the capital of the Philippines, where the plant grows.

First attested as applying to cordage (although earlier applied to matting) in 1855 in Royle, *Fibrous Plants of India*, 48.

man-of-war   an armed vessel equipped for warfare as part of a recognized navy; a *warship*. A *Portuguese man-of-war* is not an Iberian battleship but a maritime hydrozoan of the genus *Physalia*, so called because it floats on the sea's surface with a sail-like ridge of its body displayed (and its poisonous tentacles hanging down).

In its early and obsolete sense of a male warrior, first found in 1449, the expression is said to be derived from the French '*homme de guerre*'; but in its nautical sense, recorded only 35 years later, it almost certainly subsumes the use of 'man' to denote a ship (as in 'merchantman', etc). At all events, the source of 'man' is OE 'mann', from a common Teutonic root; but the similarity with the Sanskrit '*manu*' is now thought to stem in parallel from a common anterior source rather than to imply direct descent. 'War' is from the late (about 1050) OE 'wyrre', 'werre', and thence from the North-Eastern OF '*werre*', equivalent to the central OF and modern French '*guerre*'. (For further elucidation see *warship*.)

First attested in its nautical sense in 1484 by W. Cely in the *Cely Papers* (Camden Society, 1900), 144.

manrope   a rope *rigged* as a handrail for an accommodation *ladder* or *gangplank*.

From OE 'man(n)', plus 'rope'.

First attested in 1769 in Falconer, *Dictionary* (1780 edition), II: '*Tire-veilles*, the man-ropes or entering-ropes of the side.' Contrary to possible supposition, '*tire-veilles*' is not a misprint for '*tire-vieilles*': the second part of the word refers to wariness, not aged and unsteady lady passengers.

Marconi rig   *Bermuda rig*, i.e. with a triangular *foresail* and a *jib-headed mainsail* set to a tall *stayed* mast. Still the common term for Bermuda rig in the USA.

Named after the wireless telegraphy inventor Guglielmo marchese Marconi (1874–1937) because the staying system of the mast was thought to resemble that of a wireless mast.

First attested in 1912 in *Yachting Monthly*, XIII, 256/2.

marina   a dedicated yacht harbour. When first mentioned, it was described as a 'trick name for a basin'; but times change, and it would now be hard to better Desoutter's definition, in *The Boat-Owner's Practical Dictionary* (1978), 135: 'An artificial yacht harbour, sometimes totally concealed from view by bingo halls, boozing dens, and boatels, but revealing itself to the ear by the unceasing jangling of halyards on the masts of boats whose owners have long since forgotten their existence.'

Undoubtedly from 'marine, which itself is derived, via, French, from the Latin *'marinus'* and *'mare'*; said to have originated in the USA after World War II, but in fact first on printed record in the UK.

First attested in 1935 in *Yachting Monthly*, LIX, 223/2.

marine   a soldier trained to serve at sea; (as an adjective) concerned with the sea. *Marine glue* was not glue in the familiar sense, but a *caulking* compound for the seams of *laid* decks, consisting of rubber, pitch, naphtha and shellac, now superseded by other compounds. *Marine growth* consists of barnacles, weeds, and other fouling that cover a ship's *bottom*; *marine plywood* is that used for shipbuilding, made to official standards of water and heat resistance; *marine stores* are all those needed *aboard*.

Like *marina*, derived from the Latin *'marinus, 'mare'.

As an adjective describing sea-going soldiers, first attested in 1690 in Luttrell, *Brief Historical Relation*, 1678–1714 (1857), II, 1.

mariner   a seafarer; in law, anyone employed *aboard* ship. A *mariner's splice* is a *long splice* in *cable-laid* rope, finished with the *strands* of each rope *unlaid* and spliced in.

From the Anglo-French *'mariner'* (modern French *'marinier'*) and the medieval Latin *'marinarius'*.

First attested *c.* 1290 in *Early South-English Legendary* (EETS, 1887), I, 329/220.

mark   any object used as a guide for navigation; in yacht racing, one of the objects (usually *buoys*) to be *rounded*; on a *lead line*, one of the markings used to indicate depth in *fathoms*: it was the Mississippi riverboat *leadsman*'s cry of 'Mark Twain' that gave Samuel Clemens his *nom de plume*. A *mark buoy* or *marker buoy* is usually one positioned for racing.

From OE 'mearc', a boundary sign or landmark.

First attested as a navigational aid *c.* 1400 in *Sailing Directions* (Hakluyt Society), 12; as a gradation on a lead line, in 1769 in Falconer, *Dictionary* (1780 edition).

marl   to secure the *worming* and *parcelling* of a rope by winding on a tight *serving*, with a *hitch* at each turn; to *lace* with a series of *half-hitches*. See also *marline, marling*.

From the Dutch and Low German '*marlen*' and thence from the Middle Dutch '*merren*', to tie.

First attested in 1704 in Harris, *Lexicon Technicum*, 1704–10, I.

marline   small *line* of two *strands*, used for *seizing*, or to *marl*. A *marline spike* or *marlinspike* is a tapering iron spike with a sharp point used for opening the strands of a rope for *splicing*, as a lever in marling, or to ease open knots: it often features on clasp-knives and is sometimes thought to be a device for removing stones from horses' hooves. A *marline-spike hitch* is made by laying a spike through a jammed *bight* for leverage.

Probably from a confusion of two associated words, already confused in Dutch: 'marline' from the Dutch '*marlijn*' (from '*marren*', to bind) and 'marling' from the Dutch '*marling*'.

First attested in 1485 in *Naval Accounts* (Navy Records Society, 1896), 70.

marling   the action undertaken when one *marls*. A *marling hitch* is that used when a long *lashing* has to marl down a furled sail, etc., and is made by passing a rope over and under in a series of *half-hitches*.

From the same confused source as *marline*, with which it is frequently used interchangeably.

First attested in 1485 in *Naval Accounts* (Navy Records Society, 1896), 51.

maroon   to put a person ashore, usually in a remote or desolate spot, and sail away. The most famous such castaway was Alexander Selkirk (1676–1721), the model for Daniel Defoe's *Robinson Crusoe*, published in 1719, although Crusoe was *shipwrecked* whereas Selkirk was marooned (at his own request).

Adapted from the French '*marron*' – not in this case a chestnut, but a derivative of the Spanish '*cimarron*', wild or savage. 'Maroon' in the sense of a firework is unrelated to this verb: it comes from the French '*marron*' meaning chestnut. As a noun, 'maroon' (in the '*cimarron*' family tree) meant one of a group of fugitive slaves in the West Indies: this usage is recorded a century before that of the nautical verb.

First attested in 1726 in *Brice's Weekly Journal*, 1 July, 2.

marry   to join two ropes by *butting* the *unlaid* ends together (as in a *long splice*) so that they can pass through a block; to align two ropes so that both hoist or lower together, as in the case of a boat's *falls*.

An obvious figurative extension of the familiar sense of the word, which itself is adapted from the French '*marier*' and thence from the Latin '*maritare*'.

First attested in connection with a *splice* in 1815 in Falconer, *Dictionary*, enlarged by W. Burney; in the sense of parallel effort, in 1867 in Smyth, *Sailor's Word-book*.

martingale   in *square-rigged* ships, the *stay* holding down the *jib-boom*; in a sailing *dinghy*, the rope or strap running from a point on the *boom* to the *foot* of the mast, to hold the boom down – better known as the *kicking-strap* or *boom vang*.

Originally a strap arrangement fixed to the noseband, bit or reins of a horse and secured at the other end to the girth, to prevent rearing or throwing back of the head, the word was used by Rabelais in the expression '*chausses à la martingale*' to describe a variety of hose or breeches fastened at the back. Whether the hose followed the horse, i.e. whether Rabelais was mockingly applying to human dress a term from dressage, is uncertain: some suggest that the garment was worn by the Martigaux, inhabitants of the Martigues in Provence; but it seems equally possible that the Martigaux gave their name to the piece of tack. From here its nautical extension was natural. Less clear still is how the word came to mean doubling the stake after a loss at gambling in the hope of recouping, a sense that first appears in 1815. Thackeray was one of the first to advise against this hazardous system.

First attested in its nautical sense in 1794 in *The Elements and Practice of Rigging and Seamanship*, I, 233.

mast   roughly vertical pole on a vessel, on which sails may be *set*. *Mast abeam* is the phrase to be used in yacht racing by the *helmsman* of a *windward* yacht to tell one to *leeward* that she is too far back to have the right to *luff*. A *mast band* is a metal band round a wooden mast to attach rigging or prevent chafe. The *mast beam* is that fitted *forward* and *aft* of a *keel-stepped* mast. A *mast clamp* is a metal clamp hinged to a *thwart* to keep the mast in place; the *mast coat* is a waterproof cover fitted round a keel-stepped mast at deck level to prevent leaks; a *mast collar* is a metal substitute for a mast coat. A *mast gate* is either a device at the *foot* of the mast which opens to let the slides fit on to the track or, in racing *dinghies*, the bar that closes the deck-level slot through which the mast fits. The *masthead* is its top, or that part which is above the *eyes* of the rigging or, in small boats, above the *hounds*; a *masthead cutter* (or *sloop*) is one in which the *forestay* on which the *foresail luff* is *set* reaches to the masthead; a *masthead float* is a floating or inflatable device at the masthead of a *catamaran* to prevent her *turning turtle*; a *masthead knot* is a *collar knot*; a *masthead light* (*steaming light*) is the white light carried by power vessels at night or in poor visibility, showing when *under way* from dead ahead to 22.5 degrees *abaft* the *beam* on either side. *Mast hoops* are wooden hoops round the *mainmast* for attaching the *luff* of the *mainsail*; *mast partners* are strong *timbers* between the *beams* to support a mast (cf. *tabernacle*). The *mastrope, rove* through a *sheave* at the masthead, is that used for raising a lowering the mast (and sometimes a seaman). A *mast ship* was one designed to transport masts, having large square *ports* in *bows* and *stern* for loading and unloading. The *mast step* is the recess in the *keelson* in which the mast is *stepped* or fitted; the *mast track* is the metal or plastic linear device on the *after* side of the mast into which the slides of a sail's *luff* fit; *mast wedges* are wooden wedges to help secure the mast at deck level. A *made mast* is one constructed from several pieces.

From a Western Indo-German root, *'mazdo-s'*, giving OE 'maest' as well as the Latin *'malus'* (corrupted by the eighth century to the popular Latin *'mastus'*, probably the origin of OF *'mast'* and the modern French *'mât'*).

First attested in the late eighth century in *Beowulf* (edited by C.W.M. Grein, EETS, 1882), 1905.

master   originally, the officer in a *warship* responsible for navigation, with a lieutenant's rank but of subordinate command until 1814, when the rank became *commander* and the title 'master and commander', a term that lapsed late in the nineteenth century; the *captain* of a merchant vessel. The *master-at-arms* is the officer in a naval ship who is responsible for police duties; a *master mariner* is the captain of a merchant vessel who has passed the requisite examinations and holds the resultant certificate; a *master's mate*, when the master was the navigator, was one of his assistants, with the rank of *petty officer*. The *master station* is the main transmitter when a chain of stations is sending linked radio signals. A *master's ticket* is a master's certificate (see above).

From the Latin *'magister'* via OE 'maeyester' and ME 'meister', and associated with similar words in most Western European languages.

First attested in a general nautical sense *c.* 1330 in Manning, *Story of England* (Rolls Series, 1887), 12085.

mate   rank in the merchant navy just below that of *master*, but now usually called 'officer'; an assistant as in *bosum's mate*, etc.).

From a fourteenth-century word of identical spelling, adopted from the Middle Low German or Middle Dutch as an abbreviated form of *'gemate'*. companion or messmate; also no doubt associated with ME 'mette', a table companion, itself linked with 'meat'.

First attested in its nautical sense in *Naval Accounts* (Navy Records Society, 1896), 166.

Matthew Walker   a *stopper knot* for a rope's end, made by forming a *half-hitch* with each *strand* in the direction of the *lay*, then tucking them over and under – a development of the *wall knot*, traditionally tied in a rope used for the handle of a wooden bucket.

From the name of its inventor, who was condemned to death as a criminal but pardoned when he tied this knot in the middle of a length of rope, and the judge was unable either to untie it or to tie it again.

First attested in 1808 in Lever, *Sheet Anchor*, 5.

Mayday   the international distress signal given by voice radio on one of the emergency channels.

Said by many authorities to be a phonetic approximation to the French '*m'aidez*', the word seems more likely to correspond to '*venez m'aider*' with the first word omitted, since the normal form of the unexpanded imperative would be '*aidez-moi*'.

First attested in its nautical sense in 1927 in the *International Radio Telegraph Convention*, 51.

meet her   order to the *helmsman* to apply opposite *helm* to check a vessel's swing. *Meet her when she shakes* is an order to do so as the ship comes round into the wind.

From OE 'metan', itself derived from the Old Teutonic '(ga)motjan', from '*moto*', a coming together: cf. '*moot*'.

First attested in 1776 in that year's edition of Falconer, *Dictionary*.

mess   group of sailors who eat together *on board*; the place where they do so; thus to eat together. A *mess bill* is that for catering; the *mess deck* is that where the crew messes; *mess gear* is crockery, etc., used in the mess; a *messmate* is one who shares a mess; *mess traps* are the same as mess gear.

Adapted from OF '*mes*', a portion of food (cf. the modern French '*mets*' and the Greek '*mezethes*', and descended from the late Latin '*missum*', that which is sent in or set out; cf. also the German '*Messe*' and associated words). 'Mess' in the sense of muddle, confusion, or dirt is a late arrival, not found until the early nineteenth century.

First attested in a nautical context in 1536 in the *Lord Treasurer's Accounts of Scotland* (1905), VI, 450.

messenger   a *heaving line*; a small line used to guide a heavier one through a narrow space, e.g. inside a hollow mast; an endless rope used in the days of manual *capstans*, to wind round them instead of the thick and heavy *anchor cable*, to which it was *nipped*.

A figurative extension of the familiar sense, i.e. one who runs an errand or carries a despatch; the word itself comes from ME 'messager', 'messagier', from the French and OF respectively; the word 'message' itself comes from the popular Latin *'missaticum'* (also found in twelfth-century Latin) and from *'mittere'*, to send.

First attested in a nautical context in 1633 in James, *Strange and Dangerous Voyage*, 80.

middle ground   a *shoal*, *sandbank* or rock outcrop in a *fairway*, effectively dividing it in two. *Middle ground buoys* (now usually *cardinal marks*) identify such *shoals*. The *middle passage,* in the days of slave-trading, was from West Africa to the West Indies or the Southern States of America. *Middle stitching* is reinforcing a seam along its centre. The *middle watch* is that from midnight to 4.00 a.m.

From OE 'middel' plus 'ground'.

First attested in 1801, in a quotation attributed to Horatio Nelson in Duncan, *Life* (1806), 146.

midshipman   rank intermediate between naval cadet and lowest commissioned officer. *Midshipman's butter* is avocado; *midshipman's half-pay* was 'nothing a day and find for yourself'; a *midshipman's hitch* is a single *Blackwall hitch* so formed that the *bight* also rounds the *bill* of the hook; *midshipman's nuts* are broken pieces of biscuit; a *midshipman's roll* is a clumsily bundled *hammock*.

From 'mid' plus 'ship' plus 'man', obviously enough, but whether because of the station or because of the quarters of those concerned remains uncertain. The OED says: 'So called because stationed "amidships" when on duty'; Burgess, *Dictionary* (1961) says: 'So called because midshipmen's quarters were once amidships on the lower deck.' To this might be added the fact that a midshipman was intermediate between a rating and an officer.

First attested, as 'midships men', in 1626 in Smith, *Accidence*, 2; in its present form, in 1685 in *The London Gazette* No. 2054/3.

mile (nautical)   6080 feet, one sixtieth of a degree at the equator, as contrasted with the British and US terrestrial mile, which is 5280 feet.

The word is derived from the Latin *'mille'*, a thousand, i.e. a thousand paces, or approximately 4854 feet.

First attested in its nautical sense in 1632 in Lithgow, *Totall Discourse*, VIII, 362.

miss stays   to fail to *go about, luffing up* into the wind but falling back on the same *tack*.

From OE 'missan' (to fail to hit, meet, or light upon) plus *stays*.

First attested in 1691 in *The London Gazette* No. 2687/3.

mitre   the strengthened seam in a sail (especially a triangular sail) where the cloths meet at an angle, roughly bisecting the angle at the *clew* and at right angles to the *luff*, i.e. continuing the line of the *sheet*.

Generally presumed to be a figurative extension to carpentry and needlework of the early form of the ecclesiastical mitre, with a vertical band bisecting a rectilinear angle at the top. The word itself seems to have been adopted from the French *'mitre'*, which in turn is descended from the Latin *'mitra'* and the Greek *'mitra'*, a form of head-dress which the Romans considered effeminate when worn by men.

First attested in needlework in 1882 in Caulfield and Saward, *Dictionary of Needlework*, 305; in a nautical context in 1961 in Burgess, *Dictionary*, 146.

mizen or **mizzen**   the *fore-and-aft* sail hoisted on the third (*aftermost*) mast of a *square-rigger* or of a three-masted *schooner*, or on the small *after* mast of a *ketch* or a *yawl*; it is also known as the *spanker* or *driver* (no longer a *mizen-sail*); the same word may be used of the mast in question.

Believed to be adapted from the French *'misaine'*, although in modern French this is a *foresail* or *foremast*. Hatzfeld and Damesteter, in their *Dictionnaire Général* (1895–1900), record *'migenne'* c. 1381, supposedly derived from the Italian *'mezzana'*, which did mean 'mizen' in the English sense, being the feminine of the word for 'middle'. Whether this meant middle-positioned or middle-sized remains uncertain: if the former, it certainly did not refer to the main. The modern French usage is possibly deviant – it is certainly a 'false friend'.

First attested in 1465 in *Manners and Household Expenses* (Roxburghe Club, 1841), 200.

mole   a *pier* or *breakwater* protecting a harbour, and usually one against which vessels can lie.

Among the many words apparently identical, 'mole' in this sense is alone in being derived from the Latin *'moles'*, a mass (which was its original meaning in English). In its 'breakwater' sense, it may have come from Latin through the French *'mole'*, since in Italian and Spanish *'mole'* means 'mass', although the 'breakwater' sense is present in the Spanish *'muelle'*, the Portuguese *'molhe'* and the Italian *'molo'*.

First attested in this nautical sense in 1548 in Hall, *Chronicle*, 204.

molly, mollie   a fulmar or *Fulmarus glacialis*; also applied to a *Diomedea malanophrys* and other birds; a meeting (often bibu-lous) of *sea-captains* in the *cabin* of one of them when sailing in company.

A dialect word, said to be an abbreviation of *mollymawk*.

First attested as applied to birds in 1857 in Morris, *History* (1851–7), VI, 237; as denoting an evening get-together, in 1874 in Markham, *Whaling Cruise*, 112.

mollymawk   a fulmar (*Fulmarus glacialis*); also applied to other birds, including the *Diomedea melanophrys*. Sometimes mis-spelt 'mollyhawk'.

From the Dutch '*mallemok*' (from '*mal*', foolish, and '*mok*', gull): cf. the German '*Mallemuck*' and the French '*malamoque*'.

First attested in 1694 in the translation of Martens, *Observations (Several Late Voyages*, 1711), 100.

monitor   a shallow-*draft*, low-*freeboard* ironclad vessel used for coastal bombardment until World War II.

A class named after the original *Monitor*, designed in 1862 for the American Navy during the Civil War, by Captain John Ericsson.

Hence first attested in 1862, in a letter of 20 January by Ericsson, quoted in Church, *Life* (1890), I, 255: 'The ironclad intruder will thus prove a severe monitor to those leaders.'

monkey   a small sixteenth- and seventeenth-century coastal trading vessel, single-masted, with a *square sail* and sometimes also a *topsail*; a small *grog cask*; a form of double steam engine for marine use; various other marine mechanical devices, many now obsolete. A *monkey block* is a small single *block stropped* with a *swivel*; a *monkey forecastle* is a small low forecastle, open *aft* and used for stowage; a *monkey gaff* is a small gaff for the flag, hoisted or secured above the *spanker gaff*. A *monkey jacket*, once a thick, close-fitting serge garment worn on *watch*, is now the everyday jacket of officers and *petty officers*. A *monkey pump* is a straw inserted through a gimlet hole, to suck liquor from a cask; a *monkey rail* is a light rail fitted above another; a *monkey seam* (or *monk's seam*) is a flat overlapping seam made in the centre of a sail. A *monkey's fist* is a *Turk's head* on the end of a *heaving line* to make it easier to throw; a *monkey's island* is a platform on or over the *bridge*; the *monkey's orphan* was the ship's fiddler.

From the word for the simian animal, often indicating something small, neat, clever or (derisively) not quite human (see below). The word itself is of uncertain origin. In the Middle Low German version of *Reynard the Fox*, in 1498, '*Moneke*' is the name of the son of Martin the Ape, who earlier, in the four-teenth century, is called '*Monnekin*' or '*Monnequin*' in Jean de

Conde, *Li Dis d'Entendement*. The OED suggests that there may have been, apart from the proper noun, an otherwise unrecorded Middle Low German word, '*moneke*', corresponding to a Middle Dutch word, '*monnekijn*', which was a colloquialism for 'monkey', and that 'this may have been brought to England by showmen from the continent'. This putative word, the OED continues, 'would appear to be a diminutive... of some form of the Romance word which appears as early modern French *monne* (16th–17th centuries)... The origin of the Romance word has not been discovered.' A less tortuous hypothesis might conceivably be that '*monnequin*' simply meant 'manikin', implying that a monkey looked like a little man. 'Mon' for 'man' is after all a common substitution in Scotland.

The first attestation of the word in a nautical context is not, curiously, as a coastal vessel, although this is recorded by Kemp, *Oxford Companion*, 556. According to the OED, which omits that usage, the word is first attested in a maritime sense in 1750 in Blanckley, *Naval Expositor*: '*Monkey*, a Block made of Iron with a Catch, made use of in Ginns for driving Piles.' It next appears in 1794 in *The Elements and Practice of Rigging and Seamanship*, I, 80, as 'a machine for setting the arms, &c.' In 1834, in *Peter Simple*, Marryat used the word as an abbreviation for **monkey block** (see above); and in 1867, finally, Smyth, in *The Sailor's Word-book*, defined 'monkey' as 'a kind of wooden kid for grog'.

monsoon   seasonal wind, most important in the Indian and Western Pacific Oceans, caused by the summer heating and winter cooling of the land mass; the ensuing rain.

From the early modern Dutch '*monssoen*', with the same meaning, and probably derived, like all the equivalents in Romance languages, from the Arabic '*mausim*', season.

First attested in 1584 by Robert Barret in Hakluyt, *Principall Navigations* (1589), II, i, 278.

moonraker (also **moonsail**)   a small sail *set* above the *skysails* of *square-riggers* in very fair weather.

From 'moon' (from OE 'mona' and a common Teutonic root) plus 'raker' (ultimately from the OE noun 'raca', the verb being adopted from ON '*raka*'). Originally, at least as early as the eighteenth century, the term was applied to natives of Wiltshire, the story going about that some of them raked a pond trying to catch the reflection of the moon – although a Wiltshire retort was that this was the tale they told the revenue men who caught them trawling for smuggled and concealed brandy.

First attested in its nautical sense in 1829 in Jerrold, *Black-ey'd Susan*, reprinted in Booth, *English Plays* (1969), I, 173.

moor   to make fast either to a laid *mooring* or to a *quay* or *pontoon*, or by dropping two *anchors*: if only one is used, the vessel is anchored, not moored.

To *moor alongside* is to secure a boat close and parallel to another, or to a *pier*, quay or pontoon, etc. A *mooring* is a permanent arrangement of *ground tackle* laid to secure a vessel without her using her own anchors. A *mooring bitt*, *bollard* or *cleat* is one of many types of deck fitment for securing *mooring lines*; a *mooring buoy* is a large cylindrical buoy or other *marker*, attached to ground tackle, to which vessels may tie up; *mooring lines* are strong ropes with which a vessel is moored. The *mooring pennant* is the wire passed through the *hawse pipes* and round the *bow* so as to bring the *cable* round the bow and secure it to a *mooring swivel*; a *mooring pipe* is an oval casting in the *bulwarks* for the passage of the *fasts*; *mooring rights* are permission to lay and use moorings; *mooring snatching* is picking up and using a mooring without permission; a *mooring spring* is one inserted in a mooring line to prevent *snubbing* and absorb sudden shocks; a *mooring swivel* is one put in each cable to prevent a vessel's getting a *foul hawse*.

From the early modern English 'more' and probably from OE 'marian'.

First attested (in the form of 'mooring') in 1495 in *Naval Accounts* (Navy Records Society, 1896); (as 'mored') in 1497, *Ibid.*

Morse (code)   method of signalling by dots and dashes, either visual or aural, now obsolescent. The International Morse Code contains signals for accented and other letters additional to those found in English.

Named after its inventor, the American electrician Samuel Finley Breese Morse (1791–1812), who also invented the electric telegraph.

The first attestation of the word is hard to isolate, since Morse's name was very generally used to describe his evolving apparatus. Apart from periodicals, a firm but late reference is in 1858 in Prescott, *Electric Telegraph* (1860), xiv, 191.

Mother Carey's (or Cary's) chickens   stormy petrels; snow. Said to be a corruption of '*Mater cara*' (see *The Athanaeum*, 1864, 558/2: 'The sailors' slang for snow… "Mother Cary" being the *Mater cara*… of the Levantine sailors.' How birds and snow could be associated, still less confused, remains a mystery.

First attested in 1767 by Captain Carteret in Hawkesworth, *Voyages*, 1773, I, 318.

mould   in traditional boat-building, a thin, flexible length of wood used to form a pattern of the various frames for the *hull*;

in plastic (GRP) boat construction, the container in which the plastic is set; to construct by this latter method. A *moulded hull*, in traditional boat-building, is one built by bonding layers of veneer. *Moulding*, in shipbuilder's parlance, is the depth of any piece of wood; the *mould-loft* is a long building on whose floor the boat's lines can be drawn full-scale and the wood assembled accordingly.

From ME 'molde', seemingly an alteration of OF '*modle*' (modern French '*moule*'), which may be related to OF '*modelle*' (modern French '*modele*') and hence to 'model'.

First attested in 1769 in Falconer, *Dictionary* (1780 edition).

mouse a collar of *spunyarn* round a rope or wire (e.g. a *stay*) to prevent something (e.g. a running *eye*) slipping past; a mark on a rope to show when it has reached the desired position; to close the *jaws* of a hook with spunyarn to make it secure.

From the familiar word, itself from OE 'mus' and thence from common Teutonic and Indo-Germanic roots. The figurative implication is of something small and neat.

First attested in 1750 in Blanckley, *Naval Expositor*.

mud (usually plural) tracts of mud on the margin of a *tidal* river. A *mud-berth* is a hollow in the shore near the high water mark where a boat can settle and lie up; a *mud flat* is a muddy shore or bank submerged at high water; the *mud hook* is slang for the *anchor*; *mud pattens* are broad wooden pattens used for crossing soft mud; *mudlarks* are people, often children, scavenging on mud banks at low water.

From ME 'mode', 'mudde', cognate with the Middle Low German and Low German '*mudde*'.

First attested in this 'estuary' sense in 1883 in Davies, *Norfolk Broads*, I, 3.

muffled oars *oars* bound with *canvas*, etc., where they pivot (in *crutches*, in *rowlocks*, or on *thole pins*) to deaden the sound.

Probably from OF '*mofle*', '*moufle*', thick glove: cf. the English 'muff'.

First attested in this 'rowing' sense in 1761 in *The British Magazine*, II, 500.

murderer a small iron or brass handgun used until the nineteenth century against enemy boarders of a ship, with socket emplacements in various places on board.

From both the Anglo-French '*mordreur*' and the basic noun 'murder', itself derived from OE 'mordor'. The name was no doubt given to inspire reciprocal confidence and fear.

First attested in this sense in 1497 in *Naval Accounts* (Navy Records Society, 1896), 338.

mushroom anchor a special *stockless anchor* with a heavy rounded hollow *crown*, used for moorings laid in soft *mud*.

So called from its resemblance to an edible fungus, whose name in turn is adopted from the French '*mousseron*' itself usually thought to be derived from '*mousse*', moss.

First attested in 1845 in the *Encyclopaedia Metropolitana*, XIV, 548/1.

muzzler   a wind 'dead on the nose', i.e. directly against the intended course.

From the noun 'muzzle', itself derived from OF '*musel*', '*muzel*', '*mousel*', '*muisel*' (modern French '*museau*'), which in turn has its origin in the medieval Latin '*musellum*', a diminutive of the medieval Latin '*musus*' or '*musum*', snout.

First attested in this nautical sense in 1878 in Kemp, *Manual*, 359/2.

Nail-sick   leaky at the nail-holes.

From 'nail' (from OE 'naegel', 'naegl' – cf. the modern German '*Nagel*') plus 'sick' (from OE 'seoc').

First attested in 1855 in Henry David Thoreau, 'Cape Cod', published in *Putnams Magazine*, 1865 edition, viii, 145.

narrow, narrows (usually plural)   the most confined part of a *fairway*, *channel*, *sound*, *strait* or river. *The Narrow Seas* were those over which the Crown of England claimed sovereignty from about the fifteenth century until the adoption of the three-mile limit: they were the Channel, the Southern North Sea between Britain and the Netherlands, and the Irish Sea.

From the adjective, itself from OE 'nearu', 'nearo', but of otherwise doubtful etymology.

First attested in this maritime sense in 1633 in James, *Strange and Dangerous Voyage*, 106.

nautical mile   see *mile*.

navel-line (also **nave-line**)   in *square-riggers*, a rope or small *tackle* from the *main* and *foremast heads* to the *parrels* or *trusses* of the *yards*, to hold them up while the yards were *swayed up*. *Navel hoods* were thick pieces of wood to protect the *hawse-holes* from chafe; the *navel-pipe* is a metal tube through which the *anchor cable* passes to the *chain locker*.

In these combinations, 'navel' is not a misprint for 'naval', although the latter spelling later spasmodically crept in. The OED admits that its origin and meaning are 'obscure', and it does not appear other than in combination. Commenting on *navel-pipe*, Kemp, *Oxford Companion* (1976), 576, conjectures that: 'The origin of the term, it would appear, was anatomical, coming from the similarity of feeding the cable through a pipe into the chain locker with a mother feeding an unborn baby through the umbilical cord (not unlike a navel pipe) into its stomach.' If sailors were so biologically well-informed and poetically fanciful, then the origin of 'navel' in its nautical sense is indeed the familiar word, from OE 'nafela' and a common Teutonic root, and associated with 'nave', whose primary meaning was the hub of a wheel.

First attested in 1711 in Sutherland, *Ship Builder's Assistant*, 143.

neap (of *tides*)   those in the first and third quarters of the moon, when its pull is most counteracted by that of the sun, making high water lower and low water higher. To be *neaped* is to be left *aground* at this time, when the tidal range is thus decreasing and one may have to wait for the *spring tides* to float the vessel free.

From OE 'nep', but otherwise of unknown origin and obscure meaning.

First attested *c*. AD 725 in the *Corpus Glossary*, EETS, 1885; Hessels, 1890), Int., 196.

necklace   a *chain* or *strop* round a mast or *spar*, often to hold a hanging *block*.

By obvious extension from the familiar word, which in turn is composed, obviously enough, of 'neck' (from the rare OE 'hnecca', nape of neck, as distinct from 'heals', neck – cf. the German '*Hals*') plus 'lace' (from OF '*laz*', '*las*' and the popular Latin '*lacium*' – Latin '*laqueum*', a loop). The original meaning was not a trinket but a snare.

First attested in its nautical sense in 1860 in Stuart, *Catechism*, 55.

ness   promontory, cape or headland.

From OE 'naes', 'nes'. Preserved mainly but not wholly in place-names such as Dungeness, etc.

First attested in the late eighth century in *Beowulf*, 1912.

netting   spaces on the upper deck, the *forecastle*, the *poop* and the *break* of the *quarterdeck* where *hammocks* were stowed by day; a net across the *waist* of the ship on which sails could be spread as a hot-weather awning. *Splinter-netting* was a tout rope netting rigged by sailing navies between the *main* and the *mizen mast* some 12 feet above the quarterdeck to protect those below and cushion any fall of those above.

From OE 'net, 'nett' and a common Teutonic root; first recorded in the eighth century.

First attested in its nautical context in 1567 by G. Fenner in Hakluyt, *Principall Navigations* (1589), 149.

nettle (also and perhaps originally **knittle**)   small *line* for use *on board*; *yarn* of a *strand* when twisted for *pointing*; *reef point*; line of a *hammock clew*.

From the verb 'knit' (from OE 'cnyttan', originally to knot).

First attested in 1627 in Smith, *Seaman's Grammar*, v, 25, where it is spelt 'knettels'. The spelling 'nittles' is attested in 1762, and 'nettles' in 1841 in Dana, , *Seaman's Manual*, 43.

nickey   small *lugsail* boat used off the Isle of Man.

Of unknown etymology: it may be a reference to the name 'Nicholas', to rapidity and accuracy (after one of the senses of 'nick'), or even to the Dutch '*nikken*', to nod, which is otherwise unconnected with 'nick'. 'Old Nick' seems for once not to be involved.

First attested in 1883 in the *Fisheries Exhibition Catalogue*, 4th edition, 132.

niggerheads   *bollards*, and sometimes *winch* heads. A *nigger-headed* sail is one whose *leech* has acquired an inward curve.

From 'nigger' (itself an alteration of 'neger', from the French '*negre*') plus 'heads'. The term, now to be avoided, is a late figurative expression: it was also applied to various plants and rock outcrops.

First attested in this nautical sense in 1927 in Bradford, *Glossary*, 119/1.

nip   a short turn or twist in a rope or *hawser*; such a turn caught fast; pressure on a ship by two converging ice-floes; to bind two ropes together; (of ice) to squeeze a vessel. The nip of a *splice* is the part of a rope that rounds the *thimble*. A *nipper* was a short length of rope used to bind the *anchor cable* temporarily to the *messenger*, used in the days when the anchor was *weighed* round the *capstan* by hand: it was also the term for slings for the *yards* of *square-riggers*, as also for a *hammock* unable to stand on end in the *netting*, and finally for the boys or men who worked the anchor cable nippers. A *nipping turn* is the nipping of one rope to another by a *racking turn*.

The noun is derived from the verb, whose precise source is unknown, although the OED declares that it is 'apparently an ablaut-variant of the stem *nip-*, which appears in the Dutch *nijpen*' – to nip.

First attested in a nautical sense in 1667 in Davenant and Dryden, *Shakespeare's Tempest* (altered), I, I.

no man's land   in *square-riggers*, deck area where *blocks*, ropes, and *tackles* used on the *forecastle* were stowed; a space missed out when scrubbing.

The earliest use of the expression was not (as might nowadays be thought) to denote the unoccupied land between opposing battle-lines, but to describe (from the mid fourteenth century at the latest) the unowned territory outside the north city wall of London, where executions took place. How it came to mean a particular area of deck *on board* ship is uncertain: Kemp, *Oxford Companion* (1976), 599, suggests that it 'arose possibly because it is neither on the forecastle nor in the waist, nor on the port or starboard side of the ship'. It would also be a place where no one was permanently stationed or permitted to sleep.

First attested in a nautical sense in 1769 in Falconer, *Dictionary* (1780 edition).

norman   short wooden bar inserted in one of the holes of a *windlass* or *capstan* to *veer* a rope or fasten the *cable*; a preventer pin or bar through the head of a *rudder* to secure it against loss; a metal pin or bar to keep the *chain* clear and prevent its falling off.

Although this appears to be the same word as that used for an inhabitant of Normandy (as it is in Dutch and other languages), the connection is as the OED points out 'not clear'. Could there be some fanciful reference to supposedly Norman qualities – reliability, firmness? Or, more plausibly, were the devices in question of Norman origin?

First attested in a nautical sense in 1769 in Falconer, *Dictionary* (1780 edition).

nose   the *prow, bow*, or *stem* of a vessel. A *nose-ender* is a wind from dead ahead, on the nose.

Figurative use of the familiar word, which comes from OE 'nosu', with cousins in most Western European languages.

First attested in a nautical sense in 1538 in Elyot, *Dictionary*.

nothing off   order to the *helmsman* to keep as close to the wind as possible.

From the familiar word, composed (obviously enough) of 'no' (a reduced form of 'nan', 'non', from the French *'none'*) plus 'thing' (from OE 'thing', which originally meant a council – cf. the Nordic *'storting'*, big council, parliament – then a matter brought before it, then a concern, before it began to be used ambiguously and evasively, and hence very generally): the colloquialism 'he has a thing about it' is a reversion to an earlier sense of the word.

First attested as a nautical expression in 1846 in Young, *Nautical Dictionary*.

nozzer   a novice seaman or new *hand*.

Relatively recent sailor's slang, this word has three possible origins, none of them confirmed or particularly convincing. First, it may be derived from 'No, Sir'; secondly (according to Granville, *Sailors' Slang* (1962), 82/2), it may have originated in the training establishment *HMS Ganges*, where at one time the petty officer in charge of new entrants was nicknamed 'Nosey'; thirdly and least implausibly, it could be a corruption of 'novice'.

First attested in 1943 in 'Taffrail', *White Ensigns*, ii, 32.

nuggar   large, broad-*beamed*, high-*prowed*, two-masted *lateen-rigged* transport boat used on the Nile.

A direct borrowing from Arabic.

First attested in 1870 in Baker, *Ismailia* (1874 ed.), I, 173.

nun buoy   one shaped like two cones, one above the other base to base (an Eastern *cardinal mark*).

From 'nun' in the now rare sense of a child's spinning top, first attested as such in 1598 and only conjecturally related (perhaps on account of a shaped head-dress) to the name given a member of a female religious order. In its ecclesiastical usage the word is derived from OE 'nunne' and ultimately from the Latin '*nonna*' and the late Greek '*nonna*', respective feminines of '*nonnus*' and '*nonnos*', originally titles given to the elderly: cf. the Italian '*nonno*', grandfather, and '*nonna*', grandmother.

First attested in its nautical sense in 1703 in Dampier, *New Voyage*, III, I, 149.

nut   the ball on the end of the *stock* of a *fisherman*'s type *anchor*, to prevent the stock going into the ground. Over several centuries, different nautical lexicographers have offered different precise definitions. The OED, perhaps wisely, calls the ball 'A part of a ship's anchor', without specifying which.

From the familiar word, whose origin is OE 'hnutu', with a common Teutonic root, from a pre-Teutonic '*knud-*', related also to the Old Irish '*cnu*', the Gaelic '*cnu*' and the Welsh '*cneuen*', all meaning 'nut' in its familiar sense.

First attested in a nautical sense in 1627 in Smith, *Seaman's Grammar*, vii, 29.

Oakum   teased-out fibre of old *hemp* rope, tarred and used for *caulking*. Picking oakum is no longer used as a punishment, afloat or ashore.

From OE 'acumbe', off-combing. In that spelling, it was applied to the coarse part of flax that was separate in the process of hackling.

First attested in its nautical use (and something nearer its present spelling) in 1481–90 in the *Howard Household Books* (Roxburghe Club, 1844), 24.

oar   a long wooden pole used as a lever to propel a boat through the water (as distinct from a *paddle*, which has no fixed pivoting point, or a *punt*-pole, which is simply thrust against the bottom); an *oarsman* or *oarswoman*, i.e. a *rower*. *Oars* is the command to cease *pulling* and 'lay on your oars', or remain sitting upright with the *blades* of the oars horizontal.

From OE '*ar*', cognate with ON '*ar*', '*or*' and from the Old Teutonic '*aira*': its root may also survive in the Greek '*eretis*'.

First attested before AD 900 in *The Anglo-Saxon Chronicle*, year 897. The current spelling is first attested in 1582.

off   away from the land, the ship, or the wind; at a distance. *Off and on* means keeping the land by heading in and standing off; *offing* is the distance a ship keeps away from the shore; *offshore* means, in the case of a ship, at a distance from the shore or (in the case of a wind) coming from the shore. *Off soundings* means to seaward of the 100-*fathom* line; *off the wind* means further from the wind when necessary when attempting to sail *close-hauled*, or with the wind *abeam*.

Originally from OE 'of', and not completely differentiated until about 1600; the primary sense of 'of' was 'away from'.

First attested in a nautical sense in 1610 in Shakespeare, *The Tempest*, I, I, 53.

oggin   the sea. A nautical slang corruption of 'hogwash'.

First attested in 1946 in Irving, *Royal Navalese*, 126: '*Oggin*, the sea; the Drink; the Ditch. The term descends to us aitch-less from an earlier abuse of the sea as the Hogwash.'

oil bag   a porous container from which oil is allowed to seep in rough weather to calm the seas. *Oilies* or *oilskins* are protective garments, originally (from the late nineteenth century) made of *canvas* impregnated with oil, but now made from plastics. An *oily wad* is a seaman without ambition.

From early ME 'oli', 'oyle', 'oile' (from the Latin '*oleum*', oil or olive oil – the Latin '*olea*' meaning olive) plus 'bag' (from early ME 'bagge': cf. the medieval Latin '*baga*', chest.

First attested in its nautical sense in 1889 in *The Century Illustrated Magazine*, March, 710/1.

on a lay   (of a ship's *crew*) recruited for a share of the profits instead of wages.

On a split yarn means lightly secured, ready for use. *On board* is *aboard*; *on the beach* is on leave, out of work, or retired. *On the beam* is at right angles to the ship and at any distance from her; *on the bow* is between dead ahead and 40 degrees to *port* or *starboard*; *on the quarter* is between *abeam* and *astern*. *On the wind* is *close-hauled*. *Onshore* (of a wind) is blowing towards the land.

From OE 'an', on, plus 'lay' in the sense of a wager, from the verb, whose origin is OE 'lecgan': cf., for instance the German *'legen'*.

First attested in 1889–91 in *The Century Dictionary*.

open   (of a *transit*) with neither mark obscuring the other; (of a boat) undecked; to draw further apart. *Open hawse* refers to a vessel lying to two *anchors* without the *cables* becoming crossed. *Open link* is a studless *chain* link. *Open order* is a formation in which large ships are four *cables* apart.

From OE 'open' and a common Teutonic root; the 'o' was originally short, but lengthened in ME.

First attested in a nautical sense, meaning in full view, in 1478; but this usage being obsolete, the first attestation as regards a transit is in 1686 in the *London Gazette*, No.2112/4.

orlop, orlop deck   the lowest deck in a ship, beneath the lower deck.

From the Dutch *'overloop'*, a covering, since the orlop (not usually or at first considered a deck) was the floor or covering over the *hold* or over the *beams* below the turn of the *bilge*.

First attested in 1467 in *The Acts of the Parliaments of Scotland, James III* (1814 edition), 87.

otter boards   boards *rigged* with *lines* and *bridles* and *towed* under water to spread a net or keep open the mouth of a *trawl*. An *otter trawl* is a beamless trawl fitted with otters to hold it open.

From 'otter' (OE 'otr', 'ot(t)or', 'oter', from a common Teutonic root going back to the Sanskrit 'udra') plus 'board'. Originally, otter boards were used by salmon fishers to tauten their line or net as they towed it along the shore: they bore several hooks, and were so named because the animal in question was a predator of salmon.

First attested in 1901 in *The Field*, 5 January, 19/2.

outboard   beyond the rail or *bulwarks* of a vessel; outward from a vessel's *fore-and-aft* centre line; an *outboard motor* (i.e. one fitted outside the vessel, usually on the *transom*). *Out* occurs in many other nautical combinations. The *outer jib* is that in front of the inner jib; the *outfall* is the seaward end of a sewage pipe, usually marked by an *outfall buoy* or *beacon*; to *outfoot* is to best a competitor; an *outhaul* is a rope or *purchase* used to pull a sail outboard along a *spar*; to *outpoint* is to sail closer to the wind than a competitor. An *outlicker, outligger* or *outleager* was a short *boom* extended *astern* in older *square-riggers* to haul down the *mizen sheet* when the *mizen-*

mast was *stepped* too far *aft* for this to be done *inboard*; an *outrigger* is, first, a float secured outboard of a boat or *canoe* to prevent a *capsize*, or secondly a *spar* extended outboard for sails or *rigging*, or thirdly a *beam* used to secure the masts when *careening*, or finally a boat whose *rowlocks* are on outboard supports. To *outsail* is to best a competitor.

From 'out' (OE 'ut' – cf. the Dutch '*uit*', the German '*aus*', etc.) plus 'board'.

First attested in 1823 in Crabb, *Technological Dictionary*.

overboard   over the side of the ship; out of her. 'Over', like 'out', is found in many other nautical combinations. *Overcanvassed* means carrying too much sail; an *overfall* is a *wave* that breaks owing to the wind or current over a *shoal* or ridge or because of conflicting currents such as *tide-races* or *tide-rips*; an *overhand knot* is one made by passing the end of a rope over its *standing part* and up through the *bight* thus formed; *overhangs* are those parts of a vessel that extend beyond her *waterline*. To *overhaul* is to overtake, or to pull the *blocks* of a *tackle* farther apart, or to *refit* by examining and repairing. A *overhauling whip* is one used to separate the blocks of a tackle. An *overlap* occurs when the *bows* of an over-taking vessel pass the *stern* of that overtaken; *overlapping planks* are those of a *clinker-built* boat. *Over-raked* is the situation of a vessel at *anchor* in bad weather with seas breaking over her bows, often because she is on too short a *scope*. To *overstand* is to stay too long one one *tack* when *beating* towards an objective. The *overtaking light* is the compulsory stern light, white and visible for two miles from right *astern* to two *points abaft* the *beam* on either side; the *overtaking* (or give-way) vessel is one approaching another within the prescribed arc of her overtaking light, whether by night or by day. *Over the bay* is ancient seamen's slang for tipsy. *Over the masthead* was an exercise or minor penalty in old sailing ships, which involved climbing the *rigging* up one side and down the other.

From 'over' (OE 'ofer', with the later connotation of passing over the brim and spilling), plus *board*: treated as two separate words until the seventeenth century.

First attested *c.* AD 1000 in Aelfric, *Homilies* (Thorpe, 1844–6), I, 246.

oxter plates   the outer plates of a ship's *hull* riveted or welded to the *sternpost*.

From 'oxter' (OE 'oxta', 'ohsta', armpit – cf. the Latin '*axilla*', diminutive of 'axula') plus 'plates'. 'Oxter' in this sense is found as late as 1977 in Bagley, *The Enemy*, although in the following year the word had to be defined in the *Journal of the Lancashire Dialect Society*: the explanation may be that Bagley was originally a Kendal man.

First attested in 1885 in Paasch, *From Keel to Truck*, 46.

Packet, packet-boat   a mail-boat plying regularly between two *ports*, also carrying passengers and goods.

A diminutive of the thirteenth-century ME 'packe', 'pakke', a bundle or package. It remains uncertain whether 'packet' came from the French *'paquet'* or vice versa: both appear together in the sixteenth century. However, since a French diminutive of the obsolete *'paque'* would have been *'pa(c)quette'*, it seems marginally more likely that the French word is derived from the English – unless the word was an Anglo-French diminutive of 'pack'. The original meaning of 'packet' was of course the mail itelf: 'packet' in the sense of a boat is an abbreviation of 'packet-boat', whose appearance precedes that of 'packet' as a boat by more than 60 years.

First attested as 'packet-boat' in 1641 in Evelyn, *Diary*, ll October; as 'packet' meaning a boat in 1709 in Sir Richard Steele, *The Tatler*, No. 107, 1.

paddle   a short *oar* used without an fulcrum such as a *rowlock*, mainly for *rafts* and *canoes*; to use such an implement. A *paddle steamer* is one propelled by *paddle-wheels*, fitted with blades or floats and mounted either in a pair *amidships* or as a single wheel at the *stern*.

The word's origin is obscure. Since it originally meant a spade-like tool for cleaning a ploughshare or using as a trowel or hoe, some have conjectured that 'spaddle', which it was sometimes called in the seventeenth and eighteenth centuries, was its original form, a diminutive of 'spade'. But as an agricultural implement, 'paddle' appears as early as 1407, whereas 'spaddle' is not attested before 1669, and may indeed be unconnected with 'paddle', instead having links with 'spatule' which appears in or before 1425, or with 'spatula', first attested in 1525. Whatever their inter-relationship, if any, 'paddle' seems to be the oldest of all these words.

First attested as a means of propelling a boat in 1624 in Smith, *Historie*, II, 32.

Paddy's hurricane   a dead calm. *Paddy's lantern* is the moon; a *Paddy's purchase* is one with no gain and an actual power loss, as, for instance, a *line* passing over a nail.

From the pet-form of 'Padraig' or 'Patrick' plus *hurricane*:

these are only some of the many derogatory allusions to the Irish.

First attested in 1865 in Smyth, *Sailor's Word-book* (1867 edition), 514.

painter   a length of rope for securing a small boat, usually attached at the *stem*.

Unconnected with art or with the brushlike end of a frayed rope, but with no other unequivocal derivation. The OED affirms that 'Connexion with *panter*, net, snare... has been conjectured, but no corroborative evidence has been found.' Yet the original meaning of the word, in the fifteenth century, was the rope or *chain* with which the *shank* and *flukes* of the *anchor* were secured to the ship's side when it was carried at the *cathead*. This seems to confirm that the basic idea was restraint or confinement – hence a likely origin in 'pent' or 'penned' (from 'pen' and thence from the ME verb 'pennen' and the OE noun 'penn'). In the seventeenth century, the word was occasionally spelt 'penter' when used in its anchor-securing sense; but how it came to shift to its present meaning remains uncertain.

First attested in its present nautical sense in 1711 in Sutherland, *Ship Builder's Assistant*, 154.

palleting   raised platform in the magazines of old *warships* on which powder barrels were kept dry.

Two alternative etymologies are on offer. The first is 'pallet', from ME 'paillet' (cf. the dialect French '*paillet*', bundle of straw, from '*paille*', straw, and the Latin '*palea*', chaff), meaning a humble bed and then a *ballast*-locker (now obsolete in this sense). The second possible source is 'pallet', derived from the French '*palette*', diminutive of '*pale*', a spade, shovel, blade, etc.: by the eighteenth century this also meant a flat board of various kinds, including the blade of an *oar* or the float of a *paddle-wheel*.

First attested in 1815 in Falconer, *New Universal Dictionary* (ed. Burney).

palm   the broad triangular surface of the *fluke* of an *anchor*; a leather or *canvas* hand band with a hole for the thumb, plus a thimble, used in sewing sails; often known as a *sailmaker's palm*.

From the palm of the hand, which originated as ME 'paume', from the identical French word, and associated with the Latin '*palma*', which also meant the tree of the same name, whose leaves might be thought to resemble a hand with the fingers outstretched. In early English, none the less, the two words seem to be distinct, that for a palm tree being OE 'palm', 'palma', 'palme', with parallels in Old Scandinavian, Old High German, etc. Latin, in other words, appears to be the bridge, if any, between hand and tree.

First attested as applied to an anchor in 1706 in Phillips, *New World*, 6th edition, edited by J. Kersey; as a sailmaker's aid, in 1776 in Falconer, *Dictionary* (1776 edition).

pant   to vibrate or (of iron plating) to bulge in and out under the impact of the waves. A *panting beam* is one fitted *forward* to reduce vibration.

From the familiar word, whose origin remains uncertain. Common since the mid fifteenth century, it may be related to (or an abbreviation of) OF *'pantoisier'*, to be short of breath.

Although applied figuratively in the seventeenth century to waves, first attested in its present sense in 1869 in Reed, *Shipbuilding in Iron and Steel*, I, 12.

parbuckle   a device for raising or lowering a *cask*, etc., by passing the middle of a rope round a *bollard*, etc., leading the two ends under the object in question, and in effect using it like the *sheave* of the *block* to increase the pulling power.

A popular and now universal misreading of 'parbunkle', whose origin is unknown. The present spelling seems to have emerged around 1760.

First attested, in its original but now obsolete spelling, in 1626 in Smith, *Accidence*, 13; in its present spelling in 1769 in Falconer, *Dictionary* (1776 edition).

parcel   to cover a rope with *canvas*, plastic pipe, smaller rope, etc., to protect it from chafe.

From the original sense of the noun, by a devious route.

'Parcel' originally meant a part, or even a small part: its immediate origin was the French *'parcelle'*, from the Latin *'particella'*, a diminutive of the already diminutive *'particula'*, from *'pars'*, a part. The verb from the noun meant, first, to divide into 'parcels', then to put up in 'parcels', no doubt wrapping them. The OED considers that 'The connexion of sense 3 [the nautical sense] is not apparent, and it is perhaps a distinct word.' In fact, however, the notion of wrapping seems a very plausible link.

First attested in a nautical sense in 1627 in Smith, *Seaman's Grammar*, ii, 13, where it describes not wrapping a rope but covering a *caulked seam* with *canvas* and sealing it with *pitch* – a sense now obsolete.

parish-rigged   poorly or parsimoniously equipped.

From the familiar word for the administrative unit, no doubt considered in this context as the source of niggardly poor relief. The word itself originally appeared in two forms: one was 'paroche', from the Anglo-French and OF and thence from the late Latin *'parochia'*; the other was 'parosshe', from OF *'paroisse'* and thence from the popular Latin *'parocia'*. The word appears in Norman French in the *Laws* of William the Conqueror, but not in English before the thirteenth century.

First attested in 1899 in Bullen, *Sea-waif*, 163.

Parliament (or **Parliamentary**) **heel**   a makeshift way of *heeling* a ship, in the days of the sailing Navy, for instance by concentrating the weight of the guns, etc., on one side and then the other, so as to be able to clean or repair as much of the *hull* as possible without *careening* or using a *dry dock*. In 1782 the practice caused tragedy: HMS *Royal George*, undergoing a Parliament heel, tilted so far that the sea entered her lower gun-ports and she *capsized* and sank at Spithead with great loss of life. A poem by William Cowper (1731–1800), 'The Loss of the Royal George', commemorated the event with more spirit than accuracy; he also translated it into Latin as '*In Submersionem Navigii, cui Georgius Regale Nomen Inditum.*'

Obviously from the name of the British legislature (which is derived through ME from OF '*parlement*'), but why? Some believe that it denoted naval contempt for parliamentary rule, implying that a job incompletely done (cleaning only part of the *hull*) would be enough to satisfy an MP; but, according to Kemp, *Oxford Companion* (1976), 632, 'the more likely derivation is from the period of its introduction, the term coming into the British Navy during the first Anglo-Dutch War (1652–4) when England was governed by Cromwell's Parliament and when this process was much used'. This seems unconvincing, especially in view of the 115-year time-lapse between the War in question and the first record of the expression.

First attested in 1769 in Falconer, *Dictionary* (1789 edition).

parrel   a rope, wire, *collar* or similar device to attach a *yard* or the *jaws* of a *gaff*, etc., to the mast, enabling it to pivot and to be raised and lowered. *Parrel beads* are wooden beads that may be strung on a rope parrel to facilitate hoisting: they are sometimes themselves known as 'parrels'. A *parrel lashing* is a rope with an *eye* in each end for attaching a yard to a mast; a *parrel rope* is a rope parrel; *parrel trucks* are similar to parrel beads.

According to the OED, the same word as 'parel', which it describes as an aphetic form of ME 'aparail', apparel: it compares the word with the fourteenth-century OF '*parail*', rigging. A further comparison might be made with the modern French word '*appareiller*', to hoist sail.

First attested in 1485 in *Naval Accounts* (Navy Records Society, 1896), 37.

part   (of a rope or *cable*) to break. To *part brass rags* is to quarrel, the origin of the expression supposedly being the habit of shipboard friends keeping their brass-cleaning rags in a joint bag until one or the other decides otherwise: see Drury, *Tadpole* (1898), 141–2. Doubt may be cast on this explanation by the way in which the expression is often pronounced: 'They parted *brass rags*' – as if the italicised phrase intensified the sense of the verb, adding a note of high dudgeon.

A specialised but not wholly eccentric use of the verb 'part', which originally meant to divide or separate (as a comb parts the hair or a couple parts). Its origin is the French '*partir*', which in the past meant to divide as well as to leave.

First attested in its nautical sense of breaking in 1793 in Smeaton, *Narrative*, 149.

partners   pair (or more) of *timbers* secured to the deck around the places where the masts, *bitts*, *capstan*, or *Samson-post*, etc., penetrate it, for strengthening.

From the familiar word, whose origin seems to be '*parcener*', Anglo-French for partner or sharer, from OF '*parconier*': the word is first found in English, in a legal context, in the late thirteenth century. The substitution of 't' for 'c' seems to have been under the influence of 'part', and also to have occurred in the late thirteenth century.

First attested in its nautical sense in or before 1608 in Vere, *Commentaries*, in Arber (ed.), *An English Garner* (1877–96), 48.

paternoster, paternoster line   an arrangement of consecutive hooks at intervals on a *fishing line*. Burgess, *Dictionary* (1961), 157, appears to be alone in defining the word as 'A pattern of small booms as used for fishing.' Could 'booms' here be a misreading for 'hooks'?

From the first two words of the Lord's Prayer in Latin, via the rosary – the hooks being fancied to resemble its beads, and the 'paternoster bead', usually every eleventh bead, being of distinctive shape and indicating that here the Lord's Prayer is to be said.

First attested in this fishing sense in 1676 in Cotton, *Angler*, Cassell, xvi, 153.

paunch or **paunch mat** (also sometimes spelt *panch*)   thick matting made by weaving twists of *ropeyarns* together and ramming them close, used as a protection against chafe or when dragging heavy objects along the deck.

From the familiar word, whose source is ME 'panche', from Old Northern French, with counterparts in various Romance languages, including Italian ('*pancia*'), from the common Roman '*pantica*'. The OED considers that the nautical use of the word may be derived from a variant of 'paunch' spelt 'paunce' and applied to the garment covering the belly (cf. the Italian '*panciotto*', waistcoat). 'Paunce', contrary to what might be supposed, is unconnected with 'pants', which is an abbreviation of 'pantaloon' – which in turn began life not as the name for nether garments but as that of the Venetian character in Italian *commedia dell'arte*, from the *'pantalone'* mask the character wore.

First attested in its nautical sense in 1626 in Smith, *Accidence*, 15.

pawl   a short bar that (with others) slots into a toothed wheel or rack on a *winch* or *capstan* as a ratchet to prevent its running back; thus to secure a winch, etc. A *pawl-bitt* is a strong vertical post in which the pawls of a *windlass*, etc., are fixed; the *pawl-head* is that part of a capstan to which the pawls are attached; a *pawl-post* is a pawl-bitt; the *pawl rack* is a circular cast-iron plate around the capstan, secured to the deck, with notches for the pawls to fit into; a *pawl-rim* is a pawl rack.

Like 'pale' and 'pole', 'pawl' probably comes from the Latin *'palus'*, no doubt via the French *'pal'*, a stake; but unlike 'pale' and 'pole', it has no known early history in English. In Welsh the word (identically spelt) means a pole, stake or bar.

First attested in English nautical usage in 1626 in Smith, *Accidence*, 13.

pay   to fill, dress or cover with *pitch*. To *pay away*, of a vessel, is to fall away to *leeward*; to *pay debts with flying topsails* is to sail away with unpaid debts; to *pay down* is to pass a rope down. A *paying off pennant* is a very long one, hoisted to show that a ship will shortly discharge all *hands*; to *pay off* (of a vessel) is to pay away, (of a rope) is to let out, and (of a crew) to discharge. To *pay out* a rope or *cable* is to slacken it so as to secure it again in a new position, as distinct from *casting it off* altogether. To *pay round* is to turn the ship's *head*.

'Pay' in the sense of filling with pitch comes from the Old Northern French *'peier'*, the Central French *'poier'*, *'poyer'*, and ultimately from the Latin *'picare'*, from *'pix'*, pigment: the past tense of this word is 'payed'. The more familiar word 'pay', which gives rise to all the other nautical usages above, comes from ME and OF *'payer'*, which meant both to reimburse and to please: its source was the Latin *'pacare'*, to please, which in the Middle Ages came to mean also to settle up financially.

First attested in its *caulking* sense in 1627 in Smith, *Seaman's Grammar*, ii, 13; and in its other nautical sense in the same year and the same source, vii, 30.

pea   the pointed end of an *anchor*'s *fluke*.

Unconnected with the vegetable (whose name is an erroneous singular from the supposedly plural 'pease'): according to the OED, it is said to be shortened from *peak*.

First attested in 1833 in the *Penny Cyclopaedia*, I, 505/1, which corroborates the OED by adding 'Seamen by custom drop the k in *peak* and *fluke*, which they pronounce *pea* and *flue*.'

pea-jacket   a coarse thick garment formerly popular at sea.

Equally unconnected with the vegetable, 'pea-' in this context comes from the fifteenth-century 'pee', 'pe', and thence from the late Middle Dutch '*pie*', now '*pij*', a coarse woollen coat: the direct source may be the Dutch '*pij-jakker*'. Marryat, in *Poor Jack* (1840), xxii, wrote of 'a short P-jacket (so called from the abbreviation of *pilot's* jacket)'. The OED justifiably concludes that this 'appears to be a mere gratuitous surmise'.

First attested in 1721 in *The American Weekly Mercury*, 23 March, 2/2.

peak   the narrowing *hold* at the *bow* of a ship (the *forepeak*) and/or at the *stern*; the upper corner or *head* of a triangular sail, but more properly the *after* upper corner of a *gaff main-sail*; the upper end of a *gaff*; the point on the *fluke* of an *anchor* (also known as the *pea*); to raise the gaff. A *peak brail* is one attached to the peak of a sail; a *peak downhaul* is a rope *rove* through a *block* at the outer end of the gaff to haul it down; a *peak halyard* is one for hoisting the peak of a gaff; a *peak piece* is a piece of *canvas* for strengthening the peak of a sail; a *peak purchase*, in *cutters*, is one fitted to the standing peak halyards for *swaying* up tight; the *peak span* is a rope support from the mast to the peak of a gaff. *Peak tanks* are those adjoining the *stem* and *stern*, usually containing water *ballast*.

The etymology and even the pronunciation of this word or these words are complex and uncertain. The word appears to be separate from 'Peak' as in the Peak District, which may have been a proper noun, 'Peac', but if so was later confused with 'peak' in the hilly sense. The most likely ancestor of the word may be 'pike', which in eighth-century old English was spelt 'piic' and in ME 'pic' – like the French word, which Littré considers to be of Celtic origin: this word meant primarily a pick (the tool) and secondarily a mountain peak (owing to its pick-like pointed shape). In English, 'pick' has not acquired this mountainous meaning; but the Langdale Pikes are a reminder, if any be needed, that 'pike' has. 'Peak' first appears in the sixteenth century, probably as an offshoot of 'pike', since in the fifteenth century 'peked' appears as the equivalent of 'piked'. What all these related words have in common, of course, is the notion of pointedness.

First attested in the sense of a ship's hold in 1693 in Lyde (transl.), *A True and Exact Account*, reprinted in Arber (ed.), *An English Garner*, VII, 11; of a sail, in 1762–9 in Falconer,

Shipwreck, II, 387; as part of an anchor, in 1793 in Smeaton, *Narrative*, 143.

pelican hook   a *slip hook* whose tongue, shaped like a pelican's bill, is held by an easily removable link or ring: used to secure guard rails, *lifeboats*, etc.

From its resemblance to the bill of a pelican: the source of this word is the Late Latin '*pelicanus*', '*pelecanus*', itself from the Greek '*pelekan*'.

First attested in 1890 in *The Century Dictionary*.

pelorus   a large pivoted metal protractor or *compass* dial or ring, used for taking relative *barings*: it may be fitted around a compass or simply act as a 'dumb', i.e. non-magnetic compass dial. It has two sighting arms or *vanes*. '*Pelorus Jack*' was the name given to a *dolphin* which, at the end of the nineteenth century and the beginning of the twentieth, used to accompany every ship sailing through the French Pass between d'Urville Island and the mainland of South Island, New Zealand – the Westernmost part of Pelorus Sound: the New Zealand Government actually put the animal under its protection.

First attested in 1854 in Friend and Browning, *British Patent No. 2652*.

pen   space for vessels to *berth* between *piers*, *pontoons* or fingers; a covered *dock* for a naval vessel, notably a submarine. Cf. *painter*.

From OE 'penn' meaning an enclosure for animals, poultry.

First attested in a nautical sense in 1769 in Falconer, *Dictionary* (1789 edition).

pendant, pennant   a short length of rope or wire, with a *thimble spliced* into one end, on each side of the *main* and *foremasts* of a *square-rigger* just below the *shrouds*, for hooking on the main and fore *tackles*; any similar *strop* used for various jobs *aboard* and characterised by a preceding adjective; a narrow tapering *flag*.

The etymology and pronunciation of these words need explanation, as does their relationship with *pennon*. The strops described above derive their name from the French '*pendant*', hanging, found as early as the thirteenth century: it was sometimes pronounced with the 'd' sounded, but more often without. The flag sense seems to be derived from 'pennon', and is always pronounced without the 'd', as it is now most often written: but its official nautical spelling has always been 'pendant'.

First attested, as a strop, in 1485 in *Naval Accounts* (Navy Records Society, 1896), 36; as a flag, in the same year and the same source, 40.

pennon   very long coloured streamer *flown* from the *mast-*

head or *yardarms* of fifteenth and sixteenth century *warships* on state occasions.

Originally applied, in the fourteenth century, to streamers flown from knights' lances or helmets, the word is derived from OF *'penon'*; but it soon became confused with 'pendant' and 'pennant'.

First attested in a nautical sense in 1627 in Drayton, *Agincourt* (etc.), lxvii.

perch   withy, pole, or sapling marking the edge of a *channel* in shallow water, as in a river or estuary.

From the thirteenth-century French *'perche'* and thence from the Latin *'pertica'*, a pole, long staff or measuring-rod, and long commemorated in old arithmetic textbooks in the phrase 'rod, pole or perch'.

First attested in 1465 in the *Calendar of the Ancient Records of Dublin* (1889-), I, 323.

periplus   a circumnavigation; a voyage; a circuit; an instructive account of such a voyage: cf. the French *'périple'*.

Directly from the Latin, which in turn is from the Greek *'periplois'*, literally a voyage around.

First attested in Greek and Latin as early as 500 BC, but in English in 1776 in Chandler, *Travels in Greece*, 221.

petty officer   not necessarily a small-minded office-holder, but the naval equivalent of an army non-commissioned officer.

'Petty' is from late ME 'pety' and thence from the French *'petit'*, small; not until the sixteenth century did it begin to acquire the overtone of triviality, of which this and other specialized usages remain free. 'Officer' is from the Anglo-French *'officer'*, equivalent to the fourteenth-century OF and modern *'officier'*, and ultimately from the medieval Latin *'officiarius'*.

First attested in a general sense in the sixteenth century, but in its specific naval sense in 1760 in Johnston (anon.), *Chrysal*, 1822 edition, III, 14.

picaroon   a *pirate*; a pirate ship; a slave ship; to act as a pirate, to pillage.

From the Spanish *'picaron'*, augmentative of *'picaro'*, a rogue. Not to be confused with the North American 'picaroon' (from the French *'piqueron'*, a pike), meaning a pole fitted with a spike or hook for logging and/or fishing.

First attested in 1624 in Smith, *Generall Historie*, v, 184.

picket-boat   a vessel employed for reconnoitring in advance of a ship; a large utility boat carried by a *warship*.

From the French *'piquet'*, originally a stake, then specifically one to which (or a stockade within which) horses were confined; then by extension a detachment of soldiers whose mounts they were, and finally any special detachment of troops, etc., including eventually a strike picket.

First attested in 1866 in *Oregon State Journal*, 13 January, 1/4.

pieces of eight   Spanish dollars or *pesos* to the value of eight *reals* each, and marked with the figure 8. Best known as the parrot's catch-phrase in R.L. Stevenson, *Treasure Island*, 1883.

Not necessarily an Anglicisation of '*pesos*', since 'pieces' was already used for coins as early as 1526. 'Piece' originated in ME as 'pece' (sometimes also plural), from the thirteenth-century OF word of the same spelling, and thence from the late Latin '*pettia*', '*pettium*' and the early medieval Latin '*pecia*', '*petia*', '*pecium*', '*petium*', a detached portion of land.

First attested in 1610 in Jonson, *The Alchemist*, III, iii, 15.

pier   one of the supports of a bridge; a solid stone or other structure projecting into the sea or a river, to protect a harbour and form a landing-place; a *mole* or *breakwater*; more recently, a pleasure promenade, open beneath, projecting over the sea. A *pierhead jump* is a sudden and very late recruitment to a ship's company.

Although of uncertain origin, this word's ancestor appears in the twelfth century as 'per', from the medieval Latin '*pera*'. It is unlikely to be derived from OF '*piere*', stone, or from that word's Latin source, '*petra*'. However, it may just possibly be linked with the OF (Picardy and Flanders) word '*pire*', which was very rarely spelt '*piere*', and which meant a breakwater or barricade of piles, or a weir or *boom* protecting a harbour.

In its mole or breakwater sense, first attested in 1515 in *Extracts from the Council Register of the Burgh of Aberdeen 1398–1625* (Spalding Club, 1844–8), 94.

pillar buoy   a tall metal structure on a buoy to make it visible from a distance, often at the seaward end of a series of *channel buoys*.

From OF '*piler*' (modern French '*pilier*') and thence from the Latin '*pila*', a pillar, *pier*, or mass, plus *buoy*.

First attested in 1858 in *Mercantile Marine Magazine*, V, 285.

pillow   block of *timber* fixed to the deck of a sailing vessel just inside the *bow* as a support for the *bowsprit*.

Figurative extension of the familiar word, whose source is OE 'pyle', 'pylu', probably from a Western German '*pulwi*', which gave rise to the Latin '*pulvinus*', a cushion.

First attested in its nautical sense in Smith, *Accidence*, 12.

pilot   expert with local knowledge, taken on board to guide a ship into and out of a port and its approaches, or through a *channel*, river, canal, etc.; colloquially, the navigator; a book of sailing instructions for particular waters. *Pilotage* is the art of navigating in shallow coastal waters; a *pilot boat* or *cutter* (or *pilot vessel*) is one taking pilots to meet an incoming ship; the *pilot house* is the *wheelhouse*; a *pilot jack*, the Union Flag with a white border, was originally *flown* to indicate 'I need a pilot', now indicated by flying *flag* G (with yellow and blue vertical stripes).

From the early modern (sixteenth-century) French '*pillotte*' and the medieval Latin '*pilotus*'; thought to have been modified by popular etymology from similar words spelt with a 'd' in place of the 'l', and hence to be descended from the late Greek '*pidotis*', a steersman, from '*pidon*', an *oar* (but in the plural a *rudder*).

First attested, but simply as a ship's navigator, in 1530 in Palsgrave, *Lesclaircissement*, 254/1; as a temporary guide, in 1549 in Thomas, *Italie*, 74.

pinch   to *luff up* too close to the wind; to squeeze a vessel, e.g. between two bigger ones, distorting her *hull*.

From the Old Norman French '*pinchier*' (OF '*pincier*', modern French '*pincer*') – possibly nasalized from an earlier word like the Walloon '*pissi*', which resembles the obsolete Italian '*picciare*' (Venetian dialect '*pizzare*', modern Italian '*pizzicare*' – familiar in English from its past tense, indicating that a stringed instrument such as a violin is plucked), and also the early modern Dutch '*pitsen*', the Flemish '*pinssen*' and the German '*pfetzen*', all three meaning to pinch in the familiar sense.

First attested in the nautical sense of luffing in 1895 in *The Daily News*, 11 September, 5/5; in the sense of a ship's being squeezed, in 1896 by J.E. Jeaffreson in *The Westminster Gazette*, 4 August, 5/1.

pink   originally, a small *flat-bottomed* coasting and fishing vessel, later especially with a narrow *stern*; later, a small Danish *warship*. A *pink stern* was a narrowing *after* part with a rising *sheer*.

From the Middle Dutch '*pincke*', '*pinke*' (modern Dutch '*pink*'); cf. the Middle Low German, Low German, and Modern German '*Pinke*', the French '*pinque*' and the Italian '*pinco*'. The word's earlier ancestry, if any, remains unknown.

First attested in 1471 in *The Acts of the Parliament of Scotland, James III* (published in 1814), II, 100/2.

pinkie, pinky   a narrow-*sterned* fishing boat, either identical with or similar to a *pink*.

A diminutive of 'pink'.

First attested in 1843 in *The Knickerbocker*, XXII, 187.

pinnace   originally, a small, light vessel, usually two-masted and at first *square-rigged*, sometimes with a *lugsail* on the *main*, later *schooner-rigged*, used as a *tender*, scout, etc.;

subsequently, a double-banked (usually eight-*oar*ed) ship's boat for a *warship*.

Associated with the French '*pinasse*', '*pinace*', equivalent to the thirteenth-century Spanish '*pinaca*', with similar forms in Portuguese and Italian. However, the French and ME spelling and pronunciation of the word were different: 'spinace' in ME, '*espinace*' in OF, corresponding to the medieval Anglo-Latin '*spinachium*'. The resemblance to 'spinach' may not be wholly fortuitous: early etymologists linked this word with the Latin '*spina*', thinking of the vegetable's prickly seeds. Could small, busily mobile boats evoke a similar image? The Latin '*spinachium*' seems to figure in the background of both words.

First attested in its augmented form ('espynasse') in 1321–7 in *Ancient Correspondence* in the Public Record Office, LVIII, 8; in a more normal Latin form ('*pynneis*') in 1546 in Marsden (ed.), *Select Pleas* (Selden Society, 1894–7), I, 138; in English some four years later by Barton in the Surtees Society's *Miscellanea* (1888), 68.

pin-rack (also *pin-rail*)   *fife-rail*, board carrying *belaying-pins*.

From late OE 'pinne' and a common German root, plus 'rack', from the Middle Dutch '*rec*', '*reck*'.

First attested in 1875 in Knight, *Dictionary of Mechanics*.

pintle   the male element, fitting into a female *gudgeon*, on which a *rudder* pivots.

From OE 'pintel', probably a diminutive since various words in early Danish, Frisian and German lack the suffix and share the word's now obsolete meaning of penis.

First attested in its nautical sense in 1486 in *Naval Accounts* (Navy Records Society, 1896), 15.

pipe   the *boatswain's whistle*; to make a call on this. *Pipe down* is the day's final call on the whistle, the naval equivalent of 'The Last Post'. *Piping the side* is the ceremonial call (*piping aboard*) used when dignitaries come *on board*: its high and low notes were originally indications to the *crew* manoeuvring the *boatswain's chair* whereby the persons were hoisted aboard. A *pipe cot* has nothing to do with the whistle: it denotes a hinged *bunk* stretched on a frame of galvanized metal piping (in the familiar, non-nautical, but related, sense of this word).

From OE 'pipe' and the late Latin '*pipa*', each meaning a tubular musical wind instrument.

First attested in its nautical sense in 1638 in Herbert, *Relation* (second edition), 30.

piragua (also *periagua*, *pirogue*)   a dug-out *canoe*, originally Caribbean.

From the Carib and Spanish words of the same spelling: the form 'pirogue' spread under French influence.

First attested in English in 1609 in *Virginia Richly Valued*, 41.

pirate   water-borne robber, usually at sea, but also on navigable rivers, etc.

From the Latin '*pirata*' and the Greek '*peiratis*', from '*peiran*', to assault.

First attested in English (it appears in Latin in an English text of 1387) in 1426 in Lydgate (transl.), *De Guileville's (G. de) Pilgrimage* (EETS, 1899–1904), 23963.

pitch   a mixture of *tar* and resin boiled down and used for *caulking*; the plunge of the bows into a *trough* in the waves; (of a *propeller*) the distance one turn would advance it in unmoving water. *Pitch and toss* is the motion of a vessel plunging about in the waves; to *pitch-pole* is to overturn (or be overturned) *stern* over *stem* by heavy (following) seas.

Pitch as a caulking medium is from OE 'pic' and thence from the Latin '*pix*', pigment. As concerned with motion, the noun is derived from the verb and from ME 'piche', 'picche': originally it meant to drive in, as of a stake.

First attested in its caulking sense in or before AD 700 in *The Epinal Glossary* (in *Oldest English Texts*, EETS, 1885) 820; describing motion in a nautical context, in 1762–9 in Falconer, *Shipwreck*, II, 725; as applied to a propeller, in 1863 in Barry, *Dockyard Economy*, 264.

plain sailing (or **plane sailing**)   now, anything straightforward and trouble-free; originally, sailing by a *plane chart* as if the globe were flat.

'Plane' is a seventeenth-century adaptation of 'plain', to distinguish it from other senses of that word and to draw it closer to the parent Latin '*planus*', flat. 'Plain', its original spelling, is associated with OF '*plain*' both as a noun and as an adjective; the source remains the Latin '*planus*'. After the first Mercator-projection chart was produced in 1569, it became clear that sailing by a plane chart was no longer accurate, especially when far from the equator.

First attested in 1699 in Dampier, *New Voyage*, II, I, 90.

plane   to skim the water as a result of the *forward* part of the *hull*'s rising out of it at speed.

From the French '*planer*', already known in the twelfth century, and thence from the Latin '*planare*', originally to make smooth.

First attested in its nautical sense in 1914 in *Technical Report of the Advisory Committee on Aeronautics 1912–13*, 243, dealing with aeronautical floats.

plank   length of wood for covering the outside and deck *beams* of ships. *Planking* is the inside and outside casing to a ship's *frames*. To *plank it* is to sleep on deck. *Plank on edge* is long and narrow, as of certain now superseded racing boats. The *plank sheer* consists of the upper planks that form the *sheer* on a boat's side.

From ME and Old Northern French 'planke' and thence from the post-Augustan Latin *'planca'*, itself probably from a Greek root *'plak-'*.

First attested in a specifically nautical context in 1495 in *Naval Accounts* (Navy Records Society, 1896), 154.

pledget   a roll of *oakum* prepared for *caulking*, pressed into the *seam* and then *payed* with *pitch*; originally, a compress for a wound.

Of disputed origin and (at first) pronunciation as well as early spelling. Without the 'd', and if the 'g' were hard, the word might be associated with 'plug' and descended from the Middle Dutch, Middle Low German and Low German *'plagge'*, meaning among other things a rag. The apparently diminutive ending of 'pledget', however, may suggest a Romance source, possibly the Latin *'plaga'*, a wound: cf. the French *'plaie'*. But no ancestor of the word has been traced before the sixteenth century, and its seems highly likely that the link is with 'plug' and associated words in various Teutonic languages, contaminated by confusion with 'pledge', which is several centuries older.

First attested (in a medical context) *c.* 1540 in *Cyrurgyons of Mountpyller*, A j. The OED offers no nautical citations. Burgess, *Dictionary* (1961), 161, defines 'pledge' [sic] as 'A roll of oakum ready for caulking', but omits 'pledget'. Kemp (ed.), *Oxford Companion* (1976), 653, gives the fullest nautical definition, but omits any medical reference.

Plimsoll line or **mark**   mark on the sides of all British merchant ships to indicate the *draught* levels to which they may be loaded in varying conditions: tropical fresh water, fresh water, tropical sea water, summer sea water, winter sea water, winter North Atlantic. These horizontal lines are accompanied by another (level with that for summer sea water, showing summer *freeboard*), bisecting a circle and bearing the letters 'L' and 'R' (for Lloyd's Register of Shipping) or, more rarely, those of some other registration society.

Made compulsory in Britain by the Merchant Shipping Act of 1876, the mark owes its name to its proponent and champion Samuel Plimsoll, MP (1824–98).

First attested (in a slightly different form – 'Plimsoll's mark' – from its present-day version) in 1881 in *The Daily Telegraph*, 28 January.

point   one of the 32 points of the *compass*, 11 degrees and
15 minutes apart; a promontory or cape; to sail close to the wind.
To *point a rope* is to ornament its end by *unlaying* and
unstranding it as far as the *whipping*, then making a tapered
heart from the inner *strands*, *marling* them to a point, the
remaining *yarns* being twisted into *nettles;* to *point and graft*
is to decorate a rope by pointing one end and working a similar
pattern with the strands of an *eye spliced* in the other. *Pointers*
are the two end stars of the plough. To *point higher* is to sail
closer to the wind; to *point ship* is to swing the ship's *head* into
the right direction after *weighing anchor* and before gaining
way. The *points of sailing* are the various angles a boat may
make with the wind (e.g. *close-hauled, fetch, reach, broad
reach, run*). To *point up* is to point higher.

   From two or perhaps even three sources: the first associated
with the French '*point*', a minute hole or dot, the second with
the French '*pointe*', a pointed extremity, and the third a verb
indicating direction. All are clearly related in sense, but distinct;
in some other languages, different words express the different
senses (e.g. in German '*Punkt*' and '*Spitze*').

   First attested in a quasi-nautical sense, referring to points of
the compass, in or before 1500 in Arnolde, *Chronicle*, 1811
edition, 86; as a promontory, in 1553 in Eden (transl.), *Treatyse*
(ed. Arber, 1885), 32; as a verb denoting direction (e.g. 'up' or
'higher'), in 1889 in *The Century Dictionary*.

polacca, polacre   a three-masted Mediterranean *square-
rigged* (and sometimes *lateen-rigged* sailing vessel of the
seventeenth and eighteenth centuries.

   From the French '*polacre*', '*polaque*', Polish – but otherwise of
uncertain origin. As the OED remarks, 'It is difficult to understand
how a Levantine or Mediterranean vessel should be so described.'

   First attested in or before 1625 in Purchas, *Pilgrimes*, II, vi,
885.

pole   mast (usually in the phrase 'under *bare poles*').

   From OE 'pal', itself derived from the Latin '*palus*', a stake.

   First attested in this nautical sense in Sturmy, *Mariners
Magazine*, I, ii, 17.

Pompey   nickname for Portsmouth.

   The OED declares the word's origin 'unknown'. Kemp (ed.),
Oxford Companion (1976), 659, conjectures that, according to
'one theory', 'it owes its name to the fact that the local fire
brigade, known as the Pompiers, used to exercise on Southsea
Common, adjacent to the town'.

   First attested as applying to the town (and its football club)
in 1899 in *The Evening News*, 9 December, 3/6.

pongo   sailors' slang for a soldier or *marine*.

From an Angolan or Loango word, sometimes spelt '*mpongo*', applied to a large anthropoid ape.

First attested in this opprobrious sense in 1917 in 'B. Copplestone', *Lost Naval Papers*, vi, 85.

pontoon   a *flat-bottomed* boat used as a *lighter*; a special boat used to support a road or footbridge; a *caisson*; a floating structure acting as a *pier* or *quay* but rising and falling with the tide; a low flat vessel with cranes, *capstans*, *tackle*, etc., used for *careening* ships.

From the French '*ponton*', known as early as the fourteenth century as denoting a flat-bottomed boat, and thence from the Latin '*ponto*', a *punt* (a word probably descended directly from the Latin, since it appears in the tenth and eleventh centuries).

First attested in 1591 in Unton, *Correspondence* (Roxburghe Club, 1847), 266.

poop   the raised *aftermost* deck of a ship; (of a sea) to break over the *stern* of a vessel, which is then *pooped*. *Poop lanterns* are a *flagship*'s *stern lights*; the *poop royal* was a short deck above the *after* end of the poop in French and Spanish *warships* of the sailing navies, known to British shipwrights as the *topgallant poop*. From ME and OF 'pupe' (in modern French '*poupe*') and thence from the Latin '*puppis*', stern. The colloquial (originally US) 'pooped', meaning exhausted, may be derived from the nautical expression, although the OED declares its 'origin unknown'.

First attested as a nautical noun in 1489 in Caxton, *Fayttes of Armes* (translation), II, ii, 93; as a nautical verb, in 1748 in Anson, *Voyage*, III, ii, 319.

poppet   a short piece of wood used for various purposes: to support a ship's *hull* during launching; to fit into the *rowlock* of a *rowing-boat* when the *oars* are not in use, so as to strengthen the *gunwale*; or to support the end of a ship under construction. 'Poppet' originally meant a small person, but already in the seventeenth century it carried a technical sense, being used to denote one of the upright pieces in a turning lathe.

From ME 'popet', 'popette', a doll, cognate with 'puppet'.

First attested in a nautical sense *c.* 1850 in Greenwood, *Sailor's Sea-book*, 138.

popple   a strong ripple, as of a cross sea in shallow water.

Although the noun is of fairly recent date (see below), the verb (now rare) is of late medieval origin, and almost certainly onomatopoeic, comparable with the Middle Dutch and Dutch '*popelen*', to quiver or murmur, as well as with the medieval Latin '*populare*', '*papellare*', which meant only to murmur.

First attested as a verb in the thirteenth century in *Early English Alliterative Poems* (EETS, 1864–9), C, 319. The noun, although used in the fourteenth century and until the sixteenth for a bubble in boiling water, and in the seventeenth century for a swelling like a bubble, is not attested as denoting a ripple until 1875 in Buckland, *Log-book*, 80.

port   a *shore* haven and/or its town; an opening in the side of a ship; the left-hand side of a vessel (facing forward); to turn to that side; a *port* cover; a *porthole* or (to nautical purists) *scuttle*, i.e. a hinged glass window, often round, in the side of a ship. The *port establishment* is the time of *high water* at a given port in relation to the phase of the moon or to some other port. *Port fire* is a composition made up as a slow-burning signal *flare*. *Port-hand buoys* are those marking the left-hand side of a *channel* when approaching from the sea or with the main flood *tide*. A *port sail* is an old sail or *tarpaulin* slung between ship and shore when loading or unloading *cargo* above it. *Port sills* or *cills* are the timbers lining the top and bottom of gun ports in sailing *men-of-war*. On the *port tack* describes a sailing boat with the wind coming over her port side and the sails trimmed accordingly: on the *port gybe* is sometimes used to describe the same situation when the wind is *abaft* the *beam*. The *port watch* consists of half the *crew*, the other half being (surprise, surprise) the *starboard watch*.

The three strands of meaning here, although distinct, are related. As a haven, 'port' is derived from the Latin *'portus'*, a harbour. As an opening, it comes from the Latin *'porta'*, a door or gate. As the left-hand side, it may owe its origin to the fact that openings for cargo were made on the opposite side to that of the *steersman*, or starboard side; this usage long predated its official adoption in 1844 as a substitute for the previously current *larboard*; it was also the *quay* or seaport side.

First attested as a haven *c.* AD 893 in King Aelfred (transl.) *Orosius* (EETS, 1883), I, 1, 20; as an opening, in 1390 in Gower, *Confessio amantis* (R. Pauli, 1857; *English Works*, EETS, 1900), I, 197; as the left-hand side, in 1543–4 in the *Admiralty Court Examiner*, 92 (January 11), Rypper's Deposition; as a port cover, in 1627 in Smith, *Seaman's Grammar*, vi, 27; as a porthole, in 1882 in Cussans, *Heraldry*, 3rd edition, 112.

Portuguese parliament   an argument with everyone talking at once.

Opprobriously derived from the supposed uproar in the Lisbon legislature, which some monoglot British sailor may have visited and misunderstood.

First attested in 1897 in 'F.B. Williams', *On Many Seas*, 388.

posh   smart, classy.

The word belongs here only to scout a frequent and ingenious piece of almost certainly false etymology. It is often said to be derived from the letters 'P.O.S.H.', supposedly standing for 'Port Out, Starboard Home' and allegedly printed on the return tickets of first-class Peninsular and Oriental (P & O) liner passengers paying a supplement to book *cabins* on the port or Northern side when steaming out to the East and on the starboard (also Northern) side coming home, so as to avoid the heat and glare of the sun. There are many objections to this theory – not least the fact that cabins were numbered; they are comprehensively expounded by G. Chowdharay-Best in *Mariner's Mirror*, January 1971, 91–2. A far more likely source is the noun 'posh', first attested in 1830 as thieves' slang for money, and derived from the Romany word for a half, specifically a halfpenny, and by 1867 (if the same word) used to describe a swell or dandy.

If the P & O theory were right, the adjective 'posh' might have been expected to be first attested fairly soon after the opening of the Suez Canal in 1869; but – apart from a spelling 'push' by P.G. Wodehouse in 1903 (which may be a different word) – 'posh' is first attested as an adjective in 1918 in *Punch*, 25 September, 204.

post-captain   title given between about 1730 and 1824 to full *captains* in the British Navy, the courtesy title of 'Captain' being extended during that period to those in charge of lesser vessels, who would now hold the rank of *commander*. To 'give post' was to confer the rank of full captain.

The prefix comes from the French '*poste*', position, and thence from the Latin '*postum*', itself a contraction of '*positum*', the neuter past participle of '*ponere*', to place.

First attested in 1747 in an *Order-in-Council* of 10 February on the 'Rank and Precedence of Officers', 11.

powder-monkey   powder-boy,   employed   to   carry gunpowder from the powder-room to a *warship's* guns.

'Powder' from ME 'poudre', associated with the same word in French, and derived from the Latin '*pulverem*' (nominative '*pulvis*'), plus *monkey*.

First attested in 1682 in Shadwell, *John Bayes*, Ep. A iv.

praam, pram   a *flat-bottomed* Dutch or Baltic *lighter*; a flat-bottomed gunboat; a small ship's boat; a small US sailing *dinghy* much like a British Mirror; a *tender* with a *transom* at the *prow* as well as the *stern*.

Totally unconnected with 'perambulator' or its familiar contraction, but from the Dutch '*praam*', itself one of a group of almost identical words in Old Frisian, Middle Low German,

ON, French, etc. All these are derived from the Old Slavonic *'pramu'*, cognate with the Old High German *'farm'*, freight-boat or *ferry*, and related to the English word 'fare', originally meaning to travel (cf. 'thoroughfare').

First attested as a lighter in 1390–1 in Derby, *Expeditions* (Camden Society, 1894), 42; as a gunboat, in 1715 in the *London Gazette* No.5340; as a ship's boat, in 1860 in Reade, *The Eighth Commandment*, 338; as a sailing dinghy, in 1937 in the *Baltimore Sun*, 31 July, 11/8; as a tender with a cut-off *bow* (not mentioned in the OED), in 1961 in Burgess, *Dictionary*, 163.

pratique   release from *quarantine* (and, nowadays, clearance by customs).

From the French '*(libre) pratique*' in the sense of (unrestricted) interchange (and thence the Latin *'practica'*); originally spelt in English 'pratticke'.

First attested in 1609 in Biddulph, *Travels* (1612 edition), 4.

press gang   group of men under an officer employed to press men into naval service, usually in time of war.

Despite the temptation of invoking 'pressure', 'press' in this context is derived from 'prest', from the OF *'prest'* (modern French *'pret'*) a loan – referring to the advance on pay (the king's shilling) that sealed the engagement of the unwilling (or sometimes unwitting) recruits.

First attested in 1693 in Robinson, *The British Fleet* (1894), 424.

press of sail (originally *press sail*, *prest sail*, *pressing sail*) as much sail as can safely be carried.

Of unknown origin, except in so far as 'press' has the sense of effort and urgency.

First attested in 1592 in Nashe, *Four Letters Confuted* (in *Works*, ed. Grosart, 1883–5), II, 240.

preventer (originally *preventer-rope*)   additional *stay*, usually to support a mast, often as an extra *backstay*.

From the Latin *'praevenire'*, to anticipate, hinder, etc. First attested in or before 1625 in *Nomenclator Navalis* (Harleian MS 2301) and Manwayring, *Sea-mans Dictionary* (1644).

prick   to mark a position or *course* on a *chart*; a small roll of tobacco. A *pricker* is a small *marlinespike*; *prick-stitching* is a system of sewing used for heavy *canvas* or other materials, in which the needle goes through one layer and then, separately, the other: it was used for sewing an extra central seam between the two that normally join the cloths of a sail – an operation also known as *pricking*.

From OE 'prica', 'pricca', a sharp point; the roll of tobacco may have owed its name to its resemblance to the bound hair on the nape of the neck, known as *'perique'*, Louisiana French for tobacco but also surely derived from *'peruque'* and thence from the French *'perruque'*, wig. Confused as this etymology may seem, some may prefer it to the alternative theory that the tobacco roll resembled a penis.

First attested, as chartwork, *c.* 1595 in Captain Wyatt, *The Voyage of Robert Dudley* (Hakluyt Society, 1899), 21; as a tobacco roll, in 1666 in Davies of Kidwelly, *Caribbee Islands*, 190.

prime   to make ready (e.g. a *lead* before *sounding*, a pump, a cartridge); (as an adjective) tip-top or (of a seaman) fully trained. The *prime meridian* is that which passes through Greenwich; *tides* are said to be *priming* when the time between them is less than the average; a *priming iron* was a pointed iron tool with a wooden handle, used to expose the powder of a muzzle-loading cannon by thrusting it through the vent hole and puncturing (priming) the cartridge.

Probably from the Latin *'primus'*, first (since the actions described by the verb were the first to be undertaken); the source of the adjective is the same word in its competitive connotation.

First attested in a nautical context in 1513 in Douglas (transl.), *Virgill*, III, vi, 213.

privateer   a privately-owned armed vessel authorised to operate against enemy ships, especially merchant ships; a *commander* or *crew* member of such a vessel.

A development from 'private', on the same lines as 'volunteer'. 'Private' comes from the Latin *'privatus'*, meaning deprived of public office. The original expression for 'privateer' was 'private man-of-war', and the practice of issuing letters of marque, or licences, for such ships goes back as far as the late thirteenth century. Privateers were finally abolished in 1856.

First attested in 1651 in the *Calendars of State Papers*, where it was clearly a summary colloquialism; it appears in the *Papers* themselves *c.* 1664 (Lynch, *Calendars of State Papers, Colonial*, 1880, 211).

prize   ship or property captured at sea in war; contraband seized and confiscated.

Prize money is the net proceeds from the sale of ships and goods thus captured and condemned in an Admiralty Court.

Not the same word as 'prize' in the sense of a trophy or reward, which is derived from ME 'pris', 'prise' – now 'price'. In the nautical sense of booty, the word comes from the French *'prise'*, meaning either the act of seizure or the material seized. In English the word is largely obsolete except in its nautical context.

First attested in or before 1512 in Rymer, *Foedera*, (1704–35; 1816–30), XIII, 328/2.

proa   Malayan boat, now usually meaning one carrying a large triangular, often *lateen*, sail, with an *outrigger* and the ability to sail both 'forward' and 'backward' by adjusting the sail and shifting the *rudder* or *steering oar*.

From the Malay '*p(a)ra(h)u*' (sometimes spelt '*prahu*'): this word means any kind of boat.

First attested in 1582 in Lichefield (transl.), *Lopez de Castanheda*, I, xxv, 62b.

propeller   the rotating *screw* that forces a ship through the water, also known as the *wheel*.

From the Latin '*propellere*', via the verb 'propel'.

First attested in its nautical sense in 1809 in the *United States Patent Specifications* (Fulton).

proviso (as in the expression *a proviso* or *a-proviso*)   a (usually) *stern warp* attached to the *shore* in addition to an *anchor offshore*.

From the ablative absolute of the Latin '*providere*', and meaning 'it being provided that': but the logical connection remains obscure, the nearest modern colloquial equivalent perhaps being 'for if' or 'just in case'.

First attested in 1627 in Smith, *Seaman's Grammar*, ix, 45.

prow   the *fore* part of a vessel (now chiefly a literary expression); in the sixteenth and seventeenth centuries, the fore gundeck of a naval ship.

From the French '*proue*' (sometimes spelt '*proe*' in the fourteenth century) and thence from the Latin '*prora*' and the Greek '*prora*', earlier '*proira*', a prow.

First attested in 1555 in Eden (transl.) *Decades* (ed. Arber, 1885), 231.

puddening, pudding   thick padding of *yarns*, matting, rope, *coir*, etc., used wherever chafe is likely, e.g. as a *fender*. A *pudding bag* is a stocking or sleeve used as a *weather vane* or windsock; a *pudding chain* is one made of short links to run easily over a *sheave*, once used for *jib halyards* to avoid stretching; a *pudding fender* is one made of puddening or pudding in this sense.

From ME 'poding', 'puddying', almost certainly cognate with the contemporary (thirteenth-century) French '*bodin*', now '*boudin*', and initially meaning (as '*boudin*' still does) a kind of meat sausage. That sense is first attested in 1305; that of a sweet pudding not until 1544. The remoter origin of the French word is hard to determine, although it may be linked with the Italian '*boldone*' and the Latin '*botulus*', whose stem may be connected with the French '*bouder*', originally meaning to pout. There may be a link between the English word and 'pod', although the latter seems not to have emerged until the seventeenth century – a possible but far from certain common antecedent being the rare OE 'puduc', a swelling': cf. the Westphalian dialect '*puddek*', a lump or pudding.

First attested in its nautical sense (postdating the sweet course) in or before 1625 in *Nomenclator Navalis* (Harleian MS 2301) and Manwayring, *Sea-mans Dictionary* (1644), 1f, 61b.

pull   (in the Navy) to *row*.

From OE 'pullian'. Kemp (ed.), *Oxford Companion* (1976), 674, conjectures that the naval usage 'may have come about because most naval seamen at the oars in a boat are not very much concerned with the finer points of rowing, such as feathering the oar at the end of a stroke, but are more concerned with getting the blade square into the water and pulling it through with maximum force'.

First attested in this sense in 1676 in Shadwell, *The Virtuoso*, II, 20.

pulpit   originally, the *poop* of a ship; then a *harpooner's* platform; now, the metal guardrail at the *bow* of a *yacht*.

By obvious extension from the familiar word, first used in its ecclesiastical context *c*. AD 1200. The word comes from the Latin '*pulpitum*' (medieval Latin '*pulpitrum*'), a platform, pulpit; cognate with the French '*pupitre*', desk.

First attested, as meaning the poop, in 1513 in Douglas (transl.), *Virgill*, VIII, iii, 46; as a harpooner's platform in 1888 in Goode, *American Fishes*, 250; as the bow guardrail, in 1961 in Burgess, *Dictionary*, 164. This last affirms that the pulpit may be 'at the bow or stern'; but in practice the stern guardrail is now almost universally known, familiarly, as the *pushpit*.

punt   a small *flat-bottomed craft*, originally a floating platform for working on the *hull* of a ship; a wildfowler's vessel for stalking game-birds; in a general usage a craft with square ends propelled by a *pole*.

From OE 'punt', attested *c*. 1050 and thence from the Latin '*ponto*', a Gallic transport, a floating bridge or pontoon. Over the centuries, it assumed a number of forms, including 'pontonium', pontebot(s), and 'punte boots'.

First attested in its present form in 1568 in that year's edition of Withals, *Short Dictionarie*, 10a/2.

purchase   a device to increase power by means of a rope *rove* through one or more *blocks*; when two or more blocks are involved, this is known as a *tackle*, unless double or treble blocks are used, in which case they are known as twofold or threefold purchases. The word is also used to describe the mechanical advantage thus obtained.

Originally meaning the hunt (as in 'the chase'), the word is of ME origin and from OF *'porchas'*, *'pourchas'*, *'purchas'*.

First attested in 1711 in Sutherland, *Ship Builder's Assistant*, 26.

purse net, purse seine   a fishing net that can be closed like a purse, used mainly to catch *shoal* fish.

An extension from the familiar word, whose origin is OE and ME 'purs', almost certainly from the late Latin *'bursa'* (which gives rise to similar words in other Romance languages), and whose 'b' became a 'p' in English under the influence of OE 'pusa', 'posa', a bag. 'Seine' comes from OE 'seyne' and thence from the Latin *'sagena'*, a net.

'Purse net' is first attested (in this case for catching rabbits, etc.) *c.* 1410 in *The Master of Game* (Digby MS 182 etc., ed. Hahn), vii; 'purse seine' in 1870 in *The American Naturalist*, IV, 515.

purser, pusser   originally, the officer in charge of provisions and clothing; from 1825 onwards, when part of Royal Navy *crews'* wages were allowed tobe paid monthly, the purser acquired this duty too, and in 1842 was designated 'purser and paymaster', then in 1852 'paymaster'. Nowadays the rank of purser is still used in merchant ships for the officer in charge of finances and, in passenger liners, the passengers. 'Purser' is also sometimes used to denote a boat fishing with a *purse net*. 'Pusser' (with the 'u' pronounced as in 'pus', not 'puss') is the nautical pronunciation of the word, which therefore appears (rather self-consciously) with this alternative spelling. In most of the combinations below, the word has a mocking overtone, no doubt because paymasters are often thought stingy by those they pay. A *purser's crab* is a naval uniform boot; a *purser's dagger* is a seaman's clasp knife; a *purser's* or *pusser's dip* is a small candle. A *pusser's grin* is a sneer; *pusser's issue* is produce supplied by the Admiralty; a *pusser's medal* is a food stain on clothing. A *purser's name* is a false name. A *purser's* or *pusser's shirt on a handspike* is ill-fitting clothing.

From *purse*.

First attested in a nautical sense (as distinct from its earliest sense as a maker of purses) is in 1548 in the *Calendar of the Ancient Records of Dublin* (1889), I, 300.

pushpit   raised guardrail at the *stern* of a *yacht*, corresponding to the *pulpit* at the *bow*. Desoutter, in *Practical Dictionary* (1978), 160, comments: 'Some people get cross when they hear this word, but that is probably because they did not think of it themselves.'

A pun on *pulpit*.

First attested in 1964 in *English Studies*, XLV, 23.

put about   to change from one *tack* to the other. To *put back* is to retrace one's *course* in the opposite direction, or simply to go back; to *put in* is to call at (a port); to *put off* (now rare) is to set forth, but now more commonly to leave a ship by boat. To *put one's oar in* is to intervene with an opinion, possibly unwelcome. To *put out to sea* is to begin a voyage. To *put over* (of the helm) is to move it to the other side, and (of a vessel) to cross to the opposite *shore*. To *put to* is to make for (shelter or the shore). To *put the helm down* or *up* is to move the *tiller* to *leeward* or *windward* respectively.

Like many apparently simple words, 'put' is one of the most complex and versatile in the language. Its source is late OE 'putian'; and although the earlier history of this word is obscure it seems to be derived from a stem that also produced 'butt' (strike with the head) and 'putt' (as in golf); this common stem may have been 'pot-' or 'put-'. One sense of the basic word is to thrust or push relatively gently (as in 'put about'). A common nautical overtone is (almost) to go: by itself, in the late sixteenth century, the word meant to set forth, a usage since obsolete.

First attested in Smollett, *Humphry Clinker*, 8 August, 1.

putty   sticky mud under water; the ship's painter (in the sense of decorator, not rope).

In its familiar sense, the word is derived from 'pot', being its contents. As mud, this is an obvious colloquial extension; as painter and decorator, the association is with the filler.

First attested, in the sense of mud, in 1883 in Davies, *Norfolk Broads*, I, 5; in the sense of a painter and decorator, in 1946 in Irving, *Royal Navalese*, 141.

Q-boat, Q-ship   small merchant ship armed as a decoy intended to destroy enemy submarines in World War I and (until March 1941) in World War II. With few exceptions, they were not particularly successful in World War I, and none even sighted an enemy submarine in World War II, although two were sunk by torpedoes.

Arbitrary use of the letter 'Q'.

First attested in 1918 in the *Army and Navy Gazette*, 10 August, 501/1

quadrant   an obsolete instrument for measuring angles, superseded by the *sextant*; a quarter of a circle, in particular of the magnetic *compass* card; the fan-shaped casting on a *rudder* head that takes the *steering cables*.

From the Latin *'quadrans'*, a fourth part.

First attested in a nautical sense *c.* 1400 in Halliwell (ed.), *Rara Mathematica*, (1841), 58

quant   a *barge pole*, used like a *punt* pole, with a cap at the top and a prong at the bottom to prevent its sinking in the mud; to propel a boat thereby. In Kent it is also used to denote a young sapling or a walking-stick.

Thought to come from the Latin *'contus'* and the Greek *'kontos'*, a boat-pole.

First attested *c.* 1440 in *Promptorium parvulorum* (Camden Society, 1843–65), 418/2.

quarter   the side of a ship or boat between *amidships* and the *stern*, on either side; also, the direction from which a wind is blowing (e.g. 'the wind is in the south-west quarter'). Earlier, the word was also used for a quarter of a *fathom* and for that part of a *yard* that lay between the *slings* and the *yard-arm*. A *quarter badge* is a shaped protective wooden block at the extreme *after* end of a ship's side, where it meets the *transom*, often ornamentally carved. The *quarter-bill* is the nominal list of men and officers in a *warship* showing their action stations. *Quarter-blocks*, in a *yacht*, are those on deck at the two quarters through which the *main sheets* are *rove*, whereas in a *square-rigger* they were two single *blocks* on the quarters of a *yard* through which upper *clewlines* were rove; a *quarter boat* is one hoisted to *davits* on the quarter; *quarter-cloths* were strips of *canvas*, usually painted red, on the *outboard* side of the *quarter-nettings* from the *quarter galleries* to the *gangways*, to protect the *hammocks*. The *quarterdeck* is that part of the upper deck *abaft* the *mainmast* and *before* the *poop*, usually reserved for officers, from which a bridgeless ship was commanded; a *quarterdecker* is a stickler for naval etiquette. A *quarter gallery* was a small 'balcony' to each *cabin* on the quarter, communicating with the *stern* gallery. A *quarter-gunner*, in the sailing navies, was a *petty officer* assistant to the gunner. The *quarter knees* are those strengthening the points at which the *gunwale* meets the *transom*. The *quartermaster*, formerly a petty officer helping to *stow* the *hold*, *coil cables*, etc., is now concerned with the upkeep of navigational equipment and with taking the *helm* when entering of leaving harbour. The *quarter-nettings* were those at the quarters; a *quarter wind* is one that comes over either quarter; *on the quarter*, strictly speaking, is 45 degrees *abaft* the *beam* on either side; *quartering* is sailing with a quarter wind.

From twelfth-century OF *'quarter'*, *'quartier'*, and thence from the Latin *'quartarius'*, meaning the fourth part of any measure or thing.

First attested in a nautical sense in or before 1618 in Ralegh, *Royal Navy*, 10.

quay   (originally spelt 'key'): an artificial landing-place or *wharf*, usually stone, along the boundaries of a harbour for loading and unloading.

From OF *'kay'*, *'kai'*, *'cay'*, as are the German and Danish *'kai'*, the Swedish *'kaj'* and the Dutch *'kaai'* (earlier *'kad'*, *'kae'*, *'kaeye'*); cognate with these is the Spanish *'cayo'*, a *shoal* or *reef*, which was also the meaning of OF *'cay'*, *'caye'*. There is also a possible connection with the Breton *'kae'*, an embankment, and the Welsh *'cae'*, a hedge. In the seventeenth century, the familiar word 'key' was pronounced 'kay', and *'cay'* was sometimes written *'key'* – as it now usually is in the West Indies: cf. Key Largo.

First attested in its modern spelling, after the French *'quai'*, is in 1696 in Phillips, *New World* (fifth edition).

Queen staysail   small balloon-like triangular *main topmast staysail* in a *schooner yacht*.

'Queen' is from OE 'cwen' and the Gothic 'qens', woman. But the sail in question is not named for any supposedly regal qualities of its own, but after the name of the yacht for which it was designed (see below).

First attested in 1944 in Callahan, *Rigging*, 130: 'The late J. Rogers Maxwell introduced a funny little staysail on his famous schooner *Queen* and it has always been known as the queen staysail.' In 1948, in *The Rudder*, August, 58, L.F. Herreshoff added: 'Because previous staysails had to be lowered away in tacking, when my father designed the schooner Queen he did away with the triatic stay and in its place ran a stay called a "fresh water stay" between the topmast heads. This staysail with which a schooner can tack is a "Queen staysail", as it was first used on the schooner Queen.'

quiff   a labour-saving dodge or trick.

Of unknown origin – as in its other senses (a whiff of tobacco smoke, a lock of hair, a young woman): perhaps the common nuance is slightness.

First attested in its nautical sense in 1881 in *Advertiser Notes and Queries*, I, 77/2.

quilting   *paunch matting* used to protect a wooden *hull* against *drift* ice; meshed or woven rope as a container for bottles, jars, etc.

From 'quilt', which in turn is derived from twelfth-century OF *'cuilt'*, itself from the Latin *'culcita'*, a cushion: cf. OF *'coute'*, later written *'coulte'* and *'couste'*.

First attested in a nautical sense in 1776 in Falconer, *Dictionary*.

quinquereme   (of ancient ships) having five banks of *oars*.
From the Latin *'quinqueremis'* (*'quinque'*, five; *'remus'*, oar).
First attested in 1654–6 in Orrery (anon.), *Partenissa*, 1676
edition, 716.

quoin   wedge with a handle used to raise or lower gun-barrels;
wedge used to prevent *casks* shifting or rolling.
A variant of 'coin' in its primary sense of wedge or corner,
from the French *'coin'*; it acquired its sense of 'money' because
it also meant the die in which coins were moulded.
First attested in a nautical sense in 1627 in Smith, *Grammar*,
xiv, 65.

Rabbet   groove in *timber* to receive the edge of another
piece secured to it; to fit thus.
From OF *'rabat'*, *'rabbat'*, rebate; although sometimes
spelt with an 'I' in place of the 'e' it has nothing to do with the
animal.
First attested in 1404 in *Durham Account Rolls* (Surtees
Society, 1898–1901), I, 396.

rabbit   an article stolen or smuggled or both.
Even in its familiar animal sense, the word 'rabbit' is of uncertain origin: it may be that the ME form 'rabet' is the oldest; it
may be that the word originated in Northern France: cf. the
Walloon *'robett'*. Equally, the scabrous nautical slang meaning
may derive from the conjuring trick of producing a rabbit from
a top hat, or it may conceivably be a (perhaps Celtic) pronunciation of 'robbed'. An argument against this latter theory is that
a 'rabbit' may also, if rarely, be a piece of craftwork made by a
seaman to take or send *ashore*.
First attested nautically in 1929 in Bowen, *Sea Slang*, 109.

race   a fast, strong, and confused complex of *currents*
produced by a narrow *channel, shoals* or the confluence of
two *tides*; a sailing contest; (of a propeller) to run unduly fast,
for instance when lifted from the water.
From the (originally Northern) OE 'raes', a rush (of water,
etc.), associated with ON *'ras'* and the Norwegian and Swedish
dialect 'rås'. The primary meaning of the word (attested in 1325)
is the act of running, but it speedily acquired its maritime sense.
First attested in this tidal sense in 1375 in Barbour, *The Bruce*
(EETS, 1870–89; STS, 1894), III, 687.

rack (or **racking**)   a *seizing* of *marline* or similar *small stuff*
used to bind ropes together, usually in figures of eight ending
in round *turns*; to apply such.

In its familiar sense of shelf, etc., the word is of course used in nautical as well as general contexts, notably denoting a rack of *sheaves* on either side of a *bowsprit*, etc.

In its specifically nautical sense, the word's origin is obscure; but it may be derived from the torture, or instrument of torture, of the same name. If so, the verb seems to predate the noun: it probably comes from the Middle Dutch or Middle Low Dutch *'recken'* or the Old High German *'recchan'*, to stretch: the verb appears in 1433, the noun in 1460 – although the latter may be associated with the German *'Recke'*, a device for stretching wire, leather, and human beings.

First attested in its nautical sense as 'racking' in 1711 in Sutherland, *The Ship Builder's Assistant*, 143; as 'rack' in 1841 in Dana, *Seaman's Manual*, 119.

raffee   a small, often triangular sail set high on the mast of large sailing ships in light weather; a *moonraker*.

The word's origin is unknown: it has no obvious link with 'raff' or 'raffish'.

First attested in 1880 in Kemp, *Manual*, second edition, 547.

raft   a collection of *logs*, *planks*, *casks*, etc., *lashed* together, to be floated to a destination; a flat structure of such things, including skins, etc., used to transport people or things on water (e.g. a *liferaft*); to *moor* several boats side by side in a *trot*.

From ON *'rapt'* (Swedish *'raft'*, Danish *'rafte'*), meaning a rafter (which word itself comes from the same source but via OE 'raefter'). The word's primary meaning (*c.* 1420) was a *beam*, *spar*, or rafter; but this is now obsolete.

First attested, in the 'raft of logs, etc.' sense, in 1497 in *Naval Accounts* (Navy Records Society, 1896), 249; as a conveyance, in or before 1590 in Shakespeare, *Comedy of Errors*, V, I, 348; as a trot of boats, in 1976 in *Yachts and Yachting*, 20 August, 353/1.

raise   (when sailing) to come in sight of (a *light*, a ship, etc.). From ON *'reisa'*, which had most of the current English senses.

First attested in the general sense of 'to cause to appear' (cf. 'raising' ghosts) in 1382 in the *Wyclif Bible*, Zechariah, xi, 16; in the specifically nautical sense (which may be connected with how objects appear to rise above the horizon) in 1556 by W. Towrson in Hakluyt, *Principall Navigations* (1589), 98.

rake   the slope of a *bow* or a *stern* beyond the ends of the *keel*; the forward or (far more usually) backward inclination of a ship's *mast* or funnel.

The word has no direct link with that denoting a farm or garden implement, which is derived from OE 'raca', with the same meaning. The origin of 'rake' as a slope is obscure: it may be derived from the associated verb, which in turn may be linked to the Swedish '*raka*', to project, and to the Danish '*raga*' and the German '*ragen*'. However, the Swedish and Danish words are also associated with ON '*raka*', meaning to scrape with a rake; and this is the source of the verb 'rake', in the sense of enfilading with gunfire. So connection or confusion between the two families of words seems to stretch far back into their respective ancestry.

First attested as a noun in 1626 in Smith, *Accidence*, 9; as a verb in 1627 in Smith, *Seaman's Grammar*, ii, 4.

ram   solid point or beak projecting from a ship's *bow* for attacking other vessels or for breaking ice; a ship thus equipped.

Almost as old as the word denoting a male sheep (which is attested *c.* AD 825), the origin of 'ram' in its nautical sense is OE 'ram(m)', a battering-ram, attested in 897 and associated with various German equivalents such as the German '*Ramme*', a rammer, all possibly related to ON '*ramm-r*', strong – a sense which may also inform the word for a male sheep.

First attested in its nautical sense in 1865 in Tenney, *Military and Naval History*, 223/2.

ramp   to sail swiftly.

From OF '*ramper*', to creep, crawl or climb – a meaning that 'ramp' retained until the seventeenth century in the case of animals, and until the late nineteenth century and even later in the case of plants. By this time, it had come to refer to climbing plants that had got out of hand; but in parallel with this development of meanings the word also referred, from the fourteenth century onwards, to animals standing on their hind legs ('rampant') and, over the same period, to people storming about.

First attested in its nautical sense in 1872 in Blackie, *Lays*, 61.

randan, ran-dan   a system whereby three can *row* a boat straight, the *stroke* and *bow* using one *oar* each on opposite sides, while the person in the centre uses a pair of oars. Of doubly obscure origin. 'Randan' or 'ran-dan' appears as early as the eighteenth century, denoting a spree or disorderly behaviour: this may, but by no means certainly, be derived from 'random'. 'Ran-tan', an echoic term for a loud banging noise, appears in 1630, and may therefore be the source of 'ran-dan'. In 1853, in *Household Words*, 24 September, 75, Charles Dickens wrote: 'For the one word drunk... I find... beery, winey, slewed, on the ran-tan.' The OED sees no connection between these words and the term for a rowing system; but this ignores a second possibility. In about 1805, Maria Edgeworth wrote (*Works*, I, 185): 'To... go down... to Marryborough, in his dog-cart, randem-tandem.' This usage, repeated by several later writers, including Thomas Love Peacock, refers to the harnessing of three horses (instead of two) in tandem. Although 'ran-dan' was an early spelling of the rowing term, the analogy with an odd-numbered team of horses seems a much more likely source for the expression than anything to do with drunk and disorderly behaviour.

First attested in a rowing context in 1828 in *The Sporting Magazine*, XXII, 251.

range   to sail along (e.g. a coast); to come *alongside*; to lay out (*cable*, etc.) for inspection or to ensure free release.

From the French '*ranger*' in use since the twelfth century; also associated with 'rank' and 'range' as a noun.

First attested in its nautical sense of skirting a coast in 1603 in Smith, *Works* (1819), I, 108; as regards coming alongside in 1709 in the *London Gazette*, No.4521/2; as regards laying out a cable, etc., in 1833 in Marryat, *Peter Simple* (1873 edition), xv, 103.

rap full   with the sails *full* with no wrinkles, shivers or lifting. Possibly from the familiar noun and verb, which appeared in the fourteenth century and seems to be of echoic origin: the notion in this case being that a sail when full can be knocked or slapped and feel rather solid. But there is no proof of this conjecture, and there are few instances of the term's being used.

First attested in 1867 in Smyth, *Sailor's Word-book* (1867 edition).

rating   the station a person holds in a ship's company; a person of a certain *lower-deck* rank; the classification or handicap situation of a racing vessel.

From the noun 'rate' via its verb; 'rate' is from OF '*rate*' and thence from the medieval Latin '*rata*' (from the Latin '*pro rata parte*), feminine of '*ratus*', the past participle of '*reri*', to think or judge.

First attested as regards a nautical rank in 1702 in the *London Gazette*, No. 3815/3; as applied to the person rather than the rank, in 1893 in the *Westminster Gazette*, 2 December, 3/2; as regards a vessel's classification in 1891 in *The Daily News*, 16 June, 3/6.

ratlines   rope (or sometimes wooden) steps up the *shrouds* of a mast enabling those working in *square-riggers* to reach the *yard*.

Not, as might be imagined, from either 'rat' or 'lines' (suggesting a stairway for rodents), but most probably from OF '*raelingue*', '*raalingue*' – originally perhaps '*radelingue*', '*ratelingue*' – and now '*ralingue*', meaning small cordage used to strengthen the edge of a sail. In English, the word was applied first (in the late fifteenth century) to the cordage and only later to the steps made out of it.

First attested in or before 1611 in Cotgrave, *Dictionarie*.

rattle (down)   (usually with object 'the rigging') to set up or tauten the *ratlines*.

Distinct from the familiar noun and verb 'rattle', being a back-formation from 'rattling', itself a written and (more often) oral variant of 'ratline'.

First attested in 1729 in Wriglesworth, *MS Logbook of the 'Lyell'* (1730), 1 September.

razee   a sailing *warship* reduced in size by the removal of one or more upper decks.

From the French '*rasée*' (shaven), and sometimes thus spelt in English, though without the acute accent.

First attested in a nautical context in 1794 in Greville, *Diary* (1930), 14 September, 335.

reach   a fairly straight stretch of river, etc.; a point of sailing with the wind broadly on the *beam*; to sail thus. A *beam reach* has the wind on the beam; a *broad reach* has it just *abaft* the beam; a *fine reach* has it just *before* the beam.

From the familiar verb, which in turn is derived from OE 'raecan', and itself gives rise to the familiar noun.

First attested to denote a stretch of waterway in 1536 in Marsden (ed.), *Select Pleas* (Selden Society, 1894–7), I, 58. In sailing, the word once denoted a *run* on one *tack*, first attested in 1830, in Cooper, *The Water Witch*, xv; but by the twentieth century this usage had shrunk to the present more precise meaning, first attested in 1949 in the Baltimore *Sun*, 20 June, 16/1.

ready about   the command in a sailing vessel to prepare to *tack* or *go about*, followed by the command *lee-oh* as the *helm* goes *down*. *Ready for running* is the expression used for a *coil* of rope that has been prepared so that it may run our freely.

From the familiar word, whose origin is early ME 'raedi' (and similar forms) and thence from OE 'raede' and the Teutonic stem '*raid-*', denoting putting in order.

Although mostly now heard in *yachts* and *dinghies*, the phrase used to be part of larger ships' vocabulary, and is first attested in 1841 in Dana, *Seaman's Manual*, 150.

reckoning   estimate of a ship's position and distance made good since that fixed by shore or astronomical observation, based on the *log*, the *course steered*, the *tide*, etc. (Cf. *dead reckoning*).

From 'reckon', itself derived from OE 'recenian', with roots in several Teutonic and Scandinavian languages. 'Reckon' originally meant to enumerate, recite, and narrate; and 'reckoning' of course has many other more ominous overtones, including its kinship with the German '*Rechnung*', meaning among other things the bill to be paid.

First attested in its nautical sense in 1669 in Sturmy, *Mariners Magazine*, iv, I, 138.

reef   one of the portions of a sail that can be rolled or folded to reduce it in strong winds; a ridge, chain, or group of rocks, coral, etc., at or near the sea's surface; to reduce sail by taking in a reef, or several. A *reef band* is a strip of strong *canvas* sewn on to a sail in a *square-rigger* to strengthen it at the *reef points*; a *reef becket* is a loop with a *toggle* as used with a *reef line*; *reef cringles* are *thimbles* on the *leeches* of a *square-rig* sail that are hauled up to the *yard* and *lashed* to it when the sail is to be reefed, and in *fore-and-aft* sails on the *luff* and the *leech*, to become the new *tack* and *clew* when the sail is reefed. The *reef earings* are short *pendants* for hauling down and securing the cringle of a reefed sail to the *boom*. A *reef knot* is a square knot consisting of two interlinked *half hitches*, used when tying *reef points* and in general joining two ropes of roughly equal thickness. A *reef line* is a rope fixed across a sail for passing reef beckets so as to reef or *shake out* a reef quickly. *Reef points* are short lengths of *line* attached to each side of a sail for tying up its reefed portion(s); *reef tackles* are hooked into the reef cringles of a square-rigger to hoist them to the yard and make reefing easier. A *reefer* is one who reefs, and hy transference both a *midshipman* and the thick close-fitting jacket worn when reefing. *Reefing gear* describes the patent roller reefing systems used on many present-day *yachts*.

The two senses of the noun are less unrelated than they might seem. 'Reef' in its sail-reducing sense is derived from ME 'riff', 'refe', and thence also from ON '*rif*', both with the same meaning, but both ultimately likely to be a transferred sense of '*rif*', meaning a rib. 'Reef' as a ridge of rocks is no doubt derived from the same source, this time via Dutch and Middle Low German. The Danish, Norwegian and Swedish words for both kinds of 'reef' are the same, and from the same ON original.

First attested in its sail-shortening sense in 1390 in Gower, *Confessio amantis* (R. Pauli, 1857; *English Works*, EETS, 1900), III, 341; as a ridge of rocks, in 1584 in Norman (transl.), *Safegard*, 11; as a verb in the sail-shortening sense, in 1667 in Davenant and Dryden, *Shakespeare's Tempest*, I, I.

reeve   to pass a rope through the *throat* of a *block* and on to its *sheave*, or through any such aperture; the past tense and participle are 'rove'.

Of unknown origin, although sometimes said to come from the Dutch '*reven*', which means to *reef*. 'Weave' might seem a tempting comparison; but this has always meant to form a fabric by interlacing. However, a dialect word 'reeve' appears in the nineteenth century, meaning to twine, twist, wind, or unwind: so there may be a link after all.

First attested in 1627 in Smith, *Seaman's Grammar*, v, 23.

regatta   a programme of *yacht* and other aquatic races, contests, etc.

From Italian (Venetian) '*regatta*', '*regata*'; cf. French '*régate*'.

First attested (slightly distorted, as 'regatto' and referring to an event on the Grand Canal in Venice) in 1652 in *S.S. Secretaries Studie*, 265; applied to the first such English event, on the Thames on 23 June 1775, in *The Public Advertiser*, 24 May, 1775, 2/2.

relieving tackle   ropes and *blocks* used to prevent a ship's overturning when *careened*; *purchases rigged* on either side of the *tiller* to ease the strain in heavy seas.

'Relieving' comes from eleventh-century OF '*relever*' and the Latin '*relevare*', to raise again, assist, etc. 'Tackle' (in this context often pronounced 'taykle') seems to be of Low German origin: in Middle Low German '*takel*' meant equipment generally, while the same word in Low German and early modern Dutch denoted strong rope.

First attested, as regards careening, in 1769 in Falconer, *Dictionary* (1780 edition); as regards the tiller, in 1815 in W. Burney's revised edition of Falconer.

render   to ease a rope through a *block* or round a post or *bollard* to lesssen the strain; (of a rope) to pass over the *sheave* of a *block*, etc.

From OF '*rendre*' and the popular and medieval Latin '*rendere*', itself an alteration, by analogy with '*prendere*' of the classical Latin '*reddere*', to give back.

First attested in 1769 in Falconer, *Dictionary* (1780 edition).

rhumb line   an imaginary line on the earth's surface that intersects all meridians at the same angle (e.g. parallels of latitude, at 90 degrees). To keep on a constant *course* is to sail along such a line, which on a plane surface would be the shortest distance between two points – as it appears on a Mercator projection *chart*, a straight line. On the curved surface of the earth, especially over long distances, a rhumb line is not as short a course between two points as a 'great circle'; but since this involves continual changes of *compass* course, many prefer to follow the rhumb line. Only if sailing along a constant latitude, or on a meridian, is the rhumb line the same as the great circle.

From the French '*rumb*' and the Spanish and Portuguese '*rumbo*'and thence from the Latin '*rhombus*' and the Greek '*rombos*'.

'Rhumb' is first attested, in the now obsolete sense of a steady course, in 1578 and in the equally obsolete sense of a course of action, in 1666. It was used in the nineteenth century as both a *point* of the compass (its original French meaning) and the angular distance between two successive compass points (11 degrees 15 minutes). The expression 'rhumb line' itself is first attested in 1669 in Sturmy, *Mariners Magazine*, iv, v, 159.

rib   one of the *frames* or *timbers* of a vessel. *Ribs and trucks* are odds and ends; the *ribs of a parrel* (in *square-riggers*) were those separating the round *bullseyes* or *trucks* (the small round balls that acted as bearings to help the *yards* swivel on the mast when *braced*.

From OE 'rib', 'ribb', and a common Teutonic root, with similar words in most of the Germanic and Nordic languages, basically meaning the curved bones encasing the thorax, but extended, as here, to many comparable objects.

First attested in a nautical sense in 1553 in Douglas (transl.), *Virgill*, I, p, xii.

ribband   one of many long, narrow, flexible pieces of *timber* nailed or bolted to the outside of the *ribs* of a wooden vessel and to the *stem* and *sternpost* to hold the timbers in place until the deck *beams* and *stringers* are fixed. *Ribband carvel*, sometimes 'ribbon carvel', is a form of light boat construction without *athwartship frames*, timbers, or ribs, which are replaced by stringers, *splines*, or ribbands from stem to *stern* covering the inside *seams* of the *carvel planking* laid *fore-and-aft*.

Either composed, as seems likely, of 'rib' plus 'band' or a figurative use of 'ribband' for 'riband', i.e. a ribbon.

First attested (and capable of confirming either hypothesis) in 1711 in Sutherland, *Ship Builder's Assistant*, 163: 'Ribbons, or rib-bands, so called from binding the Ribs or Ship's Timber together.'

ricker   short, light *spar* or pole made from a young tree. Of uncertain origin, but perhaps from the German '*Rick*', a pole.

First attested in 1820 in Scoresby, *Artic Regions*, I, 511.

ride   to float secured; but with many variants. Thus, to *ride apeak* is to have the *bows* above the *anchor*; to *ride at* (or *to*) is to be attached to whatever holds the ship – usually the anchor; to *ride athwart* is to have the anchor out to one side (owing to *tide* or wind). A ship is said to *ride* by her *cable*. To *ride down* is either to be lowered in a *bosun's chair* or to *foot*-in the *bunt* of a sail when working on the *yards* of a *square-rigger*; to *ride easily* is to have no difficulties when anchored or *hove to*; to *ride hard* is the opposite. To *ride hawse full* is to *pitch* when at anchor to the point when the bows are submerged; to *ride out* a *gale* is to survive it at anchor or hove to; to *ride to* the wind or the tide is to be blown or carried in the direction of either while the bows are still held by the anchor. *Riders* are additional *timbers* secured between the *keelson* and the *orlop beams* of a wooden ship weakened by, e.g., *stranding*, but may also be the upper tier of *casks* in a *hold*. *Riding bitts* are those to which cable is fastened so as to ride at anchor; *riding chocks* are a bow fitting as a lead-in for the cable, with a *pawl* to prevent its running back; the *riding light* is the anchor light, an all-round white light; *riding scope* is the length of *chain* secured to the *ground scope* of *moorings*; a *riding slip* is a square safety *slip* to enable the cable to ride by it if anything *carries away* on deck; a *riding turn*, e.g. on a *sheet winch*, is a loaded turn of the rope that jams the hauling part by crossing over it under strain because it has not been *tailed*.

From OE 'ridan' and a common Teutonic root, with similar words in all the Germanic and Nordic languages, as well as French (probably from Flemish), with the primary meaning of travelling on horseback or on some other bearer or conveyance; here the nautical senses are fairly obviously figurative.

First attested, of a ship at anchor, in the eighth century in *Beowulf* (EETS, Grein, 1882), 1882.

ridge rope   *jackstay*, including one for attaching *lifelines*, but especially when used for an awning, in which case it resembles the ridge pole of a tent.

'Ridge', from a common Teutinic root, is derived from OE 'hrycg' (ME 'rigge'), which also gave birth to dialect forms 'rudge' (in the South-West), 'redge' (in Kent), and 'rig' (in Scotland and the North of England).

First attested in 1769 in Falconer, *Dictionary* (1780 edition).

rig   to fit out for sailing; the design and arrangement of a ship's masts, sails, etc., clothes. A *rigger* is a person employed on *shipboard* or in *shipyards* to deal with all the wires, ropes, and chains used to support *masts* and *yards* and to *hoist*, lower, and *trim* the sails. The *rigging* is the collective term for all these. *Running rigging* consists of the moveable rigging, e.g. *sheets*; *standing rigging* is the fixed rigging, e.g. *shrouds* and *stays*. A *rigging screw* is a small *bottle-screw* clamp for *tautening* shrouds, with two eye-bolts threaded in opposite directions into the ends of a central body which, when turned, tightens or loosens both.

The verb predates the noun, but both are of obscure origin. The Norwegian and Swedish '*rigga*' and the Danish '*rigge*' (all in nautical use) are thought by the OED to come from the English; but '*rigga*' in Norwegian also means to bind or wrap, while in Swedish dialect 'rigga på' means to harness (a horse).

First attested, as a verb, *c.* 1489 in Caxton (transl.), *Blanchardyn and Eglantine* (EETS, 1890), liv, 221; as a noun, in 1822 by Scoresby, quoted in Brewster, *Natural Magic*, 1831 (1832 edition), vi, 144.

right the helm   not to put it to *starboard*, but to put it *amidships*; to set upright a ship previously listing.

From OE 'rihtan', 'ryhtan', 'rehtan' and a common Germanic root, originally with the now obsolete meaning of to straighten, e.g. a path.

First attested in a nautical sense in 1627 in Smith, *Seaman's Grammar*, ix, 37.

rigol   a small waterway or *channel*, most often the semi-circular gutterway over a *scuttle* (or *porthole*).

From the French '*rigole*', a gutter, drain, etc. The French '*rigoler*', to laugh, used to mean to go on a debauch, so is unlikely to be echoic of the sound of water chuckling, but rather to have originally had the sense of being diverted (in both senses).

Although the word occurs in Shakespeare and was once used to mean a small furrow, its nautical use is not attested until 1961 in Burgess, *Dictionary*, 172.

rip, rip tide   a disturbed state of the sea, sometimes owing to the confluence of two *tides*, in which the tide rises as it flows and breaks in ripples.

The OED conjectures that this nautical word may be related to 'rip' in the sense of a handful of unthreshed grain; but it seems more likely to be linked with 'rip' in the sense of to tear, the verb in this case being the source of the noun. Even if so, however, mysteries remain: is it derived from the Frisian '*rippe*', to tear, or from the Flemish '*rippen*', to rip or strips off roughly? And are these linked with the Middle Dutch and Low German '*rippen*', a variant of '*reppen*', to move?

First attested in its nautical sense in 1775 in Roman, *Florida*, Appendix, 88.

rising   one of the narrow *strakes* fitted *fore and aft* inside a small *rowing* boat instead of *knees* to support the *thwarts*.

From OE 'risan' and a common Teutonic root, with no links outside the Germanic languages.

First attested in a nautical context in 1627 in Smith, *Seaman's*

Grammar, ii, 6; but this refers to supports for the decks in a ship; in the modern sense of supports for the thwarts in a rowing boat, *c.* 1850 in Greenwood, *Sailor's Sea-book*, 142.

roach   a curve cut in the edge of a sail, outward in the *leech* of a *fore-and-aft* sail, concave in the *foot* of a *square sail* (to keep it free of the *mast stays* when the *yards* are *braced* up).

The OED regards the word as 'apparently' a transferred use of 'roach' in its primary sense of the freshwater fish *Leuciscus rutilus*. Although the link is not immediately obvious, the association of 'roach' with curvature is attested as early as 1575 in George Turberville (anon.), *Venerie*, 15. Kindred expressions include 'roach-backed' and 'roach-bellied'. There is no connection with the US 'roach', a Bowdlerising abbreviation of 'cockroach' – a word almost certainly derived from the Spanish '*cucaracha*'.

First attested in its nautical sense in 1794 in *The Elements and Practice of Rigging and Seamanship*, 116.

road(s), roadstead   a sheltered piece of water near the *shore* where ships may safely *ride* at *anchor*.

Essentially the same word as the familiar 'road', whose original primary meaning (in the ninth century) was the act of riding on horseback, or a journey thus made: cf. the noun 'ride', meaning both a horseback journey and its route. By extension, 'road' came to mean the act of riding on the *waves*; and although this latter meaning (now obsolete) is not attested until about 1400, 'road' and 'roadstead' both occur, in their present nautical sense, in the fourteenth century. The source of the word itself is OE 'rad', from 'ridan', to ride; it has clear affinities with a number of similar words in Nordic and Germanic languages.

First attested in its nautical sense, as 'road', *c.* 1320 in Scott (ed.), *Sir Tristram*, 1804, 1811; STS, 1886, 801; as 'roadstead' in 1351 in the *Whitby Cartulary* (Surtees Society), II, 425.

Roaring Forties   essentially, that area of the South Indian Ocean between latitudes 40 degrees and 50 degrees South, dominated by strong winds from the West; also used more loosely of rough parts of the ocean in the corresponding Northern latitudes, notably in the Atlantic.

'Roaring' comes from the stem of OE 'rarian' and ME 'raren', both probably echoic. The sound in the latitudes in question is partly wind and partly sea.

First attested in 1883 in the *Encyclopaedia Britannica*, XVI, 146/2.

Rob Roy   a light, single-person *canoe* propelled by a double-ended *paddle*.

From the name (meaning Red Robert) of the Highland free-booter (1671–1734); John Macgregor (1825–92) thus named the canoe in which he made some notable trips.

First attested in this sense in 1886 in the title of Macgregor's book, *A Thousand Miles in the Rob Roy Canoe*.

roban, roband, robbin, robin   one of the small, sometimes plaited *lines* used at the *head* of a *square sail* to *lace* it to the *yard* or the *jackstay*.

Although often said to be a contraction of 'rope-band', this set of words is more likely to be derived from '*raband*', a now obsolete Scottish term for the same thing, cognate with similar words in Dutch, German, and Swedish.

First attested, as 'robbin', in 1497 in *Naval Accounts* (Navy Records Society, 1896), 321; as 'roband' in 1762 in Falconer, *Shipwreck*, II, 80.

rocker   the upward curvature of a *keel fore* and *aft*. *Rockered* describes a keel thus curved.

A transferred use of the word, which originally meant someone who rocked a *cradle*, and then the curved base on each side of a rocking chair. The verb from which 'rocker' is derived originated in OE 'roccian', apparently from the Teutonic stem '*rukk-*': this in turn underlies the now obsolete verb 'rich', whose primary meaning was to pull.

First attested in its nautical sense in 1876 in the *Encyclopaedia Britannica*, IV, 812/2.

rode, roding   an *anchor warp*.

The former is the older and North American term, and does not always denote a rope used for anchoring. The OED considers both versions to be 'of obscure origin'; but there would seem to be a clear connection with *ride* and especially with its offshoots *tide-rode* and *wind-rode*.

First attested in this nautical sense as 'rode' in 1679 in *Boston Records* (Registry Department, Boston, Massachusetts, 39 volumes, 1876–1909), VII (1881), 135; as 'roding' in 1897 in Kipling, *Captains Courageous*, iii, 57.

rogue's yarn   coloured *yarn* laid up in a *strand* of rope to indicate its provenance and/or manufacture.

So called because it thwarted attempts to sell stolen naval property. The word 'rogue', unconnected with the French adjective meaning arrogant, arose in the mid sixteenth century to describe one of the sturdy beggars abroad at that time. It may be related to 'roger' (pronounced with a hard 'g'), a now obsolete word of the same period denoting a beggar who pretended to be a poor Oxbridge scholar.

First attested in 1769 in Falconer, *Dictionary* (1780 edition).

rolling hitch   a *hitch* used to *tail* a small rope to a larger one, or to *bend* a rope to a *spar*: made by passing the end of the rope round the spar twice, the second time so that it *rides* over the *standing part*, as in a *clove hitch*, then bringing the end up and across through a third *turn*.

Ultimately from OF '*roler*', '*roller*', '*rouler*': the hitch has the rope 'rolling' round the spar.

First attested in 1769 in Falconer, *Dictionary*.

roove, rove   (in boat-building) a saucer-shaped copper washer that fits over the point of copper nail once the latter has been driven through, so that the point can be *clenched* or beaten down on it to rivet it tight. (The US word for the object is 'burr'.)

From ON '*ro*' (cf. the Norwegian '*ro*' and the Faroese '*rogv*') with the same sense. The rare spelling 'ruff' may suggest a link with the item of clothing.

First attested in 1406 in *Durham Account Rolls* (Surtees Society, 1898–1901), 606.

rope   cordage of more than one inch diameter, made from natural or man-made fibres or wire, plaited, braided or *laid* (*hawser-laid*) – *cable-laid* referring to hawser-laid ropes twisted or laid up the opposite way to their own *lay*. To *rope a sail* is to sew on its *boltrope*; a *rope end* was a short length of rope, usually *knotted* at the end, used as a punishment or goad; a *ropehouse* is a long building or shed in which ropes are laid by twisting; a *ropewalk* is a ropehouse.

Ropey means sub-standard. *Rope yarn* is twice-laid *yarn*, made from old rope; a *rope yarn knot* joins yarns together by splitting the end and knotting together one part of each. A *roping needle* is a large *sailmaker's needle*, with the pointed end curved, used to rope sails with *roping twine*, stout flaxen thread used for this purpose.

From OE 'rap' and a common Teutonic root, with the same meaning in a number of Germanic languages.

First attested *c*. AD 825 in the *Vespasian Psalter* (in Sweet, *Oldest English Texts*, EETS, 1885), civ, 11.

round   the curve of a *hull* (usually with *aft* or 'down' indicating where); to pass to the other side of (e.g. a cape, a *buoy*). A *round bilge* is the curved bulge of a boat's side, where the sides turn into the *bottom* without an angle or *chine*; to *round down* is to *overhaul* a suspended *tackle*. A *round house*, paradoxically, was a square or rectangular *cabin* built on the *quarterdeck* of eighteenth- and nineteenth-century passengers ships and East Indiamen, so called because one could walk round it. To *round in* is to gather horizontally the *slack* of a rope; *round line* is small three-*stranded line*. The *round of a rope* is the length of a single strand making a complete *turn*; a *round seizing* is one used to *lash* two ropes together with small line. *Round the buoys* is a colloquial term for a sailing race round a buoyed course. To *round to* is to bring a vessel up into the wind. A *round turn and two half hitches* is a *knot* commonly used to secure a rope to a post or *bollard* or to the ring of a *buoy*, or to attach *fenders* to the guard rail, the round turn being made round the fixed object and the two half hitches round the *standing part* of the rope. To *round up* is to take in the slack or a rope vertically. *Rounding* is small worn-out rope used against chafe; *rounds* are inspection. To *go round* is to *tack*.

The adjective seems to have preceded both the noun and the verb: its source is OF '*rund*', '*rond*', '*round*', and it appears in English *c.* 1290.

First attested as a nautical noun in 1769 in Falconer, *Dictionary* (1780 edition) under 'Architecture'; as a nautical verb in 1743 in Bulkeley and Cummins, *Voyage*, 60. Earlier attestations can be found for some of the combinations and phrases above.

rouse (**in** or **out**)   to *haul* in or out (or up) with force.

A nautical extension of the familiar word; but the latter itself was a technical term too, used to mean raising game in hawking or hunting. The origin of the word itself, according to the OED, is 'presumably' OF or Anglo-French, 'but the precise source is obscure.'

First attested in its nautical sense *c.* 1625 in *Nomenclator Navalis* (Harleian MS), 2301.

rove   see *reeve*.

rover   *pirate*.

Nothing to do with 'rover' in the sense of wanderer (which comes from a technical term in archery, denoting a mark selected at random): the source of 'rover' in its nautical sense is the Middle Dutch or Middle Low German '*rover*', from '*roven*', to rob (with which word it is plainly cognate). The Dutch term for pirate is '*zee-rover*'.

First attested in this sense in 1390 in Gower, *Confessio amantis* (R. Pauli, 1857; EETS, 1900), I, 359.

row   to propel a boat by *pulling oars*. A *rowlock* is strictly a space cut in a vessel's *gunwale* to take an oar, closed with a *shutter* when not in use; but the word is very often loosely used to mean a *crutch* or even a *thole pin*.

From OE 'rowan', with corresponding words in a number of other Germanic languages. The root 'ro-' also appears in OE 'rodor' (*rudder*) and in a number of other languages, including Irish and Latin, and thence in French.

First attested *c.* AD 950 in the *Lindisfarne Gospels* (The Holy Gospels, in Anglo-Saxon, etc., Skeat, 1871–87), Luke, viii, 23.

royal   the sail next above the *topgallant sail* in a *square-rigger*, for fine weather (originally known as the *topgallant-royal*); a prefix signifying upper, applied to *masts*, *stays*, etc. *Royal fishes* (or *fishes royal*) are sturgeons and whales. A *royal salute* is a 21-gun salute.

From the familiar word, which is itself derived from OF '*roial*' and thence from the Latin '*regalem*'; as the OED notes, 'The French origin of many ME and early modern uses is shown by the adjective being placed after the noun.'

First attested in its nautical sense in 1769 in Falconer, *Dictionary* (1780 edition), Appendix.

rubbing strake   a replaceable piece of half-rounded *timber*, rubber, or plastic fitted along the side of a boat on or just below the *gunwale* as a permanent *fender*.

From the familiar verb 'rub', itself derived from ME 'rubben', equivalent to the same word in Low German, which is the probable source of the Danish '*rubbe*' and the Icelandic, Norwegian, and Swedish '*rubba*' plus 'strake'.

First attested in 1875 in Bedford, *Sailor's Pocket-book*, second edition, vi, 227.

rudder   a flat vertical piece or framework of wood or metal hinged on the *sternpost* and used for *steering* the vessel. *Rudder chains* are chains sometimes fitted on either side of the rudder for emergency steering; the *rudder head* is the top of the rudder which is manoeuvred from the *tiller* or *wheel*; the *rudder port* is the hole in the *hull* which takes the *rudder stock*, which is the vertical pivoting fitment on which a *yacht*'s rudder is often hung.

From OE 'rodor', with many cognate words in Germanic and Scandinavian languages; from the same root 'ro-' as *row*.

First attested before 1303 in Manning of Brunne, *Handlyng Synne* (Roxburghe Club, 1862; EETS, 1901), 4624.

rumbo   rope stolen from a naval *dockyard*.

Of unknown etymology, this slang term just may be connected with the now obsolete word 'rumbo' meaning rum punch; equally, it may be a contraction of 'rumbowline' or 'rumbowling', an obsolete term for old rope used only when strength is not essential, and also slang for anything inferior, including *grog*. Cf. *rabbit*.

First attested as meaning stolen rope in 1846 in that year's edition of *The Swell's Night Guide*, 130/2.

run   to sail freely and easily, especially with the wind *aft*; the point of sailing with the wind *astern*; the *after* part of a ship's *bottom* as it rises and converges towards the *stern*; a distance sailed between two points or during a stated time. A *runabout* is a small open motor-boat capable of fairly high (10–15 knots) speed. To *run aground*, when sailing, is to become stuck on the *shore*, a sandbank, a *reef*, etc.; a *run ashore* is a few hours' shore leave. To *run free* is to sail with the wind well aft; to *run out to a clinch* is with all *cable out*; to *run out to sea* is to sail away from, e.g., a *lee shore*; to *run the easting down* is to make the Easterly voyage between the Cape of Good Hope and Australia along the latitudes between 40 degrees and 50 degrees South – i.e. the *Roaring Forties*. A *runner* is a stout rope *rove* through a single *block* with one end attached to a hook and the other passed round a *tackle-block*; a *runner and tackle* consist of a tackle applied to a runner; runners (in the plural) are *stays* that support the *mast* when running before the wind. A *running bowline* is one that has its *standing part* running through it as a noose. *Running by the lee*, in a *fore-and-aft* vessel, is sailing *downwind* with the *mainsail* (potentially dangerously) out to the *windward* side. A *running fix* is one obtained by taking two *bearings* of the same object with a measured interval between them; a *running knot* is made by forming a loop in a rope end and making an overhand knot in the end, containing the standing part. *Running rigging* consists of all mobile parts of the rigging, as distinct from *standing rigging* such as *shrouds* and *stays*.

Like many short, ancient and apparently simple words, 'run' has a complex history, being formed by the confluence of two originally distinct OE verbs: the strong intransitive 'rinnan' and the weak causative 'aernan', 'earnan' – a metathetic or letter-transposed form of an original '*rannjan*', which appears in other languages but is not attested in OE. Even 'rinnan' is rare; so it may well be that the two forms found in ME ('rinnen' and 'rennen') come largely from ON '*rinna*' and '*renna*'.

First attested in the sense of easy (and later specifically down-wind) sailing before1000 AD in Aelfric (Grammaticus) (transl.), *Proverbs*, ed. Grein, 1872, 186; as describing a ship's hull, before 1618 in Ralegh, *Royal Navy*, 10; as denoting a distance sailed, in 1712 in Rogers, *Cruising Voyage* (1718 edition), Introduction, 10.

S **addle**   a block of wood, hollowed appropriately and fixed to a *spar* to support another attached to it.
By natural extension from the familiar word. This in turn is from OE 'sadol', 'sadul' and a common Teutonic root, which itself may be derived from an Indo-European source.

First attested in its nautical sense in 1512–13 in *Accounts of the Lord High Treasurer of Scotland* 1473– (Scottish Record Series, 1887-), IV, 463.

sag   *drift* (both noun and verb) to *leeward*; to settle *amidships* when supported at *bow* and *stern*.

Probably from, or at least associated with, the Middle Low German '*sacken*', to subside: cf. the modern Dutch '*zakken*', the Swedish '*sacka*' and the Norwegian dailect '*sakka*'. In English, while the modern spelling is already found in the fifteenth century, the following century produced 'sacke' with the same meaning.

First attested as a nautical noun (although the nautical verb almost certainly predated it) meaning drifting, in 1580 in Hakluyt, *Principall Navigations* (1599 edition), I 436; as meaning to drift, in 1633 in James, *Strange and Dangerous Voyage*, 93; in the sense of to subside, in 1777 in Hutchinson, *Practical Seamanship*, 13.

sail   shaped piece of *canvas* or other material held *aloft* by *spars* to catch the wind and propel a vessel; to travel in such a vessel (or, loosely, any vessel); a trip in such a vessel. *Sail area* is the total area of the sails carried, according to wind strength. A *sailboard* is a single-sail craft like a long *surfboard*. The *sail burton*, in *square-riggers*, is the *purchase* running from the *heads* of the *topmasts* to the deck and used for *hoisting* sails aloft to be *bent* to the *yards*. To *sail close on a wind* is to keep *close-hauled* with sails *full* but not shaking; to *sail close to the wind* is a metaphorical variant of this, meaning to take a risk, perhaps dishonestly. *Sail cloth* is a stout canvas of flax and cotton, or any one cloth that is part of a sail; a *sail coat* or *cover* is the cover that protects a sail when it is *stowed* along the *boom*. To *sail downhill* is to *run* before a favourable wind; *sailing free* is *reaching* or running, and able to do so on either *tack*. A *sailing thwart* is either one used for *rowing* that can be removed, or a *fore-and-aft midship plank* secured to the *thwarts* as a mast support; a *sailing tiller* is one lengthened to enable the person at the *helm* to *sit out*. To *sail large* is to have the wind between the *beam* and the *quarter*, with *sheets eased* off; to *sail like a haystack* is to do so badly, perhaps losing *way*. A *sailmaker* is one skilled at manufacturing, cutting, sewing, and repairing sails; a *sailmaker's needle* is a triangular tapered needle used for working canvas; a *sailmaker's palm* is a leather pad to protect the hand when sewing sailcloth; *sailmaker's stitching* covers all types of stitching – darning, flat stitching and round sewing – used on canvas; *sailmaker's twine* is the flaxen thread used; *sailmaker's whipping* is one devised to be strong and permanent, involving the *unlaying* of two or three inches of rope end, with a *bight* of *whipping* twine over the middle *strand*, *relaying* the rope, whipping it with a long end of the twine, passing the bight up outside the whipping, tightening the short end, then attaching both ends with a *reef knot* inside the rope.

Sailmarkings are insignia sewn on both sides of a sail to show class and number. To *sail on her ear* is to be close-hauled and well *heeled* over. A *sailor* is one who sails in ships, a *seaman* with practical skill; a *sailor's best friend* is his *bunk* or *hammock*; a *sailor's farewell* is an abrupt, rude, or debt-ridden departure. A *sail plan* is a drawing showing the sizes, shapes, and positions or sails; a *sail track* is a groove on the mast in which *lugs* attached to the *luff* of a sail can travel

From OE 'seg(e)l' and a common Teutonic root; however, the only known root form '*seg-*'or '*segh-*' means to hold or conquer, so some trace the word to the root '*sek-*' (Teutonic '*seh-*'), to cut (as in the Latin '*secare*'), with the implication of cutting the sail. Tempting as this may be, it seems far-fetched: so the mystery remains.

First attested as a nautical noun *c.* AD 888 in King Aelfred (transl.), Boethius, *De Consolatione Philosophiae* (Sedgefield, 1899), xli, 3; as a nautical verb *c.* AD 893 in King Aelfred (transl.), *Orosius* (EETS, 1883), I, I, 14; in the sense of a water-borne trip in 1604 in Shakespeare, *Othello*, V, ii, 268.

St Elmo's fire   luminous corona discharge of static electricity around a ship's *mast* or *rigging*, often in stormy weather (of which some thought it presaged the end). Cf. *Corbie's aunt*, *corposant*.

The OED confidently calls this term 'a corruption, via Sant'Ermo, of the name of St Erasmus (martyrded 303), Italian bishop and patron saint of Mediterranean sailors; cf. It. *fuoco di Sant'Elmo*.' However, Kemp (ed.), *Oxford Companion* (1976), 744, points out that the name 'has also been equated with St Peter Gonzalez (c.1190–1246), a Dominican friar who accompanied Ferdinand III of Spain on his expedition against the Moors, and then devoted the remainder of his life in [sic] work to improve conditions of the seafaring people along the Spanish coasts'. Kemp also remarks that phenomenon 'is known by over fifty different names'.

First attested (without 'fire') in 1561 in Eden (transl.), *Cortes*, II, xx, 51b.

sally   to run from side to side of a vessel, usually in order to rock her into motion in light airs or to free her from *grounding*; a heave, often thus produced. A *sally port* (from the more general meaning of the word as a large exit) is either a large *port* cut in the side of a fireship or three-decker sailing *warship*, for egress in the former cae and two-way movement in the latter, or a Portsmouth Harbour landing-place reserved for the boats of men-of-war.

From the French '*saillie*', an outbreak or outburst.

First attested as a nautical verb in its rocking sense in 1825 in Brockett, *Glossary*, 181; as a nautical noun in the sense of a heave, in 1867 in Smyth, *Sailor's Word-book*.

saloon   a large *cabin* for collective use, especially by passengers in a *liner*, etc.

From the French '*salon*' and the Italian '*salone*', augmentative of '*sala*', hall. Devotees of the 1930s US singing group known as The Yacht Club Boys may recall the boast that they 'owned a sal*on*, not a sal*oon* but a sal*on*' ('a beauty parlour really à la mode').

First attested in a nautical context *c.* 1835 in Johnson (ed.), *American Advertising* (1960).

salt   a sailor, especially a veteran ('old salt'). *Salt horse* or *salt junk* is slang for salted beef; a *salting* (often plural) is a low-lying area of land covered at high *tide*, possibly from the (mainly Northern) local word 'ing', itself from ON '*eng*', a meadow.

Alluding to the saltness of the sea, from the familiar word, whose source is OE 'sealt' and a common Teutonic root, cognate with the Greek '*al-s*' and the Latin '*sal*', whence the Romance-language versions of the word.

First attested denoting a sailor in 1840 in Dana, *Two Years*, I.

salvage   payment due to those who have saved a ship and/or its *cargo*; the action of saving either or both; the property thus saved; to save it. The *salvage hawser* is a *towing line* kept ready for emergency use as stipulated by insurance policies (therefore also known as 'the insurance hawser').

From OF '*salvage*' and/or the medieval Latin '*salvagium*', itself from the Latin '*salvare*', to save.

First attested, as payment for salvage, in 1645 in Rushworth, *Historical Collections*, iv, I, 186; as denoting the action of salvage, in 1713 in *Act 13 Anne*, c.21, 2; as the property saved, in 1755 in Magens, *Insurances*, I, 356; as a verb, in 1889 in *The Times*, 25 November, 6/5. The fact that the first instance refers to payment, and that it figures in two of the others, stresses the emphasis this may take in practical cases of salvage.

sampan   small light oriental boat; the harbour type usually has an awning and a *scull* over the *stern*, while the coastal type has a single *mast* and a *junk*-type sail.

The OED declares that the word's source is the Chinese '*sanpan*' (from '*san*', three, and '*pan*', boat); but according to Kemp (ed.), *Oxford Companion* (1976), 748, 'some hold it to have a Malayan origin.'

First attested in 1620 in Cocks, *Diary* (Hakluyt Society, 83), II, 122.

sampson or **Samson post** (also *Samson's post*)   a strong wooden post now rooted in the *keel* (it was once erected temporarily on deck) and passing up through the deck to act as a *bitt* for the *anchor cable* or for *mooring* or *towing warps*, or to support a small *derrick* or the *cargo booms*.

Named after the Biblical hero: cf. *Judges*, XVI, 29.

First attested in 1769 in Falconer, *Dictionary* (1780 edition).

sand (often plural)   *shoal, sandbank*. A *sandbagger* was a now obsolete broad, shallow, *open* or partly decked American nineteenth-century racing boat which used moveable sandbags as ballast. A *sandbank* is a mound or shoal of sand formed in the sea or in a river by the action of *tides* and *currents*; a *sandbar* is a similar shoal at the mouth of a river or in a harbour. A *sand boat* is a small chassis on wheels, powered by sails, for use on large sandy areas. A *sand-glass* is an obsolete instrument for measuring time, rather like a sturdy egg-timer. *Sandpapering the anchor* is slang for putting on a show of hard work. A *sandscratcher* is a sailor, especially when *holystoning* a deck. A *sand yacht* is a large sand boat.

From OE 'sand' and a common Teutoic root; it and similar words are found in most Germanic and Nordic languages, though not in any Gothic source.

First attested in this specific nautical sense in 1495 in the *Acts of the Court of Requests* (1592), 11.

saxboard   the topmost *strake* of an *open* boat.

Probably, but obscurely, from ON '*sax*', which meant both a cutting implement and the *prow* of a ship. It has of course no connection with the abbreviation for a saxophone, although this instrument was invented by Adolphe Sax *c.* 1840, some years before 'saxboard' appeared in print.

First attested in 1857 in Colquhoun, *Companion*, 28.

scampavia   a swift sailing and *rowing warship* used most notably in the Mediterranean by the Kingdom of the two Sicilies (Sicily and Naples) during the Napoleonic Wars (1803–15).

From the two Italian words '*scampare*', to run off or decamp, and '*via*', away.

First attested long before the Napoleonic Wars, in 1723 in *The Present State of Russia* (transl.), I, 35.

scandalise   to *shorten sail*, in *fore-and-aft rig* by hauling up the *tack* and lowering the *peak* of a sail. The 'd' being originally and properly a 't' (see below), two other nautical terms may be considered with this word. *Scant* was originally applied to the wind when it was uncomfortably close to dead ahead on the *course* of a *square-rigger*, to the point at which she had to *brace* her *yards* to the maximum. *Scantlings* are the required dimensions of the various parts of a ship's *hull* (originally only the *timbers*).

Unconnected with 'scandal': the original form of the word was 'scantelise', from the noun 'scantle', a prescribed or small size or quantity, itself from the verb (now obsolete) which meant to diminish – including the diminishing of sail area.

On the word's earlier etymology, confusion and controversy abound. 'Scant', the adjective still just current in the slightly arch phrase 'scant regard', seems to be derived from ON '*skamt*', short or brief, equivalent to the Old High German '*scamm*' (which in turn may possibly bear a tenuous relationship with the modern US 'scam', racket or deceit). 'Scantle', in one of its senses (to adjust to a required measure) is possibly a back-formation from 'scantling', which in some of its later senses means a small portion; 'scantling', however, appears to be an alteration of 'scantillon', which is thought to come from OF '*escantillon*' (modern French '*échantillon*', a sample). The OED considers the etymology of this word to be 'uncertain': but the notion of smallness seems to crop up in so many of these words that a family relationship is not implausible.

First attested in its nautical mis-spelling in 1862 in Cooper, *The Yacht Sailor*, 18.

scarf   a joint whereby two pieces of *timber*, *spar*, etc., are connected end-to-end in one continuous piece by notching, bevelling, or otherwise cutting away each of them to fit the other; to make such a joint.

Totally unrelated to the familiar word for a muffler, etc., but of uncertain etymology itself. It predates the recorded appearance of its several counterparts in other Germanic languages; but its Swedish variant, '*skarf*', has a more general application and may therefore be older than the English word. The OED points out that 'the Swedish *skarf* has commonly been referred to the Teutonic root *skerb-*, *skarb-*, represented by OE scearfian (= Old High German *scarpon*, German *scharben*), to cut into shreds… ; but affinity in meaning seems wanting.' A possible link unmentioned by the OED is however with the German '*scharf*', sharp, and '*schaerfen*', to sharpen. The Teutonic root underlying 'sharp', etc., is '*skerp-*', '*skarp-*'; and this is not a million miles from that supposedly relating to the Swedish '*skarf*'. All are in any case related to the notion of cutting, and to scarf a piece of timber might be compared to sharpening its end.

First attested in a nautical sense in 1497 in *Naval Accounts* (Navy Records Society, 1896), 312.

scend   the lift imparted to the *bow* or *stern* of a vessel by the motion of the *waves*; the vertical movement of waves or *swell* against a harbour wall; to move in either of these ways. Despite its unusual spelling, suggesting a contraction of 'ascend', and the occasional insertion of an apostrophe before the 's', the word seems simply to be a variant of 'send', one of whose senses, as a noun, is a physical impetus. 'Send', first recorded as a verb, comes from a common Teutonic root, of which the OE offshoot was 'sendan'.

First attested (without the 'c') in 1625 in *Nomenclator Navalis* (Harley MS 2301; cf. Manwayring, *Sea-mans Dictionary* (1644).

schooner   a *fore-and-aft rigged* vessel with two (and some-times more) *masts*, originally carrying *square topsails* on the *foremast*, and often identified by its *rig* as, e.g. a *topsail schooner*, a *gaff schooner*, etc.

The word's etymology is romantically uncertain. Allegedly, when the first schooner was being launched, *c.* 1713 in Gloucester, Massachusetts, an onlooker exclaimed 'Oh, how she scoons!' This may have been a US adoption of the Scottish verb 'scon', which meant to make flat stones skim on the surface of water. The shipbuilder, Captain Andrew Robinson, is said to have answered 'A scooner let her be.' This tale, described as 'traditional', is recorded in a letter of 1790, quoted in Babson, *Gloucester, Mass.*, (1860), 252; but the OED, which reports it, decides that it 'looks like an invention'. Perhaps; but there is much evidence to suggest that the boats, and their name, orig-inated in Massachusetts. The original spellings lacked the 'ch' and were either 'scooner' or 'skooner'; the change to the present form, now universal, may have been under the influence of Dutch or of similar words in that language, which – like many others – adopted the name from English. The application of the word to glassware is of obscure origin, but may perhaps be a jocular allusion to the vessels described above.

First attested in its nautical sense in 1716 in *Boston Records*, XXIX, 231.

scope   the length of *anchor* rope or *cable* paid out and the area over which it may range.

A word many of whose early meanings are obsolete or rare. Its source is the Italian '*scopo*', meaning aim or purpose, and thence the Greek '*skopos*', which meant a mark for shooting at. This was also its original meaning in English. Not until the mid seventeenth century is it recorded as the intention of a proposal or law; but as meaning the range of a person's view it famously occurs *c.* 1600 in Shakespeare, Sonnet 19, line 7: 'Desiring this mans art, and that mans skope.' As the range of a subject reviewed it first appears in the early nineteenth century; but as range in a material sense it can be found in the sixteenth century.

First attested in its nautical sense in 1697 in Dampier, *New Voyage*, I, 437.

score   the groove in the *shell* of a *block* that takes the rope *strop* surrounding it; a similar groove in a *spar* to take a rope or another spar; the space uncovered in a rope when *unlaid*, e.g. to make a *long splice*.

A groove, notch, or mark seems to be the earliest meaning of the word, although this sense is not attested until the fourteenth century, whereas the sense of 'the number 20' is found before AD 1100. This seems to have been the meaning of the word's OE ancestor, 'scoru'; but that again is derived from ON '*skor*', which meant both twenty and a notch or tally. What seems most likely is that the counting of sheep, cattle, etc., was done orally in twenties, a notch being made as each group was complete.

First attested in a nautical sense in 1794 in *The Elements and Practice of Rigging and Seamanship*, I, 29.

Scotchman   wood, leather, or metal fitting to prevent chafe, notably on the *backstay* or the *shrouds*, to spare the *running rigging*; also on the deck to protect it from the *anchor cable*.

Of uncertain origin, although Kemp (ed.), *Oxford Companion* (1976), 760, considers that 'the name comes from the scotch, or notch, cut in the hide or batten along which is passed the line securing the Scotchman to the backstay or shrouds so that it does not slip'. The OED, noting the noun, declares it to be cognate with the verb 'scotch', whose now obsolete first meaning was to make an incision; but this carries the etymology little further, since the verb itself is 'of obscure origin'.

First attested in its nautical sense in 1841 in Dana, *Seaman's Manual*.

scow   a large *flat-bottomed lighter* or *punt*; (US) a small flat-bottomed racing *yacht*; a *coracle*; a tray for hoisting small items of *cargo*. To *scow an anchor* is to attach the *cable* to the anchor's *crown*, but with only a breakable *seizing* to the *ring*: then, if the anchor is *foul*, the seizing will part and (with luck) the cable will pull the anchor free. The origin of this verb sense of the word remains obscure.

From the Middle Dutch '*schouwe*' (Dutch '*schouw*'), the Low German '*schalde*' and the High German dialect '*schalte*', a punt pole or a boat thus propelled. (Cf. Schouwen – once an island, now linked to the mainland by a bridge.)

First attested as a verb, meaning to cross a river by scow, in

1749 in Douglass, *Summary*, I, 460; as a noun, in 1780 in Jefferson, *Correspondence* (in *Works*, 1859), I, 254.

screw   a boat's or ship's *propeller*. A *screw aperture* is an opening left in the *deadwood* or the *rudder* to allow the propeller to rotate; a *screw slip* is a *slip* (*cable-stopper*) embodying a *bottle-screw*; a *screw slip stopper* is a large *turn-buckle* fitted on deck to secure a *bower anchor*.

Although the original meaning of the word is a male helix, its origin seems to be OF '*escroue*', meaning its female counterpart, or nut. This OF word may also be linked to similar words in the Teutonic languages, e.g. the Middle Low German and Middle Dutch '*schruve*', corresponding to the modern Dutch '*schroef*' and the modern German '*Schraube*'. Although the OF word appears identical to that denoting a parchment scroll, origin of the modern English 'escrow', these are two different notions and words: '*escroue*' in the sense of a scroll was derived from the medieval Latin '*scroda*', which in turn came from Teutonic sources, e.g. the Old High German '*scrot*', a scrap, and the Old Teutonic '*skraudo-*', whence the English 'shred'.

First attested in its nautical sense in 1788 in Cutler, *Life*, before 1823 (1888), I, 408.

scrimshaw   the practice of engraving or carving whales' teeth, walrus tusks, etc.; articles thus decorated.

Possibly related to the military slang 'scrimshank', meaning to evade duties; but both words are in any case of obscure origin. The OED considers that 'scrimshaw' may have been influenced by the surname 'Scrimshaw'; and Kemp (ed.), *Oxford Companion* (1976), 762, declares that 'the word is believed to be derived from Admiral Scrimshaw, an expert in this work'. The approximate spellings below may seem to cast doubt on both these conjectures

First attested (in one close approximation, 'scrimshonting') in 1825–6 in *The American Neptune* (1952), XII, 104; in another, 'skrimshandering', in 1851 in Melville, *Moby Dick*, I, 14; in its present form in 1864 in Hotten, *Modern Slang*, third edition.

scuba   usually in the combinations *scuba-dive*, *scuba-diver*, *scuba-diving*): aqualung apparatus.

Acronym: Self-Contained Underwater Breathing Apparatus.

First attested in 1952 in Hahn and Lambertsen, *On Using Self Contained underwater Breathing Apparatus*, published by the United States National Academy of Science, 1.

scud   to *run* before a strong wind with reduced sail or under *bare poles*; light clouds, foam, or spray driven before such a wind; a sudden gust.

Of uncertain origin. Formally, but not in meaning, it might

seem to be related to the Middle Low German and Middle Dutch '*schudden*', to shake; in meaning, but not formally, it may bear comparison with ON '*skunda*', to hasten. Several dialects use 'scut' in the same sense of hurrying; and this may just possibly refer to the tail of a hare – especially since the earliest recorded use of 'scud', in 1532, denotes a hare's bolting. A further link may be with the verb 'scoot', which is most likely of ME origin as 'skute', cognate with ON '*skiota*', to shoot.

First attested in a nautical sense, as running before the wind, in 1582 in Stanyhurst, *Virgil* (1836; Arber), III, 85; as light driven cloud, in 1669 in Dryden and Davenant, *Shakespeare's Tempest*, 1667 (1670), I, 1; as foam or spray, in 1850 in Taylor, *Eldorado*, xxi, 143; as a gust of wind, in 1694 in Motteux (ed.), *F. Rabelais' Works, by Sir T. Urchard* [Urquhart] *and others* (etc.), v, xviii (1737), 36.

scull   an *oar* used to propel a boat by working it in figure-of-eight motion over the stern; one of a pair of light, short oars with curved *blades* used to *row* a *dinghy*, usually with one oarsman using both at once; to propel a boat by either method. A *sculler* was a small Thames river-boat of the seventeenth and eighteenth centuries, rowed by one man with a single pair of oars; *sculling about* is moving aimlessly, like debris left on deck; a *sculling hole, notch*, or *score* is the half-round aperture in the top centre of a boat's transom to take the *sculling oar*.

Of unknown origin. According to the OED, 'some' identify it with 'skull', meaning bowl or goblet, on acount of the scoop-shaped blade; but, as the OED itself says, this is very improbable – not least because the earliest use of the word refers to 'large and long oars', which were clearly not those mentioned above.

First attested, as meaning such large oars, in 1345–6 in Nicolas, *Royal Navy* (1847), II, 477; as a verb or verbal substantive, in 1624 in Smith, *Generall Historie*, vi, 225.

scupper   drain hole in the *bulwarks*, foot rail or *toe rail*; to sink.

Of uncertain derivation: some trace it to 'scoop' in its original sense of *bailer*, from both the Middle Low German '*schope*' and the Middle Dutch '*schoppe*'; others see it as an Anglo-French adaptation from OF '*escopir*', to spit. The former seems more likely. How the verb relates to the noun is a further mystery. The verb first appears as military slang for surprising and massacring in the late nineteenth century, and the OED does not even mention its use as meaning to *founder* or sink. There may be a link with *scuttle*, which has the double meaning of (as a noun) *porthole* and (as a verb) to sink by cutting holes in the *hull* or opening *seacocks*.

First attested in the combination 'scupper nail', denoting one of those securing the scupper leather (to prevent water coming *inboard*), in 1485 in the *Cely Papers* (Camden Society, 1900), 180.

scuttle   originally, and still in US usage, an opening or *hatch* in the deck or in a *bulkhead*; but now almost exclusively a round *port*, *porthole*, or *portlight* in the side of a ship to admit light and (when open) air; as a verb, to sink a ship deliberately by opening *seacocks* or blowing holes in the *hull*. A *scuttled* or *scuttle butt* was a *cask* of water with a hole cut in it, used as a source of drinking water – hence the US slang meaning of (often misleading) gossip exchanged at such a rendezvous.

The noun has two possible origins: one from the French '*écoutille*', a *hatchway*, with its related forms in other Romance languages; the other from the Dutch or Low German '*schutten*', to shut, and linked with the English 'shuttle' in a dam. The former suggestion seems to presuppose that the French word originally referred to the hatch cover as well as to the hatchway itself. The verb is derived from the noun, either because the original method of scuttling was to cut holes in the ship's hull or (as some conjecture) because the action resulted in the scuttles reaching sea-level and letting still more water in. The former seems the more likely hypothesis.

First attested in a nautical sense in 1497 in *Naval Accounts* (Navy Records Society, 1896), 323.

sea   the expanse of salt water covering 70% of the globe; an expanse of this water smaller than an ocean; a large *wave*; the *swell* in a *storm*. A *sea anchor* is a *drogue* or parachute-like contraption used to hold a ship *bow* to sea in heavy *weather*. A *seaboat* is the naval term for one of the ship's boats suspended from *davits* and not *stowed inboard*. A *sea breeze* is one blowing from sea to land, usually late in the day after the air over the land has risen owing to daytime heating. A *seacock* is a valve or tap to control the ingress or outlet of water. A *sea dog* is a veteran *sailor*. *Sea kindly* is said of a *hull* that *rides* the sea comfortably. A *sea lawyer* is a person well versed in maritime rules and regulations, often to the point of being uncooperative. *Sea* legs connote the ability to overcome the motion of the ship, including any tendency to *seasickness*. A *seaman* ('Ordinary' or 'Able') is a person who goes to sea suitably qualified; *seamanlike* is showing good *seamanship*, i.e. the practical art of handling a vessel; a *seaman's quadrant* was the earliest instrument used in the fifteenth century for measuring the altitude of a heavenly body. A *sea-mark* is any floating navigational *mark* (as distinct from a landmark, which is *ashore*). A *sea mile* is a nautical mile (6080 feet). *Sea room* is adequate space for manoeuvre at sea.

Seasickness is motion sickness afloat. A *seaway* is a deep-water *channel* or the path of heavy seas. *Seaworthy* is fit to go to sea, if necessary in heavy weather.

From OE 'sae' and a common Teutonic root giving rise to many similar words in Old Frisian, ON, Middle Low German, Middle Dutch, etc., as well as their modern counterparts.

First attested in the late eighth century in *Beowulf*, 2394.

sea-conny   a *helmsman* or *quartermaster* in a ship manned by *lascars*.

Despite appearances, this term is unlikely to be derived from *sea* plus *con*. It seems instead to be a corruption (influenced towards these words) of '*sukkani*', a Persian offshoot of the Arabic '*sukkan*', a rudder. In Portuguese, it appeared as '*socoes*' in the sixteenth century.

First attested in 1800 in the *Asiatic Annual Register*, III, 21/1.

seam   the narrow gap between *planks* forming the deck and sides of a wooden vessel; the join of the cloths from which a sail is made; thus to join them.

From OE 'seam' and a common Teutonic root going back to the Sanskrit '*syuman*: cf. the Latin '*suere*', to sew. The word's original meaning was a sewn junction of two pieces of fabric.

First attested in its nautical (deck plank) sense *c*. AD 1000 in Aelfric, *Homilies* (Thorpe, 1844–6), I, 20: this source also includes the fabric sense.

seiche   the rise and fall of water in a lake or at a *marina* not caused by *tide* but possibly due to changes in atmospheric pressure or to *waves* of very long periodicity.

From the Swiss French word of the same spelling, pronunciation, and meaning, probably in turn from the German '*Seiche*', a subsiding of water.

First attested in 1839 in Roberts, *Dictionary of Geology*.

seize   to bind (a rope to itself or another) with *small stuff*. *Seizing* is either that small stuff or the finished result.

From OF '*saisir*', '*seisir*' (modern French '*saisir*'), with the same meaning as the familiar meaning of 'seize', i.e. to take hold or possession of.

Fist attested in this nautical sense in 1644 in Manwayring, *Sea-mans Dictionary*.

selvage, selvagee   untwisted skein of rope *yarn marled* down tight to make a *strop*.

A specialized use of the familiar word sometimes spelt 'selvedge' and seemingly from 'self plus 'edge'. Similar formations exist in modern Dutch ('*selfegghe*') and Low German ('*sulfegge*').

First attested in its nautical sense in 1711 in Sutherland, *ShipBuilder's Assistant*, 133, where its spelling is 'salvages'; as 'salvagees' in 1750 in Blanckley, *Naval Expositor*. The use of 'a' instead of 'e' as the word's second letter arises from its usual nautical pronunciation, possibly also influenced by *salvage*.

semaphore   a *signalling* system whereby the extension of mechanical or human arms, often bearing *flags*, in different positions represents the various letters of the alphabet. Introduced into Britain in 1816, when Admiral Sir Home Popham's system replaced that of the Reverend Lord George Murray.

From the Greek '*sema*', a sign, plus the Greek '*phoros*', bearing, bearer (via modern Latin '*-phorus*' and French '*-phore*'). First attested in 1816 in the *Annual Register, Chron.*, 85/2.

Senhouse, Senhouse slip   a *cable stopper* for quick release, the hinged tongue going through the end link of the cable and being closed by a ring that can be knocked off; customarily used in the *chain locker* near the *clench* bolt.

'Origin unknown', says the OED; but it seems overwhelmingly likely that 'Senhouse' was the name of the slip's inventor. First attested in 1923 in the Admiralty *Manual of Seamanship*, II, ix, 163.

serang   a native *boatswain* or *captain* of a *Lascar crew*.

An Anglo-Indian term, from the Persian '*sarhang*', commander. First attested in 1799 in the *Hull Advertiser*, 21 December, 4/1.

serve   to cover a rope that has been *parcelled* by winding *spunyarn* or *marline* round it for further protection. *Service*, accordingly, is any kind of protective covering wrapped round a rope. A *serving board* is one shaped to facilitate serving; a *serving mallet* is one with a semi-circular groove fitting round the rope, and a handle round which the spunyarn is looped: as the mallet is rotated round the rope the *yarn* is tightly bound.

A distant extension of the familiar verb, whose origin is OF and modern French '*servir*' and the Latin '*servire*', with similar verbs in other Romance languages. The basic notion is 'to care for', a sense attested in or before 1586 in Sidney, *Arcadia* (Sommer's edition, 1891), III, 295. First attested in its nautical sense in 1627 in Smith, *Seaman's Grammar*, V, 25.

set   the direction of a *tidal current*; the extent to which this diverts a ship; thus to divert a ship; the position or angle of sails relative to the wind; to *hoist* and *sheet* home a sail. To *set sail* still denotes departure on a voyage, even in a purely motor vessel.

Like many apparently simple words, this has a complex

history and multiple meanings. Basically, the verb and its past participle are the origin of the noun, and this is true of its nautical uses too. The word comes from OE 'settan' and a common Teutonic root; it is cognate with similar words in most other Germanic languages, and by the fourteenth century was already confused with 'sittan', meaning to sit.

First attested in a nautical sense in the fifteenth-century *Sailing Directions* (Hakluyt Society), 11.

settee   a sharp-*prow*ed, two-*mast*ed, *lateen-rigged* Mediterranean ship of the sixteenth to nineteenth centuries (as described, for example, in Conrad, *The Arrow of Gold*.

The word has nothing to do with the piece of furniture, whose name is most probably a variant of 'settle': it comes instead from the Italian '*saettia*', which in turn is likely to be derived from '*saetta*', an arrow, since the ships were noted for their speed.

First attested in 1587 in Sanders, *Voyage to Tripoli*, C, iv.

settle   to lower a sail slightly by *easing* the *halyard*; to sink gradually.

From OE 'setlan', in turn derived from 'setl', a place of rest.

First attested in the sense of easing sail in 1626 in Smith, *Accidence*, 28; in the sense of sinking, in 1819 in Byron, *Don Juan*, II, xliv.

sewed up   (pronounced 'sued up') *stranded*.

As the pronunciation indicates, this word is distinct from that denoting needlework: it comes instead from the same complex of origins as 'sewer', in North-Eastern OF '*essewer*', '*essever*', related to the popular Latin '*exaquare*', all meaning to drain. ('Sewer' is derived from North-Eastern OF '*se(u)wiere*', a duct for the overflow from a fishpond.)

First attested *c.* 1588 in *The Defeat of the Spanish Armada* (Navy Records Society), I, 16.

sextant   optical navigational instrument for measuring vertical and horizontal angles at sea, improving on the *quadrant* (which could measure only up to 90 degrees) by being able to measure up to 120 degrees, thus enabling lunar calculation of longitude before the chronometer made this unnecessary.

From the Latin '*sextant-*', '*sextans*', a sixth part, in turn from '*sextus*', six; the instrument is so called because its graduated arc is the sixth part of a circle, subtending an angle of 60 degrees (doubled by the use of two mirrors to the full 120 degrees).

First attested in 1628 in Burton, *Melancholy*, third edition, II, ii, iv, 264.

shackle   a (usually) U-shaped metal link closed with a pin across the jaws (making it a D-shackle) used to connect lengths of chain *cable*, cables to *anchors*, *halyards* to sails, etc.; a length of chain cable between two shackles, usually 12.5 fathoms, sometimes 15.

From OE 'sceacul', a fetter, corresponding to various similar but not identical senses of similar words in Low German, Dutch, ON, etc.

First attested, in virtually its nautical sense but in a non-nautical context, in 1343 in *Durham Account Rolls* (Surtees Society, 1898–1901), 205; in a nautical context but as applied to the fastening of a *scuttle*, in 1627 in Smith, *Seaman's Grammar*, xiv, 68; as denoting a length of chain cable, in 1886 in Caulfield, *Seamanship Notes*, 4.

shake   a longitudinal split in *timber*; thus to split; a *stave* of a *cask*; the shiver of a sail when *luffed up* too close to the wind; thus to shiver; (usually with 'out') to *unfurl* or unfasten (e.g. a *reef*). To *shake a block* is to dismantle it; to *shake a cask* is to take it to pieces; to *shake a leg* is to hurry or to get up. A *shake-down* is a temporary berth; a *shake-down cruise* is one in which the *crew* becomes acclimatised. A *brace of shakes* (supposedly a couple of shivers of a sail) is a second or two. *Shakings* are odds and ends of rope and *canvas* to be unpicked to make *oakum*.

Presumably from OE 'scacan', which correspnds to the Old Saxon 'skakan', with the now obsolete meaning of 'shake' in the sense of to depart: cf. the modern colloquialism 'to split'. The corresponding Low German '*schacken*' means to shake in the familiar sense of to agitate or vibrate, as does ON '*skaka*'.

First attested in a nautical context, in the sense of unfurling, in 1549 in the *Complaynt of Scotlande* (EETS, 1872), vi, 41; as a noun meaning a split, in 1651 in White, *Rich Cabinet* (1677 edition), 29; as a verb meaning to split, in 1679 in Moxon, *Mechanick Exercises* (1703 edition), 149; as regards luffing up, in 1769 in Falconer, *Dictionary* (1780 edition), II E e e 2.

shallop   a small, light (*c.* 25-ton) vessel once *schooner-rigged* but later with *lug* sails, used for fishing or as a *tender* for sailing *men-of-war*; a large, heavy undecked boat with one or more *masts fore-and-aft rigged* or with *lug* sails; a small eighteenth-century and early nineteenth-century French coastal gunboat; a shallow-water boat with *oars* or a sail used as a tender or *dinghy*.

From the French '*chaloupe*', which may be either the source or an offshoot of the Dutch '*sloep*' (cf. *sloop*); there are similar words in German (*Schaluppe*'), Italian ('*scialuppa*') and Spanish ('chalupa').

First attested before 1578 in Lindesay of Pitscottie, *History* (STS, 1898–9), II, 278.

shanghai   to enlist a *sailor* against his will, taking him aboard under the influence of drink or drugs.

Of US origin, and derived almost certainly from the name of the Chinese seaport; why is a matter of conjecture. It may have been because this was one of the victims' distant destinations; it has been suggested, in Kemp (ed.), *Oxford Companion* (1976), 776, that the origin of the term is possibly 'the Australian word "shanghai", meaning catapult, in that the unfortunate seamen were catapulted off to sea'. The same verb is used for players eliminated from the game of darts known as 'Shanghai'; but since this usage is not attested before 1930 it seems unlikely to be the source of a nautical usage recorded some 60 years earlier.

First attested in its nautical sense in 1871 in the *New York Tribune*, 1 March, quoted in Schele De Vere, *Americanisms* (1871) 347.

shank   the long central shaft of an *anchor*. The *shank painter* is the rope or chain round the shank securing it to the ship.

A figurative extension of the familiar word for the tibia (and, jocularly, the leg or thigh), whose origin is OE 'sc(e)anca'. Similar words in other Germanic languages include the Danish '*skank*', the Low German '*schanke*', the Norwegian '*skonk*' (all meaning thigh), and the Flemish 'schank', bone.

First attested in its maritime sense in 1549 in the *Complaynt of Scotlande* (EETS, 1872), vi, 40.

shanty   a *seamen*'s work song, broadly divisible into *capstan shanties* and *halyard shanties*.

For derivation, see *chantey*.

First attested in 1867 in Clark, *Seven Years*, xvi, 165. But the practice, and examples of it, long predated the first record of the word. 'Haul the Bowline' is several centuries old, and a capstan shanty appears in the mid sixteenth-century *Complaynt of Scotlande*.

shape (a course)   to plan and put into practice.

Akin to the familiar noun, but slightly differently derived, coming from a common Teutonic source, of which the OE offshoot is 'scieppan'. In this and in similar forms in other Germanic languages the sense of the word is to create, and sometimes to fashion: cf. the modern German '*schaffen*'. Some scholars link the word's ancestors with those of a similar form that meant to draw water from a source; others, perhaps more plausibly, regard the two families of words as distinct.

First attested in this nautical sense in 1593 in Peele, *Garter*, C, 4, b.

shark's mouth   the part of an awning, canopy, or boat cover that divides to fit round the mast.

An obvious figurative extension from the name of the sea animal – which is of unknown origin. The first specimen exhibited in Britain, in 1569, was brought back by the *sailors* of Sir John Hawkins's expedition, and was called thus by them: cf. B.L., *Ballads and Broadsides* (1867), 147: 'Ther is no proper name for it that I knowe, but that sertayne men of Captayne Haukinses doth call it a sharke.' A possible link with the Australian dialect word 'schirk', sturgeon, is unproven.

First attested in 1881 in Hamersly, *Naval Encyclopaedia*.

sharp (up)   (of a *square-rigger*) *trimmed* as near as possible *fore-and-aft*.

From OE 'scearp' and a common Teutonic root: a ship thus trimmed would naturally look narrower (i.e. 'sharper').

First attested in 1669 in Sturmy, *Mariners Magazine*, I, ii, 17.

sharpie   a long, sharp-*bowed*, *flat-bottomed* sailboat originally used for fishing and oyster *dredging*, developed later as a *cruising yacht*; in the 1930s, a small *hard-chined* racing boat, *Bermuda sloop rigged*; an international class racing *dinghy* 19 foot six inches long, made an Olympic class in 1956.

From the adjective 'sharp' and thence from OE 'scearp' and a common Teutonic root.

First attested in a nautical sense in 1860 in a diary for 10 December published in 1913 in *Outing*, March, 688/2.

sheave   the wheel in a *block* that takes the rope.

Cognate with the Old Saxon 'sciva' and with a number of similar words in other Germanic languages.

First attested before 1336 in the *Accounts of the Exchequer of the King's Remembrancer* (MSS in the Public Record Office), 19/31 m.

sheepshank   a *hitch* made in a rope to shorten it temporarily: two long *bights* are formed in opposite directions and a *half hitch* made over the end of each, which may be knotted by passing the two ends of the rope through the eyes of the bights.

'Sheep' comes from OE 'sceap'; *shank* is treated above. The hitch was clearly so named because of its resemblance to a sheep's leg.

First attested in 1627 in Smith, *Seaman's Grammar*, v, 26.

sheer   an abrupt change of *course*; the upward curve of a deck towards the *bows* and *stern* (*reverse* or *hogged* sheer being a downward curve in those directions); the angle a ship takes to her *cable* when at *anchor*; to turn aside; to keep the *tiller* of an anchored ship over to one side so as to avoid *fouling* the anchor. A *sheer draught* is a design drawing of a ship showing her outline in elevation and the spacing of her *frames*; a *sheer hulk* is an old *unseaworthy* vessel fitted with *sheer legs* or *sheers*, which are two or three heavy *spars* arranged for lifting weights. To *sheer off* is to move away. A *sheer plan* is the *fore-and-aft* vertical plan of a ship to be built. *Sheer poles* are horizontal steel rods fixed to the lower ends of *shrouds*, above the *rigging screws*, to prevent their twisting. The *sheer strake* is the uppermost strake in a boat's side.

To *sheer up alongside* is to approach at an angle and gradually curve in close and parallel.

Probably from at least two sources, according to its meanings. As denoting movement by the ship, the origin may be one of the uses of the verb 'shear', in the sense of to divide: in Middle Low German, Middle High German, modern Low German, modern German and modern Dutch the corresponding word '*scheren*' carries the meaning of to depart. As describing the curve of a deck, the word's origin may be one sense of the noun 'shear', meaning the result of shearing (often a steady curve). In this connection the OED notes that the French word for a deck's curvature is '*tonture*', identical to that denoting shearing or clipping, and cognate with the English 'tonsure'.

First attested in a nautical sense, meaning to turn aside, in 1626 in Smith, *Accidence*, 19; as the curve of a deck, in 1691 in Hale, *Several New Inventions*, 121.

sheet   rope (or chain) attached to the *clew* (or, in *square* sails, the clews) of a sail to *trim* it to the wind. The *sheet-anchor* (whose etymology is uncertain) at first meant the biggest of a ship's anchors (hence its figurative sense of the most reliable resource), but has gradually come to denote a spare or reserve anchor, used only if the *bower* anchors fail to hold: this second sense is not necessarily inconsistent with the first, or indeed with the figurative sense of something to be relied on when all else has failed. A *sheet bend* or *swab hitch*, used originally for *bending* a sheet to the clew of a small sail, is made by passing the end through the *bight* or *eye*, round behind it, and back under its own *standing part*, thus *jamming* it: a second turn makes it a double sheet bend. The *sheet cable* is that attached to the sheet anchor. *Sheet clips* are metal arms in which to jam a sheet. To *sheet home* is to *haul* the sheet *taut*. A *sheet horse* is a *thwartships* slide, bar or tube along which the *block* of a sheet (usually the *main* sheet) travels.

From OE 'sceata', which like OE 'sceat' meant among other things a corner, quarter, skirt, or cloth: the apparently identical word 'sheet' in the familiar sense of a cloth seems to be derived from OE 'sciete'. But confusion remains possible, especially since 'sceat' appears in the combination 'sceatline', which seems to convey more clearly the nautical sense of 'sheet', although from its earliest recorded use onwards the word appears alone without any additional 'line'.

First attested in its nautical sense in 1336 in the *Accounts of the Exchequer of the King's Remembrancer* (MSS in the Public Record Office), 19/31 m. 4.

shelf *fore-and-aft timber* running along the top of the timbers, on which the deck boards are fixed; a *sandbank*.

A particular application of the familiar word, which is itself probably derived from the Middle Low German '*schelf*' with the same meaning, cognate with OE 'scylfe', which seems to have meant some kind of compartment. In its sense of a sandbank, the etymology of the word would seem to be clear, a figurative extension of its primary meaning: but the OED considers it 'obscure' – perhaps because of its identity of meaning with the obsolete 'shelp', attested a century earlier than the first recorded use of 'shelf' in this sense.

First attested in its shipbuilding sense in 1834–6 in the *Encyclopaedia Metropolitana*, VI, 396/a; as a sandbank in 1545 in Elyot, *Dictionary*.

shell the outer case or frame of a *block*. *Shellback* is a jocular but sometimes admiring term for an ancient mariner, supposedly encrusted with barnacles, etc.

From the familiar word, which is derived from OE 'sciell', similar to a number of cognate words in other Germanic languages, notably West Frisian, North Frisian, Middle Low German, Middle Dutch, etc., with the same range of meanings.

First attested in this specific nautical sense in 1769 in Falconer, *Dictionary* (1789 edition).

shift a change in the wind's direction, less specific than the terms *veer* and *back*; to change (clothing), a sense that the OED holds to be obsolete except in dialects, although current until recently in the Royal Navy; (of *cargo* in a *hold*) to move at random. A *shifter* is the old naval term for a cook's *mate*; a *shifting backstay* is an extra *preventer stay*; *shifting boards* are temporary *bulkheads* or partitions put in holds to prevent cargo shifting.

From ME 'schift', originally meaning to arrange, and cognate with ON '*skipti*', a division or exchange, and the Middle Swedish '*skipt*'with much the same meaning – although the Middle Swedish '*skipte*' had the added meaning of 'change', and is an obvious ancestor of the modern Swedish '*skift*', a spell of work or a relay of workpeople (as in another sense of the modern English word).

First attested in a nautical sense in 1594 in Blundevil, *Exercises* (1636 edition), vii, xxxi, 702.

ship   strictly, in the days of sail, a vessel with a *bowsprit* and
three *square-rigged masts*, each with a *topmast* and *topgallant* mast; in reality, any large *sea*-going vessel – and in OE,
also small craft; to place ready for work.
   Ship ahoy is the correct nautical hail to a vessel. *Shipboard*
was originally the side of a vessel, but survives now mainly in
the phrase 'on shipboard', a slightly pedantic variant of *on
board*. *Ship-money fleets* were those sent annually by Charles
I between 1635 and 1641 to patrol the Channel and the southern
North Sea. A *ship's company* is her *crew* excluding the officers; a *ship's cousin* is a *seaman berthed aft* but working with
the *foredeck* hands; a *ship's husband* is someone appointed
by the owners to act as agent, accountant, manager, or general
busybody. *Shipshape* (often, 'and *Bristol fashion*') is in good
seamanlike order. A *ship's number* is her four *signal* letters.
Shipworm is the wormlike Teredo mollusc. *Shipwreck* is the
total loss of a vessel on rocks, a *shoal*, land, etc.
   From OE 'scip' and a common Teutonic root; beyond the
Gothic '*skip*', however, uncertainty reigns. The Germanic word
finds Romance counterparts in the French '*esquif*' and the Italian
'*schifo*': cf. the English *skiff*.
   First attested as a noun *c*. AD 725 in the *Corpus Glossary*
(Oldest English Texts, EETS, 1885; Hessels, 1890), S 188; as
a verb in 1616 in Chapman (transl.), *Musaeus*, 352.
shiver   (of wood) to break into fragments; (of a sail) to shake;
to cause a sail to shake by *luffing up* into the wind. '*Shiver my
timbers*', expressing surprise or incredulity, is more often read
than heard.
   In origin, two separate words. That regarding the breaking
of wood is derived from a now rare noun meaning a fragment,
chip, or splinter, which comes from early ME 'scifre', cognate
with the old High German '*scivero*', with the same meaning, and
from the Teutonic root '*skif-*', to split. In the sense of shake,
'shiver' is from early ME 'chivere', whose etymology remains
obscure, although the OED conjectures that it may 'doubtfully'
be connected with early ME 'chevele' or 'chefle', to wag the
jaws or chatter: cf. 'chattering' teeth.
   First attested in the sense of breaking *c*. AD 1200 in the *Trinity
College Homilies, Second Series*, EETS, 1873), 113; in the sense
of shake, in or before 1250 in the *Old English Miscellany* (EETS,
1872), 176 (*Death*, 142).
shoal   a patch of shallow water; shallow; to become shallow.
A boat of *shoal draught draws* little water and can cross shoals
or shallows. *Shoaling* means coming from deeper to shallower
water (often inconveniently shallow). The apparently identical

word for a group or school of fish is quite distinct, derived as it is from OE 'scolu', a division of an army, and OE 'scola', a multitude: hence 'school' as an equivalent term.

From OE 'sceald' and the prehistoric *'skalda-'*, developing in parallel with OE 'scealu', which is the source of 'shallow'.

First attested in AD 839 in Birch (ed.), *Cartularium Saxonicum* (1885–93), I, 593.

shoe   boards added to the *fluke* of an *anchor* to increase its holding power; a block of wood with a recess to take the fluke of an anchor so as to protect the ship's side; a false *keel*; a metal heel fitting for a *rudder*, *capstan* bar, etc.; a base on which *sheer-legs* are placed; to fit a shoe.

All these are figurative adaptations from the familiar word, which itself is from OE 'scoh', with a common Teutonic origin and probably a pre-Teutonic ancestor in *'skouko'*, from *'skeu-'*, to cover; thus the modern German word *'Schuh'*, a covering for an extremity, is not exclusive to the foot, whence the otherwise clumsy-seeming word *'Handschuh'* for a glove.

First attested in a specifically nautical sense in 1644 in Manwayring, *Sea-mans Dictionary*, 3.

shoot   to *fore-reach*, i.e. *luff up* and make progress to *windward*; to sail (or canoe, etc.) through a dangerous passage (e.g. rapids in a river). To *shoot in stays* is to *go about* on to a new *tack* without losing *way*; to *shoot the compass* (in naval gunnery) is to shoot wide of the target; to *shoot the nets* (*drift* nets or ring nets, not a *trawl*) is to lay or *stream* them; to *shoot the sun* is to take an altitude with a *sextant*; to *shoot up* is not to inject a drug but to make progress to windward by luffing.

From the familiar word, whose original meaning was indeed to go swiftly or suddenly, and whose source is OE 'sceotan' and a common Teutonic root.

First attested in a nautical sense in 1622 in Hawkins, *Observations* (Hakluyt Society, 1847, 1878), xli, 95.

shore   the land; a strut used to prop a boat on dry land (more commonly a *leg*); thus to prop a boat; a stout *timber* used to reinforce a *bulkhead*.

Although the two senses of the word might seem to be distinct, both are derived from a pair of identical-looking sources: ME 'schore' in the case of the shoreline, and late ME 'schore' in the case of the prop. The former appears to be associated with the root of 'shear', perhaps in the sense that the shoreline is a division between earth and water. The latter 'schore' seems to be cognate with similar words of similar meaning in Middle Low German and Middle Dutch, as well as with ON *'skorda'*.

First attested in the sense of shoreline in the fourteenth

century in *Early Alliterative Poems* (EETS, 1864–9), A 230; in the sense of a prop *c.* 1440 in *Promptorium Parvulorum* (Camden Society, 1843–65), 448/1.

short allowance   petty warrant, i.e. victuals for four to feed six. *Short boards* are frequent *tacks* needed to *beat* to *windward* in a narrow *channel*; a *short sea* is one with little distance between *wave* crests. A *short splice* is one in which the ends of the two ropes to be joined are *unlaid* and *married* together with the *strands* of one alternating with those of the other, each then tucked over its adjacent strand and under the next (this tuck being made twice, or thrice if for heavy duty), the result being a thickening of the rope, by contrast with a *long splice*. A *short stay* is not a brief sojourn but an *anchor cable taut* and leading down to the anchor at an acute angle. To *shorten in* is to take in some of the anchor cable; to *shorten sail* is to reduce the area of sail *set* by *reefing*, replacing, or taking in.

From OE 'sc(e)ort', corresponding to the Old Teutonic type '*skurto-*'; but whether this is a native Teutonic form is disputed. If so, it may come from a pre-Teutonic '*skerd-*', an extension of '*sker*', to cut: cf. 'shear'. If not, the source is Latin, either through the prefixing of a sibilant (perhaps from the preceding word) to the Latin '*curtus*', or through a supposed popular Latin '*excurtus*', for which there is little evidence.

'Short allowance' is first attested in 1745 in Thomas, *True and Impartial Journal*, 3.

shoulder block   one with a squared top to its *shell*, to prevent the rope *jamming*. A *shoulder-of-mutton sail* is a triangular *Bermuda* sail. To *shoulder the anchor* is to lift it inadvertently because the *cable* is too short. The *shoulders* of a boat are at the *fore-part* of the *hull*, just *abaft* the *head*.

'Shoulder' is from OE 'sculder', corresponding to a number of similar words in other Germanic languages.

'Shoulder block' is first attested in 1794 in *The Elements and Practice of Rigging and Seamanship*, I, 156.

shove off   to push a boat away from *alongside*; to go away. From OE 'scufan' and a common Teutonic root: in its early usage (as in its continuing nautical sense) the word lacked the present general connotation of roughness.

First attested in its primary nautical sense in 1600 in Holland (transl.), *Livy*, XLI, iii, 1098.

shroud   one of a set (usually in pairs) of now wire ropes as *standing rigging* to give a *mast* lateral support. A *shroud-laid* rope is of four *strands* instead of three, laid round a central strand or heart. *Shroud plates* are *chain plates*, to which the shrouds are attached at deck level; a *shroud roller* is a loose tube enclosing a shroud to prevent chafe.

Almost certainly from the original meaning of the familiar word, before it came in the sixteenth century to mean a winding-sheet. Its initial meaning was any garment or covering; and in the fifteenth century rope shrouds were necessarily many, and thus more like a covering than a single *stay*. The origin of the word is OE 'scrud' (equivalent to *'skrud'* in ON), meaning fittings, furniture, ornament or textile fabric.

First attested in its nautical sense in 1458 in *Archaeologia* (The Society of Antiquaries of London, 1770–), XXIX, 328.

shutter   a detachable part of the *gunwale* of a wooden boat, which when removed allows an *oar* to be dropped into the *rowlock* it closes off.

From the familiar word 'shut', whose origin is OE 'scyttan' and, further back, the prehistoric *'skuttjan'*.

First attested (referring to a *punt* rather than a *rowing* boat) in 1898 in *Encyclopaedia of Sport*, II, 168/2.

shy   (of a *spinnaker*) *set* on a *close reach* rather than a *run*; (of a *wind*) almost too light to sail by.

Presumably, but rather obscurely, from the familiar word, whose origin is OE 'sceoh', timid. The only nautical sense mentioned by the OED is that relating to a wind. This might imply that the wind in question needed to be coaxed like a shy or nervous child or animal. The application to a spinnaker could then be an extension of the idea that a wind dead *astern* might erroneously be thought more helpful than one on the quarter.

First attested in a nautical sense in 1891 in *The Century Dictionary*.

sidelights   the red (*port*) and green (*starboard*) navigation *lights* that a vessel must display at night as part of her *steaming lights*: they should show from right ahead to two *points abaft* the *beam* and be visible for at least two miles.

'Side' comes from OE 'side' and a common Teutonic root; 'light' from OE 'leoht'. Words similar in formation and identical in general meaning occur in Frisian (*'sydljacht'*) and German (*'Seitenlicht'*).

First attested in 1887 in *Cassell's Encyclopaedic Dictionary*; but the British legal requirement for such lights dates back at least as far as 1862.

siding   the width of the deck *beams*.

From 'side' (and hence from OE 'side' and a common Teutonic root).

First attested in its shipbuilding sense in 1797 in the *Encylopaedia Britannica*, third edition, XVII, 399/2.

sight   a nautical astronomical altitude observation; to inspect (the *anchor* as it breaks the surface); to approach (the land from *sea*ward) so as to see it.

From OE 'sihd', cognate with similar words in other Germanic languages. The sense of 'to inspect' (regarding the anchor) was a Scottish usage from the sixteenth century, now obsolete except in this specific nautical instance.

First attested in a nautical sense in 1835 in Ross, *Narrative*, viii, 121.

signal   sign for sending a message over a distance; a message thus sent; thus to send a message. A *signal gun* is one specifically used as such; *signal letters* are the four assigned to every ship as a means of identification, and normally (if oddly) known as the *ship's number*. A *signalman* is a specialist in signals. From the French '*signal*' (OF '*seignal*', '*seignau*') and the medieval Latin '*signale*', based on the Latin '*signum*'.

First attested in a general sense in 1593 in Shakespeare, *Richard II*, I, iii, 116; in a nautical sense in 1801 in Lord Nelson's famously ignoring Admiral Sir Hyde Parker's signal to withdraw at the Battle of Copenhagen on 2 April. Strangely, the OED ignores this well-known instance, and declares that the nautical use of the word is not attested until 1816.

sill (sometimes *cill*)   horizontal structure or step at the bottom of the entrance to a *dock*, *dry dock* or *lock*; the upper and lower horizontal frames of a square *port* in a ship's side; a ridge on the *sea*bed effectively separating the waters on either side.

From OE 'syll', 'sylle', cognate with other Germanic-language words and likely to be related to the Latin '*solea*', meaning the foundation of a wattled wall: cf. also *sole* (as in *cabin sole*).

First attested in a nautical sense, in respect of a dock, in 1789 in *Transactions of the Society… for the Encouragement of Arts*, 55; in respect of a port, in 1815 in Burney (ed.), *Falconer's New Universal Dictionary*; in respect of a seabed ridge, in 1933 in *The Geographical Journal* of the Royal Geographical Society, LXXXI, 571.

silt   sediment, usually brought in by the *tide*. To *silt up* is to become clogged with silt.

From no certain source, but comparable with the Danish and Norwegian '*sylt*', as well as the Norwegian and Swedish dialect '*sylta*', meaning a salt marsh or a *sea* beach. Hence the word may originally have meant a salty deposit. This is confirmed by similar words in other Germanic languages, and notably by the Dutch adjective 'zilt', salt.

First attested *c.* 1440 in *Promptorium Parvulorum* (Camden Society, 1843–65), 77.

simoom, simoon   hot, dry, suffocating *sand-wind* that blows across the African and Asian deserts, and especially around the Red Sea, at intervals during spring and summer: cf. the 'khamsin' in Egypt and the *sirocco* in the Mediterranean.

From the Arabic *'semum'* and the root *'samm-'*, to poison.

First attested before 1790 in Bruce, *Travels*, IV, 559.

single anchor, at   *riding* at one anchor only; prepared for a quick getaway.

The *single bend* is the *sheet bend*; a *single-hander* is a small *yacht* that can be sailed by one person. To *single up* is to *cast off* all *mooring lines* except one at each end of the boat, prior to leaving. A *single whip* is a single rope *rove* through a fixed *block*.

'Single' is derived from OF *'single'*, *'sengle'*, and thence from the Latin 'singulum' (which in classical Latin was used only in the plural).

First attested, curiously, in the metaphorical sense of the anchoring phrase, in 1822 in a letter of 2 September by the diplomatist Charles Arbuthnot, a friend of the Duke of Wellington.

sinker   a weight for sinking a fishing-line, net, *sounding-line*, *buoy* or mine.

From the verb 'sink', from OE 'sincan' and a common Teutonic root.

First attested in 1844 in Maxwell, *Sports and Adventures* (1855 edition), 323.

scirocco, sirocco   hot, enervating wind that blows from the north coast of Africa across the Mediterranean: cf. *simoom*, *simoon*.

From the Italian *'scirocco'*, *'sirocco'* (occasionally *'scilocco'*), an adaptation of the Arabic *'sharq'*, east.

First attested before 1617 in Moryson, *Itinerary*, I, 2ll.

sisal   the fibre obtained from several species of *Agave*, *Fourcroya*, etc., and used for making rope.

From the name of the *port* in Yucatan via which the fibre was exported, although it also comes from Indonesia and Cuba.

First attested in 1843 in the *Penny Cyclopaedia*, XXVIII, 724/1.

sister block   one with two *sheaves* in a single plane, fitted between the first pair of *topmast shrouds* on each side of a *square-rigger* and secured below the *catharpings*; the *reef-tackle pendant* was *rove* through the upper sheave, the *topsail lift* through the lower. *Sister hooks* are clip hooks, i.e. a pair of flat overlapping hooks on a single ring, facing opposite directions, which when closed together form one *eye*. A *sister ship* is one of the same class, design, name or *line*.

'Sister' here is of course a figurative use of the familiar word, from OE 'sweoster', 'swuster'. Although the word has a common Teutonic origin, the 'w' is not present in such other Germanic languages as East, North, and West Frisian, Middle Dutch, Middle Low German, Dutch, Low German, ON, Icelandic, Danish, Norwegian and Swedish – from which one of the ME forms ('sister' as distinct from 'suster' and 'soster') is probably derived.

'Sister block' is first attested in 1794 in *The Elements and Practice of Rigging and Seamanship*, 156.

sit   to use one's body to balance a boat. This use of the word by itself is now rare.

Far more common, though ignored by the OED, is *sit out*, which means to sit on the *weather gunwale* (especially of a racing *dinghy*), usually and advisably with the feet under the *toe-strap*, to counteract *heeling* – a practice that is also current, though proportinally less effective, in bigger racing *yachts*, when a number of *crew* members will perch like starlings on the weather rail.

From OE 'sittan' and a common Teutonic type '*sitjan*' (Gothic '*sitan*'); as the word developed, it was often confused with 'set', but is now fairly clearly distinguished from it except in dialect.

First attested in its nautical sense in 1865 in *Etonia*, xi, 170.

skeet   a scoop with a long handle used to wet the decks and sides of wooden ships in very hot climates (and the sails of smaller boats); thus to wet them.

'Of obscure origin', declares the OED. It would be tempting, but implausible, to liken the word to 'scoop' – or indeed to the obsolete adverb 'skeet', meaning swiftly or easily: cf. 'scoot'. There is likewise no discernible link with 'skeet' as in 'skeet shooting'.

First attested in 1719 in Defoe, *Robinson Crusoe* (1840; Globe, 1873), II, 476.

skeg   originally (until about 1630) a short length of *keel* projecting *aft* beyond the *sternpost* to protect the *rudder*; in steam ships an extension of the *deadwood* to stop the *propellers fouling* the *ground* if the ship went *ashore* on a bank; in modern *yachts*, a protection for the *rudder*, or the metal socket that supports it; on a *sailboard* or *surfboard*, the fin.

All these nautical applications are figurative, since the word's origin is ON '*skegg*' (in Icelandic '*skegg*', in Norwegian '*skjegg*', in Swedish '*skagg*', in Danish '*skjaeg*'), all of which meant 'beard', initially of a man, then as in English, of a kind of oat.

First attested in a nautical sense before 1625 in *Nomenclator Navalis* (Harleian MS 2301); as applied to a board, in 1962 in Masters, *Surfing*, 65.

skid   a *beam* or *plank* as a protective *fender* hung over the side, as a *davit*, as a support under a ship being built, or as one of rollers to move her.

Of uncertain origin; but there may be a link with ON '*skio*' (cf. 'ski') and/or with OE 'scid', a piece of wood split off from a *timber*.

First attested in a nautical sense in 1750 in Blanckley, *Naval Expositor*, 152.

skiff   a small sea-going boat for *rowing* or sailing, originally one of a ship's working boats, *clinker-built*, but eventually used more generally for any small light boat.

Adapted from the French '*esquif*', the Spanish and Portuguese '*esquife*', and the Italian '*schifo*' – all probably derived from the old High German '*scif*', ship or boat: cf. the German '*Schiff*', and indeed the English *ship* itself.

First attested in or before 1575 in Robert Laneham, *A Letter* (Ballad Society, 1871), 13.

skimming-dish   a light fast boat that *planes* easily.

From the familiar word for the utensil used in skimming, though probably not directly, since the utensil removes the surface liquid, whereas the verb 'skim' also means to glide over it, as a planing boat more or less does. The original verb is derived from OF '*escumer*', to remove the scum – which last noun is not only associated with OF but also virtually identical with the Middle Low German '*schum*'.

First attested in its specifically nautical sense of a such a boat in 1884 in Henshall, *Camping*, ii, 15.

skin   the *planking* or outer covering of a vessel (although sometimes used for the inside planking, with the outside being called the 'case'). *Skin drag* is the friction of the water on the *hull* that slows a boat; *skin fittings* are any that necessitate piercing the hull. To *skin a sail* or *skin the bunt* is to stow a sail by laying it tightly along the *boom* or the *gaff* and rolling the bunt around it.

A figurative use of the familiar word, which is associated with ON '*skinn*' and related to the Old High German '*scindan*'. In some Germanic languages the word extended from animal hide to the bark of a tree and the peel of a fruit.

First attested in 1769 in Falconer, *Dictionary* (1780 edition).

skipjack   a US east-coast workboat, *sloop-rigged*, with a *jib-headed mainsail* and a *foresail set* on a *bowsprit*.

A remote figurative use of a term that originated in the sixteenth century or earlier, then meaning a pert and frivolous person of little brain: its components come from the verb 'skip', denoting hopping (associated with the Middle Swedish '*skoppa*', '*skuppa*') and the noun 'jack', slightly condescending for a person (from the colloquial by-name for 'John'). Intermediate senses of the word include 'jockey', a kind of toy, various types of (mainly leaping) fish, a species of beetle, and a trout-fly: the application to a boat may come from either the fish or the fly.

First attested in a nautical sense in 1887 in *Forest and Stream*, IX, 75.

skipper   strictly, a *sailor* qualified by examination to act as *Master*, but commonly applied to *captains* of relatively small craft, or indeed to those who act as such, whether competent or not. *Skipper's daughters* are high white-crested breaking *waves*.

Adapted from the Middle Dutch and Middle Low German '*schipper*', from '*schip*', a ship: similar words, some identical to the English (as in Frisian and Danish) exist in other related languages.

First attested in 1390 in Derby, *Expeditions* (Camden Society, 1894), 37.

skirt   the side or *leech* of a sail; extra fabric sewn to the *foot* of a *spinnaker* or *genoa*.

A figurative use of the familiar word, which comes from ON '*skyrta*'. In the Nordic languages, this and similar words denote 'shirt', although according to the OED the corresponding Low German '*schoert*' in some districts also meant a woman's gown. The trans-sexual shift of meaning remains a mystery.

First attested as the side of a sail in 1627 in Smith, *Seaman's Grammar, v*, 23; as an addition to the foot, in 1976 in Kemp (ed.), *Oxford Companion*, 807.

skylight   a glassed framework in a deck to admit light and, when open, air – as well as, too often, water. A *skysail* was that *set* next above the *royal* in a *square-rigger*; a *skyscraper* was the small triangular sail set above the royal.

From 'sky' (associated with ON 'sky', which meant 'cloud', as did the English word until the mid sixteenth century) plus 'light' (from OE 'lecht').

First attested in a nautical context in 1834 in Marryat, *Peter Simple*, (1863 edition), 239.

slab   any *slack* part of a sail that hangs down after the *leech lines* have been *hauled* up. A *slabline*, in a *square-rigger*, was a small *line* attached to the *main* or *fore course* and *rove* through a *block* on the lower *yard*, used to lift the *foot* of the sail and give the *helmsman* a clear view *forward* in congested waters. *Slab reefing* is a system whereby the slack of a slightly lowered sail is taken in on the *boom* in steps rather than continuously rolled: it produces 'slabs' of sail in the familiar sense of the word, but this is not the origin of the expression.

'Slab' in the nautical sense is from the Dutch '*slap*', slack – probably via the word 'slabline', from the Dutch '*slaplijn*'.

First attested in its nautical sense in 1882 in Nares, *Seamanship*, sixth edition, 12.

slack   not *taut*; that part of a rope which is loose. *Slack away* (also *slack off*) is to *ease* off a rope. *Slack in stays* means sluggish in *going about*. *Slackness* is a tendency to *fall off* the wind. *Slack tide* or *slack water* is the brief period at high or low water when little *current* flows.

From OE 'sleac', 'slaec' and a common Teutonic root; related to the Latin '*laxus*'.

First attested in a nautical sense in 1798 in *The Elements and Practice of Rigging and Seamanship*, 95.

slant   originally (and properly) a puff of wind, or slight wind; commonly, a favourable wind far enough on the *beam* to obviate sailing *close-hauled*.

Both the familiar word (which has influenced the practical meaning now given to 'slant' in its nautical sense) and the nautical word itself are related to ON '*slent*': but this seems to have been two words, or at least to have had two meanings. One was 'aslant', of which the familiar word is an aphetic form, being descended from ME 'a-slonte', 'a-slante'. The other was to dash or throw; and it is from this that the original nautical word is derived.

First attested in its nautical sense in 1596 in Ralegh, *Discoverie* (Hakluyt Society, 1848) 53.

slat   (of sails) to flap idly.

Possibly from ON '*sletta*', to slap, splash, etc.: but possibly also an autonomous onomatopoeic formation.

First attested in 1840 in Dana, *Two Years*, v.

slatch   the *slack* of any rope or *cable* lying outside the ship.

From OE 'slaec', *slack*. First attested in or before 1624 in *Nomenclator Navalis* (Harleian MS 2301), 126.

sleeper   a strong internal *timber* in a ship; one of the *knees* connecting the *transom* to the *after* timbers; one of two crosspieces over the *top* at the *masthead* used to secure it to the *cross-trees* and *trestle-trees*.

From the verb 'sleep' (from OE 'slapan'); the figurative sense may arise, via housebuilding, from the fact that in that process 'sleepers' are horizontal (i.e. recumbent), or – more fancifully

– that these timbers are internal and not normally disturbed.

First attested in a strictly nautical context in 1626 in Smith, *Accidence*, 9.

slew   to turn on its axis.

The origin of this word, originally and sometimes still spelt 'slue', is unknown even to the OED.

First attested in 1769 in Falconer, *Dictionary* (1780 edition).

slick   a smooth patch of water, e.g. in the *lee* of a *hull* or, notoriously, caused by oil spillage.

From the familiar adjective and verb, the former from ME 'slike', developing also into 'sleek', the latter from the OE '-slician', which is related to the Icelandic and Norwegian '*slikja*', to be or make sleek.

First attested in 1849 in Webster, *Private Correspondence*, II, 333.

sling   loop in a rope or chain used for *hoisting*, including those supporting a *yard* on the *mast*; to secure or hang with a sling. To *sling one's hammock* is to have time off duty to get used to a new ship; to *sling one's hook* is to move off.

A nautical use of the familiar word, which is almost certainly related to that denoting a device for throwing a missile: the latter, whose first recorded use, before 1300, only slightly predates the former (in 1323–4), is itself related to the Middle Low German '*slinge*', while the former is related to the Low German '*sling(e)*'.

First attested in a specifically nautical sense in or before 1625 in *Nomenclator Navalis* (Harleian MS, 2301).

slip   an artificial slope used as a *landing* or *launching* place; a *slip hook* (see below); to release (a slip hook, a seaboat, a *mooring* chain, etc). To *slip by the board* is to slide down the ship's side. A *slip hook* is one hinged, its tongue held in place by a ring that can be knocked off to release the hook's grip; a *slip knot* or *slippery hitch* is a *bend* used to attach a rope to a ring or *spar*, with a *bight* passed under it so that it is jammed until a jerk on it frees the whole thing. To *slip one's cable(s)* or *slip one's wind* is to die. A *slip rope* is one used as a temporary hold, ready to release when needed – as, e.g., *rove* through the ring of a *buoy* while the *anchor* is *stowed*. A *slipway* is a landing or launching slip.

The noun is comparable to the Old High German and Middle High German '*slipf*', a sliding; but all forms of the word are from or related to the verb, which seems to be adapted from the Middle Low German '*slippen*', to slip or slide. The use of the word to denote, in pottery, semi-liquid clay and water is also not necessarily unrelated, although the OED considers that its OE form is doubtful and of obscure origin: in fact, the OED itself mentions the Norwegian '*slip*', '*slipa*', meaning slime, as on fish. All these usages are slippery in every sense.

First attested in a nautical sense in 1467 in the *Ordinances of Worcester* in *English Gilds* (EETS, 1870), 374.

sloop   a *fore-and-aft rigged* sailing vessel, with one *mast* (*Bermuda* or *gaff rigged*), formerly with a long *bowsprit* and *foresail* and *topsail* as well as *mainsail* and *jib*, but now most commonly only the latter two; in the seventeenth to nineteenth centuries, a small ship of war; in World War II, an anti-submarine convoy escort vessel.

Adopted from the Dutch '*sloep*', cognate with similar words in other Germanic and Nordic languages, and itself an adoption from the French '*chaloupe*' and the Spanish '*chalupa*'. (In French, '*sloop*' or '*sloupe*' is a re-adoption from English or Dutch.)

First attested in 1629 in Foster (ed.), *English Factories* (1906–12), 1909, III, 315.

slop   a choppy sea.

The same as the familiar word for *slush*, etc., whose probable origin is OE 'sloppe', related to 'slyppe', with the sense of 'slip'.

First attested in its nautical sense in 1956 in the Baltimore *Sun*, 21November, 23/6.

slops   baggy ready-made clothing, especially *breeches*, issued to *seamen* from 1623 until the introduction of official naval uniform in 1857.

From the Middle Dutch '*slop*' (cf. the Old Icelandic '*sloppr*' and the earlier OE compound 'oferslop'): but these words refer to a loose outer garment, whereas the plural seems to have been used primarily for breeches.

First attested in a nautical context in 1691 in Maydman, *Naval Speculations*.

slush   grease or fat from meat boiled *on board*, once used for candles; later the grease used to rub on scraped *masts* and *spars*.

From the familiar word for melted snow, whose origin is obscure and may be echoic; it may be from the Danish '*slus*', with the same meaning, but does not appear in English until very much later, in the seventeenth century.

First attested in its specific nautical sense in 1756 in *The Gentleman's Magazine*, XXVI, 419.

smack   originally, a single-*masted fore-and-aft* sailing vessel *rigged* like a *sloop* or *cutter*, used as a coaster, fishing craft, or *tender*; sometimes a similar *ketch-rigged* vessel; later, any sailing fishing craft; nowadays, any small fishing boat, however propelled.

Probably adopted from the Dutch '*smak*', with kindred words in Low German, Danish, German, and Swedish. Their common source is uncertain, as is their link with similar words in French ('*semaque*'), Portuguese ('*sumaca*'), and Spanish ('*esmaque*').

First attested, in the combination 'smacke... sayle', in 1611 in Cotgrave, *Dictionarie*; as a noun by itself, in 1684 in Chamberlayne, *Angliae Notitia*, twelfth edition, II, 245.

smiting line   a small rope *made fast* to the lower end of a (normally *lateen*) *mizen yardarm*, led along the *yard* inside the ropeyarns that *stopped* the sail to the yard, and down to the *poop*: by pulling on the smiting line the *furled* sail could be loosed and *set*, by breaking the ropeyarns, without going *aloft*.

From the (no longer very) familiar word 'smite', with various meanings apart from hitting, and including smearing and throwing, which the OED considers may have been 'perhaps the original one'. This might accord with the nautical usage, since 'smiting the mizen' was a fairly abrupt and dramatic affair, as it were 'throwing' the sail into action. The OE 'smitan', which is the source of the word, certainly meant 'to throw'.

First attested in or before 1625 in *Nomenclator Navalis* (Harleian MS 2301).

smoke-boat   sailing *seaman*'s derogatory term for a *steamship*: cf. 'stinkpot', applied by some *yachtsmen* to motor-boats. A *smoke-box*, in a nautical context, was a canister containg phosphorus, carried by merchant vessels during World War I and used to lay a *smoke screen* (an artificial cloud of smoke used to hide a vessel from the enemy); a *smoke sail* is a small sail or screen erected round a *galley* funnel to divert smoke when not *under way*; a *smokestack* is a funnel.

From the familiar words: 'smoke' comes from OE 'smoca', cognate with similar words in other Germanic languages.

First attested in 1867 in Clark, *Seven Years*, xii, 116.

smuggle   to import or export clandestinely so as to avoid paying customs duty or other tax. A *smuggler* is a person or vessel doing so.

Originally 'smuckle' and apparently an import, clandestine or otherwise, from Low German ('*smukkeln*') or Dutch ('*smokkelen*'), although the slightly later form 'smuggle' echoes the Low German '*smuggeln*' and similar words in Danish, German, Norwegian, and Swedish.

First attested (26 years after the nevertheless later 'smuggler') in or before 1867 in Petty, *Political Arithmetick*, 1691 edition, IV, 84.

snap shackle   one without the normal pin but with some form of hinged closure that snaps into position, usually over a spring-loaded bar.

From the familiar word 'snap' (plus *shackle*), which is related to its equivalent in Dutch and Low German, as well as late Middle High German. The OED relates the word to the Middle High German '*snaben*' and thence to '*snabel*', a beak (in modern German '*Schnabel*'). There is no doubt an echoic element in all or many of these words.

First attested in 1974 in *The Islander*, 21 July, 11/1.

snatch   an open *lead* used to guide a rope, e.g. a *fairlead*. A *dumb snatch* is one without a roller or sheave. A *snatch block* is one with a hinged opening to enable a rope to be dropped in rather than *reeving* its whole length through the block; to *snatch a rope* is thus to use a snatch block. To *snatch a turn* is to take a quick temporary turn of a rope round a *bollard*, *cleat*, etc., so as to take the strain prior to other action, but without *making fast*.

From the familiar verb and noun, both of obscure origin but thought to be related to 'snack', also of doubtful origin but comparable with the Middle Dutch or Flemish '*snacken*', to snap (of a dog), and the Norwegian dialect '*snaka*', to snatch.

First attested in its nautical sense *c.* 1850 in Greenwood, *Sailor's Sea-book*, 98.

sneer   to strain a ship by carrying too much *canvas*.

The familiar word is of unknown and probably imitative origin: it initially meant to snort like a horse, but may be related to the North Frisian '*sneere*', to scorn. Even harder to determine is how this familiar word acquired its specific nautical sense: was it because of the sound of overstretched sails, *sheets*, *spars*, etc.? Or was the rash *skipper* thought to be sneering at fate or the elements – or at competitors? Alternatively, was it the competitors who sneered as their rival's *rigging* crashed?

First attested in 1867 in Smyth, *Sailor's Word-book*.

snob   a ship's cobbler or boot-mender.

A nautical survival of the familiar word's original meaning: subsequently, from thus meaning a person of (supposedly) low degree, it came to denote one such who aspired to gentility, and only later someone of whatever station in life who despised those regarded as inferior. The ultimate origin of the word, which began as slang, remains as obscure as that of the original person 'of low degree'.

First attested in the general sense of cobbler, without nautical connotations, in or before 1781 in Hone, *Every-day Book* (1825–7), II, 837; in its nautical context, in 1961 in Burgess, *Dictionary*, 191.

snorter, snotter   the ring or support holding the lower end of a *sprit* to the *mast*; a rope length, or length of rope with an *eye spliced* in each end, used to hold *fast*.

'Snorter' is thought by the OED to be an earlier – or otherwise variant – form of 'snotter': in both cases the origin is obscure, and not necessarily related to the familiar noun 'snort' and the over-familiar noun 'snot' – the latter having as its earliest meaning the 'snuff' of a candle, i.e. the burnt part of its wick.

First attested, as 'snorter' in its nautical sense, in 1750 in Blanckley, *Naval Expositor*, 154; as 'snotter' in its nautical sense, in 1769 in Falconer, *Dictionary* (1780 edition).

snotty   a *midshipman*.

From the familiar colloquial word, whose origin is ME 'snotte' or 'snot'; this is related to similar words of the same meaning in Danish, Dutch, Frisian, Middle Dutch, Middle Low German, and Low German. In all these languages it denotes or denoted nasal mucus. In English, its original (fourteenth-century) meaning was the 'snuff' or burnt part of the wick of a candle. This survives, if at all, only in Northern dialect, the second sense of the word having emerged in the early fifteenth century. As regards its nautical application, Hunt and Pringle, in *Service Slang* (1943), 61, declare that a midshipman is called a 'snotty' on account of 'the buttons on his sleeve, which are said to be there for a purpose not unconnected with the nickname'. But the latter may equally well (and less periphrastically) be derived from the supposed youth, rawness, and nasal incontinence of its victim, or from a general dislike of his rank.

First attested in its nautical sense in 1903 in Farmer and Henley, *Slang*, 1890–1904.

snow   a small *brig*-like sailing vessel with *main* and *foremast*, plus a small *trysail* mast *abaft* the main: used as a merchant (sometimes a fighting) ship in Europe between the sixteenth and nineteenth centuries.

Unrelated to the familiar wintry word, but adapted from the Dutch '*snauw*', whence also the Danish and Swedish '*snau*', the German '*Schnau*', '*Schnaue*', and the French '*senau*'. Beyond this, however, the word's origin is obscure. In English, despite such links, 'snow' in its nautical sense is now pronounced like the familiar word, although its early spellings included 'snaw'.

First attested in its nautical sense in 1676 in *The London Gazette* No. 1079/3.

snub   to check abruptly, as by taking a quick *turn* of a *line* round a *bollard*, or by the *anchor*'s taking a sudden hold when the ship is travelling too fast and there is too little *scope* to the *cable*. A *snubbing line* is one used for snubbing, as on the *bow* of a canal boat; a *snubbing winch* is one with a drum but no lever, and a ratchet acting as a brake on a line turned round it.

A specialised use of the familiar word, which comes from ON *'snubba'* and corresponds to the Middle Swedish *'snubba'*, *'snobba'* – all implying rebuke. In modern Norwegian and Swedish dialect *'snubba'*, as well as in the Danish *'snubbe'*, there is the sense of cutting something short and making it stumpy.

First attested in its nautical sense in 1841 in Dana, *Seaman's Manual*, 124.

snug   trim, neat, *shipshape* and prepared for heavy *weather*; (often with 'down') thus to prepare a ship.

Of doubtful origin, according to the OED. Although the word is familiar in a variety of contexts, including its use as a noun denoting a cosy room in, say, a pub, the adjective first appears in its nautical sense.

First attested *c.* 1595 in Wyatt, *Voyage* (Hakluyt Society, 1899), 58.

sny   a curve in a *plank* of wood; a *toggle* used with a *flag*.

Of obscure origin, although the OED compares it to 'sny', 'snigh', dialect verbs meaning to turn up one's nose.

First attested in its 'curve' sense in or before 1711 in Sutherland, *Ship Builder's Assistant*, 54; as a toggle, in 1961 in Burgess, *Dictionary*, 192.

soldier   to malinger, to idle. A *soldier's wind* is one that even a non-sailor can handle, since it blows on the beam and requires neither *tacking* nor sailing *close-hauled*.

From the familiar noun and verb, which in turn are derived from OF *'soudier'*, *'saudier'*, *'sodyer'*, *'soldier'*, and from OF noun *'soude'*, meaning pay (cf. the medieval Latin *'solidarius'*) – the point being that the earliest meaning of 'soldier' was a mercenary, one who served in the military for pay. Inter-service rivalry explains the derogatory use of the term by *sailors*.

First attested as a nautical verb in 1840 in Dana, *Two Years*, IV.

sole   the floor of the *cabin*, *cockpit*, or *forecastle*; the bottom lining of the *bilgeways* and of the *rudder* to bring it down to the level of the *false keel*. A *sole piece* is a *timber foot* fitted to the *heel* of a rudder and detachable as a protection if run *aground*; *sole-pieces* are also the name sometimes given to the A-brackets beyond the *sternpost* of a steam or motor vessel that help support the *propeller* shafts.

From the familiar word denoting the bottom of a foot or of a piece of footwear, which itself is derived from OF *'sole'*, the equivalent of the Provencal and Portuguese *'sola'*and the Spanish *'suela'* (cf. the Italian *'soletta'*), all linked with the popular and medieval Latin *'sola'* (in place of the classical Latin *'solea'*). Beginning as applied to the foot, the word came in the fifteenth century to be used for the foundations of the site for a city, etc., and in the seventeenth for the floor of an oven.

First attested in a nautical sense as lining *c.* 1850 in Greenwood, *Sailor's Sea-book*, 149; as a floor, in 1867 in Smyth, *The Sailor's Word-book*.

soogee-moogee, souji-mouji (and many other spellings) caustic soda in solution with other detergents for cleaning paint-work; so to use it.

Possibly related to the Hindi '*suji*', a flour made by grinding Indian wheat, and perhaps referring to the allegedly abrasive resultant mixture.

First attested in 1882 in Kemp, *A Manual*, third edition, 579.

sound   a fairly narrow *channel* of water, especially between the mainland and an island, or an inlet of the *sea*; to ascertain the depth of a channel, etc., with a *line* and *lead* or other means, e.g. an echo-*sounder*. A *sounding* is a measurement of the depth of water; a *sounding machine* is one invented by Lord Kelvin (1824–1907) whereby with piano wire running out until the *sinker* reaches the bottom the depth of water up to 100 *fathoms* can be measured at an unslackened speed of up to 16 *knots*. A *sounding pipe* is one led down through the ship to take the *sounding rod*, which is used to feel and measure depth, now usually by hydrographic surveyors. *In soundings* is close enough to the *shore* to take soundings (at roughly 100 fathoms).

Despite appearances, these are two distinct word. The noun comes from OE and Old Norwegian 'sund', meaning 'swimming' and in the latter also a *strait* (as also in Danish, Norwegian, and Swedish). The verb is of the same family as that involving audibility: its source is OF '*suner*', '*soner*' (modern French '*sonner*') and the Latin '*sonare*', from '*sonus*', a sound.

First attested as a nautical noun in or before 1300 in *King Horn* (Harleian MS, 628; as a nautical verb, *c.* 1485 in the *Digby Mysteries* (New Shakespeare Society, 1882), III, 1397.

sou'wester   a *wind* blowing from the south-west; a water-proof hat or cap, usually *oilskin* or plastic, worn for protection in wet or blustery *weather*.

Abbreviated form of 'south-wester', from OE 'sudwest'; in Britain, wind from this direction often brings rain.

First attested to denote the wind in 1838 in Hawker, *Diary* (1893), II, 157; to denote headgear, in 1837, *Ibid.*, II, 130.

spale   temporary cross-*beam* to hold the frames of a wooden vessel under construction before the permanent deck beams are fitted.

The OED considers this and its associated word 'spall' to be 'of obscure origin'; but there would seem to be a clear links with the Italian '*spalla*', shoulder, cited by the OED in connection with 'spall' as a rare word for 'shoulder' – cf. the French '*épaule*'. First attested in 1867 in Smyth, *Sailor's Word-book*.

span   a rope or wire with each end secured to, say, an object to be lifted, with a *tackle* in the middle whereby it is *hoisted*, forming a flattish inverted V; the distance between the *port* and *starboard turnbuckles* or *deadeyes*, measured over the *mast-head*, not just from side to side.

From OE 'span(n)', 'spon(n)', with similar words in other Germanic language, originally meaning the distance between the tip of the thumb and that of the little finger on a hand fully extended. In that sense, the word dates back to before AD 900.

First attested as a hoisting device in 1769 in Falconer, *Dictionary* (1780 edition); as a measurement of *rigging*, in 1846 in Young, *Nautical Dictionary*, 289.

Spanish burton   a *purchase* with two single *blocks*, the upper attached with its *standing part* forming the *strop* of the lower. The *Spanish Main* was originally used to describe the mainland of Spanish possessions in sixteenth- to eighteenth-century America, but later in that period shifted its meaning to cover the Caribbean Sea. A *Spanish reef* was a method of *reefing* the *topsails* or *topgallant* sails of *square-riggers* by lowering the *yard* to the *cap* of the *mast* – or, still more frowned on, a means of reefing the *jib* by tying a *knot* in its *head*. A *Spanish windlass* is a way of tightening a *seizing* by inserting, say, a *marline spike*, twisting it and making it fast.

From the name of the country, via OE 'Speonisc' plus *burton*. In some expressions of this kind, the 'foreign' name implies a shoddy practice; in others, exotic ingenuity.

First attested in 1829 in *Natural Philosophy, Mechanics*, II, viii, 36.

spanker   extra *gaff-rigged* sail *set* on a *mizen-mast* to benefit from a following *wind* (earlier known as a *driver*), later replacing the *mizen course*.

Not directly connnected with chastisement: the words 'spank' and 'spanking' in that sense are probably imitative of the sound, and were certainly regarded as vulgar and colloquial when they made their first recorded appearance in the eighteenth century. 'Spanker' in its nautical sense seems to be a separate word, and is associated with 'spanking', first attested in the later seventeenth century and implying size, impressiveness, etc. – as in the phrase 'spanking new' – and, a little later, lively (of a breeze), although the first recorded nautical use of this adjective post-dates that of the noun. Its origin is doubtful, but it may be related to the Danish and North Frisian '*spanke*', to strut. 'Spank' as a (rare) verb meaning to bowl merrily along is probably a back-formation from 'spanking', although the latter's first recorded nautical use postdates it too. The only possible link with 'spank' in the sense of chastisement is that both sets of words imply rapid movement.

First attested as a nautical noun in 1794 in *The Elements and Practice of Rigging and Seamanship*, 162.

spar   any wooden (or, now, metal or plastic) support used in the *rigging* of a ship, such as a *mast, yard, boom, gaff, spinnaker pole*, etc. A *spar buoy* is one topped by a vertical pole; a *spar deck* was strictly a temporary deck, but was also more loosely a *forecastle deck* or a *quarterdeck*, and now can be the upper deck of a flush-decked vessel; a *spar torpedo* was an explosive charge exploded by a contact pistol and fixed to the end of a long pole: it was developed and used during the American Civil War (1861–5), but made obsolete a decade or so later by the locomotive *torpedo*.

Adopted, possibly via OF '*esparre*', from a family of words in the Germanic languages, such as the Middle Dutch '*sparre*', denoting a rafter in a roof.

First attested in 1388 in Nicolas, *Royal Navy* (1847), II, 476.

speak (a ship)   to communicate with her by any method, including speech.

A particular and peculiar nautical use, without preposition, of the familiar word, whose origin is OE 'sprecan', which by the eleventh century had begun to lose its 'r', but is obviously cognate with the modern German '*sprechen*' and similar words in other Germanic languages.

First attested in this nautical usage in 1792 in Riddell, *Voyages*, 20.

specksioneer, specktioneer   person who directs the cutting of the blubber in a *whaler*, usually the chief *harpooner*.

A corruption of the Dutch '*speksijer*', fat or rind cutter. The word 'speck' for the blubber of a whale still survives in American and South African English: '*Speck*' in German, the normal word for bacon, also applies to fat and blubber.

First attested in or before 1820 in Scoresby, *Artic Regions*, II, 40.

spencer   a *loose-footed trysail laced* to a *gaff* and *set* on the *after* side of a *square-rigger*'s *foremast* or *mainmast*.

Possibly, but not certainly, named after one of the Spencer family, several of whose members gave their names to personal accoutrements: Charles Spencer, third Earl of Sunderland (1674–1722) to a wig; George John Spencer, second Earl Spencer (1758–1834) to a coat; Mr Knight Spencer (*fl.* 1803) to a (long superseded) lifebelt; Christopher Miner Spencer (1833–1922) to a rifle.

First attested in this nautical sense in 1840 in Dana, *Two Years*, V.

spider   a metal *outrigger* to keep a *block* clear of a *mast* or of the side of the ship. A *spider band* or *spider hoop* is a metal band round a mast, *spar*, etc., with many *eyes* welded to it, to take the *shackles* of *shrouds*, etc.; in *fore-and-aft* vessels, the band to which the *gooseneck* of the main *boom* is attached and which in *gaff-rigged* vessels may carry *belaying pins* for *halyards*. By analogy, since it often has three or more legs, with the arachnid, whose name comes from OE 'spidra', which is linked with verbs meaning to spin.

First attested in this nautical sense in 1860 in Nares, *Naval Cadet's Guide*, 5.

spile   a wooden plug, sometimes a spigot, to stop up holes; a *pile*; to shape the *timbers* of a vessel to take account of the *sheer*; to transpose a curve in a solid to a flat surface.

The noun comes from the Middle Dutch or Middle Low German '*spile*', a splinter or peg: cf. the German '*Speil*'; cf. also the English 'spill' (a splinter of wood, such as may be used for lighting a fire). In the sense of 'pile' the word may simply have lost its initial 's'. The OED gives verbs associated with these two nouns, meaning to furnish with plugs or piles respectively; but it omits the two verbs used in shipbuilding.

First attested, as a noun in the sense of plug, in 1707 in Mortimer, *Husbandry*, 573; in the sense of a pile, in 1513 in Douglas (transl.), *Virgill*, IX, x, 20.

spill   to empty a sail of *wind* wholly or partially, either by coming closer to the wind or by *easing* the *sheet*. A *spiller* is a *longline*; *spilling lines* are (or were) those *rove* round *square sails* to prevent their blowing away when the *tacks* were eased off.

From OE 'spillan' (which is related also to the synonymous OE 'spildan'), linked with a number of similar words in other Germanic languages. In English, the word's original meaning was to kill, from the tenth century until the seventeenth; thereafter this use of the word was mostly consciously archaic. The familiar meaning (of liquid overflowing or splashed) seems to date from the early fourteenth century.

First attested in its nautical sense in or before 1625 in *Nomenclator Navalis* (Harleian MS 2301).

spindrift   spray blown from the tops of cresting *waves*.

A variant of *spoondrift*, apparently owing to a local Scottish pronunciation of 'spoon'. The latter is derived from a now obsolete verb 'spoon', meaning to *run* before the *wind*, first recorded in the sixteenth century, unrelated to the early twentieth-century slang verb for courting, and according to the OED of obscure origin – although it is apparently identical in meaning to 'spoom', which would seem to be related to 'spume', whose meanings include sea foam. Unfortunately, there is no record of such a word as 'spumedrift', which would have neatly closed the gap. *Drift* is here self-explanatory.

First attested in 1600 in Melvill, *Diary*, in *Autobiography and Diary* (Wodrow Society, 1842), 169.

spinnaker large, light, three-cornered and now balloon-shaped *headsail* used when *running* or *reaching* (and in the latter case *set shy*). A *spinnaker boom* is the *spar* used to spread the *foot* of a spinnaker to *windward*; a *spinnaker chute* is a tube opening through the *foredeck*, via which the spinnaker with its *halyard* attached can be rapidly *hoisted*; a *spinnaker guy* is the *line* attached to the spinnaker's *tack* where it meets the spinnaker boom; a *spinnaker net* is a mesh of light line hoisted to prevent the spinnaker's wrapping itself round the *forestay*; a *spinnaker pole* is a spinnaker boom; a *spinnaker recovery line* is one attached to the sail's centre to enable it to be pulled back either down on to the deck or down the chute; a *spinnaker sheet* is the line attached to the *clew*; a *spinnaker sleeve* is a long sleeve of light cloth through which the spinnaker is hoisted; a *spinnaker staysail* is one *set* below the spinnaker to make the most of the *wind*; a *spinnaker topsail* is an extra topsail set on a short boom.

Said to have originated when the *yacht* 'Sphinx' (mispro-nounced 'Spinx') first carried such a sail in the Solent in 1865. But in fact Thames *barges* also carried a *jib staysail* (usually white against the tan of the other sails) which their *skippers* called 'spinnakers': see Chatterton, *Fore and Aft* (1912), vii, 233. Might the name therefore be connected with the obsolete word *spoon*, meaning to *run* before the wind (cf. *spindrift*)?

First attested in 1866 in the *Yachting Calendar and Review*, August, 84.

spirketing extra thick *strake* either at the *outboard* ends of the deck *beams* or next above the *waterways*.

Of obscure origin, possibly derived from 'spirket', East Anglian dialect for a stout peg or hook, itself possibly arising from the East Anglian 'spurk', to sprout.

First attested in 1748 in Anson, *Voyage*, II, iv, 158.

spit a long narrow headland; a long narrow submerged *shoal* projecting from the *shore*.

From OE 'spitu', meaning a spit in the roasting sense and

linked with a number of similar words in other Germanic languages; their Romance cousins include the Neapolitan dialect '*spito*', the Portuguese '*espeto*' (both meaning a roasting spit) and the French '*époi*', the points of a deer's antlers.

First attested in a maritime sense in 1673 in Hickeringill, *Gregory*, 138.

spitfire jib   a *storm jib*, small and made of heavy material, used by *yachts* in heavy *weather*.

Fairly obviously compounded from the familiar words 'spit' (from the Northern OE verb 'spittan') plus 'fire' (from OE 'fyr' and a common Teutonic source with its origins in Sanksrit. The word's literal meaning was complemented as early as the seventeenth century by figurative applications – a famous twentieth-century example being the World War II fighter aircraft.

First attested in its nautical sense in 1858 in Mayne Reid, *I Ran Away to Sea* (1859 edition), xii, 93.

Spithead nightingales   *boatswains* and their *mates*. *Spithead pheasant* is a kipper or a bloater.

From the *anchorage* off Portsmouth in the Solent, bounded by Spit Sand to the North, Horse and Dean Sand to the East, Sturbridge Shoal and the Motherbank to the South, and Ryde Middle Sand to the West. 'Nightingales' refers not to nocturnal heavy weather but to the (only fancifully birdlike) *piping* of orders: the word itself is derived from OE 'nehtegale', 'nehttgale', and thence from the Teutonic '*naht*', night, and '*galan*', to sing.

First attested in 1890 in Barrere and Leland, *Slang*, II, 283/1.

splash boards   additional *strakes* fitted above the *gunwale* for obvious reasons.

'Splash' has its origin in 'plash', known from the tenth century onwards as a noun denoting a marsh, from the sixteenth century as both a verb and a noun in the same sense as the modern 'splash', and derived from the Middle Low German and Low German '*plaschen*'. The initial 's', aptly making it sound wetter, seems to date from the eighteenth century.

First attested in a nautical context (it is also used in connection with road vehicles) in 1907 in Stewart, *Partners of Providence*, vi.

splice   to join two ropes together by interweaving their *strands* in one of a variety of ways; such a junction. In a *back splice*, the three strands are made into a *crown knot* and then tucked back into the rope; in a *cut splice*, two ends of a short piece of rope are spliced into two places in a longer rope, like a handle; in an *eye splice* the rope's end is turned back and woven into the rope to make a loop. In a *long splice* (which does not thicken the rope like a *short splice*) strands in each rope are *unlaid* at some length and the ropes are *married*, after which a strand of one rope is unlaid even more and a strand of the other is *laid* up in its place, this operation being repeated with the other rope, followed by the two other strands being cut short and tied in a *reef knot* in the middle of the rope. In the more secure, though thicker, *short splice* the strands of each rope are unlaid, the ropes married together, and the strands of each tucked under the still laid strands of the other, working against the *lay*. To *splice the main brace*, originally an arduous task deserving alcoholic reward, was to serve an extra tot of rum or *grog* to the *crew*.

Adapted from the Middle Dutch '*splissen*', whose origin is doubtful, but perhaps linked with 'split'.

First attested (in an ecclesiastical context) in 1524–5 in the *Records of St Mary at Hill,* EETS, 1905, 327; in a nautical context in or before 1625 in *Nomenclator Navalis* (Harleian MS 2301).

sponson   a permanent structure projecting from the side of a ship, including the platforms *before* and *abaft* the *paddle*-boxes of a paddle-steamer, the gun platforms of a *warship*, etc.; in *canoeing*, the permanent *buoyancy*.

Of unknown origin: there seems to be no connection with 'sponsion' or its source the Latin '*spondere*'.

First attested in 1835 in the *Nautical Magazine,* IV, 154.

spoon   to *run* before the *wind*; to *bear* down on another vessel; (rare, if not obsolete) to *set* (of a sail).

The OED considers the word's origin 'obscure'; but the connection with *spoondrift* or *spindrift* suggests a link with 'spume' – the shared notion being that of being blown along: a later spelling was indeed 'spoom'.

First attested, as running, in 1576 in Hakluyt, *Principall Navigations,* (Hakluyt Society, 1903–5), II, 206; as bearing down, in 1608 in the *Admiralty Court Examiner,* 40, 20 December; as setting a sail, in or about 1635 in Boteler, *Six Dialogues* (1685 edition), 293.

spoondrift   *spindrift.*

spreaders   struts placed in pairs *athwartships* on the mast of a *yacht* to broaden the angle of the *shrouds* or side *stays*: bars on the *bows* of a *square-rigger* to spread the *tacks* of the *fore course. Spreader lights*, often mounted on the spreaders (whence the name) are those focused on the deck, and especially around the *foot* of the *mast*, for night work.

From the verb 'spread', which in turn is derived from OE 'spraeden', with counterparts in a number of other Germanic languages, whence also some similar words in Denmark and Sweden. The ultimate origin is unknown.

First attested in a nautical sense in 1895 in *The Daily Telegraph*, 11 September, 5/5.

spring   one of a pair of diagonal *warps*, one led *forward* from near the *stern* to a *bollard* on the *quay* near the *stem*, the other led back from near the *bow* to another bollard nearer the stern, their purpose being to prevent the ship's *surging* as it would do if secured only by bow and stern *lines*. The *fore spring* is that led forward to the quay, the *back spring* the other. The same device may be used between two ships lying *alongside* each other. *Springs* in the plural, when not referring to more than one 'spring' in the above sense, denotes *spring tides*, those at which the *tidal* range is the greatest, occurring not just between winter and summer, but immediately after a full or new moon, when sun and moon both pull in the same direction, in contrast to *neaps*. To *spring* (of a *plank*) is to break loose at one end; to *spring a leak* originally meant to suffer a leak in the *hull* because a plank has sprung, but now refers to leaking for whatever reason. To *spring ship* is to point a vessel in the right direction by securing a *hawser* from the *quarter* to the *cable*, which is then *veered*.

Spring stays were spare mast stays carried by sailing *warships* to replace those shot away.

A specific application of the word in its general sense of an elastic device, which like many other senses of the word is derived from its primary meaning of a water source. Its origin is OE noun 'spring', 'spryng', rather rare in surviving texts and probably derived from the OE verb 'springan' or 'dispringan', although in surviving records this may postdate the verb – depending on the precise date assigned to *Beowulf*.

First attested in a nautical sense in 1744 in Philips, *Authentic Journal*, 156.

sprit   a long *spar* stretching diagonally across a four-sided *fore-and-aft* sail to support the *peak*, as in a Thames *barge*. A *spritsail* was originally a small square sail *set* on a *yard* under the *bowsprit* in late sixteenth-century *square-riggers* to balance the *lateen mizen*: as a *spritsail topsail* it was set on a short mast above the spritsail. Both were superseded by triangular *jibs* and *staysails* in the eighteenth century. Later, the term 'spritsail' came to be applied to a four-sided *fore-and-aft* sail set on a diagonal sprit.

Originally meaning a pole, and especially a *punt*-pole, the word is derived from OE 'spreot', associated with similar words in other Germanic languages and both 'sprout' and 'sprote'.

First attested in a nautical sense in the fourteenth century in *Early English Alliterative Poems* (EETS, 1864–9), C, 104.

sprog   (originally nautical slang) child or offspring; a new recruit.

Of obscure origin, but related to 'sprag', which in the sense of a twig or spray is first attested in 1676 and is comparable with the Swedish dialect word of the same spelling and sense. 'Sprag' is now a dialect word in English too; and in the sense of a lively young fellow it has become obsolete: it survives only as denoting a young salmon or cod. Both 'sprog' and 'sprag' are surely related to 'sprig': but this too, unfortunately, is of obscure origin, and the OED considers 'doubtful' any link between it and the Low German *'sprick'*, meaning a dry twig.

First attested, as a new recruit, in 1941 in *The New Statesman*, 30 August, 218/3; as a youngster, in 1945 in 'Tackline', *Holiday Sailor*, vii, 75.

spunyarn   coarse *line* made of several *yarns* loosely twisted and *tarred*, used for *seizing*, *serving*, and for *stopping* sails.

From 'spin' and thence OE 'spinnan', plus *yarn*.

Although recorded in a general context in the late thirteenth century, the word is first attested in a nautical context in 1627 in Smith, *Seaman's Grammar*, v, 25.

spurling gate   metal fitting on the deck through which the *cable* passes down to the *chain locker*. A *spurling line* is either a line linking the *rudder-head* to the *wheel* and operating a *tell-tale* to indicate the angle of the *rudder*, or a line *athwartships* between the foremost *shrouds*, with *thimbles spliced* into it to act as *fairleads* for the *running rigging*. A *spurling pipe* is that which encloses the cable between the *windlass* and the chain locker.

Of unknown origin: the word 'spurl' is Scottish for sprawl or scramble, and may conceivably be linked wth 'spurling' on account of the loose, clumsy, rattling fall of the cable.

First attested in 1927 in Bradford, *Glossary*, 169/2.

spurnwater   beading or *coaming* to repel water.

From the verb 'spurn', which originally meant to stumble over or kick, and whose source is OE 'spurnan', 'spornan', almost certainly related to 'spur' in the equestrian sense.

First attested in 1347–9 in the *Accounts of the Exchequer of the King's Remembrancer* (MSS in the Public Record Office), 25/32.

squall   a sudden gust of strong *wind*, often from an unexpected direction and with rain. A *black squall* is accompanied by dark clouds and often rain; a *white squall* comes with a clear sky. As a noun, of obscure origin: it may be derived from one particular use of the verb, denoting screaming, squealing or squawking – all, like this use of the verb, imitative. The OED doubts whether there is any link with various Scandinavian words with the stem '*skval-*', also imitative.

First attested in its meteorological sense in 1719 in Boyer, *Dictionnaire* (second edition), I.

square   (of the *yards* of a *square-rigger*) at right angles to the *mast* and /or the *keel*, in harbour *trim*: *square by the braces* being at right angles to the keel, *square by the lifts* at right angles to the mast (i.e. horizontal). *Square-butted*, of the yardarms of smaller square-riggers, means thick enough to have a *sheave*-hole safely cut in their ends, used for *reeving* the *braces*. A *square knot* is a *reef knot*; a *square lashing* is the over-and-under *lashing* tying two *spars* together at right angles. A *square number* is a cushy billet or job. *Square rig* is that in which rectangular sails are *set* cross-wise on *yards* suspended from the *mast* at their mid-points, as distinct from *fore-and-aft*: a *square-rigger* is a ship with such a *rig*. A *square sail* is a rectangular (seldom literally square) sail spread out by a yard at right angles to a mast. To *square yards* is to put things to rights, to settle up, or (less amicably) to get even.

From OF '*esquarre*' and the popular Latin '*exquadra*'.

First attested in a nautical sense in 1769 in Falconer, *Dictionary* (1780 edition).

staff   a light pole to carry an *ensign* or *jack*, or a *topmark* on a *buoy*.

From OE 'staef' and a common Teutonic source, traceable to a pre-Teutonic type '*stapo-*' or '*stabho-*', found in Sanskrit.

First attested in a nautical sense in 1667 in Milton, *Paradise Lost*, I, 535.

staghorn   a metal *bollard* with horizontal arms fitted in big ships for *belaying* big *hawsers* (a kind of giant *cleat*).

From two familiar words: 'stag' from OE 'stacga', 'stagga'; 'horn' from OE 'horn' and a common Teutonic source. In addition to its literal meaning, the word is also applied to plants, insects, and coral.

First attested in its nautical sense in 1923 in the revised edition of the Admiralty *Manual of Seamanship*, II, 87.

staithe   a *wharf* or embankment, usually on inland waterways.

In a now obsolete usage, the word once meant a river bank, and in this sense 'staithe' seems to be derived from OE 'staep'. In its two current but (according to the OED) local usages, it has no OE counterparts, and seems to be linked instead with ON '*stod*' – as may be confirmed by the fact that it survives in those parts of the UK where Norse influence was strong.

First attested, as a wharf, in 1338 in the *Original Chartulary of Tinmouth Monastery*, 172, in Brand, *History*, 1789, II, 255; as an embankment, in 1698 in De la Pryme, *Diary* (Surtees Society, 1870), 185.

stanchion   upright supports for the guardrails or, if longer, for an awning or even a light upper deck.

From OF *'estanchon'*, *'estancon'* (modern French *'étançon'*) and thence from the popular Latin *'stantia'*.

First attested in a nautical context in 1591 in Horsey, *Travels* (Hakluyt Society, 1856), 186.

stand   to *steer* in a certain direction. To *stand in* is to approach; to *stand off* is to keep clear; to *stand on* is to maintain *course* and speed; to *stand on and off* is to move towards and away from, e.g. the shore, essentially *jilling* about.

A *stand of tide* is a prolonged period of high water or a 'double *tide*'.

A particular use of the familiar verb (it is also thus used of *winds*, etc.); the word's origin is OE 'standan', with counterparts in several other Germanic languages.

First attested in a nautical sense in Taylor, *A Famous Fight*, in *Works* (1630), III, 39/1.

standing   (of *rigging*) fixed as distinct from *running*. A *standing lug* is a *rig* in which the *forward* end of the *yard* that carries the *lugsail* lies close and almost parallel to the *mast* so that it need not be *dipped* when *going about*. A *standing main* is a *fore-and-aft mainsail* as in a *dipping lug cutter*, its *foot bent* to a *boom*. The *standing part* of a rope or *tackle* is that which is *made fast* permanently, as distinct from the *hauling part*. *Standing rigging* is that set up permanently, such as the *shrouds* and *stays*. A *standing topping lift* is a wire span suspending a *derrick* when not in use. A *standing wave* is one on the surface that does not advance, as when a fast stream crosses a ledge just submerged.

From *stand*.

First attested in a nautical sense in or before 1625 in *Nomenclator Navalis* (Harleian MS 2301).

starboard   the right-hand side of a ship seen from *aft*, the opposite to *port*.

Starboard gybe, in *fore-and-aft* vessels, is another term for *starboard tack*, applicable when the *wind* (which is on the starboard side in both cases) comes from *abaft* the *beam*. A *starboard-hand buoy* is one marking the right-hand side of a *channel* coming in towards a harbour or up-river, or going with the main stream of a flood *tide*. *Starboard tack* is the situation of a vessel with the wind coming from her starboard side, whether *close-hauled* or not. To *starboard the helm* is to put the *tiller* to starboard: to *starboard the wheel* (usually simply, as an order, 'starboard ten' or some other number) is to put the wheel (and therefore the *rudder* and the ship's *head*) to starboard to the required number of degrees – in other words, to *steer* in the opposite direction to 'starboarding the helm'. The *starboard watch* is that half of the *crew* not on the *port watch*.

From OE 'steorbord', 'steor' meaning a steering *paddle* or rudder, which in the early Teutonic ships was operated over the right-hand side or *board*. The modern French '*tribord*', with the same meaning, is derived from OF '*estribord*', itself adapted from Germanic originals. The modern French '*babord*', meaning port, indicates the side to which the *steersman* turned his back, known in several Teutonic languages as the equivalent of 'backboard', whence the French term.

First attested *c.* AD 893 in King Aelfred (transl.), *Orosius* (EETS, 1883), I, I, 14.

starbolins   men of the *starboard watch* (*larbolins* were those of the *port watch*).

Almost certainly a corruption of 'starboardlings'.

First attested in 1769 in Falconer, *Dictionary* (1776 edition), II.

stargazer   a small extra triangular sail *set* above the *moonsail* (which was above the *skysail*) in *square-riggers*, to catch light airs.

From 'star' plus 'gazer', which are derived respectively from OE 'steorra' (and a common West Germanic root) and from (possibly) either ON '*ga*', to heed, or the Swedish dialect '*gasa*', to stare.

First attested in its nautical sense in 1867 in Smyth, *Sailor's Word-book*, 630.

start   (of an *anchor*) to *break out*; (of a *sheet* or other rope, etc.), to *ease*; (of a *cask*) to open; (of a *plank*) to loosen; to flog (obsolete, and illegal in the Royal Navy since 1809).

From ME 'sterte' and the Teutonic root '*stert-*'; but while most continental Teutonic equivalents of the word have meanings like to empty out, pour out, gush out, or rush, there may also have been a OE 'steortian' or 'stiertan', corresponding to the Middle High German '*sterzen*', to stand up stiffly. This might explain the duality of sense in the familiar, non-nautical uses of the word, i.e. both to leap and to begin.

First attested in a nautical sense, as loosening, in 1711 in Sutherland, *Ship Builder's Assistant*, 46; of an anchor, in 1744 in Philips, *Authentic Journal*, 152; as easing a rope, in 1846 in Young, *Nautical Dictionary*, 296.

starve   to slow a vessel by sailing her too close to the *wind*, otherwise known as *pinching*.

A figurative use of the familiar transitive verb, from OE 'steorfan' and a common West Germanic root; cognate with the old High German '*sterban*', whence the modern German '*sterben*', to die.

First attested in its nautical sense in 1876 in Kemp, *Manual*, 371.

station   originally, a *port*, harbour, or *roadstead*; now, a place where naval vessels are based; in shipbuilding, a cross-section of the *hull* at one of several points. A *station bill* is a list showing the places and roles of *crew* members during various manoeuvres. A *station pointer* is a navigational instrument consisting of a round protractor with three arms that can be used to transfer observed *bearings* to the *chart*, enabling the ship's position to be ascertained at their intersection.

From the twelfth-century French '*station*' and the Latin '*stationem*', from '*stare*', to stand; cf. the Spanish '*estacion*', the Portuguese '*estacao*', and the Italian '*stazione*' (station) and '*stagione*' (season).

First attested in a nautical sense in 1382 in Wyclif, *Bible* (ed. Forshall and Madden, 1850), *Genesis*, xlix, 13.

stave   a stout pole (e.g. of a *boathook*); one of the curved wooden parts forming the side of barrel; to break a *cask* into staves; to break the *planking* of a ship; to rebuild a cask. To *stave in* is to make a hole in the *hull* by knocking a *plank* inward; to *stave off* is to *fend* off with a *spar* to prevent a collision. The past tense and past participle of the verb are 'stove', although a cask is sometimes said to be 'staved'.

A back-formation, creating a singular noun from the plural 'staves' of the singular *staff*.

First attested, of a barrel, in 1398 in Travisa (transl.) *Bartholomeus*, XIX, cxxviii, 934; of breaking a cask, *c.* 1595 in Wyatt, *Voyage of Robert Dudley* (Hakluyt Society, 1899), 10; of holing a boat, in 1628 in Digby, *Journal* (Camden Society, 1868), 65; of repairing buckets, in 1627 in Smith, *Sea Grammar*, viii, 36.

stay   one of the *forward* or *aft* supports of a *mast*; to secure by this means; to bring the *head* of a vessel up to the *wind*. *At long stay* (when at *anchor*) is with the *cable* stretching at some distance from the ship, while *at short stay* means that the cable is more nearly vertical. *In stays* is *head to wind* (and stuck there); to have *missed stays* is to have fallen back on the original *tack* without *going about*. A *stayband*, the modern equivalent of the *hounds*, is a metal bar near the top of a mast with lugs to take the stays and *shrouds*. A *staysail* is a triangular *fore-and-aft* sail *hanked* to a stay and taking its name from that fact.

For once, the nautical use of the noun seems to be the primary one. It comes from OE 'staeg', corresponding to the Dutch and German *'stag'*, found also in the Scandinavian languages, and all derived from a pre-Teutonic *'stak-'* or *'stok-'*. The Germanic word was Romanised in (twelfth-century) OF as *'estai'* (modern French *'étai'*) and in the Spanish and Portuguese *'estay'*.

First attested, as a noun, before 1100 in Wright, *Vocabularies*, second edition, ed. Wuelcker (1884), 288/26 (*De Nave et Partibus eius*); as a verb meaning to bring up to the wind, in or before 1625 in *Nomenclator Navalis* (Harleian MS 2301); in the sense of securing, in 1627 in Smith, *Sea Grammar*, v, 19.

stealer   a short *plank* in the *strakes*.

From the verb 'steal' in the specal sense of omitting one or more of the usual parts in a shipbuilding structure; the original verb comes from OE 'stelan' and a common Teutonic root.

First attested in this sense in 1805 in *The Shipwright's Vade-Mecum*, 201.

steep-to   (of a *shore*) verging on the vertical.

'Steep' is from OE 'steap', which corresponds to the Middle High German noun *'stauf'*, a steep or declivity, seen in the name of the Hohenstaufen family.

First attested in 1748 in Anson, *Voyage*, II, iii, 139.

steer   to direct the *course* of a vessel by means of a *steering oar* or by a *tiller* or *wheel* connected to a *rudder*: sailing schools also teach the art of rudderless steering by adjustment of the *crew*'s position and the sails. *Steerage* was a large space below deck, originally *aft* above the propellers, used for the crew in some merchant ships and for low-fare passengers in the nine-teenth and early twentieth centuries, so named because this was where steering and steering gear were located before being brought above deck. *Steerage way* is enough *headway* for the rudder to be effective. A *steering oar*, forerunner of the rudder, was an *oar* projecting over (usually) the *starboard* side, but later over the *stern*; the *steersman* is (or was) the *helmsman*.

From OE 'stieran' and a common Teutonic root; the Old Teutonic was *'steurjan'*, from *'steuro'*, a rudder. In Gothic, the similar word *'stiurjan'* meant to establish or affirm.

First attested in or before 1122 in the *Anglo-Saxon Chronicle* (Laud MS) for the year 1046.

steeve   (of *cargo*, etc.) to pack tightly; (of a *bowsprit*) to tilt upwards; the angle a bowsprit makes with the horizon; a long *derrick* or *spar* with a *block* at the end, used for *stowing* cargo.

In its first sense the word is derived, through French and other languages, from the Latin *'stipare'* (the root of 'constipation'), to crowd or press (French *'estiver'*, Provencal *'estibar'*, Catalan '*stibar*', Portugues and Spanish '*estivar*', Italian '*stivare*'): cf. *stevedore*. As regards the senses relating to a bowsprit, two theories compete. One suggests a connection with the Scottish and dialect word 'steeve', meaning *stiff* and possibly derived from it – the notion being that a tilted bowsprit was 'stiff' (though why it should be more so than a horizontal one is unclear, unless there is an implicit phallic overtone). The other theory links the word with OF '*estive*', a ploughtail, from the Latin '*stiva*': 'not improbable' is the OED's judgment. In the sense of a loading derrick, there may be a connection with the bowsprit-related sense, but there may also be a link with the Spanish '*esteba*', which has the same meaning. Is it conceivable that both may be echoing the word 'steep'? The notion of tilting is shared.

First attested, in the sense of packing tight, in 1482 in the *Calendar of Public Rolls* (Public Record Office), Grant of 30 April (1901), 300; as regards a bowsprit, in 1644 in Manwayring, *Seamans Dictionary*, 102; as a derrick, in 1840 in Dana, *Two Years*, xxix.

stem   originally, until the late fifteenth century, the *timber* at the *bow* or *stern* of a ship into which the *planks* are butted; later, that at the bow. As a verb, to make *way*, perhaps with difficulty, against the *tide*. The *stemhead* is the top of the stem, usually capped with a metal fitting to *anchor* the *forestay* and/or act as a *fairlead* for the *cable*. The *stemson* is a curved timber behind the *apron* to support the stem.

From OE 'stemn', 'stefn', also the trunk of a tree.

First attested as a nautical noun in the later eighth century in *Beowulf* (EETS, 1882), 212; as a nautical verb, in 1593 in Shakespeare, *Henry VI, Part III*, II, vi, 36.

step   square wooden or metal fitting to take the *foot* of a *mast*; to fit the mast into its step; step-shaped break in the bottom line of a high-speed *hull*, to let the water flow break away from the hull's skin. A *stepped hull* is one thus designed.

From the OE noun 'staepe' or 'stepe' and the Old Teutonic root '*stap-*'; the verb, intertwined with the noun, comes from OE 'staeppan' or 'steppan' and the Old Teutonic '*stapjan*', '*stop-*', '*stapan-*'.

First attested as a nautical noun *c.* AD 1000 in Cockayne (ed.), *The Shrine* (1864–70), 35/15.

stern   the *after* end of a vessel. A *sternboard* is not a *transom*, but a movement in reverse, either involuntary or in order to turn the vessel's *head* where there is no room to do so while moving forward. A *sternchaser* was a gun (often a long 9-pounder) fitted in the stern to fire on pursuers. *Stern drive* is a transmission system with the engine *inboard* and the gears, shaft and *propeller* in an *outboard* unit that can be swung clear of the water like an outboard engine. A *stern-fast* is a *warp* led from *aft* for *mooring,* etc. A *stern gland* is a sleeve round the propeller shaft packed with compressible material to allow it to turn without letting water in. The *stern light* (properly, the *overtaking light*) is white, showing from dead *astern* to 22.5 degrees *abaft* the *beam* on either side. A *stern mainsheet* controls the *boom* at the *after* end rather than the centre. *Stern on* means with the stern pointing towards anything, e.g. a following *sea.* The *sternpost* is the vertical *timber* aft that carries the *rudder.* The *stern pulpit* (or *pushpit*) is that at the *after* end of a boat. The *stern sheets* are the space and benches at the after end of a boat (often a *rowing* or ship's boat). The *stern wave* is that generated towards the after end of a boat. *Sternway* is backwards movement. A *sternwheeler* is a *paddle*-steamer propelled by a single *wheel* at the stern.

One original and now obsolete meaning of the word was the vessel's *steering* gear, which was the meaning of its probable source, ON *'stjorn'*: there is no evidence for an equivalent OE 'steorn'.

First attested (and in the modern, not the obsolete sense) *c.* 1300 in *King Horn* (in Ritson (ed.), *Romances,* 1802), 935.

stevedore   one who loads or unloads *cargo* in merchant vessels. A *stevedore's knot* is a *stopper knot* made like a *figure-of-eight knot* but with more turns.

From the Spanish *'estivador'*: cf. *steeve.*

First attested in 1788 in *The Massachusetts Spy,* 10 July, 2/3.

stick   colloquial term for a *mast.*

From OE 'sticca' and the Teutonic root *'stik-'*, to pierce or prick.

First attested in this nautical sense, but without today's semi-jocular overtones, in 1802 in *The Naval Chronicle,* VIII, 517; with something approaching the current self-deprecating tone, in 1834 in Marryat, *Peter Simple,* xlvi.

stiff   (of a vessel) not easily *heeled* over; (of a breeze) strong.

From OE 'stif', the Old Teutonic type *'stifo-'*, and the pre-Teutonic *'stipo-'*, cognate with the Latin *'stipare'*, to crowd or cram: cf. *steeve.*

First attested in a nautical sense in 1627 in Smith, *Sea Grammar,* xii, 56; of a *wind, c.* 1290 in *St Brendan,* in *The Early South-English Legendary* (EETS, 1887), 232.

stirrup   one of the short ropes hanging from the *yards* to support the *footropes* in *square-riggers.*

From OE 'stigrap', climbing or foothold rope. The nautical application may, as suggested by Kemp (ed.) *Oxford Companion*

(1976), 836, be connected with the fact that footropes are sometimes known as *horses*; but the imagery seems confused, since
in this nautical context the horses hang from the stirrups.

First attested in this nautical sense in 1495 in *Naval Accounts*
(Navy Records Society, 1896), 152.

stock   the (originally wooden) horizontal cross-piece of a *fisherman's anchor*; (in the plural) the framework of blocks in
which a ship is supported while being built.

From OE 'stoc(c)', meaning a tree-stump or tree-trunk,
cognate with similar words in other Germanic languages and
derived from the Old Teutonic '*stukko*', '*stukkjo-*', whence both
the modern German '*Stock*', stick, and '*Stueck*', piece.

First attested, in its anchor connection, in 1346 in the
Accounts of the Exchequer of the King's Remembrancer (MSS in the
Public Record Office), 25/7; in its shipbuilding connection, in
1422 in the *Foreign Accounts* (MSS in the Public Record Office),
61 m 43.

stone frigate   a naval *shore* establishment.

From 'stone' (from OE 'stan' and a common Teutonic
source: cf. the modern German '*Stein*') plus *frigate* (since such
establishments were often named after frigates).

First attested in 1917 in Hainsselin, *Grand Fleet Days*, iv, 15.

stop   to secure (a sail) with small *yarn* so that it can be broken
out easily; one such *tie*; to pack a split or a small hole with *putty*,
etc. A *stopper* is a shortrope, *chain*, or other fitting used to
hold another temporarily, especially for instance to hold the
running rigging while the *fall* is being *belayed*; a *stopper
hitch*, used for this purpose, is a *rolling hitch* in which the
second *turn rides* over the fist. A *stopper knot* is any used at
the end of a rope to form a knob that will not pass through an
eye or a *fairlead*, such as a *figure-of-eight knot* at the end of
a *jib sheet*. *Stopping* is putty-like material used to fill cracks,
etc. A *stopwater* is (usually) a wooden dowel inserted between
pieces of *timber* to make the joint watertight when it swells.

From OE '(for)stoppian', one instance of a common West
German adaptation of the popular Latin or Roman '*stuppare*':
all denote stuffing or closing, e.g., the ears.

First attested in a nautical context, as *caulking*, in 1535 in
Coverdale (transl.), the *Bible*, *Ezekiel* xxvii, 9; in the sense of
temporarily restraining, in 1770 in *Philosophical Transactions of
the Royal Society*, LX, 191.

storm   a *wind* of average speed between 48 and 63 *knots*,
forces 10 and 11 on the *Beaufort scale*; from 56 to 63 knots is
termed a violent storm. *Stormbound* means not 'heading for
a storm' but unable to proceed because of it.

A *storm cone* is a black cone 3 feet high and 3 feet wide at the base, *hoisted* by *shore* stations as a *gale* (not a storm) warning, with its point upward if the gale is expected from the North, and downward if from the South: for an Easterly, a South cone is hoisted above a North, for a Westerly, a North cone is hoisted above a South. A *storm jib* is a *spitfire*; a *storm sail* is either a storm jib or a *trysail*. *Storm signals* are storm cones.

From OE 'storm' and a common Teutonic root (Old Teutonic '*sturmo-*' from the root '*stur-*', denoting stirring), but with no Gothic antecedent recorded.

First attested *c.* AD 825 in the *Vespasian Psalter* (in Sweet, *Oldest English Texts*), EETS, 1885, xlix, 3.

stove, stove in   (of a boat) damaged by something breaking in from without.

Past participle of *stave*.

First attested in 1850 in Melville, *White Jacket*, I, iv, 20.

stow   to put *cargo*, etc., in its proper place or places *on board*. To *stow thick* is to cram people in. *Stowage* is the place where something is normally kept, or the placing of *ballast* or *cargo* in a *hold*; a *stowaway* is a clandestine passenger.

From the now largely obsolete noun, preserved in place-names like Stow-on-the-Wold and originally meaning 'place'. The noun is from OE 'stow' and the Old Teutonic '*stowo-*'. Although the verb '*stouwen*' in Dutch has the same nautical meaning as 'stow' and may have influenced English usage, the OED declares that the two are 'etymologically unconnected'.

First attested in its nautical cargo sense in 1598 in Florio, *Worlde of Wordes*, under '*stipare*'.

stow-boat   a kind of boat used for sprat fishing on the East Anglian and South coasts of England.

Of obscure origin and largely local use: possibly an alteration of 'stall-boat', i.e. one at *anchor* in a fixed position, as at the mouth of a river, from OE 'steall' and the Old Teutonic '*stallo*': cf. the stalling of an engine.

First attested in 1833 in *British Channel Fisheries*, 11.

strait   a narrow stretch of water joining two *seas*, etc., and separating two pieces of land.

From ME 'streit', adapted from OF '*estreit*' (modern French '*etroit*') and derived from the Latin '*strictus*', from '*stringere*' to tighten.

First attested as a nautical noun in 1375 in Barbour, *The Bruce*, (EETS, 1870–89), III, 688.

strake   the whole of one *plank* (even if more than one, end to end) in a vessel's *hull*.

From ME 'strake' and probably the Old Teutonic root

'*strak-*', stretch. Etymologically, there seems to be no connection with 'streak', but from the sixteenth century onwards the words have been phonetically confused, and they share some meanings, the earliest in the case of 'strake' being the metal rim of a cart-wheel or a strip of iron on the left side of a plough.

First attested in its nautical sense in or before 1419 in a letter by Alcetre in Ellis (ed.), *Original Letters*, second series, I, 69.

strand   *shore* (often that part between high and low *tide* marks); to run or be run *aground*; one of the strings or *yarns* of which a rope is made; to break one such; to form a rope by twisting the strands.

There are two distinct etymologies here. Relating to the shore, the noun and verb are derived from OE 'strand', with counterparts in other Germanic and Nordic languages. Relating to rope, the source of the word remains obscure, there being no proven link either with 'strain', used in the sixteenth century with the same meaning, or with OF '*estran*', '*estren*', meaning rope.

First attested, regarding the shore, *c*. AD 1000 in *The Holy Gospels in Anglo-Saxon* (ed. Skeat, 1871–87), *Matthew* xiii, 48; regarding rope, in 1497 in *Naval Accounts* (Navy Records Society, 1896), 244.

stray line   the length of *line* (between 10 and 30 *fathoms*) between the *log* and the zero mark on the *log-line*, such extension being needed to prevent the log's responding to *eddies* in the ship's *wake*. The word has also been applied both to the *slack* of a *cable* and to the deviation of the *sounding line* from the perpendicular.

'Stray' comes from OF '*estraier*' via the Anglo-French '*estrai*', stray, carrying the familiar sense of errancy.

First attested in 1703 in Dampier, *New Voyage*, III, I, 99.

stream   to cast *overboard* from the *stern*: most often said of an *anchor buoy*, streamed before the anchor is let go, to prevent the *buoy-rope*'s *fouling* the anchor or its *cable*; also applied to fog-buoys, *logs*, *sea-anchors*, etc. A *stream anchor* is one larger than a *kedge* but smaller than a *bower*, often used by large ships as a *stern* anchor.

From the familiar noun, derived from OE 'stréam' and a common Teutonic root; not recorded in Gothic, but descended from an Old Teutonic '*straumo-z*', a pre-Teutonic '*straumo-s*', and an Indo-Germanic '*srou-*', with links to Sanskrit, Old Slav, Russian, Old Irish, and Middle Welsh.

First attested as a verb in this nautical sense in 1769 in Falconer, *Dictionary* (1780 edition).

stretch   a continuous sail on one *tack*.

The noun is from the verb, derived from OE 'streccan' and

a common West Germanic root; the original meaning was to place at full length.

First attested in this nautical sense in 1675 in Teonge, *Diary* (1825 edition), 42.

stretcher   a transverse *batten* in a *rowing* boat against which *oarsmen* brace their feet; a stouter version of the same to keep a boat's sides apart when she is *hoisted* up; a piece of wood or metal to spread the *clews* of a *hammock* when in use.

From the verb *stretch*.

First attested in a nautical sense in 1609 in Dekker, *Ravens Almanacke*, B 2.

strike   to lower (*colours*, a sail, a *burgee*, a *topmast*, etc). To *strike down* is to lower a *mast* or *yard* to the deck in a *square-rigger*, or to lower heavy goods into the *hold*, or (in sailing navies) to bring the guns down to the lower gun deck for stability's sake. To *strike soundings* is to reach the *bottom* with the deep-sea *lead*.

From OE 'striccan' and a common Western Germanic root; but the early meanings seem unrelated to the nautical sense: they include going, roving, wandering, rubbing, stroking, smearing, etc. It is therefore possible that the nautical verb, which has counterparts in Middle Low German and Middle Dutch as well as modern German, arises from a putative development from the Latin '*stringere*', to strip off (of leaves, etc.).

First attested in or before 1300 in *King Horn* (Ritson, *Romances*, II), 1013.

stringer   one of the *fore-and-aft* strengthening pieces running the length of the *hull* (formerly known as 'shelf-pieces').

From the noun 'string', derived from OE 'streng'; the noun was also in use until the mid nineteenth century with much the same meaning as 'stringer' today (in its nautical sense).

First attested in its nautical sense in 1830 in Hedderwick, *Marine Architecture*, 130.

stroke   a single *pull* of an *oar* when *rowing*; the *aftermost oarsman*, also known as the *stroke-oar*, whose timing determines that of the whole *crew*.

From the thirteenth-century ME 'strok' and the Old Teutonic '*straiko-z*', originally with its familiar, non-aquatic meaning.

First attested, as the pull of an oar, in 1583 in Howard, *Defensative*, L iij, B; as an oarsman, in 1825 in Westmacott, *The English Spy* (1825–6), 1907 edition, I, 28.

strongers   colloquial term for any harsh cleaning fluid.

From 'strong', derived from OE 'strang', 'strong', and the Old Teutonic '*strangu-*'.

First attested in 1929 in Bowen, *Sea Slang*, 135.

strop   a ring of rope, often with a *thimble* or *eye* to take a *shackle*, used to attach to a *spar* or act as a *sling* for *hoisting*.

From OE 'strop'; the form 'strap' appeared in the seventeenth century.

First attested in a nautical sense in 1357 in *Pipe Roll* 32 of Edward III, m 34/2.

strum (also *strum-box*, *strum-plate*)   filter or sieve placed over the intake end of *bilge*-pumps, etc., to prevent clogging.

Of obscure origin, and nothing to do with playing a banjo, etc.: possibly connected with *stream*, especially since the word's first use, in 1394–5, denoting a sieve used in brewing, was in the spelling 'strom': cf. similar Scandinavian and Germanic words with the sense of 'stream'.

First attested in a nautical context in 1894 in Paasch, *From Keel to Truck*, (second edition) 172/1.

stud   one of the iron bars inserted across the middle of *chain* links to strengthen them and prevent kinking.

From OE 'studu', originally meaning a prop or support.

First attested in this nautical sense in 1863 in Young, *Nautical Dictionary*, 398.

studding-sail (pronounced 'stunsail' and sometimes thus spelt) extra sail set in light airs with the *wind abaft* the *beam*, outside the *square* sails whose *yards* are extended for the purpose with *booms*, normally on the *topgallant* and *topmast* yards, the studding-sails on the latter extending across the depth of both the upper and lower *topsails*. *With stunsail set both sides* means with a girl on each arm.

Of obscure etymology. There may be a link back to the Middle Dutch or Middle Low German '*stotinge*', but this word comes from '*stoten*', to push, thrust or collide; and while the *wind* certainly pushes the studding-sails, in a square-rigger *running* or *reaching* it does the same to most of their fellows. The Dutch word '*stootlap*', sail lining, and '*stootkant*', border, may have some affinity with the English word; and OF '*estuinc*', '*estoinc*' and '*estouin*', ancestors of the now obsolete eighteenth-century '*estouine*' have the same meaning as 'studding-sail' and may be derived from '*stotinge*'. But this too is uncertain, especially since the modern French term for such a sail, '*bonnette à étui*' suggests that '*estuinc*' may be related to '*estui*', the OF form of '*étui*'. The Breton '*studincq*' is adopted from the English.

First attested in 1549 in the *Complaynt of Scotlande* (EETS, 1872), vi, 42.

S-twist   describes a rope *laid up* left-handed (cf. *Z-twist*).

From the shape of the letter and the appearance of the rope viewed from the end.

First attested in 1935 in *American Society for Testing Materials*, *Proceedings*, XXXV, I, 448.

suck the monkey   to drink from a bottle; later, to drink spirits from a coconut emptied of its milk, brought on board by West Indian women during the War of American Independence (1775–82). 'Suck' from OE 'sucan', corresponding to the Latin '*sugere*', plus *monkey*.

First attested in 1797 in Bennett, *Beggar Girl* (1813 edition), III, 253.

Sumner line (also *Sumner's position line*)   a series of positions worked out by combining astronomical observation with dead reckoning.

From its originator, the US shipmaster Thomas H. Sumner of Boston, Mass. (1807–76).

First attested in 1849 in Raper, *Navigation* (third edition), 345.

supercargo   officer *on board* a merchant ship concerned with commercial business, often on behalf of the owner; (colloquially) a disposable member of the *crew*.

Altered from the now obsolete 'supracargo', from the Spanish '*sobrecargo*', compounded of '*sobre*' (over) plus '*cargo*' (cargo).

First attested in 1697 in Dampier, *New Voyage*, 1729 editon, I, 511.

surf   the white crest of *waves* breaking on a *shore*. A *surfboard* is a long narrow board on which, usually standing (or crouching), one rides in on heavy surf. A *surf boat* is a specially built *flat-bottomed* boat, propelled by *paddles*, for landing people and goods on African and Indian beaches if there is no harbour: it is also applied to craft built for *surf-riding*, as on a surfboard.

A mysterious, possibly onomatopoeic word, this is a successor in time and meaning to 'suff', now obsolete, and equally obscure in origin: the connection between the two is also unclear.

First attested in 1685 in Hedges, *Diary* (Hakluyt Society, 1887–8), I, 182.

surge   (of a rope) to slip on a *winch* or *capstan*; that part of a capstan, etc., on which a rope surges; such slippage; to let it happen; (of a ship) to pull or jerk in a certain direction; a rhythmic *forward-and-aft* motion (such as is curbed by *springs*); an exceptional run of *sea* into a harbour.

Both the noun and the verb seem to be derived, partly through OF, from the Latin '*surgere*' to rise.

First attested in the nautical sense of slipping, in or before 1625 in *Nomenclator Navalis* (Harleian MS 2301), 139; as applying to a ship's motion, in 1839 in Darwin, *H.M.S. Beagle*, 1832–6 (1852 edition), x, 212.

swab   a mop made of rope-ends for cleaning the deck; a *lubberly sailor*; to use such a mop. A *swab-hitch* is one used for *bending* a rope's end to swabs when washing them *overboard*; a *swab-man* is (or was) a naval officer wearing epaulettes; a *swab-washer* or *swab-wringer* is one who washes or wrings out swabs; a *swabber* is one who swabs.

The noun comes from the verb, which (in this sense) is a back-formation from the noun 'swabber': this in turn is derived from the early modern Dutch '*zwabber*' and thence from the Dutch '*zwabben*', cognate with the Low German and West Frisian '*swabber*', a mop. Cf. the Norwegian and Swedish '*svabb*', also meaning a mop.

First attested in 1659 in Torriano, *Dictionary*.

swallow   the space between the *sheave* and the *shell* of a *block* through which the rope runs. To *swallow the anchor* is to retire from the *sea* and settle *ashore*.

From late OE 'geswelg'. 'swelh', a gulf or abyss: in other Germanic and Nordic languages the corresponding words carry also the overtone of devourer.

First attested *c.* 1860 in Stuart, *Catechism*, 37.

swash, swatch   originally, a *surge* of water meeting some obstacle; now, more often, a *shoal* just under water, against which it will ripple or surge at low *tide*.

A *swashway* or *swatchway* is a *channel* between swashes in the second sense of the word.

Imitative of the sound, with some influence from 'wash'.

First attested, as a surge, in 1671 in Skinner, *Etymologicon*; as a shoal, in 1961 in Burgess, *Dictionary*, 203.

sway   to *hoist*; the rhythmic side-to-side motion of a ship, as distinct from a roll, which is rotary. To *sway the main* is a colloquial expression for telling vainglorious stories.

Both from the verb, although according to the OED both are really two separate words: the first appears in the fourteenth century from ME 'sweye', the second *c.* 1500 from the Low German '*swajen*'. The first carries overtones of moving, carrying, and perhaps *weighing*, the second describes rhymthic to-and-fro motion.

First attested in a nautical sense in 1743 in Bulkeley and Cummins, *Voyage*, 15.

sweat   (of a vessel) to exploit to the utmost; (of a sail, *halyard*, etc.) to *hoist* as tightly as possible – in the days before *winches*, by taking a *turn* round a *cleat, hauling* out the *standing part* horizontally, then taking up the slack round the cleat. From the familiar word, which comes from OE 'swaetan', with counterparts in most Germanic languages: one notion perhaps being that a wet rope when taut squeezes out some of its moisture.

First attested in a nautical sense in 1890 in Russell, *An Ocean Tragedy*, I, iv, 73.

sweep   a long heavy *oar* carried in pre-engine sailing vessels for use when the *wind* failed.

Unlike the familiar noun and verb, 'sweep' in its nautical sense is derived from the dialect word 'swape', a *steering oar*, which in turn has its origin in ON '*sveip-*', indicating a sweeping, circle-wise motion: cf. 'swipe'.

First attested in its non-dialect spelling in 1800 in *The Asiatic Annual Register, Misc. Tr.*, 223/1.

swell   *waves* or undulations of the *sea* that do not break unless they meet an obstruction.

In this and other senses the noun is derived from the verb, whose source is OE 'swellan', with many counterparts in other Germanic and Nordic languages.

First attested in its nautical sense in 1606 in Shakespeare, *Anthonie, and Cleopatra*, III, ii, 49.

swift   to tighten or *make fast* with a rope or ropes drawn tight round the object or objects in question, whether a boat or ship, *capstan* bars, *rigging*, *masts*, etc. A *swifter* is a long *line* used to swift capstan bars: a *cut splice* at its centre is put on one bar, the others being secured with two *turns* each until the last, which takes the *thimble* and *point* at opposite ends of the swifter, which provides spaces between the bars for extra *hands* to use their muscles.

From an obsolete noun of identical spelling meaning the rope or ropes thus employed; this in turn seems to have come from Scandinavian or Low German: cf. ON '*svipta*', to reef, and the Dutch '*zwichten*', to take in (sails).

First attested in 1485 in *Naval Accounts* (Navy Records Society, 1896), 47.

swig   (of a rope or *halyard*) to *sweat* (i.e. *make fast* or take half a *turn* with the free end, then haul and take up the slack with the other hand).

Of unknown origin, like the familiar word for drinking; but there may be a link from this nautical sense of the word not only to 'sweat' but to 'swag' and *sway*, hence to Scandinavia, as in the Norwegian dialect '*svaga*', '*svagga*', to sway.

First attested as a nautical verb in 1794 in *The Elements and Practice of Rigging and Seamanship*, I, 176.

swing   (of a ship *moored* by the *head* or *riding* to a single *anchor*) to move from side to side with *wind* and *tide*. To *swing a cat* (as in 'no room to… ') refers to a confined space: the 'cat' may be the *cat-o'-nine-tails*, but not certainly so, and

certainly not a *catamaran*. To *swing the compass* is to turn
the boat through 360 degrees at approximately the same place
so as to take known *bearings* and compare them with the
compass readings, thereby ascertaining its *deviation* at each
point. To *swing the lead* (as distinct from *casting* or *heaving*
it) is to malinger or idle. To *swing the ship* is to swing the
compass.

From OE 'swingan', cognate with a number of similar words
in other Germanic languages; in OE, the primary meaning was
to beat or scourge.

First attested in a nautical sense in 1769 in Falconer,
Dictionary (1780 edition).

swivel block   one whose *eye* or hook will revolve (e.g. for a
main sheet). A *swivel link* is one that will turn on a self-
contained axis, inserted in a *chain* to avoid twists.

From 'swivel', from OE 'swifan', plus *block*.

First attested, as 'swivel-hooked blocks', in 1883 in *Manual
of Seamanship*, 136; as 'swivel block', in 1961 in Burgess,
Dictionary, 204.

Tabernacle   socket for the *foot* of a *mast stepped* at
deck level, and so lowerable.

From the twelfth-century French *'tabernacle'* and
thence from the Latin *'tabernaculum'*, tent, booth, shed, etc.; a
diminutive of *'taberna'*, hut or booth: cf. 'tavern' and *'taverna'*.

First attested in its nautical sense in 1877 in Knight,
Mechanics (1874–7).

table   to reinforce a sail with extra bands at *reef points* or (in
a *square* sail) at the *buntline*.

From the familiar noun, derived from OE 'tabule' and thence
from the Latin *'tabula'* – the common elements being flatness
and perhaps also strength.

First attested in its sailmaking sense in 1769 in Falconer,
Dictionary (1776 edition).

tack   originally, rope, wire, or *chain* securing the *windward*
lower corners of *courses* and *staysails* when sailing *close-
hauled*; by extension, these corners, and the corresponding
corners of *fore-and-aft* sails; a course or *board* oblique to the
wind; to take such a course; to move from one to another by
putting the ship's *head* through the *wind*; (usually in a combination like *hardtack*) food or ship's biscuit. A *tackline* is a
6-foot length of *signal halyard* used to separate groups of *flags*;
the *tack tackle* is that used for *hauling* down the tack of a sail.

With the exception of the foodstuff, whose name may have been influenced by *tackle*, the noun and the verb are both doublets of 'tache' as a noun and a verb, the latter derived from the former, which comes from fourteenth-century OF *'tache'*, a buckle or long nail. The basic notion is that of attachment, the sail being attached by its tack, and the tack being to *starboard* when on *starboard tack* (although most of the sail is then billowed out to *port*), and vice versa.

First attested, as the rope for the tack, in 1481–90 in the *Howard Household Books* (Roxburghe Club, 1844), 111; as a course or board, in 1614 by Sir Robert Dudley in *The Fortescue Papers* (Camden Society, 1871), 9; as altering course, in 1637 in Pocklington, *Altare Christianum*, 153; as the corner of a sail, in 1769 in Falconer, *Dictionary* (1789 edition); as food, in 1833 in Marryat, *Peter Simple*, xxviii.

tackle   (originally) *rigging, cordage*; (usually) one of at least a dozen varieties of *purchase* made up of ropes and *blocks*. Perhaps to distinguish such gear from fishing and other 'tackle' (and perhaps themselves from laymen), British naval personnel often pronounce the word 'taykle'. A *tackle-block* is of course a block.

From Low German, as in the Middle Low German *'takel'*, the equipment of a horseman or the *hoisting* gear of a ship; cf. the early modern Dutch *'takel'*, strong rope, *hawser*, or pulley.

First attested, as rigging, in or before 1300 in *Cursor Mundi* (EETS, 1874–92), 24944; as cordage, in 1529 in *Statutes of the Realm* 1235–1713 (Record Commission 1810–28), Act 21 of Henry VIII, c. 12, 1; as a purchase, in 153940 in *Notes and Queries* (Devon), October 1903, 238.

taffrail   the *aftermost* part of a ship's *poop*-rail. The word was also the pen-name used for his sea stories by Captain Henry Taprell Dorling (1883–1968).

A nineteenth-century alteration (i.e. corruption) of 'tafferel', derived from the Dutch *'tafereel'*, panel, picture (a diminutive of *'tafel'*, table) and originally meaning a carved panel that was part of the *stern* above the *transom*. When it came to be applied to the rail it began to be spelt as now, the '-rel' being mistaken for '-rail'.

First attested in its present spelling in 1814 in the *Chronicle* in the *Annual Register*, 176/2.

take aback   to cause a ship, through a change of *wind* or inept *helmsmanship*, to have the wind on the 'wrong'side of the sails – either with the *clew* to *windward* or pressed back against the *mast*: if this is done deliberately, the sails are said to be *laid aback*. By extension, in the familiar sense, suddenly and not always pleasurably surprised. To *take a caulk* is a colloquial expression for sleeping on deck; to *take a turn* is to pass a rope once or twice round a *cleat* to ease the strain. To *take charge* (said of the vessel itself) is to get out of control. To *take in* is to *furl, brail,* or lower a sail. To *take off* (said of *tides*) is to diminish in range after *spring tides*. To *take the ground* is to touch *bottom*. To *take up* (said of a wooden boat's *planking*) is to swell so as to close the seams.

From 'take' in one of its familiar senses plus *aback*. 'Take' comes from Late OE 'tacan', which appeared in the eleventh century, and began to supersede OE 'niman', cognate with the German *'nehmen'* and with the same sense.

First attested in 1748 in Anson, *Voyage*, II, vii, 215.

tan   to preserve sails and nets by soaking them in *cutch*.

From Late OE 'tannian', and probably thence from the medieval Latin *'tannare'*; the noun comes from the French *'tan'*, oak bark, and the Latin *'tannum'*, which may be of Celtic origin: cf. the Breton *'tann'*, oak, and the Cornish 'glas-tannen', ever-green oak, ilex. (An infusion of crushed bark from oak and other trees was used for tanning leather.)

First attested in its nautical sense in 1601 in Keymor, *Observations* (1664 edition), 7.

tar   residue obtained by the distillation of gum from pine trees, etc., used to preserve rope and the *standing rigging* of *square-riggers*; an affectionate term for a *sailor* (also Jack Tar).

From OE 'teru', with counterparts in a number of other Germanic languages, and probably a derivative of the Old Tetonic *'trewo-'*, the Gothic *'triu-'* and the Indo-European *'derw-', 'dorw-', 'dru-',* tree.

First attested in a specifically nautical context *c.* 1250 in *The Story of Genesis and Exodus* (EETS, 1865, 1873), 662; as applied to a sailor, in 1676 in Wycherley, *The Plain-dealer*, II, I, (Novel).

tarpaulin   *canvas* originally coated with *tar* to make it water-proof, now with any waterproofing agent, at first used for *sailors*' clothing, then for any protective purpose; a now largely archaic nickname for a sailor. A *tarpaulin captain* was a *captain* of a British naval vessel under the Tudors and Stuarts who had risen through the ranks. A *tarpaulin muster* was a nickname for the pooling of resources by a group of *seamen* before taking the *liberty boat*.

From *tar* plus (probably) 'pall', a vestment, from OE 'pael', 'pel', which meant a rich robe until about 1440, when it was first used to denote a cloth spread over a coffin. Since this was often black, like tar, it has been conjectured that 'tarpaulin' owes its name to the funereal comparison – although 'tar-pall' is nowhere to be found.

First attested, as a material, in 1605 in Jonson, *Volpone*, IV, I; as a nickname for seamen, in 1647 in Cleveland, *Diurnall-maker* (*Works*, 1687), 82.

taunt   having very tall *masts* and narrow sails.

A cousin to this adjective, and now even rarer, was 'ataunt', which the OED suggests was an adaptation of the French '*autant*' – highly unlikely, given the sense. A second possibility is a link with the noun, whose origin may (in the phrase 'taunt for taunt', now obsolete) be the French '*tant pour tant*', tit for tat.

Far more plausible is a connection with the early sixteenth-century non-nautical adjective 'taunt', meaning proud or high-and-mighty – a notion easily transferable to the profile of a tall, slim ship. The chronology of the word's recorded occurrences does not contradict such a lineage; the meaning of 'taunt' as a verb may seem to confirm it. First attested in 1622 in Hawkins, *Observations* (Hakluyt Society, 1847, 1878), lix, 138.

taut   tightly drawn, not *slack*; (of a ship) *trim* and strictly run; (of a person) strict and disciplined. *On a taut bowline* (of a *square-rigger*) means *close-hauled*; a *taut leech* describes a sail well *set* and *trimmed full*.

Almost certainly from ME 'togt', 'toght', 'tought', but not found with the spelling 'taught' until after 1600. The ME word seems to be descended from OE 'teohan', 'teon', to pull, which comes from the Gothic '*tiuhan*', with the same meaning: cf. the modern German '*ziehen*'. There may also be a link with ME 'tigt', tight (and with this word itself).

First attested, in the first, familiar, 'non-slack' sense, in or before 1604 in Peele, *Tale of Troy*, 256; as applied to a *seaman*, in 1829 in Jerrold, *Black-ey'd Susan*, III, ii, 43. The commonest use of the term is in the phrase 'a taut ship': cf. *Time* magazine, 29 December, 1941, 8/1.

tell-tale   originally, an extra *compass* in the *master*'s *cabin*; then a device at the *wheel* to show the *rudder*'s angle; now (but not in the OED) a strand of wool attached to a sail, or a ribbon attached to a *shroud*, to indicate local airflow.

'Tell' (from OE 'tellan') plus 'tale' (from OE 'talu') – a combination first attested in its familiar sense of informing in the early sixteenth century.

First attested in a nautical sense in 1815 in Burney (ed.) Falconer, *New Universal Dictionary*.

tender   a ship or boat employed to attend a larger one, especially to transfer *cargo*, passengers, etc.; (as an adjective and of a ship) easily *heeled* by the *wind*.

The noun is an aphetic form of 'attender', from 'attend' and thence from OF '*atendre*' and the Latin '*adtendere*'. The adjective is from the French '*tendre*', first attested in the eleventh century, and the Latin '*tenerum*', delicate.

First attested as a nautical noun in 1675 in the *London Gazette* No. 1054/2; as a nautical adjective in 1722 in Defoe, *Colonel Jacque* [*Colonel Jack*] (1840 edition), 190.

teredo   a genus of bivalve boring mollusc, especially *teredo navalis*, erroneously called the 'ship-worm' since until 1733 it was believed to be a worm.

From the Latin '*teredo*' and in turn from the Greek '*teridon*', a wood-gnawing creature (from the Greek '*ter-*', the root of '*terein*', to wear away, bore.

First attested in 1398 in Trevisa (transl.), *Bartholomeus*, Tollemache MS; Add.MS (B.M.) 27944; MS/ e Museo (Bodl.), 16; W. de Worde 1495, 1535; vii, xxiii (Bodl. MS).

Thames barge   *ketch* or *yawl-rigged* sailing *barge* with a large *spritsail*, once common in the Thames estuary. *Thames Measurement*, usually abbreviated to T.M., is a system for measuring *yachts* introduced in 1855 by the Royal Thames Yacht Club, expressed in *tonnage* but actually relating to length and *beam*, and arrived at by the following formula:

$$\frac{(L - B) \times B \times \text{one-half } B}{94}$$

where L = the length in feet from the *forward* side of the *stem* under the *bowsprit* and measured at deck level to the *after* side of the *sternpost*, while B = the *beam* in feet measured to the outside of the *hull planking*.

First attested in 1883 in *Boats of the World*, 4.

thick stuff   *timber planking* more than four inches but less than twelve inches thick.

'Thick' is from OE 'thicce', 'stuff' from ME 'stoffe'.

First attested *c.* 1850 in Greenwood, *Sailor's Sea-book*, 155.

thieves' cat   a *cat-o'-nine-tails* with three knots in each of its tails, used in some sailing navies on thieves. A *thieves' knot* is a *reef knot* deliberately tied so that the two ends finish on opposite sides, with a view to its slipping. 'Thieves' comes from OE 'thiof', 'theof': the final consonant was originally voiced, like 'f' in Welsh, or as in the present plural of 'thief'.

First attested in 1867 in Smyth, *Sailor's Word-book*.

thimble   a round or heart-shaped metal or plastic *eye* grooved on the outside to take a rope *spliced* round it.

From OE 'thymel', from 'thuma', thumb: the suffix denotes an instrument, as in 'handle', since in its familiar sense a thimble was worn as a finger stall or thumbstall. (The 'b' in the word's later forms parallels the cases of 'humble', 'nimble', etc.)

First attested in this nautical sense in 1711 in Sutherland, *Ship Builder's Assistant*, 132.

thole, thole pin   a vertical wooden or metal pin on a *rowing* boat's *gunwale*, originally used with a rope ring, later with a second pin or with a hole in the *oar*, to enable an oar to pivot when rowing; largely superseded by *crutches* or *rowlocks*.

From OE 'thol(l)', with counterparts in a number of Scandinavian and Germanic languages: in ON, *'thollr'* also meant fir-tree.

Late spellings of the English word, such as 'thoule', 'thowle', and the nineteenth-century 'thowel', seem to have been influenced by 'doule', 'dowle', which are variant spellings of 'dowel', whose source is probably the Middle Low German *'dovel'*, the plug or tap of a cask.

First attested *c*. AD 725 in the *Corpus Glossary* (Oldest English Texts, EETS, 1885), 1820.

thoroughfoot   a kink or tangle in a rope; to remedy such a problem by *coiling* the rope down and passing the end through the coil; a method of joining two ropes that both have *eye-splices* in their ends, by looping one over the other in what then looks like a loose *reef knot*.

'Thorough' is a development of OE 'thurh', through: it appears in later OE as 'thuruh'. Since an early and now obsolete form of 'thoroughfoot' was 'thoroughput', it may be that the origin of the nautical expression is the notion of 'throughput', putting through.

First attested in a nautical sense, as a tangle, in 1867 in Smyth, *Sailor's Word-book*; as a remedy, in 1961 in Burgess, *Dictionary*, 207; as a junction of two ropes, in 1976 in Kemp (ed.), *Oxford Companion*, 866–7.

thrash (to *windward*)   to *beat upwind*, especially in rough weather.

From the familiar word, whose primary meaning was to thresh – an alternative spelling still used in the mid nineteenth-century: its origin is OE 'thercan', from the Gothic *'thriskan'*, the Old Teutonic root *'thresk-'* and the Indo-European *'tresk-'*.

First attested in a nautical sense in 1830 in Hawker, *Diary* (1893), II, 15.

three figure method   system for showing *bearings* in degrees from nought to 359, using nought or double-nought for double or single figures, reading off clockwise round the *compass*, starting with North at 000 degrees. The *three mile limit* was the old limit of territorial waters round the coast of a state; *three sheets in the wind* means unsteady through drink (the implication being that even with three *sheets* instead of two a steady course would be impossible); *three sisters* was the name of an unauthorised and (from 1809) illegal instrument of punishment, consisting of three rattans bound together with waxed twine, used on the backs of *seamen* in the seventeenth and eighteenth centuries in the practice known as *starting*, i.e. (supposedly) spurring them on to greater effort.

'Three' comes from OE 'thri', 'thrie', 'thrio', 'threo', from common Teutonic and Indo-European sources; 'figure' is from the French *'figure'* and thence from the Latin *'figura'*; 'method' is from the French *'méthode'*, the Latin *'methodus'*, and the Greek *'methodos'*.

First attested (*pace* the OED, which finds only an approximation to the phrase, and that two years later) in 1976 in Kemp (ed.), *Oxford Companion*, 867.

throat   the hollow in the bend of a *knee-timber*; the *jaws* of a *gaff*; the *amidships* part of a floor *timber*; that part of a *mizen yard* close to the *mast*; the upper *foremost* part of a four-sided *fore-and-aft* sail; the *swallow* of a *block*; the curve of the *flukes* of an *anchor* near the *shank*. *Throat halyards* are those used to *hoist* the throat of a sail or the jaws of a gaff; *throat seizing* is that binding the *thimble* in the *strop* of a block, or that which binds the two parts of a rope together to form an *eye*.

All these figurative uses come from the familiar word, whose source is OE 'throte', counterpart of the Old High German *'drozza'*, from the Old Teutonic root *'thrut-'* and the Indo-European *'trud-'*.

First attested, as applied to a knee-timber, in 1711 in Sutherland, *Ship Builder's Assistant*, 165; as the gaff's jaws, in 1776 in Falconer, *Dictionary*; as part of the floor timbers, *c.* 1850 in Greenwood, *Sailor's Sea-book*, 155; as applied to a yard, in 1867 in Smyth, *Sailor's Word-book*; as part of a sail, in 1961 in Burgess, *Dictionary*, 208; as part of a block, in 1978 in Desoutter, *Practical Dictionary*, 217.

thrum   (often plural) *hempen* or woollen *yarn* in short pieces, for making mats, mops, ant-chafe pads, etc.; to sew short lengths of such to a sail or piece of *canvas* for use as a collision mat.

From the (fairly) familiar word for a fringe of threads, which comes from OE 'thrum' and thence from the Old Teutonic *'thrum-'*, *'thram-'* and the Indo-European *'trmo-'*: cf. the Latin *'terminus'*.

First attested as a nautical noun in 1466 in *Manners and Household Expenses* (Roxburghe Club, 1841), 346; as a nautical verb, in 1711 in Sutherland, *Ship Builder's Assistant*, 162.

thumb cleat   a small *cleat* with only one arm or *horn*, often fixed to a *spar* and used for jamming a rope, for example on the *boom* to secure the *outhaul* when the *foot* of the sail has been *hauled* out *taut*. A *thumb knot* is a simple *overhand knot* made by laying the end of a rope over its own part and bringing the end under and through the loop thus made.

'Thumb' is a figurative adjectival use of the familiar noun, whose origin is OE 'thuma', from the Old Teutonic '*thumon-*' and the pre-Teutonic '*tumon-*', the stout of thick finger, whichin turn is from the root '*tu-*' to swell: cf. 'tumescence'. Beyond this is the Sanskrit '*tutuma*', strong, as well as '*tumra*', fat. The 'b' was added to the ME version of the word in the late thirteenth century.

First attested in 1867 in Smyth, *Sailor's Word-book*.

thwart   the transverse seat in an open boat on which an *oarsman* may sit, though it often has a structural role too. *Thwartships* is a contraction of *athwartships*, meaning transverse(ly) in a boat.

A noun formed from the adjective and adverb meaning transverse, whose origin is early (*c.* 1200) ME 'thwert', adapted from ON '*thvert*', and beyond that from the Old Teutonic '*thwerh-*' and the Indo-European '*twerkw-*', whence the Latin '*torquere*', to twist: cf. the Sanskrit '*tarku*', a spindle. The adjective appears in English some fifty years later than the adverb, the spelling 'thwert' being replaced by 'thwart' in the fifteenth century. The noun appears in the seventeenth century, at first spelt 'thought', 'thoat', or 'thout': as 'thwart' it is not recorded until *c.* 1730. The verb acquired its familiar sense of 'to impede' (by placing something or someone – including oneself or one's men – *athwart* another's path) in the early sixteenth century.

First attested in 1721, as 'thoughts' but meaning 'thwarts', in Bailey, *Dictionary*; as 'thwarts', in 1736 in Bailey, *Dictionarium* (second edition).

ticket   (colloquially) a Merchant Service Officer's Certificate.

From the familiar, non-colloquial word, which emerged in the sixteenth century as 'tiket', an aphetic form of 'etiket', adapted from the French '*etiquet*', a little note, and the parallel '*étiquette*', from OF '*estiquette*', whose source is '*estiquer*', to stick or affix, from the Teutonic, as in the Old Low German '*stekan*', the Old High German '*stekhan*' and the German '*stechen*' – the basic notion being of a note or label affixed to something; so there is an ancient link between 'ticket' and 'to stick'.

First attested in its colloquial nautical sense in about1900 in Cutcliffe Hyne, *Master of Fortune*, (Century Supplement), i.

tidal atlas   a collection of twelve *charts* showing the *tidal* *streams* for a given area for each hour of the *flood* and *ebb*, the directions being shown by arrows and the speed in *knots* by figures (if only one, that at *springs*; if two, the higher being that at springs, the lower that at *neaps*). A *tidal basin* is a partly enclosed *dock* area, open to the rise and fall of the *tide*. A *tidal harbour* is one that can be entered or left only at some time during the flood. A *tidal stream* is the lateral displacement of water caused by the rise and fall of the tide; a *tidal wave* is an exceptionally large *wave* caused by some such phenomenon as a earthquake.

'Tidal' is from *tide*, 'atlas' from the Latin *'Atlas'* and the Greek *'Atlas'*, one of the older family of Gods who was supposed to support the pillars of the universe (as Mount Atlas in Libya was supposed to support the heavens).

First attested in 1976 in Kemp (ed.), *Oxford Companion*, 868.

tiddley, tiddly   colloquial for smart and neat; in this nautical sense it has no connection with its other, perhaps more familiar, colloquial meaning of tipsy, which may be derived from the rhyming slang 'tiddlywink', i.e. drink.

In its nautical sense, the word's origin is probably 'tidy', which originally meant 'timely' (a sense now obsolete), from ME 'tid' (time) plus 'y'.

First attested in its nautical sense in 1925 in Fraser and Gibbons, *Soldier and Sailor Words*, 281.

tide   the rise and fall of the *sea* as a result of attraction by the sun and the moon: *spring tides*, the largest, being when sun and moon are line with the earth, while *neaps*, the smallest, are when they are not. A *tide gauge* is a post in the water marked in metres or feet or both, indicating the depth either there or nearby, such as at the entrance to a lock. To *tide over* is to work the tide by *anchoring* during a contrary *tidal* flow and sailing when it becomes favourable. A *tide race* is a sharp acceleration in a tidal flow owing to a change in depth; a *tide rip* is a series of short *waves* caused by a shallow or uneven *bottom* or by the confluence of two currents. *Tide-rode* means *riding* at anchor but *swung* to it by the tide (rather than the wind). *Tide Tables*, published by the British Hydographic Department of the Navy, give annual predictions for the time and height of high and low water for every standard *port*, with tidal constants for intermediate ports.

A *tideway* is a *fairway* through which the tide *ebbs* and *flows*.

Originally meaning 'time' (as in 'Yuletide', etc.), 'tide' comes from OE 'tid', and is cognate with, among others, the modern German *'Zeit'*.

First attested in its nautical sense *c.* 1435 in the *Torrent of Portugal* (Halliwell, 1842; EETS, 1887), 1430.

tie, tier, tyer   short length of rope or canvas strip or elasticated cord, for securing a *furled* sail.

From OE 'teah', 'teax' and Old Teutonic 'taux-a', 'taux-o'.

First attested, in the now largely obsolete sense of the rope or *chain* by which a *yard* is suspended, in or before 1465 in *Manners and Household Expenses* (Roxburghe Club, 1841), 200; as a sail tie, in 1611 in Cotgrave, *Dictionarie*; as 'tyer', in 1860 in Nares, *Naval Cadet's Guide*, 81.

tight   watertight.

Seemingly an altered form of the original 'thight', attested *c.* 1375, and derived from early ON *'thehtr'*, but now confined to dialect. Both forms occur together in the 1379 *Rolls of Parliament*, but in combination; the first time 'tight' is found by itself is *c.* 1435 in the sense of thick or dense (as of a wood).

First attested in a nautical sense in 1568 in *Satirical Poems* (STS, 1891–3), xlvi, 4.

tiller   a wooden or metal bar or long handle fitting in or round the *rudder head* to turn it as required to *steer* a boat. A *tiller extension*, is a bar attached to, and swivelling at, the *forward* end of the tiller, with which a *dinghy helmsman* can control it when *sitting out*. The *tiller head* is the forward end of the tiller. *Tiller lines* are those *rigged* with *tackles* to increase the helmsman's muscular power, or without them to fix the tiller's position. *Tiller ropes*, made of rope, *chain*, or hide, are those that link the rudder head to the barrel of the *steering-wheel*, if there is no *steering*-engine interposed (as there is in big ships). *Tiller soup* is the use of the tiller, withdrawn from its housing and brandished by the *coxswain* to threaten or discipline the *crew*.

From the (*c.* 1200) OF *'telier*, originally a weaver's beam (form the medieval Latin *'telarium'*, from *'tela'*, a web), but spelt with a double 'l' to mean the grooved wooden beam of a crossbow that takes the arrow – which was also the first and now obsolete meaning of 'tiller'.

First attested in its modern, nautical sense (not shared by the French, whose equivalent is *'timon'*, *'barre'* or *'barre de gouvernail'*) in or before 1625 in *Nomenclator Navalis* (Harleian MS 230l).

tilt   awning in a small boat, often over the *stern sheets*.

Nothing to do with an inclined plane or misuse of a pinball machine, but derived from OE 'teld', a tent or canopy, the vowel change having taken place in ME, and the final consonant perhaps influenced by 'tent'.

First attested in a nautical context in 1611 in Middleton and Dekker, *The Roaring Girl*, IV, ii.

timber   one of the large wooden *ribs* of a ship, attached to the *keel*, giving the vessel its shape and strength. *Timber heads* are the tops of some vertical timbers that project above deck level. A *timber hitch*, used among other things for *towing logs*, is a means of securing a rope round a *spar* (or log) by passing it round the spar, then making a *half hitch* round itself and tucking the end three or four times in and out of the part surrounding the spar. *Timbertoes* was a nickname for someone with a wooden leg. *Shiver my timbers* is an expression of surprise or incredulity more common in sea stories than at sea.

From OE 'timber', the Old Teutonic '*tim-ra*', '*tim-ro*', and the Indo-European '*dem-ro*': cf. the Greek '*demein*', to build, and '*domos*', a house (Latin '*domus*'). The original meaning of 'timber' in English, now obsolete, was in fact construction, building, house.

First attested in this specific nautical sense in 1748 in Anson, *Voyage*, II, iv, 158.

timenoguy (pronounced 'timonoggy')   a rope stretched *taut* between different parts of a sailing ship to prevent entanglements of various kinds; a *twiddling line*, used to steady the *wheel*; a gadget.

From the French '*timon*', a tiller, plus *guy*: this explains the 'twiddling-line' sense, but does not explain the earlier usage.

First attested, as a tangle-preventer, in 1794 in *The Elements and Practice of Rigging and Seamanship*, I, 178; as in relation to the wheel, in 1867 in Smyth, *Sailor's Word-book*; as a gadget, in 1886 in Brown, *Spunyarn and Spindrift*, xxxi, 378: 'Then the names of all the other things on board a ship! I don't know half of them yet; even the sailors forget at times, and if the exact name of anything they want happens to slip from their memory, they call it a chicken-fixing, or a gadjet, or a gill-guy, or a timey-noggy, or a wim-wom – just *pro tem.*, you know.'

timoneer   a rather literary word for a *helmsman*.

From the twelfth-century French '*timonier*', with the same sense.

First attested in 1762–9 in Falconer, *Shipwreck*, II, 178.

tingle   a metal (often copper or lead) patch applied to the *hull* to stop a leak.

From ME 'tingle', a very small nail; cognate with the Middle High German '*zingel*', little tack or hook, whose Low German form would be '*tingel*'. A later meaning was a hook to support slates on a roof.

First attested in its nautical sense in 1909 in Harris and Allen (ed.), *Webster's New International Dictionary*.

tjalk   a *barge*-type Dutch *cargo* vessel dating from the seventeenth century, with *jib* and *spritsail*, but nowadays built of steel and powered by a diesel engine.

A Dutch and Low German word for a kind of ship, possibly a diminutive of '*tjal*' for '*kjal*', OE 'coel', keel.

First attested in 1861 in *Mitchell's Maritime Register*, 1417/1.

toe-rail   a low raised lip running along the outer edge of the deck. A *toe-strap* is a length of webbing strung *fore-and-aft* in a racing *dinghy* for the *crew* to hook their feet into when *sitting out*.

From the familiar words: 'toe' from OE 'ta' and the Old Teutonic '*tai(w)on*' plus 'rail' from OF '*raille*' and thence from the popular Latin '*regla*'and the Latin '*regula*'.

First attested in 1978 in Desoutter, *Practical Dictionary*, 221.

toggle   a short pin passed through the *bight* of a rope or a link in a *chain*, to hold it in place; a smaller equivalent (an elongated button) on the *hoist* of a *signal flag* or as the front fastening of a *duffel coat*.

Of obscure etymology. Said to be of nautical origin, it seems to be related to 'tuggle' (frequentative of 'tug', to pull) and to 'tagle' (entangle) – both now obsolete. 'Toggle' is unlikely to be a frequentative of 'tog', although the later seems to predate the former, because 'tog' is an abbreviation of 'togeman', 'togman' (sixteenth-century vagabonds' cant for a cloak, usually thought to be based on the Latin '*toga*'), whereas the primary meaning of 'toggle' is not to do with clothing (which came later) but related to ropes and *rigging*.

First attested in 1769–76 in Falconer, *Dictionary*.

Tom Cox's traverse   a means of appearing active while actually idle. *Tom Pepper* is old nautical slang for a liar.

From the familiar abbreviation of 'Thomas' – and presumably a once famous exponent of the art.

First attested in 1840 in Dana, *Two Years*, xii: 'Every man who has been three months at sea knows how to "work Tom Cox's traverse" – "three turns round the long-boat, and a pull as the scuttled-butt."'

ton   (at sea) a measure of capacity, not weight, based originally on the number of *tuns* (*casks* or barrels) of two pipes or four hogsheads or 252 old wine gallons that could be carried in the *hold*; now, for registered *tonnage*, 100 cubic feet; for freight, 40 cubic feet unless the total weighs more than 20 cwt.

From OE 'tunne' and OF '*tonne*', a *tun* or cask, which in ME was usually spelt 'tonne'; 'tun' was more common in the sixteenth and seventeenth centuries, while from about 1688 onwards the modern differentiation of 'ton' from 'tun' began to be customary.

First attested in a nautical context in 1379 in the *Rolls of Parliament*, III, 63/2.

tonnage   originally the charge for hiring a ship at so much per *ton* of her *cargo*, and also a tax on imports: eventually it came to mean a ship's carrying capacity, estimated (and officially adopted in 1694) by multiplying the ship's length in feet by her broadest *beam* in feet and by the depth of her hold below the main deck in feet, and dividing by 100 before 1694 and by 94 thereafter. A new measurement was introduced in 1773, known as Builders Old Measurement, using the formula:

$$\frac{(L-3/5B) \times B \times \text{one-half B}}{94}$$

where L = Length and B = maximum Beam.

This was superseded for iron-built, steam-powered ships by a system of calculating the actual below-deck capacity in cubic feet and dividing by 100, giving *gross tonnage*: *net tonnage* was derived from this by subtracting from the total capacity any space not available for cargo. Both these tonnages are known as *registered tonnages*. *Deadweight tonnage* is the number of *tons* of cargo a ship can take to *trim* the *hull* down to her *Plimsoll marks*. *Displacement tonnage* is the actual weight of the ship herself. Merchant ships are normally described by their gross or deadweight tonnage, *warships* by their displacement tonnage. *Yachts* are described by their *Thames Measurement* formula.

From *ton*.

First attested in a nautical context in 1422 in *Rolls of Parliament*, IV, 173/2.

top   platform at the *masthead*, mainly to extend the *topmast shrouds* to give more support to the *mast*, but in ships of war used by *marines* or soldiers with muskets, etc.; to raise one end of a *derrick* or *boom* with a *topping lift*.

Top-armour was red-painted *canvas* or cloth stretched around the tops of fighting ships for display and concealment. A *top-castle* was a top. *Top-chain* was that used as *slings* for the *yards* of *square-rigged warships* in addition to rope slings in case the latter were shot away. *Top-gear* is the *rigging*, sails, and *spars* of a ship; *top hamper* is all the structure above the *hull*, in cluding the *dog-house, deckhouse, companion*, rails, radar scanner, etc., all creating *windage. Top lights* are those carried by *flag officers* in warships. A *topmark* is a distinguishing mark or shape on the *staff* of a *buoy* or *beacon*; a *topmast* is that next above the lower mast. *Topmen* (in *square-riggers*) are those whose work station is on the masts and yards. A *topping lift* is a *tackle* for *hoisting* or lowering the end of a *spar* – in *yachts*, taking the weight of the *boom* while the sail is being *hoisted* or *stowed*. *Topsides* are the sides of a ship above either the main *wales* or, nowadays, the upper deck – or, in yachts, the water-level. The *topstrake* is that secured to the *gunwale*.

From OE 'top' and common West German and Nordic roots; thence from the Old Teutonic '*tuppo*'. The original meaning was a tuft or crest of hair on the head – a sense preserved in the French derivative '*toupet*' and the French-influenced English 'toupee'. The verb may be distinct from the noun.

First attested as a nautical noun *c.* 1420 in Lydgate, *Assembly* (EETS, 1896), 342; as a nautical verb, in 1549 in the *Complaynt of Scotlande* (EETS, 1872), vi, 41.

topgallant   (sometimes pronounced 't'gallant') short for top-gallant sail, i.e. one of those *set* above the *topmast* in a *square-rigger*, and therefore the highest until the introduction of *kites*. A *topgallant mast* was that *stepped* above the topmast, making the third tier of the full mast.

From *top* plus 'gallant' (from the French '*galant*', present participle of OF '*galer*', to make merry, and retaining in English the sense of dashing); the word is definitely not, as once conjectured, from 'garland'.

First attested in this nautical sense in Thomas Dallam, *Diary* 1599–1600 in *Early Voyages* (Hakluyt Society, 1893), 9.

topsail   that *set* next above the *course* (in a *square-rigger*) or next above the *mainsail* (in a *gaff-rigged fore-and-aft* vessel). A *topsail schooner* is one with *square sails* on the *foremast* only; a *topsail yard* is that on which the topsail is set.

From *top* plus *sail*.

First attested in 1399 in Langland, *Richard the Redeles* (ed. Skeat; EETS, 1867–85; 1886), IV, 72.

tosher   small open Cornish fishing boat with a high *freeboard* and firm *bilges*. A mysterious word, with no evident etymological ancestors but a number of sometimes dubious associates. 'Tosh' is first attested in 1776 as meaning neat, tidy, or trim, with a similar adverbial sense appearing four years later, followed eight years later by 'toshly' in the same sense. 'Tosh' next appears – by 1825 – as thieves' slang for items of value retrieved from drains or sewers, with 'tosher' as one who seeks such items; then, in 1859, as one who steals copper from ships' *bottoms*. In 1881 'tosh' is attested as school slang for a bath, and in 1883, also in school slang, as an intransitive verb for taking a bath and a transitive verb for splashing. By 1889, in university slang, 'tosher' has come to mean a student unattached to a college; and by 1892 'tosh' is being used to denote nonsense.

By 1912, as an abbreviation for 'tosheroon' (which, with no known etymology, dates from 1859), a 'tosh' is being used for a florin or half-a-crown. In World War II, 'tosh' was heard as a matey form of address, attested in print in 1954. The OED conjectures that 'tosher' in its nautical sense may be connected with 'tosh' in its sense of splashing – which may seem paradoxical in view of the high freeboard of the boat thus named. Was a 'tosher' thought to be neat and trim? Was it sheathed in stolen copper – or manned by totters? Further speculation seems idle.

First attested in its nautical sense in 1885 in *The Daily Telegraph*, 26 November.

touch   to sail on the *wind* (as close to it as possible).

From eleventh-century OF '*tocher*', '*tuchier*' – a softening, into merely brushing, of the Old Northern French '*toquer*', to knock: cf. the Italian '*toccare*', which means both touching and striking.

First attested in this nautical sense in 1568 in *Satirical Poems* (STS, 1891–3), xliv, 54.

tow   to *haul* another vessel through the water by means of a rope or *cable*; the action of so doing; a rope thus used; the vessel towed; the vessel towing. *Tow aft* indicates preparing to take a vessel in tow. *Towage* is the charge made for towing. *Tow forward* indicates preparing to be towed. A *towing bollard* is a portable post placed in a strong fitting, whereby the vessel may be towed; a *towing bridle* is a *catenary*, or length of cable inserted in the middle of a long tow to withstand shocks; a *towing thwart* is a boat's *foremost thwart*, made to receive a towing bollard. A *towline* or *towrope* is a *hawser* suitable for taking a vessel in tow.

The verb precedes the noun: its source is OE 'togian', to pull or drag, cognate with similar words in other Germanic and Scandinavian languages, and traceable to the Old Teutonic '*togojan*'.

First attested as a nautical verb *c.* AD 1000 in the *Passio St Margaret* in Assmann (ed.), *Angelsaechsiche Homelien* (1889), 178; as a towrope, in 1600 in that year's edition of Hakluyt, *The Principall Navigations*, III, 585; as the action of towing, in 1622 in Hawkins, *Observations* (Hakluyt Society, 1847), 226; as the vessel towed, in 1805 in Nicolas, *Dispatches and Letters of Nelson*, VII, 189; as the vessel towing, in 1874 in Bedford, *Sailor's Pocketbook*, vi, 172.

track   a ship's *wake*; her *course*; to *tow* from a towpath or along a bank; a metal strip on the *after* side of a *mast* or the upper side of a *boom* to take slides fixed respectively to the *luff* or the *foot* of a sail.

From fifteenth-century OF '*trac*' and (probably) beyond that from the Teutonic, possibly connected with the Middle Low German and Dutch '*treck*', '*trek*', meaning draught, drawing, pull, line drawn, etc. Both 'drag' and 'trek', therefore, are related to 'track'.

First attested, as a wake, in 1706 in Phillips, *New World of English Words* (ed. J. Kersey); as a course, in 1748 in Anson, *Voyage*, II, x, 240; as an act of towing, in 1727 in Hamilton, *East Indies*, II, xxxiv, 21; as a mast or boom track, in 1976 in Kemp (ed.), *Oxford Companion*, 882.

trail-board   a carved *board* on each side of a *square-rigger*, either near the *stem* (and often to support a *figurehead*) or near the stern. A *trailer* is a wheeled device on which a *yacht* can be *towed* on land by a motor vehicle; a *trailing board* is a plank or wood, metal or plastic with rear lights, indicators, and registration number, fitted behind a yacht on a trailer. The *trailing edge* is the *after* edge of a sail, *keel*, or *rudder*. To *trail oars* is to let them swing in the *rowlocks* with the *blades* floating *aft*.

'Trail' here is from an early (fifteenth-century) sense of the word, meaning a wreathed or foliated ornament: the noun itself seems to be derived from the verb, whose source appears to be late OE 'traegelian', 'traeglian', though this meant to pluck or snatch, whereas ME 'trayle', 'traille' seems identcal with the Old Northern French '*trailler*', to drag or trail (as of a boat).

'Board' here seems to combine both the OE senses of the word 'bord', i.e. a *plank* of wood and a ship's side.

First attested in 1704 in Harris, *Lexicon Technicum*, I.

trammel   a fishing net consisting of one vertically hung and weighted fine-mesh 'wall' flanked on either side by wide-mesh 'walls': the fish swims through the wide mesh, is entangled in the fine mesh, then swims out through the other wide-mesh 'wall', which effectively closes a fine-mesh 'bag' around it: hence the familiar figurative sense of the corresponding verb.

From OF '*tramail*', with similar words in Italian, Spanish and Portuguese, all derived from the late popular Latin '*tramaculum*', meaning either three-mesh or thorough-mesh, depending on whether the word be analysed as '*tri-*' plus '*maculum*' or '*tra-*' (*trans*) plus '*maculum*'.

First attested *c.* 1440 in *Promptorium parvulorum* (Camden Society, 1843–65), 499/1.

tramp, tramp steamer   *cargo*-carrying merchant vessel not on a regular route or service but plying between various *ports* as required.

An extension of the familiar noun for vagrant, although its original meaning was a heavy tread; the noun is derived from the verb, with a similar evolution of meaning; and the source of that is ME 'trampen', from the old Teutonic root '*tramp-*', a nasalised form of the Old Teutonic '*trep*', '*trap*'.

First attested in its nautical sense in 1886 in the *Shipping Gazette* of 9 July.

trampoline   the net or rope of webbing that fills part of the gap between the two *hulls* of a *catamaran*.

No one in his senses would leap up and down on this, but the word's original sense is of course in its acrobatic or recreational context, and derived from the Italian '*trampoli*', stilts.

First attested in 1978 in Desoutter, *Practical Dictionary*, 223.

transit   a *bearing* placing two objects in line with each other and the observer, used as a local navigational guide. From the Latin '*transitus*', a verbal noun from '*transire*', to cross.

First attested in 1978 in Desoutter, *Practical Dictionary*, 223.

transom   in a wooden ship, the *athwartship timbers* bolted to the *sternpost*; in a *yacht* or *dinghy*, the flat or slightly curved transverse *after* end of the *hull*, usually vertical, on which the *rudder* is hung. *Transom drive* is *stern drive*; a *transom flap* is a hinged flap in the transom of a racing *dinghy* that opens to let the water out; a *transom knee* is that *angling* the *sternpost* and the *hog*; a *transom stern* is one more or less flat, as distinct from a *canoe stern*, a *counter*, or a raked 'v'.

Originally meaning various kinds of transverse *beam*, in housebuilding among other things, the word is thought to be a corruption of the Latin '*transtrum*' with the same sense.

First attested in a nautical sense in 1545 in Elyot, *Dictionary* (third edition); in the precise modern nautical sense, in or before 1642 in Monson, *Naval Tracts* (Navy Records Society), IV, 47.

trapeze   a harness used by racing *dinghy crew* to enable them to stand on the *weather gunwale* or on a sliding *plank* and lean out to *windward* to keep the boat as upright as possible.

From the familiar gymnastic word, itself derived, through the French '*trapeze*', from the modern Latin '*trapezium*', adapted from the Greek '*trapezion*', diminutive of '*trapeza*', a table.

First attested in its nautical sense in 1961 in Burgess, *Dictionary*, 211.

traveller   a ring or other fitting that may be moved along a *horse, boom, gaff, bowsprit*, etc., or up and down a *mast*.

From the familiar word 'travel', which was originally (and perhaps understandably) identical with 'travail', ME 'travaillen' being adapted from OF *'travaillier'*, which in turn was derived from the late popular Latin *'trepaliare'*, from *'trepalium'*, an instrument of torture involving three (*'tres'*, *'tria'*) stakes (*'palii'*). The notion of torture gradually softened into suffering and then into working hard, a sense further softened in French into merely working. In English, 'travail' retained (and retains) the sense of 'toil', but 'travel' became the spelling for the notion of voyaging, developed from Anglo-French but not retained in French.

First attested in a nautical sense in 1762–9 in Falconer, *Shipwreck*, II, 258.

traverse   the zigzag *track* of a vessel sailing against the *wind*. A *traverse board* was an approximate way of 'resolving' a traverse (turning its zigzags into a single *course* and distance) by putting one of eight pegs into a series of holes bored along the points of the *compass*, one every half-hour on the bearing the ship was the following. A *traverse table* is one giving the measurement of the two sides of any right-angled triangle subtended by the hypotenuse, showing the difference of *latitude* and the *departure* (from which to find the change of *longitude*) for any distance along a *rhumb-line* course, this being the hypotenuse in question.

From the familiar (and complicated) word, derived from two contrasting OF nouns: *'travers'* from the popular Latin *'traversum'* and the Latin *'transversum'*, transverse; and *'traverse'*, from *'transvertere'*, to transvert.

First attested in its nautical sense in 1594 in Davis, *Seamans Secrets* (1607 edition), 46.

trawl   a bag-shaped net *towed* along under water, sometimes on the *seabed*, to catch fish and crustacea; thus to fish. A *trawler* is a fishing vessel designed to operate a trawl. *Trawl lines* were baited cod-fishing *lines* attached at intervals to a long line *moored* on the Grand Banks off Newfoundland and *buoyed* at each end – nothing to do with trawling as such.

Probably from the Middle Dutch *'traghel'* and thence from the Latin *'tragula'*, drag-net.

First attested, as a noun if an indistinct manuscript is read aright, in 1481–90 in the *Howard Household Books* (Roxburghe Club, 1844), 192. If, however, 'trawelle' should be read as 'tramelle', then the word is first attested as a verb, in 1561 in Eden (transl.), *Cortes*, Preface iv b.

treenail (pronounced 'trennel')   long bolt made of oak or other hardwood used to secure the *planks* of a wooden ship's sides and *bottom* to her *timbers*: when wet they would tighten, unlike metal, which might rust and loosen.

From 'tree' plus 'nail', the former from OE 'treow' and the

Old Teutonic '*trewo-*', cognate with the Sanskrit '*dru*', wood, and the Greek '*drus*', oak; 'nail' is from OE 'naegel', 'naegl', and the Gothic '*nagls*': cf. the Sanskrit '*nakhas*' and the modern German '*Nagel*'.

First attested in 1295 in the *Accounts of the Exchequer of the King's Remembrancer* (MS in the Public Record Office), Bundle 5, No. 21.

trestle-trees   *fore-and-aft* supports at the *masthead* for the *top*, the lower *cross-trees* and the *topmast*.

From 'trestle' plus 'trees': the former from ME 'trestel' from the identical word in OF (cf. the modern French '*tréteau*'), and thence from the popular Latin '*transtellum*', a diminutive of '*transtrum*', beam; 'trees' from OE 'treow' and the old Teutonic '*trewo-*', cognate with the Sanskrit '*dru*', wood, and the Greek '*drus*', oak.

First attested in or before 1625 in *Nomenclator Navalis* (Harleian MS 2301).

triatic stay   a *fore-and-aft stay* running between *masts*, for *hoisting windsails*, *flags*, or even boats.

The 'tri-' part of the word may seem to indicate something threefold: but what remains a mystery, and the word's origin remains obscure.

First attested in 1841 in Dana, *Seaman's Manual*.

trice (often with 'up')   to *hoist*, usually securing or *lashing*. A *tricing line* is one used to trice up, most often now on the *loose-footed mainsail* of a *gaff-rigged* boat. The expression 'in a trice' (first attested in the fifteenth century as 'at a trice') literally meant at one pull or tug, from 'trice' as a verb.

From the Middle Dutch '*trisen*' (modern Dutch '*trijsen*'), to hoist, associated with the Middle Dutch '*trise*', '*trijse*', a pulley or *windlass*.

First attested before 1400 in *Morte Arthure* (EETS, 1865, revised 1871), 832.

trick   a spell of duty at the *wheel* or *helm*. The *trick wheel* is the *after* auxiliary steering wheel at the *rudder head*.

From OF '*trique*', the Picard and Norman form of '*triche*', deceit, probably from the verb '*triquier*'. In modern French, '*tricher*' retains the sense of cheating, and is linked with both the Provencal '*trichar*', '*triquar*' and the Italian '*triccare*', as well as (via OF '*trecherie*', '*tricherie*') with 'treachery' in English. In modern English, however, 'trick' has many honest meanings.

First attested in its nautical sense in 1669 in Sturmy, *Mariners Magazine*, iv, I, 138.

tricolour(ed) lamp or **lantern**   a *masthead* lamp showing red in the *port* sector, green in the *starboard* sector, and white *astern*, as specified in the International Regulations for the Prevention of Collisions at Sea, 1972.

'Tricolour' is from the late Latin *'tricolor'*.

First attested, despite its familiar application to the post-Revolutionary French flag, in 1786 (as short for the *Amarantus tricolor*) in Abercrombie, *Gardener's Assistant*, 239; in a nautical context, in 1961 in Burgess, *Dictionary*, 212.

trigger   a support holding the *dogshore* in position; the dogshore itself. The *trigger bar* is the iron rod on the sloping *billboard* that keeps the *anchor* in place.

Not the familiar word, which is derived from the Dutch *'trekker'*, but more probably a derivative of ON *'tryggja'*, to make firm or secure.

First attested in its nautical sense in 1867 in Smyth, *Sailor's Word-book*.

trim   fit, sound; to fit out for sea; to make float on an even *keel*; to adjust (the sails) to the *wind*; a ship's state of readiness for sea; her *fore-and-aft* equilibrium; the difference between her *draught forward* and her draught *aft*; the adjustment of her sails; her general appearance. To *trim a jacket* was to flog its wearer. A *trim tab* is a metal plate (often one of a pair) at the *stern* of a motor-boat to lift the stern to reduce drag. To *trim the dish* is to level up a boat, especially a *rowing* boat; to *trim the tanks* is to flood or empty the *trimming tanks* (known in a submarine as auxiliary *ballast* tanks) which adjust the trim.

The noun is derived from the verb, which is associated with, and may be preceded by, the adjective – but not as regards its first recorded use. The verb comes from OE 'trymman', 'trymian', 'trumjan', to make firm or strong, apparently from the OE adjective 'trum', firm, strong, sound, etc. There is a gap in the written record in the later Middle Ages: the verb appears in the sense of 'strengthen' before AD 800, but goes underground, as it were, after the thirteenth century until 'trim' explodes into various parts of speech with a multiplicity of meanings, all current by 1550.

First attested as a nautical verb *c.* 1513 in a letter by E. Howard in Ellis (ed.), *Original Letters* (1824–46), III, I, 47; as making float on an even keel, in 1580 by H. Smith in Hakluyt, *Principall Navigations*, 1598–1600 edition, I, 448; as a noun denoting a state of readiness for sea, in 1590 in Shakespeare, *Comedy of Errors*, IV, I, 90; in the sense of adjusting sails, in 1624 in Smith, *Generall Historie*, II, 24.

trimaran   a boat with a single central *hull* (not three hulls) and a float on each side.

Formed from 'tri-' (three) plus '-maran', from *catamaran* – which might logically – but erroneously – suggest that the catamaran's two hulls were here augmented to three.

First attested in 1949 in the Baltimore *Sun* of 27 September, 22/3.

trip a short voyage; a *board* or *tack*; (of an *anchor*) to break it out of the *ground*; (of a *spar*) to tilt it; (of a floorboard, etc.) to warp or twist. A *trip hook* is one with an extra *eye* for attaching a wire that can be used to trip the hook and release the *hoist* so that the weight can be borne by the *tripping line*, strictly a small rope made fast to a *yardarm* so that the latter may be tripped or canted to the perpendicular for lowering, but now commonly used for the *buoy-rope* made *fast* to the *crown* of an anchor, and used to trip it.

Unlikely as it may seem, both the noun and verb come from the same source, primarily that of the verb: this is OF '*treper*', '*triper*', '*tripper*', meaning to strike the ground with the foot, or to hop. Although 'trip' is now a familiar noun denoting a journey on land, the OED describes it as 'apparently originally a sailor's term'.

First attested, as a voyage, in 1691 in Hale, *Several New Inventions*, 12; as a board or tack, in 1700 in Brown (transl.), *Fresny's Amusements*, 34; as a verb regarding an anchor, in 1748 in Anson, *Voyage*, II, I, 112; as regards tilting a spar, in 1840 in Dana, *Two Years*, xxiii; as regards the twisting of floorboards, in 1869 in Reed, *Shipbuilding*, ii, 23.

trireme an ancient *galley*, originally Greek but later also Roman, with three banks of *oars*.

From the Latin '*triremis*' (from '*tri-*', three, plus '*remus*', an oar): cf. the fourteenth-century French '*trireme*'.

First attested in English in 1601 in Holland (transl.), *Pliny*, VII, lvi, I, 190.

troll to fish by *trailing* a baited *line* behind a boat.

A late and chiefly at first American and Scottish use of an angling term with a number of other, non-nautical meanings: in the present sense it may be influenced by 'trail' and *trawl*. The source of the word itself, which originally meant saunter or stroll, is OF '*troller*', to seek game, and perhaps also OF '*traller*', to ramble.

First attested in its nautical, fishing sense in 1864 in Webster, *American Dictionary*.

trot a *line* of *moorings* rising at spaced intervals from a base mooring; a number of small vessels secured alongside each other.

Probably if mysteriously from the familiar word (although

'trat', of unknown origin, was used – as is 'trot' itself – to denote a long line with baited hooks hung at intervals from it). The source of the familiar word 'trot' is the twelfth-century French '*trot*', a verbal noun from '*trotter*', to trot.

First attested in a nautical sense in 1923 in the UK Admiralty *Manual of Seamanship*, (revised edition), II, 107.

truck   a round wooden capping for the *top* of a *mast*, usually fitted with *sheaves* for *flag halyards*.

There are two possible derivations: from the Latin '*trochus*' and Greek '*trochos*', a hoop; or from 'truckle', from the Anglo-French '*trocle*', '*trokle*', and thence from the Latin '*trochlea*' and Greek '*trochilia*', a sheave. Of the two, the latter seems marginally the more likely.

First attested in 1626 in Smith, *Accidence*, 13: 'The maine top gallant sayle yeard, the trucke or flagge staffe.'

trunk   a watertight shaft passing through the decks of a vessel, or (in a *dinghy*, for instance), through the *hull*, as with the *centre-board* case or the *rudder trunk*.

From the familiar word, via its sense as the trunk of a tree: its source is the twelfth-century Old (and modern) French '*tronc*' and thence the Latin '*truncum*', accusative of '*truncus*', the trunk of a body or a tree.

First attested in its nautical sense in 1862 in the *Illustrated Catalogue of the Industrial Department of the International Exhibition*, II, xii, 2/1.

truss   a *tackle* by which the centre of a *yard* was *hauled* back and secured to the *mast* in a *square-rigger*; now a metal fitting consisting of a ring and *gooseneck* with the same function.

From OF '*trusse*', '*tourse*' (modern French '*trousse*').

First attested in its nautical sense in 1296 in the *Accounts of the Exchequer of the King's Remembrancer* (MSS in the Public Record Office), 5/20 m. 5.

try   to attempt to *ride* out a *storm* by greatly reducing *canvas*, remaining in the trough of the sea, and keeping the boat's *head* to the *waves*. A *trysail* is one used for this purpose, small and robust, and *set* instead of a *mainsail*.

From the familiar word, whose original meaning was to sift, from twelfth-century OF '*trier*', with the same basic sense as the modern French word.

The sense of a judicial trial (sifting evidence) developed from this, whence arose the sense of testing and then of endeavour.

First clearly attested (there is a debatable instance in 1533) in 1556 in Hakluyt, *Principall Navigations* (1598 edition), I, 277.

tuck   the gathering of the *bottom planks* at the *after* end under the *stern*; (colloquially) a *reef* (of a sail); (of a reef) to take in. The *tuck plate*, in an iron ship, is a curved plate of the *hull* at the point where the *stern-post* is bolted to the *transom* frame. The *tuck rail*, in a wooden ship, is that which forms a *rabbet* for *caulking* the *butt* ends of the bottom planks.

The noun comes from the familiar verb, whose origin is OE 'tucian' and early ME 'tuke'. But its original, now obsolete meaning was to chastise, then to finish cloth, and then to pluck or snatch. The meaning of pleating appears only in the fifteenth century, although the noun carries that sense a century earlier.

First attested in its nautical sense in or before 1625 in *Nomenclator Navalis* (Harleian MS 2301).

tug   a small powerful vessel designed to *tow* others, especially when manoeuvring in a restricted space.

The noun, which appears in the sixteenth century meaning pulling, struggling, etc., is derived from the verb, whose source is late ME 'tuggen', and thence OE 'teo(ha)n', 'teah', 'tugon', 'togen', cognate with similar words in a number of other Germanic and Scandinavian languages, all related to the Gothic *'tiuhan'*, etc., equivalent to the Latin *'ducere'*, to lead, and represented in modern German by *'ziehen'*. Other derivatives of the same root include 'taut', 'team', 'tie', 'tight', 'tough', and 'tow'.

First attested in its modern nautical sense in 1817 in the *Chronology* of the *Annual Register*, 101.

tumblehome   the inward curve of the upper part of a ship's side.

From the two familiar words: 'tumble' from ME 'tumbel'; 'home' from OE 'ham' and a common Teutonic source. In early instances, 'home' does not always appear; and the OED gives the whole word only as an intransitive verb, not as a noun.

First attested (with these provisos) in or before 1687 in Petty, *Treatise* (in Hale, *Several New Inventions*, 1691), I, ii.

tun   a large *cask* for transporting wine, with a capacity of 252 old wine gallons, equal to four hogsheads or two pipes: the origin of the word *ton*.

From OE 'tunne' and perhaps OF *'tonne'*, but with uncertainty about its earlier ancestry.

First attested before AD 725 in the *Corpus Glossary* (Oldest Englsh Texts, EETS, 1885; Hessels, 1890), C, 945.

Turk's head   an ornamental *stopper knot* at the end of a rope, continuing a simple *manrope knot* by tucking the *strands* twice.

From the two familiar words, or which 'Turk' is derived from the French *'turc'*, the medieval Latin *'turcus'*, the Byzantine Greek *'tourkos'*, and the Persian and Arabic *'turk'*. The allusion is of course to the Turk's supposed headgear (a turban) rather than to his head, since the knot has a turban-like appearance.

First attested as a applied to a nautical knot (it was earlier applied to the melon-thistle) in 1833 in Marryat, *Peter Simple*, vi.

turn   the act of passing a rope once round a *bollard*, *cleat*, etc.; (of the *bilge*) the curve where the side meets the *bottom*; (of the *tide*) the transition from rising to falling, or vice versa. *Turnaround* is the time between arrival at a *port* and departure from it. A *turnbuckle* is a *rigging screw*. To *turn end for end* is reverse a *halyard*, etc., to minimize repeated chafe; to *turn for lowering* is to take off surplus turns from a *belayed* rope, leaving enough to *ease* it off gradually; to *turn in* is either to swing a *davit inboard* or to go to bed; to *turn in all standing* is to go to bed dressed. A *turnmark* is the mark on a *log line* whose passage over the *quarter* is a *signal* to turn the *log glass* and start counting the *knots*. To *turn out* is to swing a davit *outboard*. To *turn out of watch* is to exchange duties with a member of the opposite *watch*. To *turn to* is to begin work. To *turn turtle* (of a ship) is to be completely inverted.

Partly from the Anglo-French '*torn*', '*turn*', '*tourn*', and the equivalent of OF '*tor*', '*tour*', and thence from the latin '*turnus*' and the Greek '*tornos*'.

First attested in a nautical context in 1743 in Bulkeley and Cummins, *Voyage*, 115.

turtle-back   an arched structure over the *forward* (and sometimes the *after*) deck of a steamer as protection against heavy seas. A *turtle-boat* was a fully *decked* American craft with only six inches of *freeboard*, invented by Robert Fulton (1765–1815) and used in the 1812 Anglo-American War to *tow* explosive charges that could be swung against the sides of British *warships*. A *turtle deck* is one with a convex curve to encourage water to flow down from the centreline to the *scuppers*.

From the two familiar words: 'turtle' a corruption of the French '*tortue*' by analogy with the original English word for a turtle-dove (from OE 'turtla', first attested *c.* AD 1000, and thence from the Latin 'turtur'). The French word comes from the late popular Latin 'tortuca'. 'Back' is from OE 'baec' and a common Teutonic root. The reference is of course to the creature's arched shell.

First attested in 1881 in *The Standard*, 30 August, 2/3.

twice-laid   (of rope) made from the *yarns* of old rope; (of food) warmed up from a previous serving.

From 'twice' (whose source is late OE 'twiges') plus 'laid' (from *lay*).

First attested, as applied to rope, in 1592–3 in *Act 35 of Queen*

Elizabeth, c.8 (heading); as applied to food, in 1777 in Thicknesse, *Year's Journey*, II, xlvi, 110.

twiddling line   a light *line* once used to steady or secure the *wheel*; a line attached to the *compass* box to free the card if necessary; a line connecting larger *steering* lines to the *yoke* in a *pulling* boat; a line connecting the *rudder* to an indicator showing the *helmsman* its position.

From 'twiddle' plus *line*, the former apparently onomatopoeic, combining the sense of 'twirl' or *twist* with the belittling '-iddle' (as in 'fiddle' or 'piddle') to indicate something trifling.

First attested in a nautical sense in 1867 in Smyth, *Sailor's Word-book*.

twin-boat   a kind of motor *catamaran*, two of which were built in 1811 and 1812 for use as ferry-boats crossing the Hudson river, each consisting of two complete *hulls* joined by a deck or *bridge*. *Twin keels* properly refers to those vessels that have a *keel* on each side but not central keel, the term *bilge keel* being reserved for those with a keel on each side plus one in the centre. *Twin screws* are two propellers on separate shafts, revolving in opposite directions.

From 'twin' (from OE 'twinn') plus *boat*.

First attested *c.* 1816 in Rees, *Cyclopaedia*, under 'Steam-Engine'.

twist   one of the *strands* of a rope. A *twisted shackle* is one made so that the axis of the pin is at right angles to the plane of the *bow*.

From the familiar verb, whose stem appears to be 'twi-' in the alternative and apparently conflicting senses of 'divide' and 'combine' two elements. Both the noun and the verb are first attested in the fourteenth century with, unsurprisingly, widely different senses. That of the familiar verb appears in the fifteenth century; of the familiar noun in the sixteenth.

First attested in its nautical sense *c.* 1615 in Boteler, *Six Dialogues*, 192.

two blocks   *chock-a-block*, i.e. with no further travel possible in a *purchase* because the moving block has been *hauled* right up against the *standing* block.

A *twofold purchase* is one with its rope *rove* through two double blocks.

From 'two' (from OE 'twa') plus *block*.

First attested in 1841 in Dana, *Seaman's Manual*, 99.

Ullage   the amount of wine that has leaked or evaporated from a *cask*, leaving it partly empty and possibly spoiled; a hopeless member of the *crew*.

From the Anglo-French '*ulliage*' and OF '*oullage*', etc., based on the OF verb '*ouiller*' and the Provençal 'ulha', 'oulha', to fill up.

First attested in English, as regards casks, in 1481–90 in the *Howard Household Books* (Roxburghe Club, 1844), 288; as regards the crew, in 1901 in *The Daily Chronicle*, 23 May, 5/1.

umiak   a woman's counterpart to the *kayak*.

Eskimo or Inuit word.

First attested in English in 1769 in Falconer, *Dictionary*, 1789 edition, L b.

Una rig   *rig* for a small sailing boat consisting of a large *gaff* and *boom mainsail* or *lugsail*, *set* on a *mast stepped* well *forward*, and with no *headsail*.

Named after the first American 16-and-a-half foot racing *catboat* of this kind, tried out in 1852 and brought to Britain soon afterwards.

First attested in 1878 in Kemp, *Manual*, xvi, 171.

unbend   to untie (a *cable*, *line*, or sail).

From 'un-' plus *bend*.

First attested in 1627 in Smith, *Seaman's Grammar*, vii, 30.

unbitt   to uncoil a *cable* from the *bitts*.

From 'un-' plus *bitt*.

First attested in 1769 in Falconer, *Dictionary*, 1780 edition.

under   (of sails) with the specified sails *set*. *Under bare poles* means with no sails set; *under canvas* means being propelled only by the wind on the sails. An *undercurrent* is one below the surface. *Under foot* means under the ship's *bottom*. *Under full sail* means either with all sails set or (colloquially) tipsy.

Under hatches means below decks, off duty, under arrest, or dead and buried.

To *under-run* is to *haul* a *warp* or *hawser* over a small boat to free it from some underwater obstruction, or to separate and disentangle all the moving parts of a *tackle*. *Under sail* is the same as *under canvas*; *under sailing orders* is ordered to prepare for sea or (jocularly) dying. *Under the lee* is sheltered from the *wind*, usually by a spit or cliff of land; *under the weather* is unwell. *Undertow* is an undercurrent running counter to that above it, as in the backwash of a breaker. *Under way* is making progress through the water; *under weigh* is said of an *anchor* which is off the *bottom* and whose weight is on the *cable*.

From OE 'under', a common Teutonic root, the Gothic '*undar*' and the Sanskrit stem '*adharas*': cf. the Latin '*infra*'.

First attested in a nautical sense *c.* AD 893 in King Aelfred (transl.), *Orosius*, I, l, 021.

Union flag   the national *flag* of Great Britain and later of the United Kingdom, now often miscalled the *Union Jack*, which was originally and is strictly speaking a small Union flag *flown* as the *jack* of a ship.

From 'union' (whose source is the twelfth- and thirteenth-century French '*union*', after the Latin '*unus*', etc.) plus *flag*.

First attested in 1634 in Rymer, *Foedera*, (1704–35; 1816–30), 1732, XIX, 549/1.

unmoor   to *weigh* and *hoist* one *anchor*, leaving the ship *riding* at one only; to *cast off moorings*.

From 'un-' plus *moor*.

First attested in 1497 in *Naval Accounts* (Navy Records Society, 1896), 229.

unreeve   to pull a rope out from a *block* or *sheave*. To *unreeve one's lifeline* is to die.

From 'un-' plus *reeve*.

First attested in 1600 in Hakluyt, *Principall Navigations* (new edition), III, 847.

unrig   to dismantle both *running* and *standing rigging*.

From 'un-' plus *rig*.

First attested in its nautical sense in 1579–80 in North (transl.), *Plutarch* (1595 edition), 541.

unship   to unload from a vessel; to detach (e.g. a *mast*) from its normal fixed place. To *unship someone's grommet* is to knock someone's head off.

From 'un-' plus *ship*.

First attested in or before 1450 in the *Continuation of The Brut*, (EETS, 1906), 542.

up   to *windward*. *Up along* is from the mouth of a *channel* inwards, the opposite of *down along*. To *up anchor* is to *weigh anchor*. *Up and down* describes an anchor *cable* that has been *hove* in enough to bring the ship directly over the anchor. *Up funnel down screw*, in the early days of steam-assisted sail, meant to *furl* sails and continue on engine. *Up Ladder Lane and down Hemp Street* meant being hanged at the *yard-arm*. The *upper deck* is the highest of those running without a *break* from *stem* to *stern*. *Upperworks* are all superstructures above the upper deck. *Upstream* is against the flow of the stream. An *uptake* is a shaft orpipe to ventilate a compartment or take the smoke from a boiler to the funnel, etc. *Up the line* is a term for a few days' *shore* leave. *Up topsides* is a hail to someone on a higher physical level. *Upwind* is to *windward*.

From OE 'upp', 'up', and thence from the Gothic '*iup*': cf. the German '*auf*'.

First attested in 1591 in Ralegh, *Revenge*, B2.

Vane   a piece of bunting on a wooden frame at the *mast-head*, rather like a *yacht's burgee*, to show *wind* direction; the wind-rotated part of a self-*steering* device.

A Southern variant of 'fane', from OE 'fana' and a common Teutonic root, of which the German '*Fahne*' is an obvious descendant, unwelcomely familiar in the first line of the Nazi Horst Wessel song, '*Die Fahne hoch…* '

First attested in a nautical sense in 1706 in Ward, *Wooden World* (1708 edition), 3.

vang   one of the two ropes used to keep the *peak* of a *gaff* or *sprit* from sagging to *leeward* and twisting the sail; in the US, a *kicking strap* is known as a *boom vang*.

From OE 'fang', the act of catching or seizing: cf. the modern German '*fangen*'. In its nautical sense, the word began to be spelt with both an 'f' and a 'v' in the eighteenth century.

First attested in 1769 in Falconer, *Dictionary*, under 'Brace'.

variation   magnetic declination, or the angle between true and magnetic North, which differs from place to place and changes very slowly over time.

From OF '*variation*', '*variacion*', and thence from the Latin '*variatione*', whose source is '*variare*', to vary.

First attested in this specific sense in 1556 by Burrough in Hakluyt, *Principall Navigations* (1886 edition), III, 126.

vedette   a small naval patrol or scouting vessel; a motor *launch*.

From the identical French word, itself from the Italian '*vedetta*', probably from '*vedere*', to see. In English, in fact, the word was long pronounced 'vidette' (as if directly from the Latin '*videre*') and in the first half of the nineteenth century often thus spelt. Its original meaning in English was a sentry or military lookout.

First attested in its nautical sense in 1884 in *The Pall Mall Gazette*, 6 October, 6/1.

veer   to *pay out* a rope or *cable*; to change *course* by bringing the *stern* instead of the *bows* across the *wind*; (of wind) to change direction – clockwise in the Northern hemisphere, the opposite in the Southern. To *veer and haul* is to *slacken* and *haul* repeatedly, prior to a heavy, steady haul.

There are two different sources for the word (or words) according to meaning. In the sense of paying out, the source is the Middle Dutch '*vieren*', to let out or slacken off. In the sense of changing direction, the source is the French '*virer*', which the OED admits to be 'of obscure origin'.

First attested, as paying out, *c.* 1460 in *Pilgrims Sea-voyage* (EETS, 1867), 25; as a change of course, *c.* 1620 in Boyd, *Zion's Flowers*, 1855), 134; as a wind shift, in 1582 in Lichefield (transl.), *Castanheda*, 73.

Very (pronounced 'veery') **lights**   pyrotechnical *signals* of red, white, and green *flares* fired from a *Very* pistol.

Named after their inventor, the US naval officer Edward W. Very (1847–1910).

First attested in 1907 in *The Journal of the Military Service Institute of the United State*, XLI, 368.

vessel   (according to the *International Regulations for Preventing Collisions at Sea*) 'every description of water craft, including non-displacement craft and sea-planes, used, or capable of being used, as a means of transportation on water'; (in current practice) anything larger than a *rowing* boat and afloat either at sea or on one of the larger rivers or lakes.

Perhaps presciently, the English word also means a receptacle for liquid, etc.; but this ambiguity dates back to the Latin '*vascellum*', a small vase or a ship: its plural '*vascella*' is the source of the modern French '*vaisselle*', crockery (most commonly in the phrase '*faire la vaisselle*', do the washing-up). In English, 'vessel' has lost this collective sense, which is derived from Latin via the Anglo-French and OF '*vessele*', '*veselle*'. In its present double senses the English word is derived from the Anglo-French and OF '*vessel*', ancestor of the modern French '*vaisseau*', which shares the same double meaning.

First attested in a nautical sense in or before 1300 in *Cursor Mundi* (EETS, 1874–92), 1662.

vigia   a mark on a *chart* to denote some hidden danger such as a rock or *shoal* not yet confirmed by hydrographic survey.

From the Portuguese and Spanish '*vigia*', a lookout, and thence from the Latin '*vigilia*', watchfulness, itself from the Latin '*vigil*', awake or alert.

First attested in 1867 in Smyth, *The Sailor's Word-book*.

viol   a large *messenger* used with a *capstan* to help *weigh* the *anchor* if its *cable* was too big for the capstan.

Of unknown origin, unconnected with the musical instrument. First attested in 1627 in Smith, *Seaman's Grammar*, ii, 8.

Waft   a *flag* or *ensign* with its centre of its *fly stopped* to the *ensign staff* and used as a *signal*, originally indicating a man *overboard* but now used to invite the customs to come *aboard* and release for the *crew*'s use tobacco etc, sealed under bond.

A complex word, most of whose meanings (such as 'convoy') are now largely obsolete; in some of its senses related to 'waff' (from ON *'veifa'*) and *wave* (from OE 'wafian'), but in its present nautical sense probably derived from the Swedish *'vifta'*, fan, and its counterparts in other Scandinavian languages. There are, however, family resemblances among all of these, whose origin may be the Indo-European *'weib-'*: cf. the Latin *'vibrare'*.

First attested in this nautical sense as a flag in 1644 in Manwayring, *Sea-mans Dictionary*.

waist   the middle part of a vessel; the upper deck between the *forecastle* and the *quarterdeck*, or between the *foremast* and the *main-mast*, or between the *fore* and *after hatches*. A *waistcloth* was a decorative cloth hung on state occasions in the sixteenth and seventeenth centuries along the sides of *warships* between the forecastle and the *poop*. A *waister* was a seaman employed on relatively humble or unskilled duties in the waist of the ship, and hence by association one who was untrained, past his prime, or otherwise incompetent.

An early figurative application of the familiar anatomical word, whose source is thought to be OE 'waest', 'weahst', corresponding to ON *'vahstu-r'* and the Gothic *'wahstu-s'*, growth or size, from the Teutonic root *'wags-'* (the source of 'wax' in the sense of grow). In English the general adoption of the present spelling, as against 'wast', dates from Dr Johnson's *Dictionary*.

First attested in its nautical sense in 1495 in *Naval Accounts* (Navy Records Society, 1896), 194.

wake   the disturbed water left in the *track* of a vessel under *way*, indicating *leeway* if at an angle to the centreline of the *hull*.

Although not attested before the sixteenth century, the word is almost certainly much older and probably comes from ON *'vaku'*, a hole in the ice – the likelihood being that this word (which has many kindred in other Scandinavian and other Germanic languages) was first applied to the path through the ice made by a vessel, and then to the visible signs of a passage through water.

First attested in or before 1547 in the Harleian MS, 309, f.4.

wale   a *strake*, strip, or *plank* standing proud of the *hull* above the *waterline*, often bolted on, to prevent damage.

From OE 'walu', the mark of a lash: cf. 'weal'.

First attested in its nautical sense in 1295 in the *Accounts of the Exchequer of the King's Remembrancer* (MSS in the Public Record Office), 5/8 m. 8.

walk   to *haul* on a rope by trudging round the *capstan* with it or by pacing backwards. To *walk the plank* was to be pinioned and blindfolded, then obliged to walk along a *plank* projecting over the ship's side until one fell in the sea: this treatment is said to have been imposed by *pirates*, and on them and on mutineers.

From OE 'wealcan'; the word's first, now obsolete, meaning was to roll or toss (both transitive and intransitive). A similar OE word, 'wealcian', meaning to muffle up or to curl, may have meant also to full (cloth), which is a secondary and now obsolete or dialect sense of the verb 'walk'. Only in ME did 'walk', as recorded, begin to mean travelling about: it may have had this sense in speech before that, perhaps in ironical use.

First attested in its nautical sense in 1836 in Marryat, *The Pirate*, viii.

wall   (short for) *wall-knot*, a *stopper knot* made in the end of a rope by *unlaying* it to four or five times its circumference, then tucking each *strand* over that behind and under that in front, then again under the two strands in front and up to the centre, after which each strand is *hauled taut*, they are *whipped* together close to the *knot*, and the ends are cut off; to make such a knot.

In this sense, according to the OED, 'of obscure origin': the word seems not to be an application of the familiar word involving a barrier. Similar words meaning a double or secure knot are found in modern Danish ('*valknude*'), Norwegian and Swedish ('*valknut*'), and German ('*Waldknoten*' – probably popular etymology from '*Wald*', a wood or forest).

First attested (as 'wall knot') in 1627 in Smith, *Sea Grammar*, v, 27; as 'wall' (the noun) in 1834 in Marryat, *Peter Simple*, vi; as 'wall' (the verb) in 1883 in *A Manual of Seamanship*, 112.

wangle   to *scull* over the *stern* with a single *oar*.

In its physical sense, 'wangle' originally meant to totter, or to move unsteadily on its base (not unlike the oar of an unskilled sculler), a sense first attested in 1820 and now described as dialect; this was perhaps an altered form of 'waggle', a frequentative of 'wag', from OE 'wagian' via ME 'wagge-n'. In its more familiar sense of dishonest manoeuvring, the verb is of uncertain origin: it first appears as printer's slang in 1888.

First attested in its nautical sense in 1961 in Burgess, *Dictionary*, 218.

wardrobe   all the sails carried *on board* a racing or cruising *yacht*.

From the familiar word in its sense of a person's complete outfit of apparel; the source of the word is of course its place of storage, in OF *'warderobe'*, a North-Eastern variant of *'garderobe'*.

First attested in its nautical sense in 1976 in Kemp (ed.), *Oxford Companion*, 924.

wardroom   the naval officers' mess, once (before 1948) restricted to commissioned officers above the rank of sub-lieutenant.

From 'ward' plus 'room': the former from OE 'weard', guard; the latter from OE 'rum'. Essentially, therefore, the word is a naval cousin to the army's 'guardroom', although the latter has a much less convivial meaning.

First attested in 1758 in *The Annual Register 1758* (1791), 306/1.

warm the bell   to do something (including ending one's own *watch*) before the appointed time.

From 'warm' plus 'bell': the former from OE 'wierman' (transitive) and 'wearmian' (intransitive); the latter from OE 'belle'. The expression may arise from the belief, in the days of measuring time by a half-hour *sand-glass*, that if the glass were warmed its neck would expand to let the sand run through more quickly, shortening one's spell on duty. The expression may, however, merely mean striking the ship's bell ahead of time.

First attested in 1924 in Willis, *Royal Navy*, 116.

warp   a rope for *hauling* or *mooring* a ship; to move her by hauling; to stretch *yarn* in lengths to be *tarred*.

From the OE weaving term 'wearp', warp, and ON *'varp'*, meaning the cast of a net: cf. Danish and Swedish, in which this word also means a hauling-rope. The further source is the Old Teutonic *'warp-'*, to throw: cf. the modern German *'werfen'*.

First attested (in the combination 'warp-rope') in 1296 in the *Accounts of the Exchequer of the King's Remembrancer* (MSS in the Public Record Office), 5/20 m. 4 b.

warship   a ship armed and manned for war.

From 'war' plus *ship*: the former from the late (*c.* 1050) OE 'wyrre', 'werre', and thence from North-Eastern OF *'werre'*, the equivalent of central OF and modern French *'guerre'*, associated with the old High German *'werra'*, confusion. As the OED points out, Germanic nations in early historic times had no word for 'war' as such, while the Romance languages avoided the Latin *'bellum'*, presumably for fear of its possible confusion with *'bello-'*, beautiful.

First attested in 1533 in the *Accounts of the Lord High Treasurer of Scotland* (Scottish Record Series, 1877–), VI, 134.

wash   *surging* movement of water on the *shore* or on some object; the *surge* produced by a vessel's passage. A *washboard* in a *yacht* is a removable board (usually in two sections or more, and lockable) to seal off the entrance to the *cabin* from the *cockpit*; a *washstrake* (sometimes also 'washboard') is a removable upper *strake* fitted to the *gunwales* of some open boats to keep out spray.

From the verb, which has a common Teutonic source not recorded in Gothic: the OE verb is 'waescan', the noun 'waesc'.

First attested in its general nautical sense *c.* 1050 in the *Supplement to Aelfric's Glossary* in Thomas Wright (ed), *Vocabularies*, Second edition, ed. Wulcker (1884), 179/35.

watch   period of duty, usually of four hours, except that the evening watch from 1600 hours to 2000 hours is divided into two (the first and last) *dog watches* so that the *crew* does not keep the same watches every day; one of the (usually two) teams of officers and men who alternate periods of duty – if two, known as the *port* and *starboard* watches, if three often known as red, white, and blue; (of a navigational buoy) to be floating and working properly. The *watch and station bill* (also a *watch bill*) is the list of the crew's watches and duties; *watch and watch* is one on, one off, alternately; *watch ashore* is that below, when granted *shore* leave; a *watch buoy* is one moored near a *lightship* to check her position; the *watch on deck* is that available for duty; a *watch tackle* is a *luff tackle*. *Watch there* is a command to those operating a deep-sea hand *line*, each carrying a *coil* and calling to the man behind him when releasing its last *turn*.

From OE 'waecce', a weak feminine noun from the stem of the OE verb 'waeccan', a doublet of 'wacian', a weak verb meaning to be awake, as distinct from the strong verb 'wacen' to become awake; their Teutonic root is '*wak-*', representing a pre-Teutonic '*wag-*': cf. the Latin '*vegere*', to rouse, and '*vigere*', to be vigorous. Behind these may perhaps be detected the Indo-European root '*aweg-*': cf. the Latin '*augere*' and the Gothic '*aukan*', to increase, grow (or augment).

First attested as a spell of nautical duty (as distinct from a period of the night, attested as early as AD 1000) in 1585 in Washington (transl.), *Nicolay*, I, ii, 2; as a division of the crew, in 1626 in Smith, *Accidence*, 790; as a verb applied to a buoy, in 1633–4 in the *Admiralty Court Examiner*, 50, 21 January MS).

water ballast   water carried to stabilise an empty ship, pumped out as *cargo* is loaded; also used in some modern *yachts*. *Waterborne*, applied to a vessel, means floating: of goods, it means transported by lake, canal, river or sea.

A *water carnival* is the energetic splashy washing down of decks and *upperworks* with hoses. *Waterlaid* (of a rope) is *cable-laid*. The *waterline* is that traced by the water round a floating *hull*, or a drawing of it, or in some cases the top edge of the *boot-topping* where it meets the *topside* colour – the *light waterline* being that which the water should reach on an empty hull, the *load waterline* being that which it should reach when the ship is carrying the full load. *Waterlogged* means saturated and only just *afloat*. A *waterman* is one who plies from ship to *shore* and vice versa, or between shores, or who hires out boats; *watermanship* is the art of handling small boats with *oars* or *sculls*. *Watermarks* are those made above the waterline by oil, etc., or the *fore-and-aft* figures showing *draught*. A *waterplane* is a horizontal section through the hull at the waterline. A *water sail*, in *square-riggers*, was one *set* low down (e.g. below the lower *studding-sail* or below the *boom* of the *driver*) to catch a following *wind* in very light airs. A *waterside shark* is a shore-based person who preys on *sailors*. A *waterspout* is a funnel-shaped column in which the cloud base joins spray from the sea as a result of a *whirlwind*. To *waterstart* is to restart a *sailboard* from the water, the *wind* in the *rig* pulling the sailor up. *Watertight* is impervious to water.

Waterways are gullies or grooves to drain water away from the sides of a deck, from around a yacht's *cockpit*, or under the lids of the cockpit lockers.

From 'water' plus *ballast*: the former from a common Teutonic source, in OE 'waeter', in Old Teutonic *'watar'*: the Indo-Germanic root is *'wod-'*, which survives in the Russian *'vodka'*.

First attested in 1878 in Kemp, *Manual*, 377.

wave   a surge of water raised above the general level by the *wind*. The *Wavy Navy*, until 1956, described naval reserve officers and *ratings*, since until that date reserve officers wore wavy stripes or rings on their sleeves to indcate rank, unlike the straight stripes or rings then restricted to active service officers.

The noun, perhaps surprisingly, comes from the verb, whose origin is OE 'wafian', to undulate, and the Teutonic root *'wab-'*, the source of 'waver' and of ON *'vafe'*, doubt or uncertainty. The noun's late appearance (in the sixteenth century) is explained by the fact that until then the normal English word for a wave was 'waw', from ME 'wage', related to the OE verb 'wagian'.

First attested in its nautical sense in 1526 in Tindale (transl.), *New Testament, James*, I, 6.

way   the movement of a vessel through the water by means of her own power or the *wind* on her sails (not, that is, merely *drifting* with the *current*); (usually plural) the *timber* platforms sloping towards the water down which the *cradle* holding a ship slides when she is *launched*. *Way enough* is an order given to *rowers* to *pull* only one more *stroke*.

From OE 'weg' and a common Teutonic root: the Latin '*via*', once thought to be cognate with it, seems to come from a different source.

First attested as a ship's movement in 1663 in Davenant, *Rhodes*, Part II, I; as a slipway, in 1639 in Foster (ed.), *East India Company* (1907), 332.

wear   (of a *flag*) to *fly*; (of a sailing vessel) to bring on to the other *tack* by turning away from the *wind* and putting the *stern* through the wind (the opposite of *tacking*); (of a *fore-and-aft rigged* vessel in particular) to *gybe*.

Apparently two different words. That referring to a flag comes from OE 'werian' and has a common Teutonic root, its Old Teutonic origin being '*wazjan*' from the Indo-Germanic root '*wes-*', whence the Latin '*vestis*', a garment: the nautical expresson is a fairly straightforward extension of the familiar meaning. As a regards turning a ship, 'wear' is 'of obscure origin', according to the OED: in sense it coincides with *veer*, first attested in that sense *c.* 1620; but there seems little etymological affinity unless by confusion.

First attested in its flag connection in 1558 in Perrin, *British Flags* (1922), 88; as turning a ship, in 1614 (some six years before 'veer') in Gorges (transl.), *Lucan's Pharsalia*, v, 200.

weather   the state of the *wind* and other meteorological circumstances (e.g. heavy, fair, etc.); the side of direction from which the wind is blowing; to pass to *windward* of; to pass safely through, e.g. a *storm*. The *weather anchor* is that lying to windward; *weatherbound* is delayed by contrary winds; *weather bitted* is said of a *cable* all of which is in use, with the *inboard* end secured to the *bitts*. A *weather cloth* is a screen to protect the *crew* from wind or spray (as do the *dodgers* in a *yacht*). To *weathercock* is to have a tendency to turn *head* to wind when at *anchor* or under motor. A *weather glass* is a barometer. *Weather helm* is a tendency to *come up* into the wind, which has to be countered by keeping the tiller to windward or the *wheel* to *leeward*. *Weatherly* describes a boat that is well *trimmed*, makes little *leeway*, and can sail *close* to the wind. A *weather shore* is one lying to windward. To make *good* (or *bad*, or *heavy*) *weather* is to behave well (or badly) in a *storm*. From OE 'weder' and a common Teutonic source, and the Old Teutonic root '*wedro-m*' as well as the Indo-Germanic root '*we*', to blow. The verb is derived from the noun.

First attested, denoting windward, in 1390 in Gower, *Confessio amantis* (R. Pauli, 1857); EETS, 1900), II, 370; as passing to windward, *c.* 1595 in Wyatt, *Voyage of Robert Dudley* (Hakluyt Society), 18; as surviving a storm, in 1673 in Sir William Temple, *Observations upon the United Provinces of the Netherlands*, viii, 255; as surviving generally, in 1616 in Donne, *Sermons* (1640), xxi, 210.

weaver's knot   a *sheet bend* or a single *bend*.

From 'weaver' plus *knot*: the former from 'weave', whose source is OE 'wefan', from the Old Teutonic root '*web-*' and the Indo-Germanic '*webh-*'. The knot was used for joining threads in weaving.

First attested in 1532 in Gilbert Walker (anon.), *Manifest Detection* (Percy Society, 1850), B iij b.

weep   to leak slightly; (as a noun, in the plural) rust marks below an iron fitting.

From the familiar word, whose source is OE 'wefan', to cry aloud, from the Old Teutonic '*wopo-*'.

First attested in a nautical context in 1869 in Reed, *Shipbuilding*, I, 11.

weigh   (of the *anchor*) to break it out from the *bottom* and lift it clear.

From the familiar word, which from the earliest times carried the double sense of lifting as well as weighing: its source is OE 'wegan', from the common Teutonic root '*weg-*', the Indo-Germanic '*wegh-*' and the Sanskrit '*vah*': cf. the Latin '*vehere*', to carry, and the modern English 'vehicle'.

First attested in a nautical sense in the fourteenth century in *Early English Alliterative Poems*, 13 (EETS, 1864–9), C. 103.

well   vertical shaft protecting the pump below decks in a ship's hold; (in a fishing-boat) the tank into which the fish are thrown; any vertical aperture or hollow trunk (e.g. that through which an *outboard* motor may be shipped; (in a *yacht*) the *cockpit*. A *well deck* was one of two spaces on the main deck of older merchant ships, one between the *forecastle* and the *midships housing* which supported the *bridge*, the other between that and the *poop deck*.

From the familiar noun, originally meaning a spring, but from the tenth century onwards a pit dug in the ground to exploit one; its source is OE 'wielle', from the stem of 'weall-an', to bubble or boil up: cf. the Old High German '*wella*' and the German '*Welle*'.

First attested in a nautical sense in 1611 in Cotgrave,

Dictionarie: as a fish-tank, in 1614 in Gentleman, *England's Way*, in Arber (ed.), *An English Garner* (1877–96), IV, 19.

well-found   fully equipped.

From the adverb 'well' (from OE 'wel', 'well', a common Teutonic source, and the Golthic '*waila*' – cf. the German '*wohl*') plus 'found' (from OE 'findan', a common Teutonic source, the Teutonic root '*find-*' and the pre-Teutonic '*pent-*').

First attested in a nautical sense in 1891 in Markham, *Franklin*, 301.

whale-boat, whaler   an open boat pointed at both ends, either used for *whaling* or modelled on those that were.

From 'whale' (the sea mammal family), whose source is OE 'hwael', with a number of cognate words in other Germanic and Nordic languages, plus *boat*.

First attested, as 'whale-boat', in 1756 in Rogers, *Journals* (1769), 13; as 'whaler' in 1806 in the *Sydney Gazette*, quoted in O'Hara (anon.), *New South Wales* (1817), 270.

wharf   a wooden or stone structure alongside which ships may *berth* to load or unload *cargo*; in hydrography, an underwater scar, *shelf*, or *sandbank* on which *tides* will produce an *overfall* or *race*. *Wharfage* is the charge made for the use of a wharf; a *wharfinger* is a person in charge of, or owning, a wharf.

From late OE 'hwearf', with counterparts in various other Germanic languages, and (curiously) akin to the now obsolete word 'wharf' that meant an assembly of people: this disappeared in the thirteenth century.

First attested in a nautical sense in the eleventh century in a *Charter of Eadward* in Kemble (ed.), *Codex Diplomaticus* (1839–48), IV, 221; as a sandbank, in 1867 in Smyth, *Sailor's Word-book*. Cf. also Shakespeare, *Hamlet* (1602), I, v, 33: 'The far weede That rots it selfe in ease, on Lethe Wharfe' – seemingly a riverbank.

whifflow   a gadget, a what-you-may-call-it.

A fanciful formation.

First attested in 1961 in Burgess, *Dictionary*, 222.

wheel   circular *steering* device, often spoked, needing less effort but more skill than a *tiller*. *Wheel effect* is the sideways push of a rotating propeller: turning clockwise (when viewed from *astern*) it will send the *stern* to *starboard*, and vice versa. A *wheelhouse* is a permanent enclosed space above deck level for the *helmsman*, the *wheel*, the *steering compass* and the *helm* indicator. *Wheel-ropes* are ropes or *chains* connecting the wheel to the *rudder*.

From the familiar noun, whose source is OE 'hweogol', 'hweol', from the Old Teutonic root '*gwe(x)ula-*' and the Indo-

European '*qweqwlo-*', represented by the Sanskrit '*cakra-*', a circle or wheel.

First attested in its present nautical sense in 1743 in Bulkeley and Cummins, *Voyage*, 8.

whelps   raised *ribs* on the barrel of a *capstan* or a *winch* to help grip, and on the *after* end of a *boom* to prevent its drooping when *roller-reefed*.

According to the OED, from the familiar word for a puppy, whose OE and Old Saxon source was 'hwelp'. However, the same word was also used erroneously, from 1912 onwards, for 'welt'. Since this more closely resembles a nautical 'whelp' than does a puppy, it seems possible that the confusion may be of earlier date. The argument against such a conjecture is that 'whelp', more or less thus spelt, seems to have been in constant use from the fourteenth century onwards.

First attested in 1356 in *Pipe Roll 32 of Edward III*, m 34/1.

wherry   a light *rowing* boat, used especially to carry passengers on the *tidal* Thames in the eighteenth and nineteenth centuries, but known long before; a large, shallow-*draught* sailing *barge*, especially as used on the Norfolk Broads.

Of obscure etymology: the OED suggests – not altogether convincingly – a possible source in 'whirr', indicating rapid movement. If so, the word's ultimate origin is probably Scandinavian: cf. the Danish '*hvirre*' and the Norwegian '*hvirve*'. There may be some influence from 'ferry'. Could there be a bad pun involved? 'Wherry you goin', Sir?' is a common question.

First attested, as a rowing boat, in 1443 in the *Foreign Accounts 21 of Henry VI* in the Public Record Office, G dorso; as a barge, in or before 1589 by R. Lane in Hakluyt, *Principall Navigations*, 740.

whip   to bind twine, etc., round the end of a rope to prevent *unlaying* or fraying; such binding; a lifting *tackle* with a single rope and *block*; to use such a tackle. A *whipping* is the binding of a rope, as above. A *whipstaff*, formerly also named a whip, was a vertical rod attached to a *tiller*, before the introduction of the *wheel* in first years of the eighteenth century.

From the familiar word, both noun and verb, originally denoting quick movement and cognate with the Middle Low German and Dutch '*wippen*', but also with the Gothic '*wipja*', crown – perhaps indicating the binding sense, which is stronger in the Gothic root '*weip-*'. As the OED admits, 'The early history of this verb and its relative substantive is uncertain.'

First attested, as a verb related to binding, in 1440 in *Promptorium parvulorum* (Camden Society, 1843–65), 524/2; as the corresponding noun, in 1540 in the *Churchwarden's Accounts of Ludlow* 1540–1600 (Camden Society, 1869), 4; as a tackle, in 1769 in Falconer, *Dictionary*.

whisker   one of two *spreader spars* fitted to the *bowsprit* when this is extended by a *jib-boom*, to give it broader support by opening out the *guys*. A *whisker pole* is a spar used to hold out the *clew* of the *jib* in a *yacht* or a *dinghy* on the opposite side to the *mainsail* when *running* before the *wind*.

A figurative extension of the familiar word denoting (usually facial) hair – which itself is a figurative expression, since the original sense of the word was something used as a light brush. Its immediate source is the verb 'whisk', which is probably of Scandinavian origin: cf. the Swedish 'viska', to whisk off or sponge, and similar words in Danish and Norwegian.

First attested in its nautical sense in 1844 in Houston, *Texas*, II, 15.

whistle   (older name for) a *boatswain's pipe*; a ship's siren. A *whistle buoy* is one that emits an audible signal tone. To *whistle down the wind* is to talk pointlessly; to *whistle psalms to a taffrail* is to offer unheeded good advice; *whistling for a wind* was a superstitious practice when *becalmed*.

From OE 'hwistle', 'wuduhwistle': cf. ON *'hvisla'*, to whisper – a word thereby related to 'whistle'.

First attested in a nautical sense in 1513 in *Letters and Papers* (1913), 148: 'The boy... saw hym [the Admiral] take his whistill from aboute his neck, ... and hurlid it in to the see' – to avoid his insignia of office falling into enemy hands.

white   short for *white* squadron. The *white ensign* is a white *flag* with a red cross and a *Union flag* in the upper corner by the *hoist*, *flown* by all ships of the British Royal Navy and by members of the Royal Yacht Squadron: it was adopted in 1864 when the earlier division of the *fleet* into red, white, and blue squadrons was dropped and the red and blue *ensigns* allocated to other uses. *White horses* are *waves* whose crests are breaking. *White rope* is that which needs no tarring. A *white squall* is a tropical whirlwind heralded only by a small white cloud.

The noun comes from the familiar adjective, whose source is OE 'hwit', from the Gothic *'hweits'* and the Old Teutonic *'gwitaz'*.

First attested in this nautical sense in 1704 in Chamberlayne, *Magnae Britanniae Notitia* (1708–48), 21st edition, 572.

winch   a small horizontal or vertical *capstan*, power-driven in larger vessels, but in *yachts* usually turned by hand with a ratchet and pawl, for *halyards*, *sheets*, etc.

From late OE 'wince' and the old Teutonic *'winkjo-'*, from

the Indo-European root '*weng-*', represented also in the familiar word 'wink'.

First attested in a nautical context (although current *ashore* much earlier) in 1769 in Falconer, *Dictionary* (1776 edition).

wind   a current of air, named according to the direction whence it blows and according to its strength on the *Beaufort scale*. *Windage* is both deflection (or drag) owing to the wind and the parts of the vessel that cause it (by their size and prominence). A *windbag* is a largeish sailing ship. *Windbound* is held up by unfavourable winds; *windfall* describes strong winds blowing from the shore to the sea. A *windflag* is one *hoisted* to show wind direction, like a *burgee*. *Wind gradient* is the difference between wind speed at the surface and higher up. A *windjammer* is a non-nautical name for a *square-rigger*; a *windlipper* is a slight breeze likely to precede a strong one. *Windrode* is *riding head to wind* at *anchor*, with the wind overpowering the *tide*. A *wind-rose* (or *wind-star*) was the (poor) equivalent of the *compass* before the magnetic needle was introduced, used for wind navigation in the Mediterranean and associated with the Phoenicians; a *windsail* is a *canvas* funnel used to ventilate below decks; a *windscoop* is a metal scoop used for the same purpose. *Wind shadow* is the area in which one vessel's sails may blanket another's. *Windward* is the side or direction from which the wind blows.

From OE 'wind', the Old Teutonic '*windaz*', and the pre-Teutonic '*wentos*', cognate with the Latin '*ventus*': cf. the Sanskrit '*vata*', wind. Until the eighteenth century, the normal pronunciation was 'wined', which persisted in dialect and poetry after fashion had changed.

First attested in a specifcally nautical context in the fifteenth century in *Sailing Directions*, published by the Hakluyt Society, 13.

windlass   originally, a small *capstan* on a horizontal shaft in the *bows* for *weighing* an *anchor*; now, in smaller vessels, a powered substitute for the capstan.

Nothing to do with *wind* in the sense of an air current, or indeed with 'lass', but an alteration of the now obsolete 'windas', originally Anglo-French, from OF '*guindas*', itself in turn derived from ON '*vindass*', compounded of 'wind' (in the sense of turning or reeling in) plus 'ass', from the Gothic '*ans*', a pole. All these nouns mean winding-gear: in 'windlass' the 'l' is intrusive.

First attested *c.* 1400 in the *Laud Troy Book* (EETS, 1902–3), 12652.

wing   the part of a ship's *hold* that is nearest the side; the parts of a *paddle*-steamer's decks *before* and *abaft* the paddles; boards projecting over a vessel's sides. *Wing and wing* is another term for *goosewinging*, i.e. running before the wind with sails *set* on either side. *Wingers* are small *casks* or bundles *stowed* close to the ship's sides – or young *seamen* made the protégés of older *hands*. A *wing sail* is a rigid or semi-rigid aerofoil, sometimes with a movable flap at the *leech*.

All figurative extensions from the familiar word, whose source is the plural ME 'wenge', 'wengen', 'wenges', adapted from ON *'vaengir'*, the plural of 'vaengr' (Danish and Swedish *'vinge'*), the wing of a bird.

First attested in a nautical sense in 1730 in Wriglesworth, *MS Log-book*, 25 September; as a regards a paddle-steamer, in 1846 in Young, *Nautical Dictionary*, 370; as a projecting board, in 1906 in *The Daily Chronicle*, 19 February, 10/5.

wiring   (in a small boat) the *stringers* that support the *thwarts*.

From the familiar word, which itself comes from 'wire', whose source is OE 'wir', with cognate words in Middle Low German and ON. It was applied to non-metallic objects of long, thin shape as early as the seventeenth century.

First attested in this paticular boating sense in 1878 in Kemp, *Manual*, 380.

wishbone   a divided *spar* whose two arms are pivoted together at the *fore* end, each in a roughly parabolic or aerofoil curve, the sail being *hoisted* between the two, whose curves enable it to adopt the best aerodynamic shape; the similar *boom* of a *sailboard*. A *wishbone ketch* is one that has her *main-sail* area divided diagonally in two.

From the familiar word denoting the merrythought or furcula of a bird. 'Wish' comes from the verb, whose source is OE 'wyscan' from Old Teutonic *'wunskjan'*: cf. the Sanskrit *'vancha'*. 'Bone' comes from OE 'ban' and the Old Teutonic *'baino(m)'*.

First attested in its nautical sense in 1934 in Fox, *Sailing*, I, 54.

wonk   a novice *seaman*; a *midshipman*.

Possibly from 'wonky' (unstable), of equally obscure origin though perhaps related to the German *'wankel'*, with the general sense of fickle.

First attested, as a novice, in 1929 in Bowen, *Sea Slang*, 153; as a midshipman, in 1962 in Granville, *Sailors' Slang*, 134/1.

wooden walls   sailing *warships*. *Wooden wings* are *leeboards*. A *wood-butcher* or *wood-spoiler* is the ship's carpenter or his *mate*.

From the familiar words: 'wooden' from 'wood', whose source is OE 'widu', 'wiodu', and later 'wudu', from the Old Teutonic *'widuz'*; 'walls' from OE 'wall', a Saxon and Anglo-Frisian adoption of the Latin *'vallum'*. But the source of the expression as such is *'ksulinon teichos'*, used by Herodotus, *History*, vii, 141. The walls were not the ship's *hulls*, but their existence as a defence.

First attested in 1598 in Phillip (transl.), *Linschoten* (Hakluyt Society, 1885), Introduction.

woold   to bind rope or *chain* round a *spar* where it has split or been *fished*.

Woolding is the operation of thus binding, as well as the rope or chain used.

Possibly a back-formation from *woolding*, first attested nearly two centuries earlier. If so, its origin is late ME 'wol(l)ing', from the Middle Low German *'woling'*. If not, it comes directly into late ME from the Middle Low German *'wolen'*.

First attested in or before 1616 in Cocks, *Diary* 1615–33 (Hakluyt Society, 1883), I, 96.

work   (of a ship) to suffer from parts (e.g. *planks* and *timbers*) starting to move relative to each other, often causing leaks. The *working load* or *working strain* of a *cable* is one-sixth of its *breaking load* or *breaking strain*; *working sails* are the essential *mainsail* and *headsail*. To *work up the reckoning* is to estimate a ship's position by *dead reckoning*. To *work with the tide* is to take advantage of it.

From the familiar word, whose source is OE 'wyrcan', 'wircan', from the Old Teutonic *'werkjan'*.

First attested in this nautical sense in 1769 in Falconer, *Dictionary* (1776 edition).

worm   to fill the spiral groove in a rope or *cable* by winding *small stuff* along it, thereby making a flatter surface for *parcelling* and *serving*.

Unlikely as it seems, the nautical verb comes from the familiar noun and its verb, the link being the supposedly spiral movement of the animal, echoed in expressions like 'to worm one's way'. The source of the noun is OE 'wyrm', cognate with similar words in a number of Germanic and Nordic languages, and related to the Latin *'vermis'*.

First attested in this nautical sense in 1644 in Manwayring, *Sea-mans Dictionary*, 116.

wrack   seaweed, especially when deposited on *shore*.

Virtually the same word as *wreck*, since both at different times and places have meant both seaweed and maritime disaster or debris. 'Wrack' comes from the Middle Dutch (and now modern Dutch) '*wrak*' and the older Flemish '*wracke*', and its primary meaning, now dialect, was a foundered or crippled vessel and its remains.

First attested to mean seaweed in 1499 in *Promptorium parvulorum* (Winchester MS), EETS, 1908; with the same meaning, but spelt 'wreck', in or before 1522 in Douglas (transl.), *Virgill*, III, ix, 34.

wreck   a *foundered*, stranded, or crippled abandoned vessel, or its ruins; any such debris; to cause such. A *wreck buoy* is one to mark a wreck, now subsumed under those marking isolated dangers; a *wreck-marking* or *wreck vessel* is one performing the same function as a wreck buoy.

Virtually the same word as *wrack*, although (at least theoretically) derived from a different source – the Anglo-French '*wrec*', '*wrech*', '*wrek*' (also '*werec*', '*waerec*', '*warec*', whence OF '*varech*', '*varec*' (seaweed) and the medieval Latin '*wreccum*', '*warectum*'. But the Anglo-French word is itself from ON '*wrec*', '*wrek*', from the tem of '*wrekan*', to drive; and it seems likely that there is a link between this and other Nordic and German words associated with 'wrack'.

First attested in a nautical sense in 1097 in the *Chronicle of Romsey (William I)* in the Rolls Series, 201.

wring   (of a *mast* or *hull*) to twist.

The familiar word, from OE 'wringan', with many cognate words in other Germanic languages: cf. the Gothic '*wruggo*'a snare. The notion of twisting clearly the reflects the two-handed twisting of a wet cloth to wring it comparatively dry.

First attested in a nautical sense in 1815 in Burney (ed.), Falconer, *New Universal Dictionary*.

Xebec   small three-*masted* (originally two-masted) partly or wholly *lateen-rigged* sixteenth- to nineteenth-century Mediterranean vessel, once a fighting ship, later a merchantman.

From the French '*chebec*' and thence from the Spanish '*xabeque*', later '*jabeque*'.

First attested in 1756 in *The Gentleman's Magazine*, 409/2.

Yacht   originally a light fast sailing-ship used to convey important persons; later, any vessel other than a *dinghy* propelled by sail or power and used for pleasure *cruising* and/or *racing*. (Note: *yachtsmen* or *yachtswomen* never call their own boats 'yachts'.) A *yacht club* is one that unites devotees, promotes the sport, and organises races. *Yachting* is navigation by sailing, steam, or motor yacht. A *yachtmaster's certificate* is one issued by the Royal Yachting Association to those who have passed a practical and theoretical examination and put in a certain required number of hours at sea by day and night. A *yachtsman* or *yachtswoman* is one who owns or sails a yacht.

From the early modern Dutch '*jaght(e)*', now '*jacht*', literally a ship for chasing, a light, fast, and possibly piratical vessel, from '*jagen*', to chase or hunt.

First attested in 1557 in *The Voyage of Stephen Burrough*, in Hakluyt, *Principall Navigations*, second edition (1598), I, 294.

yankee   a light-*weather foresail set* on the *topmast stay* with its *luff* extending almost the stay's full length, narrower and higher-*clewed* than a *genoa*.

From the familiar word, of which there are several competing etymologies. They include: the Cherokee word '*eankke*' (a slave or coward); a slang word for 'excellent'; a native American corruption of 'English' ('yengee'); and a diminutive ('*Janke*') of the Dutch name '*Jan*'. The word is not used to describe such a sail in the United States.

First attested in 1912 in Heckstall-Smith and Du Boulay, *Complete Yachtsman*, vi, 152.

yard   a large wooden or metal *spar hoisted* on a *mast* horizontally or diagonally, from which sails are *set* or *flags* and *lights* may be hung. The *yardarm* is the outer end of a yard, *outboard* of the *lifts*; a *yardarm group* is a portable round shade holding a cluster or lights, hoisted when extra illumination is needed. A *yardman* is a *topman*, i.e. one who works *aloft*.

Nothing to do with an area, but from OE 'gierd', 'gyrd', 'gird', probably from the Old Teutonic '*gazdjo*' and the Gothic '*gazds*', and also probably related to the Latin '*hasta*', a spear. The original meaning was a straight slender branch.

First attested in its nautical sense, in the combination 'sail-yard', *c.* AD 725 in the *Corpus Glossary* (Oldest English Texts, EETS, 1885), 588.

yarn   spun threads of which a *strand* of a rope is composed.

From ON 'gearn', apparently from the same root as ON '*garno*', meaning guts or intestines, and related to the Greek '*chorde*', the Latin '*hira*', and the Sanskrit '*hira*', a vein.

First attested in its nautical sense, in the combination 'spun-yarn', in 1627 in Smith, *Seaman's Grammar*, v, 25.

yaw   involuntary deviation from *course* owing to *wind* and *tide*; thus to deviate, often oscillating as the *helmsman* tries to correct the movement, which may be due to a following *sea*'s limiting the effect of the *rudder*.

Of obscure origin, but possibly related to ON '*jaga*', describing the to-and-fro movement of a door on its hinges – fitting the to-and-fro motion of a yawing ship.

First attested, as a nautical noun, in 1546 in Gardiner, *Declaration*, 91; as a nautical verb, in 1586 in Melvill, *Autobiography and Diary* (Wodrow Society, 1842) 253.

yawl   a two-*masted* sailing vessel with the *mizen-mast stepped abaft* the *rudder-head* (as distinct from a *ketch*, whose mizen-mast is stepped *forward* of it); until the mid nineteenth century, a small ship's boat with four or more *oars*.

From either the Middle Low German '*jolle*' or the seventeenth-century Dutch '*jol*', described in 1708 as 'a Jutland boat'. The 'ship's boat' sense, now obsolete, preceded that of the sailing vessel, first identified as a fishing boat.

First attested, as a ship's boat, in 1670 by John Covel, *Diary*, in *Early Voyages to the Levant* (Hakluyt Society, 1893), 131; as a fishing vessel, in 1670 in Smith, *England's Improvement Reviv'd*, 254; as a sailing boat in general, in 1684 in *The London Gazette*, No. 1898/4.

yellow admiral   (before 1864) an *admiral* with no rank in the *flag* list because not belonging to the red, *white*, or blue squadrons: the need to create them grew during the Napoleonic Wars (1803–15). The *yellow flag*, *yellow jack* or *yellow peril* is the yellow *quarantine flag*, Q in the flag alphabet.

From the familiar adjective, whose source is OE 'geolu', from the Old Teutonic '*gelwa*' and the Indo-European '*ghelwo*': cf. the modern German '*gelb*' and the Latin '*helvus*', greyish-yellow.

First attested in 1788 in *Parliamentary History*, XXVII, 22.

yeoman   a junior officer, usually subordinate to a superior, in practical charge of some duty, including stores, *signals*, etc. The *yeoman of signals* is the *signalman* in charge of a *watch*.

From the familiar word (which originally meant an upper servant in a royal or noble household), whose source is the fourteenth-century ME 'yoman', 'yeman', 'yiman', probably from the ME equivalent of 'youngman'.

First attested in a nautical sense *c.* 1400 in *The Tale of Beryn* (Chaucer Society, 1876; EETS, 1909), 2997.

yoke   a fitting across a *rudder-head* in a *rowing* boat, for use in place of a *tiller*. *Yoke lines* are those held in the hand by the *helmsman* to control the yoke.

From the familiar word, whose source is OE 'geoc', from a common Teutonic root and the Gothic '*juk*', corresponding to the Latin '*jugum*'.

First attested in a nautical sense in or before 1625 in *Nomenclator Navalis* (Harleian MS 2301).

yulo, yuloh, yulow   a long *oar* or *sweep* used over the *stern* by Chinese *boatmen* to propel a *sampan* or a small *junk* by *sculling*; thus to *scull*.

From the Cantonese '*iu-lo*', to scull a boat.

First attested in 1878 in Giles, *Glossary*, 170.

Zenith   the point in the sky directly overhead. The *zenith distance* is the angle between the observer's zenith and an observed celestial body subtended at the centre of the earth.

From OF '*cenit(h)*' or medieval Latin '*cenit*', and the Arabic '*samt*' in '*samt ar-ras*', meaning path over the head.

First attested in 1387 in Trevisa (transl.), *Polychronicon* (Rolls), II, 177.

z-twist   describes rope *laid up* right-handed, as distinct from *s-twist*.

From the appearance of the *strands* as seen at a cut end.

First attested in 1935 in the *Proceedings of the American Society for Testing Materials*, XXXV, I, 448.

Zulu   a type of fishing boat formerly used in the North-East corner of Scotland, broad-*beam*ed and *carvel-built*, with a pointed and steeply *raked stern*, *rigged* with a *dipping lug foresail* and a *standing lug mizen*.

Named after the Zulu Wars (1878–9), which were being waged when the boat was introduced: 'Zulu' is of African origin.

First attested in this nautical sense in 1884 in *Highland Society, Prize Essays*, 122.

Bibliography

Abercrombie, John: *The Gardener's Assistant*, 1786
Account of Several Late Voyages and Discoveries, An, 1694 (1711)
Acts of the Parliament of Scotland, The, (1566, 1597, 1814–75)
Addison, Joseph: *Remarks on Italy*, 1705 (1733)
Admiralty, Articles concerning the Admiralty Court Examiner, The
Admiralty: *Manual of Seamanship*, Vol. II (revised), 1923
Aelfred, King: (transl.) Boethius, *De Consolatione Philosophiae*, *c*. 888
   (Sedgefield, 1899)
— (transl.) *Gregory's Pastoral Care*, *c*. 897 (EETS, 1871)
— (transl.) *Orosius*, *c*. 893 (EETS, 1883)
Aelfric: *Glossary*, *c*. 1000
— *Homilies*, *c*. 1000 (ed Benjamin Thorpe, 1844–6)
— *Proverbs*, *c*. 1000 (ed C.W.M. Grein, 1872)
Aeronautics, Technical Report of the Advisory Committee on 1912–13,
   1914
Aikin, J.: *Manchester*, 1795
American Naturalist, The, 1867–
American Neptune, The
American Society for Testing Materials, Proceedings, 1898–
American Weekly Mercury, The
Ancient Correspondence (Public Record Office)
Andreas, late 10th century (ed. John M. Kemble, 1844; Grein, 1888)
Anglo-Saxon Chronicle, The, mid 12th century (ed. Benjamin Thorpe,
   Rolls Series, 1861; John Earle, 1865; Earle and Plummer, 1892,
   1899)
Annual Register, The, 1758
Anson, George: *Voyage Round the World, compiled from his papers*, 1748
Arber, Edward (ed): *An English Garner*, 1877–96
Archaeologia: or Miscellaneous Tracts Relating to Antiquity (Society of
   Antiquaries of London, 1770–)
Army and Navy Gazette, The
Arnolde, Richard: *Chronicle (The names of the baylifs custos mairs and
   sherefs of London*, 1502 (1811)
Ash, John: *The New and Complete Dictionary of the English Language*, 1775
Asiatic Annual Register, The, 1800
Assmann, Bruno (ed): *Angelsaechsische Homelien und Heiligenleben* 1889
Athenaeumn, The, 1828–1921

B.E.: *A New Dictionary of the Terms Ancient and Modern of the Canting
   Crew* 1690

B.L. Ballads and Broadsides, 1867

Babson, J.J.: *The History of Gloucester, Mass.*, 1860

Bagley, Desmond: *The Enemy*, 1977

Bailey, C.: *The Loss of the Pegasus*, 1843

Bailey, Nathan: *An Universal Etymological English Dictionary*, 1721
— *Dictionarium Britannicum: or a More Compleat Universal Etymological English Dictionary*, 1730, 1736

Baker, Anne E.: *Glossary of Northamptonshire Words and Phrases*, 1854

Baker, Sir Samuel W.: *Ismailia*, 1870

Baltimore Sun, The, 1837–

Barbour, John: *The Bruce*, 1375 (EETS, 1870–89; STS, 1894)

Barclay, Alexander (transl.): *Sebastian Brant's Narrenschiff, The Shyp of Folys*, 1509

Baret, John: *An Alvearie or Triple (Quadruple) Dictionarie*, 1573, 1580

Barrere, Albert and Leland, C.G.: *A Dictionary of Slang, Jargon and Cant*, (1897)

Barry, Patrick: *Dockyard Economy and Naval Power*, 1863

Bartlett, John. R.: A *Dictionary of Americanisms*, 1848, 1859, 1850, 1876

Barton, Sir Andrew: *Miscellanea* (Surtees Society, 1888)

Battle of Maldon, The, 993 (Grein, 1883)

Beatson, Robert: *Naval and Military Memoirs of Great Britain*, 1790

Beck, S. William: *The Draper's Dictionary*, 1886

Bedford, Frederick G.D..: *The Sailor's Pocket-book*, 1875

Bellenden, John (transl): *Livy's History of Rome*, 1533 (1822; STS, 1901)

Bennett, Agnes Maria: *The Beggar Girl and her Benefactors*, 1797 (1813)

Bennett, F.W..: *Leaves from a Log*, 1869

Beowulf, late 8th century (EETS, 1882)

Berners, John Bourchier, 2nd Baron: *The First Volume of Syr John Froissart, of the Chronycles of Englande, Fraunce, etc.*, 1523

Beryn, The Tale of, c. 1400 (Chaucer Society, 1876; EETS, 1909)

Biddlecombe, G.: *The Art of Rigging*, 1848

Biddulph, William: *The Travels of Certaine Englishmen into Africa, Asia, etc.*, 1609 (edited by T.Lavender, 1609, 1612)

Binnell's Description of the Thames, 1584 (1758)

Birch, Thomas: *The History of the Royal Society of London*, 1756–7

Birch, Walter de Gray (ed): *Cartularium Saxonicum*, 1885–93

Blackie, John Stuart: *Lays of the Highlands*, 1872

Blackwood's Edinburgh Magazine, 1817–

Blake, John: *A Plan for Regulating the Marine System of Great Britain*, 1758

Blanckley, Thomas R.: *A Naval Expositor*, 1750

Bligh, Captain William: *Narrative of the Mutiny and Seizure of the Bounty*, 1790

Blount, Thomas: *Glossographia, or a Dictionary interpreting such hard words... as are now used*, 1656, 1661, 1670, 1674 (1681)

Blundevil, Thomas: *Exercises*, 1594 (1636)

Boats of the World, 1883

Bone, Sir David: *The Brassbounder*, 1910

Booth, Michael R.. (ed): *English Plays of the 19th Century*, (1969–73)
Boston News-Letter, The, 1704–76
Boston, Records Relating to the Early History of, 1876–1909
Boteler, Captain Nathaniel: *Six Dialogues about Sea Services, c.* 1635
    (1685)
Bourne, William: *A Regiment for the Sea*, 1574 (1577)
Bowen, Frank Charles: *Sea Slang: a Dictionary of the Old-Timers'
    Expressions and Epithets*, 1929
Bowes, Thomas (transl): *De la Primaudaye's French Academie*, 1586,
    1589, 1594
Boyd, Zachary: *Zion's Flowers, c.* 1620 *(Four Poems from,* 1855)
Boyer, Abel: *Dictionnaire François-Anglois*, 1699, 1719, 1727, 1768, 1783
Boy's Own Paper, The, 1879–
Bradford, Gershom: *A Glossary of Sea Terms*, 1927
Brand, John: *History and Antiquities of the Town and County of Newcastle-
    upon-Tyne*, 1789
Brereton, Sir William: *Travels in Holland, etc.*, 1634–5 (Chetham
    Society, 1844)
Brewster, Sir David: *Letters on Natural Magic*, 1831 (1833)
Brice's Weekly Journal, Exeter, 1725–8
*British Channel Fisheries, Report of the House of Commons Select Committee
    on*, 1833
British Magazine, The, 1760–7
Brockett, John T.: *A Glossary of North Country Words*, 1825, 1829, 1846
Brown, R.: *Spunyarn and Spindrift*, 1886
Brown, Thomas (transl): *Fresny's Amusements Serious and Comical*, 1700
Browne, William: *Britannia's Pastorals*, 1613
Bruce, James: *Travels to Discover the Source of the Nile*, 1790
Brut, The, or the Chronicles of England, Continuation of, c. 1450 (EETS,
    1906)
Buckland, Francis T.: *Log-book of a Fisherman and Zoologist*, 1875
Bulkeley, John and Cummins, J.: *A Voyage to the South-seas*, 1743
Bullen, Frank T.: *The Log of a Sea-waif*, 1899
Burchett, Josiah: *Memoirs of Transactions at Sea*, 1703 (1720)
Burgess, Francis Henry: *A Dictionary of Sailing*, 1961
Burke, Edmund: *Reflections on the Revolution in France*, 1790
Burney, William (ed): William Falconer, *A New Universal Dictionary of
    the Marine*, 1815
'Burton, Alfred' (John Mitford): *The Adventures of Johnny Newcome in
    the Navy*, 1818
Burton, Robert: *The Anatomy of Melancholy* 1621 (1624, 1628, 1638,
    1651, 1676)
Byron, George Gordon Noel, 6th Baron: *Don Juan*, 1818–24
— *The Island*, 1823

Caedmon: *Genesis* and *Exodus, c.* 670 (Grein)
Calendar of the Ancient Records of Dublin (1889–)
Calendar of Patent Rolls (Public Record Office)

Callahan, H.A.: *Rigging*, 1944
Canute, King: *Charter*, 1023
Capgrave, John: *The Chronicle of England*, 1460 (Rolls Series, 1858)
Carew, Richard: *The Survey of Cornwall*, 1602
Carpenter, Nathanael: *Geography Delineated Forth in two Bookes*, 1625 (1635)
Cassell's Encyclopaedic Dictionary, 1879–88
Cassells's Technical Educator, 1877–82
Catholicon Anglicum, An English-Latin Wordbook, c. 1483 (EETS, 1881)
Caulfield, J.M.: *Seamanship Notes*, 1886
Caulfield, Sophia S.F. and Saward, Blanche C.: *The Dictionary of Needlework*, 1882
Caxton, William (transl): *Blanchardyn and Eglantine*, 1489 (EETS, 1890)
— (transl): *The Book of Fayttes of Armes and of Chyualrie*, 1489
— *The Chronicles of England*, 1480 (1482, 1520)
— (transl): *The Historie of Jason*, 1475
Cely Papers, The: Selections from the Correspondence and Memoranda of the Cely Family, Merchants of the Staple, 1475–88 (Camden Society, 1900)
Century Dictionary, The, An Encyclopaedic Lexicon of the English Language. Prepared under the Superintendance of W.D. Whitney, 1889–91
Century Illustrated Monthly Magazine, The, 1881–
Certayne sermons, or homilies, appoynted by the kynges maiestie, to be declared and redde by all persons, vicars, or curates, every Sondaye in their churches 1547: the seconde tome of homelyes, 1563 (1859)
Chamberlayne, Edward: *Angliae Notitia: or the Present State of England*, 1667 (1707)
Chambers, Ephraim: *Cyclopaedia; or, an Universal Dictionary of Arts and Sciences*, 1728 (1738, 1741, 1751) *Supplement*, 1753
Chambers's Edinburgh Journal, 1852–4
Chambers's Journal of Popular Literature, 1854–
Chandler, Richard: *Travels in Greece*, 1776
Chapman, George (transl): *The Divine Poem of Musaeus*, 1616 (1658)
— (transl): *The Iliads* [sic] *of Homer, c.* 1611
Charles II, King: *Proclamation, 6 April 1671*
— *State Papers Domestic*
Chatterton, Edward Keble: *Fore & Aft*, 1912
Chaucer, Geoffrey: *Canterbury Tales, c.* 1386
— *The Hous of Fame, c.* 1384
Cheever, H.T.: *A Whaleman's Adventures in the Southern Ocean* (ed William Scoresby, 1850 (1859)
Chester Whitsun Plays, The, c. 1430–1500 (Shakespeare Society 1843–7; EETS, 1893)
Chowdharay-Best, G.: *Mariner's Mirror*, 1971
Christie, W.D.: *The Life of the Earl of Shaftesbury*, 1871
Church, William C.: *The Life of John Ericsson*, 1890

Churchill, John (ed): *A Collection of Voyages and Travels*, 1704
Civil Engineer and Architect's Journal, The, 1837–
Clark, G.E.: *Seven Years of a Sailor's Life*, 1867
Cleveland, John: *The Character of a Diurnall-maker*, 1654 (*Works*, 1687)
Cockayne, T. Oswald (ed): *The Shrine. A Collection of Occasional Papers on Dry Subjects*, before AD 1000 (1864–70)
Cocke Lorelles bote, c. 1515 (Percy Society, 1843)
Cocks, Richard: *Diary in Japan 1615–22* (Hakluyt Society, 1883)
Coke, John: *The Debate Betwene the Heraldes of Englande and Fraunce*, 1550 (1877)
Coker, Temple H. et al: *The Complete Dictionary of the Arts and Sciences*, 1764–6
Coleridge, Samuel Taylor: *The Rime of the Ancient Mariner*, 1798
Coles, Elisha: *An English Dictionary*, 1676
Collins, John: *Making Salt in England, c.* 1682
Colquhoun, Sir Patrick: *A Companion to the 'Oarsman's Guide'*, 1857
Colvil, Samuel: *Mock Poem, or Whiggs Supplication*, 1657 (1681)
Complaynt of Scotlande, The, 1549 (EETS, 1872)
Congreve, William: *Love for Love*, 1695
Conrad, Joseph: *The Arrow of Gold*, 1919
Cook, Captain James: *A Voyage to the Pacific Ocean in 1776–80*, 1779–80,1784
— *Voyages*, 1790
Cooper, James Fenimore: *The Red Rover*, 1827
— *The Water Witch*, 1830
Cooper, W. ('Vanderdecken'): *The Yacht Sailor: A Treatise on Practical Yachtsmanship, Cruising and Racing*, 1862
'Copplestone, B.': *Lost Naval Papers*, 1917
Corpus Glossary, c. 725 (Oldest English Texts, EETS, 1885; Hessels, 1890)
Cotgrave, Randle: *A Dictionarie of the French and English Tongues*, 1611
Cotton MSS, The, c. 1582
Cotton, Charles: *The Compleat Angler: Being Instructions how to angle for a trout or grayling in a clear stream*, 1676
Court of Requests, Acts of the
Coverdale, Miles (transl): *The Bible*, 1535
Cowell, John: *The Interpreter: or Booke containing the Signification of Words*, 1607 (1637, 1672)
Crabb, George: *Universal Technological Dictionary*, 1823
Croker, Temple H. et al.: *The Complete Dictionary of the Arts and Sciences*, 1764–6
Cromwell, Oliver: *Letters and Speeches*, 1653–8 (ed Thomas Carlyle 1845)
Cursor Mundi (The Cursor of the World, *c.* 1300. A Northumbrian Poem of the 14th Century in Four Versions (EETS, 1874–92)
Cussans, John E.: *The Handbook of Heraldry*, 1868 (1869, 1882)
Cutcliffe W. Hyne, C.J.: *The Adventures of Captain Kettle*, 1898
— *Master of Fortune, c.* 1900

Cutler, Manasseh: *Life, Journal, and Correspondence by his Grandchildren*, before 1823 (1888)
Cynewulf: *Crist*, 9th century (Grein; Gollancz, 1892)

Daily Chronicle, The, 1872–
Daily Colonist, The (of Victoria, BC) 1886–
Daily News, The, 1846–
Daily Telegraph, The, 1855–
Dampier, William: *A New Voyage round the World (Voyages and Descriptions; A Voyage to New Holland)*, 1697 (1699) 1703–9 (1729)
Dana, Richard Henry Jr: *The Seaman's Manual*, 1841
— *Two Years Before the Mast*, 1840
Darwin, Bernard: *Golf Courses of the British Isles*, 1910
Darwin, Charles: *Journal of Researches into the Geology and Natural History of the various Countries visited by H.M.S. Beagle, 1832–36*, 1839 (1845, 1852, 1879)
Davenant, Sir William: *The Siege of Rhodes*, 1656–9 (1663)
Davenant, Sir William and Dryden, John: *Shakespeare's Tempest, or the Enchanted Island* (altered), 1667 (1670)
Davies, George C.: *Norfolk Broads and Rivers*, 1883 (1884)
Davies, John (transl): A. Olearius: *Voyages and Travels of the Ambassadors sent…to the great Duke of Moscovy. Whereto are added the Travels of (J.A. de) Mandelslo from Persia into the East-Indies*, 1662
Davies of Kidwelly, John: *The History of the Caribbee Islands*, 1666
Davis, John: *The Seamans Secrets*, 1594 (1607)
Dee, John: *General and Rare Memorials Pertayning to the Perfecte Arte of Navigation*, 1577
Defeat of the Spanish Armada, The, *c.* 1588 (Navy Records Society)
Defoe, Daniel: *The History and Remarkable Life of Colonel Jacque [Colonel Jack]*, 1722 (1840)
— *The Life, Adventures, and Pyracies of the famous Captain Singleton*, 1720 (1840)
— *The Life and Strange Adventures of Robinson Crusoe*, 1719 (1840)
— *A New Voyage Round the World*, 1725 (1840)
Dekker, Thomas: *The Ravens Almanacke*, 1609
— *The Shoemaker's Holiday*, 1600
Depew, A.N..: *Gunner Depew*, 1918
Derby, Henry Earl of (later Henry IV): *Expeditions to Prussia and the Holy Land*, 1390–1 (Camden Society, 1894)
Desoutter, Denis Marcel (Denny): *The Boat-Owner's Practical Dictionary*, 1978
Destruction of Troy, The. The Gest Hystoriale of the Destruction of Troy: an alliterative romance translated from Guido de Colonna's Hystoria Troiana, *c.* 1400 (EETS, 1869–74)
Dialogue of Salomon and Saturnus, The, before 1000 (Aelfric Society, 1848; Grein, 1898)
Dibdin, Charles: *A Musical Tour*, 1788
Dickens, Charles: *American Notes for General Circulation*, 1842 (1850)

— *The Life and Adventures of Nicholas Nickleby*, 1838–9
Digby Mysteries, The. Ancient Mysteries from the Digby Manuscripts,
  c. 1485 (Abbotsford Club, 1835; New Shakespeare Society, 1882;
  EETS, 1896)
Digby, Sir Kenelm: *Journal of a Voyage into the Mediterranean*, 1628–9
  (Camden Society, 1868)
Digges, Leonard: *A Geometrical Practise named Pantometria*, 1571 (1591)
Dodsley, Robert: *A Select Collection of Old Plays*, 1744, 1780. 1825–7
  (ed William Carew Hazlitt, 1874–6)
Donne, John: *LXXX Sermons*, 1640
Douglas, Bishop Gavin (transl): *The xiii Bukes of Eneados of the Famose
  Poete Virgill*, 1513 (1553, 1710, 1874)
Douglass, William: *Summary*, 1749
Drayton, Michael: *The Battaile of Agincourt* (etc.), 1627
Drury, W.P.: *Tadpole of Archangel*, 1898
Dryden, John: *Annus Mirabilis: The Year of Wonders*, 1666
— *The Tempest*, 1670 (See Davenant and Dryden)
Duncan, Archibald: *The Life of Lord Nelson*, 1806
— *The Mariner's Chronicle*, 1804, 1810
Durham, Extracts from the Account Rolls of the Abbey of, 1278–1580
  (Surtees Society, 1898–1901)
Durham, Sacrist's Roll of, 1338

E.S.: *Britaines Busse: or a computation as well of the charge of a busse or
  herring-fishing ship as also of the gaine and profit thereby*, 1615
Early English Alliterative Poems in the West Midland Dialect, mid 14th
  century (EETS, 1864–9)
Early English Psalter, An, c. 1300 (Surtees Society, 1843–7)
Early South-English Legendary or Lives of the Saints, The, c. 1290 (EETS,
  1887)
Early Voyages to the Levant, (Hakluyt Society, 1893)
Eden, Richard (transl): *Martin Cortes' Arte of Nauigation*, 1561
— (transl): *The Decades of the Newe World or West India*, 1555
— (transl): *A Treatyse of the Newe India*, 1553 (ed Edward Arber, 1885)
Edgeworth, Maria: *Works*, 1800–49
Edinburgh, Extracts from the Records of the Burgh of, 1403–1589 (Scottish
  Burgh Records Society, 1869–82)
Edward III, King: *Pipe Rolls*
— *Statutes*
Edward the Confessor, King: *Charters*
Elements and Practice of Rigging and Seamanship, The, 1794
Ellis, Sir Henry (ed): *Original Letters Illustrative of English History*,
  1824–46
Ellis, William: *The Country Housewife's Family Companion*, 1750
Elyot, Sir Thomas: *Dictionary*, 1538, 1542, 1545
Emerson, Ralph Waldo: *English Traits*, 1856
Encyclopaedia Britannica, The, 1768–
Encyclopaedia Metropolitana, The, 1818–45

Encyclopaedia of Sport, The, 1897–8
English Gilds, before 1400 (EETS, 1870)
English Studies: a Journal of English Letters and Philology, 1919–
Entick, John: *History and Survey of London and Places Adjacent*, 1766
Epinal Glossary, The: Latin and Old English, c. 825 (Sweet, 1883; Oldest English Texts, EETS, 1885)
Erfurt Glossary, The, c. 875 (Oldest English Texts, EETS, 1885)
Etoniana Ancient and Modern, 1865
Evelyn, John: *Diary*, 1623–1705/6 (ed E.S. de Beer, 1955)
Evening News, The, 1881–1980
Examiner, The, 1710–14; 1806–36
Exchequer Accounts (Public Record Office)

Fabyan, Robert: *The Newe Cronycles of Englande and of Fraunce*, 1494 (1516)
Falconer, William: *The Shipwreck*, 1762
— *An Universal Dictionary of the Marine*, 1769 (1776)
Fiddes, Richard: *The Life of Cardinal Wolsey*, 1724 (1726)
Field, The, 1853–
Fisher, A.: *The Journal of a Voyage of Discovery*, 1821
Fisheries Great International Exhibition Catalogue, 1883
Flinders, Matthew: *A Voyage to Terra Australis*, 1814
Florio, John: *A World of Wordes, or Most Copious and Exact Dictionarie in Italian and English*, 1598
Folkingham, William: *Feudigraphia. The Synopsis or Epitome of Surveying Methodized*, 1610
Foreign Accounts (MS in Public Record Office)
Forest and Stream (A Weekly Journal of the Rod and Gun), 1973–
Fortescue Papers, The: Consisting chiefly of Letters Relating to State Affairs. Edited from MSS in possession of Hon. G.M. Fortescue (Camden Society, 1871)
Foster, William (ed): *Court Minutes of the East India Company*, 1639 (1907)
— *The English Factories in India, a Calendar of Documents in the India Office, British Museum and Public Record Office 1618–41* (1906–12)
Fox, Uffa: *Sailing, Seamanship and Yacht Construction*, 1934
Fraser, Edward and Gibbons, John: *Soldier and Sailor Words and Phrases*, 1925
Fraser, John S. and Henley, William E.: *Slang and its Analogues, Past and Present*, 1890–1904
Friend and Browning: *British Patent No. 2652*, 1854
Fryer, John: *A New Account of East India and Persia*, 1698
Fuller, Thomas: *The History of the Worthies of England*, before 1661 (1662, 1840)
Funk, I.K. and Wagnall: *A Standard Dictionary of the English Language*, 1893–5

Gabrieli's Mysterious Husband, 1801

Gardiner, Bishop Stephen: *A Declaration of such true Articles as G. Joye hath gone about to confute as false*, 1546

Garrard, William: *The Art of Warre*, before 1587 (1591)

Gascoigne, Henry B.: *Gascoigne's Path to Naval Fame*, 1825

Gates, C.M.: *Five Fur Traders*, 1933

Gentleman's Magazine, The, 1731–1868

Gentleman, Tobias: *England's Way to Win Wealth, and to Employ Ships and Mariners*, 1614 (In Edward Arber (ed) *An English Garner*, 1877–96)

Geographical Journal, The, 1893–

Giles, Herbert Allen: *A Glossary of Reference on Subjects connected with the Far East*, 1878

Glanville, Sir John: *The Voyage to Cadiz*, 1625 (Camden Society, 1883)

Glascock, W.N.: *The Naval Sketch-Book; or, The Service Afloat and Ashore*, 1826

Goode, George Brown: *American Fishes, a Popular Treatise upon the Game and Food Fishes of North America*, 1888

Gorges, Sir Arthur (transl): *Lucan's Pharsalia*, 1614

Gosson, Stephen: *The Schoole of Abuse, Containing a plesaunt inuective against poets, pipers, plaiers, iesters and such like caterpillers of a common-wealth*, 1579

Gower, John: *Confessio amantis*, 1390 (R. Pauli, 1857; English Works, EETS, 1900)

'Grand, Sarah' (Mrs M'Fall): *The Heavenly Twins*, 1893

Granville, Wilfred: *A Dictionary of Sailors' Slang*, 1962

Great Exhibition of the Works of Industry of all Nations, Official Description and Illustrated Catalogue of the, 1851

Greene, Robert: *Orpharion*, 1592 (1599)

Greene, Robert and Lodge, Thomas: *A Looking Glasse for London and England, c.* 1594 (1598)

Greenwood, James: *The Sailor's Sea-book. A Rudimentary Treatise on Navigation*, 1850

Grein, Christian W.M.: *Bibliothek der angelsaechsischen Poesie*, 1857–64 (1883–97)

— *Bibliothek der angelsaechsichen Prosa*, 1872 (1885–8)

Greville, Robert Fulke: *Diary*, 1794 (1930)

Grimstone, Edward (transl): *J. de Acosta's Naturall and Morall Historie of the East and West Indies*, 1604 (Hakluyt Society, 1880)

Grose, Francis: *A Classical Dictionary of the Vulgar Tongue*, 1785 (1796, 1823)

Hacke, William: *A Collection of Original Voyages*, 1699

Hahn and Lambertson: *On Using Self Contained Underwater Breathing Apparatus*, 1952

Hainsselin, M.T.: *Grand Fleet Days*, 1917

Hakluyt, Richard: *Divers Voyages Touching the Discouerie of America*, 1582

— *The Principall Navigations, Voiages, and Discoueries of the English Nation*, 1589

Hale, Thomas: *An Account of Several New Inventions; also a Treatise of Naval Philosophy written by Sir W. Petty*, 1691

Hall, Edward: *Chronicle (The Union of the Two Noble and Illustre Families of Lancestre and Yorke)*, 1548 (1550, 1809)

Halliwell, James O. (ed): *Rara Mathematica, c.* 1400 (1848)

Hamersly, Lewis R.: *Naval Encyclopaedia*, 1881

Hamilton, Alexander: *A New Account of the East Indies*, 1727

Hanshall, James A.: *Camping and Cruising in Florida*, 1884

Harper's New Monthly Magazine, 1850–

Harris, John: *Lexicon Technicum, or an Universal English Dictionary of Arts and Sciences*, 1704–10

Harris, W.T. and Allen, F.S. (ed): *Noah Webster's New International Dictionary of the English Language*, 1909

Hatton, Correspondence of the Family of, Being chiefly Letters addressed to Christopher first Viscount Hatton, 1601–1704 (Camden Society,1878)

Hatzfeld, Adolphe and Darmesteter, Arsène: *Dictionnaire Général de la Langue Française, avec le concours de Antoine Thomas*, 1895–1900

Havelok the Dane, The Lay of, c. 1300 (EETS, 1868; Skeat, 1902)

Hawker, Lieut.-Col. Peter: *Diary 1802–53* (1893)

Hawkesworth, John: *An Account of the Voyages undertaken for making Discoveries in the Southern Hemisphere and performed by Commodore Byron, Captain Wallis, Captain Carteret, and Captain Cook (from 1764–71)*, 1773

Hawkins, Sir Richard: *Observations in His Voiage into the South Sea*, 1593, 1622 (Hakluyt Society, 1847, 1878)

Hawksmoor, Nicholas: *An Account of London Bridge*, 1736

Heckstall-Smith, Brooke and Du Boulay: *The Complete Yachtsman*, 1912

Hedderwick, Peter: *A Treatise on Marine Architecture*, 1830

Hedges, Sir William: *Diary*, before 1701 (Hakluyt Society, 1887–8)

Henry VIII, King: *State Papers*

Henshall, James R.: *Camping and Cruising in Florida*, 1884

Herbert, Sir Thomas: *A Relation of Some Yeares Travaile Begunne Anno 1626, into Afrique and the Greater Asia 1634*, 1638 (1665, 1677)

Heywood, John: *A Dialogue conteinyng the nomber in effect of all the prouerbes in the English tongue*, 1546, 1562 (1874)

— *Epigrammes*, 1555–60, 1562

Heywood, Thomas: *A True Description of His Majesties royall Ship built at Wooll-witch*, 1637

Hickeringill, Edmund: *Gregory, Father Greybeard, with his Vizard off*, 1673

Highland Society of Scotland, Prize Essays and Transactions of, 1884

Holinshed, Raphael: *The firste Volume of the Chronicles of England, Scotlande, and Irelande*, 1577

Holland, Philemon (transl): *Livy's Romane Historie*, 1600

— (transl): *Pliny's Historie of the World, commonly called the Natural Historie*, 1601 (1634)

Holland, Sir Richard: *The Buke of the Howlat*, 1455 (Bannatyne Club, 1823)

Holme, Randle: *The Academy of Armory, or a Storehouse of Armory and Blazon*, 1688

Holyday, Barten (transl): *D.J. Juvenalis and A. Persius Flaccus*, 1661

Holy Gospels in Anglo-Saxon, The: Northumbrian and Old Mercian Versions, etc. (ed. Skeat, 1871–87)

Hone, William: *The Every-day Book*, 1825–7

Hood, Thomas: *Up the Rhine*, 1840

Hooker, John: *The Lyffe of Sir Peter Carew*, c. 1575 (in *Archaeologia*, XXVIII)

Hooker, John (alias Vowell) and Fleming, Alexander: *Continuation of* Holinshed's *Chronicles*, 1586–7 (1807–8)

Horsey, Sir Jerome: *Travels in Russia*, before 1627 (Hakluyt Society, 1856)

Hotten, John C.: *A Dictionary of Modern Slang, Cant, and Vulgar Words*, 1859, 1860, 1864, 1874

Household Words, 1850–9

Houston, Mrs M.C.: *Texas and the Gulf of Mexico; or Yachting in the New World*, 1844

Howard, Edward: *Rattlin the Reefer*, 1836

Howard, Henry, Earl of Northampton: *A Defensative against the Poyson of Supposed Phrophesies*, 1583

Howard Household Books, 1481–90 (Roxburghe Club, 1844)

Howard, Henry, Earl of Surrey: *Proem. to the 73rd Psalm*, before 1547 (Chalmers, *Works*, 1810; ed. Nott, 1815; Anglia XXIX, 1906)

Hughes, Thomas: *Tom Brown at Oxford*, 1861

Hull Advertiser and Exchange Gazette, The, 1796–

Hunt, John Leslie and Pringle, Alan George: *Service Slang*, 1943

Hutchinson, W.: *Practical Seamanship*, 1777

International Exhibition of 1862, Illustrated Catalogue of the Industrial Department of the, 1862

International Radio Telegraph Convention, 1927

Ireland, William H.(anon.): *Scribbleomania; or the Printer's Devil's Polichronicon, a Poem*, 1815

Irving, John James Cordell: *Royal Navalese: a Glossary*, 1946

Islander, The (Victoria, British Columbia), 1953–

Jackson, J.: *Journal from India*, 1799

James, Thomas: *The Strange and Dangerous Voyage of Captaine Thomas James in his intended Discovery of the Northwest Passage into the South Sea*, 1633

Jeake, Samuel (transl): *Charters of the Cinque Ports*, 1678 (1728)

Jefferson, Thomas: *Works*, 1859

Jerrold, Douglas: *Black-ey'd Susan*, 1829 (in Booth, *English Plays*, 1969)

Johnson, Myron (ed): *American Advertising 1800–1900*, 1960

Johnson, Peter: *The Encyclopedia of Yachting*, 1989

Johnston, Charles (anon.): *Chrysal; or The Adventures of a Guinea*, 1760
    (1822)
Jones, R.V.: *Most Secret War*, 1978
Jonson, Ben: *The Alchemist*, 1610 (1616)
— *Volpone, or the Fox*, 1605 (1607, 1616)
Journal of the Lancashire Dialect Society, The

Kane, Elisha K.: *Arctic Explorations: the second Grinnell Expedition in
    search of Sir John Franklin*, 1853 (1856)
Kemble, John M. (ed): *Codex Diplomaticus aevi Saxonici* (1839–48)
Kemp, Dixon: *A Manual of Yacht and Boat Sailing*, 1878 (1884,
    1895)
Kemp, Peter (ed): *The Oxford Companion to Ships and the Sea*, 1976
Kerchove, René de: *International Maritime Dictionary*, 1948
Key, A.: *The Recovery of the Gorgon*, 1844
Keymor, John: *Observations made upon the Dutch Fishinge*, 1601 (1664)
King Horn, before 1300 (in Ritson, *Metrical Romances*, II, 1802;
    Ballantine Club, 1845; EETS, 1866, 1901)
King, William: *The Art of Cookery, in Imitation of Horace's Art of Poetry*,
    1708 (1807)
Kingsley, Charles: *The Water Babies, a Fairy Tale*, 1863
Kipling, Rudyard: *Captains Courageous*, 1897
— *Life's Handicap*, 1891
Kipping, R.: *Mast-making and Rigging*, 1853
Knickerbocker, The, or New York Monthly Magazine, 1833–62
Knight, Edward H.: *The Practical Dictionary of Mechanics*, 1874–7
Kyd, Thomas (transl): *R. Garnier's Cornelia*, 1594

Lambarde, William: *A Perambulation of Kent; conteining the description,
    hystorie, and customes of that Shyre*, 1576 (1596, 1826)
Laneham, Robert: *A Letter: whearin, Part of the Entertainment vntoo the
    Queens Maiesty, at Killingwoorth Castl,...is signified, c.* 1575 (Ballad
    Society, 1871; Shakespeare Library, 1907)
Langland, William: *The Vision of William concerning Piers Plowman*,
    1360–1399 (EETS, 1867–85; 1886)
— *Richard the Redeless*, 1399 (EETS, 1867–85; 1886)
Laud Troy Book, c. 1400 (EETS, 1902–3)
Layamon: *Brut, or Chronicle of Britain, c.* 1205 (Society of Antiquaries,
    1847)
Legh, Gerard: *The Accedens of Armory*, 1562, 1568, 1576, 1597
Letters and Papers relating to the late War with France, 1513 (1913)
Lever, D.: *The Young Sea Officer's Sheet Anchor*, 1808
Levins, Peter: *Manipulus vocabulorum, A dictionarie of English and Latine
    words*, 1570 (Camden Society; EETS, 1867)
Lichefield, Nicholas (transl): *Lopez de Castanheda's First Booke of the
    Historie of the Discoverie and Conquest of the East Indies*, 1582
Ligon, Richard: *A True and Exact History of the Island of Barbados*, 1657
    (1673)

Lindesay of Pitscottie, Robert: *The Historie and Cronicles of Scotland*, c. 1578, 1728 (STS, 1898–9)
Lindisfarne Gospels, The, c. 950 (Skeat, 1871–87)
Lithgow, William: *The Totall Discourse of the Rare Adventures and Painefull Peregrinations of Long Nineteen Yeares Travayles*, 1632 (1682, 1906)
London Gazette, The, 1665–
Lord High Treasurer of Scotland, Accounts of the, 1473– (Scottish Record Series, 1887–; 1905)
Love, James: *The Mariner's Jewel*, 1692
Lubbock, Basil: *The China Clippers*, 1914
Ludlow in Shropshire, Churchwardens' Accounts of the Town of, 1540–1600 (Camden Society, 1869)
Luttrell, Narcissus: *A Brief Historical Relation of State Affairs*, 1678–1714 (1857)
Lyde, Robert (transl): *A True and Exact Account of the Retaking of a Ship called 'The Friend's Adventure of Topsham'*, 1693 (in Arber, *English Garner*, VII)
Lydgate, John (transl): *G. de Guileville's Pilgrimage of the Life of Man*, 1426 (EETS, 1899–1904)
— *The Assembly of Gods: or The Accord of Reason and Sensuality in the Fear of Death*, c. 1420 (EETS, 1896)
— *Chronicle of Troy*, 1412–20, 1513, 1555 (EETS, 1906–10)
Lynch, Col. T.: *Calendars of State Papers, Colonial, 1880.*
Lyndesay, Sir David: *The Complaynt*, 1529 (in *Works*, EETS, 1865–71)

MacGregor, John: *A Thousand Miles in the Rob Roy Canoe*, 1866
— *The Voyage Alone in the Yawl 'Rob Roy'*, 1867 (1868)
Mackenzie, Murdoch: *A Treatise on Marine Surveying*, 1774 (1819)
Magazine of Natural History, The, 1829–40
Magens, Nicolas: *An Eassay on Insurance*, 1755
Malynes, Gerard de: *Consuetudo vel lex mercatoria; or The Ancient law-merchant*, 1622
Manners and Household Expenses of England in the Thirteenth and Fifteenth Centuries (Roxburghe Club, 1841)
— *Handling Synne*, c. 1303 (Roxburghe Club, 1862; EETS, 1901)
— *Langtoft's Chronicle*, 1338 (1725, 1810)
— *The Story of England*, c. 1330 (Rolls Series, 1887)
Manual of British Rural Sports
Manual of Scientific Enquiry, A, 1849–59
Manual of Seamanship, A, 1905
Manual of Seamanship for Boys, A, 1883
Manwayring, Sir Henry: *The Sea-mans Dictionary*, before 1625 (1644)
Markham, Albert H.: *Sir John Franklin*, 1891
— *A Whaling Cruise to Baffin's Bay*, 1874
Marryat, Captain Frederick: *The Dog Fiend, or Snarley-yow*, 1837
— *The King's Own*, 1830
— *Mr Midshipman Easy*, 1836

— *The Naval Officer; or Scenes and Adventures in the Life of Frank Mildmay*, 1829
— *Newton Forster; or the Merchant Service*, 1832
— *Peter Simple*, 1834 (1836)
— *The Phantom Ship*, 1839
— *The Pirate, and the Three Cutters*, 1835
— *Poor Jack*, 1840
Marsden, Reginald G. (ed): *Select Pleas in the Court of Admiralty* (Selden Society, 1894–7)
Marston, John: *The History of Antonio and Mellida*, 1600 (1602)
Martens, F.: *Observations made in Greenland and other Northern Countries* (Translation, 1694) (in Account of Several Late Voyages)
Masefield, John: *The Bird of Dawning*, 1933
— *A Tarpaulin Muster*, 1907
Massachusetts Spy and Worcester Gazette, The, 1772–1830
Master of Game, The, c. 1410 (Digby MS, ed. Hahn)
Masters, Ted: *Surfing Made Easy*, 1962
Mather, Increase: *An Essay for the Recording of Illustrious Providences*, 1864
Maury, Matthew F.: *The Physical Geography of the Sea*, 1855
Maxwell, William Hamilton: *Sports and Adventures in the Highlands and Islands of Scotland*, 1844 (1855)
Maydman, Henry: *Naval Speculations and Maritime Politicks*, 1691
Mayne Reid, Thomas: *I Ran Away to Sea*, 1858
Meade, R.W.: *Naval Architecture*, 1869
Melvill, James: *Diary 1555–1601* (Published in *Autobiography and Diary*, Wodrow Society, 1842)
Melville, Herman: *Moby Dick or the Whale*, 1851
— *White Jacket; or the World in a Man-of-War*, 1850
Mercantile Marine Magazine and Nautical Record, The, 1854–60
Michigan Academy of Science, Arts and Letters, Papers of the
Middleton, Thomas and Dekker, Thomas: *The Roaring Girl, or Moll Cut Purse*, 1611
Military Service Institute of the United States, The Journal of
Milton, John: *Paradise Lost*, 1667
Minsheu, John: *Igeon eis tas glossas id est Ductor in linguas The Guide into Tongues etc.*, 1617 (1627)
Mitchell's Maritime Register, 1861
Monro, Robert: *His Expedition with the Worthy Scots Regiment called Mackeyes Regiment*, 1637
Monson, Sir William: *Naval Tracts*, before 1642 (Navy Records Society; in John Churchill: *Collection of Voyages and Travels*, III, 1704; 1752)
Morden, Robert: *Geography Rectified, or a Description of the World*, 1680 (1688)
More, St Thomas: *A Treatice upon the Passion of Chryste*, 1534 (1557)
Morris, Francis Orpen: *A History of British Birds*, 1851–7
Morte Arthure, or the Death of Arthur, *c.* 1400 (EETS, 1871)
Mortimer, John: *The Whole Art of Husbandry*, 1707 (1721)

Moryson, Fynes: *An Itinerary, c.* 1617
Motteux, Peter A. (ed): *F. Rabelais' Works, by Sir T. Urchard* [Urquart]
    and others, 1694 (1708, 1737)
Moxon, Joseph: *Mechanick Exercises, or the Doctrine of Handy-works,*
    1677–1700 (1683, 1703)
Murray, M.: *Shipbuilding,* 1754

Narborough, Sir John: *Journal,* 1694 (in *Account of Several Late Voyages*)
Nares, Sir George S.: *Narrative of a Voyage to the Polar Sea 1875–76,*
    1878
— *The Naval Cadet's Guide,* 1860
— *Seamanship,* 1862 (1865, 1868, 1882)
Nashe, Thomas: *Works* (ed by Alexander B. Grosart, 1883–5)
Natural Philosophy (Library of Useful Knowledge), 1829–35
Nautical Magazine
Naval Accounts and Inventories of the Reign of Henry VII, The, 1485–97
    (Navy Records Society, 1896)
Naval Chronicle, The, 1799–1818
Navy Board Letters (MS in the Public Record Office)
New Statesman, The, 1913–
New York Tribune, The, 1841–
Nicholas Papers, The, Correspondence of Sir E. Nicholas 1641–1660
    (Camden Society, 1886–1920)
Nichols, Philip: *Sir Francis Drake Revived,* 1593, 1626 (in Edward Arber,
    ed., *An English Garner,* 1877–96)
Nicolas, Sir Nicholas H.: *The Dispatches and Letters of Vice-Admiral Lord
    Viscount Nelson,* 1844–6
— *A History of the Royal Navy,* 1847
Nicolls, Thomas (transl): *The Hystory writtone by Thucidides,* 1550
Nicolson, Joseph and Burn, Richard: *The History and Antiquities of the
    Counties of Westmorland and Cumberland,* 1777
Nomenclator Navalis, c. 1625 (Harleian MS 2301)
Nordhoff, C.: *Merchant Vessel* in *Nine Years a Sailor,* 1857
Norman, Robert (transl): *The Safegard of Saylers,* 1584
North, Sir Thomas (transl): *Plutarch's Lives of the Noble Grecians and
    Romanes,* 1579 (1595, 1603, 1612, 1657, 1676, 1895)
Notes and Queries, 1850–

O'Hara ——: (anon.) *History of New South Wales,* 1817
Old English Miscellany (EETS, 1872)
Orders for the Spanish Fleet, 1588
Orders in Council
Oregon State Journal, The
Orrery, Roger Boyle, 1st Earl of (anon.): *Partenissa, a Romance,* 1654–69
    (1676)
Otway, Thomas: *The Souldier's Fortune; a comedy,* 1681
Outing, An Illustated Monthly Magazine of Recreation, 1886–
Owl and the Nightingale, The, c. 1250 (Percy Society, 1843)

Paasch, Henry: *From Keel to Truck, Marine Dictionary in English, French and German*, 1885 (1894)

Pall Mall Gazette, The, 1885–1926

Palsgrave, Jehan: *Lesclaircissement de la langue françoyse*, 1530 (1852)

Parish, William D. and Shaw, William F.: *A Dictionary of the Kentish Dialect and Provincialisms in use in the County of Kent* (English Dialect Society, 1887)

Parliamentary History

Paston Letters, The, 1422–1509 (ed. James Gairdner, 1872–5)

Pawson, Des: *The Handbook of Knots*, 1998

Peele, George: *The Honour of the Garter*, 1593

— *The Tale of Troy*, c. 1604

Pell, Daniel: *Pelagos: nec inter vivos, nec inter mortuos; or, an Improvement of the Sea*, 1659

Pelly, David: *The Illustrated Encyclopedia of World Sailing*, 1989

Pennant, G.: *Young Sailor*, 1951

Pennsylvania, Minutes of the Provincial Council of (1851–3)

Penny Cyclopaedia of the Society for the Diffuson of Useful Knowledge, 1833–43

Pepys, Samuel: *Diary*, 1660–9

Perrin, W.G.: *British Flags*, 1922

Perry, Captain John: *The State of Russia under the Present Czar*, 1716

Petty, Sir William: *Political Arithmetick, or a Discourse Concerning the Extent and Value of Lands, People, etc.*, before 1687 (1690) (in Edward Arber, *English Garner*)

Philips, John: *An Authentic Journal of the Expedition under Commodore Anson*, 1744

Phillip, William (transl): *J.H. van Linschoten his Discours of Voyages into the Easte and West Indies*, 1598 (Hakluyt Society, 1885)

Phillips, Edward: *The New World of English Words: or, A General Dictionary*, 1658 (1662, 1678, 1696, 1706)

Philological Society, The, Transactions of the, 1854–

Pilgrims Sea-voyage and Sea-sickness, The, c. 1460 (in the EETS, *The Stacions of Rome*, 1867)

Plot, Robert: *The Natural History of Oxfordshire*, 1677

Pocklington, John: *Altare Christianum; or, the Dead Vicars Plea*, 1637

Political Poems and Songs relating to English History, A Collection of (Rolls Series, 1859–61)

Pope, Alexander (transl): *Homer's Iliad*, 1715–20

Potter, John: *Archaeologiae Graecae; or, The Antiquites of Greece*, 1697–9 (1715)

Practyse of Cyrurgyons of Mountpyller, The, c. 1540

Prescott, George B.: *History, Theory and Practice of the Electric Telegraph*, 1860

Present State of Russia, The (transl) 1723

Promptorium parvulorum sive clericorum, lexicon Anglo-Latinum princeps, c. 1444 (Camden Society, 1843–65)

Pryme, Abraham De la: *Diary*, 1698 (Surtees Society, 1870)
Public Advertiser, The
Purchas, Samuel: *Hakluytus Posthumus, or Purchas his Pilgrimes, contayning a History of the World in Sea Voyages and Land Travell by Englishmen and others*, 1625–6
Putnams Magazine, 1868–70

Ralegh, Sir Walter: *The Discoverie of the...Empyre of Guiana*, 1596 (Hakluyt Society, 1848)
— *A Report of the Truth of the Fight about the Iles of Acores, this last Sommer, betwixt the Reuenge...and an Armada of the King of Spaine*, 1591
— *The Royal Navy*, 1618
Raper, H.: *The Practice of Navigation and Nautical Astronomy*, 1849
Raynalde, Thomas (transl): *(E.) Roesslin's Byrth of Mankynde, otherwyse called the Womans Booke*, 1545 (1552, 1564)
Reade, Charles: *Hard Cash*, 1863
— *The Eighth Commandment*, 1860
— *Love Me Little, Love Me Long*, 1859
Reed, Sir Edward J.: *Shipbuilding in Iron and Steel*, 1869
Rees, Abraham: *The Cyclopaedia or Universal Dictionary of Arts, etc.*, 1802–20
Richardson, Thomas: *Mercantile Marine Architecture*, 1833
Riddell, Maria: *Voyages to the Madeira and Leeward Caribbean Isles*, 1792
Ridley, Mark: *A Short Treatise of Magneticall Bodies and Motions*, 1613
Riley, Henry T.: *Memorials of London and London Life in the XIIIth, XIVth and XVth Centuries 1270–1419*, 1868
Ripon, Acts of the Chapter of the Collegiate Church of SS. Peter and Wilfred, 1452–1506 (Surtees Society, 1875)
Ritson, Joseph (ed): *Ancient English Metrical Romances*, 1802
— (ed): *Robin Hood; a Collection of All Ancient Poems, Songs and Ballads now Extant Relative to that Celebrated Outlaw*, 1795
— *A Select Collection of English Songs*, 1783
Roberts, G.: *A Dictionary of Geology*, 1839
Roberts, George: *The Four Years' Voyages of Capt. G. Roberts*, 1726
Roberts, L.: *A Map of Commerce*, 1638
Robinson, Charles Napier: *The British Fleet*, 1693
Robinson, Francis K.: *A Glossary of Words used in the Neighbourhood of Whitby* (English Dialect Society, 1876)
Roe, Sir Thomas: *The Embassy of Sir Thomas Roe to the Court of the Great Mogul, 1615–1619, as narrated in his Journal and Correspondence* (ed W. Foster, 1899)
Rogers, James E. Thorold: *A History of Agriculture and Prices in England from 1259 to 1793*, 1866–87
Rogers, Robert: *Journals of Major R. Rogers containing an Account of the Several Excursions he made...upon the Continent of North America during the late War*, 1769 (1883)
Rogers, Woodes: *A Cruising Voyage Round the World*, 1712 (1718)
Rolls of Parliament (Rotuli parliamentorum), 1278–1503 (1767–77)

Romans, Bernard: *A Concise Natural History of East and West Florida*, 1775

Romsey, *Chronicle of the Abbey of (William I)*, 1097 (Rolls Series)

Ross, Sir John: *Narrative of a Second Voyage in search of a North-west Passage and of a Residence in the Arctic Regions during the Years 1829–33*, 1835

Royal Commission on Historical Manuscripts, Reports of the

Royal Society, Philosophical Transactions of the, 1665–

Royal United Services Institute, Journal of the

Royle, John Forbes: *The Fibrous Plants of India*, 1855

Rudder, The, 1890–

Rushworth, John: *Historical Collections of Private Passages of State, Weighty Matters in Law, Remarkable Proceedings in Five Parliaments* (1659–1701)

Russell, William Clark: *Sailors' Language, a Collection of Sea-terms and their Definitions*, 1883

— *An Ocean Tragedy*, 1890

Rymer, Thomas: *Foedera, conventiones, literae, et cujuscunque generis acta publica, inter reges Angliae et alios quosvis imperatores, reges, pontefices, principes, vel communitates...ab anno 1101 ad nostra usque tempora, habita et tractata* (1705–35; 1816–30)

SS. Secretaries Studie, 1652

Sailing Directions, 15th century (Hakluyt Society, 1889)

Sailing Instructions, 1633 (MS Sloane 2682)

St James' Chronicle

St Mary at Hill, Records of. Medieval Records of a London City Church, 1420–1559 (EETS, 1905

Salesbury, William: *A Dictionary in Englyshe and Welsh*, 1547 (1877)

Sanders, T.: *A Voyage to Tripoli*, 1587

Sandys, George (transl): *Ovid's Metamorphoses*, 1621–6

Satirical Poems of the Time of the Reformation, 1565–84 (STS, 1891–3)

Schele De Vere, M.: *Americanisms: The English of the New World*, 1871 (1872)

Schult, Joachim: *The Sailing Dictionary* (translated and extensively revised by Barbara Webb, and revised for the second edition by Jeremy Howard-Williams), 1992

Scoresby, William: *An Account of the Artic Regions, with a History and Description of the Northern Whale-fishery*, 1820

— *Journal of a Voyage to the Northern Whale-fishery*, 1823

Scott, Michael: *The Cruise of the Midge 1834–35*, (1863)

— *Tom Cringle's Log*, 1829–33

Scott, Sir Walter (ed): *Sir Tristrem*, 1804 (1811)

Scribner's Magazine, 1887–

Sea Dictionary, 1708

Sears, Roebuck Catalogue, The, 1876–

Sewall, Samuel: *Diary 1674–1729* (1878–82)

Shackleton, Ernest Henry: *South: The Story of Shackleton's Last Expedition 1914–17* (1919)

Shadwell, Thomas: *The Medal of John Bayes: a Satyr against Folly and Knavery*, 1682

Shadwell, Thomas: *The Virtuoso*, 1676

Shaftesbury, Anthony Asley-Cooper, 7th Earl of: *Diary*, before 1885 (in W.D. Christie, *Life*)

Shakespeare, William: *All's Well that Ends Well* Between 1595 and 1604 (1601)

— *The Comedy of Errors*, c. 1590

— *Henry VI, Part III*, 1593

— *The Life and Death of King Richard II*, 1593

— *Sonnets*, c. 1600 (1609)

— *The Tempest*, 1610

— *The Tragedie of Anthonie, and Cleopatra*, 1606

— *The Tragedy of Hamlet, Prince of Denmark*, 1602

— *The Tragedy of Othello, the Moor of Venice*, 1604

— *Twelfe Night, or What You Will*, 1601

Shelvocke the Elder, George: *A Voyage Round the World*, 1726 (1757)

Sherwood, Robert: *English Dictionary* addition to Randle Cotgrave (q.v.)

— *A Most Copious Dictionary of the English set before the French*, 1632

Shipping Gazette, The

Shipwright's Vade-Mecum, The, 1805

Sidney, Sir Philip: *The Countess of Pembrokes Arcadia*, 1586

Sidney State Papers, The. Letters and Memorials of State in the Reigns of Mary, Elizabeth, James, Charles I, Charles II and Oliver's Usurpation, written by Sir H. Sydney, Sir P. Sydney and others (ed A. Collins, 1746)

Simmonds, Peter L.: *A Dictionary of Trade Products*, 1858

Sinclair, Sir John: *Correspondence*, 1831

Skeat, Walter William (ed): *Holy Gospels in Anglo-Saxon, The: Northumbrian and Old Mercian Versions, etc.*, c. 1000 (1871–87)

Skinner, Stephen: *Etymologicon linguae Anglicanae*, before 1667 (1671)

Smeaton, John: *A Narrative of the Building, and a Description of the Construction of the Edystone Lighthouse 1791* (1793, 1838)

Smith, Captain John: *An Accidence or the Pathway to Experience Necessary for all Young Sea-men*, 1626

— *A Description of New-England*, 1616

— *The Generall Historie of Virginia, New-England and the Summer Isles*, 1624

— *A Sea Grammar, with the Plaine Exposition of Smiths Accidence for Young Sea-men Enlarged*, 1627

— *The Seaman's Grammar* (enlarged 1653) 1692

— *Works*, before 1631 1607 (1819)

Smith, J.: *The Baroscope*, c. 1688

Smith, James: *The Panorama of Science and Art*, 1812–16

Smith, John: *England's Improvement Reviv'd*, 1670 (1673)

Smith, Simon: *Royal Fishings*, 1641

Smith, Sir Thomas: *De Recta Lingua Anglorum Scriptae*, 1568

Smollett, Tobias: *The Adventures of Peregrine Pickle*, 1751 (1779)

— *The Adventures of Roderick Random*, 1748 (1812)
— *The Adventures of Sir Launcelot Greaves*, 1762 (1793)
— *The Expedition of Humphry Clinker*, 1771
Smyth, Admiral William Henry: *The Sailor's Word-book: An Alphabetical Digest of Nautical Terms*, before 1865 (1867)
Smythe, Sir John: *Certain Discourses...concerning the Formes and Effects of Divers Sorts of Weapons, and other uerie important Matters Militarie*, 1590
Society...for the Encouragement of Arts, Manufactures and Commerce, Transactions of the, 1789
Somerset, Edward, Marquess of Worcester: *A Century of... Inventions*, 1655 (1663, 1865)
Southern Literary Messenger, The, 1834–64
Spenser, Edmund: *The Faerie Queene*, 1590–6
Sporting Magazine, The, 1793–1870
Standard, The, 1827–1916
Stanyhurst, Richard (transl): *Thee First Foure Bookes of Virgil his Aeneis translated...wyth oother poetical diuises*, 1582 (Arber, 1836)
Statutes of the Realm 1235–1713 (Record Commission, 1810–28)
Stevenson, Robert Louis: *Treasure Island*, 1883
Stewart, C.D..: *Partners of Providence*, 1907
Story of Genesis and Exodus, The, An Early English Song (EETS, 1865, 1873)
Stuart, H.: *The Novice's or Young Seaman's Catechism*, 1860
Stubbs, Bishop William (ed): *Select Charters and other Illustrations of English Constitutional History*, 1870 (1895)
Sturmy, Samuel: *The Mariners Magazine, or Sturmy's Mathematical and Practical Arts, etc.*, 1669 (1683)
Sutherland, William: *The Ship Builder's Assistant*, 1711
Swell's Night Guide, The, 1841, 1846, 1847
Swift, Jonathan: *The Journal to Stella*, 1710–1713 (1766, 1901)
Sydney Gazette, The

'Tackline': *Holiday Sailor*, 1945
'Taffrail' (Henry Taprell Dorling): *White Ensigns*, 1943
Tatler, The, 1709–11
Taylor, Bayard: *Eldorado; or, Adventures in the Path of Empire*, 1850
Taylor, John ('Water Poet'): *The Praise of Hemp-seed*, 1620
— *Works* (1630)
Temple, Sir William: *Observations upon the United Provinces of the Netherlands*, 1673
Tenney, William J.: *The Military and Naval History of the Rebellion in the United States*, 1865
Teonge, Henry: *Diary*, 1675–9 (1825)
Testamenta Eboracensia; or Wills Registered at York (Surtees Society, 1836–1902)
Thickness, Philip: *A Year's Journey through France and part of Spain*, 1777

Thomas, Pascoe: *A True and Impartial Journal of a Voyage to the South-Seas and Round the Globe under the Command of Commodore G. Anson*, 1745

Thomas, William: *The Historie of Italie*, 1549 (1561)

Tickell, Thomas: *Poetical Works*, before 1740, 1807

Time magazine, 1923–

Times, The, 1788–

Tindale, William (transl): *The New Testament*, 1526, 1534

Tomlinson, A.: *Military Journals*, 1855

Torrent of Portugal, The, c. 1435 (EETS, 1887)

Torriano, Giovanni: *A Dictionary Italian and English, formerly compiled by John Florio, now diligently revised*, 1659

Tottel, Richard: *Tottel's Miscellany (Songs and Sonettes written by the Ryght Honourable Lords Henry Howard late Earle of Surrey, and others)*, 1557 (Arber, 1870)

Trevisa, John de (transl): *Bartholomeus (de Glanville) De Proprietatibus Rerum*, 1398 (Tollemache MS; Add.MS (BM) 27944; MS e Museo (Bodl.) 16; W. de Worde, 1495)

— (transl): *Polychronicon Ranulphi Higden*, 1387 (Rolls Series 1865–86)

Trinity College Homilies (Old English Homilies of the Twelfth Century. From the MS in the Library of Trinity College, Cambridge), EETS, 1873

Turberville, George (Anon.): *The Noble Arte of Venerie or Hunting*, 1575

Turner, William H. (ed): *Selections from the Records of the City of Oxford, 1509–83*, 1880

United States Commissioner of Fish and Fisheries, Reports of (1873–1941)

United States Patent Specifications

Unton, Sir Henry: *Correspondence 1591–2* (Roxburghe Club, 1847)

Uring, The Travels of Captain N., 1726

Vere, Sir Francis: *Commentaries*, before 1609, 1596 (1657) (in Arber, *English Garner*)

Vespasian Psalter, The, c. 825 (in Sweet, Oldest English Texts, EETS, 1885)

Virginia Richly Valued, 1609

Walker, Gilbert (Anon.): *A Manifest Detection of the Most Vyle and Detestable Use of Dice-play*, 1532 (Percy Society, 1850)

Ward, Edward: *The Wooden World Dissected, in the Characters of a Ship of War*, 1706 (1708)

Washington, Thomas (transl): *N. de Nicolay's Nauigations into Turkie*, 1585

Weber, Henry W. (ed): *Metrical Romances of the 13th, 14th and 15th Centuries*, 1810

Webster, Daniel: *Private Correspondence*, c. 1852 (1857)

Webster, Noah: *An American Dictionary of the English Language. Revised and Enlarged by Chauncey A. Goodrich, New and Revised Edition*, 1864–80

Westmacott, Charles M. ('B. Blackmantle'): *The English Spy*, 1825–6 (1907)

Westminster Gazette, The, 1893–1927

Whitaker, Thomas D.: *The History and Antiquities of the Deanery of Craven in the County of York*, 1805 (1812)

Whitby Cartulary, The, 1351 (Surtees Society)

White, John: *A Rich Cabinet with a Variety of Inventions*, 1651 (1668)

'Williams, F.B.': *On Many Seas*, 1897

Willis, G.H.A.: *The Royal Navy as I Saw It*, 1924

Wills and Inventories, Illustrative of the History, Manners, Language, etc. of the Northern Counties of England, 1592 (Surtees Society, 1835)

Wines, E.C.: *Two Years in the Navy*, 1832

Winthrop, John: *The History of New England*, before 1649 (1825–6, 1853)

Withals, John: *A Shorte Dictionarie (English and Latin) for Yonge Begynners*, 1553, (1556,1568)

Wolcot, John ('Peter Pindar'): *Works*, 1782–95 (1809, 1812, 1816, 1819, 1824)

Wolsey, Cardinal: *Correspondence* (MS. Cott. Calig.)

World Wide Magazine

Worsley, F.A.: *A First Voyage in a Square-rigged Ship*, 1938

Wright, Thomas and Halliwell, J.O. (ed): *Reliquiae Antiquae: Scraps from Ancient Manuscripts* (1841–3)

Wright, Thomas and Wuelcker, R.P.: *Anglo-Saxon and Old English Vocabularies* (Second edition, 1884)

Wriglesworth, Captain W.: *MS Logbook of the 'Lyell'*, 1730

Wyatt, Captain: *The Voyage of Robert Dudley, afterwards Earl of Warwick and Leicester and Duke of Northumberland, to the West Indies, narrated by Capt. Wyatt, by himself, and by Abram Kendall, Master* (Hakluyt Society, 1899)

Wycherley, William: *The Plain-dealer*, 1676

Wyclif, John (transl): *The Holy Bible made from the Latin Vulgate*, 1382, 1388 (ed. J. Forshall and Sir F. Madden, 1850)

— *De Ecclesia, c.* 1380 (in *Selected English Works*, 1869–71)

— *Wisdom*, 1382

Yachting, 1907–

Yachting Calendar and Review, The

Yachting Monthly, 1906–

Yachts and Yachting

York Mysteries (York Plays. The Plays performed by the Crafts or Mysteries of York on the day of Corpus Christi), *c.* 1440 (1885)

Young, Arthur: *Nautical Dictionary*, 1846 (1863)